A Source Book of the Bible
for Teachers

A Source Book of the Bible for Teachers

Edited by Robert C Walton

SCM PRESS LTD

334 01562 6

First published 1970
by SCM Press Ltd
56 Bloomsbury Street London WC1
Fourth impression 1979

Filmset by Oliver Burridge Ltd, Crawley
and printed in Great Britain by
Butler & Tanner Ltd, Frome

CONTENTS

Preface   xvii

Contributors   xix

Abbreviations   xxi

Part One · Teaching the Bible: An Introduction

1   What is the Bible?   *Robert C. Walton*   3
    The arrangement of the biblical library   4
    The truth of the Bible   4

2   The Biblical Scholar and his Tools   *John Bowden*   5
    The beginnings of modern biblical scholarship   5
    What is 'criticism'?   6
    Asking the right questions   6
    Can we trust the text that we read?   7
      1   The New Testament   7
        (i) Manuscripts   7
        (ii) Making a decision   8
        (iii) Some examples   8
      2   The Old Testament   9
        (i) The Massoretic Text   9
        (ii) Other texts   9
    Who wrote the books?   9
      1   External evidence   9
      2   Internal evidence   10
    How were the books written?   10
    Before writing   11
      1   The Old Testament   11
      2   The New Testament   12
    Archaeology and the world of the Bible   12
    Technological tools   13
    Assured results?   13

Books of reference   14

Part Two · The Needs of the Pupils

1   Children Growing Up: The Role of Religion   *Ellen C. Mee*   17
    Significant and relevant changes in educational outlook in the last thirty years   17

Causes of difficulties in religious and biblical education 18
The general nature of children's growth 21
How religious and biblical 'understanding' grows 22
Development versus stagnation 24
Aspects of intellectual growth 25
The adolescent stage 27
Suggestions to those who teach the Bible 28

2   The Art of Communication   *Alan T. Dale* 30
The assignment 30
  1   What sort of help? 30
  2   The Bible as a record of experience 31
The heart of the Bible 31
The approach 32
  1   Language 32
  2   Comprehension 33
  3   Methods 34

3   The Bible in the Classroom 35

The Infant School   *Violet Madge* 35
Children's experiences and biblical truth 35
At-one-ness 36
The response to mystery 36
Personal relationships 38
Introducing biblical material 40
School experience and Bible stories 40

The Junior Stage   *Gordon Benfield* 44
Feeling and knowing 45
Possible approaches 46
  1   The 'Bible box of tricks' approach 46
  2   The 'setting the scene' approach 47
  3   The 'meeting people' or 'what were they like?' approach 47
  4   The 'Bible spectacles' approach 48
  5   The 'big question' approach 49
  6   The 'Bible-words' approach 50
  7   The 'biblical theme' approach 51
  8   The 'life-theme' approach 51
Agreed syllabuses 52
Some specific problems 52
  1   Teaching the miracles 52
  2   The passion narratives 53
  3   Real Bible or Bible stories in classroom and worship? 53

The Secondary Stage   *J. W. D. Smith* 53
The pupils we teach 53
The problem of relevance 54
Focusing on Christian faith and life 56
The theme of vocation 58
The theme of failure 59
The theme of hope 60
The theme of fulfilment 62

The Sixth Form   *Robert C. Walton*   64
    Built-in assumptions   65
       1   The Bible is one book   65
       2   The Bible is true and valuable. The Bible is untrue and irrelevant   66
       3   The Bible is a collection of ideas about God and the world. There is no
          evidence that the ideas are true   67
    Discussion in the classroom   68
    Three inescapable questions   69
       1   Identity   69
       2   Love   70
       3   Purposes   70

For further reading   71

Part Three · The Old Testament

1   Major Events in Israel's History   75

2   The Land and the People   *J. R. Bartlett*   76
    Geology   76
    Geography   77
    Climate   81
    Near Eastern ways of life   82

3   How Israel Became a Nation   *Ernest Nicholson*   84
    The origins of the Pentateuch   85
    The salvation-history in the Pentateuchal documents   87
       1   The 'J' document   87
       2   The 'E' document   89
       3   The 'D' document   91
       4   The 'P' document   93
    The historicity of the Pentateuch tradition   95

4   In the Beginning   *Robert Davidson*   96
    The background   96
    The nature of the material   97
    Content and meaning   98
       1   The hymn of creation   98
       2   The enigma of man   98
       3   Cain and Abel   99
       4   The descendants of Cain   99
       5   The beginning of the worship of Yahweh   99
       6   The first priestly genealogy – from Adam to Noah   100
       7   The prologue to the flood story   100
       8   The flood   100
       9   The covenant with Noah   100
      10   The family of Noah   101
      11   The table of the nations   101
      12   The tower of Babel   101
      13   The genealogy of the sons of Shem   101

Contents

5   The Patriarchs   *Robert Davidson*   102
    The historical question   102
    The character of the traditions   103
    The theology of the narratives   104
       1 Call or election   104
       2 Promise   105
       3 Covenant   105
       4 The presence of God   106

6   Moses   *Robert Davidson*   107
    The historical problem   107
    Extra-biblical evidence   108
    The significance of Moses   109
       1 The revelation of the character and name of God   109
       2 The exodus   110
       3 The covenant   111
       4 The Decalogue   112
    The legacy of Moses   113

7   Joshua and the Judges   *J. R. Porter*   114
    The evidence   114
       1 Biblical material   114
       2 Archaeological evidence   114
    A reconstruction of events   114
    Canaanite religion   115
    A gradual conquest   115
    Judges and the Deuteronomic history   117
    The people of Israel   118
    The tribal league   119
    The central sanctuary and the ark of the covenant   120
    The holy war   120

8   The United Monarchy   *R. N. Whybray*   121
    The evidence   121
       1 Biblical sources   121
       2 Archaeological evidence   121
    Becoming a nation   121
    Saul: the first king   122
    Saul and David   122
    The reign of David   123
    Jerusalem: capital of the kingdom   124
    The organization of the state   125
    The accession of Solomon   126

9   The Divided Kingdoms   *R. N. Whybray*   127
    The evidence   127
       1 Biblical sources   127
       2 Archaeological evidence   127
    The revolt of the northern tribes   128
    The threat from Assyria   129
    The end of Israel   131
    The kingdom of Judah   132
    The threat of Babylon   133

10   Prophecy in Israel   *R. E. Clements*   134
    The nature of early prophecy   134
    The nature of developed prophecy   136
      1   Amos   136
      2   Hosea   137
      3   Isaiah   139
      4   Micah   142
      5   Jeremiah   142
    The prophetic interpretation of history   145

11   Worship in Israel   *J. H. Eaton*   147
    Places of worship   147
    Seasons of worship   149
    Leaders of worship   150
    Sacrifices in worship   151
    Glimpses of worship   152
    The Psalms   154
      1   The journey to the festival   155
      2   Acts of penitence and purification   156
      3   The resanctification of the temple   157
      4   God's battle   158
      5   God's procession of victory   159
      6   The proclamation of God's kingship   159
      7   The speech of God   160
      8   The new year of growth   160
      9   God confirms the dynasty of David   161
    Epilogue   162

12   Wisdom in Israel   *William McKane*   162
    Wisdom in Israel and the ancient Near East   162
    Statesmen versus prophets   164
    The book of Proverbs   164
    The book of Job   166
    The book of Ecclesiastes   169
    Job and Ecclesiastes   172

13   The Exile   *H. McKeating*   173
    The evidence   173
      1   Biblical references   173
      2   Archaeological evidence   173
    Why this period is important   174
    The Neo-Babylonians   174
    The life and thought of the Jews   175
      1   In Babylon   175
      2   In Egypt   176
      3   In Palestine   176
    The coming of the Persians and the Babylonian defeat   176
    Developments in prophecy   177
      1   Ezekiel   177
      2   Deutero-Isaiah (Isaiah 40–55)   179
      3   Obadiah   182

Contents

14 The Return   *H. McKeating*   182
    The evidence   182
        1 Biblical references   182
        2 Non-biblical literature   183
        3 Archaeological evidence   183
    The Persian achievement   183
    Persian religion   184
    The rebuilding of the temple   184
    The work of Ezra and Nehemiah   185
    Judaism in the post-exilic age   187
    The literature   188
        1 The final shaping of the Pentateuch   188
        2 The book of Ruth   188
        3 The work of the Chronicler (I and II Chronicles, Ezra, Nehemiah) 189
        4 The Song of Songs   189
        5 Trito-Isaiah (Isaiah 56–66)   189
        6 The book of Joel   189
        7 The book of Jonah   190
        8 Haggai and Zechariah 1–8   190
        9 The book of Malachi   190

15 The Seleucids and the Maccabees   *J. R. Bartlett*   191
    The evidence   191
        1 Biblical references   191
        2 Extra-biblical references   191
    The coming of the Seleucid rulers   191
    The Greek way of life: 'Hellenization'   191
    Jewish resistance to Hellenization   193
    Independence   194
    The literature   195
        1 The book of Daniel   195
        2 The apocrypha   196

For further reading   198

Part Four · The New Testament

1   Rome and the Middle East   *Margaret J. Thorpe*   203
    Rome and Israel   203
    Herod the Great   203
    Tetrarchs and procurators   206
        1 Archelaus   206
        2 Philip and Antipas   207
        3 Pilate, procurator of Judaea   208
        4 Pilate and the trial of Jesus   209
    The later tetrarchs and governors   209
    The Jewish war and the fall of Jerusalem   211
    The Roman administrative system   212
    The Decapolis   213

2 Daily Life in Galilee   *Phyllis Doyle*   214
    Geography and climate   214
    Roads and hill-paths   214
    Cities, towns and villages   215
    Houses   215
    Clothes   216
    Food and drink   217
    Education   218
    Flowers and birds   219
    Two centres of Jesus' ministry   219
      1 Capernaum and its neighbourhood   219
      2 Jerusalem, the last week   220

3 Jewish Religious Life in the First Century AD   *John Bowden*   222
    Background and sources   222
    The temple   224
    Temple worship   225
    The temple staff   226
    The Law   226
    The Sadducess   227
    The Sanhedrin   227
    The scribes   228
    The Pharisees   228
    Rabbinic Judaism   229
    The synagogue   229
    Judaism in the Dispersion   231
    Qumran   231
    The Zealots   232
    The Samaritans   233

4 Accepted Ideas in First-century Palestine   *Margaret Thrall*   234
    Evil and suffering   234
    The presence of God   235
    Hopes for the future   236
    The glorious future   237

5 The Writing of the First Three Gospels   239

    What Kind of a Book is a Gospel?   *C. F. Evans*   239
    External evidence   240
    Internal evidence   241
    The Synoptic problem   242

    What Actually Happened?   *D. E. Nineham*   246
    The shape of Mark's Gospel   246
    The purpose of Mark's Gospel   247
    The stories in Matthew and Luke   249
    Interpreting the Gospels   250

    The Gospel Makers and their Message   *C. F. Evans*   253
    The Gospel according to Mark   253
    The Gospel according to Matthew   255
    The Gospel according to Luke   256

Contents

6   The Miracles   *John Bowden & Robert C. Walton*   257
        The nature of miracle   257
        Miracles and science   259
        Do miracles happen?   259
        Miracles in the Gospels   260
        The Resurrection   261
        Teaching the miracles   262
            1   Infant classes   262
            2   Junior pupils   263
            3   Senior pupils   263

7   The Ministry of Jesus   *Alan T. Dale*   264
        The evidence for the story   264
        The presuppositions of the story   265
        The background of the story   266
        The outline of the story   267
        The climax of his death   268
        His call   270
        In Galilee   271
        In retirement   273
        Near Caesarea Philippi   274
        In the south   275
        The strategy of Jesus   276
        The man behind the story   278
        The heart of the story   279
        Not the end but the beginning   280
        'Follow me!'   282

8   The Message of Jesus   *Robert C. Walton*   283
        The needs of the first Christians   283
        'The greatest artist of us all'   285
        How did Jesus teach?   286
        The originality of Jesus   286
        The parables   287
        Teaching about the kingdom   290
        Teaching about God   292
        Teaching about prayer   293
        Teaching about man   293
        Time present and time future   296
        The future of Israel   297
        The Day of Judgment   298
        Who was Jesus of Nazareth?   299
            1   Christ   299
            2   Son of man   300
            3   Son of God   300

9   Paul and his World   *C. H. Dodd*   301
        The Graeco–Roman world   301
        The empire: political and social structure   302
        Philosophy and religion   303
        Christianity in the Graeco–Roman world   304
        Paul: Jew and Roman citizen   304

The conversion of Paul   306
The first missionary journey   307
The second missionary journey   308
The third missionary journey   309
The Judaistic controversy   310
Jerusalem and Rome   311
A note on chronology   312

10   The Thought of Paul   *C. H. Dodd*   313
The Paul and his letters   313
The Jewish heritage   313
Judaism and the nations   314
The divine initiative   314
God in Christ   316
The people of God   317
Life in Christ   318
Problems of the church   319
The Spirit in the church   320
The law of the Spirit   321
The law of Christ   322
Social ethics   323
Christ, the church and the future   325

11   The Gospel According to John   *C. F. Evans*   326
Authorship and date   326
The structure of the Gospel   327
The background of the Gospel   330
  1   Synoptic Gospels   330
  2   Judaism   330
  3   Philo   331
  4   Hellenistic religion   331
Purpose and thought   332

12   The Early Church   *John Bowden*   335
The sources   335
Names and dates   335
Differences of opinion   336
The Acts of the Apostles   336
  1   Date and authorship   336
  2   Luke as a writer   336
  3   Historicity   337
  4   The chief concerns of Acts   337
  5   A later picture?   338
The ascension   338
The twelve   339
Pentecost   339
The early church   340
The seven   340
Philip   341
The conversion of Cornelius   341
Life in the early church   341
  1   The spread of the church   341

Contents

2	Gnosticism	343
3	Places of worship	344
4	Baptism and eucharist	344
5	Sabbath and Sunday	345
6	Church order	345
7	Persecution	346
8	The appeal of Christianity	348

Literature from the growing church — 349

1	The pastoral letters: I and II Timothy, Titus	349
2	Hebrews	350
3	The catholic letters: I, II and III John, I and II Peter, James, Jude	350
4	Revelation	351

13	Has the Bible Authority? *Robert C. Walton*	352
	Should the Bible be a source book in the classroom?	352
	The 'canon' of scripture	353
	The nature of biblical authority	353

For further reading — 355

Part Five · For Quick Reference

Compiled by Jean Holm

Agriculture	359		Taxes	365
Craftsmen	360		Travel	365
Dress	361		Warfare	366
Education	361		Water supplies	366
Food	361		Weights and measures	367
Games	361		Writing	367
Justice	361		Miscellaneous	369
Languages	362		The date of Jesus' birth	369
Marriage	362		The high priest's dress	369
Money	363		Jot and Tittle	369
Names – the land and the people	363		Phylacteries	369
Slavery	364		Urim and Thummim	370

MAPS

1	The Fertile Crescent	373
2	The Patriarchs in Canaan	374
3	From Egypt to Canaan	375
4	The Empire of David and Solomon	376
	The Kingdoms of Israel and Judah	
5	The Threat of Great Empires	377
6	The Struggle of the Maccabees	378
	The Kings of the North and the Kings of the South	
7	The Kingdom of Herod the Great	379

8   Palestine: the Gospels and the Acts of the Apostles   380
9   Jerusalem in the Time of Christ   381
10 The Journeys of Paul   382–3
11 Jewish Dispersion and the Christian Churches of the First Century   384

Index of Names and Subjects   387
Index of Selected Biblical References   391

PREFACE

This *Source Book of the Bible* replaces *The Teachers' Commentary* which was first published in 1932 and went through six editions before being revised and enlarged in 1955. These seven editions testify to the value of the *Commentary* as a book of reference for many thousands of professional teachers, clergy and Sunday School workers.

There are two reasons for publishing now an entirely new book, differently conceived and more relevant to the needs of those engaged in religious education in the nineteen-seventies. In the first place, many advances have been made during the past fifteen years both in Old and New Testament studies. To take three examples at random: we understand much more positively the significance and religious value of the myths and sagas which occur in the early chapters of the book of Genesis. Again, so much new light has been thrown upon the wisdom literature of Israel (the books of Proverbs, Job and Ecclesiastes) that in the *Source Book* it has been given an equal place alongside prophecy and worship in Israel. For senior pupils the wisdom literature provides exciting new material. A third example of this advance in knowledge is a more detailed understanding of the purposes and methods of the Gospel makers who compiled Mark, Matthew and Luke. However, it is almost invidious to isolate these three examples: almost every contribution contains fresh insights into literature of the Bible.

The second justification for a new book is the striking and revolutionary changes in the theory and practice of religious education. Increasingly it is 'child-centred' education which recognizes more fully and sympathetically how children grow up, and how they may grow in religious awareness, and recognizes also the doubts and perplexities, the strains and tensions to which adolescents are subjected in the contemporary world. For this reason, Part II of the book (some 45,000 words) is devoted to a series of articles on the needs of boys and girls, on the art of communication and the techniques of class-teaching at different stages of a pupil's school life. It is not without significance that the publishers did not choose as the editor a biblical scholar but one who has spent most of his working life in the field of religious education.

A source book is different from a biblical commentary. A commentary contains a number of general articles, but is in the main an introduction to, and a detailed exposition of, the chief passages of every book in the Bible. This *Source Book* has been planned on a different principle. The Old Testament articles describe the main events of Israel's history and discuss the original meaning and present-day significance of the leading ideas of the lawgivers, prophets, historians, psalmists and wisdom writers. The New Testament articles analyse the literature of the first Christians, tell what is known of the lives of Jesus of Nazareth and Paul of Tarsus, and study in some detail the message of Jesus and the thought of Paul. Thus if the reader wishes to know, for example, what the Covenant meant to the people of Israel, he will find the information here. If, on the other hand, he requires a full exposition of such a phrase as 'the covenant of an everlasting priesthood' (Num.25.13) he will need to consult a commentary on the book of Numbers. This plan will, it is hoped, serve best the requirements of teachers at the present time. The emphasis in biblical instruction today falls less upon a close study of the whole text of selected books (except for advanced examinations) and more upon the need to grasp the wide sweep of events and to enter with imagination and sympathy into the lives and beliefs of the people of the Bible.

My task as editor has been pleasant. The majority of contributors are specialists either in religious education or in biblical studies. They have all taken great care to write as simply as their subject would permit and to explain adequately the few technical terms, such as *eschatology* or *theophany*, which it was necessary to use. I owe a special debt of gratitude to the Rev. J. S. Bowden, the Editor of the Student Christian Movement Press Ltd, for constant advice, criticism and support during the three years of preparation for this book. In the long period between planning and publication the circumstances of some of those invited to contribute have changed and they have been compelled to withdraw from participation in the making of the book. Others have taken their places at short notice and to them we are especially grateful.

It would be foolish to imagine that in this *Source Book* the last word has been written either on the Bible or on religious education. The study of the literature of the Old and New Testaments will continue, and our insights into the needs of boys and girls will deepen. But it is not, I hope, presumptuous to believe that this book will contribute towards the enrichment and illumination of the religious life and religious knowledge of children at school.

Robert C Walton

CONTRIBUTORS

JOHN BARTLETT   *Lecturer in Divinity, Trinity College, Dublin*

GORDON BENFIELD   *County Religious Education Adviser for Hampshire Local Education Authority*

JOHN BOWDEN   *Editor and Managing Director, SCM Press, London*

R. E. CLEMENTS   *Lecturer in Hebrew and Old Testament, University of Cambridge*

ALAN T. DALE   *Formerly Head of the Department of Religious Education at Dudley College of Education*

ROBERT DAVIDSON   *Professor of Old Testament Languages and Literature, University of Glasgow*

C. H. DODD   *Late Professor in Divinity, University of Cambridge*

PHYLLIS DOYLE   *Formerly Senior Research Fellow, Department of Education, University of the West Indies, Jamaica*

J. H. EATON   *Senior Lecturer, Department of Theology, University of Birmingham*

C. F. EVANS   *Emeritus Professor of New Testament Studies, University of London King's College*

JEAN HOLM   *Principal Lecturer in Religious Studies, Homerton College, Cambridge*

VIOLET MADGE   *Late Senior Woman Tutor, Rolle College of Education, Exmouth*

WILLIAM MCKANE   *Professor of Hebrew and Oriental Languages, St Mary's College, University of St Andrews*

H. MCKEATING   *Lecturer in Theology, University of Nottingham*

ELLEN C. MEE   *Consultant, School Broadcasting Council, British Broadcasting Corporation; External Examiner, Institute of Education, University of London*

ERNEST NICHOLSON   *University Lecturer in Divinity and Dean of Pembroke College, Cambridge*

D. E. NINEHAM   *Warden of Keble College, Oxford*

J. R. PORTER   *Dean of Arts and Professor of Theology, University of Exeter, Canon and Prebendary of Wightring and Theological Lecturer in Chichester Cathedral*

J. W. D. SMITH   *Formerly Principal Lecturer in Religious Education at Jordanhill College of Education, Glasgow*

MARGARET J. THORPE   *Classical Mistress, Sutton High School, Sutton, Surrey*

MARGARET THRALL   *Reader in Biblical Studies, University College of North Wales, Bangor*

ROBERT C. WALTON   *Formerly Senior Producer of Religious Programmes, School Broadcasting Department, British Broadcasting Corporation*

R. N. WHYBRAY   *Reader in Theology, University of Hull*

ABBREVIATIONS

For the books of the Old Testament:

Gen.	Genesis	Eccles.	Ecclesiastes
Ex.	Exodus	S. of S.	Song of Solomon
Lev.	Leviticus	Isa.	Isaiah
Num.	Numbers	Jer.	Jeremiah
Deut.	Deuteronomy	Lam.	Lamentations
Josh.	Joshua	Ezek.	Ezekiel
Judg.	Judges	Dan.	Daniel
Ruth	Ruth	Hos.	Hosea
I Sam.	I Samuel	Joel	Joel
II Sam.	II Samuel	Amos	Amos
I Kings	I Kings	Obad.	Obadiah
II Kings	II Kings	Jonah	Jonah
I Chron.	I Chronicles	Micah	Micah
II Chron.	II Chronicles	Nahum	Nahum
Ezra	Ezra	Hab.	Habakkuk
Neh.	Nehemiah	Zeph.	Zephaniah
Esth.	Esther	Hag.	Haggai
Job	Job	Zech.	Zechariah
Ps.	Psalms	Mal.	Malachi
Prov.	Proverbs		

For the books of the New Testament:

Matt.	Matthew	I Tim.	I Timothy
Mark	Mark	II Tim.	II Timothy
Luke	Luke	Titus	Titus
John	John	Philemon	Philemon
Acts	Acts of the Apostles	Heb.	Hebrews
Rom.	Romans	James	James
I Cor.	I Corinthians	I Peter	I Peter
II Cor.	II Corinthians	II Peter	II Peter
Gal.	Galatians	I John	I John
Eph.	Ephesians	II John	II John
Phil.	Philippians	III John	III John
Col.	Colossians	Jude	Jude
I Thess.	I Thessalonians	Rev.	Revelation
II Thess.	II Thessalonians		

For Bible versions:

AV	Authorized Version, also known as KJV
KJV	King James Version, also known as AV
NEB	New English Bible
RSV	Revised Standard Version
RV	Revised Version

PART ONE

Teaching the Bible:
An Introduction

1

What is the Bible?

Robert C. Walton

'The book of books, the storehouse and magazine of life and comfort, the holy scriptures.' This is George Herbert's answer to the question which is the title of this article. He was a seventeenth-century parson and poet, a man of deep and sensitive faith, a Christian of mature understanding. Such an answer, however, is inappropriate in a twentieth-century classroom. In a secular age, to say that the Bible is 'the word of God' or that it enshrines 'divine revelation' is to use phrases which have lost their meaning. They are vague and imprecise and belong to a different world from that of a present-day audience. As teachers, it has been said, we have no right to put the word 'holy' upon the children's bibles before they have even read them. If, ultimately, confidence in the truth of the Bible is an act of faith, there is first a road of serious study and understanding to be travelled. This *Source Book of the Bible* is designed as a guide for those, especially for those teachers, who are willing to venture along that road.

What, then, is the Bible? It is not, from a literary point of view, a book, though it is normally bound between two covers, often of funereal black. Between these covers are two Testaments, the Old and the New. The Old Testament is a selection of the literature of the Israelite people over a thousand years of their history, roughly comparable to the English literature which has survived from the Anglo-Saxon Chronicle to the writings of Sir Winston Churchill. The comparison is, of course, inexact. There is a far greater volume of English literature, partly because the English suffered no foreign invasion since the Norman Conquest; still more, because since the fifteenth century books have been printed, not inscribed by hand. The New Testament is a selection of the literature of a new religion – Christianity – in the first hundred years of its existence. These selections are to some extent arbitrary, depending partly upon what chanced to escape destruction, but also upon the needs of the communities which preserved the writings. There was the wastage of the years but also deliberate acceptance and rejection.

This literature is not all 'religious' in the narrow sense of that word. In the Old Testament there are tales of long ago which, like the Norse sagas or the story of King Arthur and the Knights of the Round Table, tell of the nation's origins and reveal the inward, intuitive interpretation which the people of Israel put upon the realities of their national life. There are many historical narratives, and like any shelf of history books these vary both in accuracy and in literary quality. There are codes of law; reporting of events which today we should call 'current affairs'; protests against social injustice; poetry and songs both sacred and secular and a special kind of literature which has preserved the spoken and written message of the prophets. The New Testament begins with four brief records of the life of Jesus and the first three of these – the Gospels of Mark, Matthew and Luke – are linked together in a particular literary relationship. Some events in the early history of the Christian church are recorded in the Acts of the Apostles, and there is a selection of letters written by Paul of Tarsus and by others to warn, encourage and instruct individuals or the members of young churches, in places like Corinth, Ephesus, Philippi or Rome.

The analogy of a school or public library is a useful one in the classroom. With a little ingenuity a class could construct with dummy books or scrolls its own biblical library. In a library there are shelves for history books, others for poetry, biography, world affairs, religion, stories, myths and legends, and (in a public library) for legal works. The notable omission in the biblical library is scientific literature. The people of the Bible had no scientific understanding in the sense in which we use the word science today.

In the varied literature of the Old Testament we can read about the fluctuating fortunes of the people of Israel. They began as nomadic tribesmen, some of whom had escaped from slavery in Egypt, who slowly infiltrated into the land of Canaan until at last they possessed it. Then they changed their way of life, ceasing to be 'wandering Arameans' and settling down in fortified villages and walled towns. About 1000 BC they were welded into a single nation by a remarkable king named David, under whose leadership, and that of his son Solomon, Israel became an empire with influence and prestige in Middle-East politics. After Solomon's death the nation split into two separate kingdoms: Israel in the north and Judah in the south. The dreams of empire and world power declined and both nations were overwhelmed by more powerful neighbours. When the Old Testament ends and the New Testament begins, Israel is an unimportant outpost of the Roman empire. The ministry of Jesus was exercised, the Christian church took root, in a world dominated by Roman power.

The Arrangement of the Biblical Library

By modern standards the biblical library is arranged in a most arbitrary and confusing way. The thirty-nine books of the Old Testament are not printed in the order in which they were written, which would enable us to trace more easily the development of Israelite thought and experience. Moreover, many of the books consist of different strands of writing by different authors which, at a later stage, have been woven together by an editor. Two examples may be given. The book of Genesis, which is printed first in the Bible, consists of at least three separate strands of writing by different authors which, at a later time, were amalgamated by someone else. The earliest of these strands was probably written down about the time of David (c.1000 BC), though it tells of events which belong to a much earlier period. Another strand of tradition was later woven in with this, and Genesis was finally edited in its present form by

members of the priestly class round about 400 BC.

The second example is the book of Isaiah. It consists of three separate collections of writings. Chapters 1–39 refer mostly to events which occurred in the lifetime of the prophet Isaiah (c.740–701 BC), though there are insertions of a later date. Chapters 40–55 consist of prophecies by an unknown author living towards the end of the exile (c.542–538 BC), while chapters 55–66 contain oracles by unknown men living in Palestine about 450 BC. (Readers should consult the relevant sections of this *Source Book*, especially Part III, Sections 3, 10, 13, 14, pp. 84 ff., 139 ff., 179 ff., 189 ff.)

The Truth of the Bible

The Bible is more than 'a slab of ancient history in archaic language'. It contains many different kinds of truth. It is, in part, a source book for the history and social life of Israel, and without this information the nation's religion cannot be understood. It reflects the nation's way of life, reveals its developing standards and values, and bears witness to the head waters which nourished and sustained its soul. It is also the record of the spiritual wrestlings, questionings and affirmations of a deeply religious people, and traces their progress and their decline in thought and action towards a deeper understanding of God's purpose. It contains, in the New Testament, documents which preserve in rather fragmentary form recollections of the life and ministry, the death and resurrection of Jesus of Nazareth, interpretations of those events, and information about the early formative years of the Christian church.

At first sight it may seem that there is little of religious value in narratives which tell of kings crowned and buried or deposed and assassinated, and of armies defending frontiers or extending a nation's territory by conquest; little to stimulate man's spiritual quest in the enunciation of laws which one finds in the books of Exodus and Deuteronomy; little to help a man to worship in the often unbridled denunciations of the prophets. Let us be honest and admit that there is nickel among the gold. Yet – and it is this which makes the Bible relevant in every age and gives it unity – all these activities by which a nation lives are declared to be the direct concern of God. When a historian or chronicler records victory or defeat in battle, he sees behind the event the overruling purposes of God. When a lawyer codifies a set of laws, and includes one about safety precautions for houses with flat roofs (Deut.22.8), he is writing down 'the commandments, the statutes and the judgments of the Lord'. When a prophet denounces greed and exploitation he prefaces his stern warning with the phrase, 'Thus saith the Lord', and when he speaks of people abiding 'in a peaceful habitation, in

secure dwellings and in quiet resting places' (Isa.32.18), he is transmitting to sorely battered men and women a promise of God. This unity is the reason why the biblical library may properly be bound up as one book. Every part of this corpus of literature, whether poetry, law, or prophecy; whether recollections of the deeds and words of Jesus, or letters to young churches, speaks of the will of God, the acts of God, the purpose of God.

2

The Biblical Scholar and his Tools

John Bowden

What is the Bible? The previous section compared a seventeenth-century answer with one which might be given today. But for the same contrast, we might choose a period even nearer home. In the Bible, 'every scientific statement is infallibly accurate, all its history and narrations of every kind are without any inaccuracy'. That verdict comes from mid-Victorian England, from a popular manual much used by potential clergy, at a time when the church had a virtual monopoly on education. Doubts might be stirring, particularly as science began to raise serious problems, but a similar view was shared by the vast majority of Christians. To challenge it publicly in England was to invite personal abuse, dismissal, even legal action. *Essays and Reviews*, a collection of essays by Oxford scholars, was condemned after a petition signed by 11,000 clergy and over 150,000 laity, when its most provocative essay merely urged that the Bible should be approached like any other book. So much for the comparison between the Bible and a public library! Here was nothing less than the authoritative, inerrant word of God.

The change to a more modest assessment of the Bible has happened in just over a century, not a long time alongside its whole history. It came about because questions were asked quite unlike any others in the past. These questions

were prompted by a revolution which has affected not only the Bible, but the entire modern world.

The Beginnings of Modern Biblical Scholarship

At the end of the eighteenth century, an old world was showing signs of strain. A political and social revolution was under way, and with it came another in the realm of ideas, with new philosophical questioning and the slow development of the scientific method. Its consequence was that nothing was accepted any more simply because it was old, honoured, accepted; it all had to be tested, for the new principle was 'begin from doubt and build up knowledge on well-established foundations'. Even the Bible was not exempt.

The traditional claim was that the Bible was the word of God. The question now was: if that is so, how is it so? Is the Bible really different from other books? Is it true? Is it an accurate record? The only way to find out was to look and see, and so modern scholarship began. The chief questioners were not outsiders, but were themselves Christians, who did not hesitate to apply the strictest tests to their beliefs. This is not always recognized, but it is a tribute to the integrity of the first pioneers.

5

What Is 'Criticism'?

Professional study of the Bible by scholars is usually called 'criticism'. What is meant by the word, however, is not always clear, and it can give a misleading impression, because it has two different senses. In everyday talk, we use 'criticism' in an unfavourable sense, to mean passing a negative judgment on, finding fault with. But 'criticism' also has a more specialist sense, as when we talk about artistic, literary or musical criticism. Here the word describes a method of interpretation which draws out the qualities of a work in a systematic way, and it need have no unfavourable overtones. After all, critics often write good reviews.

Now, because of the way in which biblical criticism had to begin, challenging accepted and often dearly cherished views, and because of the sometimes unwelcome conclusions that it had to come to, it was taken very much as criticism in the unfavourable sense, and this association still clings to it. But the aim and ideal of scholarly investigation is criticism in the second sense: a systematic attempt at *understanding*, by examining and explaining the form, content and background of the Bible in the light of all available and relevant knowledge.

If he is going to understand, the critic needs to ask the right questions, those that will help him to express his subject in an undistorted way. With the Bible, finding the right questions was not easy at first, and there were some false starts before the proper approach was found.

Asking the Right Questions

As we saw, the first kind of question to appear concerned the Bible as authoritative and holy Scripture: 'Is this true?', 'Did that happen?', 'Is there a possible explanation for this?' There were great arguments about whether Genesis could be reconciled with science or whether the Israelites could have crossed the Red Sea with dry feet, or whether Moses could have written the books which bear his name, or whether Jesus could have turned water into wine. Each of these questions was discussed as though the whole fate of the Bible depended on the answer.

At the same time, however, such discussions came in the way of seeing what the Bible might be if it were allowed to speak for itself. They showed too much eagerness to make the Bible measure up to a particular set of standards. They tended to involve only a few incidents in the Bible at the expense of the rest. They were often about a principle rather than what the Bible actually contained. Above all, they ignored one all-important fact: the writers of the books of the Bible were different from us in many ways. Their world was different, their way of thinking was different, the questions they asked were different. Another approach was needed.

As they gained experience, scholars learnt to match their own questioning to that of the *world* they were investigating. They learnt that they had to do more than look at a book by itself; they had to recreate its world. It might be Palestine in the tenth century BC or Babylon in the sixth or Corinth in the first century AD; only when there was better knowledge of how people in these places and times lived and thought and spoke would the relevant parts of the Bible take their place in the new picture.

A useful illustration of this development has been given by Dr Leonard Hodgson; he comments that:

> modern zoology began when, instead of relying on Aristotelian and heraldic representations of animals in traditional bestiaries, men based their research on the observation of the actual nature and behaviour of living creatures. . . As a result of this last century's biblical studies, we are at a similar turning point in the history of Christian theology . . . A hundred years ago our forefathers looked to the Bible in the same way that mediaeval zoologists looked to Aristotle and heraldic bestiaries. To their successors' substituting of observation of actual animals corresponds our attention to the historical provenance of the biblical writings.

This meant cultivating a historical sense. That, too, has been developed only over the last century. But now it affects almost any arts subject, from music to languages, and even some of the sciences. We begin to understand a thing by looking at its origins and discovering how it came to be so.

Biblical criticism had been in progress some time before this point became clear. And in any case, it was originally in no position to reconstruct past worlds. It did not have sufficient material to do so. But this does not mean that useful and lasting work could not be done on more limited, though still important matters. Even before archaeology made its impressive contribution towards understanding the Bible, a great deal was learnt about the text of the Old and New Testaments and the literary character of the various books. As the handing down of the text of the Bible will not be discussed elsewhere in this *Source Book*, a little more space must be devoted to it here than to the rest of the critic's work, which will be amply illustrated in later sections.

Can We Trust the Text that We Read?

Editions of the Bible can be bought today in many languages; the Bible is probably the easiest book in the world to get. But there is a gap of more than 1800 years between the time when its last book was finished and the present. What has happened to the Bible down the ages? How can we be sure that what we read now corresponds to what was originally written? Printing by movable type was only invented in the fifteenth century; for a thousand and more years before that manuscripts had to be laboriously copied by hand, either through one scribe making a single copy from a manuscript in front of him, or through a scriptorium, where a lector dictated a manuscript to a small group. Ancient manuscripts were written with no space between words and with abbreviations for many common words; unintentional mistakes must have been easy. In addition, manuscripts must often have been altered deliberately, perhaps by scribes who thought that they were correcting mistakes (and whose insight was not always as good as their intentions).

The task of reaching a text as close as possible to the original and of explaining how this text was handed down is known as *textual criticism*. It is a highly complicated business and applies not only to the Bible but also to any ancient manuscript.

1. *The New Testament*

To see how strong the textual evidence for the New Testament is, it is only necessary to compare it with what the classical textual critic often has to work on. The 'bible' of the ancient Greeks, Homer's *Iliad*, is preserved in about 650 manuscripts of various kinds; the best-attested Greek tragedian, Euripides, in about 330; at the other end of the scale, the first six books of the *Annals* of Tacitus, the late first-century Roman historian, survive in only one manuscript, dating from the ninth century. On the other hand, there are over 5000 extant manuscripts of the New Testament, though many of these contain only part of it, and their age varies.

(i) *Manuscripts*

(a) *Dating*. Dating manuscripts is done by examining closely the context in which they were found, their format, the material used and the style of writing. The palaeographer, as the specialist in this kind of work is called, develops a 'feel' for dating, in the same way as the expert in antiques, but he has one independent test to help him. This is a scientific test known as the Carbon 14 process (for more details, see below). When classified, manuscripts are assigned a letter or number for easy reference.

(b) *Papyri*. The earliest text of any passage from the New Testament that we have is a papyrus fragment from the Fourth Gospel, probably dating from early in the second century. This fragment contains only a few verses, but there are more extensive papyri, covering the greater part of the New Testament, from the third century to the seventh. These are about eighty in number.

(c) *Uncials*. Parchment manuscripts are much more numerous, because they are more durable. Pride of place among them goes to the great 'uncial' manuscripts dating from the fourth century to about the tenth. They are named after the type of letters in which they are written, rather like our capitals. The two most famous of these, Codex Vaticanus and Codex Sinaiticus, only became available for detailed study in the late nineteenth century, in quite dramatic circumstances. Originally they contained all the Old Testament as well. There are 250 uncial manuscripts now extant.

(d) *Minuscules*. In the ninth century, a new style of writing was invented, of smaller letters in a running (cursive) hand, which enabled books to be written more quickly and more cheaply. This writing is called 'minuscule'. From this time onwards we have a wealth of material: over 2500 manuscripts in all.

(*e*) *Other sources.* In addition, there are almost 2000 Greek New Testament lectionaries, selections to be read on particular days of the year. Translations of the New Testament made at an early date into Syriac, Coptic, Latin, Georgian, Armenian, Gothic, Ethiopic and Old Slavonic can be used for comparison. Finally, there are New Testament quotations in the writings of Christian theologians from the second century onwards which indicate something of the text they knew.

In view of the complex variety of evidence which goes back almost to the beginning, it is unlikely that any large-scale interference with the text has gone undetected. But the complicated manuscript tradition has produced a mass of minor variants which need to be resolved. Furthermore, there may have been slight changes between the time of the originals and the dates of the earliest manuscripts we possess.

(ii) *Making a Decision*

It has been said that 'to teach another how to become a textual critic is like teaching another how to become a poet'. A full account is impossible, but here are some indications of how decisions are made.

First, manuscripts can be organized into groups or 'families', i.e., the critic can see which manuscript was copied from which. This becomes evident if, for example, an obvious error occurs at the same point in the text of two different manuscripts. Assuming that each was copied from only one manuscript, a common descent can be assumed. (The process is similar to that used in detecting forms of cheating in schools!) Later manuscripts in families, great-great-grandchildren and the like, can often be disregarded completely. This clears the air.

Four major groups are recognized and classified by geographical area:
(*a*) the *Syrian* (the Byzantine Empire: used for European Protestant translations up to the Revised Version);
(*b*) the *Western* (an early group, much given to paraphrasing);
(*c*) the *Alexandrian* (influenced by one of the great ancient literary centres);
(*d*) the *Neutral* (Codex Vaticanus and Codex Sinaiticus; so-called because this group is thought to be nearest to the originals).

After this classification, further decisions are still necessary. Mistakes are possible in the best manuscripts, and generally inferior ones sometimes preserve the truth. So decisions have to be made on individual readings, drawing on past experience of possible causes of error, and knowledge of the author and subject-matter of the writing in question. Two obvious examples are:
(*a*) The more difficult reading is to be preferred. The tendency among scribes was to make a text more understandable, and unless an obvious error has been made, the reading which is harder to make sense of is usually more likely to be original.
(*b*) Assimilation. Where, as in the first three Gospels, passages are similar, the scribe might alter, e.g., a less familiar wording in Luke to one he knew well from Matthew. Here the divergent reading is more likely to be original.

In this way, grounds for a decision are gradually built up. Time has given rise to a large and sophisticated literature about textual criticism which takes experts years to master; but it has also brought us to a position when we can be more certain about the text of the New Testament we use than ever before.

(iii) *Some Examples*

What difference does it make? A comparison of the Authorized (King James) Version with any of the newer translations will often show obvious changes. A few examples may be mentioned in passing.
(*a*) The last twelve verses of the Gospel of Mark were not originally part of the Gospel; they were added later, and the Gospel originally ended, or is irretrievably lost, after Mark 16.8 (see RSV).
(*b*) John 7.53–8.11, the story of the Woman Taken in Adultery, is an intrusion into the Fourth Gospel, though it may well be authentic material from elsewhere.
(*c*) I John 5.7 f. in the AV (KJV) is a late addition to the text, probably a reader's comment that was once written in the margin.

But there are not many 'spectaculars' like this; the majority of decisions are over much smaller questions, e.g., the description of Stephen in Acts 6.8: AV 'faith and power' becomes 'grace and power' in RSV. This is a difference in the text chosen, not in translation. Sometimes the choice is very finely balanced;

do we read 'we have peace' (RSV) or 'let us have peace' (RV) in Rom.5.1?

2. *The Old Testament*

The Old Testament can be discussed much more briefly, as the basic principles are the same. Language, background and manuscript tradition, though, are different.

(*a*) *The Massoretic text.* When a move towards the purification and consolidation of Judaism began at the end of the first century AD, attempts were made to obtain a normative text of the Hebrew Old Testament. The scholars responsible for this work took great care in transmitting their chosen text, which was accompanied by a commentary (*Massorah*). The commentary was first oral and then written in the margins; it contained statistical details about the text and notes for interpretation. These scholars were called Massoretes, and so the standard text of the Hebrew Old Testament is known as the Massoretic text. Uniformity was not complete, as there were differences over principles between rival groups of Massoretes, but basically their work was most successful, as unexpected evidence shows.

(*b*) *Other texts.* Before the rise of the Massoretic text a variety of text-forms existed, some of which have only recently come to light. Scrolls were discovered, not only at Qumran but also in a *genizah* (a storehouse for manuscripts no longer usable in worship, which were considered too sacred to be thrown away) in Cairo. Between them they may take us back as far as the second century BC. Together with ancient translations like the Greek version (Septuagint), the Samaritan version of the Law and the Syriac version (Peshitta), they show forms of the texts prior to the Massoretic process of standardization. But interesting as this new evidence is, it does not compel any far-reaching new conclusions about the reliability of the Old Testament text.

Who Wrote the Books?

Having established that he has a reasonably accurate text to work from, the critic's next concern is with the origin and background of the books of the Bible. Who wrote them, where and when? He has two ways of answering his questions. First he can see what information has been handed down about authorship and circumstances by earlier authors: this is known as *external evidence*. Secondly, he can examine the books carefully and see what their content suggests: this is known as *internal evidence*. Unfortunately the two often disagree.

1. *External Evidence*

Numerous remarks about authorship, etc., can be found in Jewish and Christian commentators. They vary from the plausible (that the Gospel of Mark was written by John Mark and contains reminiscences of the apostle Peter) to the implausible (that the text of the 'Five Books of Moses' was dictated by Ezra, through inspiration, when they had been lost at the Fall of Jerusalem). Often apparent fact and apparent fancy are combined, as when, for example, at one moment the second-century theologian Irenaeus remarks that Luke was a follower of Paul and wrote down the gospel he preached, and at the next that there must be no more and no less than four Gospels because there are four zones of the world, four winds, and four faces to the cherubim.

In particular, we have to remember the temptation there was to embellish claims about the Bible to show what a marvellous book it was, and the pressure in the case of the New Testament to demonstrate that a book was written by, or had connections with, an apostle, to qualify it for inclusion in the church's official collection (canon). If all this sounds dangerously near to forgery, we must remember the historical background; ancient literary conventions were rather different from ours.

In any case, the ancients were often quite in the dark about the origin of books which after all were not first written to be Holy Scripture. Sometimes they seem to have made their own guesses from internal evidence. In that case their external evidence is internal evidence in disguise. (Irenaeus seems to have come to his conclusion about Luke and Acts on internal evidence.) Because of this, the critic approaches external evidence suspiciously; he checks each argument carefully, and because he has better facilities for investigation than the ancients, he usually prefers to trust what he can discover from a book itself.

2. *Internal Evidence*

As he studies some of the biblical books, the critic may begin to doubt what tradition says about them. The 'Five Books of Moses' do not in fact seem to have come from him. Not only do they record his death, but they contain material apparently from a much later time. The German scholar Wellhausen described how difficult it was to read the 'historical books' of the Old Testament on the assumption that, say, Saul and David knew Leviticus; everything fell into place when he tried the theory that the Law, rather than coming from Moses, belongs to a period later than that of I Samuel–II Kings. His approach is typical of the modern scholar: he tries to construct the kind of sequence which fits the known facts and shows how one thing grows out of another.

Some conclusions from internal evidence are:

(i) Careful reading of the book attributed to Isaiah shows that it seems to come from three different periods spread over more than two hundred years. Of course, there are loose ends, but the assignment of material to two writers in addition to Isaiah makes better sense (see Part III, Sections 10, 13, 14, pp. 139 ff., 179 ff., 189 ff.).

(ii) All the letters attributed to Paul do not come from his hand. The headings of the Authorized Version assign him fourteen letters, but some are problematical. The Epistle to the Hebrews has a very different style and subject-matter from the rest (and even the external evidence is doubtful). The Epistles to Timothy and Titus also suggest a different historical setting, later than Paul's time. These are therefore usually attributed to other authors. Over Ephesians, Colossians and II Thessalonians the debate is fiercer. Some claim that these were written by disciples or imitators of Paul, others that Paul himself wrote them. Here, however, the differences are less important precisely because they are slighter; a decision either way makes little difference to our reconstruction of first-century Christianity.

Usually, however, dating and finding an appropriate background are vitally important. The way in which the biblical literature is arranged will make all the difference to our picture of the world of the Bible. And as we saw earlier, this is the critic's final aim.

How Were the Books Written?

When he has reached the probable circumstances in which a book was written, the critic tries to go further back, for it is only rarely that an author wrote as it were 'out of his head'. This happens, for example, with some of the letters of Paul, but even they refer to or draw on other material. I Corinthians is a reply to an earlier letter written to Paul from Corinth, and before that came a still earlier letter from him which is now lost. Clearly I Corinthians will mean much more if something on the file of earlier correspondence can be reconstructed. Other biblical books incorporate chunks of earlier material. Where this happens is not always easy to detect; just as the ancient world had different conventions about authorship, so too it had different conventions about quotation. Borrowings were not documented and acknowledged in footnotes as they are today; in fact, imitation was thought to be a form of flattery.

One vivid illustration of this comes from the book of Proverbs. When a document from ancient Egypt, the *Sayings of Amenemopet*, came to light in 1922, it became clear that this was the source for several chapters of Proverbs, which reproduced it almost word for word.

Investigating the sources on which authors drew is one way of finding out more about their works. The process is known as *source criticism*.

Source criticism is easier in some places than in others. As soon as the first three Gospels are set out in parallel columns it is plain that they are in some way related. Exactly what this relationship is may be more difficult to define, but the material for a solution which explains which Gospel came first and how the others made use of it is there to hand (for more details, see Part IV, Section 5, pp. 242 ff.). Similarly, I and II Chronicles draws on much of I Samuel–II Kings; what the Chronicler leaves out of the latter can be seen by a careful comparison and sheds much light on his views. In these instances, as with Proverbs and *Amenemopet*, both the 'source' and the book in which it is used still survive.

Where a book uses sources without too much alteration, it is possible to detect them even if they do not survive in their original form. In the first five books of the Bible, the Pentateuch, for example, an analysis of style and vocabulary makes it possible to detect different strands of material, each of which can be followed for some length (see Part III, Section 3, pp. 85 ff.). Within the prophetic books, it is often possible to distinguish sayings which go back to the prophet himself from the comments and additions made at later times, and even to see alternative ways in which his prophecies were first combined.

The difficulty arises when the final book is a more polished literary work in which earlier sources have been worked over and given a new form. Did the evangelist John know the Synoptic Gospels, or only a form of the tradition on which they also drew? Did he make use of other sources? It is very hard to tell. What sources did the author of Acts have? There must have been some, but his style is so good and his literary skill so great that discovering the material on which he drew is about as easy as returning a well-baked cake to its original ingredients!

Source criticism can penetrate behind a book to an earlier stage. But its aim is not just to get back as far as possible. It seeks to illuminate the whole process of the literary composition of a book: the middle and end as well as the beginning. Later material added to the original can tell us much, say, about the way in which the prophets were regarded by their followers, just as insertions discovered by textual critics can tell us a bit about what earlier generations thought as they read the Bible. Here, too, is one way of discovering the personality of a writer, as well as the tradition on which he drew.

Before Writing

Source criticism is essentially a literary process. It deals with the relationship of one document to another. But there are more ways of handing on tradition than by writing it down. Literature is usually preceded and accompanied by an oral stage in which stories, poems, hymns, proverbs, even laws, are passed on by word of mouth. Even modern civilization has its oral tradition, e.g., anecdotes and sayings, which only occasionally find their way into writing. Biblical literature begins from an oral tradition and is fed by it at numerous stages on the way.

As with the transmission of books by copying, so too with oral tradition some general

principles can be established, this time by comparison with similar cultures and parallel situations. In this way the critic can see what is likely to happen to oral material.

At the oral stage, the individual is a much less prominent figure (for how many, e.g., 'shaggy dog stories' do you know an author?). Much more influential is the life of the community and the activities in which it engages. These shape spoken material and produce distinctive forms. Hence study of the oral stage of tradition has come to be known as *form criticism*.

What a 'form' is can be illustrated from the modern world; we can recognize the difference between a joke and a limerick, a hymn and a ballad, a testimonial and a legal charge. All these are forms. Form, content and purpose even now are closely connected; a testimonial will not normally be written as a limerick nor a legal charge as a ballad (though see *Trial by Jury!*). But our society is a complex and relatively sophisticated one and so few conclusions can be drawn from forms. In a less highly developed, more structured community it is a different matter.

In the ancient Near East, forms are closely related to the life of the community. Once it is accepted that a particular form will have been determined by its place in the life of the community, we can argue back from the form (which we have) to the community life (which has passed away). This method is not an abstract one, as a check on conclusions reached is often possible from relevant archaeological evidence.

Here are some illustrations:

1. The Old Testament

(*a*) *The Pentateuch*. Here it is possible to identify by their forms riddles, work-songs, hymns, legends, prescriptions for worship and codes of law of various kinds (e.g., 'apodeictic law': 'Thou shalt (not) . . .' has a different form from 'casuistic law': 'If a man . . . then'). Like all forms, these are usually fairly brief. This helps us to see something of earliest Israelite interests and concerns.

(*b*) *The Prophetic Books*. Prophetic oracles assumed particular forms (see Part III, Section 10, pp. 134 ff.), and when we have recognized these it is possible to use the knowledge to distinguish what the prophet originally said from what has been added later.

11

(c) *The Psalms.* These differ in form (see Part III, Section 11, pp. 154 ff.): compare a hymn like Ps. 100 with a lament (Ps. 44) or a thanksgiving (Ps. 124). This helps us to reconstruct the pattern of Israelite worship.

(d) *Proverbs.* Even the collections of proverbs can be analysed by forms, which help to indicate their background and origin (see Part III, Section 12, pp. 164 ff.).

2. *The New Testament*

(a) *The Gospels.* The stories about Jesus assumed different forms depending on their use in the early church (see Part IV, Section 5, pp. 246 ff.). Compare, for example, the shape of the 'controversy stories' in Mark 2.1–3.6 with that of the 'miracle stories' in 4.35–5.43. Here, too, we can argue from the form to the use of these stories in the church.

(b) *The Epistles.* An epistle is itself a form, and by recognizing the characteristics of an epistle it is possible to distinguish real epistles (e.g., of Paul) from books like Hebrews or I John, which though named epistles are much more like sermons. Were they ever sent as letters? Within the epistles, early Christian confessions, hymns, etc. may be detected (perhaps Phil.2.5–11; I Cor.15.3 ff.).

Form criticism is inevitably a less precise approach than source criticism, but its uses have been proved.

It can also help in clarifying the character and purpose of the writers in whose work the 'forms' are included. Arrangements of individual units may be the only way in which a writer who is faithful to the tradition he has received may make his point. For example, is the order in the Gospel of Mark purely historical, or are units sometimes arranged on a different principle to put over a theological point?

When the method of form criticism is extended in an attempt to discover the intentions of the final author or editor it is known as *redaction criticism.* (This rather ugly name comes from the term used for the author/editor, 'redactor', which indicates that he is half-way between the one and the other.) As an approach, it tends to be very subjective, because of the complicated questions it has to ask, but it, too, is a promising development.

Archaeology and the World of the Bible

The methods we have looked at help the critic to understand the *Bible;* they are used hand in hand with his more general work, as a historian, in understanding the biblical *world.* Here archaeology is his chief tool.

The amazing discoveries at Qumran are the most publicized achievements of modern archaeology, but there are many more besides. Specific details will be found in the sections which follow, particularly those on the Old Testament. Numerous important sites have produced material of various kinds, bringing to life a whole new world of Palestinian, Egyptian and Mesopotamian culture. New Testament studies have been helped, too. Discoveries of second-century writings by Gnostics (a deviant form of Christianity) have been made at Nag Hammadi, in Egypt; these help us to see what happened in the obscure period between the end of the New Testament and the first 'Fathers'.

The amount of new information provided by archaeology is enormous, but it is important to see just what its limitations are. Here, too, mistakes were made at the start because this had not been realized. A comparison will show the right way and the wrong way:

1. In his excavations at Ur in the 1920s, Sir Leonard Woolley found a stratum of mud some ten feet thick and on the basis of this confidently concluded that here was evidence of Noah's flood. He was not slow to publicize this. But why should the mud be a relic of *Noah's* flood? It has no label to say so, and other explanations are far more likely. This is a hangover of the mistake mentioned earlier, the concern to *prove* the Bible right. (Werner Keller's book, *The Bible as History,* is a thoroughgoing representative of this concern.) But the Bible is not there to be vindicated; it and its world are to be understood.

2. A better illustration of the uses of archaeology is the study of Megiddo, a vital fortress in Lower Galilee from Canaanite times to the days of the Maccabees, which has been described as the most important archaeological site in Palestine. No sensational conclusions can be drawn from here to particular biblical events, but simply trying to understand what Megiddo was like at various periods deepens our knowledge of the biblical world.

Responsible archaeologists are only too anxious to point out the limitations of their work. Its contribution is usually of this latter general and indirect kind: to bring to life past cultures and their conditions. Discoveries need to be interpreted, and there is as much room for disagreement and alternative explanations here as with any complex study. Exaggerated claims ought therefore to be treated with care. Even when new written documents are found, the chances that they relate directly to the biblical narrative are slight. But once this has been said, there is much that archaeology can do and has done.

Technological Tools

From what has been said so far, it will have become clear that the critic's most important tools are his own acuteness, sympathy, imagination and insight. Like the historian and the literary critic, he must have many of the qualities of the artist. But the scientist, too, has produced aids which he can gratefully use.

Photography has transformed the study of texts. Not only is it easy to copy precious manuscripts, but photographic techniques can make difficult manuscripts more legible and even detect what lay under erasures. The Carbon 14 Process, mentioned earlier, can date accurately the age of materials by measuring the rate of emission of the rare isotope whose name it bears. Impressive resources can be marshalled for a particular project, e.g., opening the great Copper Scroll of Qumran.

Computers can be used in problems that require analysis of statistics, as in classifying manuscripts or enumerating characteristics of style. Striking conclusions have already been published, but it should be emphasized that this kind of work is very much in its infancy, and that in any case the amount of material available for the computer to work on is often too small to be significant.

Assured Results?

All these critical activities are still being actively carried on. Of course, no individual scholar would consider that he has mastered more than a very limited aspect of them; he is conscious how much the drawing of a wider picture is a co-operative effort. Unfortunately, however, there is a problem here. When individual results are put together there are often considerable disagreements. Indeed, the first thing that strikes and dismays many students is the extent to which authorities disagree. Where two scholars differ radically in their conclusions, each producing a mass of individual facts, which is the non-specialist to choose?

First, it should be remembered that the openness of biblical scholarship, the way in which it follows the same pattern as other studies, is an important guarantee of its genuineness. There is little room for biased argument and special pleading. Biblical criticism is not a 'closed shop'. In other subjects, history, philosophy, languages, even science, similar disagreements are not uncommon. So biblical scholarship does not stand entirely apart.

Where it differs is in the importance attached to its conclusions. So much has in the past been based on the Bible that changes in understanding are felt to have very far-reaching significance. But if, as is so often the case, there is just not enough evidence to come to any definite conclusion, then living with questions is the only answer. And we shall have to get used to it.

But in that case, can we be sure of anything?

It might be misleading to single out a set of assured results and present them by saying 'of this much, at least, we may be certain'. All results are only probable, though some are more probable than others, and many 'assured results' of the past have since been overturned. The reader has to make up his mind for himself; first, perhaps, as a result of the impression made by this book. Many different writers have contributed to it, by no means all of the same background or viewpoint. Is their approach convincing? Does the book as a whole add up to the beginnings of a picture which seems capable of being developed into a coherent shape? Or is it a ramshackle assemblage of doubtful ideas with little to support them?

A good deal of tension will go out of the question 'Of what can we be sure?' once the distinction drawn earlier between 'understanding' and 'proving' has been made. The Bible bears witness to God through the whole life of a particular people and the way in which it looked at the world – and life has many aspects. Begin to see that, and a great deal will fall into place of its own accord.

BOOKS OF REFERENCE

Available in paperback

Black, M. and Rowley, H. H., eds., *Peake's Commentary on the Bible*, London: Nelson, 1962.

Brown, Raymond, Fitzmyer, Joseph and Murphy, Roland E., eds., *The Jerome Biblical Commentary*, London: Geoffrey Chapman, 1969.

Hastings, J., ed., *Dictionary of the Bible*, revised by F. C. Grant and H. H. Rowley, 2nd ed., Edinburgh: T. & T. Clark, 1963.

The Interpreter's Dictionary of the Bible, 4 vols., New York: Abingdon Press, 1962.

Laymon, Charles M., ed., *The Interpreter's One-Volume Commentary on the Bible*, London: Collins, 1971.

May, H. G., ed., *Oxford Bible Atlas*, London: Oxford University Press, 1974.

Nelson's Complete Concordance of the Revised Standard Version Bible, London: Nelson, 1957.

*Richardson, A., ed., *A Theological Wordbook of the Bible*, London: SCM Press, 1950, paperback ed., 1957.

Young, R., ed., *Analytical Concordance to the Holy Bible*, London: Lutterworth Press, 1879.

These are standard books of reference. For further suggestions see the bibliographies on the Old and New Testaments at the end of Parts III and IV, pp. 198 f., 355 f. An invaluable guide to books on the Bible currently available is published annually by SCM Press: *Religion and Theology: A Select Book Guide.*

PART TWO

The Needs of the Pupils

Children Growing Up: The Role of Religion

Ellen C. Mee

Significant and Relevant Changes in Educational Outlook in the Last Thirty Years

In 1931, when junior schools for children between the ages of seven and eleven were scarcely in being, and most of those that were had little idea of where they were going, or of the standards and scope of work possible with children of this age, the Consultative Committee on the Primary School, better known as the Hadow Committee, produced a remarkable diagnosis of the principles which should animate primary education in the years to come:

> Our main care must be to supply children between the ages of seven and eleven with what is essential to their healthy growth – physical, intellectual and moral – during that particular stage of their development. . . . Life is a process of growth in which there are specific stages, each with its own specific character and needs (*The Primary School* [1931], ch. VII, para. 75).

Then again later:

> Applying these considerations we see that the curriculum is to be thought of in terms of activity and experience rather than of knowledge to be acquired and facts to be stored. Its aim should be to develop in a child the fundamental human powers and to awaken him to the fundamental interests of civilized life as far as these powers and interests lie within the compass of childhood (*ibid.*).

This statement is all the more remarkable because at that time education, except in the better infant schools, was mainly in terms of instruction, either in conveying information or in directing childrens' activity; the class was taught as a unit, the teacher dominated the situation.

Thirty-six years later, in 1967, the Central Advisory Council for Education, the Plowden Committee, reporting in *Children and their Primary Schools*, started its review of the whole of primary education by asking whether the principles advocated by Hadow had been proved true in practice. Their answer, in the light of abundant evidence, was an unqualified affirmative:

> Is there any genuine conflict between education based on children as they are, and education thought of primarily as a preparation for the future? Has 'finding out' proved to be better than 'being told'? Have methods been worked out through which discovery can be stimulated and guided, and children develop from it a coherent body of knowledge? Has the emphasis which the Hadow Report placed on individual progress been justified by the results? . . . Do children learn more through active co-operation than by passive obedience? (*Children and their Primary Schools*, para. 6).

In its conclusion the Report says:

> The appraisal we have made of the curriculum and of the methods which have proved to be most fruitful, confirm many or most of the suggestions that our predecessors made. Their insights have been justified and refined by experience. 'Finding out' has proved to be better for children than 'being told'. Children's capacity to create in words, pictorially and through many other forms of expression, is astonishing. . . . The gloomy forebodings of the decline of knowledge which would follow progressive methods have been discredited. Our review is a report of progress and a spur to more (*ibid.* para. 1233).

In those thirty-odd years between the two reports, primary education has changed so fundamentally in practice that the majority of children's lives in school are now completely different from what they were. Moreover, the range and quality of their work still astonishes those who knew the work of children of comparable age in the old unreorganized public elementary schools. At the secondary level, the trend is towards a more integrated curriculum, more closely geared to the pupils' interests and concern with the world outside school. The cultivation of their initiative and self-responsibility as one important means of developing latent abilities has been evident in the better schools for many years; and a further push in this direction was given in *Half our Future*, the Central Advisory Council's Newsom Report of 1963.

Outside the restrictive effect of examinations, in the grammar schools, the movement towards 'liberal studies', especially in the sixth forms, and a growing awareness of the interests of boys and girls in current questions in the world at large, as well as with their own personal concerns and problems, shows the same directional trend.

These changes, whether in greater or less degree, did not happen overnight, nor were they spread evenly over all the schools simultaneously, nor over the whole of the curriculum. First art, then physical education, then reading, writing and literature, then the whole range of inquiry into the world around and afar: later mathematics, later again music and, latest of all, religious education have been affected. Compared with other aspects of the curriculum, religious education is still unsure of itself, and though individual schools and teachers are gradually finding ways of work which are helping others forward, there are many, perhaps the majority, who think that religious education, which at all points involves biblical education, is failing to achieve its object. Indeed, teachers who have heard children at the top of the junior school talking freely about their beliefs in what they have been told of the Bible and religion in general bear witness to a disconcertingly wide rejection of a great deal of what the children have been taught during their previous six years of compulsory religious instruction and daily acts of worship. This rejection, though admittedly caused in perhaps a large part by

circumstances outside the school, is by no means due to them alone. The children still show disturbing ignorance of what it is thought they had learnt, much misunderstanding and attitudes which are likely to close their minds to further development. Dr Ronald Goldman's researches confirm this, though one might want to modify some of his conclusions and remedies. Teachers also report a high degree of agnosticism and disbelief in the secondary schools. Again, although this is due in part to outside influence and to the fact that pupils of this age are rightly questioning and exploring by adopting this pose or that, they themselves complain that their religious and biblical education has not been as helpful as it might have been. It has been too repetitive, too committed, takes too little account of thinking and knowledge in other fields, is too irrelevant to the circumstances of today and especially to their personal problems.

Causes of Difficulties in Religious and Biblical Education

There are four main causes of difficulty. First, the place of the subject in school; second, the nature of the subject itself; third, the current opinions and attitudes of our times which make their impact ever more continuously, raucously and effectively through modern methods of communication; fourth, the failure hitherto to relate a child's religious education to the principles and practices which have shown such great promise in recent years. This last matter is the main theme of this section. The other three can be given only brief mention.

1. *The Place of Religious Education in the School*

Religious education alone among all subjects of the curriculum is compulsory, both as worship, fixed by statute at the opening of the school day (a law more honoured in primary schools in the breach than in the observance), and as instruction, likewise required by the 1944 Act of Parliament. Add to this the fact that, except for subjects taught for examinations in secondary schools, religious education alone derives its syllabuses from outside sources, and it is not surprising that in most schools religious education has been kept isolated, while in primary schools at least the rest of the curriculum has grown together as a web of interrelated experiences. While the ways of teaching other subjects have responded more and more to the known needs and capabilities of the pupils, religious education has been hedged about by traditional methods of teaching and regarded as somehow immune from more enlightened educational thought and practice.

2. *The Nature of the Subject*

Man's relationship with God, the ways of God to man, the complex character of the Bible which is the groundwork of the Christian faith, all these are the pursuits of a lifetime, and if understanding of them is ever achieved it can be achieved only at the end of a long pilgrimage. How to guide a child's steps here demands an insight into his nature and needs, and an awareness of our own condition and a depth of knowledge which few parents or teachers have so far achieved. In a subject at once so personal and universal, so historical and immediate, dealing with issues of which the most important are incapable of logical proof, and at their most profound can be expressed only through metaphor, myth and poetry, communication is not easy, even to one's contemporaries. Children's experience in itself is limited, their language has yet to achieve the full connotation of its terms, especially its abstract terms. Their historical sense, until adolescence, is immature. Adults, including teachers, find unprejudiced discussion difficult, so stirring are the emotions involved, and so laden with the passions, fears, hopes and arguments of past and present experiences. Then, as other sections of this book show only too clearly, the Bible demands from those who use it in the education of children of any age a degree of knowledge and understanding which is hard to come by and harder still, perhaps, to make available at the right time to one's pupils.

3. *The Present Climate of Opinion*

This theme is current and continuous. To the young, especially, it seems that we live in a world of senseless contradictions. There is material affluence side by side with starvation; high idealism contrasted with violence widely spread through every country and apparently every section of society; eighty per cent of parents wanting their children to receive compulsory religious education in school while active participation in public worship declines,

and stage, screen and newspapers spread cynicism, scepticism and ridicule on religious beliefs. Never had man so much knowledge and power for good; never, it seems, was he so concerned with power to destroy or so full of devices to escape. In an age of some of the greatest discoveries, not only of science, but of history and archaeology, it is the fashion to debunk the beliefs and faith which have sustained the discoveries. We are in the 'super-market' age of big business, big colleges, big schools and big towns in which the worth of individual contributions is easily lost, while in the automation of modern industry it is all too often, as it was in Wordsworth's day, 'the power least prized is that which thinks and feels'.

Perhaps the most devastating effect of all this on young people is to make everything seem so uncertain or so unworthwhile that they are unwilling to be committed. Yet, to those who know them well, they often seem to have an inner need to be devoted to something, to espouse openly some cause greater than themselves. In their insecurity they seize on spectacular and even violent ways of making themselves feel they are doing this. On young children the effect is felt through the attitudes and behaviour of parents and other elders, whose sins, if sins they be, of drift, over-permissiveness and worldly values cannot but be visited on those they rear.

It is indeed a hard world in which to attempt to reassert the dignity of man in his relationship with God, and this obviously cannot be done by methods which succeeded in a different age. To give help on changing the methods is one of the purposes of this book.

4. *The Failure to Relate Religious Education to Recent Principles and Practices*

Some indication of what these principles and practices are has already been given in the opening paragraphs of this article by reference to recent reports. A fuller consideration of what is involved is the heart of this section, and the following paragraphs will be devoted wholly to it.

To sum up by saying that education has become 'child-centred' rather than 'subject-centred' goes some way, but is comparatively superficial. The pupil has always been the *raison d'être* of education. How the educator acts depends upon what kind of creature he believes the pupil to be, and what kind of person he wants him to become. On this rests the nature of the process of education which the educator designs.

The current tendency to slip into the metaphors of the factory and to talk of productivity, input and output, technology and use of plant cannot, or at all costs should never, blind us to the fact that education is concerned with *persons*. Even the authority of the law endorses this. Its edict is to educate every child according to 'his age, aptitudes and abilities' and in a manner likely to contribute 'towards the spiritual, moral, mental and physical development of the community'.

Because education is concerned with persons, it puts upon the educator a responsibility which he cannot abrogate – a concern with ultimate values and a duty to impart to his pupils such 'understanding' of those values as they are capable of; an understanding of the heart as well as of the head. As Professor M. V. C. Jefferys has pointed out, 'Truth is not neutral.' The Christian teacher who follows the example of Jesus leaves no doubt as to where he himself stands, though his teaching, like that of Jesus, is something much other than dogmatic assertion, and more likely to lead in the end to the pupil finding his own answers to his questions than to his accepting blindly the dogmas of authority. The Christian teacher is concerned, moreover, with a person who is an individual of ultimate worth to God, whose nature has a spiritual and enduring quality and whose involvement is not limited by terrestrial existence either during or after life. This tremendous assumption or faith cannot but stimulate and excite those teachers who hold it, nor is it surprising that many, especially the young beginners, are daunted by the supreme challenge it offers.

Educational concern with persons and with values discloses a dilemma at the root of education in this country as contrasted with that in authoritarian regimes, and one which particularly affects religious educators. The dilemma is this: there are few of us who would not wish our children to be ultimately independent in their thinking, to arrive at and live by beliefs which are grounded in their experience and which they feel they can justify, to be able to stand alone against the herd if necessary, and to take responsibility for their actions. At the same time, we hope for such conformity with, and acceptance of, other people's ways as will promote effective co-operation with them and for the acceptance of authority necessary for communal living, an authority which will hold us on our way during the days of ignorance while we explore for ourselves, though we simultaneously stimulate the continual assessment and adjustment of that authority. We expect loyalties which may involve trust beyond knowledge or experience. We seek, in fact, a subtle balance between individual integrity, communal conformity and submission to an accepted authority. This is as true in intellectual matters as in behaviour. As educators we resist terms such as 'conditioning' and 'indoctrination', though when we look frankly we have to acknowledge that the most powerful influences on our lives are not those of which we are fully, if at all, conscious. Think, argue, reason as we will, the potency is profound of suggestion, imitation, sympathy – of attitudes acquired by empathy, of sentiments and habits. These motivate our actions, and fashion the pattern of our behaviour.

We live by admiration, hope and love;
And even as these are well and wisely fixed,
In dignity of being we ascend.

Without accepting the behaviourists' doctrines of deliberate conditioning, we do in fact condition much of a young child's growth. Without admitting 'indoctrination' as that is understood in some countries, we do in fact indoctrinate. Whenever by our own behaviour in word and deed, gesture or emotional response we communicate our hopes, pleasures, fears, faith, beliefs or sense of human relations to anyone, especially to a child who loves, admires or trusts us, we are 'conditioning' and 'indoctrinating' in ways far more powerful than by precepts.

The difference, of course, between this 'conditioning' and 'indoctrinating' and that practised elsewhere is that, prodded by the horns of our educational dilemma, we also encourage our pupils to ask questions, to challenge what we say and do, to think for themselves, discuss and 'make up their own minds'. Thus we limit, though scarcely ever eliminate, our effect on the deep springs of action during a child's early years.

This complex process of education – of nurture of semi- or unconscious, largely emotional factors in a child's nature, and of continuing and gradually increasing challenge to what we have nurtured – seems in practice to promote the development of a child's growth, and to do something to prevent that most disastrous of all conditions, which is the rootlessness of insecurity coupled with stagnation of thought and ossification of creative imagination.

It might well be true that in biblical education the balance in the dilemma described here has gone wrong. There has been much authoritarian teaching with a not uncommon suggestion that to question the Bible was wrong. There have been failures to grow roots of belief by failing to develop a community life which communicates to individuals the experiences without which they cannot understand what the Bible has to teach. There has been a tendency on the one hand to impose intellectual meaning before the children are ready for it, and to withold the facts for which they were ready and which their questions show they have need of.

The General Nature of Children's Growth

There is perhaps no idea in the educational thinking of the last thirty years which has influenced practice so fundamentally as the homely fact, stated so clearly in the Hadow Report and quoted at the beginning of this article, that children grow, that all the functionings of their bodies and minds develop. Of this development there is as yet much we do not know. We are aware that growth is prompted by urges in the mind and body of the child himself, that it proceeds by interaction between him and his environment, including the human one, that is, by the interplay of his nature and the nurture which is provided for him. From this angle, education is seen as the process of nurturing good growth of the child as a whole.

The growth of a human being is an organic, not a mechanical, process. The change of educational metaphors in recent years is significant. We 'nurture' rather than 'build', speak of 'roots' rather than of 'laying foundations', 'stimulating' and 'satisfying needs' rather than 'inculcating'. Growth implies an increase in size or amount, in range and depth, but equally an increase in complexity and inter-relatedness

and of integration. 'The process of human growth,' says Professor A. Gesell, 'is continuous. All growth is based on previous growth. The growth process, therefore, is a paradoxical mixture of creation and perpetuating. The child is always becoming something new, and yet he always summates the essence of his past. His "psyche", that is "he" at the age of five [or fifteen or fifty], is the outgrowth of all that happened to him during the past number of years after birth, and the forty weeks prior to birth. For all the past was prelude.'

In this growth, trends in development tend to repeat themselves spiral-wise at three years and at five; at two-and-a-half and six; at five to seven, and at adolescence. How a child or a young boy or girl meets the challenge of later growth might well depend on how he has been guided and helped to tackle the earlier problems. Thus in religion, as in other fields of education, we are from the beginning weaving the pattern for later living.

The Ego-Ideal

Professor Jeffreys makes the point that though in the course of his several stages the physical substance of his body may change ten times or more; and though his mental and emotional attitudes may grow and adapt, and his opinions shift with experience, there remains the continuing 'he', the personality which remains recognizably itself, whose reactions, when we know the person, we feel we can predict.

From his earliest years, a child begins to form an idea of himself, and this idea or ideal or sentiment of the self has a basic influence on his development as a person. Parents and teachers find themselves encouraging it. 'Good little boys don't do this.' 'I didn't expect this of you.' 'You are surely not that kind of person.' 'I know I can trust you.' 'Yes, Tommy *would* do that.'

The ego-ideal motivates much of our conduct throughout life. 'I just couldn't do that.' 'Well, I had to.' We create, as it were, an image or legend of ourselves and we tend to live up or down to it.

We see another aspect of this development in the early appearance of children's individual ways of coping with new situations. It is almost as if they say to themselves, 'I am safe if I sit still and no one notices me.' 'I am safe if I make a loud noise and everyone notices me.' 'I am safe if I can run back to mother.' Later, perhaps, 'I am safe if I say my prayers.' 'I am safe if I don't really care about anything.' 'I am safe because I trust in God.'

This ego-ideal and its characteristic way of meeting the world gradually becomes more self-conscious, and at adolescence it is looked at objectively and with interest. 'What kind of person am I?' is not an uncommon concern, nor is the puzzling experience of the unexpected let down of what one believed about oneself. 'I can't think what came over me.' At such times the sense of kinship with the disciple Peter might be of great help. He failed in the crisis, knew the agony of self-condemnation, yet lived to be the rock on which the church was built.

During adolescence, the interest in oneself may well lead to the realization that desired achievement in this or that direction necessitates a change or development or shift of focus in the idea of the self, and through the influence of some accepted person or some compelling purpose new self-concepts emerge and seem to beget the powers necessary to uphold them. At this point there may be increased understanding of Christ's own methods of bringing about the necessary change of heart.

The conversion of the disciples is an example of this: 'I will make you fishers of men'; and the rich man who was enjoined to sell all that he had and give to the poor; and, as some would think, the paralytic who at Christ's bidding took up his bed and walked. The links with modern psychotherapy are obvious and detract nothing from the value of biblical testimony. From the Old Testament one at once thinks of the salutary rebuke to Elijah's over-weening sense of self-importance. 'Still have I left me ten thousand prophets in Israel who have not bowed the knee to Baal.'

Growth: the Paradox of its Individual Character and its General Lawfulness

On the one hand, each human being has his own rate and quality of growth. Some develop fast, others slowly; some grow healthily and seem to fulfil each stage as it comes along, thriving and blossoming in due order. Some, at one stage or another, are weakly or frustrated. It may be that the nature of this growth and its

ultimate potential is determined by our genes at birth. If it is, we cannot ever know what this potential is, so we have every reason to proceed hopefully, nurturing each child in our care towards the best he might become.

On the other hand, because we are human we all pass through the same stages in growth, and in the same order, whether the growth is physical or intellectual, and probably also in emotional, social and religious development, too. Education-wise, it follows that the needs and capacities of a group of children of the same chronological age will vary widely over a span of five years or more of development, and so will the degree of vigour of their growth on this or that side. In biblical and religious education we have hitherto taken too little account of these differences. Religious Instruction is traditionally a class-lesson, while in other fields of education there has been a widespread growth of individual and group work; 'project' and 'centre of interest' approaches have enabled children of varying abilities to contribute according to their powers while sharing in the general sense of achievement; and ways of promoting self-education are common.

But because growth is lawful, teachers and makers of Agreed Syllabuses can be aware of the characteristics of each stage of children's development, whether it occurs early or late, and be prepared for it, so that the earlier developers are not starved of the substantial and provocative challenge which they need, nor the slower ones stultified with matter and by methods beyond their capacity for response.

These educational consequences of the nature of growth are true for all aspects of development – emotional, social, imaginative as well as intellectual.

How Religious and Biblical 'Understanding' Grows

'Understanding' is printed between quotation marks because here it means much more than intellectual understanding. It embraces the whole connotation of feelings, emotive qualities, imagination, suggestions and associations as well as the thought processes, all of which are part of 'understanding'. It is the kind of 'understanding' that begets action; the kind of knowledge that becomes virtue.

If we wish to be acquainted with how children can come to understand Christianity and the Bible we must do as we do in any other subject, ask ourselves what are the experiences they have which help them to know *at first hand* what is the meaning of those terms which express the attributes of the Christian God which the Bible portrays – such terms as love, trust, forgiveness, power, awe and wonder. Only from their own experiences of these things can they 'understand' in depth, and this understanding begins long before the intellect can articulate what is 'known'.

Children's First-hand Experiences Relevant to Religious and Biblical Understanding

Probably the most fundamental experience for a young child is that of feeling secure; of being able to trust and to trust someone who will not fail him. With the person who satisfies this need, usually his mother, a young child forms a relationship vital to his growth. With this person he experiences the first delights and satisfactions of communication and the reciprocal pleasure of mutual recognition. Equally important, within the orbit of this relationship he accepts discipline and guidance, learns to accept having to do what he cannot yet know the reasons for, nor has the strength to resist. This is his first experience of love, power and authority, within which his own personality is recognized and encouraged and his unique pattern of responses is respected. He begins to feel himself a person in relation with another person whom he gradually recognizes as different from himself, and whom, later at eight or eleven, he objectifies and views critically as he does the whole relationship. At adolescence he may pull himself clear of it: if he is fortunate, to return to it later on a new footing of equality.

It is all too clear how important the quality of this experience is for the 'understanding' of what God's love, power and authority might be, and of the stages a growing child might go through in relation to it. In religious, as in other, growth, the failure of human relationships during childhood and adolescence cannot but impair growth, and teachers have great problems to solve in attempting to make up for such failures.

This inner development of emotion and attitudes begins to happen before language is acquired. When language comes, the connotations of the most potent words in it, for example, 'love', 'trust', 'help', 'I', 'you', derive their motivating power from the early experiences which give them meaning. Later experiences, whether direct or vicarious, enlarge and deepen these original meanings, but can scarcely ever erase them.

Long before he comes to school, almost every child in this country, whether from a Christian home or not, has heard of God, Jesus, angels, and perhaps of some events in the Bible, if only because of the commercial popularity of some of the Christian festivals. Christmas cards with Christian symbols adorn the mantelpiece of the atheist and agnostic, as of the Christian. Our language is shot through with biblical metaphors; Western art in thousands of reproductions is everywhere in homes and schools. Of the Christian ceremonies of christening, marriage and funeral the most neglected child knows something, and has probably dramatized them in his play. Children, therefore, soon use words such as God, Jesus, angels and so on, and from the time when they first use them must ascribe to them some sort of meaning, however vague or inaccurate.

Children's questions and their significance in showing children's development are dealt with later in this section. It can be said here that when children begin to clarify their ideas a little as to the intellectual meaning of the terms they hear, they are likely to expect explanations in terms of action – what God does, what he is for. Just as they say, 'a chair is to sit on' and 'a nose is to blow', and 'mummy is to look after us', they take note of being told that 'God made the world' and 'God loves you'. Early on, God is invoked to explain many things: 'God did it', 'God made it'. This appears all the more frequently as parents are discovered not to be omnipotent or teachers not omniscient. But these linguistic efforts at communication and expression are weak in influence compared with the sort of experiences which have been described and from which full 'meaning' at a much deeper level will gradually animate the words which are used.

To elaborate only a little of the vast amount which could be said on this theme: to a child who is subconsciously learning what love and power are from experience with a parent or teacher, there must be a great difference in effect between being told to 'shut up because I tell you to' and, 'be quiet because you'll wake the baby' or 'disturb the rest of the class'. In the one case love and power are experienced as arbitrary authority which it is disloyal to dispute; in the other as a relationship where joint purposes are accepted and whose fulfilment is a mutual concern. The relevance of this to the interpretation of Christ's teaching is clear.

Similarly, no one who has seen the traumatic effects on children of all ages in hospitals and residential homes of their parents' failure to visit them when expected, and has seen also the gradually established confidence of the five-year-old in his first days at school when his mother never fails to meet him, or be home when he arrives, can doubt where is the source of our 'understanding' of trust and trustworthiness.

A child brought up in a family or community where 'gimme' 'gimme' is the common attitude, and reward the main motive for 'good' acts, is unlikely to think of prayer except as an expression of this kind of communication and relationship with God. Similarly again, at all ages, pupils learn only from experience the difference between involvement with an authority based on fear and one based on mutual agreement in the cause of a common purpose. Hence the importance of the school community living by and living out in practice the values embodied in the words and precepts it uses.

Many children are acquainted with suffering and death. How they meet it depends on the attitude and example of their elders. It seems that if the children trust us and we are fit to do it, we can, in fact, put some of our own strength into them, sympathetically, though without lying, to soften the pain. Most people find that children accept the inevitable facts of nature with less disturbance than they show when they are 'let down' by those whom they have trusted in. The children of a widow are often less hurt than those of a divorcée. As has been said earlier, the ways in which children in their earlier years are helped to meet the ills which beset them — whether suffering and loss at home, or seeming failure at school, will have a deep effect upon their later stability. The part that religious and biblical teaching might play here again is obvious.

Development versus Stagnation

In these matters, as in much else, it is fatal to development if the attitudes and relationships which have been described remain at an infantile level. For example, 'kiss and make it well'; 'kiss and be friends' has to pass into the deeper awareness of forgiveness which involves maturer insight, sympathy, judgment and self-awareness as well as the charity born of experience. The faith and hope rooted in semi- or unconscious experience has to become articulate enough to meet the challenge of reason, and reason itself develops the humility to endure the unresolved questions of hypotheses. The failure to nurture development on the emotional as well as the intellectual side has weakened much of our religious teaching in the past. Here again, apt use of biblical material appropriate to different ages would help. Much of Christ's own teaching seems to have been directed to promote just this kind of progress. Repeatedly he made a questioner think for himself by describing some incident which showed the issues more clearly and on a different plane. 'Who is my neighbour?' is followed by the parable of the Good Samaritan: 'Which of them,' asked Jesus, 'was neighbour?' Again, he uses an incident to raise a more fundamental issue — as concerning the woman taken in adultery: 'Let him that is without sin cast the first stone.'

In the adolescent years, when self-assertive argument and intellectual analysis are paramount, and when self-respect might well be rooted in what is conceived as intellectual honesty, it might seem that for the time being the young man or woman has lost touch with the roots of his earlier life. This in fact is rarely so. At this stage there is a great deal of self-dramatization, seeing what it feels like to 'be' this or that — atheist, high church or what have you — and passion is necessary to get the full value of the experience. But all the time the terms the adolescents use have much of the meanings they have acquired through real, or through vicarious experience. Now they must be articulated and the young man or woman feel that he is 'finding out for himself'; 'justifying his own conclusions'. Above all the educator now has to respect a fully self-aware person. 'This is my life and I have to live it.' 'I've got to decide for myself.' These attitudes themselves are the product of our education. We have worked for this stalwart independence and must be prepared to cope with it.

Before indicating some general educational suggestions something must be said about intellectual growth, though without in our minds separating it from what has been said about more powerful motivating forces.

Aspects of Intellectual Growth

Much has been written in recent years about the intellectual growth of children. As has been said earlier, the research which caused the biggest stir in religious education was that of Dr Ronald Goldman, who applied the Piaget doctrines of the nature of intellectual growth to children's religious thinking, and found from his own researches that they fitted. Young children's *thinking* about the Bible and the various bits they have heard of it, and about God, Jesus, prayers, etc., follows the same pattern as their thinking in general. It moves from the unrelated, partial, fragmented and inconsistent pre-operational stage, through the stage of 'concrete situations', where nevertheless data is classified, and generalized thinking is evident, though there is often little generalization from one field of experience to another. Such generalizations and abstractions are necessarily vague and incomplete because of inexperience and ignorance as well as because of intellectual immaturity. Gradually, at about the age of ten or eleven, the capacity to think hypothetically and deductively in a more coherent and stringent manner is achieved:

> The data of thinking now changes and situations are seen in terms of propositions which may be logically true or false and these can be tested out in thought.

Goldman adds that his researches indicated that development in religious thinking was slower than in general thinking:

> One fact must be faced from our analysis of 'operational' religious thinking. It is clear that because the forms of thought used by children are childish and immature, children's religious ideas and their concepts will also be childish and immature. We should not expect anything other than this. What is disturbing is that the childish immaturities continue so

long into adolescence. A great deal of religious thinking is propositional and can therefore only be dealt with at a formal operational level of thought, to be intellectually satisfying. If thirteen to fourteen is the mental age at which this level in religious thinking is generally achieved, a great deal of time and effort may be wasted by the *instruction* in ideas which are beyond the comprehension of the child (*italics mine*).

It does not follow that other ways of learning may be inappropriate. It is not surprising that Goldman concluded that biblical teaching in the schools attempted 'too much, too soon': a conclusion which would be now widely accepted. It is necessary to emphasize that Goldman was talking about religious *thinking*, though he points out dangers in forcing emotional and imaginative responses which may lead to misunderstandings, and he warns us of the danger of boredom consequent upon the too oft-told tale.

What Goldman did not consider in any detail was the phenomenon of children's spontaneous questions. Some forty years ago Nathan and Susan Isaacs made observations on intelligent children which led them to conclude that children's questions reveal a degree of intellectual development far in advance of that which children's answers to questionnaires would now suggest. Indeed from quite young children's 'How?', 'When?', and 'What makes it?', and 'How does it work?' and especially forms of 'Why?' questions, there would seem to be indications of an awareness of generalizations and of observed inconsistencies – indeed indications of the beginnings at least of most of the *modes* of later thinking.

A study of children's questions about biblical matters is highly indicative of their state of mind. I owe most of what follows to a small group of teachers with whom I worked at the Institute of Education in London. They collected the questions which children of seven to eleven asked spontaneously, and some four hundred children from seven different schools were involved. Though without the validity of planned statistical research, the tentative indications of the findings might spur other teachers to make a similar inquiry for themselves which might throw some light on the selection and handling of biblical material. At all stages in the junior schools there seems to be an interest sufficiently great to stimulate sensible and pointed questioning. It is doubtful whether these children would have asked as many or as searching questions on any other subject in the curriculum. This might be due to the fact that religious instruction occurs daily and that the stories are generally told with a greater sense of importance and personal involvement than attaches to other subjects. There would appear to be at this stage very little boredom; and when sixth-formers remember the primary school religious instruction as boring one wonders if they have not read into it the boredom of the secondary school's repetition of primary work.

But there is plenty of evidence of unsatisfied doubt and inquiry. The same questions are asked again and again though the emphasis changes; and at ten and eleven and in the early secondary stage, as other inquiries show, a new type of question becomes insistent. The younger juniors' first concern seems to be to get the concrete, material and physical 'facts' straight in terms of their own lives. 'Was Jesus rich?' 'When did he come?' 'How long did he live?' 'Had Jesus any sisters and brothers?' 'Are angels souls of dead people?' 'Who wrote the Bible?' This last was asked by a seven-year-old. There are many questions about Jesus' physical appearance. 'Was he good at school?' 'Did he read the Bible?' The same sort of factual questions are asked about the Old Testament.

There were also many questions about how certain things happen – especially things that seem magical. 'How much magic did Jesus do?' But the idea of magic is by no means always present. A great many questions are directed at discovering how things were made or done. They are part of the general type of question, 'How do you do it?', and 'facts' are related. 'Who made God if he created everybody?' 'Can we cure the blind?' 'Is it true that Jesus rose from the dead?'

At seven and eight especially, children feel a strong need to sort out fact and fantasy. They can in their own way deal with both, but it is important for them to know which world they are in. They are also capable of appreciating the state of mind expressed in, 'We don't know as yet . . .' 'People are trying to find out and understand . . .' In religion as in science it is not too young at seven and eight to appreciate our ignorance and to begin to share the excitement of gradually getting to know more by experi-ence, thinking or finding out from books and from other people.

There is also already a human interest in motive. 'Why did God make the world?' 'Why did a disciple let Jesus down?' – part, surely, of the predominantly human and dramatic interest of this age. 'When' occurs often, probably because from seven onwards the children are emerging from the 'once upon a time' and 'long, long ago' stage and are realizing that there is some sort of sequence in the past. Here, perhaps, much more might be done to help children towards a chronological order of 'illuminated patches' of biblical history as it is in the teaching of other history.

The great interest in the Bible and its writers, its truth or otherwise, continues strongly all through and suggests that we should offer, much earlier than we do, more information on these matters, especially in answer to the questions, and if only in an incidental and informal way. To fail to give the information when it is so manifestly asked for probably accounts for much of the ignorant rejection of biblical teaching later.

On the whole, the children's intention in the early junior stage seems to be to sort out the information and stories they have heard and to fill in the gaps they sense in their understanding. They are clearly trying to interpret the stories in the light of their current experience. The gaps or inconsistencies they are aware of arise from the comparison of their own lives with those in biblical narratives, and not often from the bringing together of knowledge from different fields of learning. Generally the questions ask for a straight answer on a level and in words the child can understand, and at this stage most of the children seem willing to accept the teacher's authority.

But the older juniors, while pursuing 'facts' to get their pictures clear, probe more deeply and more widely. 'Is Buddha also a God?' 'Need we have churches when we can worship in our own homes?' But the most characteristic change is that they are bringing together their learning from many different fields and relating them so that apparent inconsistencies emerge. 'How could Jesus ascend when we have gravity?' Questions about God being in more than one place now become frequent. The dilemma of a good God and the existence of evil, war, suffering, death and the devil emerges strongly. 'Why did God make us if we are going to die?' 'Everybody says God wants peace, then why do we have war?' 'Why can't God make another world?' Quite as important is the emergence of the 'How do you know?' and 'On what evidence?' kind of question. The mere assertion by the teacher is not enough. Some of these questions are adult in form and in sense. 'How do you know there is a God?' 'How do we know that Jesus is the Son of God?' 'How do we know that there is a Holy Ghost?'

Even the most modest examination of children's questions shows that children themselves have by no means come to conclusions they sometimes seem to accept. They realize the gaps and inconsistencies in their knowledge and they want, and know they need, an explanation. It is significant that there is very little suggestion of magic or infantile fixations in the questions children ask as contrasted with the answers demanded of them in response to questions. For example, how could they be expected to explain, unaided, the parting of the Red Sea except by some magic if *explanation is demanded of them*? But in actual practice they know it needs some explanation, and they ask the question. Whether as a result they will think in terms of magic depends upon the answer they get. There is plenty of evidence of lively thought; there is at this stage a willingness and eagerness to try to understand. Both intellectually and sympathetically children are trying to enter the grown-up world. If the questions are ignored, a child becomes blasé; if they are answered in a way which offends his emerging powers of consistent and objective thinking, then rejection and scorn are not unlikely consequences, especially considering the influence of many homes.

Coupled with these considerations in the teacher's mind there must also be the awareness of primary and of many secondary pupils' inability to deal adequately with abstract generalizations on an intellectual plane. Yet such pupils may understand much through sympathy and express their understanding in ways other than in words, as is shown by the visual art created by pupils of all ages and by their own original mime and drama. A class of ten-year-olds who would have found it hard to express in prose – though perhaps they could have done much more in poetry – the meaning of the Prodigal Son left no doubt at all of their deep insight into the feelings of the characters when the whole class mimed the story. Of course the parable itself, like every worthwhile work of art, has a deeper meaning in every way as the experience grows with which to interpret it.

The Adolescent Stage

It has already been pointed out that at adolescence the desire to feel and be oneself – often to know oneself – especially through independent actions, dominates the personality. The pupils tend to fix their sights on the world outside school. Their relationships with parents and other elders are often disrupted. They rush towards what they think is freedom, but often with a daunting sense of insecurity. The questions of adolescents are therefore largely questions related directly or obliquely to their own condition of feeling, action and thought. In thought they seek logical reasons and evidence; they examine biblical material and religious thought and example to find whether it is relevant to their own problems. Under all the questioning, some of it seemingly arrogant, some sincere, even pathetic in the ill-preparedness it reveals, there is often a desire to find help and companionship of a kind that does not detract from the sensitive ego of emerging manhood and womanhood: a foothold in the shifting sands of the rather frightening uncertainty of as yet unknit adulthood.

Two examples of typical adolescent questioning can be given in their context. One is from a class of twelve-to-thirteen-year-olds during one of a series of lessons on the problems of the early church compared with those of today. Very quickly the boys and girls turned the discussion by questions about the problem of exclusiveness of small groups and the problems of others getting in or being kept out.

The boys began talking about the difficulty of accepting others with different standards, e.g., in games. Gradually 'colour' came in, and the boys talked very freely of their own experiences. One had been ducked and daubed black because he played with West Indians. Others said they got on all right, but their parents objected and 'pulled them out'. Some boys were obviously distressed by the situation and torn between what, under the school's influence, they would think right, and their parents' antagonism. This was a difficult situation for the young teacher, who made a brave effort to help the boys to see why, perhaps, the adults were less tolerant than they were, and to support the boys' more charitable outlook. Many questions were asked by the pupils of each other as well as of the teacher, 'What should I do?' It was interesting that more than once the consideration below the intellectual level of the discussion was, 'How would I feel if I was in that position?' Only towards the end, and then with great effect, did the teacher bring into the discussion a reminder of the exclusiveness of the Pharisees and Christ's attitude towards it and mention the good Samaritan.

The second example is from the discussion following a schools' broadcast from the British Broadcasting Corporation to sixth forms (*Religion in its Contemporary Context*) on *The Quest*. Through speakers of standing and extracts from literature, the question was raised as to whether human existence is

> a hopeless experience in which all struggle and endeavour is ultimately futile. Or, on the other hand, can a man travel hopefully, confident that he will arrive at a final goal? . . . Is it worth while to become involved in the enormous problems and the life-long conflicts of a rapidly changing society, to join a political party, to keep sharpened the edge of one's social conscience, to take a stand for justice and generosity, or is it more realistic to contract out and let the world go hang? There is a philosophical and religious way of posing the question: has a man's life on this minor planet a meaning which will bestow upon him a sense of purpose, or is a man's life, as the philosopher Thomas Hobbes remarked, 'nasty, brutish and short'? In a word, is there a Quest to be accomplished? (From the pupils' pamphlet accompanying the Autumn 1967 series.)

In boys' and girls' schools alike pupils' questions showed their concern, implied if not always openly disclosed, with their personal problems, especially with their concept of themselves as persons and their standing in regard to other persons. 'What is opting out, anyway?' 'What do you opt out of?' 'Society? conventionality?' 'Where does one draw the line if one breaks with society?' 'Do Hippies opt out?' It is not difficult to see here the seeking for some

guiding principle, or that appropriate biblical teaching might contribute much.

Suggestions to Those Who Teach the Bible

1. Since many children's growth in understanding biblical stories is warped by their ignorance about the nature of the Bible, in which they are interested as early as the lower junior school, steps should be taken in appropriate ways to relieve that ignorance, especially in response to the children's questions at whatever stage they are asked. The point at which some systematic teaching should be introduced is a matter for discussion, but experience would seem to point to the end of the junior school at the latest. (For the nature of the Bible see Part I, Section 1, pp. 3 ff.).

2. The message the Bible has to give is acceptable to boys and girls only in so far as its relevance to them and the affairs of their world is clear. Over recent years, in good religious education, this has meant a shift of emphasis and of starting-point. The change as it affected religious broadcasting to schools was described in the evidence submitted by the School Broadcasting Council in 1968 to the Church of England Commission on Religious Education in Schools. The change was brought about by years of experience of preparing broadcasts on the Bible and religious knowledge for children of eight up to the sixth form, and on the continuous feedback of evidence from the schools about their response and their needs. The finding corresponds closely to developments in religious education led by pioneer teachers in the schools themselves. It points out that the shift of emphasis and of starting-point from the academic subject to concern with those who are being educated is clear. With that, the producers have attempted to give the pupils information in the form in which they can understand it and at a time when they need it and can see its relevance. Instead of the once prevailing traditional and historic approaches, methods of presentation have developed which start with the experiences of the pupils themselves in the world they know. The satisfaction of the needs of the learner has come to matter more than the systematic coherence of a subject. Meanwhile, the whole scope of religious education broadcasts has widened so that in the programmes directed to older pupils especially, open-ended dis-

cussion is provoked, and many facets of opinion and experience bearing on religion are presented. Religious experiences other than those of Christians are included. The aim can be clearly seen to be communication of experience through many channels of art, literature and music as well as through information and argument. The hope is that in this way the growing boys and girls will find some stabilizing core of belief. The authoritarian attitude of the lecturer has given way to that of a more experienced, but still a fellow seeker on a pilgrimage to which, at best, young and old might be jointly committed. There is no patronage nor assumed omniscience, but a willingness on the part of those who have lived longer to disclose sincerely and frankly the beliefs, faith and hopes that living has so far enabled them to achieve. Though these sentences make no specific reference to 'teaching the Bible', what is said certainly included reference to it and is wholly applicable to it.

3. If the pupils' own experiences are to be the starting-point, it follows that biblical teaching cannot be limited to the religious instruction period. It has been shown that the most direct source of such knowledge as we have of the attributes of God is our experience of love, trust, authority and power in our lives – especially our younger lives – in everyday living.

The teaching of the Bible on the majesty of God will be influenced strongly for good or ill by how science and nature study are taught. If this teaching produces an attitude of mind in which a boy or girl feels that everything is 'explained' by experiment, or in which a pupil loses his sense of wonder in superficial explanation, the heavens will lose their power to declare the glory of God, and the divine concern in the fall of a sparrow or the beauty of lilies of the field will seem quite unimportant.

It is perhaps a pity that when the theory of evolution is propounded as an explanation of man's existence, the miracle of man's capacity to invent and apprehend that hypothesis is not realized as greater than the 'fact' of evolution itself. And whence this capacity if not from some relation with the Creator?

Art in all its forms, both as expressive of biblical events and people and as the children's own expression of their 'understanding', has a large part to play. But biblical illustration can be misleading and lead to an unfortunate fixation of ideas. Children's own pictures, models and mime are invaluable to them as expressions of what they 'understand' but cannot yet express in words. A study of children's imaginative expression, if it is truly their own and not copied, gives to a sensitive teacher a helpful insight into their state of mind.

It is unfortunate that biblical history and geography are so rarely brought into relation with other history and geography. Even at a time when disputes between Israel and the Arab countries are regularly in the headlines, very few children know that this concerns the land of the Crusades, of Jesus, of David and the rest. Moreover, wherever discussion of human motives arises, in history, geography or, especially, in literature, it would seem natural and sensible for the Bible to make its contribution. Only thus will it be woven into the stuff of learning.

4. The same consideration of children's different individual rates and quality of growth, and of the generally shared stages of it, will have to be considered in religious education as elsewhere.

5. As in other subjects, pupils of all ages need the opportunity to give their own form and expression to what they have learnt. In religious education, this will involve more than art, music, drama and writing. It will mean, also, expression in acts which are the fruits of the children's growing sense of involvement in Christian living. For this reason many schools give opportunities of service of different kinds.

6. All that has been said in this article emphasizes the need for sincerity in those who teach. Though it is all to the good that the Bible should be divested of the muffling wrappings of 'holiness' which prevent the proper appreciation of it, it is nevertheless the most remarkable storehouse of the experience of a people in their relationship with God. The teacher inevitably proclaims by his attitude to it the respect in which he holds it, and whether or not his pupils are influenced in their attitude will depend upon the effect they see it has on his life and behaviour. Only if in these ways they come to think the Bible is important and relevant to living will they really take trouble to know and understand it.

2

The Art of Communication

Alan T. Dale

The very position of this article is significant. It lies between Part I where we meet first Christian scholars dealing with the Bible and the methods used in studying it, and then in Part II children and young people in the classroom with their liveliness, courage and compassion (many of them no readers, and most of them out of touch with the Christian community), and Parts III and IV, by far the longest part of this *Source Book*, summarizing what is known about the remarkable and wide-ranging literature of the Bible. A teacher might be forgiven for feeling somewhat like Christian in *Pilgrim's Progress:* 'Then did Christian begin to be afraid, and to cast in his mind whether to go back, or to stand his ground.' 'How can we communicate all this to children and young people in any meaningful way?', the teacher asks, 'and why?' His perplexity grows when he remembers that we are dealing in this *Source Book* with only part of what he will find in any Agreed Syllabus.

It *can* be communicated, and there are genuine reasons why we should try to communicate it. But if we are to tackle effectively so intimidating a task, we must be far bolder and much more radical than we have been in answering the teacher's next questions: 'What in the Bible must I try to deal with?' and 'How am I to go about it?'.

These questions can finally be answered only in the classroom itself. 'Communication' does not take place in a vacuum. It happens (or does not happen) between *this* teacher and *these* children or young people in *this* classroom situation.

We must begin with these issues – though we cannot deal with them in detail – for we are not generalizing about an abstract theory but dealing with an urgent situation which every teacher faces in the classroom. We who teach know that, in this matter of the Bible, communication in the classroom has in many cases broken down or, rather, has not yet been achieved, for the task that began to be attempted after 1944 is one that had never really been attempted before. If we listen – really listen – to young people talking in the classroom or read about what they say in research reports, all we can say is 'What have we been doing? They haven't a clue!'

The Assignment

1. *What Sort of Help?*

Let us begin with the children and young people, ordinary young people – particularly those dealt with in *Half our Future* – with important abilities and important limitations. We want to help them to discover the Bible for themselves, not just to 'know about it', so that it means something to them personally as children or young people; and we want to help them to take their first steps towards mature religious understanding and to be able, when the time comes, to make up their own minds about religious questions as these face them in the context of their own society: to be able to say 'Yes' or 'No' for the right reasons.

It is important to emphasize the words we have just used: *discover for themselves*. There is more truth than we often care to admit in the dictum, 'You only really learn what you discover for yourself.' There is no such thing as a second-hand conviction or belief; it must be one's own. Children and young people are not really learning if all they are doing is repeating what we have told them; that way lies later scepticism or obscurantism. The question is not just, 'How can we help our pupils to grasp what the Bible is about?' (important though this question is), but, 'How can we deal with the Bible in the classroom (in Edwin Cox's words) "to help our pupils to have a religious view of life and to make up their own minds on religious questions"?' Our only justification for dealing with the Bible at all in the classroom falls within this prescription. And this is surely what the Bible itself is about.

2. *The Bible as a Record of Experience*

It is of vital importance to be clear what we are trying to do with the Bible in the classroom. In the past we have tried to tackle far too much; the 'simplification', forced on us by the school timetable and the attitudes, background, abilities and needs of the young people themselves has made us 'bitty' and often trivial in our handling of it. Was this because we did not know what we were supposed to be doing and had no 'clue' in our hands?

The importance of the Bible arises from our Christian conviction that God reveals himself to us *through human experience*; most significantly through the experience of the Hebrew and Jewish people, through the whole 'witness' of Jesus, and through the experience of those who have taken Jesus seriously. The Bible is the record of these experiences and the events to which they were a response, and to come to grips with it is to learn what 'religious conviction' (and in particular 'Christian conviction') really means. The Bible is not a report of ready-made conclusions ('Take it or leave it'), but a record of workable convictions and how they came to be held ('Doesn't this make sense to you?'). We cannot therefore by-pass it or treat it other than seriously. If this is so, we must go on as teachers to ask ourselves, 'What does an ordinary person (like the parents of our pupils and therefore the young people themselves) need to know about the Bible if he is to say "Yes" or "No" for the right reasons to the Christian way of life here and now in the twentieth century?'

Let us pause to remember two things. First, young people are seriously interested in religious questions – all the evidence points to this; but they dismiss both the Bible and the Christian community as, to quote one of them, 'a lot of rubbish'. We have to help them to discover that, whatever else it is, it is not rubbish. Secondly, we are asking of them a reading of the Bible which even adult Christians have largely ceased to undertake for themselves. We must therefore set our sights properly. We must go for *the heart of the Bible* in such a way that it captures the imagination of young people as a living and relevant book *for them,* engaged with the very questions that matter to them – as their spirit of protest shows.

The Heart of the Bible

What, then, is the heart of the Bible?

The Bible is not a textbook but a source book (our practice often assumes the former), and at its heart is a story, a genuine story about a small highland people at the mercy of powerful empires (the Old Testament), and a small scattered community at the beginning of our era whose central convictions centred on the execution of a young man (the New Testament). It is the story of people learning the hard way what our rough human experience is about and what are the things by which men really live. It is fundamentally the discovery of what love (*agape*) means, not as a sentimental attitude, but as the final nature of all relationships. It takes everything in its stride, brutality and compassion, the littleness and the greatness of ordinary men and women – it baulks nothing. It is only when we read the story closely, with the same searching concern that the outstanding people in the story themselves showed and check it up with our own experience, that we begin to understand that this is the way God revealed himself, and still reveals himself, to us, so that what becomes important to us in the story is not so much what man is doing as what God is doing.

Our business, then, is not 'to cover as much of the syllabus as possible' but to explore, as far as we can and in whatever ways we can, the story itself, so that our pupils can develop the proper attitude to it all – an attitude that may live with them.

Let us, then, set out the stages in which this exploration can be carried through, stages which can be worked out in different ways by different teachers in the light of what they know about their pupils and themselves:

1. We can begin with what I have called 'the sweep of the story' – *the real story about real people,* as real as the people of small nations in our world struggling against more powerful neighbours. It is no fairy-tale, as most of our pupils suppose it. In the Old Testament it is the rough and brutal story of a small people crushed between giant states: their escape from Egypt, the march across the desert, the capture of the highlands, the making of the nation, their political collapse and dramatic survival. In the New Testament it is the story of a young man executed on Good Friday afternoon and of what happened to his friends afterwards. What convictions the people involved in the story held they won the hard way; we shall not understand them unless we know something of what they went through. They are real convictions, something you can live by, not abstract speculations about God and Man. They held them because it was the only way they could make sense of their disastrous experience and go on living as free men. So let us first get clear the story they had to explain.

2. We can then look more closely at *the people in the story* and put them squarely in the actual world in which they lived. The young people we are dealing with can grasp more about Moses than the 'bulrushes' story, more about David than the 'Goliath' story (though this sort of thing seems often enough all that they can remember), more about Jesus than that he was some sort of magician or (in the words of one of them) 'just a very clever man who came on earth before his time', and more about Paul than that he went on three journeys, 'but nobody knows why'. Here are real people, facing real situations, asking real questions, and holding real convictions. And in talking about them, we must discuss the varied evidence on which their stories rest, whether first-hand report, tribal tradition or folk-tale. The young people ought to know something of the rigorous historical examination the biblical material has been put to. We cannot say (or assume), 'It is in the Bible', as though this was enough.

3. We can then look at *their convictions* (which we shall have already touched upon in telling their stories), for by now we hope to have stimulated our pupils' desire to go deeper. Without this seriousness nobody else's convictions can matter to us at all. Real situations demand real answers; is it because our pupils have never felt the situations of the Bible as real ones that they dismiss it so easily as fairy-tale? And we can go further still to see that the story of the Bible as a whole presents a profound understanding of our human situation. Here we come to grips with our essential work, helping young people to think and live religiously, and to realize that Christian life and thought, rooted in the Bible, is no idle dreaming but a living way of dealing with living questions. It is far from the irritating 'Don't do this!', which many of them think it is.

The Approach

If communication, where the Bible is concerned, is to have any chance of happening in the classroom with ordinary young people, we must face boldly three questions – those of language, comprehension and methods.

1. *Language*

This is our first high hurdle. Nothing really comes home to us if we are dealing with it in what, to us, is strange and unmanageable language; if, as one boy once said to me, 'The Bible's full of hard words.' Our pupils can tackle hard words, as a brief conversation with a youngster about his hobby will teach us, if they are first convinced that the whole venture means something to them here and now, something they enjoy. But they usually tackle the Bible in the classroom in adult translations – not always the most recent – and translations of the whole text at that. But if the Bible is to be a vital and inescapable story for them, they must be able to read it and explore it – and they must hear it discussed – in language they can readily follow.

I am often surprised by the words which teachers report as having caused difficulty in the classroom and hindered understanding and communication: words like 'sabbath', 'synagogue', 'Pharisees', 'Sadducees', to quote a few from the Gospels.

We must remember how important first impressions and first readings are, and how easily misunderstandings can arise. In due time, of course, if real interest is aroused we must go on to the proper words and the full text, as young people do where their serious interests are concerned. But hard words to begin with may quickly make them feel that the Bible is not for them. However inadequate in the long run, why not, for example, for the four words above, say simply 'holy day of the Jews', 'meeting house', 'religious leaders', 'rich politicians'? If we insist on stopping to explain 'hard words', especially with pupils who have trouble with reading anyway, we lose both the heart and sweep of the story and ourselves in what seem to them to be remote and meaningless details. 'It's just a queer story and it's got nothing to do with me.' Yet the bulk of the Bible was spoken or written for ordinary people (books about the Bible sometimes seem to belie this): the farmer in Shechem and the shop-keeper in Corinth. The very Greek of the New Testament was substantially the spoken language of the Mediterranean world. If the Bible is dealing with what is of enduring importance to ordinary people – everybody, everywhere – and not just to the scholar at his desk, the heart of it can and must be put into the language of ordinary people, even the limited vocabulary of young people.

Only if the Bible, as a book to be read, is open to be explored in their own language (the kind of book you can take home to read), will the young people begin to take seriously the specialized words of religious experience and see why we need to use them: words like 'repentance', 'faith', 'church', 'baptism', 'sin', 'salvation'. All these words deal with experiences that have their beginning in our relationships with one another: the first two, for instance, in 'being sorry' and 'trusting people'. The richness of these words cannot just be flung at people.

To ignore this question of language is to ask for misunderstanding and a sense of meaninglessness: 'Oh, it's something we do at school.'

2. *Comprehension*

Concern for simple language is not enough. If the range of biblical material is to be dealt with properly in the classroom, and pupils are to explore it for themselves, we must do something about the sheer bulk of it: 1300 pages in my copy, covering over a thousand years of history. Is any other school-book this size?

The Bible, as we have said, is a source book, and a source book can be explored in many ways. It brings us, in a peculiarly vivid way,

into touch with people like ourselves: asking questions, trying to make sense of our unpredictable human experience, holding testable convictions. In the Old Testament they were asking the very questions we ask today: 'What do you mean by "religion"?' 'Is there good religion and bad religion, and how do you tell the difference?' 'Does religion – even good religion – matter anyhow, and, if so, how?' Here are enduring convictions: God's presence and care, his purposes for mankind, what living in his way really means; and unanswered questions: 'Why suffering?' 'Is there a life beyond death?' 'My nation or the world?' In the New Testament we find what John Macmurray called 'The clue to history', in the whole witness of Jesus and the enlarging experience of his friends.

We who are the teachers need to be master of the whole of this story; we need to read it until, in G. M. Young's words, 'you can hear people talking'. But how are young people to begin to comprehend it?

It is essential that they approach it in their own way and go their own pace. We may summarize their needs, already more than hinted at, as these. First, they need to get the feel that it is a real story about real people. Secondly, they need help in order to explore, not the whole of the story, but the heart of it. Thirdly, they need to be helped to read it so that it captures their imagination. Fourthly, they need to be helped to see the centrality of Jesus, that he is the 'clue' not only to the Bible but to the whole human story and not least to our twentieth-century chapters of it.

In giving this help, we need to use what has been called 'the indirect approach to the Bible'. History is rather cavalierly dismissed today by young people: 'How can what happened so long ago mean anything today?' But if young people dismiss history, they are intensely concerned with moral questions. Let us begin there, then, with some issue or incident or debate in which they feel involved and move into the relevant theme or story of the Bible – not because it is in the Bible but because it is relevant. From these discussions, a more planned treatment of the Bible – what kind of book it is, its people and its themes – can be undertaken; but they will arise as answers to questions rather than as something in the school curriculum.

In answering these questions we should use the insights of modern scholarship much more boldly than we do, both its detailed analysis of the documents and its clarification of the great argument of the Bible. This makes hard work for the conscientious teacher, for books of the kind we need are all too few. But it is worthwhile.

In all this, let us remember that it is not our adult version that matters now. We must look at the Bible through young people's eyes and help them to explore it in their own way, asking their own questions and dealing with it in terms of their own needs. They don't need a digest of an adult account of the Bible – though they need the guidance of adult insights; they need to read it as *their* story. They can do it.

3. *Methods*

In handling the Bible in the classroom and approaching it at the pace of the young people themselves, we are free to use all the methods we use in the teaching of other subjects, but especially those we use in the teaching of history and literature. Our aim is to awaken the imagination of children and young people, to elicit their own responses and to help them to see the meaning of their responses. When they need information we are there to help them to find it, either by their own inquiry or by giving it to them ourselves. What we are seeking is not their acquisition of a body of knowledge as such, but their growth in critical awareness, which indoctrination can do without, but religious understanding never.

Here are a few notes – the lively teacher will not want more.

Our pupils should hear the story read aloud to them more often than they do. Let the stories make their own appeal to them; they have a dramatic quality and speak more directly to the imagination than any summary account. We want our pupils to get the flavour of the biblical writing, to realize how readable it is ('Can I take it home to read myself, sir?') and to catch something of the sweep of the story. In preparing stories for reading aloud (and they need to be prepared), we can make bold use of the information in the commentaries; we shall sometimes need to abbreviate (especially the speeches) and to make such alterations as make for continuous reading; and we shall use present-day translations. Some possibilities are:

in the Old Testament: the stories of Moses (following the 'J' narrative: see Part III, Section 3, pp. 87 ff.); of David (following the early source of the books of Samuel: see Part III, Section 8, pp. 121 ff.); of Elijah and Ahab (I Kings 19–22); the fall of Jerusalem (II Kings 24.8–25.12); the diary of Nehemiah. In the New Testament: the passion narrative (Mark 14–15); the meeting of Peter and Captain Cornelius (Acts 10.1–11.18); Paul's years in the Aegean cities (Acts 16.6–20.36); Paul's trials in Palestine (Acts 21.1–26.32).

These stories lend themselves to a more dramatic treatment where pupils can take the parts of the various characters in the story, with a reader to read the linking narrative. The whole reading should be discussed and planned beforehand (this is a real teaching situation). The tape-recorder is a useful tool here; teacher and pupils can listen together. Such presentations should lead on to creative work by the pupils; they are not an end in themselves. Then all this work can lead on to appropriate discussion, however simple or limited, where real questions can come out and the meaning of the stories for the pupils themselves be made clear.

As background to all such work, there should be good pictures and photographs on the walls; one good photograph is worth all the pious representations that so often disfigure our rooms. Remember that with modern photographs you must allow for the changes in the landscape that have taken place in the last two thousand years; for instance, in Galilee, which was wooded in Jesus's time. There are good film strips, but many bad ones; choose the factual ones, not those which try to do the pupils' work for them.

One important matter still needs to be mentioned: the poetry of the Bible. It is, when we come to think of it, amazing how much of the Bible is poetry – the words of the prophets, the hymns of the Psalms, the book of Job, the parables and poetry of Jesus; and I would add, though they are in prose, the Gospel of John (the first great comprehensive, imaginative presentation of the Christian faith) and The Revelation to John. Here we need to learn from the important developments that have been made in the teaching of poetry to children and young people. For poetry – whether in the Bible or out of it – can only be approached as poetry. How often we have turned it into dull and uninteresting prose, and destroyed it! I have known the dancing of the parables of Jesus lead to most illuminating questions and discussion – nearer to the truth of the parables than the kind of moralizing they so often get. What I would plead for here is simply that we should deal with the poetry of the Bible, aware of its central significance, as we deal with poetry elsewhere in the school.

For this raises again the most important aspect of dealing with the Bible in the classroom: it must capture the imagination of all in the room, teacher and pupil alike. It was the imaginative grasp, by all sorts of people in all sorts of ways, of the exodus story and the covenant that sustained the people of the Old Testament in their brutal experiences and made them into an enduring community. It was a similar imaginative grasp of the whole story

of Jesus, what he was, what he did and what he said, which is made clear in the passion narrative, that set his friends free from superstition and bigotry, and helped them to be critically aware of the questionable assumptions of their world and to begin to see what he meant when he talked about 'the kingdom of God' and said to ordinary men and women 'Follow me!'. In handling the Bible in the classroom we might do much less that we might do much more. Only so shall we help young people to see that this story is the clue to the twentieth century as to the first.

All we do in the classroom is 'the preparation of the Gospel'. But is not this the approach of Jesus himself, 'the most famous teacher of the Western world'? Our task is to help young people to take the first steps in the understanding of the Bible along the right road; they will walk the rest of the road by themselves.

3

The Bible in the Classroom

The Infant School · *Violet Madge*

Children's Experiences and Biblical Truth

Within the Bible itself there is guidance relevant to the education of young children. For instance, the saying of Jesus that there is 'First the blade, then the ear and then the full corn in the ear' (Mark 4.28 AV) is a reminder that full fruition is dependent upon previous phases of growth. This truth, generally accepted in other spheres of primary education, has now been endorsed by inquiries into the effectiveness of the use of the Bible in education, which have indicated that ultimate understanding may be thwarted by premature forcing. Indeed, the main concern of the teacher, with regard to introducing the Bible to young children, would seem to be that of nurturing the roots of later understanding. At the same time, the insistence of Jesus that men should become as little children if they would enter the kingdom of

God (Mark 10.15) reveals his awareness that young children by reason of their very naivety are nearer to the heart of things than their elders. They are, for example, '. . . nearer to mystery and awe, nearer to trust and dependence, nearer to hope and to the need for love' (Violet Bruce and Joan Tooke, *Lord of the Dance*, pp. ix f.).

The manner in which Jesus helped men to answer their own queries through opening their eyes to the significance of commonplace affairs is also relevant to biblical education. To Jesus, seemingly insignificant events, as the death of a sparrow, or a woman putting leaven into a lump of dough to make bread, might offer an indication of the nature of the kingdom of God. Young children, too, are alert to the smallest happenings and spontaneously through question, exploration and experiment seek for meaning in their often minute discoveries.

Anyone who has kept company with a young child will bear witness to this characteristic, provided that they have suited their steps to the steps of the child and observed and talked about the things the child noticed. Seeking truth by reflection on personal experience is, then, fundamental to biblical education. It follows that young children's first-hand discoveries of the world, themselves and other people are the roots of later appreciation of the Bible as a record of a people's search for meaning in their lives and their perception of God's presence within this experience.

At-one-ness

Part of human experience, on which the Bible is a commentary, is man's inner striving towards at-one-ness. On entering school, children are at the beginning of this striving and are coping with, as yet, not understood impulses. This fact was unusually expressed by the seven-year-old girl who lamented: 'I know what I ought to do but I don't know how to want to do it.' The inner conflict which prompted this child's statement tallied with the predicament of Paul who confessed in a letter: 'For I do not do the good I want, but the evil I do not want is what I do' (Rom.7.19). Although it is rare for young children to communicate their inner uneasiness in so direct a fashion, they do express their strivings in other ways appropriate to their phase of development and individuality. One example is the manner in which they attempt to come to terms with conflicts by working over their impressions through imitation and fantasy. This happened when a few six-year-olds, having made witch puppets, told a story to their teacher which revealed their awareness of the power of aggressive impulses:

> There were two witches
> They met three children
> They put a spell on the children and turned
>   them into monsters
> The children did not like being monsters
> They banged their heads together and
>   punched each other
> They began to dance with rage
> And suddenly they were children again
> They chased the witches and drove them
>   away.

Other creative activities by which the young attempt to unify and interpret experience include modelling, pattern and picture-making. Since the most profound religious truths may remain incommunicable, except through the emotional language of the arts, encouragement of young children's natural inclination to express themselves through these channels is an essential basis of biblical education. Indeed, to participate in creative activity is to know God, in part, and will pave the way for a more genuine appreciation of such biblical declarations as: 'O Lord, how manifold are thy works: in wisdom hast thou made them all' (Ps. 104.24 AV).

The Response to Mystery

That the mystery of creation may be a concern of young children was revealed in a conversation among six-year-olds modelling with clay. They were overheard to say:

> *Alan*   Who made God, then?
> *Gareth*   No one, he was there all the time.
> *Paul*   He must be old.
> *Shaun*   God's everywhere.
> *Alan*   Don't be daft, he can't be that big.
> *Howard*   Did God make the men of clay like
>   we did?
> *Alan*   Well, if he did he must have had a lot
>   of clay.
> *Mark*   Why didn't he make any children?
> *Deborah*   'Cos the man and the woman
>   wasn't married then.

This conversation is illuminating since it illustrates not only the questing spirit of young children but also the way in which their intellectual development and limited experience affect their attempts to interpret the mysteries which confront them.

Since the Bible is very much concerned with men's response to mystery, a sympathetic attitude to children's verbal queries must precede and accompany any introduction to its content. This may sometimes mean using the practice of Jesus in turning back the question on the inquirer that we may discover the mode of his thinking before sharing our interpretation. It may mean setting the child in the way of finding sources of further enlightenment for himself. It may mean confessing the limits of our own knowledge, or call for the introduction of an activity to deepen insights. For example, any attempt to answer the question : 'Who made the daffodils ?' is incomplete without personal involvement in planting, caring and observing the process of the growth of bulbs. Such involvement led six-year-old Margaret, on noticing that the daffodils she had planted had burst into bloom, to exclaim spontaneously : 'How very good of God.' Similarly, Graeme, peering intently at a primrose flower through a magnifying glass, murmured : 'Isn't it wonderful.' Margaret's and Graeme's emotional response of delight echoed the psalmist's acknowledgement : 'Many . . . my God are thy wonderful works' (Ps.40.5 AV), and the subsequent thanksgiving : 'O give thanks to the Lord, for he is good' (Ps.106.1). That children share with the psalmist in a joyous response to some of life's experiences is seen in quotations from a book compiled by children entitled *What is Happiness?*

Andrew declared :
  Happiness is splashing in the water.
  Happiness is going for a picnic.

Tina thought :
  Happiness is to have a friend.
  Happiness is a new baby.
  Happiness is new clothes.

Alison believed :
  Happiness is a warm, cosy blanket when you are in bed.

Spontaneous expressions of happiness were caught by another teacher who, joining a group of children in a merry mood, inquired : 'What is making you so happy?' The response gave birth to a book completed in less than half an hour, the preface reading : 'This is a happy book with all happyness.' We learn from what follows that 'all happyness' includes 'ice-cream because it is cool', 'helping Daddy', 'the cuddliness of my puppy', and 'singing'.

But it must be recognized that although there are times when children could with the psalmist exclaim : 'Thou hast put gladness into my heart' (Ps.4.7), they also know times when '. . . joy and gladness are taken away' (Isa.16.10) and they are 'tired with crying' (Ps.69.3: *Fifty Psalms: An Attempt at a New Translation*). A teacher, in suggesting the idea of a book about winter-time, made possible the acknowledgement of such emotions, which included

this simple, yet imaginative, description of the loneliness of a tree in winter :

  It is winter
  I am
  a
  lonely
  tree and my leaves
  have fallen off
  my branches and I am sad
  The birds have flown away
  The squirrels are sleepy
  And I am very, very sad.

Another child found that the elements symbolized human aggressive feelings, when following a stormy night she wrote :

  Thunder rumbling
  Winds grumbling
  They're angry
  Are you?

These children were in company with biblical writers in likening aspects of man's experience to the nature of the elements and plants : 'Man lasts no longer than grass, no longer than a wild flower he lives, one gust of wind and he is gone . . .' (Ps.103.15 f., Jerusalem Bible). Children today may come close to the fact of death through similar encounters. This happened when Walter de la Mare discovered the ephemeral nature of the frail beauty of a convolvulus :

  . . . its cool dark leaves and waxen-like simplicity awoke in me a curious wonder and delight. I plucked the flower out of the hedge to take it home to my mother. But when I came into the house it had wreathed itself into a spiral as if into a shroud. And when I realized it would never be enticed out of it again I burst into tears (*Early One Morning*, p. 45).

But young children's grief, though intense, is usually short-lived, for as C. Day Lewis has written :

  . . . pre-occupied with exploring the world through their senses, feeling no distinction between their tiny tragedies – the broken toy, the rained-off picnic – and the greater ones which press indirectly upon them, the small fatalists accept more easily than most philosophers the knowledge that what is, is (*The Buried Day*, p. 20).

This attitude was reflected in Jennifer's reaction to the death of her pet:

> Once upon a time my rabbit was very ill. Soon he died so my Dad had to bury him in are garden he was white his name was snowbal becouse he was as white as the snow before he died my Mum gave him one carrot and a drink of water but he did not want it I cried a bit.

That Jennifer felt free to share a passing sorrow with her teacher is a reminder that it is by sympathetic support, not evasion, that children may be helped towards acceptance of change and the consequent sense of loss as an inherent part of the pattern of life and the later awareness of the '. . . Father of mercies and God of all comfort' (II Cor.1.3).

At the same time, children may through observation come to sense the core of the New Testament message that apparent endings may herald beginnings. Collecting and planting seeds from faded flowers or trees or preparing leaf mould may give preliminary insights into the strange truth that life is dependent upon death, summed up by Jesus when he said: 'Unless a grain of wheat falls into the earth and dies, it remains alone; but if it dies it bears much fruit' (John 12.24). Likewise, observation of the chrysalis tomb shed by the unfolding butterfly or the broken eggshell from which the chicken has struggled afford initial entries into the inner meaning of the resurrection.

Toys that are lost, broken and beyond repair are another medium through which the young may catch glimpses of aspects of death. On the other hand, the imagination of childhood will turn discarded, broken things to creative use. Thus Marie's doll, which she made from newspaper set aside as rubbish and dressed with scraps of pretty fabric and gay ribbon cast out of her grandmother's work-basket, became her 'princess'. Here, too, was an early realization that apparent rejection may offer new creative possibilities, underlying the statement of Jesus that 'the very stone which the builders rejected has become the head of the corner' (Matt.21.42).

These descriptions of children's activities suggest how first-hand sensory, imaginative and emotional initiations may create a frame of reference for later comprehension of the metaphorical and symbolical elements of the Bible. So, too, will the encouragement of children's delight in analogy-making and poetry. The youthful imagination which turns pumpkins into fine carriages is the spring of adult symbolism, so prevalent in biblical writings. Young children realize that, as G. K. Chesterton wrote: 'Everything has in fact another side . . . viewed from that other side, a bird is a blossom broken loose from its chain of stalk, a man a quadruped begging on its hind legs, a house a giantesque hat to cover a man from the sun.' This is the side of things which tends most truly to wonder about the deeper implications of experience.

Since life is so fresh to them, wonder is a dominant aspect of young children's emotional response to experience. Because their outlook is primarily egocentric, revelations are likely to occur incidentally, being a solely personal concern. At other times there may be a group response, though not always with words. A brief, quiet, yet awesome, moment held five-year-olds spellbound when their attention was called to the imprisoned colours revealed by sunlight in raindrops hanging from the branch of a tree. 'Let's dance', was the lively suggestion of six-year-old Rachel, while she and other children were looking up through the tracery of a pink-blossomed almond tree one sunny spring morning. It was an elemental expression of worship. Since, as a fifteen-year-old girl explained, we need 'something to fill out the words with', these moments may be the starting point of 'worship in spirit and in truth', and the ground of knowing why Moses took off his shoes (Ex.3.2–5).

Personal Relationships

The Bible illustrates that man's search for meaning in life includes not only an interest in and response to the nature of the universe, but discoveries about the nature of self and other people. Indeed, the heart of Christianity is a concern about the network of personal relationships. Since to have been accepted for oneself is an essential forerunner to accepting and understanding others, adults' attitudes to children and their strivings will in turn affect the ultimate quality of their human relationships and their capacity to be open to the divine in life. Ben Vincent's reminder to house-parents of children in care that 'You are saved because you are loved' is applicable to all children. Indeed, the caring acceptance of young children is far more potent than biblical stories in aiding growth into the perception of the central biblical truth that 'We love, because he first loved us' (I John 4.19). Such caring makes possible first steps towards the imaginative insight needed for the acceptance of the commandment: 'Thou shalt love thy neighbour as thyself.' Likewise, the assurance of the psalmist: 'I called upon thee, for thou wilt answer me, O God; incline thy ear to me, hear my words' (Ps.17.6), must first be encountered in the quality of the listening response of those with whom young children commune. This is the beginning of growing into the meaning of prayer.

The seeds of such insights were sown, albeit unwittingly, when the following incidents occurred in an infant school. Claire recounted her weekend activities to her teacher, who listened with genuine interest. David, a newcomer, was encouraged towards independence as his teacher introduced him to the possibilities of sand-play. Later David was drawn into a small group admiring Roger's birthday presents. While Nicola and Anne in caring for dolls in the Wendy house felt their way into the nature of motherhood, both were developing imaginative sympathy, as were John and Phillipa in acting out the roles of doctor and nurse. Moira in the guise of a witch and Carl a Dalek were more easily able to realize and deal with their aggressiveness. John, who bumped into Jane, causing her to spill water, was quietly helped to mop it up. Patience and firmness with Robert and Jeremy who had quarrelled over the ownership of chestnuts led them to sort out the disagreement. Smiles replaced Elizabeth's tears as assistance was given in the unravelling of a tangle arising from a first knitting attempt.

That human encounters with fatherliness must precede growth into a response to 'Our Father which art in heaven' was seen in the absorption of a group of children in the items contributed by some of its members to a book 'About Fathers'. Among them were:

My father is a carpenter he macks things for me. If mummy is poorle daddy looks after her.

my father reads me storys at night time he puts me to bed sometimes I go for walks him I like going for walks with him we clim rocks and he helps me clim up.

my daddy is kind and he works hard to ern some money to buy me food and clothes daddy is gentl and big I love my daddy very very much.

When I am narte my daddy can be cros but he is nies very soon.

my father taught me to swim he held me so I did not go under the warter.

For other children the building up of the concept of caring was furthered as they talked of their experience of motherliness, coupled with the growing awareness of the ways in which other people known to them displayed a caring attitude.

My mummys hands are very gentle sometimes they get sore and get blisters. She is very kind and looks after me when I am ill I am sure I could not do without a mummy.

My mummy has helping hands because they do the cooking for us and she washis our shirts and in the morning she has our shirts redy for us and she has our breakfast redy and sends us of to school and when we come home she mack the te for us and at night she tucks us in bed.

Policemen have helping hands because they let old people across the road and he lets us across the road as well.

the doctor and nurse has careful hands she is nice to you when you are in hospital and the doctor is nice too.

Caring in which children themselves engage is another means of fostering a concern which includes 'the sparrow which falls to the ground' (Matt.10.29). The beginnings were there as Alan and Mark, who had persevered in the making of a bird-table, later in snowy weather kept it supplied with food and fresh water. Janice's excited shout, as she withdrew her hand, startled a squirrel about to peck at the peanuts she offered. When the squirrel returned, Janice was careful to restrain herself, for she had learned that 'The living ask you for food. You give it to them . . . and open your hand and they eat. . . . If you turn away they are frightened' (Ps. 104.27–29, *Fifty Psalms*).

Tracy and Diane also exercised sympathetic imagination when they cautioned a visitor: 'You can hold Tinker the rabbit but you must not touch the black guinea-pig because she's going to have babies and we keep her quiet.' Sonia and others wrote of their caring for animals:

> I love stroking animals but you must not mull them around or pick them up by their tails because it would hurt

> You must be careful not to drop the hamster because it might break its back. And all so you must not be rough with him cos you might hurt him very badley indeed.

In the same school as Sonia and her friends was Melanie, handicapped by severe muscular weakness, which prevented her from walking and affected her powers of speech. Children and teacher were troubled over Melanie's difficulty in indicating her needs. So came the successful suggestion that the children should make a flag which Melanie could wave when she required assistance.

Teachers as they mirror children's experiences in stories follow the practice of Jesus and other men of biblical times. The religious significance of stories other than biblical is that they are 'A steadying power, like a sheet anchor in a high wind, not moral at all, but something to hold to.' Fairy-tales can be told but their inherent truths about human nature will not be consciously realized until later years, when intellectual appreciation is fused with emotional insights. Thus, the story of the Sleeping Beauty carries the latent message that in spite of the apparent power of evil, love in the end overcomes. The fact that 'a man's pride shall bring him low' is contained in the adventures of Jack the Giant Killer. The essence of the Magnificat, that 'he brings to greatness humble people', is conveyed in the story of Cinderella.

Introducing Biblical Material

With a young child, then, the '. . . exploration of experience, the deepening of feeling and the extension of the horizons of his human experience' prepare for the later apprehension of biblical truth. There will be times, however, when biblical material can be introduced to young children in a meaningful manner. But in the selection several factors should be borne in mind. For instance, although biblical stories may be enjoyed in the early years, there is a risk that constant repetition may lead to bore-

dom and dulling of later comprehension of their full significance. We must also be aware of the kind of ideas which may be instilled. That it is all too easy to present confusing ideas of God and Jesus is shown in a selection of questions and comments of young children. 'Why can't I hear God speaking like Samuel did, I've tried very hard?' was the complaint of an exasperated, tearful, six-year-old girl. A five-year-old American boy expressed his bewilderment by stating: '. . . in the Bible there is a story about a flood. God promised there would never be another flood. How come there was a flood in Texas then?' Seven-year-old Michael gathered that 'God . . . rides around in jet bombers. . . . He bombs wicked Egyptians in their tents.' That Fiona was puzzled by the idea of the divinity of Jesus became clear in her query: 'Why did Jesus have two fathers? Did one die?' 'Seems like Jesus was a conjurer,' was the conclusion of a seven-year-old boy on hearing of the raising of Jairus' daughter. Another child, having heard the story of the Prodigal Son, commented: 'I do think his daddy might have gone with him.'

It is also essential to realize that for an ever increasing number of children their encounter with biblical ideas outside school may be confined to popular associations with some of the Christian festivals, weddings, christenings and funerals. As out-of-school associations are likely to be mainly superficial, there will be a tendency for children to respond positively to biblical education only if they find it ultimately intellectually acceptable. There would seem wisdom therefore in pruning the biblical material we offer in early school days, delaying its presentation until the children can more easily appreciate and discuss its historical and poetic features. Thus teachers would be well advised to consider which parts of the biblical narrative may come, at some time, to have significance for young children. Rather than following a systematic, unrelated approach, biblical references may then be introduced whenever possible alongside immediate experience, perhaps being incorporated into the usual story-time. A few examples illustrate how opportunities arose.

School Experience and Bible Stories

Six-year-old David came into the classroom

one morning eager to relate the news that one of three kittens born to his pet cat had strayed. David told how he and his father had searched for the kitten the previous evening, eventually finding him in a neighbour's garden. The kitten was carried back home, tucked inside David's coat. On returning, David placed the kitten in a basket by the sitting-room fire, where he immediately curled up against the mother cat who welcomed her baby by giving him a thorough licking. Later that morning David chose to write of this event under the title 'My Lost Kitten'. David's experience seemed to offer an opportunity to introduce the story Jesus told of the sheep which strayed. At the end of the school day the teacher recalled David's adventure by reading his story to the class, following on with the story Jesus told (Luke 15.4–6). In the following days, as may happen with children of this age, the theme was taken up by other children, including six-year-old Sheila, who told a story about 'The Little Girl who got Lost':

Once upon a time there was a little girl who got lost. She went a long way and did not know her way home. She wished she had not run away and she wished she could find her house again. After a long time she did find her house. Her mother said: 'Where have you been?' 'I ran away and got lost', said the little girl, 'I will not run away again.' The little girl's mother took her out shopping and the little girl was glad to be with her mother again.

Sheila's story, together with others, including those of the kitten and the sheep, was placed in a book which eventually came to be called *The Book of being Found*. From time to time, at the children's request, stories were read from this book when they gathered together at the end of the school day. The six-year-old boy who on one such occasion commented, 'Being found is a nice feeling', endorsed Coleridge's view that 'I meet that in the Bible which finds me'.

A broken necklace belonging to five-year-old Ann was another incident seized by a teacher. Several children helped to retrieve the beads which scattered over the classroom floor. It was some time, however, before the centre one, the largest and of a bright red colour, especially treasured by its owner, was found by a five-year-old. With the aid of an electric torch he discovered it under a cupboard. The beads were then re-threaded and Ann was happy again. During that day Ann's teacher told the story of the lost coin (Luke 15.8 f.).

Children's conversation about what they did with their friends and why they like having friends paved the way for relating how Jesus befriended Zacchaeus (Luke 19.2–8). Kevin's account records his impression:

One day there was a little man called Zaccheus. No one liked him. One day he hred some one say Jesus is cuming There was a big crood so he could not see so he climed a tree. Jesus stoped and said Come down can I cume in yor house for a cup of tea Zaccheus was so happy he said yes and they went together and had a cup of tea. Zaccheus talked with Jesus and he never pinched money again and he and Jesus became friends for keeps.

The friendly manner in which Jesus welcomed children was also recounted (Mark 10.13–16), followed by discussion as to what the children might have done when they were with Jesus. Most of the children's responses were expressed orally, but some chose to record their suggestions:

I think they askd him to tell them a story to tell what happd to him when he was a little boy They might have even bring som toys to show him I wold have askd him to tell a story about a donkey.

I expec the children askd Jesus lots of quschuns I wold

I think the children gave him flowers they pickd and sweets they had with them.

This interest in 'friendliness' later formed the theme of a shared session with the rest of the school, in which was included the thanksgivings of Jayne and Henrietta:

I am lucky to hav frends to play with mee thank you God
I am glad aboot frends so I can play ring a ring a roses and hide and seek with them

There was also Gary's plea: 'Deer god plees help my frends to be nies to me, so they will play with mee.'

The absorption of seven-year-olds in music-making with instruments they had made gave a chance to tell them of how long ago someone had written about praising with musical instruments. The children's own version of Ps.150 which they illustrated read:

Praise with the blasts of trumpets
Praise with the strings of cellos and violins
Praise with the clashings of the cymbals
Praise with the tinklings of triangles
Praise with the beating of the drums
Praise with the shaking of the shakers
Praise with singing
Praise with dancing.

The account of children's participation of praise in the first Palm Sunday events was integrated into music-making activities in another school as Easter drew near. Other seasons afford introductions to biblical narratives, the Christmas story being an obvious example. In this connection, it is important that Jesus is not relegated entirely to the 'once upon a time'. There is also need to avoid the confusion inherent in the question: 'If Jesus is born every Christmas and crucified every Good Friday, how does he grow up so quickly?'. Imaginative planning may help children to bridge these gaps. This was in mind in the suggestion that the Christmas story might be linked with the topic of birthdays. Children thinking along these lines suggested:

When Jesus was seven I think he had a party. Perhaps he invited his friends to tea and they played hide and seek.

I feed my puppy with dog biscuits. I expec Jesus had a donkey and I think but I dont know that donkeys had hay I think they did in those days.

Sometimes the sentiments of short phrases from the Bible may coincide with events, as when a class of six-year-olds had been out in search of signs of spring. During times when the children conversed about their impressions, which they had expressed in various media, the teacher shared with them poets' responses to spring-time which echoed the children's delight and included the biblical phrase: 'Lo, the winter is past . . . the flowers appear on the earth, the time of singing has come' (S. of S. 2.11 f.). Seven-year-olds' sight of a rainbow on a showery day provided a link with the reaction of a person of biblical times to a similar sight

when he enjoined: 'Look upon the rainbow, and praise him who made it; exceedingly beautiful in its brightness' (Ecclus.43.11 [Apocrypha of the Old Testament]). During excitement over a snowfall reference was made to the description of snow as '. . . white and woolly fur' (Ps.147.16, *Fifty Psalms*). On all these occasions the teacher read from her own Bible, enabling children to become familiar with the source. Previous noting of likely references made this incidental use possible.

Since children's understanding, both intellectual and emotional, develops at varying rates and is affected by their differing experience, there may be times when a teacher may think it appropriate to use biblical material usually deferred to a later stage. Thus, seven-year-olds' curiosity as to whether stories familiar to them were read to Palestinian children in the time of Jesus led to the relating of the adventures of Joseph of Old Testament times. Another opportunity presented itself through seven-year-olds' intense interest in colour. This had been stimulated by a student's provision of materials and questions, which encouraged them to explore the properties of light through a simple approach of observation, experiment and recording. An agnostic, this young woman was nevertheless deeply concerned about the religious aspect of her teaching. When reflecting on the children's responses she realized that she had tended to encourage their intellectual activity more fully than their emotional response. Among the few who had reacted mainly emotionally was Linda who had spontaneously written:

As I lay on my pillow
I saw the stars twinkling and shining
And I thought of God who made them twinkling and shining.

Taking Linda's simple expression of wonder as a preface this young teacher decided to read to the children a few phrases from Genesis about the creation of light (Gen.1.16), mentioning how they had been written many years ago when people had wondered about how light came to be. Thus it came to be that short phrases from the first chapter of Genesis appeared alongside the children's descriptions of their own discoveries and responses to light, which were expressed in both simple scientific as well as poetic terms. The study of light led some of the more intellectually able to be curious about the faculty of sight, and provision was made for them to satisfy their questioning. This point, when the children's wonder and joy in sight was so apparent, seemed to their young teacher an unanticipated opening to tell them of the blind man's joy when healed by Jesus (Mark 10.46–52). Talk ensued about the ways in which people today are helped to see by doctors and opticians and how we can help those whose sight cannot be restored. A blind woman was invited to school, accompanied by her guide dog. Prior to the visit, the seven-year-olds spent time and thought deciding what she might most enjoy. Songs and records were chosen and a group played a tune, which they had composed, with percussion instruments, while others selected articles for a game involving identification by touch. One child brought a bar of chocolate, others donated pennies from pocket money which were used to buy jonquils since 'they smells lovely'. The young woman's joyous participation made it difficult for the children to accept that she was sightless, for she possessed a perception of life independent of sensory physical sight. Intellectually most of the children's grasp of the situation was limited but because of the sensitivity of a young teacher and a blind woman the emotional impact was in the nature of a benediction.

Openings such as the one described above are likely to be rare with young children. Generally, teachers may feel it wiser to leave the miracles of Jesus for later consideration, preferring to quicken children's awareness of and delight in their physical faculties, as was apparent when Mandy exclaimed after a demonstration: 'I like spinning round and round. I call it the dizzies.'

Conversation with a teacher about things children enjoyed seeing was the prelude to the expression of those joys in picture or word-forms,

I love to see the birds fly in the sky
I love to see the cats running down the hill
It is fun to be a cat
I love butrcups
I love to see them in the fillds
I love to see the sun glittering in the sky

I love to see people making ice lollies
Theyre so very cool
I love to see the flowers
Bobbing up and down
Fireworks are a lovely sight
Glittering away
Waterfalls are pretty
As the water falls
Down into the river
Splash, splash, splish

I like to see aeroplanes
I like to see the white pattern that comes out of the engine

To encourage children in their seeing is to initiate the growth of the spirit, for as Paul observed, '. . . all that men may know of God lies plain before their eyes' (Rom.1.19 NEB). But we must remember that '. . . it often happens that what stares us in the face is the most difficult to perceive.' This is particularly true of young children and we must anticipate a time-lag between life's encounters and the grasping of meaning. Helen Keller's memory of the first time she queried the meaning of the word 'love' illuminates this point. Helen had picked some early violets and given them to her teacher, who gently spelled into Helen's hand, 'I love Helen.' 'What is love?', asked Helen. 'It is here,' replied her teacher, pointing to Helen's heart. Helen Keller reflecting on the incident writes: 'Her words puzzled me very much because I did not then understand anything unless I touched it . . . I thought it strange that my teacher could not show me love' (*The Story of My Life*, p. 32).

So we come back to the need for time to grow through personal experience, for it is in the individual's re-living of timeless truths, not a mere reverent remembering of bygone history, that the biblical story can be most fully comprehended. Only as we accept this truth will our children be free to grow towards the biblical revelation that 'It was there from the beginning; we have seen it with our own eyes; we looked upon it, and felt it with our hands; and it is of this we tell. Our theme is the word of life' (I John 1.1 NEB).

(The author wishes to thank several heads of schools for some of the illustrative material used in this article – Editor.)

The Junior Stage · *Gordon Benfield*

One has only to hint that religious education in the junior school has, in the past, been too Bible-centred and the cry will go up, 'but children love Bible stories'. Of course they do; they love stories of all kinds because stories form an immensely significant area of that wilderness of human ideas, feelings and attitudes, through which the child must wander in his search for the meaning of life. There has been, however, in the compiling of syllabuses of religious education for junior schools, a tendency to concentrate on giving to the children a thick slice of biblical knowledge without adequate reference to the total educational aim of helping them to discover and explore life. One needs only to look at the typical Agreed Syllabus produced in the late 1940s and early 1950s to recognize that, in intention, if not in fact, we have been guilty of trying to give our children too much Bible too soon. The result of this is that what has remained in the mind of the child has not always been meaningful in terms of the questioning, thinking and life-exploring which is natural to him at his limited stage of development. Hence confusion arises from half-digested notions and ill-formed concepts. All too often, through sheer desire to cover the ground fully, our biblical work has become a stumbling-block rather than a stepping-stone; it has been what so much of teaching in other areas of the curriculum can so easily become, an answering of questions which the child is incapable of asking.

If this is true, and we have recognized and accepted it in other subject areas, it does not by any means follow that the Bible should never be used in the junior school. What does follow is that we must ask more seriously how much of the Bible should be used with junior children and how and on what criteria the selection of biblical material should be made. If the danger is 'too much, too soon' we must be quite clear about 'how much, and when', and what approaches should be adopted.

The task of the religious educator in the junior school is, therefore, gradually to ease the children into a position where they can begin to understand the deep significance of scripture to those in whose lives 'God-talk' and 'God-knowledge' are vitally important and to do this in such a way that it will relate to their own searching in the area of 'God-experience'. It must be part of their God-exploring and self-exploring.

Furthermore, we now know much more than we did when Agreed Syllabuses were first drawn-up about the way children think and learn. When children think about religion, they are using the same thinking skills that they use when thinking in other fields. It came as a disturbing shock to many Christian teachers to discover from the writings of Dr Ronald Goldman that what Piaget describes as a series of fairly clear stages in the development from intuitive to full operational (abstract) thinking in normal children applies also to religious thinking. This is not the place to examine in detail the findings of Dr Goldman and other educational researchers, but we must acknowledge our indebtedness to them for reminding us of two very important considerations.

The first consideration is that children with a mental age of five to seven are almost incapable of coping *mentally* with the religious and spiritual; that those between mental ages seven and eleven are inclined to concretize in their thinking, that is to say, they are not able fully to cope with the abstract and are thus handicapped when trying to deal with religious ideas; and that it is only with a mental age of twelve plus that the child begins to handle abstract thought, and hence religious and spiritual concepts. Dr Goldman demonstrates in his writings that much of what we have often interpreted as understanding on the part of the primary school child has, in fact, been nothing more than the child giving verbalisms in answer to questions. The child has seemed to know the answer, but, when pressed, has been discovered to have only half-digested notions of what a story or saying is about.

The second consideration forced upon us as religious educators by recent research is that children learn best when the point of departure for new learning is something within their own immediate experience. One difficulty in handling biblical material with juniors has long been felt, that is, the remoteness from the child's experience of the people, language, geography and way of life which we find in the Bible. The biblical ideas and feelings, however, are not remote and many of them can be found in some degree within the child's own experience. This is therefore a good starting-point. An excellent illustration of what is in mind is contained in the *Handbook of Suggestions for Religious Education* produced by the West Riding Education Committee. A piece of work for children of seven plus is based on the theme of 'caring'. It starts with a sharing of examples of caring in children's own experience, from care for their pets and their parents', and other people's, care for them. It moves on to learning about how adults organize their care for less fortunate members of society. Only then, when the notion of caring is firmly fixed and made an issue, is a glimpse taken at caring in the Old and New Testaments from well-chosen incidents, and also from a look at the lives of some of the great characters in Christian history, including lesser-known contemporary, and preferably local, figures. This seems a good way of leading junior children into the realm of religious ideas and into the wealth of biblical material. One side advantage is that it does not rely on a chronological approach to Hebrew history; this, too, is all to the good, since it is generally accepted that the junior child has only a partially developed sense of time. It is an approach which allows him to dip into the box of biblical facts and ideas with some guide lines but, at this stage, few restrictions.

Feeling and Knowing

What has been said so far seems to dangle such a thick question mark over what has traditionally been taught in religious education that there is need for a further matter to be discussed before going on to suggest possible ways of approaching work on the Bible with junior children. We must remind ourselves that young children can often *feel* and, in one sense of the word, *know* things which they are capable neither of articulating nor of fully understanding intellectually. This is particularly true in the sphere of religious experience. A child can, through membership of a Christian family or community where religion is done as well as talked about, develop an awareness of the things of the spirit a long time before he can finally deal with his awareness in any intellectual sense. In other words, there is a *'feeling'* side of religious education which needs to be developed along with the *'thinking'* side. For this reason it is impossible to separate the work in the classroom from the junior school act of worship and whatever opportunities the children have in home or church to 'feel' about the God and Jesus of the Bible. Through all the resources of music, drama, movement, art and creative writing, it is vitally important that the child should be allowed to give expression to what he feels about God, Jesus, and the people who knew them in the Bible and the people who still know them today. A child will never know God in the fullest sense of the word simply by being able to understand the language and concepts of those who wrote about their own and other people's ideas of God. We would do well to bear this in mind when selecting material from the Bible for juniors. There is often within a biblical passage that which the child cannot fully comprehend but which, if he is allowed to feel, will add to his store of meaningful experience, if not to his store of certain knowledge. The allegory of Yahweh as the Shepherd of Israel is incredibly difficult: few, however, would deny a child's ability to feel what is meant by God watching over him as a shepherd watches over his sheep, even when he understands little about Israel's God or, for that matter, Israel's sheep and shepherds.

Bearing all this in mind, what are the possible approaches to the Bible for junior children? The following suggestions are made because they seem to be acceptable within the limits set by the child's 'readiness for religion' and also because they allow for a measure of integrated curriculum work which might avoid fixing in the mind of the child too rigid a line between the sacred and the secular. It will perhaps seem to some that the various approaches to biblical material recommended in this section require the teacher to spend too much time on too small a selection of biblical passages and that often the Bible is brought in almost as an afterthought. There is a danger here, but it is much less dangerous than dashing through every passage listed in the syllabus in such a way that young children have a wide blur of half-digested biblical knowledge, ill-formed concepts and little, if any, insight into the nature of the biblical narratives. It is more desirable at the junior stage to select passages carefully and to direct the children's research and inquiry into the hidden depths of the stories. They have their limitations at the intellectual level, but they are often capable of much more than we allow for in enthusiasm and desire to know the truth of the matter in their own terms. A top junior form meeting a chosen psalm for the first time can simply read it, enjoy the words, and possibly learn a phrase or two. Or they can ask many questions about psalms: Why were they written? What was happening to the writer? What was the feeling at the time? Do we ever feel like that? Could you give him a name or write to him back through time? Could you write a psalm about when you were feeling like that or a psalm for people in the world we know to be like that now?

If the children deal thus with one or two psalms there is a possibility that they will know how to approach a psalm when they see one! This is much more important than having met a lot of psalms in passing. Nor is any apology made for drawing this illustration from the psalms, because many of the psalms are to do with feelings, and young children know a lot about feelings if they do not know a great deal about ideas. It is surprising how children are qualified from their own limited experience to enter into the joys and sorrows of the psalmist once the historical or personal situation has been briefly outlined to provide a simple framework for the human experience (see Part III, Section 11 pp. 147 ff.).

What is true of the psalm is equally true of almost any type or form of biblical material. It is so easy to forget in religious education that we want young children to learn first and foremost about themselves, secondly about the questions that they find in themselves, thirdly about the same questions and some of the answers men have found in the Christian revelation (and at a later stage, perhaps, other revelations), and only *incidentally* about other people to whom this revelation was previously made, that is, the biblical characters. There is a tendency all too often to concentrate on the characters and their story to the exclusion of the child himself and the relevance of the narrative to him as an inquiring human being; this, let it be stressed again, is often due to a wrong selection of material. The plea, therefore, is to avoid trying to cover the whole of the Bible in the junior school and endeavour instead to ease the child into an understanding of how the Bible works so that he can use at least some parts of it in the right way.

Possible Approaches

1. *The 'Bible Box of Tricks' Approach*

This sometimes appears in a syllabus as 'What is the Bible?', or 'The Story of the Bible', but not always with the emphasis where it should be in the junior school: that is, on *discovery*. A good starting-point is a pile of old Bibles, lots of paper, paste and scissors and perhaps the adding machine for totalling chapters, pages, verses, names etc. The whole purpose of the approach is to get the young junior thoroughly at ease with the strange thick book before him that seems to be so important to so many grown-ups. How is it like other books? How is it different from other books? Who wrote it (obviously a wrong question)? How was it written, then? Why were the many bits and pieces written?

Children enjoy reading biblical names for the first time and getting their tongues round the ones they will meet again at a later stage. The examination of a Hebrew Old Testament and Greek New Testament will lead to a first look at the intricacies of translation; there are many fascinating stories easily found in books about the transmission of the text, such as Tischendorff's discovery of the Codex Sinaiticus and the jigsaw of the Dead Sea scrolls. These are full of interest for the young junior child who is not yet ready to deal with many of the ideas inside the book he has discovered. But he can at this stage learn about the various kinds of writing he will find in the Bible. He can learn, for instance, that the Bible contains legends. He might even compare a biblical legend with another legend he has read in school and find time to ask why legends were written and to what extent they contained more than, say, fairy-stories. Why did people write legends? What were they trying to say in them? He can learn that the Bible contains myth, and again begin to understand that myths are written as an attempt to explain things which cannot be put in any other way. There is much to be said for letting children write myths and legends of their own. They do in fact invent legends about their own parents without realizing that this is what they are doing, and they are quite capable of creating myths along the lines of the 'Just-so Stories'. They might write a myth, for instance, explaining why we have two ears and only one nose, or why some people have red hair. If they can leave the junior school knowing that each piece of writing in the Bible does a different job, then they will be well on the way to an intelligent understanding of the biblical text. If they have grappled with a few bits of legend surrounding selected biblical characters, looked at a myth, torn apart a parable, scratched their heads over a group of sayings, and learnt to separate these in their minds from historical narrative, they will have done at an early age what all too many people have never learnt to do with the Bible. One of the objects of this *Source Book* is to give teachers, in concise form, the necessary information to enable them to attempt this kind of work with children. It is unfortunate that so much of our biblical teaching in the past has left only one question in the minds of the young children: 'Is it true?', or, 'Did it really happen?'. What we should be leaving in their minds whenever they handle biblical material is the question, 'Why was this particular passage written?', or, 'What had been this man's experience to make him write this story in this kind of way?'. Although these seem to be questions for the advanced biblical exegete, they are nevertheless questions which the junior child can be trained to ask from the very beginning, so long as we are not over anxious to do too much text too soon.

2. *The 'Setting the Scene' Approach*

Alongside this task of gradually bringing the child to an understanding of the Bible as a varied selection of written material or 'Box of Tricks' is that of preparing children to meet the people of the Bible. The Bible is, for the junior child, one of many books about interesting and exciting people, and if he is going to understand these people properly and really 'get inside their skin' he will need to spend some time, though not as much as is often spent, learning how their pattern of life differed from his own. One sympathizes with the bishop who ended a visitation of schools by remarking, 'If I see another camel I shall scream!', yet there is much that a child living in the late twentieth-century Western world needs to know about the habits of life, customs and peculiar beliefs of people

living in the Middle East two thousand years and more ago. There is good film material available and other visual aids; with these, and with due emphasis on feeling as well as knowing, through the use of drama, art and music, the child can begin to appreciate some of the extreme pressures of life in biblical times: oppression by one big power after another, being trapped between bigger nations, good and bad harvests, belonging to a tribe, being driven from home, famine and plenty, heat and cold, richness and poverty. All these can be known and felt in imagination by the child and are as necessary a part of the scene-setting as bootbox houses and Galilean fishing-boats. The danger of too great a historical emphasis at this stage and, indeed, too great a geographical emphasis, cannot be overstressed. The lack of readiness to cope with time concepts has already been mentioned, but one doubts, too, the ability of the junior child easily to project himself into a strange culture before he fully understands his own. Hence, at this stage, the scene is adequately but not too elaborately set and the main business of meeting the people of the Bible is not pushed to one side (see Part IV, Section 2; pp. 214 ff.).

3. *The 'Meeting People' or 'What Were They Like?' Approach*

It has been suggested that for the junior child the Bible is a book about interesting people and what they did. Here, without doubt, one can so easily run into difficulty, as will be apparent on reading the subsequent commentaries in this volume dealing with the specific books containing our source material. How much do we really *know* about the key figures: patriarchs, kings and prophets in the Old Testament, disciples, apostles and even Jesus himself in the New Testament, to qualify us for introducing them to children? In some cases the answer might be that we know very little indeed, but biblical scholarship has in other cases given us quite clear portraits of many of the major characters through whom God acted in revealing himself to man. Before we begin our introduction, however, let us test in the articles provided here what we really do know and what is conjecture, and be honest in passing on this knowledge to the children. This is all part of their learning to handle the biblical material themselves.

How, then, do we introduce the people of the Bible to young children? We must be sure in the first place that we select from the biblical narratives the characters about whom we know sufficient to make them live for the children; and there are certainly plenty of these. Where there is scholarly agreement about the historical existence of a character, even allowing for differences of opinion over interpretation of detail, then we are on reasonably safe ground with junior children. Thus David is a safer choice with children than Abraham. It is difficult with the junior child to separate Abraham the person from the Abraham of Jewish legend and reverence so long transmitted in oral form. It is easier to separate David the boy, the man and the king, but to recognize at the same time what the writers were doing to David in writing about him. The children can get inside the skin of David and know they are dealing with a real person, and this they should be allowed to do by letting them *be* him in imagination and give expression to their 'David feelings' in art, free drama, and creative writing. What did it feel like to be the youngest son; to be left out; to be outlawed and persecuted; to have a friend like Jonathan? What did it feel like to be anointed king; to lose your best friend; to have a lot of power; and, above all, to feel that a powerful God had a special job that he had chosen you to do? It is much more preferable that children should really come to know a few Old and New Testament characters quite intimately in this kind of way than that they should know nothing more than the names and a few facts about a long list of biblical personalities. These people whom the children know well can then be used as points of reference in piecing together the biblical history at a later date. Possible characters for treatment in this kind of way might include, from the Old Testament: Joshua, David, Solomon, Hezekiah, Nehemiah, Isaiah, Jeremiah, and from the New Testament: Peter, Paul, Luke, Mark and Mary. It is important that the question left in the minds of the children is not so much, 'What do we know about these people?', but, 'What made them the kind of men or women they were?'. There are obvious omissions from the patriarchal narratives, but the reason for this is that of these earlier characters there are different questions to ask which junior children are not yet capable of asking. This is not to say, how-

ever, that they should not examine these earlier stories through some other approach. Junior children who have produced a tape-recorded interview with carefully selected biblical people, who have written their letters for them, felt their joy and sadness, and acted out the significant events in their lives, will have discovered a great truth. They will have discovered that the Bible is a book about how God worked through *real people*. If they can go from the junior school knowing that, they will go knowing something of great significance.

4. *The 'Bible Spectacles' Approach*

It has been stressed several times that it is better for junior children to know how to handle carefully selected biblical material than for them simply to come to know a lot of Bible stories which they will dismiss for the wrong reasons. The approach referred to here as the 'Bible Spectacles' approach is thought by many to be going beyond the capabilities of the average junior child. Experience has shown, however, that the junior child *can* become deeply aware of the difference between our view of life and that taken by those who first gave us the biblical narratives of the Old and New Testaments.

It is not difficult to imagine what is meant by 'Bible Spectacles'. It is a mental device for looking at the biblical story through the eyes of the people who first wrote or created it, or through the eyes of the people who feature in the narratives. One has, as it were, to spend time with the children gradually building up a prescription for the Bible Spectacles. The child must, when he looks through them, see a God very clearly indeed behind all that these people did and said. He must see people who had a very limited scientific understanding of the physical world and who were inclined to fill in the gaps in their scientific knowledge by carefully worked out patterns of supernatural phenomena. He must see, particularly in the Old Testament, people who thought much more in terms of the tribe or the nation than they did of the individual member of the tribe or nation. These are not too difficult for the young child to 'see', because he is himself inclined to think in similar terms or can at least remember when he did as an infant. If a child can see into the mind of the Hebrew people in this kind of way and feel something of their conviction that God was watching over them as a nation, building them up, rewarding, punishing, forgiving, rescuing, protecting – using them to show the world what he wanted men to be and do – then they are much more likely to read or listen to the stories in the right way. They will begin to ask what it is that the writer is telling us about the God who guided their nation or what he was trying to say to them through the words and actions of a particular character. It is only when they can do this that they can go a stage further and ask whether what these ancient people recognized as God's message made known to them through people and events has anything to say to us in the present day despite our being different people with a different story. Once more, the plea is to select biblical passages carefully and spend time looking quite deeply into what happened and to whom and to ask how much we can understand by putting on our 'Bible Spectacles'. Only thus will the hard literal acceptance or rejection of religious history give way to an exciting inquiry into the beliefs and experiences of the people who made, and indeed *are*, the Bible. It is surprising how top junior children can have opened up to them some of the most difficult passages by the 'Bible Spectacles' approach provided the teacher has done the necessary research. A good illustration is the story of Abraham sacrificing his son Isaac. This is much more than an account of Abraham giving the most precious thing he possessed to God, which quite rightly causes offence to the junior child, and yet so often this is where the emphasis is placed. The whole idea of sacrifice as seen by the Canaanites and the new discovery revealed by the story of Mount Moriah is only difficult for a child who is not sufficiently helped to see this through his 'Bible Spectacles'. The child who meets such a story as this, and meet it he surely will, must leave knowing that it is more than an account of how a man was going to kill his only son. He must *begin* to see it as one stage in man's groping to know what God wants in terms of obedience and that this is only one of the big questions that the Bible deals with over and over again (see Part III, Section 5, pp. 105 f.).

5. The 'Big Question' Approach

So many young people fall short in their understanding of the Bible and even reject it as a significant area for inquiry and study because they have been encouraged, through bad teaching, to search within it for answers to questions it was never asking nor seeking to answer. This is one of the more perplexing aspects of traditional Scripture teaching in schools. It is best illustrated by recalling the usual comments and questions of so many people who have been traditionally taught about the early chapters of Genesis. 'We now know the world was not made in six days', or, 'Who was there for the children of Adam and Eve to marry?'. Behind this kind of comment and question, with its implied ridicule, is a naïve assumption that the question being answered by the writers of these strange narratives was 'How did the world begin?', or 'What happened during the first few years of man's existence on the earth?'. It is the kind of naïvety and ignorance which partly led to the science versus religion controversy of the last century, and which is far from being resolved in the minds of many people who are untrained in biblical studies, including, naturally enough, a good proportion of the junior school teachers for whom this section is designed. We must be perfectly clear in our minds and make equally clear at an early stage in the minds of the children precisely to what questions we are seeking answers when we grapple with the often strange stories in the Bible. If children are going to read the Genesis stories – and it will be difficult to prevent them from knowing about these stories even if they are not taught in school – they should know also the big questions that the writers were trying to answer. They are in fact the questions that a top junior should himself be beginning to ask: 'Why are we on the earth?', 'Is there anything behind it all?', 'Did it just happen?', 'Why is it easier to be bad than to be good?'. The myths of the creation and fall deal with these very questions through the writings of men who never questioned the existence of God. These writers are not trying to find an answer; they are using words in a peculiar way to try to express the answer they already knew. A child will never find sense in these passages unless he is helped to think in this kind of way about the particular 'Big Question' behind them.

Throughout the Old Testament we have a record of men discovering bit by bit some of the answers to big questions, or, to put it another way, getting a clearer idea of God's answers until, in the New Testament, we have what a child has described as a 'one-man answer in Jesus Christ'. These big questions are:

What is man for?
How can we be good?
How can we get rid of the badness in us all?
How can we live happily?
Why do some people suffer?
What is God really like?
Does God punish people?
How does God speak to us?
Is death the end of everything?
How should we treat other people?
How can we make God happy?

These are all questions which junior children have asked, in their own words, and they are the very questions which the biblical people and biblical writers were concerned to answer. Some found an answer and some did not; some of the children will find answers and some will not. It is important, however, that we should keep reminding them and ourselves what the big questions are, and it is only when we do so that they will begin to see why the Bible has been so important a book to so many people for so long. It is because it deals with the questions that men have always asked and will only stop asking when they have ceased to be fully human. In this respect, children are remarkably human when they are given the necessary help in articulating their big questions.

6. *The 'Bible-Words' Approach*

One of the greatest difficulties in communicating the truth of the Bible to children is that the Bible was written 'from faith to faith', that is, by people who believed for people who believed. This means that there are certain 'faith-words' which, if not understood in the faith-context, make a nonsense of biblical stories to young and old. Moreover, they are the key words of biblical thought: God, Heaven, Hell, Kingdom of God, Eternal Life, Spirit, Redemption, Death, Saviour, Holy Spirit, Word of God, Angel, etc. The alarming thought for the teacher in the junior school is that these words are the subject of the deepest theological inquiry; if that is so, what hope is there that the mind of a child can ever cope with them? The answer is, surely, that a child's mind, or an adult mind for that matter, might never *fully* embrace the total significance of these verbal symbols, for that is what they are, but he can begin to 'bandy them around' in the later junior stages. A child who leaves the junior school thinking that those who talk of God are talking of 'an old, old gentleman sitting on a throne high above the clouds' is not only a victim of his own concrete thinking, but also a victim of inadequate guidance. If he is allowed to discuss 'God-ideas', he can be helped to see that all our ways of talking about God are secondary to what we and the people in the Bible *feel* about God. He can be helped to see that they had to say *something* about the God they believed in and that when they wrote about him as if he were a person they were only doing this because a person was the most important being (but a *human* being) that they knew about. Even when they used the king-image of God they were taking the idea from their own kings. There is much in God-metaphor and God-simile that children can be given to help them through the half-digested concrete images of earlier childhood if only we are prepared to allow, and perhaps be shocked or surprised by, a constant 'bandying around' or exploring of biblical words. The idea of angels is a valuable illustration. Stained glass windows, pious Bible-pictures and Christmas cards have fixed the classical angelic winged form in the children's minds. A discussion with them of the many ways that men receive 'messages' from God or the kind of people or groups of people used as his 'messengers' in everyday life is far from beyond the understanding of a young child. Any person who crashed into life and spoke of the things of God was an angel, or 'messenger' to the people of the Bible; and the complexities of Hebrew angelology is something that will be better understood at a later time if a simple open-minded approach can be adopted at the primary stage (see Part IV, Section 4, pp. 236 f.). A frequent 'stocktaking' of what we now think about key verbal symbols used in the religious language of the Bible is a most essential exercise, and teachers will prepare their own box of 'faith-words' and occasionally put one out for fresh examination. Children's thoughts must never be permitted to harden around a partial concept; when this happens they have stopped thinking religiously, and it is far more important that they should develop an ability to think religiously than that they should know a lot of biblical stories. The 'Bible-Words' approach is a valuable aid to achieving this.

7. *The 'Biblical Theme' Approach*

Several recent books and syllabuses try to overcome the 'time and culture gap' in biblical teaching by using the thematic approach. How, for instance, can a child who has no experience of a Palestinian shepherd and the way he lived with and handled his sheep be helped to understand the symbolism of Christ the Good Shepherd? One answer is to do an extensive inquiry into the whole background, not only of how shepherds lived and worked, but also of how there was gradually built up the picture-language of God caring for the flock of his people in the Old Testament through to the relationship between Christ and his disciples and Christ and his church in the New Testament. Drama and creative writing are readily usable in working out such a theme. There is a danger, especially with this particular theme, however, of labouring a point that the children can quite easily grasp, but this does not invalidate the approach. The significance of wells, rivers, and water to the people of the Bible is something which can be quite fully explored with juniors, starting from the importance of water to them and working back to its place in biblical times. This simple research can gradually be directed towards the symbolic uses of water in word and action throughout the Bible and especially in the New Testament. There could well be an extensive piece of study and research here for the enlightened teacher and class using many resources, biblical and non-biblical, and possibly integrating with work in other areas of the curriculum, particularly science. There is much to be gained from letting children see that they can ask different kinds of questions about such an ordinary thing as water. Like so many words in the Bible it has a scientific meaning and a religious meaning. The same is quite obviously true about such other words as bread, fire and wind, and the combined imagination of teacher and children, a good concordance, together with some simple scientific apparatus, can provide a fascinating area of inquiry from such heavily loaded words as these which are full of religious significance. The junior school teacher is in the wonderful position of being able to attempt integrated work of this kind and so to avoid fixing the unfortunate line of demarcation between sacred and secular in the mind of the child. The Bible often takes quite ordinary things and looks at them in a different way, but the children need to know that they are ordinary things.

A re-arrangement of material from almost any syllabus will permit the devising of imaginative biblical themes, each covering several weeks, on such topics as altars and temples (if necessary coming down to modern times), rocks and stones (literal and symbolic), mountains and hills (the events centred on these in Old Testament), dangerous journeys (many of these throughout the Bible), escapes (the whole idea of redemption), light and darkness (a most significant biblical concept).

There is always the danger that this approach can become over-contrived and over time-consuming, but good teachers are aware of these dangers and, when properly applied, the initiative and inquiry of children can be released most effectively in the working out of a biblical theme.

8. *The 'Life-Theme' Approach*

The basic principle behind what has become known as 'life-themes' is that children best learn when they start from that which is within their own experience. Many biblical concepts are difficult for young children because they are so often developed from experience far removed from that of the child. A life-theme is designed to use the child's own experience as a jumping-off point for inquiry into the deeper and fuller implications of a particular concept. A life-theme is also a means of ensuring that religious ideas are not separated from other ideas in the mind of the child. It is an appropriate approach in the modern junior school, where integrated curricula all too often embrace every subject except religious education, which is still, unhappily, remaining in its little timetable box at the beginning of the day. This could not happen, where, for example, a life-theme such as 'power' was being worked through.

'Power' would be approached by letting the children collect, draw, or write about all the powerful things they know of: pumps, engines, lights, radios, etc. They would examine powerful words and compare them with weak words.

They would collect stories about powerful people – living and dead – who have used power for good or evil, including some Old and New Testament characters. They would discuss how people have power over the lives of others and how Jesus used his power. Older juniors could discuss powers helping us to do things when we feel unable to face doing them ourselves.

It is not difficult to imagine where a life-theme of this kind could lead when the enthusiasm of teacher and child is fully released on it. As a way of leading children to look at appropriately chosen biblical material and relating what they find to the business of everyday living, the approach is extremely valuable.

Many teachers are, however, unhappy about life-theme work because it is difficult to spot where the specifically religious aspect comes in. There is reason to be cautious and to ensure in planning a theme that a true balance is kept and that children are led to *think* religiously as well as scientifically or historically. But there is an equal danger in separating the religious work from an integrated curriculum and giving children the impression that religion is not a part of real life.

Teachers who are attempting what is now becoming a widely recommended approach should see examples of themes in the newer syllabuses: for example, 'caring', 'courage', 'thankfulness', 'forgiveness', 'sacrifice', 'healing', 'light', 'barriers', 'fire', etc. It is far better, however, that groups of children should be guided by a teacher in working through a theme of their own on some given topic than that they should follow one previously worked out as a scheme of work. As an approach it can lead to many discoveries about the Bible.

Agreed Syllabuses

Some teachers will wonder to what extent it is possible to experiment with the types of approach outlined here when the religious education work in their school is laid down in an Agreed Syllabus. Two things can be said about this.

First, an Agreed Syllabus is not intended to be a scheme of work. So long as any arrangement of work does not draw on biblical material not included in the Agreed Syllabus

then it is the privilege of the individual teacher, in consultation with the head teacher, to select and arrange material bearing in mind the needs and stage of development of his or her own children. An Agreed Syllabus defines content, not methods of approach.

Secondly, many education authorities are now revising their Agreed Syllabus in the light of recent research into religious education, and the approaches and techniques outlined above, especially the thematic approaches, are being commended in the syllabuses most recently published.

Some Specific Problems

1. *Teaching the Miracles*
(see Part IV, Section 6, pp. 257 ff.)

Much of what has already been said above suggests the general approach to miracle stories. There is much to be said for leaving many of these stories as late as possible, but the better known miracle stories will be heard by children outside school, and it is essential that they should begin in the junior school to work out the proper way to understand them. The most important thing is that they should begin to ask the right, that is, religious questions about miracle narratives.

They will naturally want to know whether a miracle really happened and, if so, *how it happened*. Quite often the answer of biblical scholars is that we simply do not know. Hence the need for teaching children at an early age to ask the more important question: What kind of thing must have happened to make a person write what he did? In other words, what was the human experience of God acting that led to the particular story we have in the Bible? The second useful idea is to let children see that the miracles, especially the New Testament miracles, are really glimpses into the kind of world that God wants, or, if one likes, into the kingdom of Heaven. They are strange to us because we cannot see the full picture, but children are very capable of taking some of these glimpses or clues and filling in the pieces of the biblical jigsaw puzzle. When they can do this they are well on the way to handling the Bible in an adult way; it must never be forgotten that the Bible was not written for children. It cannot be overstressed that the detailed 'digging into' carefully selected examples of 'types' of biblical material, whether it be miracle or parable or any other type, showing children how to use it and what to look for is far more profitable in the long run than a superficial survey of all the better known stories.

2. *The Passion Narratives*

Is it good for children to dwell on the suffering of Jesus on the cross? Many teachers ask this, and the fact that schools are not normally in session for the Easter festival presents the problem of having a Good Friday without an Easter Day to follow it. Again, the key to the answer is getting children to ask the right religious questions. The fact that Jesus died must be stressed, but the details not unduly dwelt on. What is more important is that very soon afterwards he was known to be still alive in a different kind of way: the witnesses of the people who knew this to be so is what the whole of the New Testament is about. The whole purpose of studying the Gospels for young and old is to grapple with this mystery, and if the children can be led to see this before asking wrong questions about the details of the Passion narratives, they will be better able to look at the Gospels in the right way.

3. *Real Bible or Bible Stories in Classroom and Worship?*

Should children use the full text of the Bible? Again, the answer has been partly given above. They should gradually learn to handle the full text, but there are times when the story is more important than the actual wording of the Bible, and the teacher's own words or a well written story from the Bible is of more value. There are attractive Junior Bibles in many versions, and teachers' own preferences will govern choice. There is still much to be said for carefully selected passages of the Authorized Version being used for memory work at a time when this comes easily to children, even when full understanding is delayed until a much later stage. The literary and cultural heritage argument is a powerful one and difficult to refute, but there is also need to bear in mind the religious development of the child. A full discussion is not possible at this point but the advantages of a familiarity with the text of certain key passages – selected psalms, parables and sayings of Jesus – are not convincingly outweighed by the dangers of lack of understanding at the junior school stage, and many agreed syllabuses recommend a cautious use of memorizing passages. A child can often 'feel' a passage which he cannot as yet fully understand, and religious growth is not entirely a matter for understanding. This is particularly to be borne in mind in selecting biblical passages for use in school worship, and indeed in the selection of poems and other non-biblical material for use in worship.

Children *do* enjoy Bible stories. The task of the teacher in the junior schools is to give depth to this enjoyment by carefully matching the material to the child's stage of thinking and feeling, and his total experience. There is always a danger in religious education of answering questions which the children have not yet asked. Through the kinds of approach outlined above a teacher can draw out questions that are in the children waiting to be asked. Moreover, the teacher can begin to show the children how the Bible has for many men, for many years, provided answers to some of the biggest questions that have ever been asked.

The Secondary Stage · *J. W. D. Smith*

The Pupils We Teach

The junior school child's behaviour is relatively constant and predictable. He has found an acceptable identity within his limited environment. As adolescence approaches, the security and stability of that identity begins to be weakened and disturbed by new pressures and tensions. Rapid physical growth involves a period of awkwardness and readjustment. Developing sex maturity releases new emotional energy. The opportunities and responsibilities of adult life begin to stir new hopes and new fears. Horizons are widening and interests are changing. The individual ego of childhood is no longer adequate.

The adolescent must discover his true identity in that adult world which he is about to enter. He finds himself facing competition with his fellows for economic security and independence, for social approval and esteem, for the establishment of a satisfying sex relationship. The days of dependence are passing. The freedom of mature personal decision beckons but must still be won.

Primitive society provided social support and guidance during this transition period. The pattern of tribal belief and life was transmitted to each new generation under strong emotional and social pressure. In such circumstances the problem of personal identity hardly touched the surface of conscious life. Social deviants might appear occasionally but, in general, one generation followed another along the same paths towards maturity.

The poignancy of the adolescent predicament in modern society lies in the contrast between the self-perpetuating stability of primitive social life and the chaotic uncertainties of contemporary society. Few social groups are free today from the powerful solvents of mass communication. There are few stable cultures within which adolescents can find clear social guidance as they face their new tasks and responsibilities. Their eyes and ears are constantly assailed by sights and sounds which multiply their uncertainties and confuse their judgment. The adult world, as they see it, provides few signposts and offers few satisfying prospects. The revolt of youth against that world is hopeful as well as disturbing.

The secondary school has a vital pastoral responsibility for all who enter its doors. Eighty per cent of those who enter at eleven plus will be fully exposed to the pressures of adult society as young wage-earners from the age of fifteen years. The school must help to ease the strains and tensions of psychological weaning. It must help boys and girls to understand their own nature, to recognize, and accept, the possibilities and limitations of their biological and social inheritance, to discover their true identity in the wider environment into which they are moving. As they grow older many will resent and resist adult autho-

rity and guidance. Some will cling to it for security in a troubled world. All must be helped to grow beyond outward rebellion or anxious conformity towards the freedom of personal maturity and personal decision.

The problems of ego-identity in adolescence are not resolved primarily by conscious thought and personal decision. Yet knowledge and reason should inform and guide adolescent choices. Moral and religious education will proceed through every channel of human relationship within the school. Special counselling facilities are needed to provide individual guidance and to meet special needs. But more is required. Creative efforts must be made to give pupils real understanding of the Christian heritage in Western society. Its basic beliefs should be known and its moral values should be understood. Pupils may accept or reject them, but they should at least understand them.

The Problem of Relevance

The Bible is the traditional tool of moral and religious education. It was a valuable tool in earlier days when teaching was adult-directed and authoritative. Problems began to emerge when biblical scholarship raised new questions about authority and interpretation. They increased when educational theory and practice made the pupil's changing interests and capacities vital criteria in educational planning. They multiplied rapidly as the gap between the idiom of biblical thought and the secular presuppositions of modern science grew wider. They became almost insuperable when Christian belief and Christian moral standards were openly repudiated, or tacitly ignored, in large areas of the population. In these circumstances the Bible is no longer an obvious and appropriate textbook for moral and religious education in the state schools of our country.

Various attempts have been made to bridge the gulf between the Bible and contemporary life. Many modern translations and paraphrases are now available. The Revised Standard Version (RSV) is still the most valuable for general use in secondary schools. It is scholarly. It removes obscurities and errors arising from textual difficulties. It retains the literary qualities of the Authorized Version. It does, however, need to be supplemented, for many purposes, by translations which try to interpret the original meaning in a modern idiom.

Translations and paraphrases are helpful but they do not solve the problem. Alien thought-forms cannot be expressed in a modern idiom. No modern translation or paraphrase can interpret 'he saw the heavens opened and the Spirit descending upon him like a dove; and a voice came from heaven' (Mark 1.10 f.). Commentaries are needed to deal with such difficulties. Yet even the best modern commentaries make assumptions which mean little, or nothing, to many secondary school pupils. Most commentaries are written by Christians for Christians, and even the word *God* may inhibit meaningful discussion in a secondary school classroom.

Many false trails have been followed in attempting to maintain the authority of biblical truth. Attempts have been made to trace parallels between modern cosmology and the account of creation in Gen. 1. These do not stand the test of serious examination. Archaeological discoveries have been used to demonstrate the 'truth' of the Flood story and of incidents in the early history of Israel. But the findings of one generation of archaeologists may be questioned by the next generation.

More sophisticated, and more helpful, attempts have been made to show the real nature of biblical truth. These help the pupils to realize for themselves the kinds of literary material in the Bible and the different ways in which books may be 'true'. Yet such books often show a desire to buttress biblical authority. In state schools of the present day it would seem wiser to recognize that the authority of the Bible rests on personal response and is only valid within a believing community. The 'truth' of the Bible cannot be established by argument or imposed by adult authority.

Various trails have been followed in attempting to establish the relevance of the Bible in modern life. Stories from the Old and the New Testament have been presented 'in modern dress'. Parables of Jesus have been given a contemporary setting. The voice of the prophets has been related to contemporary social and international happenings. Passages from Old Testament and New Testament have been set side by side with press photographs or extracts from contemporary literature. Such attempts to establish the relevance of the Bible have one serious weakness. Some show this weakness more clearly than others, but they all seem to assume that 'the Bible' should somehow be made relevant and contemporary. This assumption deserves closer examination. The Old Testament contains many types of literature and it reflects the changing religious outlook of an ancient people during more than a thousand years of their history. The New Testament comes to us from an alien culture and its writings reflect the thought-forms of a pre-scientific age. Does the fact that these writings are contained within the Christian Bible imply that any extract from them has a unique value in itself and may be used to interpret Christian teaching?

Is the relevance of biblical truth made more evident by attempts – sometimes trivial and misguided attempts – to make extracts from biblical literature relevant and meaningful? The parable of the Good Samaritan can be retold effectively in the setting of modern violence. Is it more effective because it is taken from the literature of the New Testament? Would a parallel modern story not be equally effective? Does this use of a parable not tend to obscure biblical truth? The parables of Jesus only reveal their full significance for Christian belief when they are studied in their original life-situation.

Attempts to make biblical material meaningful and relevant need to be tested by a clear aim. The literature of the Bible has no mystic merit derived from its mere presence within the Bible. The story of Ruth is a literary masterpiece with a universal human appeal and with obvious moral values, but ancient Israelite customs obscure its meaning. Parallel stories from other literature, or from contemporary life, may sometimes be more effective and less difficult than biblical narratives. Concern for 'biblical truth' should direct us, rather, to the unity of the Bible as the sacred book of the Christian church. We must seek to make the faith and life of the church meaningful and relevant in the closing years of the twentieth century. Efforts to modernize biblical material will not necessarily help us to further that aim.

The 'life-centred' approach is the most important recent attempt to bridge the gap between biblical teaching and contemporary life. It has, however, one serious danger. The heritage of Christian belief and life should not be undervalued because of the difficulty in establishing its relevance. Dialogue in the classroom can degenerate easily into idle chatter, and will be really fruitful only on two conditions. First, the deeper, genuine concerns of pupils must come to the surface. This demands skilled and perceptive adult guidance and the use of appropriate techniques. Second, deepening insight into central Christian teaching must inform classroom discussions. It is not enough to seek biblical parallels or to rely on biblical allusions. The relevance of 'biblical truth' requires knowledge of the Bible in its Christian unity. It requires a clear grasp of basic Christian belief.

Teachers in state secondary schools should not impose such belief by adult authority. Attempts to do so are likely to meet with increasing resistance among older pupils. It is surely appropriate and desirable, however, that all secondary school pupils should have clearer knowledge of, and deeper insight into, the basic elements in Christian belief and life. Dialogue in the classroom should play an appropriate part at all stages. The whole range of modern educational techniques may also be brought into the service of religious education. The teacher should try to show Christian belief affecting life-situations and to provide opportunities for discussion and action arising from such concrete studies. Such practical approaches should be informed and enriched by systematic biblical studies at appropriate levels. Pupils in academic streams should follow a systematic course in preparation for later study of Christian origins. Those who will leave school at fifteen years of age should be helped to reach similar insights in more concrete and practical ways.

Focusing on Christian Faith and Life

New Testament writers took over the Greek word *agape* (love), and filled it with deeper meaning as they tried to interpret their experience and beliefs. The cross and the empty tomb became the symbols of their faith. The cross symbolized the suffering of perfect love in an imperfect world. The empty tomb symbolized the early Christian conviction that such love was the source of creative life and brought an eternal dimension into human existence. Such love had power to restore broken relationships, to change and renew social life and to heal the inner conflicts of human nature.

It is a striking fact that the word 'love' is widely used today in a society which pays little more than lip-service to the Christian tradition. Child psychologists use it in defining the conditions for healthy human development. Psychiatrists use it to describe the healing agent in psychotherapy. It is continually used in current debate about human relationships, about war and peace, about violence and delinquency. Dialogue in the classroom involves constant use of the word – with many divergent shades of meaning.

This fact may be a helpful pointer towards a type of curriculum which is 'faith-centred', rather than 'Bible-centred'. Non-Christians, as well as Christians, might co-operate in a curriculum which explored the meaning of *agape* in its original context. Such a curriculum could culminate, at fifth- and sixth-form level, in critical and non-partisan study of the earliest Christian documents – appropriate extracts from the Epistles preceding the Gospels. Deeper insight into the original Christian use of the word *agape* would have direct bearing on all the pressing problems of contemporary human living.

One fact would soon be obvious. The confusion in current use of the word 'love' would be seen to arise from the very nature of the word in its original Christian use. The first Christians recognized *agape* as the true norm for human living, but they knew that it was an impossible norm for the divided human will. They believed that Jesus' life, teaching and death expressed that norm in word and action. They claimed that the spirit of perfect love which they had seen in him was still at work among them. A new motive was changing and renewing their common life. 'We love,' they said, 'because he first loved us' (I John 4.19). They knew that the change was not complete and the first Christians, influenced by their Jewish background, looked for a return of Jesus their Messiah and for the beginning of God's new age.

The early expectations were not fulfilled. The followers of Jesus the Messiah had to adapt their thought and life to meet a new situation.

The standards of Christian perfection had to be reconciled with the problems and demands of daily existence in an imperfect world. The Christian spirit of love continued to inspire the Christian community and its influence permeated the life of society, but the general standards of Christian living suffered. The story of the church in later centuries has many dark pages. Still, the creative spirit lived on. Each new age brought new human problems, and the prophetic spirit of love called for new ways of living in response to new needs. Our own age has seen the breakdown of Victorian moral standards. They were not Christian standards, but they were influenced by Christian insight. Their breakdown has left society bereft of moral guidance. It has left youth without social support and direction.

Traditional Christian morality cannot be re-established among secondary school pupils by adult authority. Few would wish to see it re-established in its Victorian form. But young people need signposts and guidelines for living. They want to select their own guidelines and to erect their own signposts. They distrust the generation which they hold responsible for the world they see around them. Yet authentic Christian love retains their respect and is capable of awakening response. Non-partisan study in depth of the origin and nature of that love may be the most hopeful long-term contribution to the educational needs of our age.

What type of curriculum would prepare for this study? It would not be a Bible-centred curriculum, but it would need to use the Bible as its main source book. It would focus on the faith and life which preceded and shaped the growth of the Bible. It would try to bring out the pattern of meaning which gives unity to the Bible in Christian belief. It would illustrate that meaning from Jewish and Christian practice in the contemporary world whenever possible, and it would try to establish the relevance of that meaning in the world that pupils know.

The Bible must still be our source book, but it should cease to be our textbook. Most agreed syllabuses provide selected material from the Old Testament and the New Testament for the secondary school years. This material can be adapted, supplemented, and presented in ways that focus attention on Christian faith and life.

The focal point of the curriculum should be found in the cross and the empty tomb as symbols of the original Christian faith and life.

'We preach Christ crucified,' wrote Paul, 'a stumbling-block to Jews and folly to Gentiles' (I Cor.1.23). Words such as these send us back to the Old Testament. Why was the original Christian theme a stumbling-block to Jews? Study of the Old Testament can throw fresh light on the source and nature of Christian love. Selection of suitable material for this purpose must be determined by the pattern of meaning which the first Christians traced in the Old Testament and found fulfilled in the crucified Messiah.

Many modern writers echo Macbeth's bitter comment on human life – 'a tale told by an idiot, full of sound and fury, signifying nothing'. But the Hebrew prophets saw meaning in human life. They were aware of a word of God that sounded through the events of history and called for response from men. The destiny of men and nations was shaped by that response. God's word contained a promise of healing and renewal. Rejection of that word brought judgment and disaster. They believed that God had called Israel to be the servant of his healing purpose, and they pointed forward to a day when that purpose would be fulfilled in spite of Israel's failure. The four words *vocation, failure, hope* and *fulfilment* express the unifying themes which Christians have found in the scriptures of the Old and New Testaments. The first three words provide a simple pattern which enables the teacher to select, organize and present Old Testament material in a way which may deepen understanding of New Testament belief.

The fourth word interprets I Cor.1.23: 'We preach Christ crucified, a stumbling-block to Jews and folly to Gentiles.' It takes us to the heart of Christian teaching. Christians believed that the death of Jesus, whom they recognized as the expected Messiah, fulfilled the deepest insight and the highest hopes of the Old Testament prophets. The Roman world despised the weakness of crucified love. The Jews looked for tangible evidence of divine power. The followers of the crucified Messiah knew that 'the weakness of God' offered healing and life to men. They knew that they were 'being saved' by the power of perfect love. The teacher's task, in the Old and in the New

Testaments, is to interpret this Christian insight, latent in the Old Testament and incarnate in the New, and to show its relevance to contemporary problems of belief and life.

The Theme of Vocation

The first five books of our Old Testament are known to Jews as the *Torah* (the Law). They contain the central substance of the Jewish faith and they provide an essential background for Christian understanding. Material for study at this stage of the secondary school should be selected mainly from the books of Exodus, Numbers and Deuteronomy. While *stories* from the book of Genesis are appropriate in the primary school, serious study of the Law itself should be postponed to the top forms of the secondary school. In the earlier forms of the secondary school the teacher should use material from this part of the Old Testament as a source of insight into the Old Testament theme of vocation.

The annual Jewish festival of the Passover offers a colourful, contemporary introduction to this theme. Exodus 13.3–22 is much more useful teaching material than the narrative in Ex.12. Selected verses should be read, and attention should be concentrated on the instructions in Ex.13.8: 'And you shall tell your son on that day, "It is because of what the Lord did for me when I came out of Egypt."' 'Jews have obeyed these instructions for some three thousand years. During the annual Passover supper in a Jewish home, the question is still asked, 'Why is this night different from all other nights?'. The story of slavery and deliverance is repeated anew in the context of the sacred family meal. Teachers should try to secure information about local Jewish practice, wherever possible, and should illustrate and explain the details of the festival. Film strips and pictures may be useful with younger classes.

The sabbath service in a Jewish synagogue also helps to focus attention on the covenant faith of Israel. Pupils should know the traditional reasons for Jewish recognition of the seventh day as a sacred festival: 'For in six days the Lord made heaven and earth, the sea, and all that are in them, and rested the seventh day; therefore the Lord blessed the sabbath day and hallowed it' (Ex.20.11). They may be

familiar with the opening words of the *Shema*: 'Hear, O Israel: The Lord our God is one Lord; and you shall love the Lord your God with all your heart, and with all your soul, and with all your might' (Deut.6.4 f.). They may know that the *Shema* is repeated, like a 'creed', during the synagogue service. They may know about the *Mezuzah*, traditionally a piece of parchment inscribed with texts from the law, and its place in the life of a Jewish home. But they may not know the closing words of the *Shema*, 'I am the Lord your God, who brought you out of the land of Egypt, to be your God: I am the Lord your God' (Num.15.41). They may also be unaware of the Deuteronomic explanation of the sabbath day: 'You shall remember that you were a servant in the land of Egypt, and the Lord your God brought you out thence with a mighty hand and an outstretched arm; therefore the Lord your God commanded you to keep the sabbath day' (Deut.5.15). Revision of the earlier knowledge and the imparting of fresh information may help to build up a picture of a people who look back in gratitude to a deliverance from slavery and who acknowledge a call to a God-given vocation.

This emphasis on present-day Jewish belief and practice may help to loosen the chains of historicity which often hamper understanding of the exodus narratives. These stories belong to the Jewish acts of remembrance. They provide a thread of narrative which illustrates and supports the exodus faith. The substance of that faith is summarized helpfully in Ex.19.3–6, where Yahweh speaks to Moses on the mountain: 'You have seen what I did to the Egyptians, and how I bore you on eagles' wings and brought you to myself. Now, therefore, if you will obey my voice and keep my covenant, you shall be my own possession among all peoples; for all the earth is mine, and you shall be to me a kingdom of priests and a holy nation.' The literary form of these verses suggests a later date than that of the surrounding narratives. The central elements in Israel's faith are being traced back to divine teaching given through Moses. God had delivered Israel from Egyptian slavery and called her into *covenant* with himself. By obedience to that covenant Israel would fulfil a God-given *vocation* as a unique priestly nation. It would be their privilege to be God's chosen servant among all peoples. Very few narratives need be used in the secondary school syllabus. The theme of vocation is more important than the narratives which support it. The narratives which are used should be studied for their inner meaning.

The familiar story of the miracle at the sea (Ex.14.5–13) illustrates a contrast between prophetic faith and popular response which becomes a dominant theme in Old Testament history. In the hour of danger the Israelites want to turn back: 'When Pharaoh drew near, the people of Israel lifted up their eyes, and behold, the Egyptians were marching after them: and they were in great fear . . . and they said to Moses, "Is it because there are no graves in Egypt that you have taken us away to die in the wilderness?"' Moses, conscious of God's call (cf.Ex.2.11–3.12), urges them on: 'Fear not, stand firm, and see the salvation of the Lord, which he will work for you today.' This same contrast is evident in other stories also. Exodus 17.1–7 is a notable instance which is quoted in the New Testament (Matt.4.7; Luke 4.12). The demand for proof of God's presence is a perennial human weakness. The Old Testament writers were aware of this and they used such stories as a warning. Paul repeated the warning, but he reminded his readers of a power which could overcome such temptations: 'We must not put the Lord to the test, as some of them did and were destroyed . . . these things happened to them as a warning, but they were written down for our instruction . . . God is faithful, and . . . with the temptation will also provide the way of escape' (I Cor.10.11–13). (Further information on these themes may be found in Part III, Section 6, pp. 109 ff.).

The Theme of Failure

The books of Joshua–Judges, I and II Samuel, I and II Kings were compiled under the influence of prophetic teaching. Religious interpretation is interwoven with legend and history. II Kings 17.6–8 illustrates this very clearly. Verse 6 states a historical fact: 'In the ninth year of Hoshea the King of Assyria captured Samaria.' Verses 7 and 8 contain the compiler's interpretation of that fact: 'And this was so, because the people of Israel had sinned against the Lord their God, who had brought them up out of the land of Egypt . . .' The stories of the conquest and settlement in Canaan, the origin and division of the first Israelite kingdom, the varied fortunes and the final collapse of Israel and Judah are all told from a common standpoint. They all illustrate the fitful response and the final failure of God's chosen people. They tell of a broken covenant. The whole period is summarily described, on the eve of the Exile, in the words of Jer.7.25–28 and 22.8 f.: 'And you shall say to them, "This is the nation that did not obey the voice of the Lord their God . . . they forsook the covenant of the Lord their God." '

Many narratives from these books figure in syllabuses for junior school pupils. At the secondary stage, a fresh approach is desirable. Selected material should be used which illustrates the words of Jer.7.25 f.: 'From the day that your fathers came out of the land of Egypt to this day, I have persistently sent all my servants the prophets to them, day after day; yet they did not listen to me, or incline their ear, but stiffened their neck.' Men like Elijah, Amos, Isaiah and Jeremiah lived in times of social and international crisis. They were conscious of a call from God and they spoke or acted in his name.

The stories of Elijah, for example, belong to a critical period in the long struggle between the covenant faith of Israel and the fertility cults of Canaan. The essential contrast was not in outer forms of worship but in men's inner attitude. The rites of Baal-worship were essentially magical. They had their roots in superstitious fear and in man's desire to win security and prosperity in a mysterious and capricious universe. Baal-worshippers tried to use 'the gods' for their own ends. This same attitude persisted in the popular religion of Israel long after the struggle against polytheistic beliefs had been won. It may still be traced in popular Christian belief and practice.

The roots of Israel's covenant faith lay in gratitude and trust. Its fruit was obedience to the divine will. The prophets accused their people of ingratitude: 'Hear, O heavens, and give ear, O earth; for the Lord has spoken: "Sons have I reared and brought up, but they have rebelled against me" ' (Isa.1.2); 'What more was there to do for my vineyard that I have not done in it? When I looked for it to yield grapes, why did it yield wild grapes?'

(Isa.5.4) The prophets tried to interpret God's will in the circumstances of their own day and to remind their people of the true nature of God's demands: '. . . and what does the Lord require of you but to do justice, and to love kindness, and to walk humbly with your God' (Micah 6.8). They warned them that divine judgment would follow disobedience (cf. Amos 8.4–10).

The story of Naboth's vineyard (I Kings 21.1–20) illustrates the struggle between prophetic teaching and political realities in ninth-century Israel. It illustrates two attitudes to a perennial ethical problem. Baal-worship laid no restraint on human desires. Jezebel, the Baal-worshipper, saw no reason why a king should hesitate to take possession of a subject's property. Ahab's Israelite traditions held him back but Jezebel took action. Ahab accepted the fruits of that action and found his guilty conscience confronting him in the person of Elijah: 'Ahab said to Elijah, "Have you found me, O my enemy?" ' (I Kings 21.20a). It is an old story, but it has obvious modern illustrations. How should power be used? How can the selfish use of power be controlled in national and international life?

Elijah's historical challenge to the conscience of Israel is expressed in the well-known words of I Kings 18.21: 'How long will you go limping with two different opinions? If the Lord is God, follow him; but if Baal, then follow him.' The impression which Elijah made on his generation is evident in the wealth of legendary tales which have gathered round his name. His place in the memory of later generations is vividly illustrated by the 'cup for Elijah' which is still set on the table at the Passover supper. The Jews came to believe that one like Elijah would come again to prepare for the advent of God's perfect rule among them. The empty place at the table still symbolizes this ancient hope (cf. Mal.4.5 f.). Some of the legendary tales may be familiar to the pupils. At this stage it is important that they should recognize Elijah's significance as a prophetic voice in an hour of crisis and the place which he still holds in Jewish memories and hopes. This understanding of Elijah helps to interpret the gospel picture of John the Baptist in whom Christians recognized the expected 'Elijah'.

The prophets of the eighth and seventh centuries provide excellent teaching material for the secondary school. The following passages deserve study in their historical context: Amos 3.1–11; 5.18–24; 6.1–8; 7.10–15; 8.4–6; Isa.6.1–8; 7.1–9 (cf. II Kings 16.5–13); 30.1–5; 31.1–3; Jer.7.1–15 (cf. 26.1–15); 28.1–14. Amos appealed for social justice in an age of wealth and social change. Isaiah intervened in political affairs at two critical periods of Judah's history. Jeremiah exposed the folly of believing that worship in God's temple would guarantee God's protection. Jeremiah 28.1–14 illustrates the wishful thinking of many leading people in Judah and the uncompromising warnings of an unpopular prophet.

Older pupils should be able to study such passages from the prophets, individually or in groups, with the help of commentaries and reference books. They should find out the particular circumstances in which the words were spoken. They should discuss the teaching of the prophet in its original historical context and then consider whether there is any element in that teaching which is relevant today. What would an Amos or an Isaiah say about the social and political issues of our day? Does divine judgment always follow disobedience to divine laws? If so, what form does it take? There is ample material for rewarding study but, in the early years at least, it will be important to select sparingly and to keep the main theme clear. Our objective lies in the New Testament. (For further information on the theme of failure see Part III, Sections 9–10, pp. 127 ff., 134 ff.).

The Theme of Hope

The Hebrew prophets knew that Israel had failed, but they were confident that God's purpose in Israel's history could not fail. Hope had its roots in trust – as it still does. The theme of hope had an important place in the prophetic teaching of the exilic period. It is an important element in the book of Ezekiel. It is a central theme in the Second Isaiah (Isa.40–55). Ezekial 37 and Isa.40.1–11 might be studied together. Both passages point forward to a day of deliverance from exile. Isaiah 40 is the later passage. Cyrus of Persia was already winning victories which threatened the power of Babylonia and the prophet saw him as God's chosen instrument (his 'Messiah': cf. Isa.45.1).

Both prophets described the future vocation of their people but the descriptions differ.

Ezekiel taught that God's chosen people must separate themselves from all pagan influences (cf. Ezek. 37.23–27; 44.9). The Second Isaiah described a vocation which was outward looking and was concerned with the healing of the nations: 'I will give you as a light to the nations, that my salvation may reach to the end of the earth' (Isa. 49.6). He painted a portrait of God's perfect servant whose vocation would be fulfilled through suffering: '. . . with his stripes we are healed' (Isa. 53.5). The victories of Cyrus did provide an opportunity for Jewish return to Palestine but the actual return was slow and frustrating. In such circumstances, the teaching of Ezekiel proved to be more influential than the ideals of the Second Isaiah.

Ezra's name is still associated in Jewish tradition with the establishment of the synagogue and the acknowledgment of a sacred book. This happened around 397 BC. It marks the beginning of post-exilic Judaism. Jewish life was reorganized under the leadership of the priests and the scribes. The vision of the Second Isaiah had faded. Loyalty to the Law became all important and that loyalty was soon faced with a severe test. The victories of Alexander the Great brought Greek cultural influences to Palestine from 333 BC onwards. The Greek way of life made a powerful appeal. Many Jews, especially among the ruling classes, compromised with their own traditions and adopted Greek customs. Others stood fast by the old ways. In the second century BC, Antiochus Epiphanes, a Greek king of Syria, tried to compel the Jews to destroy their Scriptures and worship pagan gods. Faithful Jews had to choose between apostasy and death.

The annual Jewish feast of Lights (or *Hanukkah*) provides a focal point for teaching about the heroic and successful struggle for religious liberty under the leadership of Judas Maccabaeus. Information about this important period can be found in Part III, Section 15, pp. 191 ff. Details about contemporary Jewish practice should be sought locally wherever possible. The festival is held during the dark December days preceding the Christmas season. Like Christmas in northern latitudes, it has associations with the winter solstice and it is a joyous occasion. It commemorates the re-dedication of the temple after the victories of Judas Maccabaeus. Knowledge of the Maccabaean struggle throws light on the period of the Gospels. Memory of this successful revolt against the tyranny of a Greek ruler encouraged hopes of a God-sent leader who might break the power of Rome. The prevalence of such hopes may be traced in the Magnificat and the Benedictus (cf. Luke 1.51–53, 71).

The book of Daniel belongs to this period. It was written to encourage Jewish loyalty and to sustain Jewish hopes during the dark days of persecution. The tales of Daniel and his friends (Dan. 1–6) can be read in the early years of the secondary school as 'underground literature' which was intended to sustain the morale and to strengthen the resistance of loyal Jews facing the penalty of death. The spirit of these tales is epitomized in Dan. 3.16–18. They encourage loyalty but they do not guarantee deliverance from death: '. . . he will deliver us out of your hand, O king. But, if not, be it known to you, O king, that we will not serve your gods . . .' This is like the faith of Abraham who 'went out, not knowing where he was to go' (Heb. 11.8b).

Daniel 7–12 is an important biblical example of a new type of Jewish literature. The historical scene was so dark that hope for better days had burned low. But a new phase in Jewish hopes was beginning. The apocalyptic writers taught the Jews to look for a new and perfect age which would be preceded by terrible suffering and would be the result of dramatic divine action. The power of evil would be broken and God's perfect rule would begin: 'For behold, I create new heavens and a new earth' (Isa. 65.17a). Apocalyptic literature is remote, obscure and utterly alien to modern ways of thinking, but it is a very important element in New Testament thought and it should not be ignored entirely in the secondary school. Serious study of Dan. 7–12 can only be undertaken in the fifth or sixth forms, but questions about these chapters are liable to arise in earlier years. The book of Daniel is a happy hunting-ground for fringe sects.

Daniel 10.18–12.4 provides a convenient introduction to the methods of the apocalyptic writers. In the tenth chapter we read of a message given to Daniel, a traditional wise man of the sixth century BC (cf. Ezek. 14.14; 28.3) regarding the future history of the Jews. Chapter 11 gives a rapid outline of events from the sixth century onwards. The detail increases and the record becomes more accurate as the Maccabaean period approaches. Verses 21–39 describe the actions of Antiochus Epiphanes up to the point at which the book was written. In v. 40 the writer begins to look forward beyond his own day to 'the time of the end'. Historical accuracy ceases. The account of Antiochus' death does not fit the known facts. Daniel 12.1–4 describes the final deliverance of the faithful and warns Daniel to seal the book which contains the angelic message until 'the time of the end' has come. The writer of the book of Daniel believed that the sufferings of the Jews under Antiochus marked the beginning of the last days and he encouraged his people to hope for God's intervention and deliverance.

Older pupils in the academic stream should be able to gain some insight into the methods of the apocalyptic writers and the way in which they adapted age-old hopes to the needs of a new situation. They will need the help of commentaries and the guidance of their teachers. Evidence in this same passage may help teachers to deal with awkward questions from non-academic forms. Intense suffering fostered fantastic hopes of dramatic divine action. It also fed feelings of bitterness against their enemies. Both elements are evident in apocalyptic passages in the book of Joel (cf. Joel 2.28–32; 3.9–21). Apocalyptic hopes of decisive divine action would be in the minds of many who listened to Jesus' proclamation about the imminence of God's rule among men (cf. Mark 1.15). Some would hope for revenge on their oppressors and deliverance from Roman tyranny. Joel 2.28–32 is quoted in the speech attributed to Peter on the day of Pentecost (cf. Acts 2.17–21). Christians believed that God had indeed acted dramatically and decisively, although no cosmic portents and disasters had occurred. Christian writers pointed to Christ's spirit of perfect love as evidence that God's new age had begun (cf. I Cor. 13). 'We know that we have passed out of death into life, because we love the brethren,' wrote St John. (For material about the exile, see Part III, Section 13, pp. 173 ff.), and for the later history after the exile, Part III, Sections 14, 15, pp. 182 ff., 191 ff.).

The Theme of Fulfilment

The Gospel of Mark, supplemented by Luke and Matthew, offers a convenient introduction to the fulfilment theme for younger classes. Academic pupils in older forms might begin with a critical study of the speech attributed to Peter on the day of Pentecost (Acts 2.14–42). In each case it should be recognized that we are looking at historical happenings through the spectacles of early Christian belief. The opening words of the Gospel of Mark help to make this clear. The author is writing for Christians and he assumes the Christian belief that Jesus was the Messiah whom the Jews were expecting. His material is assembled and presented in ways that support and interpret Christian belief.

1. *Teaching about the Baptism and Temptation*

The Christian understanding of Jesus' baptism can be traced in the words spoken by the voice 'from heaven' (Mark 1.9–11). They echo words from Jewish Scripture. 'You are my son' can be found in Ps.2.7: the verses which follow are in line with the widespread hope that another leader like Judas Maccabaeus would arise and scatter their enemies. The words 'with thee I am well pleased' remind us of several passages in Isaiah, and especially of Isa.42.1. This is one of the 'servant passages' in which the prophet describes a servant of the Lord whose mission will be fulfilled through suffering. The contrast between popular Jewish hopes and Christian belief in a crucified Messiah is set before us at the beginning of the gospel record. The voice speaks in words which expose the ambiguity in Jewish hopes.

The contrast and the ambiguity provide a clue to the temptation narratives in Matthew and Luke. They show Jesus rejecting contemporary forms of messianic hope and setting his face towards a path which led eventually to rejection and death. The quotations from the Old Testament should be examined in their original context. Jesus' reply to the third temptation in Luke ('cast thyself down from the temple') takes us back, by way of Deut.6.16, to the incident recorded in Ex.17.1–7. The Israelites had been asking Moses to prove that God was with them. Jesus is shown rejecting the temptation to prove that he is the expected Messiah (cf. Mark 8.11–13).

2. Teaching the Parables in the Gospels

Jesus' characteristic parables were like extended similes. They were told in order to illustrate some point which had arisen in a concrete human situation. Study of the nature of the Gospel parables and of the substance of their original teaching can be undertaken fruitfully at all levels of the secondary school. Even younger pupils should be helped to put the stories in their original context and to explore their original meaning. This is not always difficult. The parables in Luke 15, for instance, are introduced by two verses which give us their probable context and help to interpret their meaning. The words *'So he told them this parable'* suggest that Jesus was correcting wrong thoughts about God which were responsible for the Pharisees' criticism.

3. Teaching the Miracles in the Gospels

Secondary school pupils usually assume that miracles are supposed to prove the truth of Christian belief about Jesus. The teacher's most important task is to expose the error in this assumption. At some point the question 'What is a miracle?' must be fully discussed. A clear contrast should be established between the popular use of the word and the biblical understanding of it. The response of faith is a necessary element in the experience of miracle. The same event may be interpreted differently by different people. Some are conscious of God's action and call it miracle. Others find a naturalistic interpretation and stop there.

Pupils will want to ask: 'What really happened?' Such questions must be discussed but they cannot be answered satisfactorily. The Gospel writers were not concerned primarily about historical details. They used memories of Jesus' deeds to illustrate Christian experience and belief. This may be illustrated readily by comparing the three Gospel accounts of Jesus' walking on the water (Matt.14.22–34; Mark 6.45–53; John 6.15–21). Factual details vary, but all three accounts illustrate Christian experience of Jesus the Messiah. It is not clear, for instance, whether the storm died away or the boat miraculously reached its destination when Jesus was received into it, but the meaning of the story is not affected by these differences. Christians knew that Christ always came to them in their hour of need: when they were willing to receive him their troubles were eased. There is an obvious echo of Ps.107.29 f.: 'he brought them to their desired haven'. Such echoes from Jewish Scripture can be traced frequently in the miracle stories. The early preachers tried to find support in such Scriptures for their claims about Jesus.

Miracle stories are not easily handled in early secondary classes. They raise questions which cannot be answered satisfactorily. They should be used sparingly at this stage. It should be possible, however, to begin directing the attention of pupils from the historical issue to the question of meaning. It is sometimes possible to suggest a 'natural' explanation, but this approach is not helpful in the long run. Even first-year pupils can be helped to recognize the link between the Christian eucharist and the feeding of the five thousand. This points their thoughts in the right direction and is far more valuable than attempts to use the story as an illustration of sharing.

4. Teaching about the Resurrection

The resurrection of the Messiah was central in early Christian belief. It came to be associated with narratives of an empty tomb and of resurrection appearances. Are such stories myth or history, symbolical or factual? This is a controversial question among contemporary theologians, and older pupils will want to discuss it. We should help all secondary pupils to recognize that the substance of the resurrection faith does not depend on the answer to this question.

Younger classes should be shown that the real evidence for belief in the resurrection lies in the facts of history. Their attention should be directed to the changed attitude of the disciples and to the emergence of a Jewish sect which believed in a crucified and risen Messiah, and developed into a universal church within the Roman empire. The first day of the week gradually eclipsed the sabbath as their sacred day and they called it 'the Lord's day'.

Older classes should be helped to understand the real substance of the resurrection faith. The followers of Jesus had seen in him a love which was free from all self-concern. In his death they recognized the perfect expression of that love. His cross became a symbol of a love which accepts the full consequence of self-centred human action. The empty tomb symbolized the power of that love to renew human life and it held the promise of a life made perfect beyond death: 'For you have died, and your life is hid with Christ in God. When Christ who is our life appears, then you also will appear with him in glory' (Col.3.3 f.).

Two serious difficulties confront the teacher who tries to make this idea of perfect love meaningful in a contemporary classroom. In the first place, 'the church round the corner' seldom looks like a body of men and women whose ways of thinking and acting are con- trolled – even imperfectly – by self-forgetful concern for their fellow-men. Perfect love may be New Testament teaching, but it is seldom obvious in popular Christian practice. The only answer to this criticism is to acknowledge that a standard of perfection tends to produce hypocrisy and compromise in an imperfect world, but to show, by contemporary examples, that it also evokes heroic response and pro- phetic leadership in every generation. At this point 'dialogue in the classroom' is an essential technique.

Even in New Testament times, the spirit of love was often defeated by the persistent power of self-interest. Self-concern was often stronger than concern for others. Paul constantly re- minded his Christian readers that a new motive was at work among them (cf. II Cor.5.14–17),

but he found it necessary also to urge them 'not to accept the grace of God in vain' (II Cor.6.1). The 'new creation' (II Cor.5.17) was not com- plete and perfect. The support of accepted moral tradition was needed then, and it always has been needed in Christian living, but the ultimate criterion is the love that men saw in Christ, and the supreme human motive is man's response to that love in trust and gratitude. Those who seek new guiding lines for action in our own day must turn back to the ultimate Christian criterion and must be conscious of the true Christian motive.

The second difficulty in seeking to make perfect love meaningful is the pervasive in- fluence of materialistic and hedonistic stan- dards. A crucified Messiah is still 'folly to the Gentiles'. At this point the natural idealism of youth is the teacher's best ally. He must seek to inform that idealism by New Testament teaching on love and law and he must seek to guide it into fruitful channels of action.

For additional material on the nature of the Gospels, see Part IV, Sections 5, pp. 239 ff., and for the ministry of Jesus, Part IV, Section 7, pp. 264 ff. The miracles are discussed in Section 6, pp. 257 ff. and the parables in Section 8, pp. 283 ff. of Part IV. For the beliefs of the first Christians, see Part IV, Section 12, pp. 335 ff.

The Sixth Form · *Robert C. Walton*

The attitudes, needs and problems of adolescent pupils have been described in considerable detail by Mrs E. C. Mee and Dr J. W. D. Smith in their articles in this part of the *Source Book* (see Sections 1 and 3, pp. 17 ff., 53 ff.) There is an additional factor which must be taken into account in considering the place of the Bible in sixth-form teaching.

Many girls and perhaps rather fewer boys entering the first-year sixth have recently taken the 'O' level examination in religious know- ledge. The very fact of being examined in this subject may destroy in many pupils any latent interest they may have had in the realities of the Christian religion. The demands of the

examiners all too often turn what could have been a fascinating and stimulating exploration into an uninspiring exercise. The nature of the 'O' level examination means that, almost inevitably, the candidates lose sight of the wood in a close study of a few trees.

Those pupils who do not enter for the 'O' level paper in religious knowledge have a parallel but somewhat different experience. The general effect of religious instruction guided by Agreed Syllabuses over four or five years has been described by H. W. Marratt:

Religion has remained something external to them, whereas we all know that if it is to be meaningful and relevant (even if the pupil does not accept it and become 'religious'), the pupil must begin to make its language his own or to explore for himself at his own level of experience the territory of religion. Clearly many pupils feel they are given a quick tour into this strange land, and although they are vaguely aware of its importance and relevance, they are there under compulsion, without any encouragement to question the guide, and so they return to normality with relief, and the territory remains foreign soil – visited but unexperienced. The sixth former is a person and rightly resents being treated as a reluctant tourist, but the fourth and second former is a person, too, and his introduction to this territory is equally important (Edwin Cox, *Sixth Form Religion*, pp. 140 f.).

All this suggests that when pupils enter the sixth form, unless they have chosen religious knowledge as one of the subjects for 'A' level, they should be given a long rest from systematic study of parts of the biblical text.

This does not mean that no work on the Bible should be attempted with sixth-form boys and girls. This false conclusion underlies the suggestion made in many of the revised Agreed Syllabuses. One recent (1968) syllabus, for example, lists the following, and only the following, sixth-form topics: men, money and sex; certain sects (i.e., Jehovah's Witnesses, the Mormons, Seventh Day Adventists, etc.); comparative religion; modern challenges to Christianity; twentieth-century Christian writers and thinkers (William Temple to Rudolf Bultmann). No doubt some, at least, of these topics will provide lively discussion and argument and, as we shall see, uninhibited discussion is a very important technique in sixth-form teaching, but to ignore the Bible completely in the last two or three years of school life does nothing to change the 'reluctant tourist' into an eager explorer who loves the land whose characteristics he has learnt to know so well.

Built-in Assumptions

One valuable starting-point in sixth-form work is to probe gently into the erroneous assumptions and prejudices concerning the Bible which boys and girls may have carried with them through their earlier school life. Even with the best of teaching it is astonishing how large can be the area of misunderstanding. In conducting some of these probes, and in the subsequent teaching, it is often helpful to bring in other specialists in the school, more particularly specialists in English and History. Three 'built-in assumptions' are here briefly discussed.

1. *The Bible is one book*. It is not. The Old Testament is a selection of the literature of the people of Israel over a thousand years of its national life. The New Testament is a selection of the literature of Christianity in the first hundred years of its existence. In the first article in this book, 'What is the Bible?' (Part 1, Section 1, pp. 3 ff.), this is worked out in detail.

This basic fact about the Bible should be taught to children in their last year in the junior school or in the first year at secondary school. No doubt this is sometimes done: one or two Agreed Syllabuses include it in the first year of secondary education. It is, of course, true that children do absorb a vague notion of different authors. There are prophets with different names and four Gospel-writers, Matthew, Mark, Luke and John. Usually, but not invariably, the distinction is drawn between the Old and New Testaments, and there are stories in the Bible as well as prophetic denunciations and the Sermon on the Mount. Nevertheless, the unexamined assumption is that the Bible must be treated as one book, to be received or rejected as a whole.

This built-in error, once it has been brought into the light, can be swiftly dealt with simply by reading aloud in a series of contrasts a historical narrative from the Old Testament, for instance, the fall of Jerusalem (Jer. 52.3b–16), followed by a modern description of the fall of Berlin. Then might follow an extract from a biblical set of laws (e.g., Deut. 22.1–4) matched with a quotation from the *Highway Code*. Poetry (an extract from Job) and a traveller's adventure (the shipwreck in Acts. 27.9 f.) with modern parallels would sufficiently complete the exposition. This might be followed by a period based on the article in this volume which discusses the biblical scholar and his tools (Part 1, Section 2, pp. 5 ff.). Here, in particular, specialists in history and in literature could contribute valuable information about the techniques used in their own disciplines.

2. *The Bible is true and valuable. The Bible is untrue and irrelevant.* Consider these contrasting opinions taken from Edwin Cox's research on *Sixth Form Religion*:

> The stories all have a meaning which is good and 'heavenly' and I feel the men who wrote them must have been inspired by God to have the ideas in the first place (p. 72).

> If the people who wrote the Old Testament were not divinely inspired, they would not have made so many prophecies about a future Messiah with such certainty (p. 74).

> The Old Testament is mainly a figment of the imagination of some poor deluded brain. The evolution of man shows this. Science and Darwin proved that man was descended from the animal. If the Old Testament writers wove such jany stories round this, heaven knows to what extent the rest is just pure fiction (p. 85).

> I think the New Testament is prejudiced – it only gives one side of the picture – and that in such flowery symbolic language that it almost cries out to be disbelieved (p. 85).

This type of comment, whether it accepts or rejects the Bible, assumes that all literature is 'true' or 'false' in one sense only, but the literature of any nation offers to its readers many different kinds of truth. The 'truth' of Isaac Newton's theory of gravitation cannot be simply equated with the 'truth' of a poem by John Donne, nor the 'truth' of C. V. Wedgwood's description of the fall of Prague in *The Thirty Years War* with the 'truth' of an Iris Murdoch novel. Even within one broad subject there are different kinds of truth. A Norse saga is a different kind of literature from Bede's *A History of the English Church and People*.

There is, in the Bible, history which is well-documented and written with a scholar's respect for facts. There is, also, as for instance in the narratives of the patriarchs, a form of literature which is known as 'saga'. A 'saga' is not well-documented history. It reveals the inward, intuitive interpretation which a community puts upon the facts of its life. It reflects

a people's historical experience much more vividly than do the official records of victories and defeats in battle, of social upheavals and political crises. A 'saga' is the form in which a people thinks of its own history and interprets the meaning of events. Thus, for example, the 'saga' of Abraham in the book of Genesis discloses the deep religious experience of a nation in its early years. This, in narrative form, is what the first Israelites knew about God and his purposes. In those purposes Israel's role was to be a blessing to all nations.

The sixth-form pupil who dismissed the Old Testament as a collection of 'jany' stories had not been taught, or had not taken in, the importance of myth in the literature of a civilization. No doubt he had in mind the myths in the book of Genesis, and probably the best way to demolish this particular road-block in the path of understanding is to embark upon a short course of study about the myths of the world, both ancient and modern. There is a built-in resistance to myth among many senior pupils, but it is foolish to despise this form of literature, and to treat the stories as if they described straightforward historical happenings is to miss their true significance. A myth is not a fairy-story like Jack and the Beanstalk, nor a legend like the tales of King Arthur and the knights of the Round Table. The subject of the great myths of the world is always a fundamental and intractable human problem. The myth states and analyses the problem not by means of a philosophical or ethical argument, but in the form of a story which captures the reader's imagination and stimulates his emotions.

It is significant that many of the finest myths are concerned with the problem of power; the peril of allowing all power to be gathered into one man's hands. Daedalus and Icarus, the myth of Faust in its various forms, are two examples. J. R. Tolkien's *The Lord of the Rings*, though not perhaps a myth in the technical sense, is also about the problem of power. (*The Lord of the Rings* is mentioned here with some hesitation because while many readers find it so fascinating that they can hardly put down the book, an equal number regard it as childish nonsense.) In various ways these myths, ancient and modern, illuminate Lord Acton's phrase, 'Power tends to corrupt and absolute power corrupts absolutely.'

The myth of Adam and Eve in the garden of Eden seems to have had several interpretations put upon it in the course of its literary history. One of these meanings – perhaps the original one – is precisely the danger of unrestricted power. Eat of the fruit of the forbidden tree and 'your eyes will be opened, and you will be like God, knowing good and evil' (Gen.3.5). It is the temptation to seize the power which rightly belongs only to deity.

There is a modern version of the myth of Eden in William Golding's well-known story, *The Lord of the Flies*, which some pupils will know. It tells of a number of schoolboys who, being evacuated by air in a future war, find themselves on an uninhabited island after their plane has crashed. The story revolves around the struggle for leadership between two boys. One is Ralph, twelve years old, strongly built, 'but there was a mildness about his mouth and eyes that proclaimed no devil'. The other is Jack, a boy with a hunter's instincts, 'and eyes turning, or ready to turn, to anger'. The parallels between the myth of Eden and *The Lord of the Flies* are close indeed. Eden is an unspoilt garden; the island is an uninhabited tropical paradise. There is a talking snake in the Genesis story and a talking pig's head in Golding's novel. In both myths innocence is lost, and both end with fire. In *The Lord of the Flies* Jack's gang sets fire to the island by mistake as they try to smoke Ralph out of his hiding place: when Adam and Eve are driven from the garden, cherubim with flaming swords guard the way to the tree of life.

3. *The Bible is a collection of ideas about God and the world. There is no evidence that the ideas are true.* How do ideas arise and how can they be tested? Apart from purely abstract theories as in some forms of mathematics and philosophy, ideas are the product of experience and by experience alone can they be validated. For the men of the Bible, living and thinking as a community rather than as individuals, experience came to them almost entirely in the form of historical events. That is why so much of the Bible – especially of the Old Testament – consists of historical narrative. This is, however, a stumbling-block not only to pupils at school, but also to adult readers of the Bible, including not a few contemporary theologians. Certainly it is difficult to find any moral enlightenment or spiritual inspiration in such a narrative as this:

In the twelfth year of Joram the son of Ahab, king of Israel, Ahaziah the son of Jehoram, king of Judah, began to reign . . . He went with Joram the son of Ahab to make war against Hazael king of Syria at Ramoth-gilead, where the Syrians wounded Joram. And king Joram returned to be healed in Jezreel of the wounds which the Syrians had given him at Ramah, when he fought against Hazael king of Syria (II Kings 8.25–29).

This is of no importance except that the persistent quarrel between Syria, Israel and Judah was one small link in the complicated chain of events which led eventually to the destruction of all three kingdoms.

Yet the emphasis on history is one, at least, of the answers to the question, 'What is the evidence that biblical ideas are true?'. The great and abiding convictions by which the Jews, on the one hand, and the Christians, on the other, have lived through the centuries, and by which they still live, were created by historical events. Events are the raw material of experience, and the biblical ideas in both the Old and the New Testaments are the fruits of that experience. In part it was an experience of deliverance, and for brief periods one of prosperity. Yet, much more it was compounded of harsh political realities – military defeats and social upheavals; suffering, exile and death. It was not in a philosopher's ivory tower, but in making bricks for Egyptian taskmasters, not in quiet contemplation but on the desert march and the battlefield, that the central powerful idea of a covenant between God and man was born (see Part III, Sections 3, 6, pp. 84 ff., 107 ff.). What this fundamental idea meant to an ordinary peasant farmer, centuries later, can be seen in the following extract from the book of Deuteronomy. At harvest time the farmer took the first fruits of his land and offered them upon God's altar and recited this formula:

'A wandering Aramean was my father; and he went down into Egypt and sojourned there, few in number; and there he became a nation, great, mighty and populous. And the Egyptians treated us harshly, and afflicted us, and laid upon us hard bondage. Then we cried to the Lord the God of our fathers, and the Lord heard our voice, and saw our affliction, our toil and our oppression; and the Lord brought us out of Egypt with a mighty hand and an outstretched arm, with great terror, with signs and wonders; and he brought us into this place and gave us this land, a land flowing with milk and honey. And behold, now I bring the first of the fruit of the ground, which thou, O Lord, hast given me' (Deut.26.5–10).

Again in the Christian religion, the theology of the early church, as it is found in the speeches recorded in the Acts of the Apostles and as it was developed in the Epistles, arose out of an historical event – the life and death of Jesus of Nazareth, and his continuing presence with the disciples and his victory over death. The ideas of the New Testament are attempts at interpreting the fact that Jesus had come, attempts to give meaning to the experience of the first Christian community:

> That which was from the beginning, which we have heard, which we have seen with our own eyes, which we have looked upon and touched with our hands . . . we proclaim also to you (I John 1.1–3).

Ideas which are born out of experience are built upon foundations of rock for those who pass through the experience. They are an example for others but not fully persuasive. They ought, however, to challenge us to examine our contemporary experience in depth and to seek for its meaning.

These three built-in assumptions – and there are others – can, if wisely handled in the classroom, be made the starting-point for an understanding of the true significance of the biblical literature. They raise, each in different ways, questions about inspiration and about revelation which need free and open discussion in the classroom. Yet, perhaps, these words are the wrong ones to use in framing the all important question. It is not the question, 'Is the Bible inspired?', or 'Is the Bible the revealed word of God?', but rather, 'What is the authority of the Bible which I as an individual freely and gladly acknowledge?'

Discussion in the Classroom

Discussion has rightly come to stay as a valuable technique in sixth-form religious education. It has developed because of the urgent needs of adolescents who are seeking to find a firm foothold in a bewildering world where the ancient landmarks have been destroyed and the modern signposts contradict each other by pointing in different directions. Discussion demands involvement, not academic interest, and certainly sixth-form boys and girls are involved in questions of personal moral behaviour, from the wisdom or foolishness of taking drugs to the ethics of pre-marital sex. They are equally involved in criticism of the society which they have inherited and which will, inevitably, to a greater or lesser degree, mould their lives. Thus they are also struggling to find answers to somewhat more abstract questions: 'What, if any, are the limits upon personal freedom?' 'Can any attitude or action be labelled "right" or "wrong"?' 'Are the promptings of conscience anything more than the subtle pressure of society to conform to fixed and socially convenient standards?'

One valuable kind of sixth-form religious education, therefore, consists of dialogue and debate in which the master or mistress takes on the dual role of chairman and of a human encyclopaedia, available for reference, and when referred to, speaking with impartiality and authority, though not with omniscience. The discussion must be free and open and seen to be free and open. It must be taken seriously by both pupils and staff or it will be worse than useless, as these comments quoted from *Sixth Form Religion* show:

> Discussions are very useful but so much depends upon the master taking you. So far this term our divinity master has torn to pieces every argument we've put forth. He's put his view forth, but I'm still very puzzled about my own conclusions (p. 136).

> During second year in the sixth form our religious instruction has been nothing but the firing by 30 boys of the most difficult questions they could think of, at a master who has heard them all before, and has the answer ready parrot-fashion. This has been an awful bore to me and of little or no value at all (p. 136).

Have debates and discussions – seriously entered into and well directed – any religious value? Surely they have, not least because they are a way of treating one another as persons; a training in respect for individuality. Yet it is easy for them to remain on a purely secular level with little Christian content apart from a few biblical allusions where these seem appropriate. Have biblical ideas and, in particular, the teaching of Jesus any significant contribution to make? Obviously it will not do to quote the Ten Commandments, yet even in the midst of forthright debate on a modern issue the Bible has its place. The teaching and example of Jesus moved at a far deeper level than conventional moral behaviour, and his understanding of human nature was profound. He is entitled to be heard in the debate.

Three Inescapable Questions

The three questions are: (*a*) Who am I? (*b*) What is my place in society? (*c*) What am I here for? The first is the question of identity, the second the question of love and the third the question of purpose. They are inescapable, because though we may never formulate the answers in words, they will be answered by the way we live. It is valuable to raise them deliberately with a sixth form and to seek answers which can be expressed in words and passed on to others. Identity, love, purpose: it would be possible to build a year's sixth-form syllabus around these three questions. The discussions would no doubt range far and wide and bring in many contemporary issues, but the starting-point of the teacher's own thinking and his constant standard of reference would be the New Testament.

1. *Identity*

Jesus was a permissive teacher in a very restrictive society. Where others said 'no' he said 'yes'. Why was Jewish society in the first century AD so restrictive? The answer lies in the Great War, the war of the Maccabees (167 BC), when the successors of Alexander the Great tried to impose Greek culture upon the Jewish people. Out of this struggle arose the party of the Pharisees (see Part III, Section 15 and Part IV, Section 3, pp. 193 f. and 228 f.).

In the first century AD, when the Romans ruled in Palestine, it was Graeco-Roman culture which was the enemy of the Jewish way of life. In the time of Jesus there was a Roman theatre and a Roman hippodrome in Jerusalem and another theatre at Scythopolis (one of the ten towns known as the Decapolis), which was only about ten miles from Nazareth (see Part IV, Section I pp. 213 f.). It was the infiltration of Graeco-Roman culture which made the Pharisees so restrictive. To obey the Mosaic Law in every detail, to keep the sabbath holy, to avoid all contact with non-Jews was, they thought, the only way to preserve the nation's identity, to remain the people of God. This, though it led to a most restrictive pattern of life, was not unworthy. It was patriotic, it was loyal to the past, it preserved purity of morals, and yet, in large measure, Jesus rejected it. He did so because he believed passionately in the identity of individuals, because ordinary men and women must be given freedom to answer for themselves the question, 'Who am I?'. The essence of the reply of Jesus to the opposition of the Pharisees was precisely that a man has his own life to live and it must be lived his way. He said in effect:

> My disciples and I have begun a new life together and that means a new kind of religion. There are times when you can't bring together the new and the old. If you tear a hole in an old coat you don't sew on a patch of new unshrunk cloth. If you do the patch will tear away from the coat, the new from the old, and leave a bigger hole. And you don't put new wine into old wineskins. The new wine will burst the old wineskins and both the wine and the skins will be lost. No, if the wine is new, you must use new wineskins (see Mark 2.18–22).

Against this background the discussion could be guided in three directions:

(*a*) What should be our attitude to the tensions which exist in our society between the restrictive and permissive forces? (Notice how far Jesus 'conformed' and how far he broke away.)

(*b*) What does it mean to say:
(i) 'I am a man'; 'I am a woman'? An attempt at an answer will be biological, psychological, sociological, but also spiritual. (ii) 'I am not just a man or a woman. I'm me. I have my own life to live and it isn't any old life. It's *my* life'? What does individual personality involve and how is it nurtured and trained?

(*c*) What is involved in claiming to live one's own life? It involves moral judgments which have to be made, including the moral judgment upon ourselves.

2. *Love*

What is my place in society? A frequent starting-point in this area of discussion is family relationships and then moving outward to the wider world. The snag is that the discussion gets bogged down at the start by heart-rending stories about ghastly parents, and when the class has been shifted away from that it is stuck with boy-meets-girl situations. A better technique, perhaps, is to start with the widest circle of love relationships: with the needs of the homeless, with our responsibility towards emerging countries, with race relationships. The urgent question for most young people is, of course, sex relationships, but it is valuable to set that problem in the widest possible context of Christian love. All the virtues which are needed to build an harmonious relationship between (say) black and white within one community – patience, a desire to understand, a refusal to exploit, sympathy and tolerance – are the virtues out of which are constructed a happy courtship and a lasting marriage.

At some point in this discussion the idea of a mediator can be introduced. There is, of course, a theological doctrine testifying to the 'way of access' through Christ to God, but here the point is that Jesus during his life in Galilee and Judaea strove to be a mediator between conflicting groups in society. A mediator is one who 'stands in the middle'; in between opposing forces, in between quarrelsome individuals, seeking always to reconcile them. Jesus stood in the middle between Jew and Samaritan and between Jew and Roman, and it is legitimate to wonder how he handled other potential squabbles. There is evidence that the disciples were sometimes at loggerheads. What was the reconciling power which kept Simon the one-time Zealot revolutionary and Matthew the ex-tax collector in the same company?

It is the testimony of the evangelists, especially Luke, that Jesus had a special regard and limitless compassion for the 'outsiders' of society. This is illustrated in the Gospels by his attitude to 'tax collectors and sinners' (in this context 'sinner' is a synonym for 'outsider'). And there were other outsiders. Luke records that as Jesus travelled about the towns and villages of Galilee he was accompanied not only by the twelve disciples but also by

some women who had been healed of evil spirits and infirmities: Mary, called Magdalene, from whom seven demons had gone out, and Joanna, the wife of Chuza, Herod's steward and Susanna, and many others, who provided for them out of their means (Luke 8.1–3).

That a travelling Rabbi should be accompanied by women is surprising enough, but two of the women, Mary of Magdala and Joanna the wife of Chuza, Herod's steward, were outsiders in a particular sense. There is no evidence that Mary of Magdala had been a prostitute. The text says that Jesus had cast out from her seven demons, which means that she had suffered from a severe mental breakdown. This in itself would make Mary an 'outsider'; one under the judgment of God. Joanna, as the wife of Herod's steward, probably lived in Tiberias, a Roman city which no strict Jew would enter. She and her husband would be branded as traitors by the orthodox, as was Matthew the tax-collector. Yet Jesus admitted Mary and Joanna to his friendship. It is a point worth developing in the midst of those interminable discussions on the relationship between men and women. But beware of speculations about the inner emotional life of Jesus. On this the Gospels are entirely silent and to guess and weave fantasies is both misleading and unscholarly.

3. *Purposes*

Two questions are involved here: (a) one's own personal desires, hopes and intentions and (b) the possibility that there is a pattern or purpose in the universe which may shape one's own life and overrule one's own plans.

On the personal level, there is obviously no omnibus purpose for everyone, and it is fruitful to discuss some of the many ways in which one's life can be spent. The good life can be lived on several different levels from the level of quiet domesticity to the level of heroism. There is a useful illustration of the point in the different solutions arrived at by Edward and Lavinia on the one hand and Celia Coplestone on the other, in T. S. Eliot's play, *The Cocktail Party*. There is also the question of the proper balance between an individual's hopes and desires and the purposes of the society in which we live. Where do we take our stand between the opposite poles of anarchism and wage-slavery?

Is there a purpose beyond our own personal purposes, a predetermined pattern not of our making, a shape not to be disregarded but accepted? In spite of the difficulties of defining such a purpose, and of finding evidence for such a predetermined shape, men always seem to return to the idea. There have been utopias by the dozen, and men still design them, usually in scientific terms. There was the nineteenth-century notion of inevitable progress, which some still believe in in spite of the shattering experiences of the twentieth century. There is the Marxist doctrine of the inevitable defeat of capitalism and 'the withering away of the state'.

There is also the Christian concept of the kingdom of God (see Part IV, Section 8, pp. 290 ff.), and a study of this leads on to a man's personal response to Jesus. Perhaps this response can be spoken of openly in the sixth form, perhaps not. Maybe the imperatives can be uttered, 'Seek first the kingdom of God,' 'Follow me.' Perhaps they must be left unsaid until they speak for themselves.

FOR FURTHER READING

Available in paperback

A. *General*

Allport, G. W., *The Individual and his Religion*, New York: Collier-Macmillan, 1962.
*Dale, Alan T., *The Bible in the Classroom*, London: Oxford University Press, 1972.
*Erikson, Erik H., *Childhood and Society*, London: Penguin Books, 1965.
Goldman, R., *Religious Thinking from Childhood to Adolescence*, London: Routledge, 1964.
*Goldman, R., *Readiness for Religion*, London: Routledge, 1965.
*Grimmitt, M., *What can I do in RE?*, Great Wakering: Mayhew McCrimmon, 1973.
*Hadfield, J. A., *Childhood and Adolescence*, London: Pelican Books, 1962.

B. *Infant and Primary*

Children and Their Primary Schools, vol. 1, London: H.M. Stationery Office, 1966.
Dean, J., *Religious Education for Children*, London: Ward Lock, 1971.
*Holm, J., *Teaching Religion in School*, London: Oxford University Press, 1975.
*Lee, R. S., *Your Growing Child and Religion*, London: Penguin Books, 1965.
Loukes, H., *Friends and Their Children*, London: Harrap, 1958.
*Madge, V., *Children in Search of Meaning*, London: SCM Press, 1965.
*Madge, V., *Introducing Young Children to Jesus*, London: SCM Press, 1971.

C. *Junior*

Goldman, R., ed. *What is the Bible?*, London: Hart-Davis, 1966 (four books for use in class and a teacher's book).
*Hubery, D. S., *Christian Education and the Bible*, Oxford: Religious Education Press, 1967.

D. *Senior and Sixth Form*

Alves, C., *Religion and the Secondary School*, London: SCM Press, 1968.
*Copley, T. and Easton, D., *A Bedside Book for RE Teachers*, London: SCM Press, 1975.
*Copley, T. and Easton D., *What they never told you about RE*, London: SCM Press, 1974.
*Cox, E., *Changing Aims in Religious Education*, London: Routledge, 1966.
*Evening, M., *Approaches to RE*, London: Hodder & Stoughton, 1972.
*Laing, R. D., *The Divided Self*, London: Penguin Books, 1967.
*Loukes, H., *Teenage Religion*, London: SCM Press, 1961.
Religious Education in Secondary Schools, Schools Council Working Paper 36, London: Evans/Methuen Educational, 1971.
Robinson, R., and Chapman, J., *Images of Life*, London: SCM Press, 1973.
*Smith, J. W. D., *Religion and Secular Education*, Edinburgh: St Andrew Press, 1975.
Young, R. W., *Everybody's Business*, London: Oxford University Press, 1968.

The Old Testament

1 · Major Events in Israel's History

Period or date BC	Biblical events	Political background (Israel's neighbours and enemies)	Biblical references	Section in Source Book Part III
c.2000–1500	Sagas about the Patriarchs: Abraham, Isaac, Jacob, Joseph	Mesopotamia; Canaan; Egypt	Gen.11.31–50	Section 5, pp. 102 ff.
c.1300	*Israel in Egypt* The escape from Egypt; the desert march; the covenant at Sinai; leadership of Moses	Egypt	Exodus	Section 6, pp. 107 ff.
c.1200–1000	*'The Promised Land'* The gradual conquest of Palestine; the rule of the judges; the tribal league	Various tribes in Palestine; Egypt	Joshua; Judges; I Sam.1–7	Section 7, pp. 114 ff.
c.1020–922	*The United Monarchy* Saul, David, Solomon Jerusalem becomes David's capital city Writing down of 'J' and 'E' traditions	Palestinian tribes: especially the Philistines; Kingdoms of Damascus, Hamath and Tyre	I Sam.8–31; II Samuel; I Kings 1–11	Section 8, pp. 121 ff. Section 3, pp. 87 ff.
922–587	*The Divided Kingdoms* Israel and Judah The prophets Writing down of 'D' tradition	Egypt; Assyria; Babylon	I Kings 12–22 II Kings 1–25 (II Chron.10–36) Deuteronomy	Section 9, pp. 127 ff. Section 10, pp. 134 ff. Section 3, pp. 91 ff.
587–537	*The Exile in Babylon* Prophets of the exile	Babylon; Persia	II Kings 25 Jer.39–44; Ezekiel; II Isaiah (ch.40–55)	Section 13, pp. 173 ff.
537	*The Return from Exile* Rebuilding of the temple and Jerusalem Writing down of 'P' tradition	Persia	Haggai; Zech.1–8; Ezra 1–6	Section 14, pp. 182 ff. Section 3, pp. 93 ff.
312–63	The Seleucids and the Maccabees	Macedonian Empire of Alexander the Great; the Seleucid Empire	I and II Maccabees (Apocrypha); Daniel	Section 15, pp. 191 ff.
63	*Rome* Jerusalem captured by Pompey	Rome		Section 15, p. 195

2

The Land and the People

J. R. Bartlett

(A simpler description of the geographical features will be found in Part IV, Section 2, pp. 214 ff.).

Any teacher of the Old Testament knows that if Abraham as a person is remote, the story can be brought to life by the use of geography. Abraham starts in Ur of the Chaldees and travels round the Fertile Crescent as far as Egypt, and one of the undoubted attractions of the Bible is that it is set in such a fascinating land. 'Mesopotamia' and 'Canaan' are not names found in the political atlases, but they are part of the deep-seated mental picture which every Christian and perhaps nearly every western European has of the Near East. They are names which arouse feeling. It will help our teaching considerably, however, if we can show how 'Mesopotamia' and 'Canaan' by their very geographical peculiarities helped to shape the history of Abraham and his descendants, and so acquired for us a more than merely geographical meaning.

Geology

Geography begins with geology. At the heart of this whole area – sometimes called the 'Near' East, sometimes the 'Middle' East, and sometimes more accurately 'South-west Asia' – lies the plateau of Arabia. This was once part of a large block called by the geologists 'Gondwanaland'. To the north and west of this block lay a sea which we call Tethys, of which the present Mediterranean Sea is a remnant. The coast-line of this sea fluctuated, sometimes extending far into what is now the land east and south-east of the Dead Sea, and leaving behind on top of the sandstone layers of the Primary and Secondary geological ages a layer of limestone. The sandstone can be seen round Petra, south-east of the Dead Sea, and the limestone in the hills round Jerusalem. Another layer of much softer limestone ('Senonian chalk') followed, and this has worn away to leave some

of the mountain passes of the modern Israel. On top of this came a third, harder layer of limestone, now seen, for example, between Mt Carmel and Samaria, or in the mountains east of the Jordan.

However, in the Tertiary period the seabed of Tethys, which was based on less resistant rock than Gondwanaland, was forced up by pressure acting from the north, and was pushed and folded into mountain chains against the unyielding edge of Gondwanaland. At the same time the Gondwanaland platform itself fractured in several places, dividing roughly into what is now Africa, Arabia, India and western Australia. At its edges, the platform warped and sometimes actually 'faulted' or broke, and the sedimentary limestone deposits on top folded upwards. In this way the present shape of 'Canaan' was produced, the faults being clearly seen, for example, in the Jordan valley, or the division of Upper and Lower Galilee, or the canyons of the trans-Jordan region. Later, volcanic activity east of the Jordan and the Red Sea, and sediment building up the coast-line and the Jordan valley contributed to the shaping of the land.

Further east, the basic platform did not get overlaid by deposits from the sea. When the platform fractured, the part which became Arabia tilted slightly, so that its western edge was higher than its eastern, and a trough was formed at the base of the Iranian mountains which the Euphrates and Tigris rivers have slowly filled with alluvium.

It can be seen, then, that Mesopotamia and Canaan belong together to one geologically related area. The frontier between eastern and western powers has crossed this region many times in the course of history; and on either side of this region the flora and fauna of Africa and Asia show many similarities (e.g., the

African and Asian elephant). This, too, is an area of routes and backwaters; thus such communities as the Maronites in Lebanon, the Druses in Gilead, and the Samaritans in the central hills west of the Jordan have retreated for security to the heights, by-passed by the main routes of the 'Fertile Crescent'. The Mediterranean coast of this region is famous as a bridge between Asia and Africa, and this feature of south-west Asia has clearly helped the rise of its civilizations.

Geography

1. *Mesopotamia*

When Abraham travelled from Ur to Haran, he passed from one distinct geographical region to another. For 'Mesopotamia' (strictly, the land between the Tigris and the Euphrates, but often used of a wider area) is composed of two regions. The northern region is the 'island'

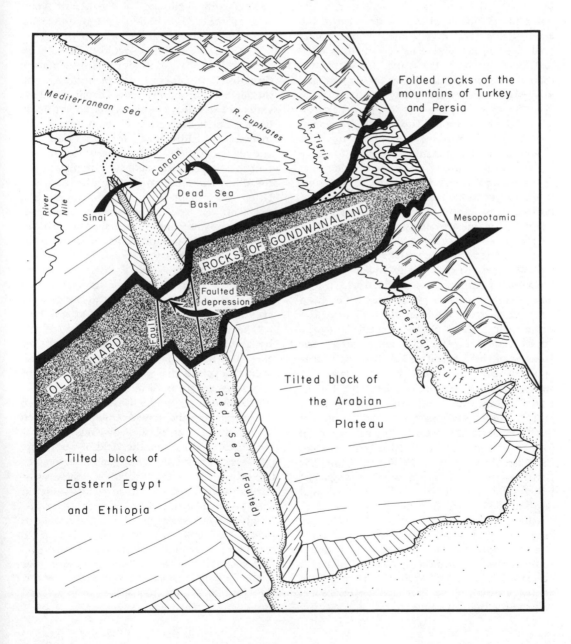

between the two great rivers, beginning where they, deriving the bulk of their waters from the snows of Armenia and Kurdistan, cut through the Kurdish scarp to the basic plateau of the Arabian massif. The plateau slopes southwards, dropping from about 1300 feet above sea level at the base of the scarp to about 200 feet at the edge of the southern, Delta, region a little north of Baghdad. On the plateau the two rivers flow across hard limestone, often between cliffs, and the riverbeds have moved very little in the course of time, so that the mounds of ancient cities still lie close to the river banks. The Zagros hills, whose waters feed the Tigris, receive more rain than areas further west, and so the Tigris, though shorter than the Euphrates, is a faster flowing stream, bringing down nearly fifty per cent more alluvium than the Euphrates. The plain between the Zagros hills and the Tigris was the home of the Assyrians, and the rainfall, rising from twelve inches per annum in the plain to thirty inches in the foothills, made for rich harvests of grain and orchard fruit (and nowadays, tobacco), even without artificial irrigation. Further west, between the two great rivers, the valley plains are narrow and the soil often barren or eroded. Cultivation therefore tends to be restricted (as in the case of the Nile valley) largely to river banks. In ancient times there was a certain amount of artificial irrigation here, and recently there have been attempts to store the river flood waters, and irrigate large tracts of land, especially in the upper valleys of the Balik and Khabur, tributaries of the Euphrates. But this steppe area between the two rivers was important in antiquity; Haran lay on the Balik (Gen.11.31 f.; 12.4 f.), Gozan on the Khabur (II Kings 17.6; 18.11), Carchemish on the upper Euphrates (Isa.10.9; Jer.46.2), commanding an important ford for traffic between the Mediterranean and the East, Pitru (perhaps Pethor of Num.22.5; Deut.23.4) a little lower down, and Mari just below the confluence of the Khabur and Euphrates. In the fifteenth and fourteenth centuries BC this was the region of the Hurrian kingdom of Mitanni, later taken over by the Aramaeans; hence the land was called Paddan-Aram (Gen.28.2: *padanu* in Assyrian denoted a measure of land) or Aram-naharaim ('Aram of the two rivers', i.e., perhaps the Euphrates and the Khabur; Ps.60, title).

The Delta region of the south – ancient Sumer and Akkad, Babylon, biblical Shinar, with Elam away to the east – was quite a distinct area. It was formed by river silt being deposited on the slowly sinking bedrock of the plateau. Here the rivers have frequently changed their courses, and the ruins of ancient cities past which the Euphrates once flowed, such as Babylon, Nippur, Shuruppak, Uruk, Larsa, Ur, now lie in the desert well away from the river. The southern end of this region is swamp land, inhabited by the Marsh Arabs who use the reeds to build their huts and boats, and hunt the wild boar and wild fowl.

In this Delta region agriculture has always depended on irrigation, for there is a mere three to eight inches of rain each winter, and the main water supply comes from the flood waters of the rivers between March and May. But the floods have always been unpredictable in quantity, badly timed for agriculture (too late for winter crops and too early for summer crops), and irrigation has been complicated by the silting up of the canals and salination. The latter is Mesopotamia's greatest agricultural problem: the land becomes saline from evaporation of water spread out over the fields, or from salt in the ground water brought to the surface by capillary action. There is not enough rainfall to wash the salt away, and drainage is hampered by the impermeability of the soil. A recent study of the Diyala river area has shown that between 2400 and 1700 BC the wheat harvest fell to nothing and the barley yield fell from twenty-eight bushels per acre to ten. A temple archive from Lagash (c.2400 BC) states that salt had made part of the temple's territory unfit for agriculture, and we are reminded of Judg.9.45 where Abimelech 'razed the city and sowed it with salt' to end settlement at that place. However, until the land became too saline, the yield of barley and wheat is said to have been as good as in modern Canadian fields, and in c.2000 BC measures of barley were used as measures of value in Mesopotamia. In this southern area grew the highly nutritious date palm, as it did not north of Baghdad, and thus the staple foods of the area were flour and dates; a variety of vegetables and fruits can also be grown here – for example, onions, cucumbers, marrows, beans, figs, apricots, and nowadays tobacco and various narcotics.

2. *The Levant*

West of Haran, perhaps at Carchemish (modern Jerablus, a mere hundred miles from the Mediterranean *via* the oasis of Aleppo), Abraham would reach the Euphrates. Crossing this, he would enter the Levant, the 400 miles long by sixty miles broad coastal strip of mountains stretching down to Gaza and the southern end of the Dead Sea. The area is divided from west to east into four zones, each traceable the whole length of the area – a coastal plain, the central mountain range, the rift valley, and a second chain of hills east of the rift. From north to south the land is divided by several crossrifts into separate blocks, and the only zone which has a continuous north-south route is that east of the rift, where one can use the 'Haj' (pilgrim) route (perhaps described in Gen.14.5 ff.) along the desert edge of the mountains. We can best picture the area in three main sections.

(i) In the northern section, the Orontes river flows north down the rift valley and then turns south-west through Antakya (Antioch of the New Testament) to meet the sea. (The ancient port of Seleucia, from which Paul sailed, was seven miles further north.) West of the Orontes lies the main mountain range, consisting here of Jebel Akra (5500 feet; the Old Testament Mt Zaphon, the mountain of the north, cf. Isa.14.13 ff.; Ezek.28.14, 16; Pss.48.2; 68.15 f.; 89.12; and the home of the Canaanite pantheon headed by the god El and worshipped at Ugarit nearby) and Jebel Ansariya (4500 feet). Though these mountains are high, the interior is easily reached from the sea, and the nearness of the Euphrates has ensured the importance of the region as a land bridge between the Mediterranean and the east. The climatic influence of the Mediterranean, too, penetrates deeply here, bringing ten inches of rain per annum to Aleppo and upper Mesopotamia, making the cultivation of cereals possible.

(ii) The Lebanon ('white mountain') and anti-Lebanon range rise immediately south of the west-east gap between Tripoli and Homs, and from here until we reach Galilee there is no easy east-west communication. From north to south communication is little easier, for the rift valley offers only a difficult passage southwards into the upper Jordan valley, and

a route south down the Litani is blocked by deep gorges at the elbow of this river. But this is a fertile region, well forested, and rich in grain and fruit in the valleys, because it takes all the rain moving east from the Mediterranean. The lands around Damascus, too, are well watered from the rains, dews and snows of the mountains, and produce a large amount of fruit – walnuts, apricots, apples, vines, olives and also wheat.

(iii) South of this Lebanon region we reach the land we have come to know variously as Palestine (after the Philistines who settled mainly in its south-west corner), Canaan (after the purple dye and the pre-Israelite merchants of the coastal cities who traded it), and Israel (after the Jewish people). Christians think of it as the 'Holy Land', and geographers think of it in terms of Cis-jordan (i.e., 'this side of Jordan') and Trans-jordan. Like the rest of the Levant, it can be divided into four zones from west to east, broken by various cross-rifts.

(*a*) East of the Jordan the mountains rise steeply out of the rift valley and fall away gently to the desert. In the north, east of the Sea of Galilee, rise the volcanic Jebel ed-Druz and Jebel Hauran, with large lava fields to their west, the Old Testament area of Bashan, famous for its oaks and cattle. South across the River Yarmuk is the well forested Ajlun, among whose trees David's son Absalom was killed (II Sam.18.6 ff.). This area became known as Gilead, but the term perhaps originally referred to a mountain just south of the Nahr ez-Zerka (Old Testament, Jabbok), the valley in which Jacob made his covenant with Laban, met Esau, and wrestled with God (Gen.31–32). South of Gilead we come to the fertile plain called *ham'-mishor* (Josh.13.9; 20.8), whose possession was a matter of dispute between Israel and Moab (cf. Judg.11.12 ff.), the slopes of Pisgah of which Mt Nebo was part (Num.21.20; Deut.34.1), the sheep country of Moab with its city Kir-hareseth (II Kings 3), and the mountains of Edom to its south. The Israelite part of this Trans-jordan territory could be summed up (Josh.20.8) by the three areas of the table-land (*mishor*), Gilead, and Bashan. The country of Ammon lay on the east of the area between the Arnon and the Jabbok. The whole length of this Trans-jordan country from Syria to Edom was traversed by the 'King's Highway' (Num.21.22), which is still an important route.

(*b*) The rift valley now descends about 3000 feet to reach its lowest point in the Dead Sea, whose surface is 1292 feet below sea level, and whose bed at the northern end is 1300 feet lower still. This section of the rift, about 100 miles long, is drained by the Jordan (the name probably means 'the descender'), which rises on the south-west slopes of Mt Hermon and descends rapidly into Lake Huleh, seven feet above sea level (perhaps 'the waters of Merom', Josh. 11.5, 7), slowly piling silt against the basalt dam which forms the southern edge of the lake, and creating round it papyrus filled marshes. The river then drops steeply for a distance of ten and a half miles to the Sea of Galilee, or Tiberias, 682 feet below sea level. It was also called 'the sea of Chinnereth' (Num.34.11) or 'the waters of Gennesaret' (from Gennasar on its western side, I Macc.11.67). A large non-Jewish population lived here in such towns as Tiberias (built by Herod Antipas in honour of the Roman emperor) and the towns of the Decapolis (Mark 5.20; 7.31). The Decapolis was a league of ten Graeco-Roman cities south-east of the Sea of Galilee, formed in the first century BC for reasons of commerce and mutual defence against their Jewish neighbours. The Jordan now falls 600 feet in about sixty-five miles (as the crow flies; the actual course of the river is about 200 miles) through tropical thickets (the 'pride' of the Jordan, Jer.12.5; 49.19) where boar are still hunted. On either side of this lie desolate badlands of ash-grey marl, and beyond that, on the higher slopes of the valley, fields and pastures. The whole valley floor is called in the Old Testament the 'Arabah' (i.e., the desert; cf. II Sam.4.7). The valley widens at Beisan (biblical Bethshan), where the Jezreel valley runs into it, narrows to a width of two miles just north of the confluence of the Jabbok, and slowly widens to twelve miles' width towards the north end of the Dead Sea. Here the valley plain was called 'the round' (Gen.13.10 ff.; II Sam.18.23). To the west were the plains of Jericho, and to the east the plains of Moab. To the south was the Sea of the Arabah, or the Sea of Salt; the name 'Dead Sea' was coined or popularized by Jerome, and the modern Arabic name is 'the sea of Lot'. On its north-western shore on the edge of the barren hills of the wilderness of Judaea lay the settlement of the now famous community of Qumran. South of the Sea the rift valley continued, dividing biblical Edom from Judah, and reaching the Red Sea at Ezion-geber, Solomon's port (I Kings 9.26).

(*c*) West of the Jordan, the mountains are higher towards the south, and get more rain on the western slopes than on the east – geographical facts with economic consequences which have often affected political boundaries. In the north, Upper Galilee did not play much part in Old Testament history, though it was settled by the tribe of Naphtali. The important city hereabouts was Hazor, destroyed in the thirteenth century BC and re-settled by the Israelites, and later destroyed by Syrians and Assyrians; it commanded the route south between upper Galilee and the Jordan. Lower Galilee, the land of the tribes of Zebulun and Issachar, was a much more populous area, consisting of hills under 2000 feet high, broken in every direction by faults, well watered and productive except in the south-west and south-east corners. In southern Lower Galilee Mt Tabor is prominent, from which Barak's forces swept down to destroy Sisera's army (Judg. 4.6 ff.), and where Gideon destroyed the Midianites (Judg.7.1; 8.18). 'Galilee' means 'ring', though whether this refers to cities or the physical features of the area is not clear; its large non-Israelite population earned it the name from early times of 'Galilee of the Gentiles' (Isa.9.1).

Immediately south of Galilee is one of the most important features of the land – the plain of Esdraelon, through which the Kishon (Judg.5.21) flows north-west to the sea between Galilee and Carmel, and the plain of Jezreel, through which the Jalud flows east to the Jordan, rising from the spring of Harod (Judg.7.1). The watershed is only about 300 feet above sea level, and thus the two plains make a unique pass between the Mediterranean and the Jordan. On the southern edge a low ridge runs north-west from the hills of Samaria to Mt Carmel, crossed by the main Egypt-Damascus road. At Megiddo this road meets the road running along the plains, so Megiddo has been a key point in many campaigns (cf. Judg.5.19; II Kings 23.29 ff.). The Armageddon of Rev.16.16 ('mount Megiddo') was thus an appropriate symbolic name for the final battle between the forces of good and evil.

To the south of Esdraelon rise the hills of Israel. The northern half of these hills, settled by Manasseh, is lower than the southern half, settled by Ephraim, and has no clearly recognizable frontiers. Samaria became its chief city (I Kings 16.24). The area is a basin, with Mt Carmel and Mt Gilboa and the higher mountains of Ephraim and Judah forming the edges on the north-west, north-east and south, with limestone hills like Mts Ebal and Gerizim pushed up in the middle, between which lie Jacob's well (John 4.6) and Old Testament Shechem. The towns here were in valleys, not on the heights. South of Shechem the road rises steeply up the watershed into the highlands of Ephraim ('Mt Ephraim'), which top 3000 feet and contained such important places as Shiloh (I Sam.1) and Bethel. The road through these places from Megiddo *via* Dothan and Shechem is mentioned in Judg.20.31 f.; 21.19; it went south along the watershed through Jerusalem to Hebron and Beersheba, and so on to Egypt.

It is not always appreciated that Jerusalem lies on the very northern border of the Judaean hill country, which stretched fifty miles 'from Geba to Beersheba' (II Kings 23.8). Indeed, Jerusalem only became attached to Judah when David captured it and ruled both Judah and Israel from a centrally situated capital. Before this time, 'Bethlehem in Judah' was perhaps the northernmost Judaean town (Judg.19.1ff.). The central and highest point of the region lies at Hebron, and Beersheba, at the foot of the mountains to the south-west of Hebron, marks the transition to the desert of the Negeb. To the west, the Judaean hills drop steeply, with deep valleys cut by erosion into the fault-line; west of this a sunken mountain plateau forms rolling foothills about 1000 feet high, increasing in breadth as they get further south. To the east, the hills drop through a barren wilderness towards the Dead Sea, in sharp contrast to the more fertile land west of the main watershed. These southern regions are well portrayed in the story of David's years as a raiding bedouin chief, enemy of Saul and dubious ally of Achish of Gath in I Sam.20–II Sam.2, until his coronation at Hebron as king of Judah.

(*d*) Lastly, we come to the zone of the coastal plains. North of Mt Carmel, this was the territory of the tribe of Asher. South of Carmel, the plain widened southwards, and was originally occupied by Philistines and other kindred 'Sea-peoples', probably being incorporated into the kingdom of Judah after David's defeat of the Philistines (see the province list of I Kings 4.7 ff.). Between the Philistine plain and the mountains is the low limestone plateau known as the 'Shephelah' (from a word meaning 'to make low'), where the tribe of Dan, to which Samson belonged, first settled, a richly fertile, well wooded buffer zone, crossed by the valley of Aijalon, down which the Philistines fled after their defeat at Michmash (I Sam.14.31), and the valley of Sorek, the scene of some of Samson's exploits (Judg.13 ff.), and the valley of Elah, where Goliath was killed (I Sam.17). The coast itself is flat, without natural harbours; at Caesarea and Joppa reefs running out into the sea were used to build up artificial harbours, but not by the Israelites, who found access to the sea difficult from their mountains, and were no great sailors. Jonah had to take a foreign ship from Joppa.

Climate

Near Eastern and European ways of life differ largely because their climates differ. In winter, from October to May, masses of humid air move into the Near East *via* the Mediterranean from the Atlantic. These winter cyclones bring rain; the Mediterranean seaboard is well watered, north Mesopotamia and the foothills north-east of the Tigris receive some rain, but beyond Mecca there is no rain. This westerly airstream is responsible for the 'former rains' (Deut.11.14; Jer.5.24, etc.) of early winter; but this airstream draws in behind it cold air from the north which heats up as it meets the Near East and becomes unstable, producing showers and even snow in mountain areas. This begins about Christmas time, and culminates in the 'latter rains' of March and April, which are a result of the turbulence from the heating-up in spring of the cold winter air. Without the former rains, the farmer could not plough and sow his ground, and without the latter rains the crops would not ripen. In the spring, north Africa and the southern desert areas of the Near East heat up, and the resulting air pressure causes hot, sand-laden winds to blow (cf. Jer.4.11; Isa.27.8; Jonah 4.8; Luke 12.55), which can scorch and destroy the grass and crops if it comes too soon. The summer climate depends on air from the monsoons of the Indian Ocean, which gets steadily drier as it moves north-west across the land-mass. Thus from May to October is a dry season throughout most of south-west Asia, and the water supply comes from whatever has been stored in wells or cisterns (Deut.6.11; II Kings 18.31; Jer.38.6), or from the rivers. In some parts, snow is stored in caves, and carried down to the towns later in the year.

All this naturally affects the region's vegetation, which has either to adapt itself to the summer season (like the vine, whose roots spread just below the surface to get the dew, or the bulbs of the anemones, the iris and lily which lie dormant for the summer), or to complete its growth season in the winter. Thus cereals are sown in autumn, harvested from April to June, and their seeds survive to germinate the following year. Different areas, however, have different types of vegetation: by the rivers grow the date palm, willow and poplar trees; in the mountains the evergreen, coniferous and deciduous trees; in the desert the thorn bushes and various grasses; in the steppe a variety of shrubs and grasses, especially the broom (I Kings 19.5); but it is in the Mediterranean climate of the Levant that the richest variety of fruits and cereals, trees and grasses may be found. But in this region considerable damage has been done over the centuries by the cutting down of the trees for fuel, and by the ceaseless cropping of the grass by goats. Woods of oak and beech, cedar and pine have been replaced by scrub; the soil has been eroded, thus lowering the water-table, making the water run-off easier, and making renewed growth more difficult. Over the last five or six thousand years these and other factors of human mismanagement such as misrule and war, rather than any noticeable change of climate, have been responsible for the visible decay of once thriving Near Eastern civilizations.

Near Eastern Ways of Life

In the ancient Near East as elsewhere, the main forms of life, in general order of development, were nomadic, agricultural, and urban, all much influenced by the geographic and climatic conditions. The bedouin shepherd, the country farmer and the town trader have flourished side by side in the Near East, only recently joined by the cosmopolitan cities and their business men, brought to the Near East by the discovery of oil.

1. *Nomadic*

Social conditions create the modern gypsies and wandering tinkers, but the desert creates the bedouin nomad of the Near East. This people derived its living by hunting, by grazing flocks of sheep, goats and cattle, or camels, on the sparse herbage (and thus constantly seeking new pastures), and by raiding both fellow-nomads and settled farmers. In Jerusalem to this day the shopkeeper will despise his bedouin customer as uncouth, and the bedouin will despise the shopkeeper as effete, and in ancient Israel there seems to have been something of both attitudes. There were Jews (including the Rechabite sect) who looked back with respect and nostalgia to Israel's wilderness days or to the period of the patriarchs as the formative period of Israel's great tradition (cf., e.g., Jer.35.6 ff.; Josh.24.2 ff.), perhaps fearing the effect of the Canaanite way of life with its agricultural deities and fertility cults on Israel's loyalty to Yahweh (see Hos.2). On the other hand, there were Jews for whom the desert was a place to avoid, the haunt of demons, where the sin-laden scapegoat was sent to wander (Lev. 16.22). But Israel's ancestors may not have been true desert nomads. The patriarchs were perhaps ass-nomads, moving backwards and forwards with their flocks to the desert fringes in winter and the hill country in summer. A famous tomb-painting from *c*.1900 BC shows a group of ass-nomads entering Egypt (always the nomad's refuge in hard times), wearing gaily coloured clothing and carrying bows, spears, a sort of lyre, and what are perhaps bellows, indicating that this group were wandering tinkers by trade. But the Bible illustrates most clearly one basic feature of nomad life – family solidarity. In the desert the family is the natural community, and even when Israel settled in towns she never entirely forgot this, as the long genealogies of the Bible and many of the laws (e.g., of blood revenge; cf. Num. 35.19, 24) show.

2. *Agricultural*

The laws of the Old Testament 'Book of the Covenant' (Ex.21–23) reflect largely agricultural societies. In ancient Israel, the earliest calendars known to us are given in terms of the agricultural year. A tenth-century BC verse inscription from Gezer describes the farmer's annual programme, beginning in late autumn:

> His two months are (olive) harvest,
> His two months are planting (grain),
> His two months are late planting;
> His month is hoeing up of flax,
> His month is harvest of barley,
> His month is harvest and feasting;
> His two months are vine-tending,
> His month is summer fruit.

The Book of the Covenant mentions as the three important seasons of the year the feast of Unleavened Bread (the barley harvest in April), the feast of First-fruits (or of Weeks, i.e. seven weeks later; the wheat harvest in May/June), and the feast of Ingathering at the end of the year (or Tabernacles, the autumn vintage feast, cf. Judg.21.19 ff.). These feasts have had a long history of re-interpretation, and are now celebrated by the church as Easter, Whitsun and Harvest Festival.

In both Mesopotamia and Israel, sheep, goats, oxen and asses played a large part in agriculture, being bred for meat, milk, and wool and for labour. In Gen.31.38 ff. Jacob describes the perils of minding the flocks; Deut.22.10 legislates against maltreatment of ox and ass at threshing time. Moab, east of the Dead Sea (II Kings 3.4), was famous for sheep and wool, and Bashan (Ps.22.12) for cattle.

In theory, the land of Israel was Yahweh's, and could not be sold in perpetuity (Lev.25.23); it was also said that God gave Israel the land as an inheritance, and each tribe, clan and family had its portion of the inheritance. Under the monarchy, the increase of trade led to the growth of rich land-owners who bought out the poorer farmers when forced to sell in time of need. But when Ahab tried to buy Naboth's vineyard, Naboth refused because it was the inheritance of his fathers (I Kings 21.3). Micah denounced the wealthy who coveted fields, and stole a man's inheritance (Micah 2.2). The land was, and is, of religious significance to Israel.

3. Urban

Neither in Mesopotamia nor in Israel was there a sharp distinction between city and country, for the city was an agricultural centre, a large part of whose population worked in the fields, and whose surrounding villages were known as 'her daughters' (e.g., Josh.15.32;

Num.21.25). The oldest settlement yet discovered in the Near East is Jericho, where *c*.7800 BC Mesolithic hunters built near a stream what may have been a sanctuary. By *c*.7000 BC a stone wall and a tower defended the site. But it is not until the fourth millennium BC that we find such walled cities in Mesopotamia, and in the third millennium the city-state, with its wall, its temple built on a platform, and its irrigation system, was the basis of Sumerian society. Mud-brick buildings may be seen today in the Jordan valley, but up in the hills of Israel cities could be built of the limestone – easily cut, and gleaming white in the sun – and records written on potsherds (*ostraca*). But both Mesopotamia and Israel used stone for more important records and monuments.

The site of an ancient city was largely determined by the needs of defence, the availability of water, and the importance of the place on a route or at a crossroads or as a control point for the surrounding agricultural land. Cities could be small, like David's Jerusalem (eleven acres), or large, like Hazor (175 acres), but all would have their temple or sanctuary ('high place', cf. I Sam.9.13 ff.), and their gate, a space just inside the main gate where people met for gossip, business or judicial purposes (cf. Ruth 4.1; II Sam.15.2; Job 29.7, etc.). The king would have his palace, often an acropolis or tower close to the temple (cf. Judg.9.46; I Kings 7.1–12; Ezek.43.8); the people's houses would cluster round without real plan or streets (until the Hellenistic period). They had flat roofs of beams, covered with brushwood or laths, topped with clay, often needing renewal, on which flax could be dried (Josh.2.6), or even an upper chamber built (cf. II Kings 4.10: this one had a bed, table, chair and lamp).

The city, then as now, was the natural centre for trade, industry, and cultural activities. I Kings 20.34 refers to trading quarters set up by diplomatic agreement in Samaria and Damascus. At biblical Debir archaeological evidence of a dye-works and textile industry has been found. Ezion-geber on the Gulf of Aqabah (I Kings 9.26) was important for both trade and its copper industry. The court at Jerusalem seems to have been a centre of literary activity, especially in the time of Solomon (cf. I Kings 4.29 ff.), and Jerusalem's cultural centrality was naturally bound up with the prime importance for Israel of the temple, especially after the exile.

Geology, geography and climate, forming and influencing desert, field and city, provide the background of the Old Testament, which shows us men and women reacting and responding with varying degrees of faith to that background and the events which came from it. A feeling for that background makes the men and their message real to us. Perhaps the greatest student of this background was George Adam Smith, who wrote in the introduction to *The Historical Geography of the Holy Land* the following words:

> What is needed by the reader or teacher of the Bible is some idea of the outlines of Palestine – its shape and disposition; its plains, passes and mountains; its rains, winds and temperatures; its colours, lights and shades. Students of the Bible desire to see a background and to feel an atmosphere; to discover from 'the lie of the land' why the history took certain lines and the prophecy and the gospel were expressed in certain styles; to learn what geography has to contribute to questions of biblical criticism; above all, to discern between what physical nature contributed to the religious development of Israel, and what was the product of moral and spiritual forces. On this last point the geography of the Holy Land reaches its highest interest.

3

How Israel Became a Nation

Ernest Nicholson

The Old Testament record of how Israel became a nation is contained in the first five books of the Bible, the Pentateuch. The composition of these books is traditionally ascribed to Moses who stands out in them as the central figure involved in the crucial events of exodus and the covenant ceremony on Mt Sinai, which Israel looked back upon as having called her into existence as the people of God. The investigation of these books in modern scholarship, however, has made it clear that this traditional view of their authorship cannot be sustained. On the contrary, it is now widely agreed that the Pentateuch comprises several originally separate documents which were composed in considerably differing periods of Israel's history and only gradually woven together into the corpus of literature which they now constitute. The Pentateuch can thus no longer be regarded as offering an eye-witness account of such events as the exodus, the covenant on Mt Sinai, the wilderness wandering and the preparation for the conquest of the land of Canaan; indeed, it has emerged that even the earliest of the documents which it comprises was composed at a time several centuries removed from these events.

This does not mean that these documents are of little use for the task of reconstructing the history of the origins of Israel. On the contrary, in each instance they contain many traditions and much material which are of great antiquity and of considerable relevance for the modern historian of early Israel. The point is, however, that the authors of the documents in question were not merely concerned with recording the facts of history; they were not mere chroniclers. Rather, they sought to present an interpretation of the events of Israel's origins for the generation in which they lived. In this way they must be regarded as historians even though the history which they wrote differs in many important respects from modern historiography. The main difference is that for them the course of history was directed by God, not just in the sense that he was believed to be the ultimate reality behind history, but that he actively intervened in the affairs of men and nations in order to fulfil his divine purposes. The history which they wrote was thus salvation-history, that is, the history of God's saving acts on behalf of his people Israel.

The Origins of the Pentateuch

One of the most permanent contributions of scholars of the nineteenth century to biblical studies was their isolation of four main documents in the Pentateuch and the chronological order in which they arranged them. The four main documents thus isolated are designated by the letters J, E, D and P. The simplest to isolate is 'D' since it consists for the most part of the book of Deuteronomy with its very distinctive style and theological point of view. The Priestly document ('P') is also relatively easy to discern and there has been widespread agreement on its contents. It also has an easily recognizable style and displays many characteristic features such as its fondness for genealogies. It also contains an elaborate description of Israel's sacral institutions, the origins of which are traced back to creation and primaeval history but chiefly to the work of Moses at Sinai. When these two documents have been removed what remains is a general narrative which is composite. The most important document in this general narrative is known as 'J' since it regards the divine name Yahweh (= Jehovah) as having been known since primaeval times and in addition shows a keen interest in the southern tribe Judah. The author of this document is accordingly usually referred to as the Yahwist. The 'J' strand in this general narrative is extensive and in many places can be isolated from the surrounding material with reasonable certainty. Thus, for example, the creation story complex in Gen.1–3 can be divided into a 'P' story (Gen.1–2.4a) and a 'J' narrative (Gen.2.4b–3). But it is not always so easy to isolate 'J', for it has been closely interwoven with a second document in this general narrative, a document known as 'E' because it uses the name *Elohim* for God up to the revelation of the divine name Yahweh to Moses, and in addition shows an interest in northern Israel (Ephraim). The presence of these two sources in this general narrative in the Pentateuch is perhaps best illustrated by the story of the maltreatment of Joseph by his brothers in Gen.37. In part of the story Joseph is cast into a pit and left to die but is then found by a band of passing Midianites who bring him to Egypt and sell him into slavery. The strand of the narrative which relates this is 'E'. On the other hand, the same chapter relates that he was actually sold by his brothers to some passing Ishmaelites and this derives from the 'J' source. Furthermore, the 'E' source describes the patriarch Reuben (the ancestor who gave his name to one of the future northern Israelite tribes) as the one who saved Joseph from death while the 'J' source with its southern, Judaean orientation depicts the patriarch Judah as having done so. By postulating the presence of two originally separate documents, which have been closely interwoven in this narrative, some sense can be made of what is otherwise a story producing not a little confusion for the modern reader. We may note, however, that such a separation of 'J' from 'E' is not always possible and for this reason scholars often refer to the material in the Pentateuch apart from 'D' and 'P' as 'JE'.

The date of the documents was determined largely with reference to 'D', for at an early stage in the scholarly investigation of the Pentateuch, Deuteronomy (in its original form) was identified with the book of the law found in the temple in 621 BC and made the basis of a reformation by Josiah (II Kings 22–23). On the basis of this and other arguments it was concluded that Deuteronomy was composed in the seventh century BC. It was then concluded by comparing the documents that 'D' represented an advancement upon 'JE', one of the main considerations being that Deuteronomy demands the centralization of the cult to one sanctuary while 'JE' still thinks in terms of a multiplicity of sanctuaries where Israel worships God. On the other hand it was very widely agreed that the Priestly document simply presupposes such centralization of worship and belongs to a later period than 'D' in which centralization still appears to be a major concern to be set forth as forcibly as possible. Accordingly, on these and other grounds it was established that 'JE' preceded 'D' and that 'P' followed it so that the chronological order of the documents is 'J', 'E', 'D' and 'P'.

In spite of various attempts to discredit it, this theory still commands the assent of the majority of Old Testament scholars. At the same time some of the grounds on which it was arrived at, as well as the assessment of the documents by older scholars for the understanding of the origins and emergence of Israel as the people of God, have been rejected or considerably modified during the past generation. In particular it has become increasingly clear that the documents are not to be regarded as largely the *ad hoc* creations of their individual authors in which they have reflected for the most part the views on the faith of Israel peculiar to their own particular age. On the contrary, it is now widely accepted that underlying the documents are traditions and material of great antiquity and this has brought with it a great deal of interest and research into the pre-literary stage of the documents and the various literary units which they contain. Thus, for example, Deuteronomy can now no longer be regarded as the work of an author who sought to set out in a programmatic form the implications for Israel's religion of the ethical teaching of the great eighth-century prophets. It is seen rather as the literary formulation at a relatively late period of traditions and legal material which point for their origins to very varied periods in Israel's history, in some instances the earliest period. Similarly, the Priestly document, though providing us with much information about Israel's religion as it developed in the exilic and post-exilic period, contains traditions and material of great age and value for our understanding of Israel's history and religion in much earlier periods.

While, however, increasing attention has been devoted to the pre-literary history of individual units of material and traditions in the Pentateuch in recent years, most significant of all has been the investigation of the emergence of what may be referred to as the Pentateuch tradition. By this is meant the basic schema of the Pentateuch as a whole comprising a number of themes which the various documents present or at least presuppose wholly or partly. This schema is as follows: (1) God who created the world and man (2) called Israel's ancestors and promised them the land of Canaan, (3) delivered their descendants from bondage in Egypt and (4) entered into covenant with them on the sacred mountain of Sinai, after which (5) he led them in the wilderness for forty years and finally (6) brought them into the promised land. The last of these themes is not actually recorded in the Pentateuch but is contained in the book of Joshua and Judg.1. It seems clear, however, that the book of Joshua is to be related to the book of Deuteronomy as the continuation of the latter while it is probable that Judg.1 contains at least partially the 'J' conquest narrative. Furthermore, 'J' and 'E' both point forward to

the entry into the land as the fulfilment of a promise made by God to Israel's ancestors and for this reason also the conquest theme must be regarded as belonging to the basic Pentateuch tradition. These themes taken together constitute the framework of the Pentateuch and present a summary of Israel's salvation-history of which the Pentateuch as a whole presents an elaborate record.

The question which now arises is the origin of this schema. The earliest of the Pentateuchal sources, 'J', follows it step by step and most probably it is to the author of this document that it owes its present form. Nevertheless, there are strong grounds for believing that he was not responsible for its creation *in toto* and that this schema represents only an expansion, albeit a significant expansion, of a schema which had already taken shape and developed at an earlier time.

In attempting to ascertain the form of this earlier schema attention has been directed above all to a short passage in Deut.26.5–10 which, with the exception of a few secondarily inserted phrases, is regarded by many scholars as an old *credo* which briefly summarizes the history of salvation which Israel regarded as having called her into existence as God's people. In this chapter in Deuteronomy we are told that when a worshipper came to the shrine to offer to Yahweh a basket of the first fruits of the harvest he made the following confession:

A wandering Aramaean was my father; and he went down into Egypt and sojourned there, few in number; and there he became a nation, great, mighty, and populous. And the Egyptians treated us harshly, and afflicted us, and laid upon us hard bondage. Then we cried to the Lord, the God of our fathers, and the Lord heard our voice, and saw our affliction, our toil, and our oppression; and the Lord brought us out of Egypt with a mighty hand and an outstretched arm, with great terror, with signs and wonders; and he brought us into this place and gave us this land flowing with milk and honey. And behold, now I bring the first of the fruit of the ground, which thou, O Lord, hast given me.

It is clear that already this old creed presents an outline of the salvation-history and for this reason it has often been referred to as the

Pentateuch or Hexateuch in miniature. There are, however, two striking omissions. First of all, the saving history as here recited contains no reference to the creation or primaeval history; it begins with the patriarchs. Secondly, there is no mention of the momentous events at Mt Sinai where the making of the covenant, so central to Israel's faith, took place. How are we to account for these omissions?

The absence of the creation theme with its related primaeval history may be explained quite simply on the grounds that it was not brought into the framework of the salvation-history until a relatively late stage in the development of Israel's faith. In fact while there is no need to doubt that creation stories circulated in Israel at a very early time it is very probable that it was the Yahwist who first linked this theme with the salvation-history as it is outlined in the old *credo*. This finds some further support in the fact that this theme is not contained in the second oldest of the Pentateuchal documents, 'E', which otherwise follows closely the same schema as the 'J' document. That is to say, the schema of the salvation-history which both 'J' and 'E' presuppose began not with creation and the primaeval history but with the patriarchs.

But what of the Sinai covenant then? Is it possible that it was also the Yahwist who first linked this theme with the *credo* themes? This suggestion has been made, but it is much more likely that in this instance the *credo* themes and the Sinai theme were already united in the basic schema which the Yahwist employed in writing his epic. The absence of the Sinai theme from the old creed is possibly due to the manner in which the themes were used liturgically; the recitation of God's mighty deeds on Israel's behalf may have formed the introduction to a Sinai covenant festival held annually in early Israel. Indeed such festivals may well have provided the occasion for recalling the events which were believed to have made the covenant possible or which at least witnessed to that covenant as forming the unique relationship between God and his people Israel. In this way Israel's cult would have lent itself to the creation of a national epic which not only would have united the basic themes of the salvation-history – the call of the patriarchs, bondage and exodus, the covenant on Sinai, the traditions about the wandering in the wilderness,

and the gift of the promised land – but would also have included a not inconsiderable filling out of these themes with other relevant material.

Something approaching this view has been argued by the German scholar Martin Noth who believes that during the period of the 'judges', when the tribes of Israel constituted a tribal league, a national epic designated by him as 'G' (= *Grundlage*), containing a history of the saving acts of Yahweh on behalf of Israel, was created. It is argued that it was this source – whether oral or written cannot be decided – which the authors of 'J' and 'E' separately employed in writing their own histories of how Israel became a nation and that this explains the well-known similarity between these two documents both in the basic schema which they follow and the traditions and sagas which they share.

This means that there is a much longer history behind the Pentateuch than scholars formerly believed. More important still, it indicates that in the earliest period of her existence Israel already confessed her faith in her God Yahweh as a God who had acted mightily on her behalf, calling her into existence and making her his people. And it is this confession which forms the very heart of the Pentateuch and which each of the documents in its own individual manner is concerned to describe and proclaim. The story of how Israel became a nation is, as far as the Pentateuch is concerned, the history of salvation. We must now turn to an examination of each of the four main documents to see just how each one of them in its own age interpreted and presented this salvation-history.

The Salvation-History in the Pentateuchal Documents

1. *The 'J' Document*

The earliest literary strand in the Pentateuch is, as we have noted, the 'J' document. There are a number of indications that this document originated in Judah such as, for example, the interest it shows in the old southern sanctuary of Hebron with which the patriarch Abraham is closely associated (cf. Gen.13.18 and 18.1) and the prominence of the patriarch Judah in the cycle of Joseph stories in Gen.37. In addition, the saying concerning Judah in the 'Blessing of Jacob' (Gen.49.8 ff.) seems to presuppose the place of supremacy attained by the house of Judah under David. This in turn affords an indication of the period in which 'J' was composed, for although it has sometimes been dated as late as 850 BC it is much more probable that it was written during the David-Solomonic period. It reflects a spirit of national confidence and fulfilment which can be fully understood against the background of national ascendancy achieved under David and Solomon, rather than against the background of the period after the disruption of the state in 922 BC. Probably, therefore, the 'J' document was composed about 950 BC.

We have seen that the author of 'J' in composing his work was dependent upon an earlier Israelite national epic ('G') which already contained the main themes of the salvation-history from the call of the patriarchs to the entry into the land of Canaan, together with much old material which had been assembled during the period of the judges and fitted within the framework of that epic. But the Yahwist did not simply reproduce this early Israelite epic; on the contrary, he expanded its framework by including the primaeval history and at the same time employed the material which it and other sources placed at his disposal in such a manner as to set forth his own theological interpretation of the salvation-history.

The Yahwist's narrative of the primaeval history begins with creation (Gen.2.4b–25) and the fall of man (Gen.3), and continues with the story of Cain and Abel (Gen.4), the stories of Noah and the flood and the rebirth of civilization after the flood (Gen.5–10 where 'J' and 'P' are blended), and the episode of the tower of Babel which brings the primaeval history to its dismal end (Gen.11.1–9). In prefacing his epic of Israel's salvation-history with the primaeval history the Yahwist sought to achieve several theological objectives. In the first place he affirmed that Yahweh was not only the God of Israel but Creator of the world and Lord of all the peoples of the earth. He also placed the history of his own people within the context of world history in general from the beginning and, more important still, asserted that Israel's election and redemption by God was not merely of national significance but of universal significance, since it was through Abraham and his descendants that God wished to bring salvation 'to all the families of the earth' (cf. Gen.12.3).

Throughout his narrative of the primaeval history, however, the Yahwist describes in bold colours man's sinfulness and persistent and increasing rebellion against God. At the same time, while at every stage God's judgment upon man is fully narrated, the Yahwist stresses throughout God's tender care for his creature and his will to save: Yahweh perceives man's loneliness and creates woman as 'a helper fit for him' (Gen.2.18); having pronounced judgment upon Adam and Eve for their rebellion against him, he makes them garments to conceal their nakedness (Gen.3.21); Cain is cursed for murdering his brother Abel but is graciously given a protective mark by Yahweh (Gen.4.15); man's sin becomes such that Yahweh destroys the world but even then acts to save by preserving Noah through whom a new beginning can be achieved (Gen.6.5–8; 7.1–5); and when, even after this, things once more go from bad to worse and man's sinfulness once again asserted itself (Gen.11), here again Yahweh's judgment is accompanied by a new act of grace through which he purposes to save, for though the primaeval history comes to an end in dismal failure it is immediately followed by the call of Abraham through whom Yahweh's saving activity acquires a new direction (Gen.12).

Genesis 12–50, which includes also much material from 'E' and 'P', presents the history of the patriarchs and as such marks the beginning of Israel's salvation-history proper. It is probable that stories about the patriarchs were already contained in the early Israelite epic 'G'; their importance as recipients of divine promises of land would have assured them a firm place in the salvation-history at an early stage. Nevertheless, the Yahwist has skilfully emphasized the element of promise throughout his work in which it becomes one of the two poles, promise and fulfilment, around which the epic as a whole is composed.

Thus Abraham receives the promise (Gen.12 and 15) which is in turn renewed to his son Isaac (Gen.26) and then his grandson Jacob (Gen.28.10 ff.), who becomes the father of the twelve patriarchs whose descendants constitute the tribes of Israel. The Yahwist stresses the tenacity of the promise and God's will to fulfil his word by describing throughout the work a series of crises in which the promise was placed in jeopardy and preserved only through the gracious intervention of Yahweh. Thus having received the promise Abraham is forced immediately to leave the land in which it is to be fulfilled to go to Egypt in a time of famine (Gen.12.10 ff.). In Egypt Sarah, who is to be the mother of Abraham's 'seed', is taken into Pharaoh's harem. But Yahweh intervenes and the patriarch returns with his wife to the land of Canaan (Gen.12.17 ff.). Here, however, yet another crisis arises, for the strife between the herdsmen of Abraham and Lot raises the possibility that Abraham will again have to leave the promised land. But Lot chooses the land to the east and Abraham remains in Canaan (Gen.13.3 ff.). The future of the promise is likewise challenged in the case of Isaac, Abraham's son and the heir to the divine promise. In this instance the crisis arises because Isaac cannot have a wife from the Canaanites among whom he lives. But again Yahweh graciously intervenes and one of his own kindred from Aram, Rebekah, becomes his wife (Gen.24). Rebekah's barrenness, which presents yet another challenge to the promise, is overcome by Yahweh and she bears two sons, Esau and Jacob (Gen.25.21 ff.). Jacob, who by cunning strategy robs his brother of his birthright and becomes heir to the promise of blessing (Gen.25.27 ff.; 27.1 ff.), is forced to leave the promised land but while in exile acquires two wives, Leah and Rachel, and is eventually led back to the promised land, having regained Esau's favour (Gen.29 ff.). And this pattern of crisis and deliverance continues with the eventual bondage of Jacob's descendants in Egypt when as never before the promise is acutely called in question but once again reactivated by Yahweh who calls Moses and delivers his people from slavery. During the period in the wilderness Israel's own sin (cf. Num.14) jeopardizes the promise, but after some years of wandering, inflicted in judgment upon Israel for her rebellion, Yahweh is able to let his people enter the promised land.

A brief sketch such as this cannot hope to do justice to the Yahwist's achievement. But perhaps enough has been said to provide at least the outlines of the breadth of vision and dimension of his theology. Two aspects of the history of salvation which he wrote are particularly worthy of emphasis. In the first place he transcended the older and narrower presentation of the salvation-history by seeing it and describing it as having been orientated not merely towards Israel but as being part of God's universal plan to bring salvation to all the peoples of the world. Israel was indeed Yahweh's peculiar people, but as such the agent through which he purposed to gather all men to himself. As we have seen, it was mainly by composing the primaeval history that the Yahwist succeeded in adding this dimension to the salvation-history. And secondly, from beginning to end the Yahwist's epic asserts that no matter what obstacles human weakness and sinfulness may create, God's will to save emerges triumphantly; through all the vicissitudes of time and the persistent attempts of men and nations to frustrate his purposes, Yahweh's word is established.

The Yahwist's achievement is further illuminated when the period in which he composed his epic is recalled, for he wrote at a time when the old tribal system of early Israel had all but disappeared and Israel was established as a national state under David and Solomon to play a role in the international affairs of the world in which it existed. Israel was now exposed to ideas and cultural movements from far beyond the borders of the little land in which she had settled, and the international atmosphere in which she now found herself, especially during the reign of Solomon, must have threatened to render the old faith inadequate if not altogether irrelevant. It was the noblest achievement of the Yahwist that he presented an interpretation of Israel's history and her divine election so as to make them relevant to the new situation in which she now found herself; there was a larger world around Israel now, and that, as the Yahwist saw it, was itself all part of the unfolding drama of salvation. This means that the Yahwist was not just narrating what was long past; he was not looking backwards. Rather, his work pointed forward. God had called the fathers and given their descendants the land. There was indeed fulfilment in this. But the process of salvation goes on so that the element of promise and expectation is still there. The Yahwist's epic thus points forward to the full realization of God's blessing upon the world.

2. *The 'E' Document*

The second oldest document in the Pentateuch is the 'E' or Elohistic strand, so designated because it employs the word *Elohim* for God in the period before Moses to whom the divine name Yahweh was first revealed (Ex.3). It is generally agreed that the 'E' document was eventually combined with 'J' by an editor who made the latter the basis of his work and used only selections from 'E' to supplement it. For this reason the quantity of 'E' material in the Pentateuch is somewhat less than 'J', which means that it is more difficult to assess the theological purpose and achievement of the author of the original 'E' document.

There are a number of indications that 'E' originated in northern Israel. Thus, for example, 'E' material is prominent in the cycle of stories about the predominantly northern figure Joseph (Gen.37 ff.), and in the story of Joseph's maltreatment by his brother it is Reuben, the patriarch of one of the future northern tribes, who takes the lead in protecting him, while, as we have seen, according to the 'J' document it is Judah (Gen.37). Similarly, interest is shown in Ephraim, one of the most influential of the northern tribes (cf. Gen.48.20). In addition, northern sanctuaries such as Bethel and Shechem figure prominently in 'E'. Furthermore, the patriarch Jacob, closely associated with the sanctuary at Bethel (cf. Gen.28 'JE'), comes more to the forefront in the 'E' narrative, while Abraham, so prominent in 'J', recedes somewhat. The 'E' document knows nothing of the story of Abraham and Lot (Gen.13) or the stories about Sodom and Gomorrah (Gen.18–19), while the story about Judah, Shua and Tamar in Gen.38 contains no 'E' material.

One of the most striking differences between 'E' and 'J' is that 'E' contains no primaeval history (Gen.1–11 comprises only 'J' and 'P' material). In this respect 'E' lacks the universal dimension of 'J' and does not share the same belief in the divine commission of Israel as the agent through which Yahweh's blessing would come to the nations. Instead, 'E' begins with the call of Abraham and from here onwards follows the course of events described by 'J'. In this respect 'E' is therefore closer to the basic Pentateuch tradition ('G'), the themes of which it, like 'J', elaborates.

A further characteristic feature of 'E' is its tendency to widen the distance between God and man. There is a more sophisticated concept of God in 'E' than we find in 'J' in which Yahweh comes down and 'walks in the garden in the cool of the day' (Gen.3.8). In 'E' God is thought of as dwelling in heaven and mediating his will to man through angels (cf. Gen.28.12) or in dreams and visions (cf. Gen.20.3). And with this stress on the otherness of God comes a corresponding heightening of the wonders and miracles which he performs; the 'E' material in Ex.7–10 ('J', 'E' and 'P') augments the miraculous element in the plagues inflicted upon Egypt.

Yet another feature of the 'E' document which marks it off from 'J' is the emphasis which it places upon the figure of Moses. It was to Moses, according to 'E' (cf. Ex.3), that the divine name Yahweh was first revealed, while 'E' also has supplied many of the details about Moses's early life and call in Ex.2 ff. The uniqueness of Moses is stressed in other ways also. Thus the distance drawn in 'E' between God and man and the necessity for intermediaries throws the mediating role of Moses into prominence. Moses in 'E' is in fact the great mediator with whom God spoke 'mouth to mouth'; he is the prophet *par excellence* (cf. Num.12.7 f.). We may also observe in this connection that the author of 'E' was keenly interested in prophets and prophecy (cf. Num.11.25 ff.).

Also characteristic of 'E' is the emphasis it places upon the exclusiveness of Israel as the people of Yahweh; Israel is to be to God 'a kingdom of priests and a holy nation' (Ex.19.6). The limitation of the use of the name Yahweh to the post-Mosaic period evidences this. But it is particularly in evidence in the polemic in 'E' against pagan cults (cf. Gen.35.2,4; Ex.19.5 ff.; 32.21). It is probable that we have here further indications of the northern background of 'E', for while Judah was by no means free from the danger of the influence of Canaanite religious and cultic practices, it seems that the real threat to Israel's worship of Yahweh was centred in northern Israel. Here the main concentration of the old Canaanite population was to be found and here the predominantly agricultural environment lent itself to Baal worship with its emphasis on fertility cults. We may note also that the northern prophet Hosea was deeply concerned with the influence of Canaanite cults at Israel's northern sanctuaries (cf. Hos.2;4;10), while the Deuteronomic authors who also probably came from the northern kingdom show themselves to have been acutely concerned with pagan cults.

The period in which 'E' was written is diffi-cult to determine. It is widely accepted that it was composed during the monarchical period in northern Israel, but whether at the beginning of it under Jeroboam I or towards the end of it under Jeroboam II is not agreed. The polemic against pagan cults more than echoes the struggle of Elijah against the worship of Baal in northern Israel, but such a struggle had already been going on even before this. Perhaps the fact that there is no hint of the threat of the Assyrians which began in the mid-eighth cen-tury may be taken as an indication that the 'E' document was composed in the earlier part of the history of the northern kingdom and the period of comparative calm in the early years of the eighth century has been plausibly sug-gested by a number of scholars.

Like the Yahwist, the Elohist author com-posed his epic as a history of salvation. But he cannot be said to have achieved the same breadth of vision and theological dimension as the Yah-wist. This is particularly evident in the absence in 'E' of the primaeval history which, as we have seen, occupies a place of great theological significance in 'J'. The 'E' document is more nationalistic in character and the emphasis throughout is on the exclusiveness of Israel as Yahweh's people among the nations. The limita-tion of the use of the divine name Yahweh to the post-Mosaic period itself stresses this and the conservative element which pervades the work as well as the acute fear of the influence of or challenge of pagan cults further throw it into prominence. The universalism which we found in 'J' is absent and the saving activity of God is orientated towards Israel alone.

In defence of the Elohist, however, it must be borne in mind that he lived in an age and environment in which Yahwism was struggling for nothing less than its survival against the increasing popularity of Canaanite religion in the northern kingdom of Israel. In such a situation the emphasis which he placed upon the exclusiveness of Israel as the covenant people of Yahweh to whom alone their allegiance was due was of extreme necessity and was patently justified. Furthermore, in stressing Yahweh's otherness he shows himself to have been one not just concerned with coining a more exalted concept of God but with asserting his holiness and divine sovereignty over against the squalid fertility rites of the Canaanite wor-ship of Baal. He sought to break through the superstitious practices of pagan cults and point to a God who could not be manipulated by such practices but whose grace had throughout the past been extended in love to his people and was still directed towards them. It was against this background and with these intentions that the Elohist presented his interpretation of Israel's salvation-history.

3. The 'D' Document

The book of Deuteronomy ('D') is the third of the four main documents which the Pentateuch comprises. This book purports to be Moses' farewell address to Israel just before his death and on the eve of the entry of the tribes into the promised land. This traditional view of its origin and composition can no longer be accepted, however, and it has become clear that the book of Deuteronomy as it now stands is the final product of a long history, both with regard to much of the material which it em-bodies and individual traditions to which it gives expression as well as the literary stages through which it has developed.

Since the work of the German scholar W. M. L. De Wette in the early nineteenth century it has been widely agreed that the 'book of the law' which, according to II Kings 22, was discovered in the temple in Jerusalem in the eighteenth year of the reign of Josiah (621 BC) was the book of Deuteronomy in its original form. The question of the contents of this original book has been much discussed, but more recently the view has been widely favoured that it comprised substantially chs. 5–26 and 28 of the present book of Deutero-nomy. The latest date for the composition of this original book is clearly 621 BC while the earliest is very probably c.700 BC, since one of the dominant characteristics of Deuteronomy is the demand for the centralization of the cult to one sanctuary, a demand which, as far as we know, was first introduced by Hezekiah as part of a reformation which he carried through in the late eighth century BC (cf. II Kings 18.4,22).

The process whereby the original book was expanded into the book of Deuteronomy in its present form is no longer possible to ascertain in all its details. It is possible that the book was periodically read within a liturgical context, perhaps as part of a covenant renewal festival (cf. Deut.31.9 ff.), and this may have provided the occasion for the addition of further material. But there is every reason to believe that much of the later material in the book (chs.1–4;27 and much of 29–34) was added by the author of a history influenced by Deuteronomistic ideas. This presents a history of Israel from Moses and the giving of the law (Deuteronomy) through the period of the conquest of Canaan (Joshua), the period of the judges (Judg.1–I Sam.7) and the monarchical period down to the fall of the northern kingdom in 721 BC and the state of Judah in 586 BC with the ensuing exile (I Sam.8–II Kings 25). Since, however, the book as a whole displays a remarkable uniformity of outlook, the authors of the original book and the later Deuteronomistic historians very probably belonged to one and the same 'circle of tradition'; for our purposes the book may be considered as a whole.

Unlike the documents 'J' and 'E' which we have examined briefly above, Deuteronomy does not present an extended narrative of the history of salvation from the creation or the call of the patriarchs onwards. Instead it centres on the Sinai covenant of which it purports to be a restatement made by Moses after the forty years of wandering in the wilderness, which followed the original covenant ceremony on Mt Sinai. This does not mean, however, that the salvation-history is of no importance in Deuteronomy; on the contrary, throughout the book it is presupposed and briefly summarized as that which called Israel into being as God's people and was as such the very basis of the covenant. It was also the record of Yahweh's grace towards Israel to which she is here called upon to respond in faithful adherence to the solemn responsibilities which the covenant placed upon her.

In its main theme as well as in its manner of presentation and the actual form which it takes, Deuteronomy is the covenant document *par excellence* in the Old Testament. As such its overall purpose is to call Israel to a full realization of her election as the people of Yahweh and the solemn obligations which this placed upon her. Accordingly, the main part of the book is a presentation of the laws governing the covenant (Deut.12–26), and the very distinctive homiletic style in which they are couched, as well as the hortatory introduction to them (Deut.5–11) and the formulation of blessings and curses which follow them (Deut.28), are all aimed at pressing home upon the minds and consciences of those to whom they were addressed the urgent necessity of obedience and faithfulness to them.

The nature of Deuteronomy and the purpose for which it was composed can be fully appreciated only when the particular period in which it made its appearance is borne in mind. At the time when the Deuteronomic authors worked the northern kingdom had already been destroyed and the best of its population exiled, while the Judaean state which had providentially escaped this disaster was in grave danger of becoming totally apostate largely due to the extreme paganizing practices which had evidently seized hold of national life during the reign of Manasseh in the first half of the seventh century BC. For those who composed Deuteronomy the problem was nothing less than the very survival of Israel as the people of Yahweh and it was in an attempt to meet the dangers which this posed that they drew up their programme of reform and renewal.

In attempting to meet the grave challenge which the age in which they lived presented, the Deuteronomic authors sought above all to assert the separateness of Israel as the people of Yahweh to whom alone their allegiance was due. To this end the book is on the one hand permeated through and through with the solemn warning against the danger of Israel becoming 'like the nations round about' by adopting their cultic and religious practices and other institutions, while on the other hand Israel's own worship of Yahweh is now brought under the strictest possible control.

The separateness of Israel among the nations is expressed in a number of ways in Deuteronomy. It is crystallized in Deut.7.6 which formulates the biblical doctrine of the election:

> For you are a holy people to the Lord your God; the Lord your God has chosen you to be a people for his own possession out of all the peoples that are on the face of the earth.

And this belief in divine election permeates the whole book forming the basis for faithfulness to Yahweh and obedience to the covenant law (cf. Deut.4.32 ff.; 6.20 ff.; 8.1 ff. etc.). It finds further expression in the warnings against entering into relationships with the nations among whom Israel is to settle in the land of Canaan (cf. Deut.7.1 ff.; 12.24 ff.; 20.16 ff.). In this respect attention must also be drawn to the marked martial spirit which pervades the book both in the form of individual laws concerning the conduct of war (cf. Deut.20; 21.10 ff.; 23.9 ff.) as well as in a number of passages exhorting Israel not to fear the peoples who shall oppose their entry into the promised land, and promising that Yahweh will himself go before Israel to fight for them (cf. Deut.7.17 ff.; 9.1 ff.; 11.22 ff.). At the time when Deuteronomy was composed the possibility of armed conflict with the inhabitants of Canaan did not exist and the idea of exterminating them was completely unreal. What these martial passages seek to do is to reinforce the demand for Israel's separateness from the nations among whom she dwelt and to protect her life as Yahweh's people against the influences of foreign culture and religion. This is further emphasized by the amount of polemic in the book against the cultic institutions and practices of the Canaanites. Israel is commanded not only to have nothing to do with them but to root them out and destroy them (cf. Deut.7.25 ff.; 12.2 ff.); any attempts to go after other gods will bring judgment upon Israel. At the same time Israel's own worship of Yahweh is brought under strict control and to this end the Deuteronomic authors formulated one of the most far reaching laws in the whole book, the law demanding the centralization of the cult at one sanctuary only which stands at the very beginning of the presentation of the covenant laws and which occurs frequently throughout the law code (Deut.12.2 ff.; 15–16).

Not only, however, does Deuteronomy attempt to control Israel's relationships with other peoples and to guard against pagan influences and to protect Israel's worship of Yahweh, it also seeks to control other aspects of her life as Yahweh's people. Thus the book contains laws to regulate the functions of important officers (judges, kings, priests, prophets in Deut.16–18), procedure in the law courts for criminal cases (Deut.19–21), and family relationships (Deut.21–22). Altogether the book attempts to regulate all aspects of Israel's life, and the motivation for this and the goal to which it was directed was to call Israel to a full realization of her role as Yahweh's holy people and to render her acceptable in his sight.

If we were to sum up the total requirement which Deuteronomy demanded of Israel we could not do better than the book itself which

right at the outset and in addition to the ten commandments sets forth the *Shema* which calls for love of Yahweh in a radical manner:

Hear, O Israel: The Lord our God is one Lord; and you shall love the Lord your God with all your heart, and with all your soul, and with all your might (Deut.6.4).

4. *The 'P' Document*

The fourth and final document which makes up the Pentateuch is the Priestly document ('P'), the distinctive features, style and theological outlook of which render it relatively easy to isolate from the surrounding material. In addition, its relation to the other sources makes it clear that 'P' provides the framework of the Pentateuch as we now have it.

Like 'J' and 'E', the Priestly document narrates the history of salvation and in doing so presents its own interpretation of that history. The author began, like the Yahwist, with creation and the primaeval history and it is to him that we owe the first creation story (Gen.1–2.4a), which sets forth the different stages of creation, all of which are attributed to the creative word and command of God. Creation reaches its climax in the creation of the first man and woman (not, as in 'J', the first man and then the first woman). The framework of the primaeval history is provided by a series of genealogies ('generations') which culminate in the genealogy of the immediate circle to which Israel belonged (Terah the father of Abraham in Gen.11.10 ff.). The primaeval history in 'P' is tersely presented with the exception of the flood story which is narrated in some detail and ends with the giving of the 'Noachian commandments' in Gen.9.1–7. The Priestly document then proceeds, like 'J' and 'E', to narrate the history of the patriarchs where again the framework is provided by a series of genealogies, in this instance the genealogies of Ishmael (Gen.25.12–17), Isaac (Gen.25.19), Esau (Gen.36,1–30), and Jacob (Gen.37.1). This is followed by the history of Jacob's descendants in Egypt, their bondage there and God's awareness of their plight at the hands of the Egyptians. At this point Moses is called (Ex.6) and, as in 'E', the divine name Yahweh is first revealed to him. There follows a description of the exodus from Egypt and the march through the wilderness to the sacred mountain of Sinai where the legislation which is to govern the life of Israel is given to Moses by Yahweh. The 'P' document then briefly describes the forty years wandering in the wilderness and the preparation for the conquest of the promised land.

The date of the composition of the Priestly document has generally been arrived at on the basis of a comparison between some of its dominant aspects and the demands and characteristics of both Deuteronomy and Ezek.40–48. Thus in 'P' the centralization of worship is taken for granted and this probably indicates that 'P' post-dates Deuteronomy in which such centralization still requires the strongest possible emphasis. Ezekiel 40–48, which belongs to the exilic period and contains plans for the future rebuilding of the temple and the ordering of its worship, knows of no high priest and designates the Levitical house of Zadok as the priests who will serve at the altar. In the post-exilic period, however, there was a high priest and the priests who served at the altar in the second temple were the sons of Aaron, all of which accords with the legislation concerning these matters in 'P'. On these grounds, therefore, it is widely agreed that the Priestly document was composed in the early post-exilic period though it seems clear that this was only the final product of a process which began and developed already in the exilic period itself.

The purpose and significance of 'P' are revealed clearly in the stages through which it traces the salvation-history and the great amount of priestly and cultic legislation which it contains. Its main object was to present a systematic view of the origin and working of the great theocratic institutions of Israel which recognized God as the divine and only ruler, and the nation as the 'congregation' of God. Like 'E', the Priestly document postpones the revelation of the divine name of Yahweh until Moses. It admits no cult in the early period: Noah does not offer any sacrifice after the flood (as in 'J'; cf. Gen.8.20 f.), nor do the patriarchs build altars and offer sacrifices. No offering is recorded until Aaron and his sons are prepared to make sacrifice in Lev.8. Nevertheless, the Priestly author skilfully makes preparation all the way through for the establishment of the sacral institutions of the congregation: the order of creation has its ritual significance, for here the heavenly bodies serve to mark the festal times and seasons (Gen.1.14); after the creation of the world and nature in six days

God keeps the sabbath (Gen.2.2); primitive humanity is vegetarian (Gen.1.29) but after the flood the new race is to be carniverous, subject, however, to the prohibition of eating the blood in which lay the life (Gen.9.3 f.). A further advance is made with Abraham when the covenant promising him the land of Canaan is sealed with the sign of circumcision (Gen.17), while the future possession of the promised land is symbolized by the cave at Machpelah in which lie three generations of patriarchs (Gen.25.8 ff.; 49.29 ff.). Yet another step is taken when the Passover ritual is instituted on the eve of the exodus from Egypt (Ex.12.1–20) and rules were added defining the conditions under which slaves and strangers were to be entitled to partake in it (the limits of the congregation being thus incidentally defined). Everything moves forward to the detailed and expansive legislation concerning Israel's worship of God given at Sinai by Moses and recorded in Ex.25–30; 35–46; in Leviticus and much of Numbers.

The account of the revelation of the institutions of the theocratic community Israel and the sacral legislation which is to govern its life as the 'congregation of Yahweh' takes up over half the Priestly document. On Mt Sinai Moses receives instructions for the building of the tabernacle and the sacred vestments of the priesthood (Ex.25–31; 35–40). Subsequently, detailed regulations concerning sacrifices and offerings are presented (Lev.1–16). At this point the Priestly author has incorporated an originally separate document (the so-called Holiness Code, 'H', in Lev.17–26 which was probably composed in the exilic period) in order to supplement the legislation already given. There follows a series of detailed laws which are to govern the life and worship of the congregation around the tabernacle 'in the camp' (Num.1–9). In this way the salvation-history reaches its climax; from creation onwards it moves, in the Priestly document, towards the establishment of the congregation of Yahweh and the legislation and institutions which are to govern its life and the communion which it is to enjoy with God, all of which is already summed up in Ex.29.44 ff.:

I will consecrate the tent of meeting and the altar; Aaron also and his sons I will consecrate, to serve me as priests. And I will dwell among the people of Israel, and will be their

God. And they shall know that I am the Lord their God, who brought them forth out of the land of Egypt that I might dwell among them; I am the Lord their God.

The theological conceptions of 'P' are in many respects quite different from those characteristic of 'J' and 'E'. The transcendence of God is emphasized and the actions of God are not described as if they were those of men (anthropomorphism). Apart from a few passages in which God addresses or 'appears' to individuals (Noah, Abraham, Jacob) he is approached solely through the priests and the cultic rituals. For the wilderness period the manifestation of God is effected by his 'glory' which 'dwells' on Mt Sinai (Ex.24.16) and fills the tabernacle when it has been erected (Ex.40.34). The cloud which conceals God is permanent; when the camp breaks up it ascends. Characteristic of 'P' also is the place which it affords to the conceptions of sin offering and atonement (Lev.16).

This peculiar emphasis of 'P' on the sacral institutions and legislation of the congregation can be fully appreciated only when the particular period in which it originated is borne in mind. As in other documents of the Pentateuch, here also there is much material and several traditions which derive from much earlier periods than that in which the author of 'P' lived and worked. Thus, for example, the tabernacle as described in 'P' is based to some extent on the traditions of the old 'tent of meeting' of the wilderness period and to some extent on the pre-exilic temple in Jerusalem. Furthermore, much of the legislation, for example, Lev.18, belongs to a very early period in the history of Israel. But, again as in the other documents, the author is here not concerned merely with describing what is past, for in recording the salvation-history in the manner in which he does he is in fact thinking of the present and the future requirements of Israel as the people of God. Working in the exilic and post-exilic period the authors of 'P' have sought to present for their generation their own interpretation of Israel's election and the system which God gave Israel for the ordering of their life as his chosen people. Israel's election had been called seriously into question in the tragedy of the destruction of Judah and the temple and the ensuing exile; here the Priestly authors have proclaimed the renewal

of Israel's life as the congregation and the solemn obligations which this imposed upon her; she is to be the holy people of Yahweh who alone is her God.

The Historicity of the Pentateuch Tradition

From our brief discussion in the foregoing pages it has emerged that the individual documents of the Pentateuch assert that God called Israel's ancestors and promised them the land of Canaan, delivered their descendants from bondage in Egypt, made a covenant with them on Mt Sinai, led them through the wilderness for forty years, and finally brought them into the promised land. We saw also that in two of the documents, 'J' and 'P', this salvation-history is prefaced by a description of the primaeval history beginning with creation and narrating man's rebellion against his Creator, the destruction of the world by the flood, the renewed sinfulness of man after the flood, and the circumstances which led to the call of the first patriarch of Israel, Abraham. The question to which we must now turn is the historicity of the basic story of the Pentateuch as here outlined.

It is clear to begin with that Gen.1–9 cannot any longer be accepted as providing an accurate description of the origin and early history of the world and mankind (see Part III, Section 4, pp. 98 ff.), yet the basic assertions of Gen.1–2 remain true today: namely that man is a finite being and the creature of God against whom he rebels, thus alienating himself from his true life in communion with his Creator, and that man accordingly stands under judgment and is in need of grace and salvation. It is for this reason that they are of abiding value and not because of the information which they are so often thought to shed on the origins of the cosmos.

What then of the salvation-history proper, that is, those events beginning with the call of Abraham and culminating in the entry into the land of Canaan which Israel looked back upon as having called her into being as the people of Yahweh? Modern scholarship leaves us in no doubt that here we are dealing with historical personalities and events, for few today deny that the patriarchs Abraham, Isaac and Jacob did exist and that events such as the exodus, the covenant ceremony on Mt Sinai and the entry into the land of Canaan by Israel's ancestors did happen.

It is now widely agreed that Israel as a group of twelve tribes came into existence only on the soil of Canaan and comprised clans and groups of clans or individual tribes which had little or no relationship with each other prior to their entry into the land. Furthermore, almost certainly the entry into Canaan of the disparate elements which were eventually united to form Israel took place over a considerable period of time. It is probable that traditions and historical events which had originally been separate, that is, the property of the originally separate clans and tribes, were united to become traditions and historical events belonging to all Israel. In other words, Israel as one people living in one land and worshipping one God traced her history back through a common historical experience to a common ancestry.

Thus it is probable that the patriarchs Abraham, Isaac and Jacob were, from a historical point of view, originally unrelated to each other but were the revered founders and ancestors of originally separate clans. When, however, these clans were absorbed into the totality Israel their separate patriachal traditions became traditions of Israel as a whole, and since the tribes of Israel eventually came to believe that they had a common origin and history, so also Abraham, Isaac and Jacob became related as father, son and grandson.

If all this is accepted, then clearly the origins of the tribes of Israel and the process whereby they became a nation living in the land of Canaan were much more complex than is suggested by the relatively straightforward account of them which forms the basis of the salvation-history narrated in the Pentateuch and elsewhere in the Old Testament. But this does not make nonsense of the salvation-history. The salvation-history witnesses primarily not to the 'bare facts' of history but to the faith of men who believed that God was concerned with the life of man and has acted and continues to act to bring salvation to man. It was in this sense, as we have seen, that the authors of the Pentateuchal documents understood the salvation-history and it is in this sense that it continues to be meaningful for us today.

4

In the Beginning

Robert Davidson

Old Testament history begins with Abraham whose westward pilgrimage from Mesopotamia to Canaan is recorded in Gen.12. What then of Gen.1–11? These chapters are the prologue to that history, with much the same function as the prologue to Shakespeare's Henry V.

1. The prologue is written *after* the main lines of the action are already known. Behind Gen.1–11 lie the story of Abraham, the exodus, the settlement in Canaan and all the knowledge Israel gained, through these events, of God in living encounter with man.

2. The prologue is an appeal to the imagina-tion, to the imagination of faith, to grasp that what was being played out on the narrow stage of Israel was of significance for all time and for all men. Within the history of one particular people there was encounter with the God who is the Lord of all history and the source of all life.

The Background

Increasing knowledge of the religions and literature of the ancient Near East makes it clear that the authors of Gen.1–11 are handling themes of common currency, particularly in

Mesopotamia. (For the authors 'J' and 'P' see Part III, Section 3, pp. 87 ff., 93 ff.) To take three examples:

1. The Creation Hymn (Gen.1–2.4b) has marked affinities with the Mesopotamian Creation Epic *Enuma Elish*. The sequence of creative acts is the same in both documents. From cosmic matter and primaeval chaos come light, the firmament, dry land, the heavenly luminaries and man, in that order. Thereafter in *Enuma Elish* the gods rest and celebrate (cf. Gen.2.2).

2. The mysterious tree of life in Gen.2.9; 3.24 recalls the Epic of Gilgamesh with its plant of life whose name is 'man becomes young in old age'. Moreover, this plant is stolen from Gilgamesh by a serpent.

3. The flood story in Gen.6–8 has many echoes of the flood story in Tablet XI of the Epic of Gilgamesh – the construction of a boat coated with pitch, the sending forth of birds to see whether the flood waters have subsided, the sacrifice to the gods after the waters have abated.

The similarities are unmistakable, but the differences are equally striking. Behind most of Shakespeare's historical plays lie Holinshead's Chronicles. All that we mean by the genius of Shakespeare, however, consists in what he pours into the bare historical outline he inherits. Genesis 1–11 handles well-known themes; but they come to us reminted in the crucible of Israel's distinctive faith and from the hands of creative writers nurtured in that faith.

The Nature of the Material

These chapters are not historical, if by historical we mean the record of certain events that once happened at a particular time and place. The background Mesopotamian material is religious mythology. What is meant by myth? 'Myth' as a word has become debased in common currency where it usually means something devoid of truth or reality: mere fantasy. It should be self-evident that this is not what is meant by describing Gen.1–11 as myth. More seriously, the word is used with a wide range of meanings in modern theology. In some cases it seems to be little more than a convenient term for religious language. Two more precise meanings of 'myth' are relevant to Gen.1–11.

1. 'Myth is to be defined as a complex of stories – some no doubt fact, and some fantasy – which, for various reasons, human beings have regarded as demonstrations of the inner meaning of the universe and of human life.' Such 'story-myths' occur in two forms. They may be traditional, popular, handed down from generation to generation, their ultimate origin lost in the mists of antiquity. On the other hand they may be the conscious creation of a great teacher. He may draw on traditional material, but he uses it for his own purposes. The myth of the prisoners in the cave in Book VII of Plato's Republic is a good example. And the purpose of such myths? 'You are describing a strange scene and stranger prisoners,' says Glaucon to Socrates; to which Socrates replies, 'They resemble us.' Thus it would be wrong to ask where or when Adam and Eve lived. Adam is not the first man. He is 'Everyman', the 'Everyman' in us. Arguments about the dimensions or seaworthiness of Noah's ark are irrelevant. The story points to the ever present realities of the judgment and mercy of God. The background to such 'story-myths' may be fantasy, e.g., the garden of Eden; or it may be fact, e.g., the memory of catastrophic flooding, a not uncommon happening in southern Mesopotamia.

2. The ancient Near East was familiar with myth in another sense. Myth is what is said as certain religious rites are performed by and on behalf of the community. It declares in words what the ritual is designed to ensure through action. It is the word element in the sacrament. The purpose of such myths and accompanying ritual is severely practical. The 'Creation Myth' is not speculation about the origin of things, its concern is with the everyday needs of man and society, with the forces which support and threaten existence, order and chaos, life and death, fertility and drought. At the New Year festival, the triumph of order over primaeval chaos is re-enacted, re-lived, because only thus could there be any assurance of the well-being of the community throughout the coming year. Was there such a New Year festival in ancient Israel? Many scholars believe that the feast of Tabernacles (Deut.16.13; Lev.23.34) was such a festival. It has been argued that Gen.1 originates in such a festival, the seven days of creation corresponding to the seven days of the festival.

Although myth and ritual are initially part of an indivisible whole, it is possible for the myth to survive long after the ritual has lost its power. Indeed it may be known simply as literature in a culture which does not accept the ritual. Echoes of an original ritual setting may be discernible in the background of some of the material of Gen.1–11. It is doubtful whether any of it is organically related to ritual in its present form.

Content and Meaning

Genesis 1–11 fall into certain clearly defined sections, each of which contributes to the meaning of the whole.

1. *The Hymn of Creation* (1–2.4a)

This is Priestly teaching in Israel at its finest. It is hymn-like, carefully schematized, making effective use of recurring words and phrases, e.g., 'God said . . . and it was so', 'So evening and morning came . . .'. Its purpose is neither historical nor scientific. It is written by faith for faith.

A good deal of myth and ritual is concerned with the natural forces that shape man's life. In myth, however, such forces are never regarded as objects; they are always personalized as gods and goddesses. In Canaanite mythology the interplay of fertility and drought is the conflict between *Baal*, the god of the fertilizing rain and his enemy *Mot* (Death). In the Babylonian *Enuma Elish* the struggle is between *Tiamat*, primeval chaos, and *Marduk*, the champion of the gods. Just as there are many different and conflicting phenomena surrounding man, so there is an inevitable polytheism in such myths.

In contrast, Gen.1 is uncompromisingly monotheistic. The Hebrew word for 'the deep' (*tehōm*) in 1.2 is sometimes claimed to be a reflection of Babylonian Tiamat. At best it is a literary echo. The entire theme of creation coming by way of conflict between rival gods has been excised. Here there is but one God who speaks, and his word is effective to create. The same point is made in 1.14–19. Instead of speaking about sun and moon, the hymn refers to 'the greater light' and 'the lesser light'. Sun and moon were common objects of worship in the ancient Near East. It is as if the hymn is deliberately demythologizing them. It refuses

to name them directly and insists that they share in the finitude of all created things. More importantly, the God of Gen.1 is not one of the phenomena of nature, not even 'Nature' with a capital N. He is wholly other, 'transcendent', standing over and against the world; the source of all its life, yet never to be equated with anything in it. The word 'create' (*bārā*) used throughout this chapter is only used in the Old Testament of God and his activity. Nothing in the world may be equated with the divine. But neither is the world in any sense the enemy of God. All is part of his good creation (cf. the summarizing verdict in 1.31). This includes man, the apex of the creation pyramid.

When the hymn comes to man (1.26), the form of expression changes. It becomes more personal: 'Let us' instead of 'Let there be'. The plural 'us' (cf. 3.22; 11.7) probably derives from the mythology of the divine council which the supreme god consults when important decisions are to be taken. But in the hymn, that is no more than a literary allusion; the plural 'Let us' switches immediately to the singular in 1.27: 'So God created . . . he created . . .'. Man is made *'in our image, after our likeness'* (1.26, cf. 1.27). The key word is 'image', 'likeness' being a more general term which merely emphasizes the image concept. But what does the image of God mean? Every age has tended to read into this phrase its own highest ideal of man, whether that is thought of in terms of the immortality of the soul or the possession of reason. In context in Gen.1, the phrase 'the image of God' seems to be defined by the words which follow. Just as God is Lord over all creation, so man exercises under God a secondary lordship over the rest of creation (cf. Ps.8). Inherent in such delegated lordship, however, is the thought that man is responsible to God for the way in which he exercises this lordship.

The concluding stanza of the hymn (2.2 f.) provides ultimate theological justification for the weekly keeping of sabbath. It traces it back to something in the very nature of God.

2. *The Enigma of Man* (2.4b–3)

Here the 'J' source takes us into the world of 'story-myth'. When such stories provide explanations of curious phenomena in the world, they are called *aetiological myths* (Greek *aition,* explanation, cause). Many explanations of different depth and interest may be offered within the one story. One native South African story, for instance, which is centrally concerned with why men die, also explains why the hare has a cleft lip and always seems to be on the run, why hare's flesh is taboo, and why the moon has marks on its face.

This section of Genesis has some curiously rough edges, which may reflect once independent stories – two accounts of man placed in the garden (2.8, 15), two accounts of the clothing of man (3.7, 21), two trees, the tree of life and the tree of the knowledge of good and evil. It must, however, be read as a whole. It suggests answers to many questions – why the serpent is such an odd creature (3.14); why the instinctive antipathy between man and serpent (3.15); why the pain in child birth (3.16); why the farmer's lot is so hard (3.17–19); why marriage and the different sexes (2.20–25). All these 'whys', however, are peripheral to the central thrust of the story. It is not another creation story. The barren desert (2.4b–7), fertilized by supernatural water (the mist, 2.6), is a very different picture from the primeval watery chaos of Gen.1. It is merely the setting for man (Hebrew *ādām*), the 'earthling' formed from 'the earth' (Hebrew *adāmāh*). Shaped by a divine potter, this man becomes a living being or creature (*not* soul), when God breathes into him the breath of life (2.7). This man is placed in a position of responsibility in the garden of Eden, almost certainly a mythical garden paradise. All attempts to unravel the geographical references in 2.10–14 come at some point to a dead end.

The 'tree of the knowledge of good and evil' in this garden has provoked endless discussion. 'Good and evil' are perhaps best interpreted to mean 'everything' (cf. our use of the opposites 'hot or cold' to mean any temperature). The temptation which dangles before man is that of grasping at a totality of knowledge which is the prerogative of God. Once possessing all knowledge he would know the whereabouts of the tree of life, and thus be in danger of trespassing upon another divine prerogative, immortality. When temptation conquers, all goes wrong. The garden of delight becomes the garden of disenchantment. Childlike trust is replaced by the guilty conscience. Harmony turns to friction. The life of rewarding toil becomes the irksome struggle for existence. Death enters the scene.

The psychological insight in the story is profound. Note the subtlety of temptation (3.1–6), the 'passing of the buck' mentality (3.12–14). But the heart of the story is theological, that basic sin in man's nature which mars his world. He is a creature in rebellion against his Creator. He refuses to accept that he himself is not omniscient or the centre of the universe. Like Gen.1, this section knows of the greatness of man. His lordship is indicated by the way in which man gives names to the other creatures (2.19 f.). But this lordship, as Israel had every reason to know, is a marred lordship.

3. *Cain and Abel* (4.1–16)

Certain curious features of this story – the different types of sacrifice (vv.3 f.), sin crouching, demon-like, at the door (v.7), the blood crying from the ground (v.11), the mark placed on Cain (v.14) – have been traced back in origin to tribal customs and Babylonian ritual practice. In context, however, the meaning is plain. From rebellion against God, man progresses to fratricide. Here is the fatal legacy of man's self-assertiveness – murder, and murder capped by a classic denial of responsibility. 'Am I my brother's keeper?' (v.9). But if man disclaims responsibility, God does not. The mark on Cain is a protective mark. Cain is punished; he is banished to wander (Nod, v.16, means wandering) on the face of the earth, but he can never wander beyond the protection of God. God does not wash his hands even of rebellious man.

4. *The Descendants of Cain* (4.17–24)

In terms of the family of Cain, various facets of cultural life are introduced – city civilization (v.17), the tent-dwelling herdsmen (v.12), music (v.21), and the metal working smiths (v.22). The Kenites, the descendants according to tradition of Cain, remained intinerant smiths.

Verses 23 f. preserve an ancient song which breathes the proud code of honour of the desert, the spirit of blood revenge. Perhaps in the mind of 'J', it is further illustration of human aggressiveness.

5. *The Beginning of the Worship of Yahweh* (4.25 f.)

This passage fits ill with Ex.3.13–15 ('E') and 6.3 ('P'), the latter passage specifically stating that worship of God under the name of *Yahweh* (the Lord) began at the exodus. The universalizing intention in Gen.1–11 is here at work. The worship of Yahweh was always the faith of the true line of mankind.

6. *The First Priestly Genealogy – from Adam to Noah* (ch.5)

The Priestly writer stresses the continuity of history by way of genealogies. Abnormally long life spans, much longer than in this list, are assigned to ancient worthies in Mesopotamian tradition. No real theological significance can be read into the numbers which, in any case, vary considerably in the different versions of the Old Testament, Hebrew, Samaritan and Greek. Enoch, the seventh in the list with 365 years, is of interest, since the seventh in the list of Babylonian pre-flood worthies was a devotee of the sun god, and skilled in the art of divination. If 'P' knew this tradition, it is significant that for one skilled in divination he has substituted a man who 'walked with God', an exemplar of true faith.

7. *The Prologue to the Flood Story – the Sons of God and the Daughters of Men* (6.1–4)

Stories of intercourse between gods and mortal women are common enough in religious mythology. Nor is it surprising that the offspring of such unions should be regarded as giants, the Nephilim (v.4). But this piece of pagan mythology is given new meaning by placing it as a prologue to the flood story. It now becomes an illustration of the evil which infects not only men, but even celestial beings. It points to a cosmic, demonic dimension to evil which more than justifies the judgment to come.

8. *The Flood* (6.5–8.22)

The flood story (a fusion of 'J' and 'P' traditions) has many points of contact with Mesopotamian flood traditions, which survive most complete in Tablet XI of the Epic of Gilgamesh. There Noah's counterpart is Utnapishtim. The biblical narrative, however, is distinctive. Its motivation is strictly ethical (6.5–7); no such reason is given in Mesopotamian tradition. Its ethos is monotheistic whereas the Mesopotamian story is polytheistic. The Gilgamesh parallel to 8.21 reads:

The gods smelled the savour,
    the gods smelled the sweet savour,
the gods crowded like flies round the sacrifice.

The ethical spirit and monotheistic conception of God, however, just scratch the surface of the basic difference. The entire orientation of the narrative is different. The flood story in the Gilgamesh Epic comes within the setting of a man's search for elusive immortality. The flood story in Genesis underscores some of the basic themes of Israel's faith.

(*a*) *The reality of judgment.* The seriousness with which God views the chaos sin brings into the world is expressed in the decision to wipe out the evil-infected age. Man bent on a 'Rake's Progress' can only progress to destruction.

(*b*) *Salvation.* Judgment is not God's last or only word. One man, Noah, finds favour in the eyes of God (6.8), is regarded as being 'in the right' with God (6.9; 7.1), 'blameless' he walked with God (6.9). As one age dies, engulfed in the surging waters, a new age is born, a new age grounded in a divine promise of the lasting stability of the natural order (8.21 f.).

9. *The Covenant with Noah* (9.1–17) 'P'

In the new age, the age of Israel's historical existence, God's original command to man 'Be fruitful and multiply' (Gen.1.28) is repeated. Part of the harmony in nature, however, has disappeared. Man is no longer vegetarian (contrast 1.29). Two specific checks are placed upon what man may with impunity do.

(i) He is not to eat flesh with the blood in it. This ancient ritual taboo is based on the equation of the blood with life (cf. Lev.17.11–14; Deut.12.23). Orthodox Jews still eat only 'Kosher' meat in the light of this ordinance.

(ii) The sanctity of human life is stressed in an ancient sacral, legal formula, 'The shedder of blood in man, by man shall his blood be shed.' This sanctity is rooted in man's kinship with God (the image of God) according to the Priestly author; and man is held responsible for the punishment of murder.

(iii) The new age is above all the *covenant* age. A covenant (*berith*) is a treaty or agreement between two parties (cf. Gen.31.44; I Sam.18.3). Within the context of Israel's faith, however, covenant has a distinctive meaning. The initiative always comes from God; it is he who establishes his covenant (cf. 6.18; 9.9–11; 15). It is his gift to man. As such, the covenant contains an element of promise, the promise in 6.18 that Noah will survive when all else perishes; the promise in 9.9 f. that never again will the earth be destroyed; the promise that God will always remember (9.15 f.).

The same emphasis appears in the way the writer deals with the bow in the cloud (9.12–17). In certain mythologies, the rainbow is the bow of the warrior storm god hung up in the sky after the defeat of his enemies. Israel may have known this myth. Here, however, the bow is merely a 'sign', a 'sign' not to man but to God, a sign which guarantees that God will always remember his covenant and covenant promises. Upon the utter dependability of God, Israel staked her faith.

10. *The Family of Noah – Curse and Blessing* (9.18–29) 'P'

The Noah of this episode is curiously different from the Noah of the flood. He is the first to plant a vineyard, and the first to succumb to over-indulgence in its produce. This episode is used by the writer to say something about the history and destiny of the peoples who struggled for possession of the land of Canaan. The three sons of Noah, Ham (Canaan), Shem and Japheth, represent three peoples whose destiny is fixed by the curse and blessing of father Noah. 'Curse' and 'blessing' are for the Old Testament not merely words. They are solemn, sacred, power-charged words, which work themselves out inexorably in events. Canaan, the indigenous inhabitants of the land prior to the Hebrew settlement, are to be abject slaves (v.25). Instead of Shem, the ancestor of the Hebrews, being blessed, it is Yahweh, the God of Shem, who is blessed (v.26). Although this expression is not paralleled elsewhere in the Old Testament, it probably reflects the writer's conviction that the true blessing of the Hebrews lay in their worship of Yahweh. In v.27 the word 'enlarge' (Hebrew *japht*) is a play on the name Japheth. The reference here is not wholly clear, but probably it is to the Philistines who, although never in alliance with the Hebrews, struggled with them for possession of Canaan in the twelfth century BC.

11. *The Table of the Nations* (ch.10) 'P'

This chapter has been well described as 'a pioneering effort among the ethnographic attempts of the ancient world'. The threefold division of peoples is neither strictly linguistic nor ethnic. It is mainly geographical. Some of the names still defy reasonable explanation. What is remarkable is that all the nations of the then known world, from the Black Sea and the Aegean region in the north to Somaliland in the south, from the Iranian plateau in the east to the western Mediterranean, are gathered together as if they were the fulfilment of the command to Noah: 'Be fruitful and multiply' (9.1). All are one and under the providence of one God.

12. *The Tower of Babel* (11.1–9) 'J'

Like Gen.2–3, this story has aetiological (explanatory) elements. It attempts to explain why, in this one world, there is such a diversity of languages. It gives a popular and quite unscientific explanation of the name Babel, linking it with Hebrew *bālal*, confuse. In fact, 'Babel' means 'the gate of God'. But the aetiological element does not take us to the core of the story. The setting is unmistakably Mesopotamia. Behind it is the memory of contact with the great temple towers or ziggurats. These Mesopotamian cathedrals, with names that sometimes stressed the link between earth and heaven, were the ultimate expressions of man's piety. But not to the Bible writer. Here he sees man's pride, his self-assertiveness, his fatal attempt to seek for self-made security apart from God. The result is disaster, confusion, the fragmentation of the world.

13. *The Genealogy of the Sons of Shem* (11.10–32)

Against this background, one family group, Shem and his descendants, are singled out because they are to be the bearers of new hope for all humanity. This line of Shem (the Semitic peoples) leads directly to Abraham, with whom Hebrew history begins. In a few bold strokes, the prologue has introduced the main themes of the Old Testament faith. God is the transcendent Lord of all creation and all history. Man, part of the finitude of creation, is made in God's image to share in this lordship.

But man is a rebel who progresses inevitably to destruction and confusion under the judgment of God. Even in the midst of judgment, however, God never renounces rebellious man; he protects, he renews, he binds himself to man in promise.

5

The Patriarchs

Robert Davidson

The patriarchal narratives in Gen.12–50 divide into blocks of material which centre on the four main patriarchal figures:

1 Abraham (12–25.18)
2 Isaac (26)
3 Jacob (25.19–33; 27–35)
4 Joseph (37; 39–50).

Of these four, Isaac is a shadowy figure, briefly mentioned, little more than a link between Abraham and Jacob. The Joseph stories, very different in character from the other narratives, are likewise a link, a link between the patriarchal period and the exodus traditions.

The 'documentary hypothesis' finds in these chapters a fusion of the three main narrative sources in the Pentateuch, 'J', 'E', and 'P' (see Part III, Section 3, pp. 85 ff.). It is not always easy to be certain of the breakdown of the narratives into these different sources. It is probably more important to begin by asking what lies behind all the sources. Each of them draws on the old traditions which must have circulated from generation to generation by word of mouth for centuries before they ever achieved written form. Many of these traditions must have been wholly independent of one another. They achieved their unity only as 'Israel' found her national unity, and traditions, once the possession of separate tribal groups, became the heritage of all Israel. We cannot regard these chapters as a straightforward chronological record of the history and the religion of the patriarchal age. What then is their value historically and theologically?

The Historical Question

So long as the world of the ancient Near East between 2000–1500 BC was a virtual blank as far as extra-biblical material was concerned, it was possible to treat the patriarchal narratives with marked scepticism. At best, they were a reading back, into idealized ancestors, of the beliefs and customs of later Israel. Some scholars went much further and dissolved all the patriarchs into gods or tribal symbols. Increasingly, new historical data for this period has become available, and with new knowledge, the need to revise this attitude of scepticism. Illustrations of the kind of evidence accumulating from two archeological sites, Mari and Nuzu, will suffice.

1. *Mari* in north-west Mesopotamia was, in the eighteenth century BC, a powerful Amorite (or proto-Aramaean) kingdom. Names similar in type to those found in the patriarchal narratives appear in many documents from Mari. These documents are engraved on tablets, made of hard-baked mud. We hear, for example, of the 'banuiamina', sons of the right hand (south); the Hebrew form is Benjamin (Gen.38.15, etc.). Social and political customs, for instance census taking, are also very similar at Mari and in the Old Testament. Since the Genesis tradition traces the coming of Abraham from Haran, in precisely the same area of north-west Mesopotamia (Gen.12.4), it is reasonable to think of Abraham and his family as belonging to one or other of the Amorite groups, whose presence at this period in different parts of the ancient Near East is amply documented.

2. Further down the Mesopotamian valley at *Nuzu* there was, in the middle of the second millennium BC, an important Hurrian community. These 'Hurri' (Old Testament: Horites, Gen.14.6; 36.20 ff.) seem to have come from the mountains of Armenia. Documents from Nuzu contain some remarkable parallels in social customs to features in the patriarchal narratives which are not easily explicable in the light of later Old Testament law and custom.

(i) Three times in Genesis, the story is told of a patriarch passing off a wife as his sister (12.10–20; 20; 26.1–11). One form of marriage contract at Nuzu provides for a man to adopt his wife as his sister. Although the Genesis narratives no longer understand the incidents in this light, the Nuzu type wife-sister relationship may underlie the stories.

(ii) In certain cases at Nuzu property could pass, not to the eldest son, but to a daughter's husband. Legal proof of this was the handing over of the 'household god' images. Rachel's conduct in Gen. 31.19 ff. when she stole 'her father's household gods' becomes clear. She was furthering Jacob's claim to part of Laban's property.

(iii) Two types of heir are recognized in Nuzu law, the direct heir (*aplu*) and the indirect heir (*ewirru*), who may be an adopted slave. If, after an *ewirru* is designated heir, a direct heir is born, the *ewirru* loses his legal rights. This seems to be the situation in Gen.15.3 where Abraham's heir is Eleazar, a slave born in his household. This Eleazar disappears when Isaac, the direct heir, is born.

(iv) At Nuzu a childless wife was under obligation to provide her husband with a concubine. This explains Sarah's action in Gen.16.1 ff.

Mari and Nuzu, as well as Babylonian, Hittite, Canaanite and Egyptian sources from various periods in the second millennium BC refer to a certain category of people as *Habiru*. The meaning of this term is still widely disputed. It is a descriptive word – 'mercenaries', 'refugees', 'donkey caravaners' have been suggested. It seems likely that there is some link between this term and the description of Abraham as *the Hebrew* (Gen.14.13). With one exception, all references to 'Hebrews' in the Old Testament occur in passages which refer to events prior to 1000 BC.

All this evidence points to the conclusion that historically, culturally and socially, the patriarchal narratives fit meaningfully into the world of the ancient Near East at about 2000–1500 BC, and into no other milieu, earlier or later. Whatever these narratives may be, they are not merely the romanticizing products of a later age.

The Character of the Traditions

Can we then call these narratives 'history'? It depends what we mean by history. Genesis 12–50 do not contain a record of significant public, political and social events. Very little of the political history of this period can be gleaned from them; and what there is is often incidental. An exception is Gen.14 which does preserve the memory of an expedition by four northern and eastern potentates against communities in the region of the Dead Sea. It faces the historian, however, with difficult questions. The identity of the kings involved is by no means certain. It is best to treat these narratives in the main as *sagas*. Sagas, transmitted from generation to generation by word of mouth, are stories which preserve the memory of the movements and adventures of tribal groups, and of the note-worthy deeds of tribal heroes. Sagas often concern themselves with quite trifling personal incidents, domestic intrigue, family quarrels, love and jealousy. Sagas preserve and reflect a way of life, a set of values. They mirror the way in which a community thinks about itself and its own past. As such they are of immeasurable historical value, even when they do not record historical events. In most cases there is a solid substratum of historical fact in the saga, but the task of penetrating to it is not always easy. Even when focusing upon individuals, such sagas may be retelling the fortunes and exploits of tribal groups. The Jacob-Esau stories (25.21–34; 27.32 f.) are a good example of this. The 'Jacob' of these incidents represents 'the sons of Jacob' (Israelites), Esau represents the Edomites. In the birth story, God says to Rebekah, 'Two nations are in your womb, and two peoples, born of you, shall be divided' (25.23). On the other hand, sagas may genuinely retain the memory of the exploits of individuals. This seems to be true in the main of the Abraham sagas. There is no good reason to regard Abraham as a tribal symbol.

Not all the material in Gen.12–50, however, is saga. There are passages which contain *aetiological* (explanatory) *legends*. Of these, many are *cult legends* explaining the origin of the worship of Yahweh, the god of Israel, at particular shrines in the land of Canaan. Prominent among such cult legends are those associated with Hebron (13.18), Shechem (12.6 f.; 33.18–20) and Bethel (28.19–21). Such holy places were centres of worship long before the Hebrews entered the land of Canaan. The narratives reflect a successful Hebrew religious take-over bid, the original Canaanite deity being grafted into Hebrew religion or simply being replaced by the Hebrew god, Yahweh. Thus Gen.33.20 speaks of a sacred stone at Shechem called El Elohe-Israel, i.e. El (the supreme Canaanite deity), the god of Israel; while Gen.14.22 identifies Yahweh with El Elyon (El Most High), the god worshipped in the pre-Israelite cult at Jerusalem. The fact that such stories are called legends does not mean that they lack all historical reference. There is no reason to suppose that the story in Gen.31.45–50 was invented to explain the boundary stone; the boundary stone may be the witness to a historical event. Nor is there any reason to doubt that a Hebrew patriarch may have had an authentic encounter with this god at or near a Canaanite sanctuary (32.24–31).

The Joseph story (37; 39–50) stands on its own. It is neither saga nor legend. Instead of a series of loosely connected episodes, we have a carefully constructed short story which builds up to a dramatic climax. Instead of narratives which speak at point after point of God making himself known to the patriarch, the interest is focused on the character, motives and actions of the human agents. The religious emphasis, although present, is unobtrusive. The local Egyptian colouring of the story is authentic. The story of Joseph's entanglement with Potiphar's wife is basically similar in plot to the Egyptian 'Tale of Two Brothers'. Throughout, it breathes the atmosphere of the 'wisdom' tradition in Israel (see Part III, Section 12, pp. 162 ff.). What the origin of these chapters is and whether they originally had any organic relationship to the rest of the patriarchal traditions are questions difficult to answer.

A rich variety of material, very different in character and purpose, is thus discernible in Gen.12–50 – fragments of historical records, sagas both tribal and personal, explanatory legends, the Joseph story. That the end product is not an impossible hotch-potch is the result of a unity which has been given to this material by Hebrew writers who have used it for their own purposes to witness to the God of Israel's faith and the mystery of his choice of Israel to be his people. Genesis 12–50 is like a collection of pearls, gathered from different oyster beds. Each pearl has its own value, its own character; but all have been matched and strung together by master craftsmen to find new lustre in a new setting.

The Theology of the Narratives

The prologue stories in Gen.1–11 close with a family tree which narrows world history down to one tribal group, the sons of Shem, and within that group, to the person of Abraham, son of Terah (Gen.11.31). At this point, Old Testament history begins; but it is history of a peculiar kind, narrated in terms of God's activity and God's purposes. This is made immediately clear in 'J''s introduction to the Abraham sagas in 12.1–3. Certain basic themes are sounded.

1. *Call or Election*

Whatever political or economic factors controlled the movements of the Amorites in the ancient Near East *c.*2000–1500 BC, this man Abraham moves in response to a call from Yahweh (the Lord):

Now the Lord said to Abram, 'Go from your country and your kindred and your father's house to the land that I will show you' (12.1).

No explanation is given as to why the call came to this man. It is left as mystery, rooted solely in the initiative of God. It is a call which looks for a response of obedience; but it is not a call which comes because of the prior goodness or merit of Abraham. The patriarchs are not idealized figures. Abraham twice resorts to deceit to save his own skin (12.10–20; 20); Isaac follows suit (ch.26). With good reason popular saga connected Jacob's name (original meaning 'may God protect') with the Hebrew words for 'heel' (25.26) and 'supplant' (27.36, cf. Hos. 12.4). Jacob had nothing to learn in the art of 'one-up-manship', as the Jacob-Esau and the Jacob-Laban stories make plain. Joseph in his childhood and youth must have been an insufferable prig (ch.37). Yet it is precisely to such men that God's call comes; it is through them that God's purposes are forwarded. Israel had few illusions about her own goodness, but even fewer about the reality of God's call.

2. *Promise*

Associated with this call there is a twofold promise.

(i) The promise of 'land' (i.e. Canaan) and a future 'great nation' (12.2, cf. 12.7). This promise echoes throughout the patriarchal narratives. It is repeated at significant crisis points in Abraham's life (13.14–17; 15.4–7; 18.18; 22.17); it is confirmed to Isaac (26.2–4, 24), to Jacob (28.3 f., 13–15; 35.11 f.) and to Joseph (48.15 f.). The change of the name from Abram to Abraham (17.5) – the forms are probably merely dialectal variants – is popularly explained by reference to this promise. This is a promise repeatedly called into question by events. The land of Canaan remains occupied by other peoples. Famine forces Abraham to leave this land and go down to Egypt (12.10). Jacob is sent back to north-west Mesopotamia (ch.28). The narrative closes with Jacob's burial, according to his wish, in a plot of land in Canaan purchased by Abraham. The Canaanites, however, are firmly in possession of the land, while Abraham's descendants find themselves in Egypt (ch.50). The promise of a great nation is hazarded by Sarah's barrenness beyond the normal age of child-bearing (18.11 ff.). Isaac, upon whom all Abraham's hopes focus, becomes the source of Abraham's greatest testing. Genesis 22, the sacrifice of Isaac, is a good example of the theological purpose of the narratives. Taken by itself, it could be a legend explaining the name of a place (22.14) or why human sacrifice, practised at certain Canaanite sanctuaries, had been replaced by animal sacrifice in Hebrew religion. But the opening words of the chapter make it perfectly clear that the incident is to be read as the supreme test of Abraham's faith. It is so because what God asks jeopardizes the promise which God has made. If Isaac dies, there will be no great nation. The opposite side of this 'promise'-coin is the demand made upon man to live trusting in the promise even when circumstances seem to threaten it (cf. 15.6; 17.1). This is faith. Again and again in the narratives it is solely God's initiative and God's intervention which keep the promise in being, sometimes in unexpected ways. Compare Joseph's words to his brothers, 'God sent me before you to preserve life' (45.5).

The strongly God-centred emphasis surrounding the promise of land and a great nation prevented, or ought to have prevented, Israel from thinking of her destiny in purely imperialistic or political terms.

(ii) On the other hand, there is the promise of blessing to come through Abraham's descendants to other nations. The destiny of other nations is linked for good and for ill, in blessing and in curse, to that of Israel. 'By you all the families of the earth shall bless themselves' (12.3). What Abraham becomes under God is to be the desire of all nations. They will use his name in invoking blessing upon themselves. This note of universal promise is repeated at 22.18 and 26.4.

These two aspects of the promise, the one inward looking, the other outward looking, were often to be in tension in the history of Israel. It was only too easy for Israel to forget that what she was, she was for the sake of others.

3. *Covenant*

Many of the strands we have touched upon in call and promise are gathered together under the concept of the covenant (see Part III, Section 4, pp. 100 f.). The tradition of a covenant between God and Abraham appears in two forms in Genesis, the one in 15.7–21 ('J'), the other in 17.1–14 ('P'). Both traditions lay stress upon the fact that the covenant is rooted in God's self-revelation and initiative. The 'J' tradition begins with a formula in which God identifies himself and declares his past mighty acts.

> I am Yahweh your God who brought you from Ur of the Chaldees to give you the land to possess (15.7, cf. Ex.20.1; Deut.5.6).

The narrative goes on to describe an ancient ritual for covenant making which lies behind one of the common Hebrew expressions for making a covenant, namely 'to cut a covenant'. The contracting parties pass between the severed halves of sacrificial animals or birds. They thus bind themselves to one another, and invoke upon themselves a fate similar to that of the victims if they violate the solemn terms of the covenant (cf. Jer.34.18 f.). In the mysterious and awesome imagery of this narrative, however, only one of the contracting parties participates in the ritual. While Abraham lies in the grip of a deep sleep, Yahweh, in the symbols of smoke (a smoking oven) and fire (a torch), passes between the severed victims. It is thus Yahweh who initiates the covenant, who binds himself to Abraham to fulfil his promise of the possession of the land. The 'P' tradition in 17.1–14 makes the same point by its repeated emphasis upon 'my covenant':

I will make my covenant between me and you   (17.2.7).

My covenant is with you   (17.4,9,13).

The speaker in each case is God. What is offered to Abraham is an 'everlasting covenant' (17.7) which binds God to be for ever the God of Abraham and of his descendants. In this tradition, circumcision is introduced as the 'sign' of the covenant. It is not the condition for belonging to the covenant people; it is simply the outward sign that a man does belong to that people. Circumcision was commonly practised among many of the peoples of the ancient Near East and beyond. Usually it is a rite associated with puberty or marriage. It is characteristic of the Old Testament that it takes such a practice and baptizes it into the faith of Israel, where it becomes the sign of a lasting theological truth (cf. the 'bow' in Gen.9.8 ff.).

Both 'J' and 'P' covenant traditions point towards the future (15.13 ff.): 'J' to the fact that the promised possession of the land will only come after a long period (400 years) of apparent frustration; 'P' (17.6) to the coming of nations and kings out of the line of Abraham. These elements in the tradition may represent a reading back into the past of hopes fulfilled in the establishment of the Davidic kingdom. Whatever their origin, they point to the unity of all Israel's history under the sovereignty of the one God.

4. *The Presence of God*

Throughout the Abraham, Isaac and Jacob sagas there is a repeated emphasis upon *theophany*, the appearing of God to the patriarchs in one form or another. Many such theophanies occur in close proximity to holy places and sanctuaries (e.g., Gen.12.6 f.; 18.1 ff.; 28.10 ff.). Sometimes the narrative simply says Yahweh or God 'appeared' (cf. 17.1); sometimes it is the word of Yahweh that comes (15.1); sometimes God's presence is revealed in a dream, an emphasis which is usually thought to be characteristic of the 'E' source (e.g., 20.3; 28.13); sometimes it is the angel (or messenger) of Yahweh who appears (e.g., 16.7 ff.; 19.1 ff.; 21.17 ff.; 22.15 ff.); sometimes God appears, at first unrecognized, in human form (e.g., 18.1 ff.; 32.4 ff.). Behind certain of these theophanies lie ancient cult legends which at one time had no reference to the patriarchs of Israel or to their God. Genesis 32.24 ff., the mysterious story of Jacob's nocturnal wrestling, is a good case in point. Its origin is probably a legend about a demonic night assailant who disputed the passage of the ford Jabbok. Whatever their origin, such stories communicate a lively sense of the continuing encounter between God and man in the patriarchal era.

The names of God in the narratives point in the same direction. Many of them are divine titles, familiar in Canaanite religion before the Hebrews entered the land. This is true of numerous divine titles in which the first element is 'El, the supreme God'; e.g., El Shaddai (17.1): God of the Mountain, El Olam (21.33): Everlasting God, El Elyon (14.22): God Most High, El Bethel (31.13; 35.7): the God Bethel. There is, however, another category of divine names which links God to a patriarch. Thus God is 'the God of Abraham and the God of Nahor' (31.53); he is the Fear (or Kinsman) of Isaac (31.42,53), the Mighty One of Jacob (49.24). All such titles indicate a relationship between God and a particular person, usually the head of a clan-group. This emphasis upon personal revelation and personal relationship with God seems an authentic element in the religious experience of Israel's patriarchal forefathers.

The patriarchal narratives will always be a happy hunting ground for the social anthropologist and the religious historian. Behind the present form of narratives lie many old, and in certain respects primitive, traditions, some of which have been uneasily assimilated into Israel's faith. In their present form, however, the narratives breathe a rich spirituality. There will always be differences of opinion as to how much of this spirituality is a reading back into patriarchal times of a knowledge of God which only came to Israel later in her pilgrimage. At every point in that pilgrimage we come up against the mystery of God's initiative and self-revelation. Why should this not have as its starting-point, as Old Testament tradition affirms, the moment when a man called Abraham left north-west Mesopotamia in response to a call from God?

6

Moses

Robert Davidson

Moses is a key figure in the history and religion of Israel. He is regarded as the ideal prophet, the true servant of God, the trustworthy mediator of God's word to the people (Num.12.1–8; Deut.18.15–22). In later Jewish tradition, the supremely authoritative section of the Old Testament – *TORAH*, the Law (Genesis, Exodus, Leviticus, Numbers and Deuteronomy) – is known as the five books of Moses. To him the Old Testament traces back much that came into Israel only later and from a variety of sources. To him is ascribed the calendar of the religious year with its fixed festivals (Ex.23.14 ff.; 34.22–24; Lev.23; Deut.14); the entire cultic system with its sacrifices, offerings and priestly ministrants; the various codes of law, the earliest of which, the 'Book of the Covenant' (Ex.20.22–23.33), already presupposes the settled agricultural life in Canaan (cf. the Holiness Code, Lev.17–26, and the Deuteronomic Code, Deut.12–26). So important for Israel were the events associated with Moses, that all Israel was regarded as participating in these events (cf. the figures given in Ex.12.13 and the census lists in Num.1 and 26). Historically this is incredible, but theologically it is true in the same sense as one may speak of all Christians being 'there' at Calvary and the Empty Tomb. Moses was not given this dominant position without good reason. Much that was distinctive in Israel's faith, much that was to be decisive for Israel's later history was there, in at least seminal form, in the revelation that came to Moses and in the events of Moses' time.

The Historical Problem

The very centrality of Moses in tradition, however, poses serious historical problems.

1. The events recorded, the institutions described in the sources which lie behind Exodus, Leviticus, Numbers and Deuteronomy, were never in Israel cold historical facts. They are handed down to us across centuries of retelling and reliving in family worship and in the liturgies of the community. They speak of the mystery and wonder of God's mighty acts on behalf of his people, of a past which had no significance in Israel apart from faith. This does not mean that we are faced with a 'take it or leave it' choice with respect to narratives steeped in the supernatural and the miraculous. The Old Testament is never naïve enough to believe that God's presence in the world is to be equated with the supernatural. The kind of questions raised are well illustrated in the story of the plagues which afflicted Egypt as narrated in Ex.7–12. With the notable exception of the final climactic blow, the death of the first-born in every Egyptian household, all the plagues are well authenticated as natural phenomena which occur in the Nile valley. The quails and manna in the wilderness (Ex.16), the water spurting forth from the rock (Ex.17) similarly admit of a natural explanation. What seems naturally explicable and what remains inexplicable are both equally God-centred in the narratives. It is impossible to eliminate the sense of wonder from the tradition.

2. The narratives tell a connected story in each part of which Moses has a crucial role to play. Beginning with the harsh enslavement of the Hebrews in Egypt, they lead us through the wonder of deliverance from bondage to the encounter with God and the making of the covenant at the sacred mountain. The subsequent years of frustration and wandering in the wilderness come to a climax with the children of Israel poised on the verge of entry into the land of promise. There at Mt Nebo, looking out across the Jordan valley to Canaanite Jericho, Moses dies (Deut.34). Many scholars believe that, as in the case of the patriarchal narratives, this connected story is the result of the bringing together, into the religious and litarary treasury of later Israel, of once separate traditions belonging to different tribal groups. In particular, on the basis of the omission of all

references to the covenant at Mt Sinai in many credal passages which refer to the deliverance from Egypt (e.g., Deut.26.5–11; Josh.24.2–12), it has been argued that originally there was no historical link between the stories of the exodus from Egypt and the covenant at Mt Sinai. The arguments for this division of the traditions are hardly conclusive. Even if they were, it remains true that from a very early date, the tenth century BC with the 'J' source, the link between the exodus and Mt Sinai had been made and was to be significant for the subsequent faith of Israel.

Whatever the problems posed for the historian by the narratives, the centrality of the personality of Moses can hardly be denied unless the traditions are drastically rewritten.

Extra-biblical Evidence

At points where we can bring extra-biblical evidence to bear, it tends to corroborate the basic authenticity of the narratives.

1. Legend may have contributed its share to the stories about the infant Moses. The very name Moses, however, fits in well with the Egyptian background. Although Old Testament tradition links the name Moses with the Hebrew verb *mashah*, to draw up (Ex.2.10), the name in fact comes from an Egyptian root meaning 'beget'. It is found frequently, added to the name of a god, in Egyptian personal names, e.g., Thut-mosis, Ra-messes. Other names belonging to the family of Levi have also Egyptian associations.

2. Exodus 1.11 speaks of the Hebrew slaves building for Pharaoh the store cities of Pithom and Raamses. Both these towns are in the Nile Delta region. Raamses is almost certainly Avaris, rebuilt as the royal capital of the vigorous nineteenth Egyptian dynasty. It was called 'the house of Ramesses' by Ramesses II (thirteenth century BC), the second ruler of that dynasty. Egyptian texts of the period provide ample documentation of *Apiru* (*Habiru*: see Part III, Section 5, p. 103) working as slaves on royal building projects. The name 'house of Ramesses' soon disappears from Egyptian texts and after the eleventh century it is always referred to as Tanis. It seems that the narratives at this point have drawn on authentic pre-eleventh-century BC tradition.

3. Two dates have been frequently canvassed for the exodus.

(i) Fifteenth century BC. This fits in well with the evidence of the fifteenth-century Amarna letters. In these letters, Egyptian satellite rulers of Canaanite city states send repeated appeals for help to the ruling Pharaoh. They allege intrigue and counter-intrigue against one another and make reference to attacks by Habiru. This date can also claim support in biblical tradition. I Kings 6.1 states that the fourth year of Solomon's reign, i.e., 958 BC, was the 480th year after the people of Israel came out of the land of Egypt.

(ii) The main thrust of present evidence, however, points to the thirteenth century BC. This fits in well with the reference in Ex.1.11 (see above). Further, the story in Num.20–21 of the Israelites seeking permission from the Edomites to travel north along the King's Highway assumes a fair degree of Edomite settlement in the area. Archaeological evidence, however, reveals no trace of settlement in the region for centuries prior to the thirteenth century BC. Any date for the exodus is inevitably related to the date of the subsequent settlement in Canaan. There is evidence of severe destruction of several Canaanite cities in the late thirteenth century including Debir and Lachish in the south (Josh.10.31 ff.), Bethel in the centre (if Bethel is to be equated, as seems likely, with the Ai of Josh.8) and Hazor in the north (Josh.11). There is, of course, no conclusive proof that it was invading Hebrews who inflicted such destruction, but where archaeological evidence and biblical traditions seem to illumine each other, it is hypercritical to deny a link between them.

The evidence from Jericho, which was once thought to support a fifteenth-century date, now needs radical revision in the light of the latest excavations at the site. The supposedly fifteenth-century walls are centuries earlier. Little or no evidence remains of Jericho of the early Israelite period, the site having been heavily eroded. If the 480 years of I Kings 6.1 is intended to be a round figure for twelve generations, then according to our calculations, this would be nearer 300 years, which again suggests the thirteenth century. Israelite elements seem to have been in the process of settling in Canaan by the late thirteenth century. The Egyptian Pharaoh Merneptah celebrated a successful Canaanite campaign by erecting in 1220 BC a victory stele on which the name 'Israel' appears.

The Significance of Moses

By the very nature of the case, we must deal with probabilities rather than certainties when we discuss the historical background to the age of Moses. The Old Testament has no hesitations, however, about the significance it assigns to Moses.

1. *The Revelation of the Character and Name of God*

Moses, although brought up in the Egyptian court, retained his sense of identity with his enslaved fellow-countrymen. He slew an Egyptian taskmaster whom he had seen mal-treating a Hebrew slave (Ex.2.11–21). In consequence he fled to Midianite territory where, near the 'mountain of God', he had an encounter with God which was to be decisive, not only for his own life, but for the future of his people. At a mysteriously burning bush, he was confronted by a god who revealed himself as the 'God of your father, the God of Abraham, the God of Isaac and the God of Jacob' (Ex.3.6). In many respects, this encounter resembles the divine appearances in the patriarchal narratives. There is the same sense of direct personal relationship, a relationship enshrouded in mystery. Moses stands on 'holy ground'. The word 'holy' denotes separateness, that which belongs peculiarly to God. When applied to God it indicated the essential difference between God and even the best and greatest of men, the divine 'otherness' which evokes from man a response of reverent awe. Yet this 'otherness' is not remoteness. This God is concerned about the oppression of the people (Ex.3.7,16,17). These two aspects of God's character are held together in later Old Testament thinking by the description of God as 'the Holy One of Israel' (cf. Isa.1.4; 5.9,24; Ps.71.22). Moses' experience also points forward to later prophetic experience. His encounter with God is not an end in itself, not an invitation to share in mystical union with God. It issues in a word of command which commits Moses to action and obedience, a word of command from which Moses at first shrinks (Ex.4; cf. Isa.6; Jer.1).

Linked with this encounter there is the revelation of the name YHWH. The Priestly narrative in Ex.6.2 f. specifically claims that this is the revelation of a new name, not known to the patriarchs. The original meaning and even the pronunciation of these four consonants YHWH are matters of considerable dispute. Some have traced the name back beyond Moses to the worship of the Kenites or Midianites. The evidence for this lies mainly in the relationship between Moses and his father-in-law Jethro, the priest of Midian (see Ex.3; 18.10–12, 13–27). This is possible, but it is a case of explaining the unknown by an even greater unknown, since nothing is really known of the religion of the Kenites in pre-Mosaic times. Old Testament scholarship today usually renders the name *Yahweh*, which is probably as near as we can get to the original pronunciation. Most modern English translations use 'the *Lord*' (AV had Jehovah, which is an impossible form which was first coined in the Middle Ages). Whatever its origin, the narrative in Ex.3.13 ff. links it with the Hebrew verb HYH, 'to be' or 'to become'. 'God said to Moses "I am who I am" [or "I will be who I will be"]. And he said "Say this to the people of Israel '*I am*' [or 'I will be'] has sent me to you"' (Ex.3.14). YHWH therefore means 'He is' or 'He will be'. It is also possible that it may be a causative form 'He causes to be'. The emphasis is upon a God whose character is essentially dynamic and active. But the form of the statement '*I am who I am*' also indicates a certain reserve or mystery. The request to know God's name is a request to know his nature. The reply declares that God cannot be known in the sense of being neatly defined or labelled. He is a God who is and will be known through his active presence in the history of his people. The definition of his name is a challenge to go on into the unknown future with only one assurance: 'I will be with you' (Ex.3.12). The fact of the presence of Yahweh is stressed in various ways in the narratives of the period of the wandering in the wilderness. He is present in the pillar of cloud by day and fire by night that accompanies the Israelites (Ex.13.21; 14.19 f.), and in the 'tent of meeting' which, according to the earliest tradition in Ex.33, was a sanctuary outside the encampment where Yahweh could be consulted by his people. A sacred box, the ark, embodied Yahweh's presence. Numbers 10.35 preserves a very old tradition which addresses this ark as Yahweh: 'When it moved, Moses said, "Arise Yahweh, and let thy enemies be scattered" . . . and when it rested, he said, "Return, Yahweh, to the ten thousand thousands of Israel."' Yahweh is therefore a pilgrim God present with his people. He is henceforth for Israel a God known by what he does. Prophets and psalmists, historians and poets all witness to this dynamic presence in Israel's history, in mercy and in judgment, in national triumph and in national disaster.

It is important to notice that Moses' encounter with God and the revelation of the name YHWH come before the deliverance of the people from enslavement in Egypt. This gives Moses the standpoint of faith from which to declare what is going to happen, and from which to interpret the meaning of what does happen. Whatever took place at the exodus, it was not something self-explanatory as an 'act of God' to anyone who lived through it. Moses taught the people to accept it as God's action on their behalf, because of a faith in God which he already had. In this Moses is the precursor of the great pro-phetic traditions in the Old Testament, men who appear in response to a call from God at moments of crisis in the nation's history, and challenge the nation to see what is happening as the outworking of the purposes of the living God.

2. *The Exodus*

The exodus from Egypt is central to the faith of the Old Testament. If there is one description of God which, above all others, is characteristic of the God of the Old Testament, it is this: 'I am Yahweh your God who brought you out of the land of Egypt.' The prophets are the heralds of this God:

I brought you up out of the land of Egypt (Amos 2.10; cf. Jer.2.6).

When Israel was a child, I loved him,
    and out of Egypt I called my son (Hos.11.1).

Psalmists praise this God:

Thy way was through the sea,
    thy paths through the great waters,
    yet thy footprints were unseen.
Thou didst lead thy people like a flock
    by the hand of Moses and Aaron
    (Ps.77.19 f.; cf. Pss.66.6; 78.11 ff.;
    136.10 f.).

When a son asked his father the meaning of the commandments binding on Israel, the father is instructed to reply:

We were Pharaoh's slaves in Egypt, and Yahweh brought us out of Egypt with a mighty hand, and Yahweh showed signs and wonders, great and grievous, against Egypt and against Pharaoh and all his household before our eyes . . .' (Deut.6.21 f.; cf. Ex.20.2; Deut.5.6).

The significance of the exodus for faith is unquestionable; what actually happened was probably sober enough. A group of Hebrew slaves under the leadership of Moses left Egypt. They safely negotiated a stretch of water called the Sea of Reeds (not the Red Sea). The location of the Sea of Reeds is uncertain; the likelihood is that it lay in the general region of what is now the Suez canal or further east along the Mediterranean coast at Lake Sirbonis. The earliest narrative strand 'J' speaks of a strong east wind blowing all night to push the water back (Ex.14.21–28). The pursuing Egyptian chariots stuck in the soft sand and were drowned by the returning water. Naturally, Egyptian records have nothing to say about what was at most, from their point of view, a minor frontier incident. In the Old Testament, however, this is never an escape bid engineered by Moses, but always a mighty act of God in which he delivered his people out of enslave-ment. What is probably the earliest Old Testament witness to the event, the triumph-song of Miriam, grasps the essence of what happened:

Sing to Yahweh, for he has triumphed
    gloriously,
the horse and the rider he has thrown into the
    sea (Ex.15.21; cf. 15.1).

This was Yahweh's victory over his enemies, a victory on behalf of his oppressed people. That it was so interpreted from the beginning must be attributed to the prior revelation of God's purposes given to Moses. The exodus is the heart of the Old Testament gospel, the good news of what God has done.

Just as the memory of central events in the New Testament gospel was preserved in the worship of the early Christian community, so the exodus was handed down in Israel in one great family religious festival 'Passover'. Alone among the festivals of the Hebrew religious year, Passover goes back beyond the time of settlement in Canaan, back in all probability beyond the exodus. In origin, Passover is the festival of a pastoral community. Celebrated in the spring, at full moon in the first month of the year, it contains a rite, the smearing of the blood of a lamb on the tent posts, which was probably designed to ward off demons of destruction or infertility. The lamb is roasted in nomadic fashion and eaten with desert food, unleavened bread seasoned with bitter herbs. The participants in the meal are ready to move at a moment's notice to defend the flock, belt fastened, sandals on feet, staff in hand. All of this is explicable without any reference to the exodus. But, just as Christmas has gathered to itself many pagan customs to give them new meaning in Christ, so Passover finds a new meaning in the Old Testament through being linked to the exodus. The name of the festival 'Pesah', a word of very uncertain meaning, is linked in the earliest source, 'J', with Yahweh's 'passing over' (Hebrew: *pasah*) the blood-smeared lintels of Hebrew homes when the destroying angel smote Egypt (Ex.12.21–27). In the 'P' tradition in Ex.12.11, the fastened belt, sandalled feet and staff in hand are memorials of the haste with which the Hebrews left Egypt at God's command. In Deut.16.3, the unleavened bread is called the 'bread of affliction', again a memorial of the people's flight in haste from Egyptian bondage. The date of the celebration is the month of Abib (April: 'the month of the green ears of corn'), 'for in the month of Abib Yahweh your God brought you out of Egypt by night' (Deut.16.1; cf. Ex.23.14 ff.; 34.18).

Passover is an illustration of something that happened to most of the festivals of the Hebrew year. Festivals such as *Massoth* (Unleavened Bread), *Qasir* (Harvest) and *Asiph* (Ingathering) are native to the agricultural life of Canaan. But whatever their origin, the Old Testament gives them a historical reference, and in most cases that historical reference is to the exodus or the events associated with it. *Asiph*, for example, is the great harvest thanksgiving festival. The farmer's work for the year is successfully completed; the mood is one of unrestrained rejoicing. In Deut.16.13, however, this festival is called *Sukkoth* (Huts). The origin of these 'huts' is disputed. Some find here a

reference to the sacred booth in which the marriage between the god and goddess of fertility was consummated, others think the 'huts' are the temporary shelters which Palestinian agricultural workers from time immemorial have erected in the fields at harvest time to give shelter from the sun in the heat of the day. According to Lev.23.42 f. these 'huts' or 'booths' have a different significance: 'You shall dwell in booths for seven days; all that are native in Israel shall dwell in booths that your generations may know that I made the people dwell in booths when I brought them out of the land of Egypt. I am Yahweh your God.'

3. *The Covenant*

Closely associated with the exodus in Old Testament tradition is the story of how the Israelites journeyed to a mountain where there was ratified a covenant between Yahweh and the people. Much is uncertain about this mountain of Israel's destiny. Its very name is variously given in tradition. Two of the sources ('E' and 'D') consistently refer to it as Horeb, two ('J' and 'P') call it Sinai. Its location is likewise in dispute. Tradition places it near to the southern tip of the Sinai peninsula at the Jebel Musa (mountain of Moses). Many scholars hold to a much more northerly location near Kadesh (Ex.15.12), while others place it further east beyond the Gulf of Aqaba. This latter location is based mainly on the supposition that the language describing God's coming to his people on the mountain implies volcanic activity. Exodus 19.16–18 speaks of thunder, lightning, thick cloud, trumpet blast, smoke like the smoke of a kiln. The language might equally refer to a violent mountain storm. It is doubtful, however, whether we ought to press literally words and images which are traditionally associated with the divine appearances (cf. the covenant with Abraham, Gen.15). The tradition as to what happened at the mountain is exceedingly complex. There are three different appearances (Ex.19–20; 24.10–18; 34) and with each there are associated laws and regulations, governing worship and social relationships within the community. Many of these regulations are obviously of later date. What is the authentic historical kernel in all this?

First we can assert with confidence that at this mountain a group of Hebrew refugee slaves from Egypt became conscious of their destiny as 'the people of God' through a covenant ceremony. The covenant ritual is described in Ex.24.4–8. It involves sacrifice and the sprinkling of half the blood upon the altar, symbol of God's presence, and half upon the people. God and people are now bound together in one common life. In one respect this covenant ceremony echoes the covenant traditions in the patriarchal narratives. The emphasis is heavily upon God's initiative. It is God who comes to the people in the awesome imagery of the mountain scene. When Moses sprinkles the blood upon the people he declares, 'Behold the blood of the covenant which Yahweh has made with you' (Ex.24.8). Exodus 34 contains what has been called a 'Ritual Decalogue' prescribing the religious acts to be observed by the community throughout the year. Its emphasis in terms of initiative is one-sided. No ceremony of covenant ratification is described, but this is a covenant which Yahweh makes (cf. Ex.34.10, 27). In another respect, however, this covenant is different from those in the patriarchal narratives. It is made by God no longer with one man such as Abraham, but with a community. The covenant is not between God and Moses. Moses simply acts as the priestly mediator in a covenant that binds God and people. Henceforth Yahweh is the God of Israel, and Israel the people of Yahweh. This means that Israel is no longer merely a tribal or racial group, but a religious community, committed to a certain kind of loyalty to a God who had chosen them to be his people.

Two points are worth stressing about the covenant bond.

(i) It is in no sense a natural or inevitable relationship based on any ties of kinship between God and people. Rather is it a relationship of grace. It was inaugurated at a particular time and place in history as the outworking of God's revealed compassion for an oppressed people. Its continuance, therefore, depends solely upon the consistency of character of this God who had chosen Israel, upon what the Old Testament repeatedly refers to as the *hesed*, steadfast love, and the faithfulness of God·(cf. Ex.34.6·f.)

(ii) Although there is a historical 'once and for all' aspect about this covenant, its significance is not tied to any one point of time in Israel's history. Since it called the people to commitment, it is a covenant which, from the side of the people, must be accepted anew by each succeeding generation. Every generation was present or ought to be present at Mt Sinai. The book of Deuteronomy speaks for every generation of the faithful in later Israel when it declares, 'Yahweh our God made a covenant with us at Horeb. Not with our fathers did Yahweh make this covenant, but with us who are all of us here alive this day' (Deut.5.2 f.).

4. *The Decalogue*

The various laws and regulations associated with the divine appearances in the exodus tradition are attempts to spell out for Israel the implications of this covenant relationship. The only element in them with any claim to be Mosaic is the Decalogue, the Ten Words. They come down to us in two versions, Ex.20.2–17 ('E') and Deut.5.6–10, both of them probably later theological variants of an original shorter form. The theological expansion is evident in the different reasons alleged for the observance of the sabbath: the Exodus version rooting it in the creation tradition of Gen. I, Deuteronomy making it a sacrament of the deliverance from Egyptian bondage. Many scholars regard the Decalogue as a distillation of the teaching of the great prophets of Israel and no earlier in date than the exile of the sixth century BC. There are, however, no compelling reasons against it being in essence of Mosaic origin. In context, the Decalogue is distinctive because it consists of words addressed by God to the people, in contrast to the surrounding ordinances, regulations and statutes. Such ordinances are, in the main, in the form of 'case law' of a type common to the great law codes of the ancient Near East – the ordinance concerning Hebrew slaves in Ex.21.1–11 is a good example. The Decalogue throughout is in the form of direct address from God to the people. This has been compared with Hittite treaty documents of the fourteenth and thirteenth century BC. Such treaty documents begin with a prologue in which the Great King identifies himself and lists his beneficent acts towards his vassal people. The obligations upon loyal vassals are then listed. They include no dealings with the king's enemies and the fulfilment of all duties incumbent upon the king's subjects. The form of the Decalogue is remarkably similar. The prologue identifies God, 'I am Yahweh your God'; it declares his gracious deeds on behalf of the people: 'who brought you out of the land of Egypt out of the house of bondage'. Obligations are then laid upon the people, including the demand for exclusive loyalty to Yahweh, and the following of a code of conduct befitting Yahweh's people. Later Assyrian treaty documents have provided further close parallels notable to elements in the book of Deuteronomy. We may therefore think of the covenant at Mt Sinai as a treaty covenant, establishing the kingship of Yahweh over his subject people. The Decalogue is the charter document of this treaty.

The character of Yahweh revealed in the Decalogue is remarkable. There is the demand for *an exclusive loyalty*: 'no other gods "before" or "besides" or "in preference to" me'. In a world of many pantheons where gods and goddesses had their places in appropriate family groups, Yahweh was to stand alone in his people's loyalty. There is the demand for *imageless worship*. In a world where gods and goddesses were represented in myriad forms – human, animal, bird, fish – there was to be no representation of Yahweh. Deuteronomy 4.15 ff. see this as a safeguard to the element of mystery in the nature of Yahweh. The people saw no form on the day that Yahweh spoke to them at Horeb out of the midst of the fire.

There is the demand to take the claims of Yahweh with *utter seriousness*. 'Not to take the name of Yahweh your God in vain' is far more than the prohibition of equivocal oaths. The best commentary on it is Josh.24.19–22 where Joshua warns the people against any glib or light-hearted pledge of loyalty to Yahweh. There is the demand to keep *sabbath*. The origin of and background to sabbath are obscure. The essential character of sabbath in the Old Testament, however, is that of a day which belongs to Yahweh, a tithe on time, proclaiming Yahweh's lordship over all time.

The last six demands are concerned with regulating human relationships within the covenant community. These six words focus attention on the character of the worshipper and the community in which he lives. They deal with what the prophets were later to summarize

as 'justice' and 'righteousness'. If we take an organic link between religion and morality, both social and personal, for granted, it is only because we stand within a Judaic-Christian heritage which stems from the Decalogue. It was not always so in the world of the ancient Near East, where religion often centred on the forces of nature rather than on the demand for righteousness.

According to Deut.10.1–5 these Ten Words inscribed on stone tablets were placed in the ark and carried with the people on their pilgrimage from the mountain to Canaan, the land of promise.

The Legacy of Moses

Considerable discussion has centred upon whether, and in what sense, Moses can be described as a monotheist. Partly this is a question of terminology. Monotheism, in the sense of a theological or philosophical doctrine that there is in fact only one divine reality in the universe, had no relevance to Moses' situation. With belief, however, in a God who shapes the forces of nature and history, who brooks no rival, who has no female consort, who demands the exclusive loyalty of a people, monotheism of a practical kind is there in seminal form. It has been well said that the poet-prophet author of Isa.40–55, many centuries later, was but pushing Mosaic religion to its logical conclusion when he unequivocally declared:

Turn to me and be saved, all the ends of the earth, for I am God and there is no other (Isa.45.22; cf. 44.6–8).

The history of Israel's religion from the time of the settlement in Canaan is a history of conflict: conflict between the many who demanded a 'Comprehensive Religious Insurance' policy covering the gods of Canaan as well as Yahweh and the few who stood for the exclusive claims of Yahweh; conflict between those who thought of religion basically in cultic terms and those who never lost sight of the essentially ethical element in Hebrew faith; conflict between the many who viewed Yahweh as the private patron saint of Israel and the few who saw judgment upon Israel springing inevitably out of the demanding nature of Israel's God.

That it was a history of conflict, not merely compromise; that a distinctive Yahwistic faith survived instead of being assimilated into the religious culture of Canaan, that it outlived the political disintegration of the Hebrew states; this is the legacy of the revelation that came to Moses, and the decisive shape that revelation gave to Israel's faith.

7

Joshua and the Judges

J. R. Porter

The Evidence

1. *Biblical Material*

This is to be found almost exclusively in the Old Testament books called 'Joshua' and 'Judges'. The former is concerned with the career of Joshua after the death of Moses; the latter covers the period from the death of Joshua to the emergence of Saul as the first king of Israel somewhere about 1000 BC. At first sight, the picture of the events given in these books appears comparatively straightforward. Under the leadership of Joshua, the twelve tribes of Israel that have come out of Egypt invade Palestine and conquer the whole country in a short space of time, as the result of three rapid campaigns – against the central part of the land (Josh.1–9), against the south (Josh.10) and against the north (Josh.11). As a result, Joshua is able immediately to divide Palestine among the twelve tribes, each of which settles in its allotted area (Josh.13–21). The book of Joshua fittingly concludes at ch. 24 with the account of a great ceremony in which, at Joshua's direction, all the tribes pledge themselves to the sole worship of the God Yahweh. After the death of Joshua, the nation broke this solemn obligation and began to worship other gods: as a result, they incurred divine judgment, which took the form of their falling under the rule of foreign enemies (Judg.2.6–3.6). When this happened, the nation repented, in consequence of which Yahweh chose a 'judge' ('ruler' conveys better the sense of the original) who first led the people to victory over their oppressors and then governed Israel during his lifetime. After his death, Israel again fell away from

Yahweh: the same sequence of events occurred and the same pattern was repeated many times (Judg.3–16). Samuel was the last of these 'judges' and it was through his agency that a new system of government, the monarchy, was introduced.

2. *Archaeological Evidence*

The evidence provided by the excavation of Palestinian sites is often adduced to support the biblical picture of a speedy and violent conquest of the whole country by the Israelites under Joshua. This evidence shows that there was a tremendous destruction of four towns mentioned in the conquest narrative as being destroyed by the Israelites, and that in each case the town was destroyed between 1300 and 1200 BC, and most probably in the latter half of the century. The towns in question are: in the south of Palestine, Lachish (Josh.10.31 f.) and Debir (Josh.10.38 f.); in the centre, Bethel (Judg.1.22–26); in the north, Hazor (Josh.11.10–13). Thus, the biblical tradition and the archaeological evidence appear to agree that these places were all violently destroyed and within a comparatively brief span of time.

A Reconstruction of Events

When both the biblical records and the archaeological evidence are examined more closely the picture appears a good deal more complicated.

The first chapter of the book of Judges gives a markedly different account of the Israelite occupation of Palestine from that to be found in the book of Joshua. First, this account makes it clear that in a number of areas the Israelites were able merely to settle down alongside the already existing inhabitants, the peoples called Canaanites and Amorites (see, e.g., Judg.1.29, 31 f.), and that, even where they became the dominant power, they did not attempt to expel or exterminate the native population (Judg.1.21, 27 f., 30, 33–35). Most of the places referred to in this connection are towns and this would appear accurately to reflect the contemporary situation. Palestine at this period consisted mainly of a number of independent city-states, usually ruled over by a king and generally situated in the plains. It would seem that for a long time the area of Israelite occupation was restricted to the hilly districts and did not extend to the plains (so Judg.1.9). The Canaanite cities retained their independence and only became incorporated in the organization of Israel with the establishment of an Israelite state when kingship was introduced. Relations between the incoming Israelites and these cities no doubt varied from place to place. Often they would be hostile, which accounts for the traditions of attacks on cities that are to be found in the book of Joshua. On the other hand, Judg.1 indicates that the two groups frequently lived side by side in a state of relatively peaceful cohabitation and there are instances of actual confederations between them. Such is the reality behind the story in Josh.9 of how four Canaanite cities made a treaty of alliance (which is what the word 'covenant' means in this chapter) with the Israelites. In Judg.8.29 f.; 9, we seem to have the picture of a similar alliance, cemented by inter-marriage, between the tribe of Manasseh and the still Canaanite city of Shechem which continued the worship of its own special god (see Judg.9.4, 27, 46). A similar marriage relationship between the tribe of Benjamin and the city of Shiloh is probably the real explanation of the story in Judg.21.19–23. The continued existence of Canaanite populations, and the friendly relations of the Israelites with them in many cases, meant that the newcomers were often tempted to worship Canaanite deities or to fuse them with their own god, Yahweh, and to introduce Canaanite religious practices into his worship.

Canaanite Religion

The Canaanites worshipped a group of gods, of whom the chief were El, the creator deity and the head of the group, Baal, the young storm-god and most active member of the group, and three goddesses, Anath, Ashtaroth and Asherah, all of whom were consorts of Baal. Canaanite religion was basically concerned with fertility, with securing a plentiful supply of crops, animals and children. The 'myths' or stories about the gods' doings all have this as their underlying theme and it seems likely that these stories were enacted year by year, in a kind of sacred drama, to bring about the fruitfulness and prosperity of the country and thus to ensure the people's continuing existence. It is not hard to see why this sort of religion appealed so strongly to the Israelites. It was concerned with survival and rooted in the soil and agriculture of Palestine: the problem for the Israelites was to survive in a strange country and to adapt themselves to the new agricultural way of life, in contrast to their previous semi-nomadic existence. Agriculture was the affair of the Canaanite gods: it was natural, therefore, for the Israelite farmer to turn to them for help or to invest Yahweh with their functions. Whatever may be thought of the worship of deities other than Yahweh – and the Old Testament universally condemns it – the development by which such a god as El was assimilated to Yahweh was not wholly bad. For it brought about a widening and deepening of the whole idea of Yahweh. He came to be seen as the Creator, the Lord of all nature as well as Lord of the history of a particular people. Thus the seed which was to grow into the idea of one universal God was already planted in this early period of Israel's history.

A Gradual Conquest

The first chapter of Judges (in contrast to the book of Joshua) suggests that the occupation of Palestine was not carried out by a single operation of all the tribes acting together under a united leadership. Rather, in this chapter, we have a picture of individual tribes, or even smaller groups, acting independently of one another, each one moving separately into a particular area on its own initiative. In a number of cases, exploits which elsewhere are attributed to all Israel are here presented as the work of a single tribe: thus, in Josh.10.36–39 Hebron and Debir are captured by a united nation under the leadership of Joshua; in Judg.1.8–15 Hebron is taken by the tribe of Judah and Debir by a small clan represented as an individual, Othniel, without any mention of Joshua at all. Further, on closer examination, even the book of Joshua tends to confirm that this picture of a piece-meal settlement in Palestine probably corresponds to what actually happened. The account of the wholesale conquest of the country is in fact confined to Josh.10–11 and is in very general terms. By contrast, in chs. 1–9, which are in much greater detail, the territory said to be conquered or occupied is limited to the area belonging to the tribe of Benjamin alone. It may well be that the kernel of the book of Joshua was originally the tribe of Benjamin's own account of how it came to possess its own particular territory. It would thus be parallel to the individual tribal traditions of settlement to be found in Judg.1 and elsewhere. Joshua himself was perhaps to begin with just the local Israelite leader in this region: he seems to have originated not from Egypt but from the neighbouring hill country, where his family held property and where he was buried (Josh.24.30).

At this point, the archaeological evidence must also be looked at again. We saw that, from the fact of the destruction of certain towns, it has been held that there was actually a sudden and fairly rapid Israelite conquest of Palestine within the period 1300–1200 BC. There are three points to be noted in connection with this. First, there is no *direct* evidence from archaeology that these particular towns, or indeed any others, were destroyed by the Israelites. Most excavated Palestinian cities suffered frequent destructions between 2000–1000 BC and not all these can be attributed to the Israelite tribes: we simply do not know who was responsible. Secondly, the archaeological evidence from some cities which are said in the Bible to have been taken by the Israelites does not allow their destruction to be placed in the century 1300–1200 BC. To refer to the most striking examples, Joshua and the Israelites are said to have captured and burned the cities of Jericho and Ai (Josh.6–8). But the latest excavations show that the site of Jericho was probably unoccupied, and certainly did not possess a city wall, during the century in question, while Ai had been left abandoned some hundreds of years before. Thirdly, there is the evidence of the Amarna letters, so called

because they were discovered at Amarna in Egypt. These are letters written somewhere between 1450 and 1350 BC to the king of Egypt from the rulers of various Canaanite cities. Some of them mention attacks on cities in Palestine by a people called the *Habiru*, and this word is probably closely connected with the name *Hebrew*. It is not possible simply to equate what is said of the *Habiru* disturbances with the biblical record of the Israelite conquest, as has sometimes been done, but it seems likely that there is some link between the two and that the *Habiru* movement probably was a part, though not the whole, of what we call the Israelite conquest and settlement of Palestine.

Taken in conjunction with the biblical witness to the piecemeal character of the Israelite occupation of Canaan, the archaeological evidence, too, suggests that the 'conquest' was probably a very slow and gradual process, extending over some hundreds of years and by no means completed even during the period covered by the books of Joshua and Judges. The difficulties and discrepancies of the Old Testament narrative, some of which have been mentioned, can probably best be accounted for by some such reconstruction as the following. To begin with, we have to think of a number of separate groups, though no doubt of much the same racial stock, which formed the basis of the later Israelite tribes. Each of these, at different times and in different circumstances, pushed into Canaan from the desert region on its eastern border and settled down there, and each group preserved its own tradition of how this happened. What we have in the Bible is, in the first place, the collecting together of these often very divergent tribal recollections, and this came about when the various tribes joined together on the soil of Palestine to form the entity which the Bible calls 'Israel'.

In the second place, the different traditions of conquest and settlement are in the Old Testament unified and harmonized, and again it is perhaps possible to suggest how this happened. One or more of the groups, though not all, that came to constitute 'Israel' migrated to Egypt and eventually experienced the events of the exodus and the desert wanderings. It was this group's tradition of those events which became the dominant one in Israel and was adopted by all the other groups as part of their own tribal history. That this was possible, it may be surmized, was because of the tremendous effect of Yahweh's greatness made on those who heard of his mighty works at the exodus. The different tribal groups came to see that the God who had been active in the deliverance from Egypt was in fact the one who had also led them in their own migrations to Palestine: that is, acceptance of the exodus tradition also meant recognition of Yahweh. Perhaps we can see signs of the process we have just outlined at work behind the narrative in Josh.24, although this chapter has no doubt been worked over by editors of varying dates. Here a great assembly of the tribes of Israel gathers together at the holy place of Shechem, but it is clearly stated that their ancestors were not Yahweh-worshippers (v. 2) nor are many of them now (vv. 14 f.). The purpose of Joshua's speech is to win over the whole body to the worship of Yahweh, who is the God of his own group (v.15). This he does by reciting a statement of Yahweh's saving acts in history up to the occupation of the Promised Land (vv. 3–13). The statement includes mention of Yahweh's care of Abraham, Jacob and Esau (vv. 3–4), and these patriarchal names almost certainly represent originally independent groups. Thus once separate histories of particular groups are here linked with the exodus tradition and with the God of the exodus. The climax is reached when all the people recognize Yahweh and make their own his deliverance of them from Egypt and his settling of them in Canaan (vv. 16–18). Finally, Joshua makes a covenant (v. 25), a solemn agreement which joins all the tribes together in a common service to the one God, Yahweh. Joshua 24, therefore, does seem closely to reflect the manner in which we have suggested the different tribal traditions came together.

Judges and the Deuteronomic History

We saw that, in its present form, the book of Judges presents the nation as a whole, and the judges appear as rulers over the entire people, succeeding one another in chronological succession. But closer study shows that this presentation is the result of the final editing of the book, the purpose of which was to give a particular interpretation to the much older material which the editor used and to set out a particular understanding of Israel's history. It is now widely accepted that this editing was done by the school of writers who produced the book of Deuteronomy and were guided by its outlook, and that the books of Joshua and Judges now form part of a much larger work, a 'Deuteronomic history', recounting the story of the nation from the settlement in Palestine to the fall of Jerusalem at the end of II Kings, for which Deuteronomy is the introduction and the programme. The Deuteronomic school always views Israel as a single whole, so that all the laws of Deuteronomy are given to the nation as one unit. Again, the Deuteronomic literature has a very definite purpose and a very distinctive theological position. Its writers were also preachers who wanted to convince the people of the need to remain faithful to Yahweh and they tried to achieve this by constantly driving home the point that disobedience to Yahweh automatically involved national disaster and vice versa. Both these characteristics are very marked in the book of Judges, but, as we have already partly seen, they represent an *interpretation* of historical events rather than an accurate picture of conditions in the age before the rise of the monarchy. When we look at the actual stories of the judges which the editor used, such narratives as those of Ehud (Judg.3), Gideon (Judg.6–8), Jephthah (Judg.11–12) or Samson (Judg.13–16), we can see that these are about the popular heroes of particular tribes and particular localities, who emerged to save their own group when it was threatened with attack by some other neighbouring people. The exploits of the judges were on a comparatively small scale and probably they were often contemporary with one another, active in different parts of the country at the same time. The judge was not even the regular or permanent leader of his group, in which authority normally resided in the 'elders' (see, e.g., Judg.11.5 f.), the senior men whose wisdom and experience fitted them for controlling the affairs of the tribe and for settling legal disputes between its individual members. Rather, the judge appeared in response to a grave crisis, almost always a dangerous external attack, which the elders could not cope with, and when his task was successfully completed he retired again to his ordinary life. He was marked out for his calling when he was possessed by the 'spirit of Yahweh' (see, e.g., Judg.6.34), a violent seizure which enabled him to perform superhuman feats of strength and military prowess. The Israelite judge is thus an example of a kind of leadership characteristic of simple societies and which is often described by the term *charismatic*, from the Greek word *charisma*, a gift: the judge was one who had the 'gift' of Yahweh's spirit, and he was therefore very close to the prophet. Hence it is not surprising that the institution of the judges disappeared with the formation of the Israelite state, when the overriding authority which he had temporarily possessed was permanently transferred to the figure of the king. So the book of Judges, too, gives a picture of the Israelites at this period divided into comparatively small and separate groups, occupying only restricted areas of the country and maintaining a precarious existence in the face of the threat from other groups pushing into Palestine as they themselves had previously done. (See also Part III, Section 3, pp. 91 ff.)

The People of Israel

Yet the fortunes of individual groups is not the whole story. As well as each particular tribe, and however different the past history of any one tribe may have been from that of any other, it seems clear it was at this time possible to recognize something called 'Israel', as a living reality over and above the individual tribes. We now have to go on to say something of the actual life of the tribe on the one hand and of Israel on the other, and to consider the relationship between them.

The individual tribes seem to have gained their form and identity as the result of the actual process of occupying specific territories in Palestine and growing into settled communities there. In not a few cases, we can see fairly clearly how the nature of the country and its inhabitants were the decisive factor in the formation of particular tribes. So, some tribal names seem to derive from the geographical area where the tribe settled, such as Ephraim from 'Mount Ephraim': again, the tribe of Judah seems to be much more a confederation than a single unit, built up by the joining together of Israelites with a number of other small groups living in the southern part of Palestine. The organization of a tribe was that of a simple agricultural community, but even the simplest society must have some rules for common living and it is the emergence of these, at the very beginning of national life in Palestine, which is one of the

most interesting features of this time. There are a number of such laws, in various parts of the Old Testament, which seem to take their rise in this early period, and perhaps the most important collection of them is to be found in Ex.21–23, which are often referred to as the 'Book of the Covenant'. Three points, among many, may be singled out for attention.

1. The regulations of the Book of the Covenant are clearly concerned with an agricultural, farming community, not a semi-nomadic one. They deal with cattle, with corn, with fields and vineyards, and the people are living in well-built houses.

2. When the Book of the Covenant is examined, it can be seen to consist of two distinct types of laws. For the moment, only one of these types will be discussed because it is this type which seems to be most directly concerned with the daily life of the local community. The type in question is commonly termed *casuistic law*, from the Latin *casus*, a case, and it is so called because it first states a typical case and then draws a principle of general application from it. Casuistic laws can be easily recognized from their opening formula: 'When a man does so and so.' A considerable number of law codes from the ancient Near Eastern world are known, from which it can be seen that this type of law was commonly used throughout the area which formed the background to Israelite life. Hence it is reasonable to think that the Israelites in Palestine may have borrowed these laws from their Canaanite neighbours: it was part of their adaptation to their new way of life. By their nature, these laws were based on custom, and sprang from the needs and problems of everyday social life.

3. The public religious life of each tribe centred on one or more holy places in its neighbourhood, and it is with these local shrines that many of the regulations about worship were originally concerned. These holy places were of greater or lesser elaboration and reputation and drew their worshippers from wider or narrower areas, but each had its own priesthood of some kind, although there was as yet no idea of a single hereditary priestly family such as came to be the case later on in Israel. It is also clear that the great majority of these sanctuaries long pre-dated the Hebrew settlement and that the Israelites took them over from, or often even shared them with, the

Canaanites. The heart of the tribe's worship were the three annual feasts of 'Unleavened Bread', of 'Harvest' and of 'Ingathering' mentioned in Ex.23.14–17. 'Feast' here properly means 'pilgrimage' and these were occasions when all males had to be present at the shrine: this is the reason why the Israelite festival most familiar to us, the Passover, is not included among them, for this was not kept publicly at the sanctuary but at home. All these feasts are linked with key moments in the farmer's year. Their original purpose was to secure the divine blessing on the basic needs of human life. The same is true of the original meaning of the presentation of the first-fruits (Ex.23.19) and of the first-born (Ex.22.29–30) and accounts for the central place given to these observances in the regulations. Here again we can see how close at this time were the basic concerns of popular Israelite religion to those of Canaanite worship.

The Tribal League

Over and above the local pattern of family and tribe, there was a wider grouping to which all the tribes belonged and to which the Old Testament gives the name 'Israel'. This was a league of tribes, built on bodies of people and not on a territorial area as were many of the states of the ancient world: so, whatever the word 'Israel' may originally have implied, it early became the alternative name of a person, Jacob, from whom all the tribes were supposed to have been descended. It would be wrong to think of the tribal league as being anything like so well-defined or so closely-knit as a state, whether ancient or modern, but it did have its central organization and functionaries. Modern scholars often use the word *amphictyony* to describe what Israel was like in the centuries before the establishment of the monarchy. This is a Greek term meaning 'those who dwell round about', a league of near neighbours. In the classical world, it denoted a distinctive organization, a group of twelve or six tribes who were united together because they worshipped at a common sanctuary, with each tribe being responsible for the upkeep of this central sanctuary for one or two months in the year. It would be dangerous to think of pre-monarchic Israel as conforming very closely to the classical *amphictyony*. Whether the twelve-tribe system was a

reality, at any rate at this time, is doubtful – in the very early poem, known as the 'Song of Deborah', for example, in Judg.5, there are at best only ten tribes mentioned – and there is no clear evidence in Israel for each tribe in turn being responsible for the monthly upkeep of a central sanctuary. Nevertheless, there are enough similarities to make it illuminating to apply the term *amphictyony* to early Israel, as long as it is not pressed too far.

As we have seen, the tribes were held together by a covenant which bound them to worship Yahweh alone: the basis of the Israelite league was the religious obligation of this covenant. But it was necessary from time to time to remind the Israelites of their convenantal obligations and also to make these known to succeeding generations. Thus there would seem to have come into being an annual ceremony, attended by all the tribes, when the covenant was solemnly renewed. On this occasion, the terms of the covenant – the demands of Yahweh – were read out to the people, who then undertook to observe them. These demands are what is meant by 'law' in the Old Testament and there all the different law-codes are represented as expressions of the will of the covenant God. In the period with which we are concerned, we can probably see the character of the covenant law in a second type of legal material found in the Book of the Covenant, which is often called *apodictic*, a word meaning 'absolute', something which admits of no exception. *Apodictic law* is recognizable by the formula 'thou shalt' or 'thou shalt not': because it expressed the will of Yahweh, it could not be modified by changing circumstances as could casuistic law. A description of the ceremony at which the terms of the covenant were read out is in Deut.31.9–13, though here the reading of the law takes place at seven-year intervals. Here the law is entrusted for keeping and reading to the priests and the elders, but there may also have been a single individual who, as the covenant mediator, was responsible for transmitting the law, and this person may be the source of some features in the biblical picture of such figures as Moses and Joshua. He may also have had the functions of a judge in the proper sense, settling disputes which were too difficult for the local elders (see Deut.17.8–13). Judg.10.1–5 and 12.8–15 is perhaps a list of such central judges.

The Central Sanctuary and the Ark of the Covenant

The renewal of the covenant implies a sanctuary where the ceremony took place and where a copy of the law was kept. This sanctuary did not replace the local shrine, but its distinguishing feature was that it was a central place where the tribes all assembled on solemn occasions. In the books of Joshua and Judges, we read of various shrines at which the tribal league came together and it is possible that different places were the site of the central sanctuary at different times during this long period. But, towards its end, the central sanctuary seems to have been firmly established at Shiloh, about which we learn a great deal from the first three chapters of I Samuel. There, we find that the main celebration was a great harvest festival in the autumn to which people came from considerable distances on pilgrimage (I Sam.1): this is the festival which is known elsewhere in the Old Testament as the 'feast of Tabernacles' and it should be noted that this was also the occasion of the reading out of the law (see Deut.31.10).

At Shiloh, we find a priesthood which had the special responsibility of looking after the ark, which, at this time, was the chief religious symbol for the Israelite nation. The exact nature of the ark is much disputed, and no doubt it meant different things at different times, but it is always closely associated with the covenant and the tribal league; indeed, in the Old Testament it is very frequently described as the 'ark of the covenant'. Sometimes the reason for this title is given as being that the ark was a kind of container in which the copy of the covenant law was kept (so Deut.31.26): but perhaps the ark was rather the symbol of the covenant God and the community in fellowship with him. So we find the title 'the ark of the covenant of Yahweh of hosts' (I Sam.4.4), where the word 'hosts'

probably refers to the massed gathering of the tribes of Israel. Above all, the ark, as many Old Testament passages show, represented the living, active presence of Yahweh among his chosen people, so that it could sometimes be virtually identified with him (see I Sam.4.6–8). Yahweh was felt to be specially active on behalf of his people when, the ark going at their head, he led them out to victory against their enemies (see Num.10.35); and here we come to what, apart from the renewal of the covenant, was at this period the chief function of the tribal league.

The Holy War

Not all wars – for example, battles between individual Israelite tribes – were 'holy': the holy war was fought by Yahweh's people and in his name against foreign enemies and their gods. Its distinctive feature was that Yahweh was considered to be the actual leader of the Israelite forces and he alone won the victory by sending a panic on the enemy which decisively routed them (see Judg.7.22). Therefore all the spoils of battle belonged not to Israel but to Yahweh: Israel could not enjoy them in any way; they all, human captives as well as animals and material objects, had to be offered to him in sacrifice (see Josh.6.17–21).

Such was the inspiration by which Israel fought its wars of conquest in Palestine. We may feel that it is almost blasphemous to call such warfare 'holy', but we need to understand the outlook of a people who believed that Yahweh had promised them possession of the land of Canaan and that he would fulfil his promise in the real situation of war and conquest. The institution of the 'holy war' is another example of the fact that it was a common loyalty to Yahweh which was the real bond holding together the tribal league, and a genuine expression of Israel's faith in this early period that its entire existence and success belonged solely to him.

8

The United Monarchy

R. N. Whybray

The Evidence

1. *Biblical Sources*

(i) The main narrative source for this period is I and II Samuel; I Kings 1–11. This contains an unusually large amount of thoroughly reliable information, especially for the reigns of David and Solomon, although a skilled critical examination is necessary to distinguish history from legend, saga and later religious or nationalist comment.

(ii) The other narrative source, I Chron.10–29; II Chron.1–9, is much less reliable. In its general outline it follows the account in Samuel–Kings for the reigns of David and Solomon, but it deliberately omits large sections of material in order to create an idealistic picture of these two kings, and adds much new material, especially concerning David's supposed preparations for the building of the temple and for the organizing of its worship, which is generally held to be wholly or almost wholly unhistorical. Chronicles was written many centuries after the events which it describes.

2. *Archaeological Evidence*

The chief contribution of archaeology to the study of this period is a negative, though useful one: discoveries which specifically confirm details of the biblical narrative are few, but the discoveries which have been made are completely compatible with the biblical statements. Discoveries which can be directly related to the biblical narrative include the discovery of a small citadel of the period at Gibeah, Saul's capital; Solomonic fortifications at Megiddo and elsewhere; and buildings at Ezion-geber on the Red Sea where Solomon established his shipyards and seaport. A copper refinery, also at Ezion-geber, provides us with one piece of information about Solomon's activities not found in the biblical narrative. Finally the plan and furnishings of a number of temples of the period excavated in Syria and Palestine confirm the description of Solomon's temple in I Kings.

Becoming a Nation

The 'Israel' of the tribal league was not yet a nation. Although there had been moments of crisis in the past when something like a feeling of nationhood had momentarily united the tribes, there had been no external pressure sufficiently prolonged to allow this tendency to develop.

About the middle of the twelfth century this impetus towards nationhood was provided by the Philistines, a non-Semitic people which had originally formed part of a great wave of migrating peoples which swept down the eastern coast of the Mediterranean from the north in the late thirteenth century, destroying whatever lay in its path. This mass movement had been checked, though with great difficulty, by the Egyptians; and when it broke up, some of its constituent groups settled in a small district bordering on the southern coast of Palestine, probably under Egyptian auspices. This occurred shortly after the arrival of the central Israelite tribes under Joshua. Egyptian dominance of Syria and Palestine was rapidly collapsing; and the Philistines began to advance from their original base. They soon obtained control of a large part of Palestine, not only in the plains where the Canaanite cities mainly lay, but also in the Israelite hill country.

Our information about the early stages of this process is very incomplete. According to the biblical narrative Israel suffered an initial defeat (I Sam.4.1–10), but then found a leader in Samuel, who inflicted total and lasting defeat on the Philistines simply by asking as Moses did before him for divine assistance (I Sam.7.7–14). This story cannot be historical, for two reasons: first it assumes a degree of national cohesion which did not then exist, and secondly it fails to explain why only a few years later Israel was still completely under Philistine control (I Sam.13.2–7, 19–23).

The role of Samuel has evidently been greatly exaggerated. The actual facts are difficult to assess; but it is probable that there was some movement towards national unity during this period, and that Samuel was closely associated with this. Probably he was recognized as head of the religious assembly of the tribes, and from this position played a decisive part in creating an awareness that the time had come for a greater degree of political unity. The multiple traditions which associate him with the institution of the monarchy (I Sam.8; 9.1–10. 25; 11.12–15) can hardly be without a historical basis.

The statement in I Sam.8.5,20 that the elders of Israel came to Samuel and asked him to 'appoint for us a king to govern us like all the nations' and to 'go out before us and fight our battles' has the ring of authenticity about it. This amounted to a recognition by the tribal leaders that only the establishment of a permanent military commander who would be authorized to enforce obedience from all the tribes could save them from the Philistines. That they should turn to the surrounding nations for the model of the new institution was natural. But it was equally natural that they should want to combine the new office with their own traditional kind of leadership. Consequently, from the very moment of the institution of a monarchy in Israel there was a tension between conflicting ideas of what the monarchy should be. The words of Samuel in I Sam.8.11–18 show a realistic grasp of political realities: a military leader to whom such extensive powers were to be given would never be content to be a military leader only: he would have to be a king 'like all the nations', having power over his subjects in other aspects of their lives besides war; and this would always create the danger of tyranny. It seems that this danger was recognized from the beginning, and that some Israelites thought it to be an even greater danger than that of Philistine domination (I Sam.10.27): hence the hesitations and opposition of which we read in these chapters.

Saul: The First King

The decision was taken; and, perhaps about the year 1020 BC, Saul was chosen as the first king. There are several conflicting accounts of the manner of his selection (I Sam.9.1–10.16; 10.17–24; 11.1–15), but all agree that he was designated by God; it is also taken for granted that his tenure of office depended on continued divine approval. Nothing is said at this stage about any dynastic principle: it was Saul, not his family, who was appointed.

At first all went well. We read of successful attacks by Saul and his son Jonathan against Philistine forces (I Sam.13.2–7, 15b–23; 14.1–23, 31–35, 52). But our information is very incomplete. These battles may have been little more than local skirmishes against occupying forces. Whether Saul ever securely held any large tract of territory we do not know; certainly the statement in I Sam.14.47 that he inflicted defeats on the neighbouring states of Moab, Ammon, Edom and Zobah can hardly be correct. The impression given by the narrative as a whole is one of a reign wholly occupied with a war of independence (cf. I Sam.14.52) which ultimately ended in total defeat for Israel, with the Philistine power once more supreme (I Sam.31). Probably there were moments of success and times of defeat – the situation was evidently a fluid one. The absence of any details about the establishment of a permanent administrative system in Israel is also significant, in that it suggests that Saul's 'kingdom' was at best a precarious one, and that there was never any respite from war which would have made consolidation possible.

Saul and David

The ultimate failure of Saul's reign was due to three main causes: his quarrel with Samuel (I Sam.13.8–15; 15.10–35) and the priesthood (I Sam.22.11–19); the split in loyalties due to the emergence of David as a rival; and the deterioration of Saul's own character. These are mutually related. Behind the accounts of Saul's dispute with Samuel there almost certainly lie reasons other than those which are given to us: the real nature of Saul's 'disobedience' to God was probably that he was not content to remain under the tutelage of Samuel but was determined to have freedom of action. It is clear also from I Sam.20.31 that he came to regard his office as hereditary, and intended to found a dynasty; and the statement in I Sam.14.52 that 'when Saul saw any strong man, or any valiant man, he attached him to himself' shows that he attempted to build up a *corps d'élite* loyal to himself and independent of the tribal organization.

But to have made enemies of Samuel and of the priests, representatives of the old order, who still exercised great influence, proved fatal to his position. His mental deterioration (I Sam.16.14 and subsequent stories), whether the result of his failures or independent in origin, made him increasingly incapable of competent leadership.

Both of these things played into the hands of the upstart David, who was one of the young men especially recruited by Saul. It was Saul's misfortune to have in his entourage a man of such outstanding ability, who had no difficulty in exploiting the situation. The stories of David's relations with Saul are so patently concerned to convince the reader of David's unswerving loyalty and disinterestedness that we can be sure that the opposite was the case. The realistic Jonathan understood quite clearly that David both intended to be, and would be, king (I Sam.20.13b–17).

David's outstanding qualities as a military commander soon won for him great popularity (I Sam.18.6–9), and equally made him an object of suspicion to Saul. Eventually there was an open breach between the two, and David became a fugitive, fleeing from place to place and ultimately driven to seek refuge with the Philistine Achish king of Gath. The stories concerning this period of David's life reveal him as almost uncannily astute. He built up a useful band of followers amounting to a private army (I Sam.22.2; 23–31 *passim*), acquired great possessions in Judah by an astute marriage (I Sam.25), and while in the employ of Achish succeeded in preparing the way for the future by establishing friendly relations with the Judaeans while at the same time convincing Achish that he was making enemies of them (I Sam.27.8–12). He also had the good sense to bide his time.

The opportunity for David came when the Philistines inflicted a decisive defeat on Israel at the battle of Mount Gilboa (c.1000 BC), in which both Saul and Jonathan were killed (I Sam.31). The Israelite kingdom, it seemed, was at an end. But the Philistines reckoned without David.

The Reign of David

After the battle the Israelites were leaderless and Philistine power unchallenged. It is therefore clear – although the biblical narrative leaves the reader to infer this – that David's first steps towards national leadership were taken under Philistine auspices. They thought that they had every reason to trust him, and no doubt approved of his first action, which was to advance upon Hebron, the chief city of Judah (II Sam.2.2–4). They were unaware that to the Judaeans David was more of a national hero than a traitor, and that they needed no show of force to choose him as their king. To the Philistines, this 'kingship' of David's was a title without substance: he was their vassal, governing Judah on their behalf. But all the time David was laying plans to give it substance, and also to extend it.

The Philistines continued to look on with approval while David carried on hostilities against what remained of the forces of Saul. Abner, Saul's cousin and commander-in-chief, had withdrawn to Mahanaim to the east of the Jordan, beyond the reach of the Philistines, and had there set up an Israelite kingdom with Ishbosheth (or Ishbaal) as puppet king (II Sam.2.8–10). But after military successes and some strokes of good fortune had removed both Abner and his protégé (II Sam.2.12–4.12), David accepted the invitation of the local elders to become king of the north and east also (II Sam.5.1–3). That they should have submitted themselves to the rule of the enemy of Saul shows a realism and sense of national unity which came as a complete surprise to the Philistines. When they realized that they had been outwitted, and that David had established an independent rule over the whole of Israelite territory under their very noses, they hastily assembled a large army; but they were too late: they were resoundingly defeated (II Sam.5.17–25). Their empire had been swept away almost overnight by a man who, though admittedly he had had his share of good luck, had won his way to power through sheer intellectual ability.

David spent the next few years in consolidating his position. His defeat of the Philistines was decisive, but he did not annex their home territory: he left them still independent but powerless to harm him (II Sam.8.1). But he went on to conquer the neighbouring states of Moab, Edom and Ammon, and the Aramaean kingdoms of Zobah and Damascus (II Sam.8; 10.15–19; 12.26–31) in such short order that more distant states such as Hamath and Tyre, recognizing the fact that a new and formidable power had appeared in Palestine, hastened to establish friendly relations with him. Others no doubt followed suit: no foreign power ever attacked Israel during David's lifetime.

Apart from the story of David's capture of Jerusalem we are not told what happened to the city states of Canaan. Some of these (e.g., Bethshan, I Sam.31.10) had been conquered by the Philistines; others had presumably remained independent until now. But from this point in the biblical narrative there is no further mention of them except, later, as cities in Israel. We may therefore assume that they capitulated to David. It is unlikely that he would have tolerated independent enclaves within his home territory when he set out on his foreign campaigns.

Thus an entirely new situation was created. Only a few years previously, 'Israel' had consisted of a few loosely organized tribes under foreign domination; there was now an Israelite empire stretching from the border of Egypt to the Euphrates. Its creator, David, was to rule it for forty years (c.1000–961; cf. II Sam.5.4 f.).

Jerusalem: Capital of the Kingdom

Internally also David took some shrewd steps to consolidate his position. He captured Jerusalem, using only his private army (II Sam.5.6–9; this event probably took place later than the biblical narrative suggests), and transferred his capital there. He thus not only secured an extremely strong fortified city as the centre of his government, but at the same time forestalled possible tribal jealousies: ruling from Hebron, he might have seemed to the northern tribes like a Judaean usurper; but Jerusalem had no tribal connections at all. David was determined to be regarded as impartially king of 'all Israel'. As later events were to show, he was not entirely successful in this attempt to secure the loyalty of the north; but for the time he succeeded well enough.

Even more astute was his transfer to Jerusalem of the ark of God. This sacred object, once the rallying-point of the tribal league, had

earlier been captured by the Philistines; and in spite of the story of its return to Israelite territory (I Sam.6) it is probable that it had remained ever since within Philistine control: it plays no part in the stories of the reign of Saul. But it evidently still had the power to command the old loyalties. By placing it permanently in his new capital, David made a shrewd move to strengthen Israelite loyalty to himself and to allay the suspicions which many conservative Israelites must have had that he intended to sweep away old traditions and institutions and to establish a new type of monarchy on a pagan model. By this action he showed himself to be after all a pious Israelite of the old type, concerned above all to restore and maintain the old institutions and to give to the old tribal league a permanent centre where the traditional worship of the God of Israel would be carried on as before.

He was greatly assisted in this policy by the fact of his immense and – as it must have seemed – miraculous success in everything which he did: no-one, it was believed, could be so successful without a special degree of divine favour. This is, indeed, the constant theme of almost all the stories which are told of him; and it was expressed as a 'theological dogma' in II Sam.7 where God is represented as confirming David's position as the divinely appointed leader through whom God's will for his people has been achieved.

That David firmly believed himself to be the servant of the God of Israel there is no reason to doubt. At the same time he was well aware that his kingdom was a composite one, composed of Canaanites as well as Israelites. The co-operation of the Canaanites was not only essential for the safety of the state, but also potentially of great benefit to it. Heirs of centuries of civilized urban life, they were superior to the Israelites in the arts both of war and of peace. Unassimilated, they constituted a serious danger; assimilated, they provided David with much needed administrators and military experts. In return for their loyalty, David seems to have left them to continue their own local administration, and to a very considerable extent to practise their own religious traditions.

Thus in his religious policy David steered a sagacious middle course. At Jerusalem, the worship of the God of Israel centred upon the ark was modified by elements taken from the pre-Israelite Canaanite cult. Canaanites who worshipped there would thus not feel that the worship was something entirely strange, imposed by a foreign conqueror. A similar policy, even more 'liberal', was adopted in the other former Canaanite cities, and the worship of the gods of Canaan, thus tolerated, continued to flourish throughout the period of the monarchy. David, although he believed himself to be under the especial protection of the God of Israel, was no religious fanatic; and this fact contributed not a little to his success.

The Organization of the State

The monarchical system established by David was thus a very different thing from the *ad hoc* rule of Saul. As a powerful political state, Israel now rapidly developed institutions which were politically necessary but entirely new to the Israelites, and which in many ways resembled those of Israel's neighbours. Efficient government required a professional civil service. David recruited this partly from native (Israelite and Canaanite) sources; but he also found it necessary to employ skilled scribes from other countries who had greater experience of administration, especially from Egypt. This central government at Jerusalem provided the king with advice on political problems, in the wisdom tradition of the ancient Near East; it also administered justice under the king as chief judge, collected taxes and dues, organized a state labour force, kept administrative records, and dealt with foreign affairs, maintaining a diplomatic correspondence with foreign powers and negotiating international treaties (see Part III, Section 12, pp. 162 ff.).

These administrative developments had far-reaching consequences. In particular they facilitated the development of greater social distinctions than Israelite society had ever known before. The Canaanite cities were already accustomed to a highly stratified social structure; but this was the first time that the freeborn Israelites had experienced rule by a wealthy, urban ruling class whose interests were far from identical with their own. In the reigns of David and Solomon Jerusalem became a wealthy, cosmopolitan city in which this ruling class enjoyed a standard of living beyond anything which could have been dreamed of; but, apart from the fact that they were now free from

foreign oppression, the ordinary Israelite population, which still consisted mainly of farmers, hardly felt the benefits of Israel's new imperial status.

Supreme above the new upper class stood the king. Whatever the divine sanctions by which he claimed to rule, and however much he might rely on the loyalty of the ordinary Israelite, one of the main sources of his power was his professional army, which owed him a purely personal loyalty. Many of its members were foreigners who had no reason for loyalty to Israel or to its God (II Sam.8.18; 11; 15.18–22; 20.7, 23). It was these 'servants of David' who, during Absalom's rebellion, defeated the rebels (significantly referred to as 'the men of Israel'), and restored David to the throne (II Sam.18.7).

His position secured by this personal army, David was able to a considerable extent to play the part of an oriental monarch, gathering round him a court which imitated the splendour and ceremonial of foreign courts, and tending to become isolated from the common people (II Sam.15.3 f.).

He was, however, too shrewd to allow this tendency to go too far. He knew that ultimately he could not retain his throne without the loyalty and affection of his people, and also that too great a departure from the old Israelite social and religious traditions would put his throne in danger. It is unlikely that the Israelite monarchy, at this or at any other time, succumbed to the temptation of claiming for itself that semi-divine character which was characteristic of some of the other monarchies of the time. It is true that both in the narrative sources and also in the Psalms and elsewhere we find phrases (such as 'the king is like the angel of God to discern good and evil', II Sam.14.17; the divine word to David, 'You are my son, today I have begotten you', Ps.2.7) which seem to suggest that this was so; but we have to distinguish between high-flown language and actual political realities. David was certainly, like Saul, 'the Lord's anointed', the man who because of his especial relationship with God had brought 'salvation' to his people; but there were too many men in his entourage who knew the facts of his rise to power, such as the old general, Joab (II Sam.19.5–7), for any more extravagant notions about his office to gain currency.

David did, however, firmly adopt one aspect of the monarchical concept which hardly accorded with Israelite ideas of charismatic leaders, that is, men chosen personally by God: the principle of a hereditary monarchy. We have already seen that Saul also had intended that his son Jonathan should succeed him. Under David the principle seems to have been taken for granted, and it was given religious sanction in the divine promise to David in II Sam.7.

However, neither David's own position nor the future of his family was really secure. The very power and prosperity of the Israelite state made it an attractive prize for the would-be usurper; and such men found no lack of disaffection which could be made to serve their purposes. There were those who had remained loyal to Saul and his family and regarded David as a usurper and murderer (e.g., Shimei, II Sam.16.5–8); there were those who disapproved of David's arrogant and sinful actions such as his adultery with Bathsheba and his murder of Uriah; in the north there were those who resented being ruled by a man of Judah; and there were those who felt that the old religious and social traditions were being overthrown. First David's own son, Absalom, and then a man called Sheba, of Saul's tribe of Benjamin, exploiting these feelings of discontent, rose in rebellion (II Sam.15–20). Although both rebellions were crushed, the feelings of discontent remained.

The Accession of Solomon

The situation in the later part of the reign was complicated by uncertainty with regard to the succession to the throne. David had a number of wives, several of whom had borne him sons. In the hereditary monarchies of the ancient Near East there was no rule that the eldest son must succeed: the king had the right to choose his own heir, and it was obviously desirable that this should be done in good time. After the death of Absalom there remained Adonijah and Solomon, half-brothers, as obvious candidates. Between them David, now old and feeble, was unable to make up his mind. Their rivalry caused a dangerous cleavage between the leading men in the state; but Adonijah made a false move, and paid for it with his life, dragging down with him some of the most important personalities of the reign which was now ending. Solomon was king; but he had to begin his reign with a bloodbath (I Kings 2).

The reign of Solomon (961–922), in spite of the splendid outward appearances, was a period of stagnation and of the beginning of decline. This was probably inevitable: even another David could probably not have succeeded in holding together the heterogeneous empire for a second generation; and Solomon was far from being a second David.

On the economic plane things might have continued to go well. Although the agricultural resources of Israel were not great, it was well placed in other respects. Possession of the Canaanite plain had given David control of the only land route linking Egypt in the south, Mesopotamia in the east, and Asia Minor in the north; and Solomon ensured his control over it by extensive fortifications of the key cities (I Kings 4.26; 9.15–19; 10.26). He was thus able, like his father, to derive considerable wealth by levying tolls and by import-export activities of his own (I Kings 10.28 f.). He also established, with the help of his Tyrian ally, a lucrative sea trade, based on a seaport which he built at Ezion-geber on the Red Sea; and he mined and refined copper in Edom, presumably partly for export. There was also trade with Egypt (I Kings 10.29), Tyre, the Sabaeans of South Arabia (I Kings 10.2,13) and elsewhere.

These activities undoubtedly brought considerable profit to Israel (cf.I Kings 10). But Solomon succumbed to a fatal *folie de grandeur*, attempting to imitate the splendours of Egypt and Mesopotamia by erecting buildings of great magnificence. Since Israel possessed neither the necessary materials nor skill, he had to import these from Hiram of Tyre, and as a consequence found himself in financial difficulties (I Kings 9.10–14). At the same time he did much to alienate popular support by not only burdening his people with the support of an extravagant court (I Kings 4.7–19, 22 f.), but also extending the forced labour scheme which David had begun to such an extent that it seriously impaired agricultural efficiency (I Kings 5.13–18).

The empire began to break up. Judah remained loyal, and the Canaanite cities gave no trouble; but Edom and Damascus revolted, re-establishing their independence and becoming dangerous enemies (I Kings 11.14–25); and the northern tribes of Israel produced a leader, Jeroboam, who, when his first attempt at revolt proved unsuccessful, retired to Egypt where he was given protection and bided his time (I Kings 11.26–40).

Solomon's most enduring achievement was the building of the temple at Jerusalem. But he certainly can have had no inkling of the importance which this was to have in later times. The building of the temple was, from one point of view, merely the corollary of David's bringing of the ark to Jerusalem: Solomon provided a magnificent shrine for it. From another point of view it was simply one example of Solomon's extravagance. Since it was designed and furnished by Phoenician craftsmen (I Kings 7.13 ff.), it is likely that the most immediate religious consequence of its construction was to increase the Canaanite element in Israel's worship.

Solomon is praised in several biblical passages for his wisdom (I Kings 3.9–14, 16–28; 4.29–34; 10.1–10). In only one of these passages does 'wisdom' mean statesmanship. Solomon may have been wise in other respects, but statesmanship was certainly not one of them. The early promise of political greatness for Israel was not fulfilled.

Nevertheless, Israel during the reigns of David and Solomon had undergone fundamental changes which would never be reversed. It had been brought into the world not only of international politics, but also of international culture. This expressed itself chiefly in literature, of which the most remarkable example is the so-called 'Succession Narrative' (II Sam.9–20; I Kings 1;2) in which characters and events at David's court are described with unequalled brilliance and subtlety. The striking advance in literary craftsmanship shown in this literary masterpiece over all earlier efforts in the same *genre* clearly indicates the extent of Israel's cultural transformation. Much of this was undoubtedly due to the influence of the Canaanite cities and of Egypt, but the Israelite literature of this period is by no means merely imitative: its authors applied the newly acquired techniques and insights to their own historical traditions, in which the new confident, national spirit inspired by the achievements of David had given them a new pride.

9
The Divided Kingdoms
R. N. Whybray

The Evidence

1. *Biblical Sources*

(i) The main biblical narrative source for this period is I Kings 12–II Kings 25. It is based mainly on reliable documents to which the compilers have added their own comments, chiefly moral and religious judgments on the various kings. Some stories, however, especially those concerning Elijah, Elisha and Isaiah, are derived from less objective sources and present a rather idealized picture.

(ii) The second narrative source, II Chron. 10–36, mainly follows Kings, but confines itself to the southern kingdom (Judah). Where it differs from Kings it also tends to present an idealized picture, although in a few instances it probably preserves accurate information

not available to the compilers of Kings. The books of the prophets Isaiah (chs. 1–39), Jeremiah, Hosea, Amos and Micah are also valuable as they depict the social and religious conditions of Israel and Judah during this period; their words need, however, to be disentangled from later and irrelevant material (see Part III, Section 10, pp. 136 ff.).

2. *Archaeological Evidence*

A vast quantity of written sources dealing with the international setting of the history of Israel has been discovered. Egyptian, Assyrian and Babylonian records have provided a very full account of the history of those empires, including their relations with the Israelite kingdoms. In a few instances they contain independent accounts of events described in the biblical narrative. Besides these sources the Moabite Stone, erected by Mesha, king of Moab, gives that king's version of his relations with Israel, also described in II Kings 1.1; 3.4 ff. From Palestine itself come two texts, written in Hebrew: the Siloam Inscription, written by Hezekiah's engineers inside a water tunnel (cf. II Kings 20.20), and the Lachish Letters, a correspondence between Judaean army officers during the campaign which ended with the fall of Jerusalem to the Babylonians. The excavation of Samaria, the Israelite capital built by Omri, brought to light the Samaria Ivories, probably part of the decoration of Ahab's palace, the 'ivory house' of I Kings 22.39.

The Revolt of the Northern Tribes

The political history of Israel during this period (922–587) is a story of increasingly rapid decline, punctuated by brief periods of partial recovery but ending in total annihilation. This fate befell not only Israel but all her neighbours as well. The rise of new centres of imperialism in Mesopotamia probably made this inevitable, though it was accelerated by the foolish policies frequently pursued by the victims.

Rehoboam (922–915), the son and successor of Solomon, either was unaware of, or chose to ignore, the weakness of his position in the northern part of his kingdom. On his accession he brusquely rejected the demands for reform made by the northern tribes; and at once all their resentment at being ruled by a Judaean, which had already manifested itself under David and Solomon, came to a head. The northern tribes declared their independence, and selected Jeroboam, their former champion, who had just returned from exile in Egypt, as their first king (I Kings 12.1–20).

The new kingdom took for itself the name of Israel, which had previously been used to designate the whole undivided kingdom; the remnant in the south, which remained loyal to the dynasty of David, became known as Judah. With this division into two separate kingdoms, at first bitterly hostile to one another, the era of Israelite glory was over.

Of the two kingdoms, Israel was both the larger and the more prosperous. It included most of the larger Canaanite cities, the main trade routes, and the best land on both sides of the Jordan, including the former kingdom of

Moab. Judah by comparison was a small state in the hills, remote from the main roads and from the sources of wealth. This remote position was to prove to be both favourable and unfavourable to Judah: unfavourable in that it was inevitably overshadowed by Israel, whether as an enemy, or, later, as a junior partner; favourable in that, being both strategically and economically less important to the great empires, it was able to survive for more than a century longer than its northern neighbour.

The monarchy thus established in (northern) Israel was somewhat different in character from that of Judah. The Judaeans remained loyal to the house of David to the very end; apart from the usurper Athaliah, no-one other than a descendant of David ever sat on the throne of Judah. But in Israel the election of Jeroboam by the assembly (I Kings 12.20) seems to have been a conscious attempt to return to the old idea of kingship as an office conferred on an individual in view of his personal merit. Whether the kings of Israel were regarded primarily as elected by the people or designated by God is not clear: in some cases the biblical narrative seems to suggest the former, in others the latter. In practice neither principle was strictly observed: many kings attempted to found dynasties, some – especially Omri and Jehu – successfully; on the other hand the fact that of all the kings of Israel only half came to the throne by dynastic succession shows that the dynastic principle was never fully accepted. The effect of this uncertainty about the succession was to make the kingdom of Israel extremely unstable: no less than eight of its nineteen kings obtained the throne through the assassination of their predecessors.

Like David, Jeroboam (922–901) made certain religious changes in an attempt to strengthen his position (I Kings 12.26–33). In order to discourage the annual pilgrimages which his subjects continued to make, in spite of the political schism, to Jerusalem, he established two royal temples of his own, choosing for this purpose the ancient sanctuaries of Bethel and Dan, where the God of Israel had been worshipped for centuries. Here, as a kind of compensation for the ark, he set up golden bull images. These were probably not intended to represent pagan deities, but to be used for the worship of the God of Israel; but they did later become centres of a debased, if not wholly pagan, worship (Hos.8.5 f.; 10.5; 13.2).

During this time the political vacuum in the Near East which had made it possible for David to establish his empire had continued to favour the independence of the Israelite kingdoms. Egypt, it is true, still hoped to re-establish its former empire in Syria and Palestine; and a few years after the division of the Israelite kingdoms its king, Shishak, invaded Palestine and devastated large parts of both Judah (I Kings 14.25 f.) and Israel (according to his own statement). But this was an isolated, though painful, incident and had no permanent results. Egypt's age of imperial power was over.

For some years there was also no threat from the other traditional centre of imperial power, Mesopotamia. Babylonia was hopelessly weak, and Assyria in a temporary state of decline from which she only began to recover at the end of the tenth century. Nearer at hand, the Aramaean kingdoms to the north of Israel were not yet ready for hostile action.

But in the ninth century the situation began to change. The first recorded interference of the Aramaean kingdom of Damascus in Israelite affairs well illustrates the fatal effects of the division of the Israelite kingdoms. Asa of Judah (913–873), hard pressed by an attack by Baasha of Israel (900–877), formed an alliance with Benhadad of Damascus and invited him to attack Israel, which he did with considerable success (I Kings 15.18–21). This was the beginning of a long history of alliances, intrigues and counter-intrigues between these three states which was to continue until Damascus was swept away by the Assyrians in 732 (I Kings 20; 22; II Kings 5–7; 8.28 f.; 10.32 f.; 12.17 f.; 13.3–7, 22–25; 14.28; 15.37; 16.5–9). Mainly it was a struggle between Israel and Damascus for the possession of territory lying between them in the north and north-east. On more than one occasion one or other of the two states came close to annihilation by the other.

The Threat from Assyria

These squabbles between small states were serious enough in themselves; but they were suicidal in view of the threat soon posed for them all by the growth of the power of Assyria. Assyrian expansion began with Adad-nirari II (912–890); but it was not until the reign of Asshur-nasir-pal II (883–859) that the Assyrians turned their attention to the west. By 877 Asshur-nasir-pal's successive campaigns had taken him as far as the Mediterranean coast, and opened the way south towards southern Syria and Palestine.

Israel seems first to have become aware of the danger after the accession of his successor Shalmaneser III (859–824), who continued his predecessor's policy. For a few years Benhadad of Damascus and Ahab of Israel dropped their quarrel, and joined with other neighbouring states in a coalition against Assyria. We learn from Shalmaneser's own account of his campaigns that Ahab was one of the leaders of the coalition, and that when the Assyrians met the allied forces in Syria at Qarqar on the river Orontes (853), his was one of the largest of the allied contingents.

Shalmaneser claimed the battle as a victory; but in fact it appears to have been indecisive, and temporarily to have checked further Assyrian advances. For the time being the threat seemed to have abated. But neither Israel nor Damascus had learned its lesson. Instead of maintaining the coalition by a permanent defensive treaty, they reverted to a state of intermittent mutual warfare, and so were unready for the new threat when it came.

Israel was at this time relatively powerful. Omri (876–869) was a military commander who seized the throne after a period of dynastic conflict (I Kings 16.8–22). Although the compilers of the books of Kings found little concrete to say about him (I Kings 16.23–28), he was one of the more able Israelite kings, and his policies were continued by his son Ahab (869–850), who, however, was constantly involved in wars with Damascus. In these wars, which continued to the end of the dynasty, the successive kings of Judah, Jehoshaphat (873–849), Jehoram (849–842) and Ahaziah (842) appear as the allies, willing or unwilling, of Israel.

The books of Kings devote a great deal of space (I Kings 16.29–22.40) to the reign of Ahab because of his religious apostasy and tyrannical behaviour, against which the prophet Elijah waged a vigorous campaign. Seen through the eyes of fervent admirers of the prophet, the character of Ahab appears far blacker than it actually was. Omri and Ahab, as kings of some consequence in the contemporary world, were necessarily subject, for political reasons, to influences of various kinds from the neighbouring states, and their wise renewal of David's policy of alliance with the powerful Phoenician state of Tyre had been sealed by Ahab's marriage to Jezebel, the daughter of the king of Tyre (I Kings 16.31). Jezebel was a woman of great determination, inspired with an ambition to introduce the religion and customs of her own people into Israel. According to the Elijah stories (I Kings 17–19; 21) she came near to exterminating the worship of the God of Israel in favour of that of Melqart, the god of Tyre (known to the Old Testament simply as 'Baal'). But this is certainly an exaggeration. It is clear that Ahab regarded himself as a worshipper of the God of Israel: not only did he on occasion recognize (if unwillingly) the authority of Elijah, but more significantly he gave to two of his sons (Ahaziah and Jehoram) names which imply devotion to the God of Israel. The truth of the matter is probably that under the influence of Jezebel he permitted or encouraged the worship of other gods as well, a policy which was by no means without precedent in Israel.

Of Ahab's tyranny the only specific example given to us is the story of Naboth's vineyard (I Kings 21), in which Ahab is represented as weak rather than tyrannical, allowing his ruthless and foreign wife to commit murder in order to obtain a piece of property which the owner had refused to sell. This story doubtless illustrates a tendency of Israelite kings towards autocratic rule; but it is important to notice that, as in the case of David and Uriah, the queen was obliged to carry out her crime by secret methods, and that when the deed became known it was regarded as an outrage. This shows that, even in the time of Ahab, tyranny in Israel was an exception and had not yet been accepted as normal.

The stories of Elijah and his successor Elisha show that the policies and actions of the kings of the dynasty of Omri were nevertheless regarded by an increasingly influential body of prophets as an apostasy from true religion which justified its overthrow. This came to pass in 842 with the murder of king Jehoram, Ahab's second son, by an army officer, Jehu, at the instigation of Elisha (II Kings 9.1–13).

Jehu (842–815) was placed on the throne because he was a fanatical champion of the God of Israel. He did not disappoint his sponsors. Besides Jehoram and Jezebel, he killed the whole of Ahab's family and all his associates, Ahaziah, the king of Judah, and his family and all the priests of Baal in Israel (II Kings 9.14–10.14; 10.18–27). No trace was left of the old regime. One learns with some relief that these 'pious deeds' were regarded with horror rather than admiration by a later prophet of greater sensibility than Elisha (Hos.1.4).

The reaction against religious apostasy had its counterpart in Judah, though not immediately. After the murder of Ahaziah there followed a six-years' usurpation of the throne by his mother Athaliah (842–837), who may have been the daughter of Ahab and Jezebel, although this is not certain (cf. II Kings 8.26). She used Jehu's methods – the extermination of the royal family – to achieve an opposite end, the establishment in Judah of the worship of Baal (II Kings 11.1–3). On this occasion it was not a prophet but a priest, Jehoiada, who put an end to the apostasy. Athaliah and the priests of Baal were executed, the sole surviving descendant of David, Joash (837–800), placed on the throne, and the return to the faith of the God of Israel inaugurated by a solemn covenant between God, the king and the people (II Kings 11.4–20). But neither of these 'restorations' was to keep Israel or Judah permanently loyal to the God of Israel.

These events were followed by a period of weakness both in Israel and Judah. The Assyrians, in spite of their check at Qarqar, still remained a menace: Jehu was forced at one time, as we know from Assyrian sources, to acknowledge the overlordship of Shalmaneser, and Judah also suffered serious defeats and loss of territory at the hands of Hazael of Damascus (II Kings 12.17 f.).

Both countries were, however, to enjoy one final period of prosperity. Damascus, Israel's traditional enemy, was crippled by the Assyrian king Adad-nirari III (811–783) in 802, and thereafter Assyria left Syria and Palestine in peace for half a century. During the long reigns of Jeroboam II (786–746) in Israel and Uzziah (Azariah) (783–742) in Judah, both countries made a swift recovery. Jeroboam recovered the whole of his northern and trans-Jordanian territory at the expense of Damascus and Hamath, pushing his northern frontier back to that of Solomon (II Kings 14.25, 28). He may also have recovered control of Moab, which had been lost to Israel after the death of Ahab. Judah had already reconquered Edom in the reign of Amaziah (800–783; II Kings 14.7, 22) and went on under Uzziah to further conquests (II Chron.26.6–15). The two kingdoms together were now almost as extensive as Solomon's empire had been.

These successes, which restored to Israel and Judah their former sources of wealth, brought in their train a sudden new prosperity with inevitable social consequences. Once more the new wealth went into the pockets of a small privileged class, while the majority of the population found itself exploited to an unprecedented degree. These social changes are fully documented in the teaching of four contemporary prophets: Isaiah and Micah in Judah, and Amos and Hosea in Israel (see Part III, Section 10, pp. 136 ff.). The wealthy classes controlled the processes of law and so were able to prevent the under-privileged from obtaining redress when they were squeezed out of their holdings and forced to become the hired labourers or even slaves of the new proprietors, who in this way built up huge farms whose produce was used to support them in luxury (cf. Isa.3.16 f.; 5.8–12; 28.1–8; 32.9–14; Amos 2.6–8; 4.1–3; 5.10–13; Micah 2). Most of these arrogant magnates saw, or pretended to see, no incompatibility between their actions and their professions of religious faith: they regarded religion and ethics as two separate spheres, unrelated to one another. For them, religion was mainly a matter of the assiduous performance of cultic duties – by no means free, especially in Israel, from corrupt and pagan elements – in recognition of a God who, they believed, had guaranteed permanent safety and prosperity to his chosen people (cf. Isa.1.12–23; 29.13–16; Amos 5.21–24; Micah 3.9–12).

The prophets of this time startled and scandalized their hearers by proclaiming the unheard-of message that the God of Israel, after vain attempts to persuade his people to reform their ways, would withdraw his protection from his people and, becoming their enemy, bring about the destruction of the two kingdoms. These predictions were fulfilled; and, in the case of Israel, with very little delay.

The End of Israel

The dynasty of Jehu had lasted almost exactly a century (842–745). Six months after the death of Jeroboam in 746, it came to an abrupt end. Jeroboam's son and successor Zechariah was murdered by an usurper, Shallum, who a month later was himself murdered by Menahem (II Kings 15.10–14). Israel now lapsed into a state of disintegration, political, religious and social, which is well chronicled by the prophet Hosea. Of its last five kings, three were assassinated. Law and order broke down. And this collapse coincided with the active return of Assyria to Syria and Palestine, and in a new mood: no longer content to bully the small states into submission, but bent on permanent conquest. The inaugurator of this new policy was Tiglath-pileser III (745–727). During the reign of Menahem (745–738) he invaded Syria and the coastal cities of Phoenicia and annexed some territory which he put under direct Assyrian rule. Menahem escaped this fate by the payment of tribute (II Kings 15.19 f.). But such acknowledgment of Assyrian overlordship was now intended to be permanent. The Assyrian frontier was now very close, and Tiglath-pileser clearly would not tolerate disloyalty.

Nevertheless, hopes of resistance were not yet dead; and a few years later one of Menahem's successors, Pekah (737–732), formed an anti-Assyrian alliance with Rezin of Damascus. Jotham of Judah (742–735), the son of Uzziah, was invited to join the coalition, but refused. Pekah and Rezin then took the fatal step of trying to force Judah to join. Ahaz of Judah (735–715), who had now succeeded his father Jotham, was faced simultaneously with one attack by Israel and Damascus and another by the Edomites, who at this point rose in rebellion; and in spite of the warning of the prophet Isaiah he felt obliged to turn to Assyria for help. This involved the acknowledgment of vassal status; but it brought the desired relief. Tiglath-pileser attacked Damascus and Israel, abolishing the kingdom of Damascus altogether and in 732 annexing a large part of the territory of Israel (II Kings 15.29; 16.5–9; Isa.7.1–17). Pekah had now been murdered by the usurper Hoshea, who immediately surrendered to Assyria and was permitted to retain the remaining territory as vassal (II Kings 15.30; 17.3).

But Israel still continued its disastrous policies. Some years later, soon after the accession to the Assyrian throne of Shalmaneser V (727–722), Hoshea committed the incredible folly of withholding tribute from Assyria and making a treaty with 'So, king of Egypt' (II Kings 17.4), a petty local ruler of part of Egypt, which at that time had fallen into a state of anarchy. Such an ally was quite useless against the might of Assyria, and Shalmaneser made the final move. He attacked Israel in 724 and besieged the capital, Samaria. After a siege of more than two years, in the course of which Shalmaneser died and was succeeded by Sargon II (722–705), Samaria fell; and Sargon put an end to the kingdom of Israel. Following a policy which had been instituted by Tiglath-pileser for preventing further rebellions among conquered peoples, he deported a large number of the inhabitants to other parts of his empire, and replaced them with people of other races (II Kings 17.5 f., 24).

The Kingdom of Judah

Judah was now left alone. During the century which followed, the fear of Assyria continued to dominate the actions of the little states which remained in and around Palestine. The policies of the kings of Judah fluctuated wildly according to their assessments at various times of the possibility of adopting an attitude of defiance. It is important to observe that their foreign and religious policies went hand in hand. Assyrian domination meant the acceptance of the worship of the Assyrian gods side by side with that of Yahweh, and was also marked by a decline in moral standards and social justice; rebellion against Assyria was accompanied by a revival of national pride which led to religious reform and greater justice.

The details of these fluctuations are fairly clearly set out in II Kings, although the Assyrian records are needed for a full picture, and in one case at least – Hezekiah's rebellion and Sennacherib's suppression of it – there remains considerable doubt about the exact course of events.

Ahaz, having placed himself under Assyrian protection, remained loyal to his overlord all his life, and as a consequence was forced to introduce Assyrian religious practices into the temple (II Kings 16.10–18). His son Hezekiah

(715–687), however, encouraged by what he took to be signs of an Assyrian collapse, joined forces with other states and attempted to assert his independence (II Kings 18.7). At the same time he instituted a religious reform, purging the temple of alien cult-objects of all kinds (II Kings 18.4). But his rebellion was crushed by the Assyrian king Sennacherib (705–681; II Kings 18.13–16; Isa.36.1).

Hezekiah's death was followed by a period of forty-seven years during which Assyrian power, under Esarhaddon (681–669) and Asshurbanapal (669–631), was at its height, and Hezekiah's son Manasseh (687–642) and grandson Amon (642–640) accepted the Assyrian yoke. In contrast with the reign of Hezekiah, this was a time when the religion of Israel reached its lowest ebb, and the people of Judah were subjected to a cruel tyranny, hardly less severe than if they had been directly ruled by the Assyrians (II Kings 21.1–16).

The reign of Josiah (640–609), the son of Amon, was as great a contrast to those of his father and grandfather as can be imagined, and recalled that of his great-grandfather Hezekiah. Josiah is the only king of Judah who is praised without reservation by the compilers of the books of Kings (II Kings 22.2; 23.25). Like Hezekiah, he reasserted Judah's political independence; but this time the action seemed to be justified by political facts. After the death of Ashurbanapal in 631 the long dominance of Assyria had come to an end. Its last two kings were not of the calibre of their predecessors, and the collapse was very swift. Its two capitals, Ashur and Nineveh, fell to the combined attacks of Babylonians and Medes in 614 and 612 respectively, and a last attempt at resistance at Haran failed in 609. Assyria was no more.

Some years before the final collapse of Assyria, Josiah took advantage of its weakened condition and not only restored the independence of Judah but also regained some of the territory of the former kingdom of Israel. He was intensely devoted to the service of the God of Israel, and carried out a religious reform which is said to have been suggested to him by the reading of a law-book, generally believed to be related to Deuteronomy, which was discovered in the temple (II Kings 22.3–23.24). The reform was much more thorough than that of Hezekiah. Not only was the temple once more cleansed of alien rites and the worship of the God of Israel fully restored; sacrificial worship was now confined to this one place alone, and all other sanctuaries, whether Israelite or pagan, were abolished throughout both Judah and the newly acquired territories. The life of the nation was re-established as far as possible in accordance with ancient Israelite traditions.

Josiah has the unique distinction of being praised by the prophet Jeremiah as one who 'did justice and righteousness' and 'judged the cause of the poor and needy' (Jer.22.15 f.).

His religious reform, whose principles were preserved and developed during the years of exile by the Deuteronomic school of religious thinkers, eventually proved to be one of the most significant events in the religious history of Israel. But its immediate effectiveness as national policy depended on the person of Josiah himself, and in this sense it perished with him.

The Threat of Babylon

No new golden age for Judah had dawned. The collapse of Assyria was not followed by a political vacuum. The bulk of the Assyrian empire fell immediately to the Medes and the Babylonians, while the south-western districts – Syria and Palestine – became the object of a conflict between Babylonia and Egypt, which after a period of Assyrian rule had now recovered sufficiently to make its last attempt at empire under Neco II (609–593). Recognizing that the real enemy was now Babylonia, Neco marched north in 609 to go to the aid of Assyria. Josiah foolishly attempted to stop him as he passed through Palestine, and at Megiddo Judah was defeated and Josiah killed (II Kings 23.29). Judaean independence was once more at an end, and Judah passed again under foreign control, this time that of Egypt. Neco deposed Jehoahaz, the son of Josiah, who had assumed the throne, and replaced him by his brother Eliakim, whom he renamed Jehoiakim (II Kings 23.30–35).

Jehoiakim (609–598) was thus from the first a vassal king. But before long his overlord Neco was decisively defeated at the battle of Carchemish (605), Egyptian hopes of empire came abruptly to an end, and Judah fell into the hands of the Babylonians under Nebuchadnezzar (605–562). Jehoiakim was confirmed in his office (II Kings 24.1).

Jehoiakim proved to combine the cruelty and religious apostasy of a Manasseh with the foolhardiness of a Hezekiah or a Josiah. Despite the defeat of Neco, Egypt was still plotting the overthrow of Babylonia, and there was a party at Jerusalem which believed that this could be achieved, and that it would be to the advantage of Judah. The intrigues with Egypt were discovered (II Kings 24.1), and in 597 Nebuchadnezzar arrived in Judah and besieged Jerusalem, which surrendered to him. Meanwhile Jehoiakim had died, and his son Jehoiachin was deported to Babylon together with a great number of the upper classes of society, while his uncle Mattaniah, his name changed to Zedekiah, was placed on the throne as a puppet king.

Even this disaster did not bring the Judaeans to their senses. The 'new men' who were now appointed to the offices of state were worthless even by comparison with their predecessors: the prophet Jeremiah did not recognize their authority at all. The king was weak and unable to control them. Within ten years news of further intrigue with Egypt came to the ears of Nebuchadnezzar, who now determined to put an end to the kingdom of Judah once and for all. In 588 the Babylonians invaded; the whole country was devastated and its cities destroyed. In 587 Jerusalem itself was captured and destroyed, together with the temple. King Zedekiah was forced to witness the execution of his sons, and along with many of his people was taken to Babylonia (II Kings 25.1–21).

So the Jewish people was torn in two. It is difficult to say which part was in worse plight: the exiles in Babylonia, deprived, it seemed, of the hope of ever returning to their homes, or the wretched lower classes, left mainly to their own devices in a land devastated, its crops ruined and its houses destroyed, a prey to hunger and disease and to the depredations of wild beasts and of the Edomite tribes from the south who now invaded the land, eager to revenge themselves on the Judaeans who had been their oppressors in the past.

10

Prophecy in Israel

R. E. Clements

(Note: The historical background to the prophets is described in Part III, Sections 7, 8 and 9, pp. 114–133.)

The Nature of Early Prophecy

Already in the historical accounts of early Israel we are introduced to certain prophets and seers who were active both in Israel itself and among its neighbours. Numbers 22–24 describes how a Moabite seer, Balaam, was called to pronounce a deadly curse against Israel, but was unable to do so under God's restraint, and instead responded by uttering a prophecy declaring the future greatness and prosperity of Israel as a nation. Besides this evidence from within the Bible of a Moabite prophet there are references in non-biblical texts to prophets in Phoenicia and at Mari in Mesopotamia, which show that prophecy was not unique to Israel, and certainly did not originate within it.

Within Israel the political interest of prophecy is revealed by the part played by the prophet Samuel in foretelling the rise to kingship of both Saul and David (I Sam.9.15 ff.; 16.1–13). In these two cases, even though the accounts were certainly drawn up after the respective rulers had assumed the throne, the message given by the prophet was a way of setting the divine authority upon the separate claims of kingship of the two men. The word of the prophet not only predicted the future, but interpreted it by affirming what did, and what did not, lie within the divine purpose.

In view of this political activity of prophets, it is not surprising to find that they came to be attached very closely to David, both in his period as an outlaw and afterwards in the Jerusalem court. The seer Gad appears as a special confidant and adviser to David when he was being hunted by Saul (I Sam.22.5), urging a particular course of action on the basis of a claim to a divinely given understanding of the outcome of events. Later he became a person of influence in David's court, assuming the role of a court prophet, and appearing as a judge of David's actions (II Sam.24.10–17). He was responsible for advising David to build an altar on the threshing floor of Araunah (II Sam.24.18–25), and in this way was concerned with the choice of the site where the temple of Jerusalem came to be built (II Chron.3.1). Even better known in David's court is the prophet Nathan, who twice intervened very decisively in matters of state. On the first occasion, after David's disgraceful affair with Bathsheba, Nathan declared God's condemnation of David's action, and foretold a punishment upon him (II Sam.12.1–15). In this we can see very well the two parts which go to make up the typical saying of a prophet. There is an interpretation of a situation, in this case David's sin with Bathsheba and his virtual murder of Uriah, which is followed by a threat foretelling future trouble and setbacks as a punishment for these actions. David will be involved in fighting to the end of his days, he will suffer a rebellion in his own family, and the child born from his illicit affair with Bathsheba will die (II Sam.12.10–14). Together these threats make up a comprehensive sequence of punishments which the further history bears out in its tragic details. These two elements, a prediction of future events and an explanation, or motive, showing why such events will take place, are the basic ingredients of prophecy.

The second recorded occasion of Nathan's intervention in David's personal history is of a very different character (II Sam.7). Here he appears as a defender of the early traditions of Israel's religion, voicing God's opposition to

David's proposal to build a temple, and promising instead that God will build a house (= dynasty) for David. The prophet's message here is of a very positive kind, providing a religious foundation for the political claims of the Davidic dynasty to rule as kings over Israel. Later this prophetic message was to provide the basis for the messianic hope of Judaism. Prophetic utterances therefore were not always necessarily of a threatening kind, but could take a very positive and affirmative form.

From these descriptions of the activities and preaching of prophets in Israel's early days we can form an instructive picture of their work. Their purpose was first and foremost to foretell the future, and this predictive element can never be removed from their preaching. This set them in rivalry to other means of foretelling future events which enjoyed considerable popularity in the ancient world: the consultation of omens (augury); the inquiry of departed spirits (necromancy) and the interpretation of the movements of the stars and planets (astrology), cf. Deut.18.9–22. In fact in Israel these other more impersonal means of inquiry into the future were almost entirely displaced by the prophets, who claimed to foresee events through their immediate communion with God. Such techniques of divination came to be rejected by the official representatives of Israel's religion, even though some popular attachment to them remained.

In regard to the prophet's status we find that both Gad and Nathan were closely attached to David's court, and were almost certainly paid a regular remuneration by the king. So also Balaam's close association with Balak, the king of Moab, suggests that he, too, was in the pay of the Moabite royal court, which highlights still further the extraordinary and unexpected nature of his message. The indications are, therefore, that all these prophets operated in close association with the monarchy, and that prophets were often attached to existing religious and political institutions. This is borne out still further by other Old Testament evidence. Saul's close link with bands of prophets (I Sam.10.5–13; 19.20–24) shows that the latter could be formed into organized companies who apparently lived and worked together, not unlike the monastic communities of later years. The mention of

their appearing close by sanctuaries suggests that they had a permanent home, or camp, there, and thus formed a prophetic guild living as a self-supporting religious community. These prophetic companies of Saul's time reveal another distinctive feature of the prophetic activity in their irrational and frenzied behaviour. I Samuel 10.5 indicates that they could prophesy to the accompaniment of musical instruments, and I Sam.19.24 reveals that Saul, after being seized by the prophetic spirit, stripped off his clothes and lay naked for a day and a night. This strange and uncontrolled behaviour is more fully illustrated in the story of Elijah's contest with the prophets of Baal on Mount Carmel (I Kings 18.20–40), when the prophets of Baal reinforced their prayers with a wild dance in which they cut themselves with knives. Such a psychological state is usually termed 'ecstasy', meaning 'being beside oneself'. Quite a variety of forms of abnormal behaviour are covered by such a term, not all of which are appropriate to prophesying, but essentially it signifies the extraordinary appearance which such prophets gave of being 'possessed' by another spirit. Whether all prophesying was performed in this manner is hard to tell. Most probably it was not, but in any case the manner of delivery does not greatly affect the content of the message, although it undoubtedly affected the popular attitude towards the prophets. Hosea 9.7 reveals the ordinary man's distrust of this extraordinary behaviour in repeating the popular saying 'The prophet is a fool, the man of the spirit is mad'.

Bearing in mind this picture of the nature of the activities of Israel's prophets, we can see the fascinating way in which the author of the great history of the Israelite kingdoms (Joshua–II Kings) has made use of such figures to interpret events (cf. I Kings 13.1–10 with II Kings 23.15–18). There is a remarkably adept interweaving of prophetic assurances of hope (e.g., Nathan's prophecy in II Sam.7) with prophetic announcements of doom (e.g., Nathan's condemnation of David in II Sam.12.1–15), which could easily at times have appeared contradictory in the hands of a less skilful writer. Instead of clumsiness, however, the author achieves a compelling picture of the hidden activity of God which operates behind human affairs and events. God's purposes, man's sinful disobedience, and the hopes and ambitions of a whole nation, are all taken up in a continuing story of that nation's history which is seen as the working out of a divine purpose. Victory and defeat are both seen to arise out of the attitudes which men adopt towards God and his known will.

The Nature of Developed Prophecy

With the appearance of Amos a new form of prophecy arose in Israel, which is distinguished by the fact that, instead of a brief account of the prophet's work recorded in a historical narrative, we have a separate book, collecting together his sayings and containing a few brief biographical details about him. This emergence of written prophecy was a new departure with Amos, and clearly marks a significant stage in the making of the Old Testament. It can only be explained by the particular character of Amos' message and that of the great prophets who followed him. It is improbable that Amos himself wrote down his words, and more likely that hearers and disciples of his did so, because of the intrinsic importance of what he had to say, and also because the political and religious leaders to whom it was addressed rejected it (Amos 7.10–17). In view of the unbelief with which Amos' message was received, he himself may have taken the first steps to see that it was remembered and recorded so that when its threats were realized the people would know that he had spoken the truth.

1. *Amos*

Amos prophesied in the northern kingdom, Israel, towards the end of the reign of Jeroboam II (786–746 BC). Although a native of Tekoa in Judah (Amos 1.1), he made a dramatic appearance at the ancient sanctuary of Bethel, and proclaimed there the coming downfall of the northern kingdom, with its royal house (Amos 7.7–9). This would be the end of the kingdom of Israel (Amos 8.2; cf. 5.2), and this disaster is described in terms which foretell a military defeat, with Israel's citizens being carried off into exile (Amos 4.2–4; 6.7 f.). Nowhere does Amos say precisely who the enemy will be who will carry out this threat, although he invites Egypt and Assyria to come as spectators (3.9). In a series of five visions

(7.1–3, 4–6, 7–9; 8.1–3; 9.1–4) this threat of the destruction and 'end' of Israel is signified. The first two foretell natural disasters which are called off after the prophet pleads with God. The remaining visions imply an impending military defeat and occupation of the land. It is possible that the fifth vision, threatening the destruction of a sanctuary (Bethel?), was thought to have been fulfilled by the earthquake which occurred two years after Amos had prophesied (1.1).

We have already noted from the example of Nathan that prophets could threaten disaster, so that this prediction of doom by Amos was not in itself a new departure within prophecy. What does appear to have been new was the threat of such utter doom upon both the dynasty and political existence of Israel. The extent of the threat was unprecedented, and undoubtedly contributed to its being remembered and written down. So far as its fulfilment is concerned, the decades after Amos had preached witnessed the resurgence of the imperial ambitions of Assyria in the west, which gave a political focus and reality to his warnings. When the final downfall of the northern kingdom came, with the destruction of Samaria in 721 BC, Amos' threats had been turned into a fearful reality.

Although the visions of a coming catastrophe contained the vital core of Amos' message, they say nothing to explain the reasons for it. For this we have to look elsewhere in the prophet's preaching to those oracles where he attacks the social conditions and conduct of Israel. Here we find that it is especially injustice which calls forth his bitterest attacks. The people 'sell the righteous for silver' (Amos 2.6), which must refer to the selling of people, usually women and children, into slavery in order to pay off personal debts. The immorality which the prophet condemns (2.7) probably refers primarily to the abuse of female slaves, who were not being granted the moral protection demanded by the law (cf. Ex.21.7–11). In particular Amos implies that the administration of justice had broken down so that by bribery and the popular indifference the wealthier citizens could manipulate the law to their own advantage and to the oppression of the poor (Amos 5.10 f., 15).

In the face of this undercutting of the basic supports of morality and justice Amos saw the organized worship of Israel as a useless sham (5.4 f., 21–24). Even worse, it positively hindered any redress of the wrongs being committed because it encouraged a sense of security and complacency. While the hymns sung in worship declared such assurances as 'The Lord of Hosts is with us' (Ps.46.7), the truth was that God was about to exact a terrible punishment from such people for their abuse of elementary justice. Only if the prevalent lack of justice were amended would God be with the people in reality (Amos 5.14). Thus Amos found himself thrown into opposition to the historic traditions of worship and priesthood which governed the religious life of the people. Not only was this traditional religion failing to make known the truth that no worship could please God which was divorced from the elementary demands of right and justice, but it even encouraged a misplaced sense of security and divine approval. Thus Amos championed a new and radical emphasis within the traditional pattern of Israel's religion, setting justice and right dealing above the more formal conventions of organized worship (5.21–24). To those who looked eagerly forward to the coming 'Day of the Lord', the great New Year's Day of the Autumn Festival, Amos warned that it would mean darkness and not light (5.18–20). Those who expected to celebrate in hymn and ritual service the righteous kingship of God would find that the divine righteousness fell in judgment upon them. The people could not praise God for a justice which they refused to apply to themselves and their own behaviour.

The sharpness with which Amos predicted the coming downfall of the northern kingdom, Israel, is matched by the simple clarity with which he interpreted and explained it. Far from this disaster signifying a divine indifference to his people, it would reveal the reality and intensity of God's concern that Israel should be his people (3.2). Such a message was perhaps not surprisingly rejected by Amaziah, the chief priest of the great sanctuary of Bethel where Amos proclaimed it (7.10–13). Amaziah had Amos formally expelled from the kingdom, maligning him as a greedy scaremonger who was concerned to frighten people into paying him generously, though he was in reality motivated by nothing deeper than a narrow patriotism for his native Judah. In defence

Amos could only appeal to the divine source and authority of his message. We are left to assume that Amos was deported to Judah, his life alone being spared by the fact that a traditional religious regard for prophets saved him from being executed for treason (cf. Jer.26.16).

2. *Hosea*

Shortly after Amos' sudden appearance at Bethel, which must have occurred sometime during the decade 760–750 BC, another prophet appeared in the northern kingdom, this time a native of that country. His name was Hosea, and, unlike Amos whose activity probably lasted no longer than a year or two, he prophesied at intervals for a period of about twenty years (c.750–730 BC, cf. Hos.1.1). In upbringing, temperament and religious background he was a very different person from Amos, yet the overall substance of his message had much in common with that of the prophet from Tekoa. Most striking of all, chs.1–3 of the book of Hosea concern the significance of the prophet's marriage and the children that were born to him. Two events are recorded: in ch.1 there is a biographical account, recorded in the third person style, of God's command to the prophet to marry 'a wife of harlotry' (1.2), whose name is Gomer. In ch.3 we have an autobiographical account of a further command to the prophet to marry an unnamed woman, who is an adulteress (3.1). A majority of scholars accept that this woman must also be Gomer, and that this event must have concerned the same marriage as mentioned in ch.1, but at a later stage. This carries the implication that Hosea had either divorced Gomer for her unfaithfulness, or more probably that Gomer had left Hosea without actually being divorced by him. She had then fallen into slavery from which Hosea bought her back. This certainly appears to be the intended interpretation of the present structure of the book, since Hos.2, which interprets Hosea's marriage as symbolic of God's relationship to Israel, hints at divorce (2.2), or separation, and points to a desire on the part of the unfaithful wife to return to her husband (2.7). Those scholars who regard the woman of ch.3 as someone other than Gomer, a view which is certainly not impossible, do tend to weaken the force of the marriage symbolism which expresses the permanence of the divine love for Israel, and to overrule the lines of interpretation which are indicated by ch.2.

There are several aspects of Hosea's marriage to Gomer which remain unclear. The main features and religious importance of the marriage for the prophet are not in doubt. At the time when Hosea married her, Gomer could already be called 'a wife of harlotry', which must be taken literally, and not be regarded simply as the prophet's later reflection on the character of the woman whom he had taken to be a pure and innocent girl at the time of his marriage to her. It probably indicates that she was a woman who had taken part in the immoral rites of Baal in which the worshippers imitated the divine marriage of Baal with his consort the goddess Anat. By doing so the worshipper sought to activate the creative and fertilizing powers of nature in order to ensure rain and fertility in the fields and among the flocks and herds. Such immorality, practised in the very name of religion, epitomized the extent of Israel's turning away from God, and is roundly condemned by Hosea (4.13–15, 18; 5.3 f.; 6.10; 7.4; 9.1,10). By himself marrying a woman who had shared in such a perverted religion, Hosea was made to realize the full shame of Israel's behaviour. God's command to Hosea, however, was not only to marry Gomer, but to have 'children of harlotry', who would be a testimony to Israel's gross behaviour. In consequence the main part of the story of Hosea's marriage is concerned with recording the births of his three children, and the symbolic names which the prophet gave to them (Hos. 1.3–11). The message of the prophet, therefore, was not so much conveyed by his marriage, as has often been suggested, but by his children whose names warned of the coming divine judgment. The first child was called *Jezreel*, recalling to Israel the violent revolution by which Jehu had assumed the crown of Israel (II Kings 9–10), and threatening punishment upon Jeroboam II, who was of the dynasty of Jehu (cf. Amos 7.11). The second child, a daughter, bore the name *Not Pitied*, indicating that God could no longer take pity on his people Israel, but had reached the time when he must punish them (cf. Amos 7.8). The third child was called *Not My People*, declaring that God now disowned Israel from being his people, and that he revoked the very promise of the covenant 'You shall be my

people, and I will be your God' (cf. Amos 8.1). The message of Hosea, therefore, in its essential character was not unlike that of Amos in that it was a warning of the coming disaster to the northern kingdom, Israel, including a threat against the throne of Jeroboam II. At times the military character of this disaster is clearly hinted at, with pictures of the desolation of the land (Hos.5.9), the death of its inhabitants (7.16) and the deportation of others into exile (9.6; 11.5). Most directly, however, Hosea threatens disaster as the just and inevitable punishment for Israel's sins, insisting earnestly that sin carries with it its own retributive punishment. 'They sow the wind and they shall reap the whirlwind' (Hos.8.7).

In explaining why Israel was faced with this coming catastrophe we find in Hosea, as in Amos, a bitter attack upon the people for their neglect of elementary justice (4.2; 5.1; 6.8 f.; 8.12). More deeply, however, this lack of justice is itself traced back by Hosea to a 'spirit of harlotry' (4.12; 5.4) within the people. Israel is the bride of God, but has dealt faithlessly with her husband and has forsaken him for her lovers, the Baals (2.8,13,17; 7.16; 11.2; 13.1). These were the various local forms of the great god Baal-Hadad, who was worshipped by the Canaanites as the controller of storms and rain, the giver of life and fertility, and the great warrior among the gods. He was acclaimed as king of the gods, superior in strength and vitality to all the other gods, and the conqueror of the dread powers of death. In particular, as we have already seen, the ritual devotion to Baal included among its rites the practice of sacred prostitution, in which young women sacrificed their virginity to Baal. Hosea could thus include a literal, as well as metaphorical, significance in his condemnation of Israel's harlotry and unfaithfulness to God. As in Amos, Hosea, too, condemns the formal worship of Israel's sanctuaries as a useless pretence at love and loyalty to God which had no real substance (6.6; 7.14; 8.13). Israel's worship is idolatry (4.17), and in particular the bull-calf images of Bethel and Samaria are singled out for attack (8.5; 10.5; 13.2). What the people regarded as symbols of divine strength and vigour were in reality nothing but occasions of disloyalty to the true God.

Where Amos had given little word of hope for Israel's future, Hosea is more positive and re-assuring. While disaster threatened the nation in the immediate future, this would provide the opportunity for God to begin again with his people. Here the metaphor of Israel as the bride of God becomes very significant, especially when it is related to the symbolic action of the prophet in restoring his wife from slavery as recorded in ch. 3. As Hosea could still love his own faithless wife, so God could not give up his love for wayward Israel. The most moving expression of this enduring divine love, however, is given, not in relation to the metaphor of marriage, but to that of Israel as God's son (Hos.11.1–9). The coming punish ment of the nation is thus seen by the prophet not as an end, but as the opportunity for a new beginning. As the historical origin of the nation had taken the form of a deliverance from Egypt and a journey through the wilderness (Hos. 11.1,5; 2.15), so Israel would have to go back to the wilderness, and to enter the land afresh (2.14 f.). This time the settlement in the land would be the entering of Israel into a new hope and a new and faithful relationship to God (2.16–23). Significantly the very names of Hosea's children, which had warned of the coming judgment, would then take on a new meaning as indicative of God's mercy and patient love (2.22 f.).

We see both in Amos and Hosea a very sombre message of doom, alleviated in Hosea particularly by a strong insistence that the love of God for his people is such that he will not allow his last word to Israel to be one of judgment. In neither prophet, however, is a specific political danger referred to as the source of the coming judgment. While Amos can speak of exile to 'Harmon' (Amos 4.3), which is not otherwise identifiable, and Hosea threatens deportation to both Egypt and Assyria (Hos.9.6), there is no direct reference to the coming down-fall of the northern kingdom as an event to be brought about by Assyria. In reality, however, there can be no doubt that the Assyrian menace to Israel in the mid-eighth century, culminating in the siege and fall of Samaria in 721 BC, represented the fulfilment of the warnings of the two prophets. It is in the preaching of Isaiah, who began to prophesy c.746 BC, and who continued his prophetic ministry at least until the end of the century, that we have a very clear and direct reference to the Assyrians as the agents of God's punishment upon Israel.

3. *Isaiah*

What is immediately striking with Isaiah is the distinctive religious and cultural back-ground which distinguishes him from Amos and Hosea. The latter two prophets had both proclaimed their warnings in the northern kingdom, even though Amos was from Tekoa in the far south of Judah. They both reflect the rural background of life in Israel, with its tradi-tional adherence to the old ideals of tribal society and family life. In Hosea the particular political and religious emphases of the northern kingdom are apparent, with a scathing hostility towards the monarchy as a divinely ordained institution (Hos. 5.1; 8.4; 10.3,7,15; 13.10 f.), which reflects the unhappy experience of the kingship among the northern tribes. In Isaiah, however, the upbringing of the prophet in the city environment of Jerusalem is very apparent. Here two great events stood out in the city's history, and served to mould its religious under-standing. David had brought the ancient ark of God into Jerusalem, and set it permanently there, making Mount Zion the site for a temple of the God of Israel. From the religious view-point this was interpreted as God's election of Mount Zion to be his dwelling-place. The second major event was Nathan's prophecy that David's sons would retain a divinely appointed kingship over Israel (II Sam.7). This meant the divine election of the Davidic dynasty to provide the kings of Israel. These two great events, with their abiding religious significance, were celebrated in the hymns sung in the Jerusalem temple (cf. esp. Pss.78.67–72; 132). Jerusalem was 'the city of the great king' (Ps.48.2), referring to God's temple there, and from it his presence shone forth in splendour (Ps.50.2). It was also the city of David, through whom the divine justice was administered to Israel (Pss.89.19–37; 132.11 f. See Part III, Section 11, p. 154 ff.). These two focal points of the religious background of Jerusalem find a prominent place in the preaching of Isaiah, who is the prophet of Jerusalem in a very special way. He views Israel as a divinely governed state with its centre at Jerusalem, where the presence of God is made known.

Isaiah's call to be a prophet (Isa.6) came to him while he was worshipping in the Jerusalem temple, and the emphasis which it placed upon God's status as the divine 'King' of Israel suggests that this may have been during the Autumn Festival, which particularly stressed this aspect of God's power and authority. What is most startling in the commission which accompanied Isaiah's call is the warning of the great disaster which was about to befall the land (6.11–13). This can only have meant a military defeat of Judah with the accompanying devastation of cities and the countryside. The terms in which this commission is given, and the cry of alarm and despondency which it called forth from the prophet (6.11), indicate the severity and extent of this coming catastrophe (cf. esp. 6.13). There can therefore be no doubt that Isaiah began to preach a similar message to the earlier prophets, warning of the danger in which Judah stood and foretelling an impending defeat and conquest of the land. In explanation of these events Isaiah followed Amos in pointing to the injustice, violence and dishonesty which marred the life of the people (1.4,21–23). Even Jerusalem, which prided itself on its good administration of law and regarded itself as a city of righteousness and faithfulness, had become filled with every kind of wrong.

Not many years after Isaiah had received his call to be a prophet, a major political crisis occurred in Judah (735–732 BC). Uzziah, the king whose death had occurred in the year of Isaiah's call, had been staunchly anti-Assyrian in his policy, participating in an alliance of minor kingdoms for mutual defence against Assyria. His son Jotham, who reigned for a brief period, continued this policy, but it was reversed when his early death put Ahaz on the throne. Ahaz preferred to seek a compromise agreement with Assyria rather than accept the risks of the existing treaties with neighbouring kingdoms. As a result, two of these kingdoms, the Aramaean kingdom of Damascus and the northern kingdom, Israel, took military action against Judah, intending to depose Ahaz and to place a puppet ruler, who is referred to as the son of Tabeel (Isa.7.6), on the throne of Judah. Things soon went badly for Ahaz, and Jerusalem was reduced to a state of siege. Ahaz was in panic and planned a strong appeal to Assyria (Isa.7.1 f.). Isaiah, with his son Shear-Jashub, met Ahaz to assure him that the attack by the Israelite-Aramaean alliance would come to nothing, and to give him some sign in confirmation of this (7.3–11). Ahaz refused to seek any such sign, perhaps because he had already

decided his policy, and may already have sent his appeal to Assyria. Isaiah then promised his own distinctive sign that a child would shortly be born whose name, Immanuel, would affirm the presence of God with Israel, with its implication of divine defence and protection. This child, whose birth was expected in the near future, appears most probably to have been a child of the king's, whose birth at this time of crisis would serve to re-affirm God's promise that only David's descendants should sit upon the throne of David in Jerusalem (7.12–17).

The key idea which underlies the prophet's thinking is expressed in 7.9:

> If you will not believe, surely you shall not be established.

Since Jerusalem was a city built upon the two great promises of divine support for David and the dwelling of the divine presence in the temple there, Ahaz was displaying a complete lack of faith in God by his appeal to Assyria. Thus the very assurances upon which his kingdom rested would be to him warnings of judgment because of his unbelief. With striking paradox, therefore, Isaiah warned Ahaz that the Assyrians would come, but would not in the outcome prove to be his deliverers, as he hoped, but his tormentors (7.7; 8.5–8). In fact the result of Ahaz's appeal was an Assyrian expedition to Israel which compelled the Aramaeans and Israelites to lift the siege of Jerusalem, and enforced a settlement of the dispute which left the borders of Israel seriously curtailed. Thus the already divided kingdoms of Israel and Judah fell further apart, and the first major step in the political ruination of the northern kingdom took place (on the conflict between the prophet and the king, see Part III, Section 12, p. 164).

In Isaiah the threats of coming disaster for Israel and Judah are specifically linked with the rise of the Assyrian empire. Assyria is the rod of God's anger, which he is using to punish his erring people Israel (Isa.10.5 f.). This in itself is a remarkable interpretation of faith, since the Assyrians regarded themselves as the servants of their god Ashur, and they ascribed all their victories to him. In their view the conquest of other nations was to bring greater honour to their god by bringing more people under his power. For Isaiah this was nothing but an arrogant illusion, since in reality the God of Israel was using them for purposes which they did not discern, and which therefore included the possibility that not only Israel and Judah, but in turn Assyria also would be punished for their violence and pride (10.7–19). At what point Isaiah began to proclaim this turn in the fortunes of Assyria, and to predict the sudden and dramatic intervention of God to humiliate and punish them, is not clear. Most probably it was not until Assyria had destroyed the northern kingdom of Israel and carried off many of her people as exiles in 721 BC (II Kings 17). With this defeat the Assyrian hold upon Judah also became tighter.

Although we cannot be sure at what point in his prophetic career Isaiah became convinced that God planned to inflict a humiliating defeat upon the Assyrians in Judah, the intensity of this conviction and its central place in his message cannot be doubted. For the prophet it supplemented his earlier warnings of the punishment which the Assyrians would bring upon Judah and Jerusalem, rather than cancelled them out. The nature and motive of this changed pattern of coming events is well described by the prophet: 'When the Lord has finished all his work on Mount Zion and on Jerusalem he will punish the arrogant boasting of the king of Assyria and his haughty pride' (Isa.10.12).

The form that this defeat of the Assyrians would take is described in different ways by the prophet. God would trample upon the Assyrians to remove their yoke from Judah (Isa.14.24–26). He would rebuke them, and they would flee away (17.12–14). He would terrify them with thunder, earthquake and great noise (29.5–8). The point that is firmly insisted upon is that it would be God, and not men, who would bring this defeat upon the Assyrians (31.4 f.; 10.33 f.), and there is a hint that this defeat would be caused by a sickness among the Assyrian soldiers (10.16–19). In this way God would be fulfilling his plan of punishing in turn the arrogant Assyrians who boasted that their victories were the consequence of their own greatness. In foretelling this crushing divine blow upon the Assyrian armies on the soil of Judah, Isaiah was able to use and re-apply ancient hymns which celebrated God's power and victory on behalf of his people (Pss.46; 48; 76). In this way Isaiah referred the imagery of the hymns to a specific historical situation, and interpreted it of a particular military threat to Judah.

In order to appreciate the relevance of this prophetic interpretation of the situation it is necessary to consider the main outlines of what took place. After the Assyrian action to prevent the suppression of Judah by the Aramaeans and Israelites in 732 the borders of Israel were greatly reduced, and conditions of subservience to Assyria imposed. In 724 the Israelites joined a rebellion against Assyria and invited more drastic punishment upon themselves. After a long siege Samaria fell to the Assyrians in 721, and large sections of the population of the northern kingdom were deported. At this time Ahaz was no longer on the throne of Judah, having been succeeded by his son Hezekiah. For a time Hezekiah continued his father's policy of submission to Assyria in return for protection, but then he, too, was tempted into joining an anti-Assyrian coalition, and into taking active steps of hostility towards his Assyrian overlord. Sennacherib, the Assyrian king, sought to inflict swift punishment upon Judah. He marched through the land, besieging and capturing Lachish, and then enforcing a siege against Jerusalem (701 BC). What happened next is not exactly clear, although it is described in detail in II Kings 18–19; Isa.36–37. From Assyrian records it is certain that Sennacherib compelled Hezekiah to capitulate and imposed heavy and humiliating demands upon him, although Jerusalem was not destroyed and Hezekiah retained his throne. It is possible that this unexpected leniency was itself regarded by the general populace as a remarkable vindication of Isaiah's preaching. Since, however, there are accounts of two deputations to Hezekiah, many scholars accept that Sennacherib relented of his leniency and later returned in an unsuccessful attempt to enforce harsh terms upon Jerusalem. Whatever the precise course of events, which now present an almost insoluble historical problem, the citizens of Judah celebrated a remarkable deliverance, and came to regard Isaiah's prophecies as having been fulfilled. Thus Isaiah, as the prophet of Zion, came to be remembered especially as a preacher of divine deliverance for Jerusalem. This must, however, be related to the very severe warnings of coming judgment with which he began his ministry.

In a famous oracle the hope of God's righteous rule from Jerusalem is presented by Isaiah (Isa.2.2–4). Since this prophecy also re-appears in the prophet Micah (Micah 4.1–4), its authenticity has often been questioned. Yet it may well have originated with Isaiah. The picture which it draws of the future age of peace, in which many nations will be united in the worship of the Lord God of Israel, is an adaptation of a traditional image of Jerusalem as a kingdom of peace, perhaps stemming from the time of David's empire. This ancient hope was undoubtedly at one time that of Jerusalem as the capital of a great empire, but with Isaiah it has been transformed into a more spiritual conception. Similarly the tradition of the Davidic kingship has been taken up and re-applied by the prophet in Isa.9.2–7; 11.1–9 to present a picture of the coming ruler of God's people. How this was related to the existing monarchy of Judah, and whether it was in any way intended to foretell the refounding of the Davidic dynasty is not wholly clear.

4. *Micah*

We have the work of another Judaean prophet, who was contemporary with Isaiah, in the book of Micah. The nucleus of his message is to be found in chs. 1–3 of his book, where it is predominantly a warning of coming disaster for both Israel and Judah. That the northern kingdom had not yet fallen to the Assyrians is evident from 1.6, where the destruction of Samaria is foretold. In 2.1–5 there is a sharp rebuke against the wealthy landowners of Jerusalem, where we have a prophetic threat that their estates will be ravaged, and the owners evicted from them. The prediction in 2.5 that the land will afterwards be re-allocated by the old tribal system of division by line for a limited period points us to a situation in which the city landowners of Jerusalem had been unscrupulous in taking advantage of the different legal systems of land tenure that operated in the cities of Israel and Judah from that which applied to the rural areas (cf. Isa.5.8–10; Lev.25.29–34). In Micah 3.5–8 there is a vigorous condemnation of certain prophets who deceive the people by their assurances of 'peace', when they are well paid for their preaching, but who threaten war against anyone who fails to reward them sufficiently. This is one of the earliest references that we have to

the existence of false prophets in Israel (cf. I Kings 22.5–28), and it is significant that their falsity is especially linked with their prophecies of 'peace', and their dishonourable professionalism. In punishment for these offences Micah threatened that even Jerusalem itself would be destroyed, and the temple left in ruins (Micah 3.9–12). That this oracle caused much consternation is clear from the way in which it was still recalled a century later (Jer.26.18), when a similar threat of the destruction of the temple was made by Jeremiah. Since we do not know exactly when Micah delivered his threat it is impossible to know precisely how it relates to the preaching of Isaiah. We must not suppose, however, that all the prophets proclaimed a uniform message, or that we can fit their preaching together into a consistent pattern.

5. *Jeremiah*

The next of the really outstanding prophets of the Old Testament was Jeremiah, who received his call to prophesy in 626 BC, three-quarters of a century after the great Assyrian crisis towards the close of Isaiah's ministry. Born in Anathoth, a small village five miles north of Jerusalem, of priestly parents, Jeremiah appears as a sensitive and discerning personality, whose work brought him persecution and forced him into isolation, reducing him near to despair. The book of Jeremiah is formed from large collections of material which reflect the history of their preservation. Of first importance is the collection of prophecies in chs. 1–25, which contains the most characteristic of the prophet's oracles, although it is difficult, and sometimes impossible, to date many of them. Chapters 26–30 and 34–45 form a 'biography' of Jeremiah, and since this concludes with a personal message for Baruch, the friend and scribe of the prophet, it is reasonable to assume that Baruch played a part in preserving this information about the prophet's life, although he may not have been the final author of it. Into this 'biography' there has been inserted a collection of assurances for Israel's future in chs. 31–33, which is often called 'the Book of Consolation'. Most of the remaining chapters of Jeremiah contain prophecies against foreign nations.

Jeremiah's priestly links with Anathoth are of interest since this was the town to which the priest Abiathar, who had been a close friend and adviser to David, had been banished by Solomon (I Kings 2.26 f.). The likelihood is that Jeremiah was a direct descendant of this historic priestly family.

When Jeremiah received his call to be a prophet (Jer.1.4–10), Josiah was on the throne of Judah, and almost a complete century had passed since the northern kingdom had been swallowed up in the Assyrian empire. During this long period of political survival Judah had remained a vassal state of Assyria. Nevertheless the mere fact of survival, in contrast to the sad fate of the northern kingdom, had greatly strengthened the popular belief that a special divine favour was being shown to Jerusalem for the sake of David, who had first made it an Israelite city, and because God had chosen Mount Zion for his divine dwelling-place. A mixture of patriotic pride and religious fervour lent to the city a unique importance in the minds of its citizens. In consequence the belief was encouraged among the people that God could certainly be relied upon to maintain his protection of the temple and of the city in which it stood.

Jeremiah's first prophecies were warnings that military and political disaster would soon overtake the land (1.11–16; 4.5–8; 6.22 f.); Jerusalem would be besieged and destruction would come at the hands of a mysterious foe from the north. The obscure way in which this enemy is described has caused much discussion, and several scholars have linked it with an invasion by marauding bands of Scythians from the north which the Greek historian Herodotus mentions from this period (Herodotus, *Histories*, 1.105 f.). Since, however, there is no reference to such an invasion in the historical books of the Old Testament, the reality of it is thrown in doubt. Most probably Jeremiah himself was at first not clear about the precise political nature of the threat to Judah, and alluded vaguely to 'the foe from the north' on the basis of older prophetic imagery. Since these warnings came at a time when Judah felt secure under the umbrella of Assyria, Jeremiah's threat gained added sharpness.

When we look to see how Jeremiah justified this impending catastrophe upon Judah we find a very close similarity with Hosea. Both prophets repeatedly accuse Israel of being the unfaithful bride of God, and point specifically to the worship of Baal with its immoral practices in support of this (cf. Jer.2.1–8; 2.20–25, 33–37; 3.1–5, 19 f., etc.). The contacts between Jeremiah and Hosea are sufficient to suggest that the later prophet was familiar with an account of the earlier prophet's message, and reflected upon it in his own prophecies. If anything the accusation against Israel that it has been unfaithful becomes even more poignant and challenging in Jeremiah's oracles.

One of the most memorable of them was a threat of the coming destruction of the temple, which would not, contrary to the popular belief, be safeguarded by the divine protection (Jer.7.1–15). Because of the sins of the people (Jer.7.9), even the ancient promise that God would always dwell within his temple (I Kings 8.13; Ps.132.13 f.) had come to mean nothing. Jeremiah himself was forbidden to pray for such a people (Jer.7.16–20; 14.11 f.), since to intercede for such hardened sinners could only be to no purpose. The personal consequences of this temple sermon for Jeremiah are described in ch. 26, where we learn that certain priests and prophets sought to have Jeremiah put to death for treason (26.10 f.). However, the earlier (unfulfilled) threat of Micah was recalled by a number of the princes, who pointed out that Jeremiah had not spoken of his own will, but in the name of God (26.16–23). In the outcome the intervention of Ahikam ben Shaphan, an influential and pious government official, secured Jeremiah's release (26.24). Already in 11.21–23 we are told how some of Jeremiah's own townspeople, the men of Anathoth, sought unsuccessfully to kill him. Neither the occasion nor the reasons for this plot are given, but it has been suggested that it may have been a consequence of Jeremiah's initial support for the religious reforms instituted by King Hezekiah which would have been resented by the priests of Anathoth because it deprived them of their livelihood.

The strong hostility and threats against his life which Jeremiah encountered brought tension and a prolonged spiritual crisis in his own life. Jeremiah rebelled against his own sufferings and came to feel that they were all in vain, since the threats of judgment upon Jerusalem failed to materialize. In a number of passages, often called Jeremiah's 'confessions', the prophet gives vent to his own feelings and complaints (Jer.11.18–23; 12.1–6; 15.10–12, 15–21;

17.12–18; 18.18–23; 20.7–18). In the most out-spoken and despairing of these utterances Jeremiah openly accused God of having deceived him and of having made him into a laughing-stock. Yet when the prophet made up his mind that he would not prophesy any more, he could not restrain himself from doing so, since the message of God was like a fire shut up inside him (20.7–12). All that he could do was to plead for vengeance upon his enemies.

The reign of Josiah came to a tragic end in 609 BC when the king was killed at Megiddo by the Egyptian Pharaoh Necho, and for a brief period Shallum ruled until he was deported to Egypt (Jer.22.10–12). By this time the Assyrian empire was in ruins and the capital Nineveh had fallen to the Babylonians and Medes in 612 BC. The passing of Assyrian power, with its reputation for brutality and violence, did not go uncelebrated in Judah and the prophet Nahum offers a vivid picture of the sense of divine justice which accompanied the expectation of Nineveh's fall. Thus Nahum gave voice to the more nationalistic feelings of Israel. Yet the end of Assyrian power did not result in any lessening of foreign domination of Judah. Jehoiakim was placed on the throne of Judah instead of Shallum by the Egyptians, and his reign was marked by oppression and bloodshed. Jeremiah condemns him as an evil tyrant over his people (Jer.22.13–19). In 605 BC control of Judah passed into the power of Babylonia, and Jehoiakim secured himself before his new masters by a transfer of loyalty. It is in this year that a major event occurred in Jeremiah's ministry, recounted in Jer.36. The prophet was personally debarred from entering the temple, and so he employed Baruch to write out a scroll, at his dictation, containing his prophecies of coming disaster upon Jerusalem. Baruch then read out this scroll in the temple on a fast day, when a large crowd would be present. The year in which this occurred strongly points to the view that Jeremiah was now openly interpreting his earlier warnings of 'the foe from the north, as referring to Babylon. Baruch was greeted with the same kind of hostility that had earlier been shown personally to Jeremiah. The scroll was confiscated and taken to the royal palace, where its contents were read out to Jehoiakim the king, who promptly cut up and burnt the leather roll as a sign of his disdain. When he learnt of this Jeremiah simply had a

second, even longer, scroll written by Baruch.

In 601 BC Jehoiakim rebelled against the king of Babylon, inviting severe retaliation. This came in 598 when Jerusalem was besieged and forced to capitulate. Before the final blow fell, however, Jehoiakim died, leaving his son Jehoiachin to face the wrath of the Babylonians. The surrender terms were severe: the king was taken as a hostage to Babylon, along with several thousand of the leading citizens of the land, and his uncle Zedekiah was placed upon the throne as a Babylonian puppet ruler.

Jeremiah now actively campaigned for complete and utter submission to the Babylonians. He regarded it as the will of God that 'all the nations' should serve the king of Babylon (Jer.27.1–11). At this time the voices of certain nationalistic prophets were raised to encourage further rebellion against Babylon, and Jeremiah vigorously opposed them and their policies (Jer.27.14 f.). A remarkable and distinctive example of this confrontation of views is recorded in Jer.28. A nationalistic prophet, by name Hananiah, foretold that within two years the Babylonian yoke would be removed. At first Jeremiah appears to have accepted the possibility that Hananiah's words would prove true, until a prophetic message from God reassured him of the folly of such nationalistic hopes (28.12–17). Not only did Jeremiah reaffirm that God willed complete submission to the Babylonians, but he now also foretold the imminent death of Hananiah, apparently in punishment for his having deceived the people in God's name.

Zedekiah appears not to have been altogether inattentive to Jeremiah's preaching (Jer.37), but he finally allowed himself to be persuaded into joining an anti-Babylonian revolt (589 BC). Inevitably stern and overwhelming retribution came. Jerusalem was besieged and destroyed in 587 BC, and Zedekiah was forced to witness the death of his own sons before himself being blinded and exiled. Throughout the siege Jeremiah consistently urged the people to surrender, even encouraging individuals to desert to the Babylonian camp (Jer.38).

After the fall of the city Jeremiah was given the choice of either going to Babylon with the exiles or staying, and he chose the latter course. He seems well content to have accepted the governorship of Gedaliah whom the Babylonians now installed as controller of the Province in place of a king (Jer.40.1–12). It may be that at this time he felt most certain of the coming renewal of Israel, and of the divine grace which would bring into being a new covenant with Israel and Judah (Jer.30–31). We cannot, however, be at all sure of the date of these assurances in 'the Book of Consolation'.

The period of Gedaliah's governorship was brief, and he was tragically murdered by a member of the royal house named Ishmael, who afterwards escaped to the Ammonites. The remainder of the people were afraid of further Babylonian reprisals, and fled to Egypt, forcing Jeremiah to accompany them, in spite of his advice not to go and his warnings that to do so would only result in their own ultimate death and destruction (Jer.42.1–17). The last oracles that we hear from him came from his place of enforced exile in Egypt, where he was still rebuking his fellow Jews for their disobedience and idolatry (Jer.43.8–13; 44).

With the fall of Jerusalem in 587 the last surviving political entity of the old nation of Israel broke up into separate, and politically subservient, communities. Many of the old nation were in exile in Babylon, where we hear more of their activities from the prophets Ezekiel and Deutero-Isaiah. Some had fled to Egypt and probably other countries where their ultimate fate is unknown. A large number remained in the land of Judah to face the pitiful sufferings of a devastated land, and to seek to build up afresh the conditions and means of a stable social and economic life. The appalling conditions are well described in the book of Lamentations, which is not from Jeremiah, but an anonymous poet, or group of poets, who lived in Judah during the period following Jerusalem's destruction. Aside from the horror of famine and disease, brought about by the ravages of war, there was the theological problem of finding some divine meaning or explanation for catastrophe. Why had God disowned his people (Lam.2.5), his sanctuary (Lam.2.7) and his chosen king of the line of David (Lam.4.20)? Only by accepting the interpretation given by the great prophets that it was a divine punishment for Israel's sins could sense be made out of such an appalling situation.

The Prophetic Interpretation of History

Although, as we saw at the beginning, prophets were not unique to Israel, no other nation seems ever to have been so deeply indebted to them as was Israel. Furthermore, in Israel the greatest period of such prophetic influence extended over no more than two centuries, stretching from the middle of the eighth to shortly after the middle of the sixth centuries BC. Again, although very many prophets were active during this period, it is only the work of a few individuals from among them which has had a lasting influence upon human history. By these few, whom we name the 'classical' or 'writing' prophets, a significant transformation of the religion of Israel was brought about.

The prophets laid great stress upon their divine 'call', which placed the authority for what they said upon God, and so looked beyond their own feelings or desires. They worked in quite a different way from the modern politician, philosopher or sociologist in their reflections upon the character and destiny of the society in which they lived. They were not looking for intrinsic laws of cause and effect which could be seen to operate in the affairs of men, but were threatening the direct personal intervention of God in judgment upon his elect people. They ascribed their message to divine inspiration, and not to their own thoughts about the future state of the world in which they lived. It was this awareness of divine authority and commission which enabled the prophets to face rejection, opposition and persecution from their compatriots. It also left them free from any self-interested professionalism and from any formal ties with the great religious and political institutions of Israel.

The prophets stand out for their remarkably detailed knowledge of international affairs, and for their awareness of the policies and diplomacy of Jerusalem and Samarian courts. They displayed a political interest which assumed from the start that God was deeply concerned about the social and political realities of life in Israel. They argued that God was exercising a controlling influence upon international affairs, and that in encountering their political fate Israel and Judah were being brought face to face with God (cf. Amos 4.12). Disaster and defeat were his judgments, deliverance and victory were his salvation. Most prominently, however, it is the negative aspect of judgment which looms largest in the prophets' preaching, making their threat a continued rebuke against political pride and military arrogance, and sharply condemning Israel's religious complacency.

In giving their interpretation of events the prophets used various pictorial images to describe the historical situation in which Israel was placed. Most dramatically Hosea pictures Israel as the bride of God (Hos.2.1 ff.), who has wilfully become unfaithful by turning to other lovers, the Baal gods. The coming judgment will be God's divorce of his faithless wife (Hos.2.2 f.). This same marriage metaphor is taken up later by Jeremiah (Jer.2.2 ff.). Such pictorial language provided a vivid and dramatic interpretation of Israel's historical situation, and provided a sharp moral condemnation in explanation of the coming catastrophe.

Another popular metaphor is that of the lawsuit in which the prophet pictures Israel as summoned to account for its behaviour in a court of law (Isa.1.2–20; Micah 6.1–5). Israel is accused of disloyalty to God, of having broken its pledges to him, and of countless acts of disobedience. The time has come for God to act, and to call his erring people to judgment. In this metaphor God is both the plaintiff and judge, while heaven and earth are called upon to act as witnesses of Israel's offences. In this lawsuit imagery there are several striking similarities between God's case against Israel and the kind of ultimatum which a reigning emperor would deliver to a vassal ruler whom he suspected of treason and disloyalty. Thus the covenant between God and Israel shows certain similarities with treaties between imperial and vassal states.

In their descriptions of the coming divine judgments upon Israel the prophets naturally drew upon conventional knowledge of life and affairs. Their widely used imagery of battle and defeat was drawn from their knowledge of contemporary military practice. Essentially it was the certainty of judgment, rather than its precise details, which the prophets foretold. Nahum could describe the violent overthrow of Nineveh, although in the event the capture of the city by the Babylonian armies was virtually unopposed (612 BC). The moral significance was of far greater importance than the literal accuracy of the details of the fulfilment of prophecy, so that such a situation in no way lessens the religious 'truth' of what the prophets said. It was not simply their ability to predict the future, but their power to interpret it, which gave to the prophets their greatness. They related past, present and future in a consistent story of God's concern for his chosen people Israel, and they interpreted this story in accordance with the moral purpose for which Israel was called. They did not therefore exclude other nations from their field of vision. Jeremiah was specifically called to be a 'prophet to the nations' (Jer.1.5), and this was certainly also true of Amos and Isaiah. The prophets interpreted Israel's history in relation to a universal purpose of God for which Israel's election had meaning. The very notion that Israel should be judged received significance in the context of God's wider concern for the welfare of all nations, and Israel's responsibility to be a light and a witness to them.

Our ultimate evaluation of the prophets' message cannot therefore be reached simply by asking whether what the prophets threatened for Israel came 'true'. Rather their 'truth' lies deeper in the realm of spiritual and moral understanding. Is the prophets' interpretation of Israel's downfall more convincing than the arrogant religious claims of contemporary Assyrian and Babylonian nationalism, or than the suggestion that it was a purely meaningless historical accident? The spiritual fruits of the prophetic interpretation in terms of humility in the face of suffering, spiritual sensitivity and a passionate concern for social justice, encourage us to believe that the prophets did preach 'truth'. This truth is not only applicable to Israel, and to the distinctive circumstances which prevailed in the eighth to the sixth centuries BC, but to a wider area of life. It concerns us also, since we also are faced with questions of nationalism, social injustice and widespread beliefs in the divinely given supremacy of certain nations and races. By their moral interpretation of the belief in Israel's national election, the prophets warned against any selfish or material conception of it. The 'truth' of prophecy can speak to us in our own situation, with our national hopes, our social needs and problems, and our personal responsibilities to one another. It is a truth which can give us insight into the meaning and purpose of life, and of the divine government of the world in which that life is lived.

11

Worship in Israel

J. H. Eaton

Places of Worship

While the territory of Israel contained many holy places, there was from the first a tendency to centralize the main festivals in one designated sanctuary. This followed from the nature of the religion as a union between God and the entire society. For a major festival it was appropriate that (in principle) the whole people should assemble as one in the place where God, in some mysterious way, would make his presence known to them. From far and near the worshippers would converge with cattle and harvest produce for their offerings; in orderly fashion they would take up temporary stations to spend perhaps a week or more in the vicinity of the sanctuary. Traditions about a tent-sanctuary suggest that in the early period the assembly may have been convened in a desert region, forming a great camp of tents. But during most of the era before the monarchy, the place of central assembly was by a town in the centre of the land. The choice varied from time to time – Shechem in the early days, Shiloh at the end; other places which had their turn included Bethel, Mizpah, and Gilgal near the Jordan crossing. Such important sanctuaries have often bequeathed to the Old Testament their own peculiar traditions reflecting stories of their origins and local customs. Sometimes these places returned to prominence in later periods; the oldest has proved the most enduring, for the Samaritans have continued to celebrate the Passover on Mount Gerizim above Shechem to this day.

Sacred buildings were relatively slight, since much of the proceedings took place in surrounding open courts, for example, the sacrifices burnt on altars. The ancient practice of setting up tall stones was continued; such pillars were said to be witnesses of Israel's pledges to God, reminders of her commitment in the covenant. But the most important symbol of the central sanctuary was the ark of the covenant, a portable chest which apparently contained tablets inscribed with the laws of the covenant and which was also imagined as a footstool before God's throne, a sign of his invisible but powerful presence.

The Philistines captured the ark in battle and proceeded to devastate its sanctuary at Shiloh. The stories about its return to Israel and how David eventually brought it to the newly conquered city of Jerusalem (c.1000 BC) seem to derive from the Jerusalem sanctuary's own account of its foundation; that this account was re-enacted at Jerusalem in regular services of reconsecration may be concluded also from Ps.132 (see below). As the new home of the ark, Jerusalem was now able to rise to predominance as Israel's place of worship. The ark made it the focus of the religion of all the tribes, while in addition it was the seat of David's dynasty, which claimed an everlasting commission to rule with and for divine right. A millennium of pre-Israelite tradition had already invested the place with a rich ideology (cf. Gen.14.18–20). The new circumstances brought a potent synthesis of ideas in which the old Israelite conception of God was decisive, though developed in new directions.

Some ceremonies used to be performed at the spring of Gihon in the valley below Jerusalem's east wall. From here one could ascend the hill which overlooked the city of David from the north. This may have been the 'high place' used for worship by the pre-Israelite population; at all events, it was chosen by David as the area for his sanctuary, though he did not himself erect important buildings on it. This latter step was taken by his son Solomon who constructed an impressive complex of temple and royal buildings set in spacious courts.

The temple itself was an oblong building consisting of three rooms in a line from east to west. The entrance was at the eastern end, and outside it were two great free-standing pillars. These were made of bronze and crowned with ornamented capitals; they were named 'Jachin' and 'Boaz', but their significance remains disputed. The entrance gave access to the first of the temple's three rooms, the porch or entrance hall. Passing through this, one entered the second and much the largest room, a kind of nave. Here were found a gold altar for incense, two sets of five candelabra, and a gold table bearing twelve loaves and more incense; the loaves were the 'shewbread', a sign of the covenant of the twelve tribes before the face of God. Beyond this room and approached up a flight of steps was the 'most holy place' or 'holy of holies'. Here in thick darkness were the symbols of God's presence: the ark and the two cherubs, human-headed animal figures with wings outstretched above the ark, representing the heavenly attendants and throne-bearers of God. It is likely that this third room centred over the ancient holy rock, the summit of the hill, as does the Muslim Dome of the Rock today.

Against the outside of the north, west and south walls of the temple was built a series of quite small rooms in three low storeys. These were for the use of the temple staff and for storage. The main altar for sacrifices was probably situated in the open court to the east of the temple. Also in the court was a bronze platform from which the king led the prayers. Other items in the open included an enormous bronze basin of water resting on twelve figures of oxen, and ten smaller basins on wheeled stands. These may have served partly for ceremonial washing, partly in some ritual as symbolic of the sources of rain.

While many details of the temple's construction and furnishing remain obscure, its significance as the 'house of God' is clear enough. Here God was said to dwell, an invisibly enthroned presence. It was as though this holy place became mysteriously identical with the heavenly abode, or as though God filled it with an extension of his own person (in biblical terms, 'putting his name there'). And so the place could be regarded poetically as the summit of all creation constructed by God himself, as the paradise-centre, or as a rocky nucleus of the cosmos standing firm amidst chaotic seas.

With these developments, Jerusalem's role as 'the city of God', the supreme 'joy of the whole earth' (Ps.48), was well established, and her royal festivals had great influence on the

form of the people's devotion. When the northern provinces broke with Solomon's successor (*c*.931 BC), their rebel king Jeroboam gave the honour of principal sanctuary to Bethel near his southern border, supplemented in the north by Dan near the Jordan's springs. He timed their chief festival (in the autumn) a month later than Jerusalem's, as though not to risk direct competition. He appointed new priests and for signs of the divine presence he provided bull-images. In all this, as with David and his successors, we see how the kings had chief responsibility for the conduct of worship, the priests being generally subordinate.

Mention of the bull-images reminds us that the severe standards of the religion descended from Moses were often threatened by other religions in the environment, at whose sanctuaries might be found images of gods, male and female sacred prostitutes, and sacrifices of children. Sometimes Jerusalem itself succumbed to such influences, particularly when the area was dominated by Assyria and Babylonia. But there were also times of reformation, and the reforms of the Judaean kings Hezekiah and Josiah included the restriction of worship to the Jerusalem temple alone. Josiah's drastic suppression of other cults (*c*.622 BC) established Jerusalem's position as the sole sanctuary, a status further confirmed in the years following the exile. (The rival sister-religion of the Samaritans persisted at Shechem, however, and we know of two cases where Jews in Egypt had their own temple for a time, at Elephantine and Leontopolis.)

The centuries of Jerusalem's sole legitimacy also saw the growth of Jewish settlements abroad. Obviously the chances of making pilgrimage to her festivals would not be enough to sustain the religion of such a far-flung community. In addition to the central sacrificial cult, it was necessary to allow practices of prayer and instruction in local gatherings. We have a few glimpses of such gatherings in the exile, but the well-organized system of local synagogues is not clearly attested until towards New Testament times.

Solomon's temple was razed to the ground by the Babylonians in 587 BC. But their successors, the Persians, supported its refounding. The second temple, less splendid, was dedicated in 515 BC. Soon we hear of a period of stagnation and cynicism which affected many priests (Mal.1.6 f.). Notable reforms, however, were achieved under Nehemiah and Ezra some time after 445 BC. Under the Hellenistic empire of Antiochus Epiphanes (175–163 BC), the temple was for a few years forced into the style of the imperial religion and the laws of Moses were suppressed. With the triumph of the Maccabees, orthodoxy was restored. The temple prospered. Herod the Great, great certainly in his buildings, sought to please his Jewish subjects by undertaking a magnificent reconstruction (20 BC). One of the wonders of the world, it had scarcely been completed when it was destroyed in the war against Rome (AD 70). But the vast area of its courts and parts of their outer walls remain clearly in evidence today. The ancient memories seem to live on in the beautiful Muslim shrines and earnest worship which still adorn the courts; the summit of living rock is gracefully sheltered by the Dome of the Rock, as once it may have been by Solomon's 'most holy place'. Nearby, Jewish pilgrims still pray at the outer wall of the court, the 'Wailing Wall', and Christians of all races venerate the site of Jesus' sacrifice. Thus tangibly, but also in the realm of the human mind, Jerusalem lives on as the supreme place of worship, the 'city of God', the symbol of Paradise.

Seasons of Worship

In spite of variations in emphasis through a long history, Israelite worship generally retained a pattern of three pilgrimage festivals a year, which were understood to have been directly ordained by God. They were anchored in the agricultural seasons, but were also interpreted as commemorative renewals of the great events in which the community's life and religion had originated.

The festival in March–April was really a combination of two observances, the night of *Passover* and the week of *Unleavened Bread*. The Passover may go back to a protective ceremony carried out by semi-nomadic shepherds before their annual migration from the desert towards the cultivated fringes; on a night of full-moon a lamb was consumed in each tent-family and the equipment smeared with the blood to ward off evil, before the camp was broken up in haste. For Israel it became a commemoration of the night when God brought death to the land of her oppressors and passed over the Israelite households marked with the sacrificial blood, who then departed in haste with their flocks (Ex.12). The Passover in itself was an observance in the family circle rather than a pilgrimage festival, and it is accordingly not mentioned in early festival calendars. It comes into prominence towards the end of the monarchy, when it is linked with the pilgrimage festival of Unleavened Bread. This latter was a week originally in celebration of the earliest harvesting, that of the barley; the first cuttings, and first-born animals too, would be presented in the sanctuary, so that the rest could be taken for human use without arrogance. The week was marked by a ban on leaven, as though to avoid contaminating the new crop with the old. When the festival came to be interpreted as a commemoration of the exodus, the unleavened bread suggested the haste of the meal in Passover night.

In May–June fell the festival of *Weeks*, so called because it was counted seven weeks after the preceding festival. It is also called Harvest, and in fact it marked the harvest of wheat with offerings of the first cuttings. Originally a one-day observance, it was later expanded to a week. It was slower than the other festivals to be interpreted as a commemoration of Israel's early history, but eventually, before New Testament times, it was related to the making of the covenant.

In September–October fell the autumnal festival sometimes called *Ingathering* or *Tabernacles*. The late fruit harvest was completed and all produce had to be taken in and stored as the long summer drought might soon end. Ancient festivities included the dancing of maidens in the vineyards and the drinking of wine. The 'tabernacles' or booths, in which the pilgrims resided, originated in the temporary shelters of branches erected in the harvest fields and vineyards. But they came to be equated with the tents of the ancestors in the desert, as the festival was used to commemorate the Exodus and the revelation on Mount Sinai. Although this festival is listed third and its month eventually counted as the seventh (as in the Babylonian calendar), it fell at the time of the new agricultural year in Canaan. It is interesting that an inscription of about the twelfth century BC found at Gezer lists 'Ingathering' as the first of the activities of the agricultural year. A great concern of the festival, then, would be to pray that the imminent rainy season, the indispensable prelude to cultivation and growth, should not fail, as it sometimes did. (Note the reflection of this festal theme in Zech.14.16 f. The Mishnah, a commentary on the Jewish Law, tells us that water was brought up each day of the festival from the spring Gihon and poured over the altar – an acted prayer for rain.) In general, then, this season was a time to look again at the foundations of life, to seek cleansing and renewed relationship with God, and the gifts of life that could then ensue.

The indications are that this festival was the most important of the three at least until the end of the monarchy. As celebrated by the league of tribes at Shechem, Shiloh, etc, it served especially to reinforce their commitment to the covenant. As celebrated at Jerusalem under the kings, it served in addition to show the place of the Davidic ruler and of Jerusalem in God's designs. The hymns of the Jerusalem festival represented God especially as the true king of all creation, subduing all harmful and turbulent forces and richly blessing the processes of life. Just as an element of drama was used (and still is) to re-create the experience of the Passover night, so too the special themes of the autumnal festival were dramatized in ceremonial movements and recitations. The malevolent forces were represented once more as overthrown, the purposes of God with David and Jerusalem confirmed again, while the worshippers hailed God as the eternal king newly revealed. By such drama, the traditions of ancient salvation became a living part of the present joy of the festival. And because of the contrast with the actual sorry state of things, this festival experience of perfection had also a prophetic quality, pointing forward to a new era of salvation still to come.

In addition to the great pilgrimage festivals, there were many other regular observances. At the temple the priests presented offerings every morning and evening. There were additional offerings for the weekly rest-day, the *sabbath*, and for the first day of every month, the day of the new moon. Great events might be commemorated on their anniversaries, as was the Babylonians' destruction of the temple; two commemorations of the later period are still observed: *Hanukkah*, which celebrates the reconsecration of the temple in 164 BC under Judas Maccabaeus, and *Purim*, which remembers the deliverance described in rather embellished form in the book of Esther. In times of crisis (war, famine, etc.) a special day of prayer was decreed, and the people gathered at the sanctuary to implore divine intervention.

The observance of the *sabbath* was not specially bound to the rites at the sanctuary; it was a matter of resting in one's house 'to the Lord', giving rest also to servants and beasts of burden, and imitating God's rest in the creation story (Gen.2.2 f.). Such consecrated rest was a holding back of domineering tendencies and acquisitiveness; the one day devoted to God signified basically that all days belonged to him and were held in trust. This intention emerges clearly in other observances related to the sabbath, – the sabbath year and the year of Jubilees. The *sabbath year* was practised probably in the early period, before agriculture had become such a central part of the tribal economy. Every seventh year the land was left uncultivated, its free growth being left for the poor; other acts of restoration were added, the annulling of debts, the freeing of slaves, and perhaps also some redistribution of land. Similar practices characterized the *year of Jubilees*, which was the fiftieth year, marking the completion of seven sabbath years. In the conditions of a complex economy, these sabbatical years fell into neglect, but they had represented a noble ideal: recognition of the sovereign rights of God, the checking of man's thrust to self-aggrandizement, a new deal for the poor and down-trodden, consideration for the other species of life on the planet.

Little is known about set times of individual prayer. Muslims observe three or five set times of prayer daily and bow down in the direction of Mecca. The Jews had similar observances, praying at morning, noon, and evening, and turning towards the 'most holy place' of the temple.

Leaders of Worship

The Davidic kings held the chief authority over the affairs of the temple. They were supreme not only in material matters, but also in leading the national worship. After the end of the monarchy the senior priest of the temple, the 'high priest', gradually acquired much of the dignity that had belonged to the king.

All sanctuaries had a staff of sacred officials. Such offices were largely hereditary, and as various family guilds developed, there was a complicated history of rivalries. The original lay tribe of Levi was probably distinct from an ancient priestly order called 'Levites'; these Levites seem to have been priests among the invading Israelites and functioned around the ark. They could not always establish themselves against sanctuary staffs of other origins (descended from pre-Israelite worship, or appointed by Davidic or northern kings, etc.). The priestly clan of Zadok prevailed over them at Jerusalem, and in the north, too, they were ousted by men appointed by the rebel king Jeroboam. It is thought that they still continued to cherish their ancient traditions descended from Moses and were able to influence the reforms of Josiah. In post-exilic Jerusalem, however, they were firmly accorded an inferior status as guardians and musicians.

The priest was an expert authority on matters for which special sacred knowledge was required. He gave guidance and decisions both on matters of religious ceremony and also in hard cases of ordinary law; he was the exponent of the laws of God. His pronouncements might rest on the basis of priestly traditions or be reached by the casting of the sacred lot ('Urim and Thummim'), which in some way yielded an oracular decision on the question propounded. He was a father and counsellor to God's people. The proceedings at the sanctuary were his special care, including the sacrifices. He lived by receiving a share of the people's offerings. However, sacrifice was not the principal task of his office, and especially in early times certain sacrifices might be offered by any head of the family.

The authorities of the Jerusalem temple under the monarchy included prophets as well as priests. Moreover, the prophetic books contain much material related to worship (hymns, laments, etc.), just as the texts of worship in the psalms contain prophetic oracles. It is notable, too, that minor priestly orders of the later temple are often depicted as inspired prophets. All in all, it is clear that while prophecy was not restricted to service in the sanctuaries, it had an important role

there. Prophets had a place there alongside the priests as ministers of God. Mediators of revelation like the priests, they were distinguished in that their very personalities were the means of inspiration; exalted states of consciousness gave them perceptions beyond the ordinary. Pilgrims to the sanctuaries would consult them and seek a word from God by them. Even in the formal ceremonies of worship they seem to have had a part, especially in bringing divine messages to the assembly through their sudden inspiration. Sometimes a great prophet might take the lead in renewing the covenant with God, in the manner of a Moses, Samuel or Elijah (see Part III, Section 10, pp. 139–145).

Another speciality among the servants of the sanctuary was that of music and chanting. There were hereditary guilds, connected closely with the priests and prophets, who composed and sang the poetic hymns and prayers and executed the carefully prescribed musical accompaniment. Our book of psalms is largely a deposit of their traditions.

Sacrifices in Worship

A prominent feature of worship was the presentation of offerings from the produce of fields and flocks. It is difficult to win a clear picture of the types of offering and their significances, as a great variety of traditions and developments has been woven together in our present sources. The central idea is that of relationship; the presentation and acceptance of the offerings are a visible sign of the bond between God and his worshippers. In response to God's own direction, his people present their gifts in costly obedience. Their offerings mean in part a self-giving, an act of self-deprivation in honour of the God to whom all belongs. Thus they give themselves in their gifts and are accepted. Such gestures of relationship imply the removal of any barrier that might have existed; the idea of the removal of sin is thus present with all the offerings, although some are explicitly concerned with this.

Distinguishing the main types roughly, we may note first those which especially had the nature of gifts. These might be vegetable or animal, and were generally burnt on the altar, as it were sent up to heaven in the form of smoke. They were sometimes offered with intercessions or in fulfilment of a vow. They expressed dependence, reverence, gratitude. With these we can consider the first-fruits of the crops and the first-born of animals, offered in acknowledgment of God's first claim as the true lord and disposer of all creation; only then was the way open for ordinary human use of these species. A primitive Canaanite custom of including also the first-born of human beings was replaced in Israel by the system of 'redemption': the child, like the whole race, belonged to God, but his life was spared and replaced by the sacrifice of an animal.

Then there were sacrifices which had the character of fellowship-meals. Originally all slaughter of animals was reserved for sacred ceremonies, a restriction which had to be abandoned when the numerous local shrines were abolished. Groups of worshippers would share in the meal at the sanctuary after the best parts of the beast had first been offered to God by fire. Such a sacred banquet signified the closest ties of trust between the deity and his worshippers, and between one worshipper and another. It is not surprising, then, that such sacrifices accompanied rites of covenant-making (Ex.24.3 f.; Ps.50.3). 'Sacrifices of thanks-giving' might have the character either of gifts or of communion meals, but they were specially designed as an occasion for testimony to some specific deliverance. Such offerings might be in fulfilment of promises made in the time of need.

Finally, we may note the sacrifices which were particularly related to purification and atonement: the sin-offering and the guilt-offering. With these the worshipper prayed for the removal of his sin and impurity. Such purification was especially the theme of the Day of Atonement, when expiatory sacrifices were made for sanctuary, leader and people. This was the occasion of the peculiar rite described in Lev.16.20–22, when a goat was driven into the wilderness, symbolically carrying into oblivion the year's burden of sin.

There were times when the worshippers distorted the purpose of sacrifices. They had to be warned not to suppose that God needed them as food, nor that abundant sacrifices could obscure God's moral requirements. Some prophets indeed yearned for the days before sacrifice, under Canaanite influence, had come

to such proportions. Nevertheless, the system represented much of value. Above all it demonstrated the costly basis of fellowship between God and man.

Glimpses of Worship

The narratives of the Old Testament frequently give us valuable glimpses of worship. Some outstanding examples are noted in the following paragraphs.

The ancient sagas of Genesis acquired a rich multiplicity of meaning through their long history, and part of this meaning is often related to customs of worship. Thus the story of Cain and Abel (Gen.4.2–7) shows two types: the semi-nomadic shepherds who sacrifice their first-born animals, sending up the choicest portions in fire on the altar, and the settled cultivators whose offering is from the produce of their fields. The former proudly think of their simple mode of life as more pleasing to God. In some way an indication is given to the worshippers (through the word of the priest?) whether the deity accepts or rejects their offering; it is fundamental that the acceptance depends on well-doing.

Again, in the profound story of Abraham's sacrifice (Gen.22), we can detect how the practice at some sanctuary of sparing the first-born child by offering instead a lamb, was justified by reference to Abraham. The willingness to give all is thus still asserted, while it is recognized that child-sacrifice is not the will of God.

The story of Jacob's dream (Gen.28.10–22) contains elements from the traditions of the ancient sanctuary of Bethel, traditions which explained to worshippers its wonderful credentials. Its anointed stone was a sign of God's presence; the place was a gateway of heaven, a place of direct communication between heaven and earth, symbolized perhaps by some stair-like building suggestive of a ladder up to heaven. The story of Jacob's experience thus gave the worshipper at Bethel confidence that here his prayers would reach heaven; here God himself was near.

Several stories of Joshua reflect customs of worship. The crossing of the Jordan (Josh.3–4) is depicted as a religious ceremony ending at the sanctuary of Gilgal and commemorating the crossing of the Red Sea in the exodus. One can trace here a regular observance around Passover time (Josh.5.11), with a procession of the ark over the Jordan and ceremonies around the sacred pillars, the intention being to re-enact the exodus scene. Close to Gilgal were found the ruins of Jericho; the famous story of the capture of Jericho (Josh.6) may have developed out of similar festal processions, the priests bearing the ark round the ruined site in commemoration of the conquest of Canaan.

The story of the tribal assembly in Josh.24 seems to have been shaped by the proceedings of regular festivals in the tribal period. From it we can see how representatives of all the twelve tribes assembled at Shechem. There was a presiding figure who, in the tradition of Moses and Joshua, mediated between God and Israel in the renewing of the covenant. He relays words of God in the manner of a prophet. The assembly understands that God himself has come to confront them and speak through the mouth of the mediator. In this way God's speech begins by recalling his dealings with the fathers, calling, saving and establishing them in Canaan. The mediator adds his own exhortation, calling upon the assembled Israel to renounce all other cults and enter into God's exclusive covenant. The assembly expresses assent. The leader gives further exhortations, stressing the formidable nature of the under-taking, and the congregation further responds with assent: 'We will serve the Lord. He is our God.' Their decision is then solemnly attested like an oath. Some ceremony marks the putting away of other gods (burial or destruction of images?) and the covenant is formally con-cluded. The leader rehearses the covenant laws, and a sacred stone is regarded as a witness that the people have pledged themselves to keep them. The leader then dismisses the assembly, no doubt with a blessing.

A further glimpse of these ancient ceremonies is afforded by Deut.27. The scene again is Shechem and the leader in the tradition of Moses is again prominent with his exhortations. But a picturesque detail is added. The obliga-tions of the law are underlined by the division of the assembly on to the over-looking moun-tain-sides. One party stands on Mount Gerizim to the south of Shechem's natural amphi-theatre, while priests among them pronounce blessings to take effect on the obedient (cf. Deut.28.1–6). The other party stands on Mount Ebal to the north, where priests declare calamity for the unfaithful; the sins listed are especially those which easily escape human detection (27.15 f.). To each curse the con-gregation answers 'Amen'.

Valuable glimpses into the annual festivals are also given by the story of the birth of Samuel (I Sam.1–2). In particular we see the occasion from the angle of a pious family of pilgrims and their domestic problems. Once every year, probably in the autumn, they make pilgrimage to the festival at Shiloh, where the presence of God as 'the Lord of hosts' was marked by the ark. The head of the family sacrificed; the fat portion was to be presented by fire to the Lord, the rest boiled in a cauldron in preparation for a sacred meal. Parts would then be due to the priests, and the rest was to be carefully apportioned to each member of the family. As it happened, the sons of the chief priest were greedily disregarding the law, taking more than their share, and even before the part for God had been presented; their misconduct with the sacred women may reflect the influence of Canaanite religion, in which sacred prostitutes had a place. Signi-ficantly, however, the corruption of the authorities did not prevent the pious pilgrims from valuing the festival as a true encounter with God. As the autumnal festival was the time to pray for the new year of fertility and growth in fields and flocks, so also prayer was made for the blessing of the human family, and the childless wife would make an earnest plea. Hannah's prayer is strengthened by a vow (I Sam.1.11). The aged senior priest, seated in honour by the entrance of the temple, mistook her emotional praying for drunkenness, since much wine flowed at that festival. But realizing his error, he was able to give her an indication that God had accepted her prayer (1.17, translate 'will grant'). The story thus illustrates how a family, and indeed an individual, found place for personal needs within the framework of the national festival. Soon judgment was to fall on the insolent priests; even the atoning power of sacrifice could not avail for so great an offence (3.14).

In I Sam.4–6 and II Sam.6 it seems that the historian has drawn on the sacred story which went with a regular ceremony celebrating and renewing the foundation of Jerusalem's sanc-tuary (see below on Ps.132, pp. 157 f.). In II Sam.6

we see how the progress of the ark along its various stations was accompanied by dancing, music and sacrifice. The participants represent the entire people, and the king himself takes the leading priestly role, dressed in the priestly apron ('ephod'), dancing with all his might, sacrificing, pronouncing the benediction. The procession of the ark up to the sanctuary seems to symbolize the triumphant ascent of God, fresh from the rout of his foes, to his heavenly palace; the ark deposited under the wings of the cherubs points to the mysterious sanctuary-presence of the Lord of hosts enthroned in glory (6.2). The much later passage, I Chron.15–16, pictures the ceremonies with more interest in the psalms and music used on such occasions.

In II Chron.20 we have a good example of a holy convocation in face of a crisis. King Jehoshaphat (873–849 BC), hearing of an enemy advancing from the south, decreed a fast and a national assembly for worship and intercession at the temple. The king took the lead in offering persuasive prayer. One of the temple ministers was then inspired to deliver an oracle promising victory. The service ended with prostration 'before the Lord' and the loudest possible hymn-singing. As the army went out to battle next day, the king declared that if they believed the word of God given by the prophet, they would succeed, as in fact they did.

Shortly after 445 BC, a special service was held to dedicate the encompassing walls of Jerusalem which the new governor Nehemiah had built. As described in Neh.12.3 f., the arrangements for the service were ordered by the governor. Two parties of notables were formed, each headed by sacred choirs and musicians. After ceremonies of purification, the double procession was commenced from the middle of the western wall. One party proceeded along the top of the wall southwards, while the other likewise moved northwards. Eventually they met on the eastern side, turning into the temple there. Sacrifices were offered and hymns were sung with the greatest volume. One may see here how such an encompassing procession is meant to trace out an area of God's blessing; the city's rampart is made a wall of divine salvation.

Finally, we may note a vivid glimpse of worship around 200 BC. In the Apocrypha, Ecclus.50, we hear of a high priest, to whom falls the duty of the earlier kings to maintain the temple buildings. Not less than royal is the splendour of his appearance as he leads the ceremonies on the Day of Atonement, emerging from the innermost shrine like a luminary in the heavens. The glowing description reflects the author's joy in worship as much as the actual spectacle. We hear of the high priest robing afresh and mounting to the altar in the open court. Assisted by a company of priests, he burns sacrifices to the Lord on the altar and pours out a wine-offering at the base. The priests shout and blow trumpets. The presence of God is now most keenly sensed, and the people fall on their faces. The singers sing psalms. Prayers are raised. The people bow again as the high priest concludes with a benediction; his lips convey a blessing 'from the Most High'.

The Psalms

The psalms deserve a special place in the present study. As poetic pieces generally intoned or chanted in worship, they often reflect ceremonies which they accompanied, and even more, the thoughts and beliefs which filled the minds of the worshippers. While the setting of many psalms in festal worship is clear, the exact contexts and sequences remain uncertain. In spite of many disputed points, however, it will be seen that the psalms do reveal the main ingredients of the festal experience; the grouping of the psalms below relates especially to the autumnal festival in royal Jerusalem.

The chief feature of the poetry of the psalms is called 'parallelism'; most verses fall into two (sometimes three) parts, which are parallel in thought and expression. In one type ('synonymous') the two parts are saying the same thing in different words: 'O come let us sing to the Lord/let us make a joyful noise to the rock of our salvation.' In the second type ('antithetic'), the duplication takes the form of a contrast: 'The Lord lifts up the downtrodden/ he casts the wicked to the ground.' In a third type ('synthetic' or 'formal'), the twofold structure is maintained, but in fact there is only a single statement: 'I have set my king/on Zion my holy hill.' Yet another variety has been called 'stair-like'; the second part repeats some words from the first and then adds a fresh element: 'Ascribe to the Lord O heavenly beings/ascribe to the Lord glory and strength,' or 'The voice of the Lord breaks the cedars/the Lord breaks the cedars of Lebanon.' However, many other variations are possible, and the patterns can also be woven through groups of verses (e.g., Pss.114.1 f.; 124.1–5).

Little agreement has been reached on how the Hebrew poets used metre. Their use of parallelism, however, imposed a disciplined rhythm of thought, which produces, even in English translation, some balance and rhythm of sound. Each part of the Hebrew verse has about three principal words, and even in English the lines are still fairly brief: 'He gives snow like wool/he scatters hoar frost like ashes,' or 'The Lord is near to all who call upon him/to all who call upon him in truth.'

Parallelism enables the poet to achieve various effects. The repetition may express emphasis or excitement. It helps to clarify the thought. It gives variations of pace, the progress of thought being sometimes held back by sheer repetition, then hurried on with single statements. Sometimes the first part leaves you guessing, and satisfaction comes only at the very end: 'Than the thunders of the great waters/than the lordly breakers of the sea/more mighty on high is the Lord' (Ps.93.4).

The wording of Hebrew poetry is unpretentious. Qualifying adjectives in the original are rare; a genitive relation is preferred: 'king of glory', 'fountain of life', 'oil of gladness', 'beasts of the forest'. Traditional vocabulary is used again and again. Especially common are the apparently moral terms, which usually revolve around the notion of covenant or established bond of goodwill: 'steadfast-love', 'mercy', 'truth', 'peace', 'righteous(ness)', 'faithful(ness)', 'upright', 'saints', etc. Correct interpretation here depends on remembering the background of covenant thought (especially religion as a covenant of the king or nation with God) and on consideration of the context. Thus the various 'moral' qualities will usually refer to fidelity to covenantal promises or loyalty to the other partner. The words for states of happiness and well-being likewise refer to the harmony arising from a sound covenant relationship. Good passages for practice in such interpretation are Pss.18.20–25; 85.7–13 (including personification); 89.1–5, 14–16; 101.1 f.; 136. A difficulty of translation is that in themselves the verbs are ambiguous in time-reference; the choice of past, present or future in English depends on the interpretation of the whole context, and sometimes uncertainty persists (cf. below on Ps.101, p. 162).

Most psalms have superscriptions. Since these are problematic in meaning and origin, they are best left aside in the present study.

1. *The Journey to the Festival*

Prominent in the experience of Israelite worshippers was the journey, often long, to the central sanctuary. Hardship was offset by the fellowship along the way and above all by the anticipation of a festival so rich in meaning. There are several psalms which some scholars think were sung on the journey. Although their place seems rather to have been within the festival, such psalms certainly tell us something about the pilgrimage and arrival.

Psalm 122

1–2. The keynote is gladness, the thrill of entering the presence of God by visiting 'the house of the Lord'. The singer expresses the typical feelings when the pilgrims from a particular area joined together to commence their journey. Translate: 'Our feet are now standing . . .'; this expresses the wonder of finding oneself at last within the holy city. (RSV here relates the psalm to the end of the festival.)

3–5. The psalm now addresses Jerusalem appreciatively. A stirring sight from the encompassing mountains, the compactly walled city seems to symbolize the fellowship of the worshippers. It is loved not for any outer grandeur, but as the place God has chosen as the centre for all Israel to converge and invoke his name (and hence his presence) in the festival; the place from which his healthful order ('judgment') should radiate, especially through the rule of the successors of David.

6–9. The worshippers are exhorted to pray for Jerusalem, for her safety and well-being. There is much play here on sounds and meaning, several words echoing 'Jerusalem', especially *šālōm,* 'peace'. The love of this particular city exceeds ordinary affection; it is cherished as the focus of communion between men and God.

155

Psalm 84

1–3. The singer expresses the emotion of pilgrims approaching the temple at Jerusalem. They come like men weak with thirst to a spring of living water, or like a bird which finds the perfect nesting-place.

4–7. As the preceding admiration of the temple is really a way of praising God, so now is the appreciation of the good fortune of the temple's ministers (v.4) and of the pilgrims (vv.5–7). The pilgrims' journey may be arduous, but the strength which will be given in the great meeting with God is already reaching them in advance. Their minds are set on the 'highways to Zion (= Jerusalem)', probably the sacred route up the temple hill used by the festal processions. Whether there was an actual place called 'Baca' is not sure, but in any case the reference is to a drought-stricken region. The belief was that where the pilgrims passed, God would soon give the blessing which was prayed for especially at this autumn festival, the 'early rain' which would begin the new year of growth. Toiling onward, 'they go from strength to strength' as they draw near to the place where God will be 'seen'. In the religions which used statues of the gods, the climax of the festival was the unveiling of the image. In Israel such images were forbidden; the divine presence was invisible to all but an inspired prophet (e.g., Isa.6). But the sense of God's nearness in the worship was still so strong, that the old concrete language of 'seeing' (him, his face, his beauty, etc.) was still used.

8–9. Prayer is offered that God should look favourably upon the king ('our shield', 'thine anointed'). The phrase 'God of Jacob' emphasizes the tradition of the old association of the twelve tribes, which David carefully carried over into Jerusalem's worship.

10–12. The conclusion returns to praise of God, partly again by way of admiring the happiness of those close to him. The contrast is better if 'doorkeeper' is not a reference to the high sacred office, but to some lowly station, perhaps even to beggars by the temple gate. The blessings which God bestows in his temple, however, are only for those who 'walk uprightly' – in integrity. The basic requirement is 'trust', a deep committal to God. All in all, the psalm gives an excellent conspectus of the features of the autumnal festival under the Davidic kings: the great central shrine, heir of the old covenant traditions; praise of God as king; his self-disclosure; his rich gifts, especially rain; prayer for the dynasty.

Psalm 15

1. Ancient sanctuaries had rules about fitness for admission. In this psalm, which may be connected with ceremonies of entry, some of the requirements for taking part in temple worship are rehearsed, the emphasis being on a sincere and fair way of living. A direct question on the matter is put to God; his answer will be given back through his ministers (for this procedure cf. Mal.2.5–7; Zech.7.1 f.; II Sam.21.1; Micah 6.6–8).

2–5. The answer is in ten parts, like the Ten Commandments. (i) God's worshipper must live in whole-hearted loyalty to God, doing his will. (ii) His words must be sincere. (iii) He does not spread slander. (iv) He does no harm to his fellow. (v) He does not throw cruel words at him. (vi) He does not 'go along with' evil men (or translate v.4a 'In his own eyes he is small and of no reputation'). (vii) He honours true followers of God. (viii) He keeps his promises, even to his own disadvantage. (ix) He does not exact interest on a loan he has made to an impoverished family. (x) No bribe can buy his assistance in condemning the innocent. God's answer concludes that one who so lives will not only be welcome to the temple; he will never be 'moved' – cast down to destruction. As when his feet stand on the rock of the temple hill, so his whole life will be lived on an unshakable basis. Such then were the teachings put before those who would come to the festival as guests in God's 'tent' or 'house'.

2. *Acts of Penitence and Purification*

We have seen that the worshippers had a vivid belief that they were coming before the face of God, and also that his standards for human conduct were high. They could not come without trepidation because of their unworthiness. Confession of sin and prayer for forgiveness were therefore among the early proceedings of the festival. There were ceremonies which expressed the divine grace of purification and atonement.

Psalm 130

1–6. A leading voice prays for all the people, crying to the Lord from 'the depths', the

Underworld which in the imagination stands for the lowest condition – corruption, darkness and death. The appeal is for the divine forgiveness, which alone enables sinful man to stand and to worship. All concentrate in faith and yearning for the coming of God with his word of reconciliation, which was perhaps to be expressed in the ceremonies as dawn broke. 'Watchmen' were posted to signal the rise of the sun above the eastern mountains, the moment for the dawn sacrifice.

7–8. The singer now addresses the worshippers, who represent the entire society. He urges them to wait trustingly for the Lord. The long vigil in the festival is a model of the religious life: men endure long ordeals of suffering, holding to the hope in the faithfulness of God as redeemer. He will at last deliver them from the slavery of sin.

Psalm 51

1–2. In asking for his own cleansing, the representative leader has in mind the healing of all the community (v. 18). He believes that God alone can wash away the stain of his sins.

3–5. He confesses his sinfulness in the general terms suitable for public prayer repeated regularly. He faces it squarely and recognizes it as in essence a breaking of faith with God. That he was born in sin (v. 5) means that he feels his whole existence to be marked by it; he is sinful in the roots of his being, so that only a miracle can redeem him.

6–9. He resumes his prayer for forgiveness and purification. Verse 7 refers to a ceremony of purification in which water was sprinkled from sprigs of the hyssop; under such outward gestures were signified the will and power of God to purify and restore his people. The 'broken bones' mean the state of sorrow and punishment which is to be transformed.

10–12. Corresponding to his earlier recognition of the deep pervasiveness of his sin, he describes the restoration for which he continues to pray as virtually a new creation. The inner man, all the inner forces of his being, must be made new. The reference to God's 'holy Spirit' and 'presence' refer to the divine presence in the temple and so in the centre of God's covenanted people; a continuing union with his world, which draws it into his own perfection. Israel's leader prays that he may be made fit for this union and not cast out; may

divine aid direct and sustain him, ennobling his soul (v. 12b).

13–15. He promises that when he is restored and cleansed of his guilt ('bloodguiltiness'), he will testify openly to God's saving power, leading many to follow the same way to healing.

16–19. Some scholars think that these verses reflect the exilic period when the usual sacrifices were suspended; a service of lamentation is offered instead, until the rebuilding of the temple will permit a return to normal. We can, however, give an explanation which fits the usual services. The singer asserts that the sacrifice of animals is not enough in itself to make atonement for sin (only for accidental errors, according to Num.15.22–31). The people must also offer true repentance, a readiness to be remade according to God's will. If God accepts them and gives them joy, they will offer many sacrifices in glad testimony, a service pleasing to him (v. 18 'rebuild': rather 'build up', 'make prosperous').

3. *The Resanctification of the Temple*

The rites of purification were applied to the temple as well as the people. As the festival progressed, they could sing again: 'Holiness adorns thy house' (Ps.93.5). The ground of communion with God was thus re-established; he had made firm again the foundations of happy life. The temple and 'Zion' (the holy city) could again be described as clothed in holy splendour.

Psalm 132

1–5. Part of the ceremonies renewing the sanctuary was, it seems, a re-enactment of David's bringing the ark to Jerusalem (II Sam.6). This psalm goes with the re-enactment. It begins by praying that in favour of David's dynasty may be counted the self-denying zeal with which David had set himself to secure a sanctuary fit for the ark and the presence of God.

6–7. The voices here seem to take the role of David's men who had been sent to find the ark. They report back how they heard of it in 'Ephrathah' and found it in 'the fields of Jaar'. Ephrathah may be a name of David's hometown, Bethlehem; or, like the fields of Jaar, it may be in the area of Kiriath-jearim, where the ark had been residing (I Sam.7.2). In response to this news, the cry goes up to hurry to the place and make obeisance before this symbol of the divine presence.

8–10. Having now come before the ark in an outlying place, the company begins the procession with sacrifices, singing and dancing into Jerusalem. As the priests lift the ark, they echo the ancient prayer, 'Arise O Lord!' (Num.10.35). Prayer is made for the priests, for the whole covenanted society (RSV 'saints') and for the present heir on David's throne.

11–18. In answer to the prayer, the prophetic ministers declare the oracle of God. As he has chosen David's dynasty, so also he has chosen Zion. This is where the ark must be taken; this is to be the pre-eminent place of the divine presence, the centre of communion and blessing. The metaphors of the bull's horn and the lamp in v. 17 denote the victorious strength and salvation which God will send through the house of David.

Psalm 87

1–3. The temple is again pure and beautiful, founded by God and chosen by him above all other Israelite sanctuaries. And now to this 'city of God', an oracle is to be spoken, 'glorious things', divine words heavy with meaning for her destiny.

4–7. God is envisaged as writing up the roll of the citizens of his kingdom, recording for each one the name and home-city. The 'citizens' mentioned are personified peoples, and they include some who had once been enemies, such as 'Rahab' (= Egypt). Representing all peoples, they are all recorded in God's register as natives of Zion! Thus the psalm declares that Jerusalem is the nucleus of God's universal society, into which are to be gathered all peoples, even former foes. The singing and dancing of the present festival will then be taken up by them all, praising Zion as the fountain of divine life, the spring of Paradise (cf. Gen. 2.10).

4. God's Battle

Underlying all the joyful songs which were sung in God's honour at the festival is the thought that he appears fresh from a victory. The battle he has waged is a poetic construction, serving to commemorate and renew God's mighty work of creation and ancient salvation. The poetic drama of the festival imagines that all the forces which would harm life have even

now risen up together to make chaos and misery prevail, but God has routed them. This poetic vision embraces both what we should call 'Nature' and 'History'. It understands the battle as the mighty deeds of the Creator against a dragon-like chaos, a dark and raging ocean; but also as God's victory over raging nations. Thus year by year, the worshippers dramatically reassert the basis of their hope in all aspects of life – the power and goodness of God, the king of all. In addition to the following psalms, we may note the theme of the battle underlying creation in 74.12–17; 89.5–18; 93.3 f.; 104.7–9.

Psalm 46

1–3. The chaos-powers are imagined as beating upon the world of life. The earth rocks (RSV 'change'), the mountains tremble, as the ocean rises with demonic rage. The worshippers declare their faith in the victory of God who is 'very present' in Zion.

4–7. Zion stands firm in the midst of all these assaults; she is pictured as the source of the Paradise river, the centre of the holy power of life, because God is in her. The kingdoms of the world are imagined as joining to attack her, but at the break of morning God will save her (v.5). At his mighty word of rebuke, the enemies collapse.

8–11. The singer surveys the scene after the battle. He has a vision of the whole earth at peace, all weapons smashed and burnt. He sees the Lord exalted in victory and hears his word 'Be still and know that I am God'. The people of God's city triumphantly proclaim the confidence they have through him.

Psalm 48

1–3. Praise is offered for the deliverance signified in the dramatic ceremonies. The fortress-sanctuary of Zion stands once more serene and beautiful, the dwelling of God, the fount of joy for all the living order. ('In the far north': originally a term denoting a Phoenician sacred mountain, but applied now to Jerusalem.)

4–7. It had been imagined how the kings of the nations had swept up to assault God's city, but were overwhelmed by the sight of his glory. His desert wind had smashed their fleets of massive ships. (This image seems to be another adaptation from Phoenicia. 'Ships of Tarshish' may be large vessels developed for the mining trade. See Part III, Section 8, p. 126.)

8–9. The ceremonies have somehow represented this model of deliverance to the ears and eyes of the worshippers. In the temple there has been an acted parable of God's fidelity to his undertakings in the covenant ('we have thought on': rather 'we have made a likeness of').

10–11. The salvation of Zion is thought of as decisive for that of the whole world. The glory of the victorious God shines out far and wide, and his right hand holds the sceptre of victory over all the cosmos.

12–14. The lesson is to be further weighed as a procession winds about the city's unharmed ramparts. Its message is to be recounted through succeeding generations. The God with whom they are covenanted is worthy of all trust; he will lead them to victory over all evil. (Very similar is Ps. 76.)

5. *God's Procession of Victory*

The symbolic victory just treated was further celebrated by a procession up the hill and into the temple like the victory march of a warrior king leading captives and spoil, heralded by messengers, and greeted by dancing and singing women (cf. Ps. 68).

Psalm 24

1–2 The procession approaches the temple gates, dramatically representing the victory-march of God the triumphant king. The victory is here seen in terms of creation: having subdued the primaeval ocean and made it serviceable to life, he has made firm in its midst the inhabited world. Accordingly, he alone is the Lord and Owner of all life.

3–6. At the gates there are exchanges between the procession and the guardians of the threshold. As in Ps. 15, conditions for entry are declared. In v. 3 the inquiry seems to be put from the procession. The guardians answer in vv. 4 f., and perhaps v. 6: worshippers will receive the blessing in the festival if they are doers of right, not worshipping false gods, honouring their commitments. Verse 6, however, may be a confirmatory response from the procession.

7–10. The leader of the procession now calls for the opening of the gates to admit 'the King of glory', the invisible presence being indicated by the ark. The doors are called 'eternal' (RSV 'ancient') because they correspond to the gates

of the heavenly palace. 'Who is the King of glory?' ask the guardians, and are answered by the citation of the special Israelite name for God ('Yahweh') and his titles as supreme conqueror (v. 8). The repetition of this dialogue in vv. 9 f. gives opportunity for still greater emphasis: God as revealed in Israel, he alone is the Creator and Monarch of the cosmos.

6. *The Proclamation of God's Kingship*

With the ark installed once more on Zion, the worshippers' minds are held by the conception of the invisible Lord enthroned above this 'footstool'. By the mighty deeds commemorated earlier, he has established his kingdom; the enemies of life have been put to flight. His victory march was already in celebration of his kingship, but now there is a special proclamation of it, as he is imagined as taking the throne in his temple-palace, manifest to his acclaiming subjects in his robes of glory. Trumpet blasts, prostration, and concerted shouts of homage mark the great moment. The psalms proclaim, 'The Lord now reigns!' or 'has commenced his reign!' It is the experience of God's kingdom as newly begun, a new era, a new world. (In addition to the following psalms, one may connect 29 and 96–100, and more generally 33; 103–4; 145–150.)

Psalm 93

1–2. The formula of proclamation resounds at the outset. The heavenly king is portrayed as radiant in the power which has secured the creation. The drama of worship is presenting eternal realities, established before time itself (v. 2).

3–5. The battle presupposed by the present scene is recalled – the quelling of the waves of chaos, the victory underlying creation. His supremacy asserted, the Creator-king issues 'decrees' which direct and control the elements of the cosmos. The temple is beautiful again with 'holiness', the divine life-power.

Psalm 47

1–5. God has gone up to his temple-throne amid acclamation and the sound of trumpets. All peoples are invited to join in the clapping and cheering. He has exerted his tremendous power (RSV 'is terrible'), establishing his supreme sovereignty. The preceding battle is here linked with the Israelite conquest of

Canaan, but this is seen as part of God's good design for all men.

6–9. Again the call to praise goes out, ecstatically repetitive. The proclamation of the enthronement insists also on God's universal supremacy. Accordingly the worshippers who now give him homage are understood as representative not just of one nation, but of all peoples and rulers ('shields').

7. *The Speech of God*

The enthroned Creator-king now speaks words vibrant with power to effect his will. As we have seen (Ps. 93.5), his creative decrees direct the elements of the cosmos. He also speaks words of promise, warning and judgment to all his subjects (cf. Pss. 75 and 82). Especially does he speak to his covenanted people Israel, as he did on Mount Sinai; and the covenant is thus renewed.

Psalm 95

1–7a. The situation here is as in the previous section. Acclaim is given to God revealed as enthroned Creator. All other powers have been subjugated (v. 3). The worshippers prostrate themselves before the symbols of his throne, conscious of being covenanted under his shepherd-like reign.

7b–11. The prophet who is to utter God's own words introduces them with an earnest, though hardly optimistic wish that the worshippers will take them to heart. The speech of God begins at v. 8. It is a warning that the people should not be insensitive to his will and quick to rebel and disbelieve as was the generation of Moses' time. Strong language (v. 10) expresses how that conduct had brought judgment, exclusion from the promised land. (Meribah and Massah were halting-places in the desert; there are various traditions about what happened there, Ex.15.25; 17.1–7; Num.20.1–13: Deut. 32.51.)

Psalm 81

1–5a. Again the manifest God is acclaimed by the festal throng with shouts and songs and instruments. (According to the calendar of later times, v. 3 would refer to fanfares first on New Year's Day and then at the beginning of Tabernacles a fortnight later; there have been various attempts to explain the Hebrew as referring to only one of these days.) The psalm

stresses that the festival is ordained by God. The prominence of the traditions of the exodus and covenant suggests that the psalm has descended from the days before the monarchy.

5b–16. The prophet first indicates his inspiration, whereby he has heard a mysterious heavenly voice. From v.6 he delivers God's own speech. God recalls his salvation of the people from slavery ('Meribah': see Ps. 95.8, previous column). On the basis of this salvation, he has become their covenanted Lord. He forbids them other gods. He promises them all good things. He yearns that they would walk in his ways and not become estranged like the first generation. The echoing of the words of the revelation on Mount Sinai (especially vv. 9 f.) indicates how this festival renews for the worshippers the original event. Today they also stand before God and can choose to follow him in the way of true life. (A similar psalm is Ps.50.)

8. *The New Year of Growth*

In the land of Canaan a summer drought extends from about May till October. If the following year is to yield crops and pasturage, the winter rains must fall abundantly and in good time. To the ancient inhabitants it seemed that the autumn and winter storms were indeed a war of deliverance waged from heaven. Hence the autumnal festival's themes of God's appearing in triumph were linked with the need for rains and fertility. The worshippers pray that God, who in the service has shown himself king over all the elements, will once again command the rains and give growth and fertility.

Psalm 65

1–4. The opening hymn shows how the festal worship is marked by praise, fulfilment of sacrificial vows, forgiveness of sins, and a drawing close to God to receive blessings.

5–8. The psalm acknowledges the mighty deeds of God as Creator-king, the victory over chaos-seas and raging nations which establishes a joyful cosmos. This is the saving event which the festival has already represented.

9–13. The coming of God now experienced in the festival is seen as the time when he determines the course of the new year and makes preparation for its growth (v. 9). Verse 10 is better translated as a prayer: 'Water its furrows . . .'. The new year is now inaugurated ('crowned') as one to be characterized by God's bounty. The processions with the ark are like the riding of God's storm-chariot through the skies; in its wake will follow a lush growth. Verses 12 f. give a future prospect: soon the parched hills will flow with rain, and a wonderful verdure will quickly appear.

Psalm 126

1–3. The theme is miraculous transformation from national misery to joyful life. The reference here may be primarily to political events. The psalm prepares persuasively for its later petition by recalling how the earlier deliverance spread the fame of Israel's God among the nations.

4–6. The prayer for a new transformation is marked by thoughts of the change in the seasons. The people ask for their circumstances to be transformed as marvellously as the dry desert gullies when they run with winter floods and spring with grass and flowers. Verses 5 f. are perhaps a prophetic speech of assurance: 'Those who sow . . . shall reap . . .'. As harvesting was celebrated with rites of rejoicing, so in ancient times rites of lamentation accompanied the burial of the seed.

Psalm 127

1–2. The worshippers are instructed that only as God is in their work can it prosper. The references to daily tasks may also allude to festal themes: the welfare of this 'house' of the temple, of the city of Zion, and of the fields. (In v. 2 we may render: 'in their sleep'.)

3–5. The pilgrims desire the gift of children, especially sons, who gave much prestige and family strength. They are taught that these are in the gift of the Lord.

Psalm 128

1–4. Blessings are pronounced over worshippers who follow God's teachings. Their fields will yield well. Their wives, too, will bear many children.

5–6. Such are the blessings that go out from the divine presence in Zion, bestowing upon a faithful community long and fruitful life.

9. *God Confirms the Dynasty of David*

If the festival saw the renewal of fundamental things, the office of the Davidic kings could not be left out. For the royal office had become one of the great elements in Israelite religious thought; the king was said to have been raised up over mankind to be God's viceroy on earth, equipped with holy wisdom and insight; God's covenant with David had entered the foundations of the faith of the community worshipping at Jerusalem. Accordingly, a number of psalms seem to have belonged to festal ceremonies which set forth the nature of the king's office. Such annual ceremonies probably repeated elements from the king's first coronation and so renewed the efficacy of his reign. Like the other parts of the festival, they seem to have had a dramatic character. A preliminary statement of God's covenant with his king is followed by a time of testing and humiliation. The drama shows the king at the mercy of evil forces, until God, being satisfied with his humility, trust and obedience, thunders to his rescue and then confirms him in glory on his throne. Such a ritual drama can be traced through Pss.2; 89; 101; 18; 21; 72 and 110, and others, such as 22 and 144, may have been used in similar rites.

Psalm 2

1–3. The scene is of a general rejection of the kingship of God and of 'his anointed', the Davidic king whom he deputes to rule on earth. Just as the sacred drama had represented a general assault by wicked kings on Zion (Pss.46 and 48 above), so now it portrays a similar insurrection against God's ruler.

4–6. But the prophetic speaker, perhaps the king himself, declares that God mocks their presumption and speaks a word of power to confound them. This word is simply a statement that God himself has installed the Davidic ruler; he is God's king set on God's holy mountain. The implication is that no powers will therefore prevail against him.

7–9. The king gives further evidence of the strength of his position. He quotes from the 'decree', a document presented at his installation. It records an oracle to the effect that this king is adopted by God as his 'son', the unique representative of God's kingdom on earth. The oracle confers on him a privilege of effective prayer; the very ends of the earth will be granted to him; he will be able to break rebellion with his royal sceptre as a man might smash jars of earthenware. (In Egypt, jars inscribed with the names of potential rebels were smashed or buried to signify the Pharaoh's supremacy.)

10–11. He warns the rebels and advises them to make their submission while there is still time.

Psalm 101

1–2a. The ceremonies will have shown the king brought low before his foes. Before God delivers him, he is required to make a statement about the righteousness of his rule. According to RSV, he has to vow to rule justly. We could otherwise translate the psalm as a statement that he has so ruled in the past year, altering the tenses from vv. 2b–8 to the past. Either way, he is pleading that God should come to deliver him from his ordeal: 'Oh when wilt thou come to me?'

2b–8. The king must especially be concerned to have as his ministers worthy men. Corrupt officials must be banished from his palace. He is pictured like the Arabian rulers who sit to dispense justice early every morning.

Psalm 21

1–7. The continuing drama has portrayed God's approval of the king. He has rescued him and now causes him to be enthroned and crowned. The singer thanks God for all that the preceding acts have signified – the answering of the king's prayer of distress, the confirmation in power of life and majesty by virtue of his reliance on God.

8–13. A prophet speaks over the king the divine promise of success. In v.13 a concluding prayer asks God to manifest his sovereignty in the days ahead, acknowledging that all power is his alone.

Epilogue

Our study of the psalms will have suggested how many great themes of later theology were first fashioned in Israelite worship. It is amazing how the psalms are prophetic of later developments. The festivals not only commemorated and represented the great moment of salvation from the past. With prophetic vision they looked deep into the nature of things and so into the ultimate destiny of the cosmos under God. Their declarations about the kingdom of God and his 'Anointed' (Hebrew 'Messiah', Greek 'Christ') live on in later Jewish teachings and in the Christian gospel.

12

Wisdom in Israel

William McKane

Wisdom in Israel and the Ancient Near East

The Old Testament wisdom tradition is a larger subject than the wisdom literature of the Old Testament. This is because the wise men were statesmen and administrators as well as men of letters and exerted great influence on the affairs of Judah from the time of David to the fall of the Judaean state. These wise men are also called 'scribes', and they belong to an educated class which was international in character and was recognizable in terms of its ethos and its role throughout the ancient Near East. They are the products of a higher education whose aim was to inculcate a rigorous mental discipline and to provide hard-headed and clear-thinking men to fill important diplomatic and administrative offices in the state.

The title of 'scribe' was given to such high officials in Egypt and that of 'scribe' or 'secretary' to their counterparts in Babylonia and Assyria. For instance, we read in an Aramaic papyrus of a man named Ahikar, who is represented as an Assyrian official, who is called 'a sagacious and keen-witted secretary', and is also counsellor of all Assyria and bearer of the seal, on whose advice Sennacherib, king of Assyria, leans. The title 'scribe' or 'secretary' does not, in these circumstances, simply mean that the person so entitled is a 'writer', nor does it show that the office which he discharges is one which calls principally for linguistic skills. It does, however, indicate that without these skills a man did not have what were regarded as essential qualifications for office, and it is a reminder that the mastery of the Egyptian hieroglyphic and the Sumerian-Babylonian cuneiform scripts required intellectual concentration of a high order. The same technical sense of 'scribe' is attested for the Old Testament as the following passages show.

In II Sam.8.16–18 and 20.23–25 there are official lists of the leading members of David's establishment, ecclesiastical, civil and military. Of the two political officials named, one Seraiah has the title 'scribe' or 'secretary', and there is no doubt that, like Ahikar, he is a secretary of state, and that both he and Jehoshaphat ('the recorder') are of the highest rank. Further information about other high officials of David is given by I Chron.27.32–34. Jonathan, David's uncle, and Ahithophel have the title 'counsellor'; Ahithophel is the 'king's counsellor', whereas Jonathan along with Jehiel is a counsellor to the king's sons. Jonathan has one of the fundamental intellectual virtues of the professional political adviser in that he is perceptive and lucid. He was also a 'scribe', and this should be taken in the general sense that he belonged to the educated class of officials rather than as a reference to his tenure of a particular, high, political office. Hushai is also mentioned in the Chronicles passage as occupying the advisory office of 'king's friend', the post held by Zabud in Solomon's reign (I Kings 4.5). The testimony of this passage that Ahithophel and Hushai were leading statesmen in the reign of David is supported by the influence of both as policy-makers in the Ahithophel-Absalom story (II Sam.15–17).

Solomon's principal officials, civil, military and ecclesiastical, are called 'statesmen' and the hereditary principle is seen to apply in both civil and ecclesiastical spheres. The office of secretary which had been occupied by Seraiah appears to be held jointly by his two sons (I Kings 4.1–6). The list is larger than those coming from David's reign, and this reflects the more complicated organization of Solomon's state. Azariah, the son of Nathan, is said to have control of 'the officials'. These are probably the twelve officials appointed by Solomon over all Israel (I Kings 4.7), each of whom was res-

ponsible for the provisioning of the royal household for one month of the year. Ahishar who is 'over the House' holds an office which still existed in the reign of Hezekiah (II Kings 18.18; Isa.36.3). The degree of centralized control which was exercised by Solomon brought into existence a cadre of officials who had close associations with Jerusalem and the court and to whom administration and diplomacy were entrusted. These correspond to the 'scribes' who filled comparable offices in Egypt and elsewhere in the ancient Near East. They were a class specially educated for the responsibility of high office, and it may be that a school for 'scribes' had been founded by Solomon in Jerusalem with a view to meeting the demands for able officials created by the structure of his state.

In II Kings 12.4–16 a 'royal secretary' acts with the high priest in counting and removing money which has been collected in a box for the fabric of the temple. This royal secretary should be equated with the secretary of David's administration (II Sam.8.17 and 20.25). This is indicated by the circumstance that later, in the reign of Josiah, Shaphan, who was certainly a secretary of state, was sent to Hilkiah, the high priest, in order to find out how much money was in this box (II Kings 22.3 ff.). The offices mentioned in II Kings 18.18 (Isa.36.3) are familiar from the previous lists. Shebna is 'secretary', Joah is 'recorder' and Eliakim is 'over the house' ('house' referring to palace and not temple). These three were apparently the king's leading advisers and made up the inner circle of government. The 'secretary' of Jer.36.11 f. is one of the statesmen, and the cabinet meeting takes place in his room. He is to be identified with the 'secretary' of the lists and he acts here as the king's first minister. The 'secretary' in Jer.37.15 f. (Jonathan) is also associated with the statesmen, and it is reasonable to conclude that he is the holder of the same office which has changed hands in the interval (in 36.11 f., Elishama is 'secretary').

These 'scribes' or statesmen were at the centre of government and affairs in Israel and Judah from the time of David to the end of the monarchy. Their prestige and reputation as weighty counsellors is reflected in the story of Ahithophel, whose judgment was so impeccable that his words were placed on the same level as the word of God (II Sam.16.23). David is convinced that Ahithophel will give Absalom the very best advice and that he himself has no hope of retrieving his position unless he can confound the wisdom of Ahithophel. This David does by planting Hushai in Absalom's war cabinet. Hushai's deliberately bad advice and the unperceptiveness of the elders of Israel bring about the rejection of Ahithophel's advice, which was the best that Absalom could have had (II Sam.17). Diplomacy and administration had become a profession in Judah and were in the hands of a class of men who understood internationally accepted protocol, and who had their own professional standards of efficiency, conscientiousness and integrity.

Statesmen versus Prophets

This, however, posed profound problems for those who still claimed the totality of Judah's life for God and who believed that God's word still offered comprehensive guidance for its direction. The scribes or statesmen or wise men claimed that it was their business to direct the internal and external affairs of Judah, that this was within the sphere of their professional competence and responsibility, and that they alone were equipped by education and expertise to take decisions on which the well-being and even survival of the nation depended. But the prophets, who were bearers of the word of God, could not concede a monopoly of policy to the wise men on those issues which affected the future of the community most crucially. Otherwise they would seem to be condemned to ineffectiveness. Their authoritative word was to be ruled out of order wherever the issues were important. They were to be left with a narrow and insignificant sphere of operations. Yet Judah was God's community and they were his accredited spokesmen, and who better than they to issue directives to the nation in relation to the great matters of the moment?

The conflict between political wisdom and prophetic authority is best attested in the books of Isaiah and Jeremiah. Isaiah's demand to Ahaz in the face of the threat to Jerusalem offered by a Syro-Ephraimite coalition was the negation of orthodox political wisdom (Isa.7, see Part III, Section 10, pp. 140); yet it is in accord with the consistent attitude of Isaiah and Jeremiah in so far as it involves a repudiation of diplomacy and foreign alliances. Judah must do nothing at all at this moment when her existence is threatened. It is not a time for diplomatic initiatives or for military bargains; it is a time to wait on God and depend absolutely on him. Here is a policy to shock the professionals; a radical concept of faith in God which leaves no room for self-help. It is not to be wondered at that Ahaz and his advisers would not take the risk. Jeremiah, too, was deeply concerned to influence the foreign policy of Judah, and the extent and seriousness of his implication in these matters may be judged by the hostility which he encountered from kings and statesmen (Jer.36–39). He was regarded as a serious political threat, a dangerous enemy of the state who had to be restrained by imprisonment and threatened by death. His opposition to all intrigues with Egypt and his counsel that submission should be made to Babylon finally brought him to a place of loneliness and disrepute, where he was under suspicion as a deserter and was thought to have undermined the morale of the community in the face of the enemy.

This conflict has to be described from the side of these professional statesmen no less than from the prophetic side. The explanation is not that the wise men were irreligious or anti-religious, any more than Ahaz was irreligious because he was unable to identify himself with Isaiah's radical concept of faith in God. The wise men were loyal to religion according to their understanding, but they were not prepared to give credence to the revealed word of a prophet in relation to affairs which they believed to be within the province of their professional competence and political judgment. They had their own canons of conscientiousness and integrity and they would not surrender these to a word of God spoken by a prophet.

The Book of Proverbs

There are different kinds of material in the book of Proverbs and these can be correlated with genres of wisdom literature in Egypt and Babylonia. The form of Prov.1–9; 22.17–24.22 and 31.1–9 is that of the *Instruction* of which there are a number of Egyptian examples. In the case of Prov.22.17–23.11, there would appear to be a literary dependence on the Egyptian

Teaching (or *Instruction*) of Amenemope. In Egypt, the *Instruction,* as its name suggests, was concerned to cultivate in apprentice officials the mental attitudes and manners which made for effectiveness and success in the service of the state. Its home was the school, where it was the instrument of an education whose goal was intellectual rigour and nicety of judgment and discrimination. It is an attractive conjecture that the genre found its way into Israel in the reign of Solomon in order to fulfil a similar educational function, and that in Jerusalem as well as Egypt it was an instrument for the education of 'scribes'.

There is, however, only a little evidence of this in the contents of Proverbs. On the whole the Israelite *Instruction* is not concerned with the education of officials, but with the instruction of the community and especially of the young men. There is a prudential emphasis in the teaching and the dangers of sexual indiscipline are a great matter. The foreign woman, strange, alluring and freed from all restraints, is regarded as a particular menace and her house is represented as the gateway to the underworld (2.18). The 'my son' address is an indication of the fundamental place of parental wisdom, but also of the kind of relation existing between teacher and pupil in the classroom, where the teacher claims a quasi-parental authority. In certain passages in Prov.1–9, however, the parent or teacher is replaced as spokesman by a personified wisdom.

1. *The Character of Wisdom*

Wisdom – thought of as feminine – is portrayed with the characteristics and speech of a wisdom teacher or a prophet (Prov.1.20 ff.). Elsewhere there is the possibility that she has been created as a rival to the seductive queen of a fertility cult (especially ch.9). In Prov.8 the personification of wisdom embraces both the concerns of political wisdom and the wisdom whose subject is the wonders of God's created works. On the one hand, wisdom asserts that through her God effectively formulates and executes his plans for the nations (Prov.8.14–16), and this is comparable to the claim which the prophets make for God as counsellor and executive. On the other hand, she establishes for herself a special place in the counsels of God in connection with the creation of the world.

Wisdom was beside God as his confidant(?) before the world was created. This is a further development of a recognizable trend in the wisdom tradition to regard the mystery and incomprehensibility of God's created works as the supreme manifestation of his wisdom. It is here that man is left far behind and feels his mystification and impotence. Although Proverbs, for the most part, represents an earlier stage of the wisdom tradition than Job and Ecclesiastes, this personification of wisdom in Prov.8 in relation to the creation of the world has the appearance of lateness. It is a step beyond the assertion that God's creative works are the supreme manifestation of his wisdom. It is the making of wisdom into a person and the assertion that she is with God before the creation of the world. How this is to be evaluated is a matter of great difficulty and uncertainty, but it would seem to be more than a mere literary device. Wisdom does not now consist in the demonstration of the divine intelligence and power in the creation of the world. The mystery of wisdom deepens and her distance from the world and from men is increased. Already before the world was made wisdom was the companion and confidant of God.

2. *Proverbial Maxims*

Apart from the longer poems in Prov.30 and 31.10–31, the remainder of the book is, for the most part, made up of wisdom sentences. Three main divisions of the material can be made.

(i) There are those sentences which embody a this-worldly, hard-headed wisdom from which any trace of moralism or piety is absent. They are addressed to the individual, and it is his success, prosperity and well-being which they seek to safeguard. They define mental attitudes and a prudential morality which the individual had better cultivate, because they are the marks of the wise man and will bring him success and safety as a member of a community.

(ii) Other sentences also discourse on the individual but they have social implications. They are about the anti-social, malevolent man whose activities are deliberately destructive of his community and injurious to relations between man and man. They discuss this behaviour both in respect of its bad effects on the community and the threat which it poses to its existence, and also its destructive

165

consequences for the misanthropic man himself. Man is made for society and for constructive, beneficent relationships with his neighbour, and if he dedicates himself to hate and malice he is a man with a sick mind. The health of the mind is conditional on creative social intercourse. This is a condition of integration, but the effect of deliberate and systematic misanthropy is disintegration.

(iii) The third group differs from the other two in that it admits the language of piety and moralism. These are the sentences in which a doctrine of theodicy comes to expression, in which it is asserted that God rewards the righteous man and punishes the wicked man, and that righteousness is therefore an infallible guarantee of well-being and prosperity. The word 'theodicy' means that God enforces justice effectively so that the righteous man gets his reward and the wicked man his punishment. In association with this there is a moralistic vocabulary, righteous and wicked, upright and devious, good and bad, reliable and treacherous. Here the wisdom sentence in its antithetic form expresses the tidiness and barren finality of a doctrine which has settled all the problems of human existence.

It has been customary for criticism to arrange these wisdom sentences into collections and to discover a relative chronology for the collections. The value of this exercise is limited. A more profitable way of looking at these sentences is to regard them as a deposit of Israelite wisdom and to examine them with a view to discovering what they tell us about the history of the wisdom tradition.

The wisdom sentence is a literary product, characterized by finish and polish. It is an attempt to make an observation or state a general truth in a memorable, concise way. The popular proverb, on the other hand, need not have a high degree of formal organization. This is true, for example, of the popular proverb, 'Is Saul also among the prophets?' (I Sam.10.11 f. [19.24]). Such a proverb is applicable and apt in any situation where there seems to be a lack of accord between a person and the situation in which he appears, where there is a strong incongruity in his behaviour. All that is required to preserve its contemporaneity and freshness is the ability to discern that a particular situation is right for the comment, 'Is Saul also among the prophets?'

Other examples of popular proverbs in the Old Testament are Gen.10.9; I Sam.24.14; I Kings 20.11; Jer.31.29 (Ezek.18.2); Ezek.12.22; 16.44. Only a few wisdom sentences in the book of Proverbs have this proverbial quality (10.5; 13.4,7; 16.26; 20.4; 24.27; 26.13, 15, 27; 27.7).

The Book of Job

The book of Job consists of a prologue (chs. 1–2), cycles of speeches involving Job, and his three friends Eliphaz, Bildad and Zophar (chs. 3–31), the speeches of Elihu (32–37), the speeches of Yahweh, Israel's God (chs. 38–41), Job's repentance (42.1–6) and his restoration (the epilogue, 42.7–17). There are formidable critical problems, but Job gives more evidence than any other book in the Old Testament of creative literary endeavour and artistic management. It is clear, for example, that a deliberate attempt is being made to carry forward the discussion of a difficult theological problem (the unmerited suffering of a righteous man) by means of an arrangement whereby Job and his so-called friends engage in a kind of conversation or debate. The debate may on examination not prove to be particularly convincing. One gets the impression that all of the speakers are bad listeners. Certainly the friends appear to be incapable of taking the point which Job is making. Job's settled conviction that they, on their part, have nothing to say to him is more understandable. This inability of Job and his friends to speak to one another may not be an artistic defect, but rather part of the effect which is striven after. Given the circumstances of these conversations and the character of the participants, these are exactly the kind of desultory exchanges for which we may look. The fact is that they cannot speak to one another; they are not on speaking terms. Instead, they lecture one another, but that is a different matter.

The most pressing critical problem, given this evidence of a work of art in the main part of the book, is how to reconcile this attempt to devise a literary mode for a serious treatment of a theological problem with the presuppositions of the prologue and the epilogue. The speeches of Elihu, whether they are original to the body of the work or subsequent, do not constitute so formidable a problem. The speeches of Yahweh and the account of Job's repentance are more troublesome. It is, however, in the prologue and the epilogue that the difficulties are sharpest. The representation of the prologue, that Job's sufferings are attributable to the licence given by God to Satan in a heavenly court to test Job's motives, destroys the seriousness of the debate in the body of the work, and the effects of the epilogue, with its account of Job's restoration to reputation and wealth, are even more devastating. The epilogue does not have a heavenly setting and is not clearly a resumption of the prologue. Job's eventual good fortune is in fact in accord with the orthodox prognostications of Eliphaz, Bildad and Zophar (8.5–7; 11.13–19; 22.21–30).

Then again the Job of the prologue is a different person from the tragic character in the body of the work. He does not rail against the day of his birth, nor long for death, nor charge God with relentless persecution, nor deny that God is a righteous judge. When he loses possessions and family he exclaims: 'Naked I came out of my mother's womb, and naked shall I return; The Lord gave, and the Lord has taken away; blessed be the name of the Lord.' When he becomes a diseased wretch and his wife invites him to curse God he replies: 'If we accept good from God, shall we not also accept evil?' Here there is no hint of rebellion or despair. There is only the serene resignation of the pious man.

1. *The Speeches of Elihu*

Although Elihu is himself convinced of the originality of his contribution and makes a point of dissociating himself both from Job and from the friends, he does not have very much to add. He is a younger man who relies on inspiration rather than on experience. He does not, however, thereby distinguish himself completely from the other three, for Eliphaz, too, had claimed to be a visionary (4.12 f.). Elihu, like the friends, maintains that God is a righteous judge who rewards virtue and punishes wickedness (36.5 f.). He repudiates Job's claim to be righteous and denies that God is a persecutor who has relentlessly harried Job. His most original contribution is his allegation that Job's attitude to God has engendered a kind of deafness. Awareness of sin is only given in a moment of revelation, and Job, because of his determination to take God to task, has no hope of hearing the God whose

silence he condemns. He has abandoned himself to anguished protest and eloquent denunciation and, if so, he must not complain that God does not speak to him. The resounding protest that God does not answer is the reason why God does not answer. The fault is with Job and not with God (35.12 f.). Elihu, like the friends, appeals to the staggering dimensions of God's creative works, to the complexity and terror of the world which is the supreme expression of his wisdom, in order to crush Job with this account of intelligence and power, and to induce in him behaviour towards God proportionate to his creaturehood.

This is not an appeal which is peculiar to Elihu. It is a strain of thought which runs through the speeches of the friends, which is developed in the poem of ch. 28, and which receives lengthy and involved treatment in the divine speeches. These speeches add nothing new. God dwells on modes of wisdom which the friends and Elihu regard as the final answer to Job's pretensions. God, too, would make Job's mind reel as he recounts the vast operations of his intelligence, and describes the terrible and mysterious creatures whom he has made. But Job has conceded this all the way through. He has not doubted that he is impotent, that the totality of God's creation and creatures defeats his efforts at comprehension. This indeed is part of what he has asserted. He has always been puzzled and tortured and despairing.

2. *The Three Friends*

It is unwise to assume that the sympathies of the author are totally identified with his principal character and that he has created Eliphaz, Bildad and Zophar as wooden and pompous spokesmen of an empty orthodoxy. A close examination of the lines which he has given them does not bear this out. Their thought may be very ordinary, they may offer Job a stone when he asks for bread, but there is nothing ordinary or prosaic about the language in which their thoughts find expression. The poet whose imaginative power is discernible in the language of Job has not denied to Job's protagonists the same recourse to striking imagery and proverbial power. Is there not perhaps something to be said for Job's opponents? Less, no doubt, than is to be said for Job, yet their words are not simply empty. Is it not perhaps the ambiguity of the problem and the desire to explore this ambiguity which has commended the pattern of speech and reply to the author? Job and the other three are not in complete disagreement, but the defenders of orthodoxy are so earnest and anxious that they do not appear to be aware that this is so. In so far as the three friends are concerned to emphasize the unsearchable character of God and of his creative works, in so far as they ascribe to him in connexion with his ordering of created things and creatures an intelligence and power which man cannot match, they are not at odds with Job.

3. *The Majesty of God*

Job, too, is struck with terror and bewilderment. Thus in ch.9 Job observes that there is no need for Eliphaz and Bildad to recite to him the majesty and mystery of God the Creator. He knows this and acknowledges it. Again when Zophar (11.7 f.) describes the transcendent, unsearchable God, Job replies that he accepts this (11.7 f.), and that it is because he accepts it that he cannot believe in God as one who sees that man gets justice, that the righteous man is rewarded and the wicked man punished. It is because he agrees with them and they seem incapable of grasping this or appreciating what its implications are for Job in his personal agony, that he loses all patience with them and denounces them as liars and quacks (13.4). Again he is in accord with them in their understanding of the marks of a man who has fulfilled himself, on whom God's blessing rests. Bildad's description of the fate of the wicked man implies that the righteous man may expect a stable home, reputation, long life and posterity (18.14–19), and it is this reputation and esteem of whose loss Job complains (19.14 f.). He, too, appeared to be well-set for a climax of attainment, his weight and influence in the community matched by his material prosperity, but now he is the object of contempt and ridicule (chs. 30–31).

4. *Is God Just?*

The three friends are unanimous that God is a just judge and that he metes out to every man his deserts. If this is so, Job's reversal of fortune can only be explained in terms of his sinfulness. God punishes sin and Job has got what he deserved. This is the main emphasis,

but along with it there is the subsidiary thought that Job's suffering may be a corrective discipline (so Eliphaz, 5.17 f.). This is no more acceptable to Job than the main contention; nor will he accept the proposition that the apparent prosperity of the wicked can be explained by the circumstance that retribution may be delayed (21.19). Against the main charge, Job vigorously maintains that he is a just, merciful and compassionate man who has always acted out of a deep sense of social concern, with a tender conscience for the poor and weak, not vindictive nor an idolator (ch. 31). When Eliphaz makes specific charges against Job (22.6 f.), he counters these by giving a firm and convincing account of his social morality. However distraught and despairing and tortured he may be, he has no doubt at all that he is a righteous man according to the definition of social morality which is accepted by Eliphaz, Bildad and Zophar. What Job can no longer believe and what they insist that he must go on believing is that such righteousness is a guarantee of well-being and prosperity, because it is God's order which he enforces by rewarding those who live by it and punishing those who break it. This is contradicted by Job's experience; it is disproved by his suffering and anguish. In these circumstances, the defence of orthodoxy undertaken by the three can mean nothing to him, and this is what he keeps on saying. The three theorize, but he is the one who suffers and their nicely calculated theology does not touch him in his pain and despair. The reality for him is that God is a relentless persecutor who harries him without respite (6.1 f.; 7.11 f.; 10; 13.24 f.; 16.12). Why should God whose power and majesty Job freely acknowledges take it upon himself to hound a frail man such as himself? For man's life is fleeting, and unlike nature he is not renewed (14.1 f.). The depths of his despair cannot be plumbed. He wishes that he had never been born, that he had been an abortion rather than a live-birth (3.1 f.). He longs for the swift release of death (17.1 f.).

The problem which comes alive in Job's suffering and tragic perplexity is constituted by two poles of the Old Testament wisdom tradition. There is the this-worldliness and earthiness of wisdom well-represented in the book of Proverbs, and the theodicy by which God's imprimatur is stamped on it. The theodicy states that God sees to it that the righteous prosper and the wicked are punished. It is the best of all possible worlds for the righteous man. The other pole is constituted by the recital of God's creative works as evidence of his wisdom and power (cf. Isa.40.12 f.; Job 28), where the emphasis is on God's transcendence, on the area of mystery in which he is shrouded and on the awe and terror which is evoked by the disparity of powers as between God and man. The transcendent God is the unsearchable God and the God whom man cannot bring to account, and the question may then be raised whether the tidy scheme of theodicy which implies so transparent an understanding of God's ways with man and with the world is not in jeopardy. For Job, this question is inescapable. He can believe in the transcendent, mysterious God whose ways with men are past finding out, but he can no longer believe in the God who takes a personal interest in every man and sees to it that he suffers no injustice.

This is the burden of his complaint against the three friends and this is the gravamen of his charge against God. Hence he says of God: 'The truth is that he is not a man like myself that I might answer him, that we might go to law together' (9.32 f.). Again, addressing God, he says: 'Remove thy hand from upon me, and may thy terror not crush me. Then call and I will answer, or else I will speak and thou shalt reply. How many are my iniquities and sins? Make me to know my transgression and my sin' (13.21–23). Is God a dark Power which terrorizes Job into abject hopelessness, or is the model of a Judge a meaningful one? Job can no longer believe that it is meaningful. He knows how judicial proceedings are ordered and how a judge may be expected to behave. He would have access to a judge and would be able to put his case to him, to engage in argument and to persuade him to the best of his ability of the justice of his case. But God is not accessible and so not amenable to argument. Job can no longer believe that God is both far and near as his orthodox friends maintain. If his remoteness and mystery are to be extolled, the pedestrian clarity of the doctrine of theodicy must be given up, and men must resign themselves to the conclusion that they know much less about God's ways than they had supposed. No longer can they maintain that the morality of their society is Yahweh's moral

order and that righteousness, as they define it, is a guarantee of well-being and prosperity.

The other way in which Job proceeds in his argument with the three is to say to them: Very well, I shall take the model of God as the righteous judge seriously, and, in that case, I have not the slightest doubt that my arguments are irrefutable and that I would be acquitted if I were given a hearing (ch. 23). If God is indeed a judge, he has shown no regard for justice in his dealings with Job and must be indicted: 'Know, then, that it is God who has done me wrong and who has encompassed me with his net. If I cry out "Violence", I receive no reply, in vain do I cry for help; there is no justice. He has blocked my path so that I cannot get through, and upon my paths he has set darkness. Of my glory he has stripped me and the crown he has removed from my head' (19.6–9). 'By God who has set aside my right and by the Almighty who has embittered my soul! So long as my spirit remains inviolate in me and the breath of God is in my nostrils, my lips shall not speak any falsehood, nor my tongue utter a lie. Far be it from me to admit that you are right; until I die I will not renounce my integrity' (27.2–5).

The Book of Ecclesiastes

'God is great,' says Elihu, 'and we do not know how great, the number of his years is unsearchable' (Job 36.26). This is not so far removed from the theme of the book of Ecclesiastes, in which the consequences of having to do with a God who is ultimately unknowable and inscrutable are explored.

Ecclesiastes is a different kind of book from Job, because there is not a suffering, despairing man crying out for an explanation at its centre. In the book of Job the integrity of an individual is at stake, but Ecclesiastes has nothing of this personal drama, and is rather a colder, more deliberate essay in scepticism in which the author is sufficiently composed and settled in his conclusions to appear in the role of a teacher – to give advice to others on what they may expect from life. Job does not have the leisure or the composure to instruct. He is too immersed in his own anguish to undertake the tasks of a teacher. Everything that he says emerges from the fires of his suffering. He does not transcend, nor has he any interest in transcending, the circumstances of perplexity and outrage in which he is engulfed.

Yet the affinity between the two books is not far to seek. Both indicate that a 'crisis of wisdom' had been reached in the Old Testament, just as it had manifested itself in the wisdom literature of the ancient Near East in Egypt and Babylonia. Two Babylonian compositions, *The Babylonian Theodicy* and *I Will Praise the Lord of Wisdom*, throw doubt in different ways on the existence of a moral order, and even the possibility of intuiting moral values, and pessimism comes to the surface in Egypt in the *Instruction* of Amenemhet. Both Job and Ecclesiastes are late representatives of the Old Testament wisdom tradition, and it is more important to establish this than to allocate dates to them. Even if the figure of the patriarch Job in the prologue is based on an old folk-tale, the folk-tale itself has little bearing on the evaluation of the book of Job. For it is the body of the book which is decisive and the Job who speaks to the friends is not the Job of the prologue. His reaction to personal disaster and suffering is different, and the mode of life which he indicates when he discusses his loss of status and esteem reflects the role of a senior citizen and counsellor in a municipality and not the antique and rustic grandeur of a patriarchal way of life. What can be said with some certainty is that Job and Ecclesiastes are later than Proverbs, because what appears in Proverbs as premises which may not be questioned or conclusions which are finally settled emerge in Job and Ecclesiastes as problems around which discussion rages.

There are sentences in Proverbs in which the dogma that God rewards the righteous man and punishes the wicked man are repeated again and again with a pedestrian precision. But it is this doctrine of theodicy to which Job will not bow. As we have seen, it is the validity and the meaningfulness of conceiving God as a judge which is called in question by Job and Ecclesiastes. Does it make sense to speak about God as a righteous judge? Can I in truth have access to him as a judge? Can I argue my case with him if I seem to be the victim of injustice? It makes sense to talk about a judge and judicial proceedings when one is describing the legal machinery which exists in a community for the trying of cases and the redress of grievances. Here, indeed, there is a judge to whom one has

access and whom one can address; here conversation, speaking and listening, is a possibility and there are intelligible principles which guide a judge towards his decision. What is meant by judge and justice is understood in this context, But can this be transferred to God and elevated into theology? The answer of Job is a passionate negative and the answer of Ecclesiastes is a cool, sceptical negative.

The dating of Job in the fifth or fourth century and of Ecclesiastes in the third century accords with these indications. The ascription of authorship to Solomon in the case of Ecclesiastes has probably the same significance as in the book of Proverbs. It is not an indication of authorship, but a pointer to the type of literature contained in these books and the close relationship between those who produced this literature and the court.

'Vanity of Vanities'

God is brought very near by the doctrine of theodicy, for the community's morality is his morality; the man who deserves well-being enjoys well-being. But is it true that this is the best of all possible worlds for the righteous man? Is this a dogma which is detached from the confusion and the ambiguities and the injustices of our human situation? Job out of his own bewilderment and outrage is persuaded that this must be so. It is not then surprising that a Job or an Ecclesiastes should focus attention on the God who is far away, who is other than man and who is regarded with wonder, awe and terror, in order to undermine the trite and empty tidiness of the doctrine of theodicy. Man is left behind in his attempt to comprehend the ways of this God, the creator of heaven and earth, and the maker of the dread Behemoth (Job 40.15 f.). Ecclesiastes can be understood as taking its departure from what is a well-established feature of the wisdom tradition and probing its implications so as to call in question or demolish the structures of orthodoxy.

Everything, according to Ecclesiastes, is vanity or emptiness, and sustained human effort does not produce enduring results and is not consolidated into lasting achievement and gain. Man's frailty and fleeting life is mocked by the cyclic character of nature and the monotonously regular repetition of its processes which is infallibly maintained. All this underlines the futility of man's existence, for he can do nothing to modify or change its natural setting. The rhythms cannot be checked or disturbed; the processes are irreversible and they take no account of man's aspirations. The circular processes of nature have always operated and they are unaffected by the brief life-span of a man.

The writer of Ecclesiastes, unlike Job, does not speak out of the anguish of a personal tragedy. His tones are not those of passionate protest and repudiation. He is able to offer a cold, coherent analysis of how he has reached his conclusion that human life is emptied of permanent values and achievements. He had himself used the tools of a wise man in order to explore the character of historical existence ('all that is done under the sun') and he had found it a vexatious and profitless enterprise. His discovery had been that all the events and experiences in which man participates are nothingness and a striving after wind (i.e., empty pursuits). Even wisdom is impotent and ineffective, because vexation grows in proportion to wisdom and increased knowledge produces an increase in pain (1.12–18).

No relief is to be had from a feverish search for pleasure; a deliberate cultivation of gaiety or the adoption of a reveller's way of life will not even be a palliative. This, too, is emptiness. Nevertheless, pleasure is the only experience accessible to man which can be turned to gain, and it only can rescue his existence from total emptiness. The author had carried out an experiment of seeking pleasure and permitting himself indiscretion without abandoning prudence. Hence he acquired a sufficient fortune, built houses, laid out gardens, was waited on by servants and maintained singers for his diversion and entertainment. The only gain which he had from the entire undertaking was the pleasure which it gave him: 'For my heart found pleasure in all my toil and this was my reward for all my toil' (2.1–11).

The wise man appears to have a great advantage over the fool, and yet one fate is reserved for both, and death destroys the disparity between wise man and fool, effectively nullifying whatever advantages obtained to wisdom. Both wise man and fool are destined for oblivion, and the fruits of a man's toil may be frittered away by a fool who inherits from him. Hence there is no escaping despair, and the best course open to a man is to eat and drink

and take pleasure from his toil (i.e., 'in return for his toil' not 'in his toil' as RSV translates in 2.24; 3.13; 5.18 f.; 8.15). But then not every man is capable of enjoying himself. Some are constitutionally incapable of experiencing pleasure and for them life is entirely empty (2.12–26).

There is the accent of predestination in the teaching of Ecclesiastes. Human activity has the same fixed and pre-ordained pattern as has nature (3.1–8). Whatever God has made is unalterable, and no new factor can emerge to give a different direction to existence. The vexatiousness of man's position is constituted by the fact that God has put eternity in his heart. That is to say, man is dissatisfied with a fragmentary understanding of his world, but he has been denied the capacity for comprehension and is doomed to perplexity and futility. A feature of the world in which man lives is the confusion of moral values inherent in it. There is a total lack of definition, a blurring or obscuring of moral distinctions, a confounding of all moral judgments. Good and bad are entangled and cannot be extricated from each other (3.1–16). Life does not have the order presupposed by the orthodox account of the operations of God's justice. If God imposes a test on men, it is not a moral test. It is to show them that they are indistinguishable from the beasts, that both die the same death, both come from the dust and return to dust (3.19–22).

When the actual conditions of life are examined, it is disclosed that there is no moral order and that it is power and not righteousness which counts. The oppressed may have righteousness on their side, but there is no redress for them because the oppressor has the power. Hence (cf. Job 3), since life is dominated by force, the dead are better off than the living, but better than both is he who was never born (4.1–3). This, however, is contradicted by 9.4 f., which declares that death is worse than life. The living are at least aware that they will die, but the dead have no awareness or emotions. At this point the structure of the author's thinking is more or less complete, and what follows consists of further illustrations of the futility of life. Thus in 6.3–6 he observes that if a man lives to a great age and has one hundred children (long life and posterity are the accepted marks of the man who enjoys God's blessing), but is incapable of experiencing pleasure, he is worse off than a miscarriage (cf. Job 3.16) which never emerged alive from the darkness of the womb (6.3–6).

In ch. 7 and the succeeding chapters there is discussion about the inequities of human existence and the lack of a moral order. The righteous man perishes with his righteousness, but the wicked man enjoys a long life for the practice of wickedness (7.15). There is no point in striving too intently to be either righteous or wise, but, on the other hand, a man should not go out of his way to commit evil or play the fool, since this may bring about an untimely death. 'Untimely' relates to the predestinarianism of the book, that is, the assertion that every life has a term fixed by God (7.16 f.). Further reflections on the problem of justice include the remark that the wicked go in and out of the (Jerusalem) temple and pass as worthy citizens in the city where they have practised their wickedness. In the end they are safely and honourably buried. When it is seen that a swift retribution does not operate against such men, evil-doers are encouraged to persist in their evil (8.10 f.).

Chapter 12 is a recapitulation of the main findings of the book. 'Remember your Creator in the days of your youth' (v.1) is a doubtful rendering, since the command does not seem to be consistent with what follows which is more in keeping with the scepticism of Ecclesiastes. There is something to be said for the translation: 'Remember your vigour in the days of your youth', which means, make the most of your youth and vigour, for youth quickly departs and then there is only the sadness of growing old. This involves no alteration of the text. There follows a poetic account of a man's melancholy fate, a dwelling on the sad inevitability of death which brings with it cessation and oblivion (vv.2–6). Therefore take as much enjoyment as you can from life before 'the silver cord is snapped or the golden bowl is crushed to pulp, or the pitcher is shattered at the fountain, or the wheel crushed at the cistern, and the dust returns to the earth where it was, and the spirit returns to God who gave it. Vanities of vanity, says the Preacher, all is vanity' (vv. 6–8).

The foregoing account has ignored the presence in the book of verses which give expression to traditional formulations of wisdom. It has been argued that these are evidences of tension or conflict in the mind of the author, and that his mind moved between acceptance and rejection of conventional forms of belief and piety. In the case, however, of such verses as 3.17; 7.18b; 8.5; 11.9b; 12.12–14, the view that these are pious attempts to correct heretical tendencies in the author would seem to be correct. Thus 12.13 urges fear of Yahweh and obedience to his commandments, and would appear to discourage the kind of speculation for which the author has shown a fondness, and v. 14, 'God will bring every deed into judgment', reintroduces a doctrine of reward and retribution which the author has categorically denied. Similarly, 8.12 f. looks like a pious rejoinder to the attack on the doctrine of theodicy in 8.10 f.

Job and Ecclesiastes

Thus the resemblances and the differences between Job and Ecclesiastes emerge. In both there is a rejection of a doctrine of theodicy and in both there is an acceptance that God is shrouded in mystery and is past finding out. The scepticism of Ecclesiastes is the more general, the more cerebral, but that of Job is the more human and the more compelling. Ecclesiastes' scepticism is more desolating in its comprehensiveness and in the weariness of its tone. It does not come out of a crisis situation in which a sympathetic human being is driven towards disintegration and despair. It betrays rather the tired accents of one who has not suffered greatly but whose world is filled with an unbearable grayness and lack of definition. Nor is his mysterious God described in the same way. Job's description of the unsearchable God whose wisdom is shown in his creative works is also part of the conception of God shared by Eliphaz, Bildad and Zophar, and appears in the speeches of Yahweh himself. But these stirring descriptions, which are a well-established emphasis of Old Testament wisdom, do not contribute to Ecclesiastes' portrait of the inscrutable God. His God is more desiccated, more abstract and more unbearable. Nature in its regularity is a witness to the fixed and unalterable patterns of existence to which man is also subject. A man cannot know why God has ordered his existence in just this way. He can know only that he has done it and that no escape or deviation is possible. As for the world in which he lives, it is one in which no moral judgments are possible, where wisdom can achieve little and where pleasure is the only positive experience, always provided that you are one of those to whom God has given the capacity for pleasure.

It is in the sadness evoked by death that the difference between Ecclesiastes and Job is most marked. Job still associates himself with the this-worldly concept of fulfilment and there is no evidence that he regards this as defective or hollow. The man who has achieved honour, reputation, wealth, children, a long life is not haunted by death. Death does not threaten the fulfilment and maturity of his existence. It is contained within the concept of fulfilment. It is part of the blessedness that after the summit has been reached there should be this gentle descent into Sheol. It is part of the joy and

contentment of a full life. In contrast, death has become a source of anxiety and proof of futility in the book of Ecclesiastes and this is a great change. The older religion with its this-worldly character and its acceptance of the boundary of death satisfied the individual only if he had the support of a community in which the worship and service of God came to effective expression. It may be that this condition was no longer fulfilled in the time when Ecclesiastes was written, and that the individual could no longer find a fulfilment which gave him communal support and permitted him to die without the fear of futility and emptiness. It is thus consonant with a date in the latter half of the third century, when religion and corporate values were challenged by Hellenism, before the revival of Jewish nationalism under the Maccabees.

13

The Exile

H. McKeating

The Evidence

1. *Biblical References*

II Kings 25 describes the revolt of Zedekiah and its results. It includes a brief account of the murder of Gedaliah, the Jewish governor whom the Babylonians had set in authority after the fall of Jerusalem, and of the subsequent flight to Egypt of the members of his court (including a reluctant Jeremiah). It ends with Jehoiachin's release from prison in Babylonia.

Jeremiah 39–44 is a longer account of the same, except that it omits any reference to the release of Jehoiachin and adds some prophecies uttered by Jeremiah in Egypt.

Jeremiah 24, the parable of the figs, and *Jeremiah 29*, the prophet's letter to the exiles, actually come from the period before 586, but are important for four reasons: (i) the parable of the figs expresses an attitude that became standard in Jewish interpretations of the exile: that the exiled fraction of the people were the

faithful and the Palestinian remainder the worthless; (ii) they mention the prophecy of restoration after seventy years, which was a very potent one; (iii) they show something of what conditions were like in exile; (iv) they illustrate again the prophetic interpretation of the event of the exile.

Lamentations. Though traditionally known as the Lamentations of Jeremiah, the book has no genuine connection with that prophet. It is a set of five poems (corresponding to the five chapters) lamenting the fall of Jerusalem and mostly composed when the memory of the disaster was still fresh. All but the last are alphabetic acrostics.

Deutero-Isaiah and Ezekiel. Deutero-Isaiah means Isaiah chs. 40–55. For selected passages from these prophets see below.

2. *Archaeological Evidence*

Excavated sites in Palestine produce no dramatic revelations bearing on the period of the exile itself. They simply confirm the general picture of a poor and under-populated land.

Excavations of Mesopotamian cities, especially Babylon, have given us a fairly full picture of life there, and have provided texts of various sorts with information about the background events of the period.

The Weidner Tablets, dug up in the royal palace at Babylon, are administrative documents which record, among other things, the allowances paid to Jehoiachin, king of Judah in exile.

There are two important accounts of the reign of Nabonidus, ending in Cyrus' rise to power; these are the Nabonidus Chronicle and the Verse Account of Nabonidus. These were both written after the accession of Cyrus and by Cyrus' supporters. We do not expect their picture of Nabonidus, therefore, to be sympathetic.

On Cyrus himself we have information in plenty. There is the Cyrus Cylinder, a kind of clay barrel found in Babylon, and as secondary sources the works of Xenophon *(Cyropaedia)*, Herodotus, and other Greek historians, such as Diodorus Siculus, Ctesias and Arrian. To these we may add Josephus, *Antiquities* 10.8; 10.9; and 10.11,1–2.

We have information about the Jews in Egypt in the Elephantine Papyri, described below.

Why This Period is Important

The exile, dated from 586–538 BC, marks a dramatic upheaval is Israel's fortunes and a radical change in her constitution and status. Israel's history revolves round the two events of exodus and exile. In the exodus and subsequent events she was constituted a nation. At the exile she ceased to be one in the accepted sense. She lost her political independence, and apart from a brief period under the Maccabees, she did not regain it until AD 1947. The exile, too, marks the beginning of the dispersion of much of her population (the diaspora). Her people were scattered, and not only to Babylon.

The astonishing thing is that she did not lose her identity. Israel had developed, or developed in exile, a culture which proved resistant to the most powerful erosive forces. Her peculiar religion played a major part in this. Israel's unique conception of God goes hand in hand with a unique conception of her national identity.

According to the way in which ancient peoples thought, the defeat and break up of the state ought to have been accepted as conclusive evidence of the failure of the national deity and to have led to the collapse of the national culture. Assyria's identity and culture did not survive her defeat at Carchemish in 605.

Israel refused to accept this as the logic of events. The fact that she did so is to be laid largely to the credit of the prophets. They had prepared her for the catastrophe not only by predicting it, but by interpreting it, before the event. They had asserted *ad nauseam* that it would take place not in spite of the efforts of the national God, but precisely because he would himself bring it about. They interpreted it in advance as a punishment for sin. Instead, therefore, of regarding the exile as evidence for the failure of Yahweh, Israel was able to see it as a vindication of the prophets' view of his character.

It must be appreciated that the religious structures which bound Israel together, and which showed themselves in subsequent ages to be so resistant to erosion, are not, in the form in which they are familiar to us, older than the exile itself. They were largely created at this very period, to meet the need of holding together the depressed and scattered people. Institutions like the law, the ritual of circumcision, sabbath-keeping, and many of the others that make up what we recognize as Jewish culture, either came into being at this point, or came into prominence only now. Circumcision, for example, though it had been practised from remote antiquity, had not previously been thought of as *distinctive*. And if the Old Testament as we now have it presents all these things as part of the normative religion of Israel, that is because the Old Testament itself is substantially a product of the exilic age.

The Neo-Babylonians

The Neo-Babylonian Empire arose at the end of the seventh century. (It is called *Neo*-Babylonian to distinguish it from Babylon's earlier period of empire in the eighteenth to sixteenth centuries BC, inaugurated by the famous Hammurabi). In alliance with the Medes, the Babylonians overthrew the reigning world power,

Assyria. Under king Nabopolassar they took the Assyrian capital, Nineveh, in 612 BC, and finished the job in 605, at the battle of Carchemish, when Nebuchadnezzar convincingly defeated an Assyrian-Egyptian alliance.

Nebuchadnezzar was the principal ruler of the Neo-Babylonian dynasty, reigning for over forty years. It was he who destroyed Jerusalem and deported the Jews in 597 and 586. His attempt to include Egypt in his empire, however, eventually failed.

His chief work was the rebuilding of Babylon. He restored the temple of Marduk, Babylon's patron deity, built a magnificent palace for himself, and also constructed the famous 'hanging gardens', which were reckoned as one of the 'seven wonders of the world'.

The achievements of his two immediate successors were modest. The third, and last, was Nabonidus, about whom so many contradictory things are said that it is impossible to do more than guess his true character or the real reasons for his policies.

Babylonian religion was an impressive affair, full of splendid and rich ceremonial, and festivals in which the gods were carried in procession along raised processional highways, and along the canals in ships. The New Year festival, in spring, when the king 'took the hand of Marduk' and led him in procession, was of great importance. The ritual of this feast seems to have included an enactment of the drama of creation, in which the god Marduk fights the chaos monster; a death and resurrection of the god; a sacred marriage between god and goddess (enacted by the king and a priestess) and a ritual abasement of the king, followed by his restoration to dignity. Babylonian religion was also much concerned with the procuring of oracles and foretelling the future.

All these features may profitably be borne in mind when reading biblical texts written during the exile, especially Deutero-Isaiah.

The Life and Thought of the Jews

1. *In Babylon*

The old phrase 'Babylonian captivity' is a misnomer. The Jewish exiles were not captives in the accepted sense of that word. They had freedom of association and considerable freedom of movement, as Ezekiel makes clear (e.g., 8.1; 14.1; 20.1 ff.). They were allowed to communicate with their homeland and receive communications from there (Jer.29). They must have been free to take jobs and make money and own property, for when the opportunity came to return, many of them had adjusted themselves only too well to Babylonian life and had no desire to leave. They seem to have been free to practise their own religion, in so far as it could be practised at such a remote distance from their only legitimate sanctuary. The existence of 'elders' suggests not only that they were gathered in separate Jewish communities, but also that these communities may have had a measure of self-government.

The numbers involved were not large. Jeremiah 52.28 ff. gives a total for all the deportations of 4600. II Kings 24.14,16 mentions figures of 10,000 and 8000 for the deportation in 597. Even if we accept the higher figure, the Babylonian exiles cannot have been more than a tiny fraction of the population of the country.

The exiles did, however, include most of the nation's leaders, and they themselves were acutely conscious of their status as 'the good figs' (Jer.24). They saw themselves as the true inheritors and guardians of Israel's traditions. They therefore felt themselves competent to work out a new and reformed system of religious faith and practice, and eventually to force this new order on the Palestinians. All this, however, came later, and really falls within the compass of the next section.

There was a new seriousness about religion. The prophetic criticisms of pre-exilic religion were accepted and assimilated. A new orthodoxy was created. Cut off from the temple cultus, the exiles reacted in two ways: they concocted idealistic schemes for the reform and re-establishment of the cult (this is the motive not only behind Ezek.40–48 but behind much of the Priestly writing also – see Part III, Section 3, pp. 93 ff.). At the same time they evolved institutions which made them less dependent on the cult in practice. It is interesting to note that after the final destruction of the temple in AD 70, the Rabbis reacted in a similar way, regulating the temple ritual in minute detail, but at the same time working out the means which enabled Judaism to do without it.

The Deuteronomic reform had partly prepared the exiles for this adjustment. In restricting sacrificial worship to Jerusalem it effectively cut off many Jews from the cultus for the greater part of the year. Deuteronomy itself therefore had already tried to fill the religious gap by encouraging the study of sacred law in the context of family life (Deut.11.18–20, cf. 6.6–9).

In order that their corporate religious life should have some way of expressing itself, the exiles seem to have created the synagogue. We have no direct evidence of its existence during the exile, but all the circumstantial evidence points to its origin in this period (see further in Part IV, Section 3, pp. 229 ff.).

2. *In Egypt*

That there were substantial communities of Jews in Egypt is clear from Jer.44, and also from the Elephantiné Papyri. The Elephantiné Papyri are a cache of letters and legal documents discovered at Yeb in Upper Egypt. They emanate from a Jewish military colony. The documents date from the fifth century but the community was older.

When did these colonies in Egypt originate? Many of the Egyptian exiles probably went there after 597 and 586. Jeremiah himself was part of an even later wave of refugees. But it is possible that some may have fled there as early as 722, when Samaria fell to the Assyrians. The religious practices of the Elephantiné Jews suggest that they knew nothing of the Deuteronomic reform (see Part III, Section 3, pp. 91 ff.). They had a temple there, and offered sacrifice, and they worshipped other gods besides Yahweh, including a feminine consort of his. We have no evidence about whether the other Jewish colonies in Egypt adhered to this unreformed religion.

However large their numbers may have been (and we cannot even guess them), the Egyptian exiles were not influential in the way the Babylonian ones became, not, at any rate, within our period. However, a strong Jewish community did survive in Egypt until well into the Christian era. And during the Greek period Egyptian Judaism, under the leadership of Alexandria, developed a distinctive culture and theology of its own.

3. *In Palestine*

We do not know for certain what steps the Babylonians took after Gedaliah's murder, though it has been plausibly suggested that there was a further small deportation. It seems that the land was subsequently governed from Samaria. When the Persians took over the Babylonian Empire they certainly regarded Judah as part of the province centred on Samaria.

It looks as if some of Israel's neighbours, especially the Edomites, infiltrated into her territory at this juncture and took over much of her land. On this subject and the feelings it aroused see below on the book of Obadiah (p. 182). The Jews' intense hatred of the Edomites (later called Idumaeans) dates from this period. One of the things which Herod the Great failed to live down was his Idumaean origin.

The Palestinians continued for a long time as a depressed community, depressed both economically and psychologically. Nevertheless, the picture of them which is presented in some of our biblical sources, notably I and II Chronicles, Ezra, Nehemiah, need not be accepted with unreserved credulity. Not only was the Chronicler biased in favour of the Babylonian exiles, who he thought were the only true and faithful Israel, but virtually all our biblical materials have been edited by men who shared this view. The idea that the Palestinians were at best apathetic and at worst prone to apostasy may not be entirely just. It may merely reflect the exiles' later discovery that the Palestinians had a mind of their own, and that they were less than enthusiastic about having a reform of their religion dictated to them by upstarts returned from Babylon (see II Chron.36.11–21).

The Coming of the Persians and the Babylonian Defeat

The Babylonian Empire (more properly the Neo-Babylonian Empire) did not last long. Its end is quickly told. Its last ruler was Nabonidus, who seems to have been unpopular. He antagonized the priesthood, possibly by attempting religious reforms. He also spent much of his time away from the capital, and failed to return even for the important New Year Festival, in which the king's rôle was vital.

Cyrus, the conqueror of Babylon, was originally a vassal of the Medes, the ruler of a minor kingdom called Anshan, whose precise location is dubious. He rebelled against his overlord, Astyages, and became master of the Median Empire. He defeated the powerful Croesus of Lydia in 546. He next moved on Babylon.

Nabonidus, still absent from his capital, was cut off and defeated by Cyrus' general Gobryas. Cyrus occupied Babylon peacefully in 538, being welcomed by its priesthood and taking the throne as representative of Marduk, Babylon's own god. II Isaiah prophesied this conquest (see Isa.46.1 f.; 47; and 43.14 in RSV translation). But his prophecies were not fulfilled in the manner in which he expected them to be.

Cyrus himself was an outstanding personality, both as a general and as a ruler. A considerable mythology arose around him. Anyone who could be given the title 'messiah' by a Hebrew prophet (Isa.45.1) and at the same time be extolled by a Greek historian (Xenophon) as a paragon of Hellenistic virtue must have been a remarkable man.

As a general his great weapon was unexpectedness. He moved his armies much faster than was common (Isa.41.2 f.), so that his enemies often found him on their doorsteps while they were still thinking of mobilizing. He acknowledged few of the rules of war, and once attacked, for example, after his opponent had called off his campaign for the winter.

As a ruler his policies were enlightened. Before his time the idea of holding an empire was to place garrisons at strategic points and demand the payment of taxes. To 'rebel' meant to refuse payment, and at the death of an emperor his successor usually had to conquer his empire afresh. Cyrus set about seriously the task of governing the lands which he had conquered.

More about the Persian achievement and about Jewish life under their rule is given in Part III, Section 14, pp. 182 ff. For the present, all that needs to be said is that Cyrus, instead of attempting to crush subject peoples and rob them of their individuality, encouraged their culture and favoured their religions. He fulfilled II Isaiah's expectation that he would allow the exiles to return.

Developments in Prophecy

Prophecy was transformed during the period of the exile. Although it had been vindicated by the exile, its day was nearly done. Ezekiel and Deutero-Isaiah are the last really great exponents of it. In their hands it has already changed significantly. It has already become a *literary* phenomenon. Ezekiel (though not II Isaiah) also heralds another change. In him prophecy has become much more pro-cultic. He takes a positive attitude to worship and is interested in the temple ritual. Prophecy also becomes much more optimistic. The pre-exilic prophets whose words have been preserved for us were principally prophets of doom. Ezekiel's pre-exilic oracles are typical doom oracles. After 586, which occurs in the middle of his career, he suddenly becomes a prophet of hope. II Isaiah, whose career was entirely after 586, is optimistic throughout. It is true that these hopeful prophecies were not all very successful ones. Later prophets are less sanguine. When prophecy passed into limbo its mantle fell upon the apocalyptists, and we may detect in Ezekiel the beginnings of an apocalyptic style, in his curious symbolism and imagery.

Prophecy's failure lay in its inability to interpret the continued depression of post-exilic Israel. Now that Israel was reformed and faithful, she ought, according to prophetic theory, to be rewarded by prosperity and independence. The earlier prophets of doom had mostly gone on to predict restoration, salvation after the punishment. The fulfilment of their threats had proved them true prophets. Why, then, were their promises not fulfilled, too? What, too, of the covenantal promises, especially the promise to David of eternal kingship for his dynasty? Had Yahweh's word become void?

These questions were answered by a resort to eschatology. The fulfilment of the prophecies and of the covenantal promises had merely been postponed. And the more depressing the present seemed to be, the more highly coloured were the pictures of the blessed future which the seers envisaged. This turn of ideas is already beginning in II Isaiah. Whether his work contains any genuine eschatology, in the sense of looking to an end of the world and of the cosmic order, may be disputed. What is certainly true is that he paints a romantic, extravagantly poetic picture of the future, and this may well be a response to the disappointments which, on the mundane level, his prophecies met with.

1. Ezekiel

(i) *Selected Passages* (these will be referred to or commented on in the body of the text) chs. 1–5; 8; 11; 12.1–16; 16; 18; 20.1–44; 23; 33.1–20; 37.

(ii) *Critical Questions*

How much of the book of Ezekiel is by the prophet himself? Since the end of the nineteenth century, many radical views have been advanced, but the more radical critics have failed to produce any agreed picture. Now it is common to accept that Ezekiel is responsible for most of the material in the book, though it contains enough problems to suggest that it was collected and edited by another hand, and that the editor possessed much of the material in two forms. It is still common to reject Ezekiel's authorship of the last nine chapters, though the present writer is inclined to accept these, too.

Where did Ezekiel prophesy? The book assumes that he went to Babylon in 597 with the first deportation and did all his prophesying there. This raises difficulties. He seems to be vividly aware of what is going on in Jerusalem (8; 11.1–13). But any alternative theory raises difficulties, too, and the view is taken here that the book is correct in suggesting that Ezekiel did not leave Babylon after 597. Our answer to this question makes little difference to what we think of Ezekiel's ideas. It does make a difference to our estimate of his admittedly extraordinary psychology.

(iii) *Ezekiel's Personality*

Ezekiel's book is full of visionary experiences and weird symbolic actions. These help to give us the impression that he was the oddest of the prophets. But is this really so? Perhaps the other prophets had similar experiences, but were less explicit about them. Is Ezekiel's vision in chs. 1–3 different in kind from that in Isa.6, or only more elaborately described? Ezekiel indulges in complicated play-acting of the siege of the city and the captivity of its people (4; 12.1–16). According to Isa.20, a similar performance of Isaiah's lasted three years. Ezekiel's symbolic action in cutting off his hair and dividing it into three portions is quite bizarre (ch. 5). Is it any more so than Jeremiah's dealings with the loincloth (Jer. 13.1–11)?

What is really odd about Ezekiel is not that he is a visionary of a very extreme type, but that he is also a rational, even prosaic person. His mystical and rational personalities do not alternate with one another. They seem actually to be combined. Most mystics, if they attempt to describe their visions at all, resort naturally to poetry, to suggestion. Ezekiel resorts to cataloguing. St John the Divine had a vision of the holy city, and he describes it poetically as 'coming down out of heaven like a bride adorned for her husband' (Rev.21.2). Ezekiel, when he saw his vision of the new Jerusalem, took out his tape measure and set down its dimensions (Ezek.40.1 ff.).

Ezekiel is a dual personality in another sense. He is both a prophet and a priest. It is tempting to connect these two functions with his two selves, the visionary and the pedant – tempting but superficial.

(iv) *Ezekiel's Message*

Although the first deportation had already taken place before Ezekiel began to prophesy, he still speaks, at first, like a pre-exilic prophet. The catastrophe of 597 had as yet taught the nation nothing. Chapter 8 is a fairly typical catalogue of the prevalent sins. Note that the ones which Ezekiel picks out are primarily cultic, concerned with ritual rather than with morals. Ezekiel's priestly interests are coming out here.

During this phase of his activities no one takes the prophet seriously. He does not expect them to. Then why prophesy at all? He does it, he says, in order to 'deliver his own soul'. He has a moral responsibility to discharge, whether people listen or not (see 3.4–8, 17–21; and 33.1–9). The latter passage contains Ezekiel's famous parable of the Watchman.

Earlier prophets, e.g., Hosea and Jeremiah, interpreted Israel's history as a tragic failure to fulfil the promise of her honeymoon period with Yahweh in the wilderness, her time of faithfulness. Ezekiel denies that there ever was such a period of faithfulness. Chapter 20.1–44 is a prosaic re-interpretation of history to prove his point, and chs.16 and 23 make the same point metaphorically.

After 586 Ezekiel's problem is no longer that people will not take him seriously. They now take him so seriously that they have lost all hope. If, as the prophet says, their fathers have been sinners since the beginning, what is the good of repenting *now*? Good behaviour at this late stage is not going to counterbalance all that huge deadweight of wrongdoing.

The prophet replies with his elaborate discussion of personal responsibility (18;

33.10–20). This is often cited as setting out an uncompromising individualism. But to say so is to miss the main point. Ezekiel's argument is not that each man must stand on his own moral feet, but that each *generation* must stand on its own feet. To this extent Ezekiel is still thinking in corporate and national terms. Put in this uncompromising form, Ezekiel's statement is not theologically acceptable. The generations do suffer for each other's sins. But prophets are not primarily theologians. They are preachers answering people's spiritual needs. In the historical context Ezekiel's argument makes excellent sense.

Ezekiel is convinced, then, of the radical nature of Israel's corruption. She merits (and after 586 has received) radical punishment. If she has any future it can only be through an equally radical intervention of grace. Now his doctrine of grace is the key to Ezekiel's whole thought, even its most unpleasant-sounding aspects. The miraculous quality of the restoration is well brought out in ch.37, the vision of the valley of dry bones. There is, of course, no thought here of individual resurrection or life after death. It is national restoration which is spoken of.

Ezekiel repeatedly says that God will save 'for his name's sake', or 'that his name might not be profaned'. At first sight this seems to mean that Ezekiel's God is a forbidding character who saves Israel not for any love he bears her, but out of concern for his own reputation. In the context of Ezekiel's thinking this can hardly be the correct interpretation. What the prophet is saying is that God saves Israel not because of what *she* is, but because of what *he* is. 'For my name's sake' means, 'Because that's the kind of person I am'. Chapter 16 makes it clear that he does love Israel, worthless as she is.

Israel as she is lacks the capacity to respond to God's affection. God himself must bestow that capacity. Ezekiel takes up an image of Jeremiah's when he speaks of the gift of the new heart (11.14–21).

Whereas the pre-exilic prophets on the whole were critical of the cult, and at best displayed little positive interest in it, Ezekiel's attention is much engaged by it. This is not an accidental consequence of his priesthood. It is bound up with his theology and especially with his doctrine of grace. To the earlier prophets repentance was what mattered, not sacrifices. Their theme is what man must do to put himself right: self-reform. Sacrifice, to them, is an attempt to evade the moral issue. Ezekiel, by contrast, has little faith in Israel's capacity for self-reform. God himself must make up her deficiencies, and the cult is the means by which he does this. Sacrifice, therefore, is not an alternative to repentance, but an expression of it. It is not a means whereby man tries to procure forgiveness, but a means whereby God offers it. Ezekiel therefore plans for the restoration of sacrifice, and all the other ritual which he finds so meaningful. His interpretation of the cultus became normative in the post-exilic period, and was taken up especially by the Priestly writer.

Ezekiel is throughout overcome by the sense of God's reality and holiness. Some of his most bizarre passages are really attempts to express this, the most notable being his call vision in chs.1–3.

One has the constant impression when reading Ezekiel that here is a man who has not found the appropriate vehicle for the expression of his thought. The Hebrew literary tradition was not well adapted to convey the kind of things which Ezekiel wished to say, and he failed to break through to any new literary forms by which to say them. His message suffers, because he has not mastered his medium. Deutero-Isaiah succeeds exactly where Ezekiel fails.

2. *Deutero-Isaiah (Isaiah 40–55)*

Deutero-Isaiah (or II Isaiah) is the name given to the unknown author of Isa.40–55, an exilic prophet.

Selected Passages (referred to or commented on below) chs. 40; 41; 42.18–20; 44.21–28; 45.1–13; 47; 51.1–11; 55. The so called Servant Songs, which will be dealt with separately, are 42.1–9; 49.1–6; 50.4–9; 52.13–53.12.

(i) *Critical Questions*

These chapters have been analysed in a number of ways, but there is little doubt that the bulk of the material comes from a single author. Some scholars hold that the Servant Songs are from a different hand, but this is the only possible exception of any substance. It is also clear that unlike most prophetic literature these chapters do not consist of short oracles, but of long poems. How many, and how long they are is disputed.

It seems established that the first part of the work, up to ch.48, was written in Babylon, when Cyrus was already active, but before his capture of Babylon in 538. The prophet speaks much of Cyrus in these chapters, and pins his hopes on him. Chapter 45.1–13 is his longest discussion of Cyrus' work and status (but cf. 41.1–4, 25). He hails Cyrus as messiah (45.1: most versions render the word here as 'anointed'), and says that his success is given him by Yahweh. Yet (45.4) this is not because Cyrus himself is anything to Yahweh. It is for Israel's sake. Cyrus' job is to free Israel (45.13). Verses 9–13 seem to be forestalling possible objections to this theory of Cyrus' messianic status. God is entitled to use his creatures as he sees fit. The imagery suggests that Cyrus is a mere tool in God's hand.

The prophet sees Cyrus as avenging Israel by destroying and humiliating Babylon. Chapter 47 is a lengthy exposition of this theme. These prophecies were unfulfilled. Cyrus was welcomed by Babylon with open arms.

Chapters 49–55 seem to have been written after 538. The prophet is partly disappointed. Cyrus is never mentioned now. The prophet's hope seems to be placed instead in a figure who is called 'the servant of the Lord'. It is possible that ch. 40 was written last of all, as an introduction to the entire corpus. It gathers up the themes from the rest of the work, and seems to be trying to come to terms with the disappointment which otherwise appears only in the second part of the prophecy.

(ii) *The Man and his Methods*

We do not know Deutero-Isaiah's name. We have no knowledge of his circumstances, or of even one single incident of his life. We have the content of his message, but we do not know how he received it. In all these respects he is as great a contrast with Ezekiel as could be conceived. He also differs from Ezekiel in that he works out dramatically new literary forms to enable him to express his insights. He exploits the capacity of poetic imagery to convey several different ideas at once: to say one thing while recalling or echoing another.

Chapter 51 usefully illustrates several features of II Isaiah's use of imagery: vv. 9–11 employ the image of the dividing of the waters.

The common Near-Eastern creation myth saw God as having created the world by dividing the waters of chaos. (This still appears in the Priestly account, Gen.1.6–8.) Rahab in Isa.51.9 is one of the names of the personified chaos monster. Yahweh had also saved Israel from Egypt by dividing the waters of the Red Sea. The promised return from exile is constantly spoken of in terms which recall both these events (cf. 43.15 ff.). The return itself involves no dividing of waters, but it does, like the exodus, involve a passage of the wilderness (41.17–20; 43.19 f.; 49.10 f.).

Chapter 51 also illustrates a rarer feature of II Isaiah's imagery, his recalling the paradise myth (51.3) and his use of eschatological language (51.6).

In all this the prophet is not merely playing with words, he is making a theological point. God's saving acts can be understood each in terms of the others. Each can only be fully understood when seen as part of the series. God is always doing 'new things', which only his prophets can predict, yet when they occur they are seen to be in character. II Isaiah thus stresses at the same time God's originality and his consistency. They are not incompatible. And the practical point of all this is that God is to be trusted. He is to be trusted in the particular concrete circumstance of the exile. He who could create the world and bring Israel out of Egypt can surely bring her out of Babylon.

(iii) *Deutero-Isaiah's Message*

Babylonian religion was characterized by an elaborate and colourful polytheism, and by very free use of divining, astrology, and other superstitions. II Isaiah's work, correspondingly, is militantly monotheistic and contemptuous of idols, and at the same time is bitingly critical of divination, gleefully contrasting its unreliability with the reliability of Yahweh's prophets. Chapter 41.21–29 illustrates both themes and their interrelation.

Yahweh is the only God, and he is the God who both saves and creates. II Isaiah uses words like 'create', 'make', 'form', 'save', 'redeem', as if they were virtually interchangeable. Theologically they *are* interchangeable, for all express different aspects of the activity of the one God. The unity of God is reflected in the unity of history (which includes creation).

We shall understand II Isaiah better if we remember that as he wrote the Priestly writer was preparing his great work. The Priestly writer combines his own creation account, in which God is said to 'create', with that of the Yahwist, for whom God 'forms' or 'makes' his creatures. And he presents that dual account of creation as the first step in a story of redemption, as part of history.

The Priestly writer and II Isaiah agree in two other respects. First, in their doctrine of the divine word. According to 'P', 'God *said* . . . And it was so.' II Isaiah in ch. 55 explains the Priestly writer's thinking here perfectly. But significantly he draws a practical and limited conclusion. If Yahweh's word is like that, cannot he be trusted to bring us back from Babylon? Second, they agree in their universalism. The Priestly writer works on a broad canvas. Salvation may be *through* Abraham and Israel, but it is *for* the world. Both the Priestly writer and II Isaiah were in exile thrown into close contact with foreigners and their culture. They could not have been insensitive to them, and could not conceive of God being insensitive to them. In 49.6 f. the prophet is ordained to be a light not only to Israel, but to the nations.

(iv) *The Servant Songs*

These are among the most discussed passages in the Old Testament. Some scholars prefer to treat them apart from their context, holding either that they were composed by someone other than II Isaiah, or that they were composed by the prophet as independent poems and inserted into the body of the work later. The chief argument for this view is that the figure of the servant who appears in the songs seems to be different from the servant who is referred to elsewhere. This is true, but it must also be noted that the servant's character also differs from song to song, and further, that the word 'servant' is not used consistently outside the songs either. Outside the songs the servant is usually Israel, and she is called 'servant' because she is God's special possession to whom he has a special obligation (41.8 f.; 44.21). But in 42.18–20, Israel the servant is Israel the inadequate. And in 44.26 the servant is not Israel at all, but the prophet. Within the songs there is the same oscillation between the servant as Israel (49.3) and the servant as an individual, which he must surely be in the last song, if not in the third.

But within the songs there is development of another kind in the servant's character. The first song (42.1–9) sets out the servant's destiny to be a kind of messiah to the world. There is nothing pessimistic in it (it is the only song to appear in the pre-538 BC half of the work). The second song (49.1–6) emphasizes the servant's preparation by God, but in 49.4 he shows himself conscious of the difficulties of the task. In the third song (50.4–9), he perceives that he must accept suffering as a necessary concomitant of the task to be done. In the final song (52.13–53.12), the suffering is given redemptive value. Perhaps here the acceptance of suffering is no longer a mere consequence of the task. It is the task itself.

In these songs the prophet is trying to come to terms with his experience of suffering and failure, both in his own life and that of the nation. In learning what to do with his own distress he tries to show his people how to regard theirs. That they failed to rise to this destiny goes without saying.

Disputes have raged around the question, Who is the servant? This is really two questions. It can be taken to mean, Where did the prophet get the idea of the servant? Put in this form the question can be answered. He clearly has in mind the sufferings of his nation in exile. Very likely he has suffered himself. He is almost certainly influenced by the experiences of his fellow prophets, and especially Jeremiah. The songs might almost be taken as commentary on Jeremiah's career. He may well have in the back of his mind the common Near-Eastern myth of the suffering king, who is ritually abased, only to rise again bringing salvation for his people. He may likewise be affected by the myth of the dying and rising saviour god. He may also have thought of the past heroes of his race who suffered for their people, especially Moses (see Ex.32.32) and possibly even Hezekiah and Jehoiachin. All these, and others, have been at some time identified as the servant. And all these suggestions could be at least partly right.

But the question, Who is the servant?, can also be interpreted, Who is to fulfil the task of the servant? Is it for the nation, or a messianic king, or a prophet, or who else? In this form the question cannot be given a direct answer. Perhaps the prophet himself could not have answered it. II Isaiah is not concerned so much with the person of the servant as with the office. He is writing about servanthood. Whatever the servant's identity, this is what he will have to do and to be. He must give his back to the smiters, and his cheeks to those who pluck out the beard. He must not hide his face from shame and spitting. He must be despised and rejected, and offer himself as an offering for sin. Whoever is willing to do this, whether the nation as a whole, or a group within the nation, a king or a prophet, or any other individual present or to come, will have taken on himself the office and

form of the servant.

3. *Obadiah*

This short work appears to date from the exilic period. It is concerned almost exclusively with Edom (which it often refers to as 'Esau'). The Edomites took advantage of Judah's plight during the exile (vv. 10–14) and the prophet foresees divine punishment for them (vv. 1–9). He looks forward to the day of the Lord (vv. 15–21) when all nations shall be judged and Judah and Israel restored.

14

The Return

H. McKeating

The Evidence

1. *Biblical References*

We are concerned with two complex series of events. These are often confused, so we shall keep them rigorously separate from the start. First, there are the events concerned with the return of some Jews from exile at the end of the sixth century, immediately following Cyrus' conquest of Babylon, and the subsequent rebuilding of the temple.

Our primary sources here are the book of Haggai and chs. 1–8 of Zechariah (the rest of Zechariah is a later composition). The prophets Haggai and Zechariah were intimately concerned with the temple rebuilding and their words are likely to have been written down shortly after the event. They are thus first-hand sources, but not systematic historical accounts.

Our chief secondary source is Ezra 1–6. This does purport to be a systematic historical account. The books we now call I and II Chronicles, Ezra and Nehemiah are parts of a single continuous literary work. Its author is usually referred to as 'The Chronicler'. Up to the end of II Chronicles we can check his account against other sources (e.g., Samuel and

Kings) and perceive how freely he treats them. In Ezra we can check him only against Haggai and Zech. 1–8. In Nehemiah we cannot check him at all. The value of his account is variable. In Ezra it is certainly confused and self-contradictory, but contains bits which may well be authentic.

We must also reckon with the apocryphal book I Esdras (see Part III, Section 15, p. 197). It contains much material taken direct from Ezra, but sometimes exhibits significant variations.

The second complex of events starts in the middle of the fifth century (about 150 years later) and centres on Ezra's reform and Nehemiah's rebuilding of the walls.

Primary sources: none.

Our secondary sources are Ezra 7–10 and Nehemiah. Ezra 7–10 again shows signs of confusion, but Nehemiah consists largely of a first-person account which may well represent an original Memoirs of Nehemiah. If we could be certain of this it would rank as a primary source.

I Esdras is again relevant.

There is other literature in the Old Testament which dates from this period (see below under

Literature). Much of it is not the kind that helps with historical reconstruction (e.g., Jonah and Song of Songs) and much that in principle might help (e.g., III Isaiah, or Trito-Isaiah) is so difficult to date precisely that it is historically unusable. But even apart from books specifically mentioned here, most of the Old Testament was put into its present form in this period (see Part III, Section 3, pp. 85 ff.).

2. *Non-biblical Literature*

Josephus (*Antiquities*, 11.1–5) is usually relying on biblical accounts and is not an independent witness. The background history of Persia is well covered by the Greek historians, Xenophon, Herodotus and Thucydides. Throughout much of our period the Persians were meeting trouble from the Greeks. The epic battles of Plataea and Marathon in 490 BC, and Thermopylae and Salamis in 480, fall about half-way between Zerubbabel's rebuilding of the temple and Nehemiah's rebuilding of the walls.

3. *Archaeological Evidence*

Many Persian cities have been excavated, providing ample information on Persian history and culture: Susa (cf. Neh.1.1), Ecbatana (Ezra 6.2), Babylon, Erech and Pasargadae among others. From Persepolis the Treasury Tablets give detailed information about Persian financial administration. The accounts of a large business firm called Murashu Sons discovered at Nippur incidentally mention many Jewish names.

The tombs of the Persian kings at Naqsh-i-Rustam are a mine of information. Important among inscriptions is that at Behistun, dramatically placed on a cliff face and recording how Darius I quelled the opposition at the beginning of his reign.

In Palestine, remains from the Persian period have been found on numerous sites. They show that for most of this period the country was neither very prosperous nor well populated. Evidence of the destruction and abandonment of Bethel in the sixth century and of Tell-en-Nasbeh and Megiddo in the fourth shows not only that times were unsettled, but that violent events took place of which our literary sources say nothing.

The Elephantiné papyri (see Part III, Section 13, p. 176) are again important, and enable us to fix the date of Nehemiah. Nehemiah's opponent Sanballat is mentioned in them, and elsewhere. Another adversary, Geshem the Arabian, is also mentioned twice in texts from this period.

The Persian Achievement

The history of Persia is too complicated to outline here. We need only concern ourselves with the following kings: Cyrus founded the empire, took Babylon in 538 and allowed the Jews to go home. His next successor but one was Darius I (522–486 BC), who usurped the throne and practically had to reconquer his empire, but proved a strong king. In his reign the temple at Jerusalem was rebuilt. Much later we have Artaxerxes I (465–424 BC), in whose reign Nehemiah came to Jerusalem. Ezra, too, is stated to have returned in his reign, but if this is an error we must reckon Ezra to the reign of Artaxerxes II, in the first half of the following century.

The Persians were great imperial administrators. Their organization was initiated by Cyrus but built up by his successors, especially Darius I. It allowed a large measure of local autonomy and encouraged local culture (e.g., local religions). It at least contrived to give the impression that it was governing people for their own good. The administration depended on swift communication. A network of fast roads connected all parts of the Empire, and the imperial postal service could relay messages non-stop and at high speed, through having teams of horses and messengers posted at the ready at intervals of a few miles along all major roads. The Persians established a *lingua franca*, Aramaic, throughout their domains. In Palestine and Syria it quickly became the vernacular. Soon after Ezra's time Hebrew was relegated to the status of a learned tongue. It was not re-established as the vernacular in Palestine until after the Second World War.

The Empire was divided into 'satrapies', each with its Satrap, who was like a powerful minor king. But there were clever checks and balances. Some of the Satrap's most important court officials were not responsible to him but directly to the great king. These included his chief financial officer and the general-in-charge of the garrison in the Satrap's own capital. The Satrap was also subject to inspection by a travelling inquisitor called 'the king's eye'.

Persian Religion

Up to the beginning of the Persian period, the religion which held sway in Mesopotamia was for all practical purposes the same polytheistic faith which had been established there by the Sumerians soon after 3000 BC. The Persians, being Indo-Europeans, had a different polytheism of their own, but made no attempt to disturb the existing cults.

Zoroastrianism seems to have originated in the sixth century BC in Persia itself. By the time of Darius I it was the state religion. Its adoption, however, made no difference to official Persian tolerance of other religions.

Early Zoroastrianism may be described either as monotheism with strong tendencies towards dualism, or as dualism with strong tendencies towards monotheism. The good God (called Ahura Mazda or Ormazd) and the evil one (Ahriman) are almost evenly matched. Both have creative power. But the good is destined to win, and the true believer must side firmly with the good.

A simplification and rationalization of the old Persian polytheism lies behind Zoroaster's system, and after his death much of the polytheism came back, albeit in covert form. A rich angelology and demonology developed. Originally Zoroastrianism was purely moralistic. A man stands or falls by the balance between his righteous and unrighteous acts. There is no room for forgiveness or divine grace.

It is generally agreed that later Judaism owes a good deal to Zoroastrianism.

The Rebuilding of the Temple

We have already distinguished primary and secondary sources, and noted the confusion in the latter. The sensible procedure therefore is to see first what we can learn from our primary sources and then allow the secondary ones to fill out the picture. Where they supply additional facts we may cautiously accept their testimony, but we must not allow them to *correct* the primary sources.

Haggai's carefully dated prophecies are all from 'the second year of Darius' (520 BC), and therefore eighteen years after Cyrus's conquest of Babylon. He graphically pictures the economic depression of the Jerusalem community (1.6; 2.16). The leaders of this community are Zerubbabel (the lay leader) and Joshua (the high priest). The book begins by hinting at discussions about whether to rebuild the temple and the general feeling is that the time is inappropriate (1.2). The common-sense answer evidently was that the community could not afford it. Haggai asserts that their priorities are wrong. If they would put the service of God first, then the economy would sort itself out, with God's help.

There have been convulsions in international politics and Haggai expects more (2.6–9). These were the disturbances at the beginning of Darius's reign, recorded on the Behistun Rock. In this shaking of the Empire Haggai sees Israel's chance of freedom, and even dominion (2.6–9). Zerubbabel (who seems to have been of Davidic ancestry) is given messianic status, and a great future is predicted for him in the age that is about to dawn (2.21–23). Haggai's advice was taken and the work of rebuilding the temple begun (2.18).

Zechariah writes a little later. His first vision is dated a month earlier than Haggai's last oracle and the rest spread over three years. He confirms Haggai's picture at every point. He reports the same depression (8.10). He, too, is in favour of the rebuilding, which has already begun (4.9 f.), and is convinced that prosperity will result (8.9–13; cf. 1.16 f.). Like Haggai he expects more than mere prosperity (8.1–7). See 2.1–13, where one element in the glorious future is to be the gathering in of the dispersed Jews.

The expected unrest has come to nothing (1.11 f.), but the prophet does not despair, for the future is still assured. The priesthood is to be purified in the person of Joshua (ch. 3). The messiah is to come (3.8). According to ch. 4 it looks as if that messiah is to be Zerubbabel (cf. Hag.2.21 ff.).

We deduce, then, that the foundations of the new temple were laid in 520 BC, by a Jerusalem community which could not well afford the project; that the leaders were Joshua and Zerubbabel, and that they were prompted and supported by Haggai and Zechariah. We also know that their economic and political expectations were sadly disappointed, for other post-exilic literature (e.g., III Isaiah and Malachi) makes this quite clear.

Note the omissions. Nothing is said of any exiles who had returned from Babylon, and there is no suggestion that anyone except the local Palestinian community had a hand in the work. Neither is anything reported of any earlier attempt to rebuild the temple.

What does our secondary source in Ezra 1–6 tell us? It records that in 538, when Cyrus conquered Babylon, he let the Jews return to Jerusalem and rebuild the temple (Ezra 1.2–4). They returned with enthusiasm (1.5 ff.) under the leadership of Sheshbazzar (1.11). In ch. 3, suddenly, Sheshbazzar's name is simply dropped from the story. Without introduction Zerubbabel and Joshua appear as leaders. They begin to re-use the temple site (3.1–6) and soon lay the foundations for a new building (3.7 ff.). In ch. 4 they are opposed by some people called 'the adversaries of Judah and Benjamin', who successfully prevent any further progress until the reign of Darius.

In Ezra 5, encouraged by the prophets Haggai and Zechariah, the returned exiles make a fresh start. This brings a renewed attack from the adversaries, who try to stir up trouble with the Persian authorities. In the course of the controversy the history of the project is re-stated. Sheshbazzar is now credited with the earlier attempt (5.14–16) and it is said that since his day the work has never stopped (5.16). The decree of Cyrus is quoted (6.1–5), this time in Aramaic. This convinces the authorities and the work is completed in 518 (6.15).

This agrees with Haggai and Zech.1–8 in stating that the successful rebuilding began in 520; that Joshua and Zerubbabel were the leaders; and that Haggai and Zechariah supported the venture.

It disagrees only in recording an earlier, unsuccessful attempt in the reign of Cyrus. The account of this is suspicious. The Chronicler is in two minds as to who was responsible, Sheshbazzar or Zerubbabel, and contradicts himself about whether the adversaries brought the work to a halt or only slowed it down.

The Chronicler also gives two accounts of Cyrus' decree ordering the return. The Hebrew version (Ezra 1.1–5) gives permission to return but no express permission to rebuild. The Aramaic (Ezra 6.1–5) gives permission to rebuild but no express leave to return.

In spite of these discrepancies a return under Cyrus is inherently likely. II Isaiah confidently expects one, and it is in line with what is known of Cyrus' policies. The information that it was led by the otherwise unknown Sheshbazzar may be accepted.

Permission to rebuild the temple is by no means unlikely either. The Aramaic decree is regarded by many as an authentic document. The Elephantiné papyri relating to a Jewish temple in Egypt show that the Persians did interest themselves in such buildings, and in the worship and ritual practices of subject communities. However, if such an attempt was actually made in Cyrus' reign, the Chronicler manifestly knows no facts about it whatever. He has transferred what he knows about Zerubbabel's rebuilding back into Cyrus' reign.

I suggest that if permission to rebuild was given by Cyrus it was never acted on, or that the attempt to act on it was so insignificant that Haggai and Zechariah could ignore it. The Chronicler, is, however, obliged to posit that a serious effort was made. He cannot conceive that his darling returned exiles, in whom the true faith burned, could have done anything other than rebuild the temple as soon as they arrived in Jerusalem. Unfortunately he has to come to terms with the known fact that the existing temple was built by Zerubbabel in the reign of Darius. So he invents reasons why the exiles were unable to carry their project through, and he fails to make those reasons quite consistent.

Comparison with Haggai and Zech.1–8 suggests that the Chronicler has magnified the part played by the exiles. He suggests that they undertook the work alone and rejected offers of local help (4.2 f.). Haggai and Zechariah reflect no knowledge of such tensions within the community, though the accounts of Ezra and Nehemiah show that they did arise later, nearer the Chronicler's own time.

The Work of Ezra and Nehemiah

Dates: Ezra and Nehemiah came back to Jerusalem from Babylon at different times. The Chronicler says both came in the reign of 'Artaxerxes', Ezra in the seventh year (Ezra 7.7) and Nehemiah in the twentieth (Neh.1.1; 2.1). Now there were several kings of that name. However, by referring across to the Elephantiné papyri, which give dated references to prominent people mentioned in Nehemiah's memoirs, we can confirm that his activities took place in the reign of Artaxerxes I and that his coming to Jerusalem was in 444 BC.

But there are three principal dates suggested for Ezra. The Chronicler himself clearly thinks that Ezra came before Nehemiah, in the reign of the same king, i.e., in 458. Many scholars believe that the Chronicler is wrong about this, and that Ezra came after Nehemiah in the reign of Artaxerxes II. This gives a date for Ezra's arrival of 398 BC, nearly half a century later than Nehemiah.

A third view is that the Chronicler has, after all, got the right king but the wrong year, and that Ezra arrived in the *thirty*-seventh year of Artaxerxes I: i.e., later than Nehemiah but not much later (428 BC).

The arguments cannot be gone into here. Suffice it is to say that the question remains an open one. The view taken here is the traditional one, that Ezra arrived in 458. On this view the course of events would be as follows:

Ezra, who was a priest and a scribe, came to Jerusalem bringing with him 'the book of the law of Moses' (Neh.8.1). This may have been the entire Pentateuch, or only part of it – the Priestly writing. This law was the expression of the new religious synthesis which had been worked out in exile. It was Ezra's mission to get the Palestinians to conform to it.

The exact status of Ezra's authority is in doubt. According to Ezra 7.25 f. he was given some political powers, but he was assuredly not made governor. Judah seems still to have been within the province governed from Samaria. Ezra may therefore have lacked the power to carry through the reforms he wished.

But there may have been more personal reasons for failure. Ezra seems to have been a pious but impractical idealist (see his behaviour in the affair of the bodyguard, Ezra 8.21–23). When he met opposition his reaction was to tear his hair (literally) and 'make a scene' (Ezra 9.3). It is interesting to compare Nehemiah's reaction in almost precisely similar circumstances (Neh.13.25).

Acceptance of the traditional dating does involve the conclusion that Ezra's work was a failure. Some of the provisions of his law were successfully resisted. His breaking up of mixed marriages (Ezra 9–10) seems not to have been permanent, for Nehemiah had to tackle the question all over again, in a less high-handed

manner (Neh.13.24–27). It is likely that he antagonized the local population; and the authorities in Samaria, who had no wish to see Jerusalem re-established as a political or religious centre, will hardly have been slow to oppose him as they later opposed Nehemiah.

It may be conjectured that this resulted in an attack on Jerusalem of which the Chronicler says nothing. Nehemiah's grief at hearing of the plight of Jerusalem (Neh.1) certainly suggests a *recent* catastrophe. In this attack the walls had again been broken down. When had these walls been rebuilt? Either they were rebuilt under Zerubbabel or were in process of construction by Ezra himself. Ezra 4.7–23 gives an account of how an attempt to rebuild the walls in the reign of Artaxerxes was frustrated by the local authorities, backed up by a decision of the Persian king.

Nehemiah learns of the failure of Ezra's mission from his brother Hanani (Neh.1). He gets himself appointed governor (see 5.14) and it looks as if at this point Judah is taken out of the jurisdiction of the authorities in Samaria.

Nehemiah rouses the people to repair the walls, and finishes the work in face of ridicule (Neh.4.1–6), threats (4.7–23) and a treacherous offer to come to terms (6.1–5). There were subsequent threats to report the matter to the Persian authorities (6.6–9) and to assassinate Nehemiah himself (6.10–14). This last seems to have been a roundabout attempt to discredit Nehemiah by getting him to seek asylum in the temple, where he had no right to be, for he was doubtless a eunuch. Nehemiah also had to tackle the community's economic troubles (Neh.5).

He was obliged to build up the population of the city by drafting in people from the countryside (Neh.7.4 f.; 11.1 f), because the existing population was inadequate for the city's defence. He brought back the Levites from secular employment to their religious duties, and regulated the payment of tithes (13.10–14; cf. 13.30 f.). He enforced observance of the sabbath (13.15–22). He took active measures against any further contracting of mixed marriages (13.23–27).

Nehemiah after some time returned to Persia, but later came back for a second period of office.

If the traditional dating of Ezra is correct, Ezra must have been in Jerusalem all the time

Nehemiah was doing his work, yet the two are rarely mentioned together (only in Neh.8.9; 12.26). In fact, where they do appear together in the account of Ezra's reading of the law (Neh.8.9) the name of Nehemiah is probably an erroneous addition (I Esdras omits it). This eighth chapter quite probably refers to events that took place before Nehemiah's arrival, and is thus out of chronological order. If Ezra had succeeded only in antagonizing people it need not surprise us that he remained in the background and left the work to the more diplomatic Nehemiah.

Nehemiah should in many ways appeal to twentieth-century readers. Though religious, he is not in the bad sense pious. He frequently reports that he prayed, but the prayers are usually brief and practical (2.4; 4.4 f.; 5.19; 6.9,14). He is very much a practical man; an astute politician, good not only at organizing but at handling all kinds of people; he gets things done. But he is no mere pragmatist. He is above all a man of principle. He knows when to be diplomatic, but he also knows when to stand his ground (see Neh.6.3 for a magisterial reply). He gives the impression of great confidence, but it is not self-confidence. It flows from his absolute conviction that he is doing what God has called him to do (Neh.2.20a; 4.19 f.).

All this, however, was accomplished at a cost. Measures were taken against mixed marriages and against foreign elements generally. These foreign elements were in some cases, it seems, just Israelites from further north. We may guess that a number of the undesirables were merely Palestinian Jews who refused to conform to the returned exiles' religious leadership.

It is commonly said that all this, though it looks unpleasant, was necessary in the circumstances, for otherwise religion could not have been kept pure. This comes close to conceding that the end justifies the means. If a religion cannot be kept pure except by such means as these, then the sooner it is adulterated the better. Exclusivism, wherever it is found (cf. Neh.2.20b) and whatever the ostensible reason for it, is always a horrid thing, a very horrid thing.

There was a universalistic movement in the post-exilic age. It was begun by II Isaiah and carried on worthily by III Isaiah, and by the authors of Jonah and Ruth. If this, rather than the Ezra-Nehemiah movement, had prevailed, who is to say that this would have produced religious disaster?

Judaism in the Post-exilic Age

From Ezra's time onwards Judaism became a religion of law. Piety consisted in the study of it and in obedience to it. The scholar, the interpreter of the law, thus became as important as the priest, and in the long run, more so. Correspondingly the synagogue, where the law was studied, rivalled and eventually replaced the temple. A body of interpretative tradition and comment grew up, and soon came to be regarded as almost as sacred as the written law itself (this is the 'tradition of the elders' mentioned in Matt.15.2 ff. and parallels). The legend developed that at the same time as God delivered the written law to Moses on Sinai he delivered the oral tradition too, and that this had been handed down in unbroken succession.

The written law was of course what stands in the Pentateuch. It consists of high moral precepts (e.g., Lev.19.1–18) and a good deal of cultic prescription, which to our minds seems of far less value (cf. Lev.19.5–8; 19.19). The faithful Jew was expected to know and to keep all these regulations, observing festivals, paying tithes and making other offerings, keeping sabbath and dietary restrictions as punctiliously as he refrained from murder, theft and adultery.

The law prescribed the cult, and it was a cult subtly different from the pre-exilic one. It was more solemn; it took sin more seriously. It allowed expiation by sacrifice and other means, but expiation was only possible for those who had made amends, material amends, for their offences (Lev.6.1–7).

Many of the cultic laws could only be observed in Palestine. The Jews of the diaspora, who were now more numerous than the Palestinians, were expected to fulfil what they could. Palestinian Judaism was still regarded as the norm.

The emphasis on the cult naturally gave the priests a prominent role. But other factors tended in the same direction. The nation, now without a king, and ruled from a foreign centre, had no native head of state but the high priest. Just as, in pre-exilic times, there had been no high priest, for high-priestly functions were fulfilled by the king, so now, lacking a king, many royal attributes and prerogatives were assumed by the high priesthood.

Not everyone accepted this new orthodoxy. Already in the time of Nehemiah a rift with the Samaritan community was widening and the Samaritans developed a religious orthodoxy of their own, which was in some respects quite different from that of the Jews (see Part IV, Section 3, p. 233).

The Literature

1. *The Final Shaping of the Pentateuch*

The development of the Pentateuch has been dealt with elsewhere in this volume (Part III, Section 3, pp. 85 ff.). It is sufficient to note here that it received its definitive shape during the exile or the early post-exilic period, in Babylon, and that it was brought back to the homeland. It seems reasonable to connect the work of Ezra with this bringing of the Pentateuch to Palestine, though whether this means we can boldly equate Ezra's law book with the Pentateuch in its entirety is open to question.

2. *The Book of Ruth*

For convenience the book of Ruth is dealt with at this point, though the belief that it was written in the early post-exilic period is not unchallenged.

The heroine, Ruth, is a Moabite woman (Moab being on the opposite side of the Dead Sea from Israel) and the genealogy at the end of the book makes her an ancestress of David. If the book really was written around the time when Ezra and his party were taking such exception to marriage with foreign women this point can hardly have gone unnoticed, though it is now fashionable to doubt whether this was the reason for the book's publication.

Be that as it may, it is certainly not the *only* point of the story. It is a story that begins sadly, but ends with devotion and patience rewarded.

It is set in the period of the judges, when there was no central government. The only security an individual had was in the strength of his family or tribe. A man therefore had a duty to his poorer relatives, however distant. He was expected to avenge them if they were wronged, to support them if they went bankrupt, and marry the widow of his childless relative so that property could be kept in the family and the family name carried on. This protecting kinsman was called the 'redeemer'. A woman, especially, was in a difficult and exposed position if left alone. She needed a husband, and a family to belong to, and children who would look after her when she became old.

When Naomi, living in a foreign country, is bereaved of all her family she does the natural thing, she goes home. But Ruth, in going with her, is hazarding everything. The 'sensible' thing would have been to stay in Moab and find another husband. But she follows Naomi, because Naomi needs her, and because they share a common grief.

In Israel she is an immigrant. Neither she nor Naomi have any livelihood, and Ruth makes what she can by gleaning. The right of the poor to gleaning was part of Israel's rough and ready social security system (cf. Lev.19.9 f.).

Boaz shows his virtue not merely in appreciating Ruth's devotion to Naomi. He accepts his duty as a kinsman to this immigrant who was not strictly a member of his family, but who had come to count herself as one.

The other kinsman (in ch. 4) is willing to accept the advantages of kinship and take up the option on Naomi's old property, but not its obligations – the upkeep and protection of Ruth. We are not to suppose, however, that to Boaz himself the duty of marrying Ruth was an unwelcome one.

The book's universalism is not confined to the genealogy at the end. Ruth is a proselyte (1.16 f.); she accepts Israel's faith and throws in her lot with the chosen people. The book does not merely argue, it *assumes* that she is entitled to all the benefits of membership, even to the point of becoming ancestress to the Messiah. The Magnificat would be as appropriate in the mouth of Ruth as in that of Mary.

In another respect the book of Ruth is universalistic. The Old Testament often gives the impression that Israel's faith is male-centred and male-dominated. It is a wrong impression, and Ruth is one of the books which helps to correct it. Ruth, the very prototype of the gentile who becomes one of the elect, is a woman. This is an interesting foreshadowing of the prominent part played by women both in the proselytizing movement in later Judaism and in the spread of the Christian gospel.

3. *The Work of the Chronicler*
(I and II Chronicles, Ezra and Nehemiah)

A good deal has already been said about the Chronicler's writings, but looking at them purely as historical sources. As such they have serious deficiencies. But the Chronicler did not intend to write an historical source book. He intended to write theology, and he wrote it in the way in which Israel's thinkers customarily wrote theology, i.e., by re-telling the history of his race.

His scope is wide. He begins with the creation and ends with the work of Ezra and Nehemiah. His coverage of the period is very uneven. He gets from Adam to the death of Saul in nine chapters, mostly of genealogy. But he spends twenty-eight chapters on the reigns of David and Solomon. He not only misses out a great deal which the earlier literature includes, he also makes significant additions. Many of these additions concern the temple and its worship, and especially the work of the Levites. Every historical event is explained in accordance with a very rigid theory of reward and punishment, and the Chronicler has no qualms about emending the facts to fit his scheme. The wicked king Manasseh had a long reign, so the Chronicler invents a spurious repentance to account for the fact. The good king Josiah was killed in his youth, so a sin has to be invented (and a very curious sin it is) to explain his death away.

God's control of events is direct and detailed. Men have little to do but trust and pray. Nearly all the Chronicler's battles are won by squads of Levites hurling no more lethal missiles than psalms of praise.

The Chronicler's theology, though he often expresses it in crude or naïve ways, is throughout a theology of faith; of confidence in the divine control of history; of conviction that if men would but trust and praise him everything would be all right. Its expression may amuse or infuriate us, but its content should not be despised.

4. *The Song of Songs*

The title means 'the best song of all'. It is unlikely to have any genuine connection with Solomon. In origin it is almost certainly purely secular. It has been analysed in various ways but is most likely a collection of love songs. It owes its place in the canon and its subsequent

popularity in both Jewish and Christian circles to the fact that it was interpreted allegorically. Its imagery, though attractive, is rather alien to our western traditions of romantic literature, though we can see why it appealed so strongly to frustrated mediaeval monks.

5. *Trito-Isaiah (Isaiah 56–66)*

These chapters clearly have much in common with II Isaiah, and worthily continue the tradition of the Isaiah school of prophets. The commonest view is that these oracles do not all come from the same hand, or from quite the same period, but that they are mostly later than II Isaiah and reflect conditions in Palestine after the return.

They betray an interest in the cult that II Isaiah does not display; e.g., 56.1–8 appeals for more care in observing the sabbath. Compare ch. 58, which in addition denounces insincerity in worship.

II Isaiah's universalism is, however, taken up, and 56.3–8 anticipates that eunuchs and foreigners will be acceptable in the Lord's temple. Verse 7 finds an important echo in the New Testament (Matt.21.13) as does 61.1 ff. (Luke 4.18 f.). Chapter 60 preaches a less attractive form of universalism but its themes and phrases have been taken up by an extraordinary variety of writings: vv. 19 f. in Revelation, vv. 21 f. as a keyword in the Jewish 'Sayings of the Fathers', vv. 1 f. in Handel's 'Messiah', and v. 5b in the title of a famous work on economics – Adam Smith's *Wealth of Nations*. These, and some other passages, are as fine as anything in prophecy. See, for instance, Isa.57.14–20 on humility, and 58.3–12 on right religion. The latter is very Amos-like in its tone. Chapter 63.1–6 has also resounded down the years, as the text for the 'Battle Hymn of the Republic'. It is perhaps better appreciated for its sonority than for its sentiments.

6. *The Book of Joel*

Joel is a problematical book. It is usually taken to date from the post-exilic period, though the arguments are not entirely conclusive and some eminent scholars prefer an earlier date. It is also difficult to say what *kind* of writing it is, and to specify the setting and purpose for which it was intended.

It appears to consist of prophecies delivered on the occasion of a devastating plague of locusts. The prophet sees the plague as God's judgment and calls for demonstrations of penitence (1.13 f.; 2.12–17). However, he seems to see even more in it than this, for he represents the locusts as God's army, and sees in their attack a foretaste of the day of the Lord (1.6; 2.2–11). He promises salvation (2.20–27), but then, from 2.28 onwards, he reverts to eschatology and the day of judgment.

It has been suggested that a prophecy originally delivered for the particular occasion of a locust plague has been adapted as a liturgical document, i.e. for use in worship on subsequent occasions, and given an eschatological significance, perhaps by the addition of 2.28–3.21. Chapter 2.28–32 is, of course, a famous passage, which the New Testament writers see as fulfilled at Pentecost.

7. *The Book of Jonah*

The book of Jonah is pure fiction. It is perhaps the only book in the Bible which is actually meant to be funny, though it is humorous with a deadly serious purpose. It destroys racism and nationalism and exclusivism by poking fun at it. Its technique is that of the *reductio ad absurdum*. The racist and religious exclusivist is forced by the logic of his own position (and such people are often as strong on their own kind of logic as they are short on humour) to set himself above God. Jonah, in the name of his religion, rejects God's call. And if you grant his religious premises he is doing the logical thing. He does so because he, Jonah, personally disapproves of God's offering of salvation to foreigners. He is the only man in the Bible who *accuses* God of being merciful (4.1 f.). The author is realistic enough to present Jonah as remaining unconvinced to the end.

We cannot be very precise about the date at which the book was written, but the religious background against which it must be placed is only too obvious.

8. *Haggai and Zechariah 1–8*

The value of these books as historical evidence has been sufficiently dealt with above. Their religious outlook, however, requires further comment.

We see in them very clearly the new, positive attitude which post-exilic prophecy takes towards the cult. To get one's worship right is the first priority; all else will be put right in consequence. This is a fine sentiment, and not to be despised as a superficial concentration on the externals of religion. It does, however, raise acute problems. The builders of our mediaeval cathedrals would have agreed wholeheartedly with Haggai's priorities. Can we, in the age of cost-benefit analysis, do the same? Granted that we ought to worship God in the best possible way, is it an acceptable expression of this aim to erect splendid buildings which strain the economic resources of the religious community?

Even if we concede that Haggai's priorities are right, is he appealing to unworthy motives in suggesting that the rebuilding of the temple will pay off in economic terms? (2.18 f.).

I do not think that the answers to any of these questions are self-evident.

Zechariah 1–8 calls for another comment. Chapters 1–6 consist of a series of visions. We have not space to deal here with the interpretation of these, but their method of putting across the prophetic message is noteworthy. The visions are of fantastic and dreamlike type, and in some of them an angel appears as interpreter. They are not a completely new phenomenon in prophecy. Ezekiel, at least, had already produced something like them, but they are very close to the methods of apocalyptic. A glance at Daniel 8 and 10 will confirm this.

9. *The Book of Malachi*

This book comes from another unnamed prophet. 'Malachi' means simply 'my messenger'. It certainly falls within our period, though in spite of its position in the canon it is by no means the last of the Old Testament books to be written.

In common with most post-exilic prophecy it is very concerned about the cult. The sins it condemns are priestly negligence (1.6–2.9) and the bringing of inadequate tithes and sacrifices (3.8–12, cf. 1.8 and 1.13 f.).

It is also very much on the defensive. It is clear that the community is not prosperous. Earlier prophetic promises of glory, or even comfort, have gone unfulfilled. In 2.17–3.5 the prophet asserts, in the face of doubters, that notwithstanding the delay, the day of judgment and salvation really is near (cf. 4.1–6).

Unique to the prophet is his condemnation of divorce (2.13–16). In the New Testament, 3.1 and 4.5 f. are taken as prophecies of the coming of John the Baptist.

15

The Seleucids and the Maccabees

J. R. Bartlett

This section describes Jewish history from 312 to 63 BC. This was a period when the Palestinian Jews attempted to establish their own independent state and live according to their own religious conscience, and the Jews abroad were forced to work out for themselves how they should live and how they should express their faith in order to bear clear witness to their faith in the alien and often cultured world about them. It is these issues that matter, not the details of the battles of the Maccabees.

The Evidence

1. *Biblical Reference*

The book of Daniel was written about 164 BC and reflects the struggle against the Seleucids. The stories told about Daniel, however, are set in Babylon in the time of Nebuchadnezzar (605–562 BC). The device of setting stories in an earlier age was sometimes adopted by writers in times of danger or when they had something unpopular to say, though for a different explanation see under *The Book of Daniel* below (pp. 195 f.).

2. *Extra-biblical References*

The Apocrypha is a selection of writings which did not find a place in the Jewish canon of scripture. Of the writings included in the Apocrypha, the most important for teachers is I Maccabees, which gives a reliable and factual history of the period. II Maccabees is history interpreted from a particular religious standpoint and is much less reliable.

The Coming of the Seleucid Rulers

The Seleucids take their name from Seleucus, one of the officers of Alexander the Great. In 312 BC, Seleucus established himself as ruler over the eastern part of Alexander's empire; in 301 BC he gained most of what is now Turkey, and for better control of his new empire founded Antioch in Syria as his capital, naming it after

his father, and Seleucia as its port (cf. Acts 11.19; 13.4). Seleucus' rival, Ptolemy, who on Alexander's death had seized Egypt, had meanwhile annexed Palestine, thus starting the struggle between 'the kings of the north' and 'the kings of the south', described in Daniel 11. For nearly a century Palestine was the battleground of these opposing forces and was frequently conquered and reconquered. The struggle ended in 198 BC when the Seleucid Antiochus III took all Palestine and sealed a treaty by betrothing his daughter Cleopatra to Ptolemy V (Dan.11.15–17).

The Greek Way of Life: 'Hellenization'

Palestine now belonged to the Seleucids, but Ptolemaic rule had left its legacy to the Jews. There had been Jews in Egypt since Jeremiah's day (Jer.43.5 ff.), and in 312 BC, Ptolemy I had settled captives from Jerusalem, Judaea and Samaria in Alexandria, where they were greatly affected by the Greek way of life. According to the Letter of Aristeas, a document probably written by a Hellenistic Jew *c.*150–100 BC, Ptolemy II had the Hebrew Scriptures translated into Greek at Alexandria for the benefit of the new library; in fact, the translation was probably made for the benefit of the new Greek-speaking Jews of the city. Here, too, the philosopher Aristobulus (second century BC), the author of the Wisdom of Solomon (first century BC), and the Jewish philosopher Philo (first century AD) all made different attempts to show that Greek and Jewish ways of thought could be used to illuminate each other (for the Wisdom of Solomon, see p. 197 below).

Judaea itself was also affected by the Hellenistic way of life, which was founded on the Greek *polis* (city), with its urban civilization and its emphasis on the training of young men in athletic and literary prowess. The Jews were surrounded by the Hellenistic cities of Egypt, of Nabataea, Transjordan, Phoenicia and Philistia, and there were Greek colonies at Acre (called

Ptolemais), Bethshan (called Scythopolis), and Samaria (later called Sebaste). There was a Greek colony in southern Judaea itself, at Marisa. From official Egyptian correspondence we hear of one Tobiah (probably descended from Tobiah the Ammonite of Nehemiah's day, Neh.2.10) in charge of an Egyptian military colony in Transjordan. His son Joseph, nephew of the high priest Onias II, succeeded in becoming the official Egyptian tax-collector in Palestine. Joseph's son Hyrcanus succeeded to the business by bribing Ptolemy, though he thereby alienated his father and the high priest Simon II, and had to retire to the family estates in Transjordan. It was leading families such as these who by their contact with the ruling classes of Judaea's neighbours mediated Hellenism to the Jews, and it was a high priest, Jason, who introduced the gymnasium and the Greek games to Jerusalem (II Macc.4.12 ff.).

However, reaction to this trend came early, as we can see from works like Tobit and Ecclesiasticus (see below, pp. 196 f.), which preached a distinctive Jewish piety. But the Seleucids in 198 BC took over a country which was neither unaware of nor altogether hostile to the possibilities afforded by Hellenism. Nor was Antiochus III hostile to the Jews and their religion; when he annexed Judaea he promised to restore the damaged Jerusalem, provide materials for temple sacrifices, allow self-government, and make some generous tax concessions. We are told that he used Jews (whom he called 'guardians of our interests' and allowed to keep their own laws) as occupying troops holding Lydia and Phrygia for him.

Antiochus III died in 187 BC, leaving Seleucus IV to mend the finances shattered by Antiochus's unsuccessful attempts at empire-building in Asia Minor and Greece and by the fines imposed by the Romans (cf. Dan.11.18). One expedient was the tax-gathering mission of Heliodorus and his attempt to raid the temple treasury at Jerusalem (II Macc.3; Dan.11.20). Meanwhile Rome had supported the Ptolemies against the Seleucids, playing one off against the other; Armenia and Parthia were breaking away from the Seleucid empire; and in 175 BC the throne was seized by Antiochus, the son of Antiochus III. Antiochus had learned Western ways from his early exile as a hostage in Rome and from his freedom in Athens where, though a stranger, he had actually been elected chief

magistrate; and on reaching the Syrian throne his policy was to unify Greek and oriental in one empire and one culture. Thus he encouraged immigration from Hellenistic cities to cities of his own empire; he conferred the Greek title and honour of 'city' on oriental towns such as Babylon and Hamath; and he tried to forge a common religious bond for his empire by equating the Greek Zeus with the Syrian Baal-Hadad and eventually by claiming that he as king was the god's human manifestation. Such a claim would not bother Greeks – Alexander had made similar claims – but was blasphemy to Jews, and to them this policy was the more outrageous because associated with the king's support of ungodly and unlawful high priests.

In 175 BC Jason (the name is a Greek form of the Hebrew Joshua), brother of the legitimate high priest Onias III, offered Antiochus 440 talents for the high priesthood, and 150 more for the right 'to establish a gymnasium and a body of youth for it, and to enrol the men of Jerusalem as citizens of Antioch' (II Macc.4.9). Perhaps, ambition apart, Jason was promoting a policy of integrating the Jews into the Hellenistic empire of Antiochus on the same terms as 'the Gentiles round about us' (I Macc.1.11) and of making Jerusalem a privileged Hellenistic city of Antiochus' empire. From Antiochus' viewpoint, a Hellenized Jerusalem, integrated into his empire, was an important buffer state against Egypt and Antiochus visited Jerusalem with this in mind, was magnificently received, and perhaps reassured (II Macc.4.21 f.).

In 171 BC, however, Menelaus outbid Jason for the high priest's office, and took his place. He did not belong to the legitimate high priestly family, and so to secure his position he had the legitimate high priest Onias III, who was in exile near Antioch, murdered (Dan.9.26; II Macc.4.23 ff.). In 169 BC, Antiochus IV campaigned in Egypt; on his return Menelaus let him plunder the temple (I Macc.1.20 ff.; Dan. 11.25 ff.). The next year Jason attacked Jerusalem in an attempt to remove Menelaus, and Antiochus, ejected from Egypt by the Romans ('the ships of Kittim', Dan.11.30), supposing that Judaea was in revolt, took Jerusalem, profaning temple and fortress (Dan.11.30 f.), slaughtering large numbers of people, and leaving a governor, 'Philip, by birth a Phrygian and in character more barbarous than the man who appointed him' (II Macc.5.22). Then Apollonius was sent (167 BC), who sacked Jerusalem, pulled down its walls, and established a garrison (I Macc.1.29–40; II Macc.5.24–26), which in spite of all attempts, military and diplomatic, to oust it remained there till 142 BC (I Macc.14.36).

Antiochus now decreed (I Macc.1.4ff.) that 'all should be one people, and that each should give up his customs', and he wrote to the Jews directing them, on pain of death,

> to follow customs strange to the land, to forbid burnt offerings and sacrifices and drink offerings in the sanctuary, to profane sabbaths and feasts, to defile the sanctuary and the priests, to build altars and sacred precincts and shrines for idols, to sacrifice swine and unclean animals, and to leave their sons uncircumcised.

II Macc.6.1 f. says that 'the king sent an Athenian senator to compel the Jews to forsake the laws of their fathers and cease to live by the laws of God, and also to pollute the temple in Jerusalem and call it the temple of the Olympian Zeus'. In December 167 BC the temple was desecrated by the erection of a 'desolating sacrilege upon the altar of burnt offering' (I Macc.1.54; Dan.11.31 ff.) – probably the erection of a heathen altar is meant. The miseries that some Jews suffered out of loyalty to the Law are vividly described in I Macc.1 and II Macc.6.7 ff. It seems that in the interests of peace and unity in his empire, Antiochus was trying to abolish Jewish nationalism. He probably underestimated Jewish feeling, supposing that their attitude to religion was much the same as that of the Greeks, and over-estimated Jewish support for his attempt to introduce Hellenistic culture, perhaps here being misled by Menelaus.

Jewish Resistance to Hellenization

It is important to realize that there were different reactions among the Jews to Hellenization. Not all opposed it. There were *Hellenists* even among the priests (II Macc.4.13 ff.), who supported Antiochus from policy or perhaps from weak-mindedness. The high priests Jason, Menelaus, and Alcimus were men of the world, ready to compromise. Secondly, there were the *Hasidim*, 'the pious', who in contrast to those who 'abandoned the holy covenant' for a

covenant with the Gentiles were 'mighty warriors of Israel' and 'chose to die rather than profane the holy covenant' (I Macc.1.63). The *Hasidim* at first took to passive resistance, but many of them joined the more militant Maccabees until religious liberty was regained. From the *Hasidim* developed in different directions the *Pharisees*, who fostered a lay spirituality for the whole nation, thus ensuring Israel's continuity after the destruction of Jerusalem by the Romans in AD 70, and the *Essenes* and the related *Qumran community*, who broke away from the official orthodoxy of the temple and priesthood in the belief that the future lay with the elect, separated from the pollutions of the world.

The fiercest reaction to Antiochus' policy came from Mattathias of Modein and his sons and their followers, known as the *Maccabees* after the third son Judas, who soon took the lead and acquired the nick-name 'Maccabee' from a Hebrew word meaning 'hammer'. When in 166 BC the people of Modein, twenty miles north-west of Jerusalem, were required to offer pagan sacrifices, Mattathias killed a Jew who was prepared to do this, killed the king's officer, tore down the altar, and fled to the hills with his sons and 'many who were seeking righteousness and justice'. A group of them were attacked on the sabbath and died rather than break the law by defending themselves; but it was then decided that self-defence on the sabbath was allowable in the circumstances. More people, including some of the *Hasidim*, joined the Maccabees, who organized an army, destroyed altars, forcibly circumcised babies, and campaigned against Hellenizing Jews and persecuting Gentiles alike (I Macc.2.1–48).

Mattathias soon died, and Judas took his place. The first aim was the regaining of freedom to obey the Jewish law, and the recovery and purification of the temple. This was achieved by two seasons' fighting in the years 166 and 165 BC (I Macc.3.10–4.35). Exactly three years after pagan sacrifice had first been offered on the old altar, a new altar was dedicated and a new annual Feast of Dedication appointed (December 164 BC). The Maccabees fortified the temple area and garrisoned it, and did the same for the town of Bethzur to the south (I Macc.4.36–61).

In 163 BC Judas campaigned to help Jews resident among the surrounding Gentiles (I

Macc.5). The Syrians counter-attacked success-fully, but the death of Antiochus forced the Syrians to offer terms to the Jews, allowing them to 'live by their laws as they did before' (I Macc.6.59). The death of Menelaus, and the accession to the high priesthood of Alcimus (a Greek form of the Hebrew Eliakim), who was at least a member of the priestly house of Aaron, meant victory to people like the *Hasidim*. The Maccabees, however, opposed the Hellenizing Alcimus, and defeated the Syrian army sent to support him at Adasa on March 17, 160 BC; the day was thereafter kept as a festival (I Macc.7; II Macc.15). II Maccabees ends with this victory, clearly regarding it as the climax of the war. But two months later the Syrians killed Judas in battle and re-occupied Judaea (I Macc.9). The Maccabees fled to the wilderness to regroup under Jonathan, Judas' youngest brother. In 159 BC Alcimus died, leaving the high priest-hood vacant, and the Syrians departed. 'The land of Judah had rest for two years' (I Macc.9.57).

It was a peace of exhaustion which satisfied no-one. The Maccabees now wanted nothing less than political freedom; and the *Hasidim*, who would have been happy with religious freedom, had been disillusioned when Alcimus began his high priesthood by murdering sixty of their number (I Macc.7.12 ff.). This dis-illusionment may have led to the withdrawal about this time of a group of *Hasidim* to settle in a closed community at Qumran. The Hellen-ists did not feel secure while the Maccabees were free to harry them from the wilderness. They asked the Syrian general Bacchides to capture Jonathan (157 BC), but Bacchides was beaten and made a final peace with Jonathan, who settled at Michmash, a stronghold north-east of Jerusalem (I Macc.9.73), and like the judges of old 'began to judge the people, and he destroyed the ungodly out of Israel'. The Maccabees had won.

Independence

From now until the arrival of the Romans in 63 BC, Judaea was virtually independent. The Seleucid empire was weakening as to the east the Parthians became more powerful and at home rivals contended for the throne. In 142 BC 'the yoke of the Gentiles was removed from Israel, and the people began to write in their documents and contracts, "In the first year of Simon the great high priest and commander and leader of the Jews" ' (I Macc.13.41 f.). It was seen as the first year of a new era.

In 134 BC Simon and his sons Judas and Mattathias were killed near Jericho by Simon's ambitious son-in-law Ptolemy. However, Simon's son John, in command of the army near Gezer, heard the news in time to reach Jerusalem before Ptolemy, and was welcomed as high priest and ruler (I Macc.16.11–22). The Seleucid king successfully attacked Jerusalem, but in 128 BC was killed by the Parthians, and thereafter the internal struggles of the Seleucid empire preserved the Jews from further moles-tation.

It was the people in Jerusalem, not the king in Antioch, who made John Hyrcanus ruler and high priest; but the precedent for such an appointment lay in the use the Seleucid rulers had made of the high-priestly office, and it is hardly surprising that Hyrcanus and his suc-cessors ruled like Seleucids. Hyrcanus used mercenary troops to capture territory in southern Judaea, Moab and Samaria; he des-troyed the Samaritan temple on Mount Gerizim and forcibly circumcised the Idumaeans into the Jewish faith. Naturally the Pharisees – descendants of the *Hasidim* – objected to his political rather than his spiritual aims, and to the combination of priestly and civil rule in one person (particularly in one of neither Davidic nor Aaronic descent). Hyrcanus therefore sup-ported the Sadducean party (for whom see Part IV, Section 3, p. 227).

In 104–103 BC Aristobulus I ruled briefly as high priest, starving his mother to death, killing his brother Antigonus, and adding Galilee and Ituraea to the Jewish state. In 103 BC his widow made his brother Alexander Jannaeus king and high priest, and married him. (Jannaeus was probably the first of his family to take the official title of 'king'.) He seized parts of Trans-jordan and Samaria, deliberately judaizing all the conquered Hellenistic cities. But his be-haviour as high priest alienated the Pharisees; civil war broke out which Jannaeus finally won in spite of the entry of Demetrius III of Syria on the Pharisees' side. Jannaeus killed 6000 rebels, and strengthened his position by building the forts of Alexandrium, Machaerus and Masada. Meanwhile the Nabataeans of Petra under Aretas were becoming powerful; they defeated

Jannaeus near Lydda, forcing him to come to terms with them. Their main interest was in the trade route across southern Judaea.

In 76 BC, Jannaeus' widow Alexandra Salome inherited the throne. Following Jannaeus' advice to make peace with the Pharisees, she appointed her son Hyrcanus II as high priest. His brother Aristobulus led the Sadducees, who had military control of the land. When Salome died in 67 BC, Aristobulus defeated Hyrcanus and became king and high priest. Hyrcanus gained the not entirely disinterested support of Antipater of Idumaea and Aretas of Nabataea, defeated Aristobulus and besieged him in Jerusalem. At this point the Roman general Pompey the Great, fresh from his conquest of Pontus and Armenia, arrived in Syria. Pompey took Jerusalem and removed Aristobulus to Rome, leaving Hyrcanus as high priest. It was Antipater, however, who gained most, for the Romans at first relied on him for stable government and later gave him the official title of procurator of Judaea. This family, under the Romans, ruled Palestine; Antipater's son was Herod the Great, and among his grandsons was Herod Antipas, tetrarch of Galilee in the time of Jesus. Once again, religious and political authority had become separated; and it is noticeable that even in the independent Jewish state the combination of religious and political authority in one man was not always popular. Church and State have always been uneasy partners; this Jewish attempt to combine the two is of abiding interest.

The Literature

The issues and events outlined above are all reflected in the literature of the time, especially in the book of Daniel and in the Apocrypha.

1. *The Book of Daniel*

This was written about 164 BC at the height of the Maccabaean struggle. Chapter 11 describes the history of the Seleucids up to Antiochus IV, the details of whose death are wrongly given. The author was probably writing just before Antiochus died; description of events changes to prediction at this point. But why did the author use the figure of Daniel, a wise man of old (see Ezek.14.14,20; 28.3), and set the narrative in the time of Nebuchadnezzar (605–562 BC)? Why did he

later, from ch. 8, pretend to be Daniel himself? A righteous figure Daniel is known as far back as the fourteenth century BC. It is often said that this device of 'pseudonymity' was used for safety in difficult times, and that while the Jews would recognize Antiochus in the figure of Nebuchadnezzar, the Seleucid officials would not. But this motive is unconvincing; Daniel was hardly 'published' like a modern work – it was meant only for the eyes of the faithful few – and even if it were, why should not the author simply remain anonymous? The answer is that Daniel belongs to 'apocalyptic' literature. Apocalyptic books claim to be revelations (*apokalupto* is Greek for 'I reveal') of divine secrets made to famous figures of the past – such as Enoch, Abraham, Ezra, and Daniel – who subsequently wrote down the revelation in secret books (see II Esdras 14). Thus the book is ascribed to Daniel because it belonged to the apocalyptic tradition which was traced back to Daniel, in much the same way as wisdom literature was ascribed to Solomon and psalms to David. Apocalyptic writers believed that in view of the approaching end, the revelations made must now at last be divulged to the faithful. Divulged, they describe past, present and near future events in enigmatic and symbolic terms (cf. Mark 13.14, 'let him that readeth understand'). Such terms, however, were not designed to conceal the message from foreign eyes (though they would have that effect), but to convey the mystery of God's dealings. The symbolism had its roots in Old Testament tradition and ancient Near Eastern mythology. The message of these writers is that in spite of present troubles men must remain faithful, for God's purpose will soon triumph. These books were clearly relevant to the Jews under their Seleucid and Roman masters; many survive, others are lost, and some previously unknown examples have appeared among the literature found at Qumran.

The writer of Daniel, then, wrote with a message for the Maccabaean age. Thus ch. 1 encourages the Jews to keep their food laws, showing Daniel and his friends on a restricted diet to be wiser than the well-fed youths of the king's court;

Chapter 2 shows Nebuchadnezzar's dream of a mountain boulder crushing an image of gold, silver, brass, iron and clay, which Daniel interprets to mean that the kingdom of God will suddenly crush the kingdoms of the Ptolemies and Seleucids and their predecessors;

Chapter 3, telling the story of Shadrach, Meshach, Abednego and the fiery furnace, ridicules image-worship and shows the ultimate triumph of those tortured for their faith;

Chapter 4, in which Nebuchadnezzar is reduced to eating grass like an ox, reminds the Jews that even men like Antiochus are subject to the rule of God, for 'those who walk in pride he is able to abase' (v. 37);

Chapter 5 shows the doom of Belshazzar and his empire for its idolatry (v. 23), a message of hope to Jews suffering Antiochus' idolatry;

Chapter 6 praises Daniel's obedience to the Law in defiance of an edict reminiscent of Antiochus' edict; Daniel's deliverance and his accusers' fate in the lions' jaws conveyed an obvious message;

Chapter 7 is a vision showing how the four beasts, symbolizing the kingdoms of the world (the 'little horn' of the fourth beast being Antiochus' kingdom), lose their authority, while the 'son of man', symbolizing, in contrast to the beasts, the people of Israel (or its heavenly representatives), is invested with an eternal kingdom;

Chapter 8 describes Daniel's vision of the ram (the Persian empire), the goat (Alexander the Great), from whose four horns (the empires which followed Alexander's death) came a little horn (Antiochus IV), 'a king of fierce countenance' who will do God's people great harm but will be destroyed (vv. 23–25);

Chapter 9 contains a long national 'general confession' put into Daniel's mouth, followed by Gabriel's reassurance that in these final years the persecuting prince will suffer the wrath of God;

Chapters 10–12 contain Daniel's last vision, which describes the Seleucid empire (11.2–20) and especially Antiochus' career and persecution of the Jews (11.21–40), predicts his death (11.41–45), and encourages the *Hasidim* who have suffered for their faith by promising deliverance for God's people and a resurrection to shame or glory for 'many of them that sleep' (probably those who have died on either side in the recent struggles), 'the wise' and 'they that turn many to righteousness' (? the *Hasidim*) being especially singled out for glory. The beginning and end of the vision (10.1–11.1; 12.5–13) set these events in the context of a

heavenly war between the kingdom of God and the powers of evil, represented by the guardian angels of different countries (cf. 10.13).

It can now be seen that Daniel, ridiculing idolatry, encouraging faithfulness, promising the end of worldly empires, was supremely relevant to its time (see I Macc.2.60, where Mattathias himself quotes Daniel as an example to be followed). Daniel is a book produced out of the struggle between two rival ways of life, one seeking to impose itself on the other in order to destroy the independent spirit of a small nation. Such a situation has its parallels today; what sort of modern parallels are there to the book of Daniel?

2. *The Apocrypha*

Apocrypha means 'hidden away', and these books were so named because they were thought either too profound or not orthodox enough for the general reader. The Apocrypha contains those books included in the Greek translation of the Jewish Bible made at Alexandria but not found in the Hebrew Bible. The more interesting and important passages are asterisked. All the books express in their different ways Jewish reactions to the issues and events of these centuries.

Of immediate importance as historical records are *I and II Maccabees. I Maccabees,* originally written in Hebrew in Hyrcanus' time (134–104 BC), uses eye-witness accounts and official documents to give a reliable and factual history sympathizing with the Maccabees rather than the *Hasidim.* The author describes the sufferings of persecution or the glory of battle in simple, factual sentences; but the result is vivid and moving. Read, e.g., 1.41–64,* 6.28–47. *II Maccabees,* summarizing the late second-century BC work of Jason of Cyrene, is Greek both in language and approach. (Read 2.19–32,* the original introduction.) II Maccabees sympathizes with the *Hasidim* against the Maccabees, emphasizing martyrdom and the resurrection hope (see ch. 7*), sabbath-keeping, and festivals of Dedication (1.18 f.; 10.1 ff.) and Nicanor's Day (15.36). II Maccabees is interested in the lessons to be learned from history rather than in the events themselves; L. H. Brockington describes the work as 'caricature with a great deal of truth in it'.

Ecclesiasticus is teaching; Ben Sira (*c.*180 BC) instructs his pupils how to live according to the Law, which he equates with wisdom. Ben Sira's attitude is well seen in 37.16–39.11*, where of all wise men he that 'meditateth in the law of the Most High' is the wisest. His shining example was the high priest Simon II (see ch. 50). *Judith* is a story, told to encourage Jews to resist invaders who threaten to profane the sanctuary (4.12) – perhaps Holofernes was originally the Persian Orofernes, a general of Artaxerxes III (358–338 BC). But the emphasis on prayer, sabbath-keeping, festivals, circumcision, ceremonial cleanliness even in time of war would all have been relevant to the Maccabees. From a much later period, the end of the first century AD, comes *Baruch*, which probably reflects the Jewish War of AD 66–70 (see 4.5–5.9), and II *Esdras*, of which chs. 3–14 are an apocalypse apparently relating to 586 BC, but in fact dealing with the events of the first century BC. The legend of ch. 14 tries to put apocalyptic tradition on a par with the Law as Scripture, assigning it to secret traditions given by God to Moses on Mount Sinai. This may reflect the problem that arose after the destruction of Jerusalem of deciding which books were to be received as true guardians of Jewish tradition and belief (see Part 4, Section 13, pp. 353 ff.).

These books were most probably written in Palestine; but some apocryphal books show the reaction of Jews abroad to Hellenistic and other influences around them. The story of *Tobit* underlined for such Jews the importance of traditional practices such as giving alms, paying tithes and dues, keeping the feasts, supporting widows and orphans, refraining from Gentile foods, washing before eating, marrying within one's kin, and generally keeping the Mosaic law. 'The Letter of Jeremiah' (*Baruch* 6) is an attack on idol-worship by a fourth or third century Babylonian Jew – an attack repeated more humorously by *Bel and the Dragon**, one of the Greek Bible's additions to the book of Daniel. Other additions are *Susanna**, perhaps just a didactic story from the first century BC; the *Prayer of Azariah*, which, mentioning the loss of prince, prophet, leader and sacrifice,

may be from Maccabaean times; the *Song of the Three Young Men*, perhaps an old hymn, with no intrinsic relevance to the fate of the three young men. The *Book of Esther*, too, received additions when it was translated into Greek in the first century BC. Clearly, Alexandria in Egypt, where the Greek Bible was translated, was the scene of much Jewish literary activity, and *I Esdras* is another possible example of this, being a Greek translation of a Hebrew or Aramaic literary cousin of the books Ezra-Nehemiah. It contains much of Ezra-Nehemiah's material (differently arranged), though omitting Nehemiah's memoirs and adding the story of the Three Guardsmen (3.1–4.46*).

The greatest example of Jewish writing from Alexandria is the *Wisdom of Solomon*. Addressed to rulers who are going astray (highly placed Jews affected by Hellenism?) the book combines both Greek and Jewish beliefs (e.g., the immortality of the soul and the resurrection of the body, 3.1,7*), and describes the Jewish figure of 'wisdom', God's helper at creation and the revealer of God's mysteries (cf. Prov.8), in terms of the Greek *pneuma* (divine spirit) or *logos* (word or thought linking the divine being and the world; see 7.21 ff.*; 9.1,17; 16.12; 18.15 f.). The book is in part an attack on the attitudes of Ecclesiastes (see, e.g., Wisd.2), a book also attributed to Solomon (Eccles.1.1). The Wisdom of Solomon was clearly well known to New Testament writers, especially Paul: see Rom. 1.20–32 (Wisd.14.22–31); Rom.9.21 (Wisd. 15.7); II Cor.5.4 (Wisd.9.15); Heb.1.3 (Wisd. 7.26). Today perhaps the best known passage is Wisd.3.1–9*.

One work remains – the *Prayer of Manasseh*, probably from Palestine but impossible to date accurately. It may come from one of the *Hasidim*, or it may be the prayer written in 'the Chronicles of the Seers' (II Chron.33.19), expressly for Manasseh. Whatever its origin, it is a genuinely humble prayer which we are glad to have among the 'other books' which 'the Church doth read for example of life and instruction of manners'.

FOR FURTHER READING

Available in paperback

A. *General*

*Anderson, B. W., *The Living World of the Old Testament*, London: Longmans, 1969.

*Anderson, G. W., *The History and Religion of Israel*, London: Oxford University Press, 1966.

*Anderson, G. W., *A Critical Introduction to the Old Testament*, London: Duckworth, 1959.

*Baly, D., *The Geography of the Bible*, 2nd ed., London: Lutterworth, 1974.

*Bowden, John, *What about the Old Testament?*, London: SCM Press, 1969.

Bright, John, *A History of Israel*, 2nd ed., London: SCM Press, 1970.

Eichrodt, W., *Theology of the Old Testament*, 2 vols., London: SCM Press, 1961, 1967.

Heaton, E. W., *Everyday Life in Old Testament Times*, London: Batsford, 1956.

Herrmann, S., *A History of Israel in Old Testament Times*, London: SCM Press, 1975.

*Köhler, L., *Hebrew Man*, London: SCM Press, 1957.

*Lace, O. Jessie, *Understanding the Old Testament*, London: Cambridge University Press, 1972.

*Mellor, Enid, ed., *The Making of the Old Testament*, London: Cambridge University Press, 1972.

Noth, M., *The History of Israel*, 2nd ed., London: A. & C. Black, 1960.

Saggs, H. W. F., *Everyday Life in Babylonia and Assyria*, London: Batsford, 1965.

*Smith, George Adam, *The Historical Geography of the Holy Land*, London: Fontana Books, 1966.

Thomas, D. W., ed., *Archaeology and Old Testament Study*, London: Oxford University Press, 1967.

*Vaux, R. de, *Ancient Israel*, London: Darton, Longman & Todd, 1961.

Wiseman, D. J., ed., *Peoples of Old Testament Times*, London: Oxford University Press, 1973.

Wiseman, D., ed., *Photo-Guide to the Old Testament*, Berkhamstead: Lion, 1973.

Short but comprehensive commentaries on most Old Testament books will be found in the Torch Bible Commentaries (London: SCM Press, various dates and authors, most are available in paperbacks); and a series of commentaries on the New English Bible Old Testament is published by Cambridge University Press.

B. *From the Patriarchs to the Exile*

Clements, R. E., *God and Temple*, Oxford: Basil Blackwell, 1965.

*Davidson, R., *The Old Testament*, London: Hodder & Stoughton, 1964.

Gray, John, *Joshua, Judges and Ruth* (Century Bible), London: Nelson, 1967.

Heaton, E. W., *The Hebrew Kingdoms* (New Clarendon Bible), London: Oxford University Press, 1968.

Heaton, F. W., *Solomon's New Men*, London: Thames & Hudson, 1974.

*Herrmann, S., *Israel in Egypt*, London: SCM Press, 1973.

McKenzie, J. L., *The World of the Judges*, London: Geoffrey Chapman, 1967.

*Mayes, A. D. H., *Israel in the Period of the Judges*, London: SCM Press, 1974.

*Otwell, J. H., *A New Approach to the Old Testament* (the four traditions), London: SCM Press, 1968.

*Rad, G. von, *Moses*, London: Lutterworth, 1959.

Rad, G. von, *Old Testament Theology*, vol. 1, London: SCM Press, 1975.

*Soggin, A., *When the Judges Ruled*, London: Lutterworth, 1965.

C. *Prophecy, Worship and Wisdom in Israel*

*Clements, R. E., *Prophecy and Covenant*, London: SCM Press, 1965.

*Clements, R. E., *Prophecy and Tradition*, Oxford: Basil Blackwell, 1975.

Eaton, J. H., *Psalms: Introduction and Commentary* (Torch Bible Commentary), London: SCM Press, 1967.

*Fohrer, Georg, *History of Israelite Religion*, London: SPCK, 1973.

*Heaton, E. W., *The Old Testament Prophets*, London: Penguin Books, 1951.

Lindblom, J., *Prophecy in Ancient Israel*, Oxford: Basil Blackwell, 1962.

McKane, W., *Proverbs: A New Approach*, London: SCM Press, 1970.

Parrot, A., *The Temple of Jerusalem*, London: SCM Press, 1951.

Ringgren, H., *Israelite Religion*, London: SPCK, 1966.

Rowley, H. H., *Worship in Ancient Israel*, London: SPCK, 1967.

*Snaith, N. H., *The Book of Job*, London: SCM Press, 1968.

*Rad, G., von, *Wisdom in Israel*, London: SCM Press, 1972.

*Rad, G., von, *The Message of the Prophets*, London: SCM Press, 1968.

Vaux, R. de, *Studies in Old Testament Sacrifice*, Cardiff: University Press of Wales, 1964.

Vriezen, T. C., *The Religion of Ancient Israel*, London: Lutterworth, 1961.

*Zimmerli, W., *The Law and the Prophets*, Oxford: Basil Blackwell, 1965.

D. *The Exile and After*

*Ackroyd, Peter R., *Exile and Restoration*, London: SCM Press, 1968.

*Ackroyd, P. R., *Israel under Babylon and Persia*, London: Oxford University Press, 1970.

*Bruce, F. F., *Israel and the Nations*, Exeter: Paternoster Press, 1963.

*Coggins, R. J., *Samaritans and Jews*, Oxford: Basil Blackwell, 1975.

Dancy, J., *A Commentary on Maccabees I*, Oxford: Blackwell, 1954.

*Heaton, E. W., *The Book of Daniel* (Torch Bible Commentary), London: SCM Press, 1956.

Hengel, M., *Judaism and Hellenism*, 2 vols., London: SCM Press, 1974.

*Hengel, M., *Victory over Violence*, London: SPCK, 1973.

*Koch, Klaus, *The Rediscovery of Apocalyptic*, London: SCM Press, 1972.

*Russell, D. S., *Between the Testaments*, London: SCM Press, 1964.

*Russell, D. S., *The Jews from Alexander to Herod*, London: Oxford University Press, 1967.

199

PART FOUR

The New Testament

1

Rome and the Middle East

Margaret J. Thorpe

The chief source for this period is the Jewish historian, Josephus, who was born in AD 37 and lived until at least AD 100. A modern translation of his History of the Jewish War, *which records Jewish history from 167 BC to AD 73, is available in the Penguin Classics series.*

Rome and Israel

By 63 BC Rome had acquired thirteen provinces, from Spain in the west to Cilicia in the east. In that year the Roman general Pompey, who had been campaigning in Asia Minor, created the new provinces of Bithynia with Pontus and Syria. From Syria, Pompey planned a campaign against the rich kingdom of the Nabataean Arabs, with its capital at Petra, but before he could embark on this he was led to intervene in Jewish affairs. Since 67 there had been civil war in Judaea between Hyrcanus and Aristobulus, the two sons of the late king and high priest, Alexander Jannaeus (see Part III, Section 15, p. 195). The history of the Jews under the leadership of this family, the Hasmoneans, had been expansionist; in particular, the kingdom of Judaea now included Idumaea to the south and Galilee to the north, and the inhabitants of these areas were compelled to adopt the Jewish faith. Now, Hyrcanus, the elder brother, was high priest and was to become king when his mother Queen Alexandra died. Aristobulus, however, who was the more forceful character, had seized most of the country and was challenging this settlement. The matter was brought to Pompey's attention at Damascus, and he condemned Aristobulus and confirmed the settlement.

Aristobulus prepared for war and, after once agreeing to surrender but breaking his promise, was besieged in the temple at Jerusalem. This first Roman siege of Jerusalem lasted three months, and, when it ended, the Gentile Pompey entered the Holy of Holies in triumph, but from religious scruples did not touch the vast treasures of the temple. He again confirmed Hyrcanus in the office of high priest, but did not make him king.

The general shape of Pompey's settlement of the East was dictated by two factors, the presence on the Euphrates frontier of the growing power of Parthia and a typically Roman reluctance to extend direct control further than was necessary. Syria was thus the only area under direct Roman rule, though even within this province there were self-governing enclaves, such as the league of ten cities known as the Decapolis. Dependent upon Syria, however, were a number of client kingdoms, areas still under the control of their native rulers, who were obliged as allies of Rome to assist in the defence of the frontier. To the south of Syria there were three such kingdoms, the Nabataean, the Ituraean, and the Jewish, which was greatly reduced in size by the loss of certain areas, such as Joppa, Jamnia, and Samaria, which had been Jewish for many generations.

Herod the Great

The man responsible for Pompey's supporting Hyrcanus was Antipater, the father of Herod the Great. He was an Arab, though Jewish by faith, being a member of the leading family among the Idumaeans (or Edomites). Like his father, he served as governor of Idumaea within the Jewish kingdom, but, more important, he was the power behind Hyrcanus' throne. He already enjoyed friendly relations with the Nabataeans and had married a princess from their country. Now, however, he realized that, with the establishment of Roman control over Syria, the conditions of political life in the Near East were totally changed: from now on it was only through co-operation with Rome that Judaea could hope to preserve any freedom of action; opposition to Rome would lead to utter ruin. This pro-Roman policy was to be the basis of his own success and that of his son Herod.

It was not an easy policy. There were elements in Judaea opposed to it, to whom the various members of Aristobulus' family would seem natural leaders. There was the possibility of a clash between his Nabataean sympathies and his pro-Roman policy. Above all, there was the fact that Rome did not speak with one voice, for this was the beginning of the period of anarchy and civil war at Rome that was to last for some thirty years. Antipater dealt successfully with all these difficulties.

In 49 BC, when war broke out between Pompey and Caesar, Antipater naturally supported the former, and his defeat and death a year later faced him with a major crisis. Luckily for him, Caesar found himself in considerable difficulties in Alexandria, where he had intervened in civil war on behalf of Cleopatra; both in the military and in the diplomatic field Antipater rendered him valuable service and was duly rewarded. Caesar confirmed Hyrcanus' position as high priest and as ethnarch (President of the Jewish nation – the title king was in abeyance). Antipater received Roman citizenship and was appointed procurator of Judaea, thus becoming the official representative of Roman power in the kingdom and its effective ruler, as Hyrcanus was now little more than a figurehead. To assist in running the state, Antipater made his eldest son, Phasael, prefect of Jerusalem and his second son, Herod, governor of Galilee.

Herod was now twenty-six; he was tall and handsome in appearance, an able speaker, and according to Josephus, 'over-flowing with energy'; moreover, he already had considerable experience both of Romans – ten years earlier he had rapidly struck up a friendship with Mark Antony – and of the Arabs and Jews among whom he had been brought up. He seized the opportunity now offered him in his first official appointment with typical vigour by hunting down a group of bandits who were infesting the border-land between Syria and Galilee. As a mark of his gratitude the governor of Syria added Samaria and parts of Syria to the area under Herod's control.

The murder of Caesar in 44 brought Antipater and his family into peril once again. Faced with opposition in Rome, the chief assassins, Brutus and Cassius, left Italy to enlist support in the east for their war against Mark Antony and Octavian. Cassius demanded seven hundred talents from the Jews, and, although this was more than they could afford, Antipater persuaded them to agree and divided the sum between the various regions of Judaea. The first to secure his quota was Herod, who thus won the favour of Cassius, and soon after Cassius gave him temporary command of all Syria 'as they hoped for valuable assistance from him'.

The defeat of Brutus and Cassius at Philippi in 42 thus necessitated another display of political dexterity by Herod and Phasael; the situation was the more difficult as Antipater had been murdered a year before, and the legal position of his sons was unclear. It says much for Herod's personality that he was able to confront the victorious Antony in the presence of a large hostile delegation and to recover his firm friendship; a few months later he and Phasael were appointed tetrarchs of Judaea. (The word 'tetrarch' is familiar to readers of the New Testament. It originally meant the ruler of a fourth part, but then came to indicate the ruler of any area, though usually one who did not enjoy full sovereignty.) Hyrcanus remained high priest and ethnarch, but effective power lay with the brothers, who would co-operate closely with the Romans.

One reason for Antony's ready support for Herod and Phasael was the continuing Parthian threat. In 53 the Roman general Crassus had attacked Parthia but had suffered a crushing defeat at Carrhae. Antony now planned a second expedition, but in 40, before he could act, the Parthians invaded Syria. With them came Antigonus, the son of Aristobulus and pretender to the Hasmonean throne. He attracted strong support from the Jews, and within a short time Judaea was in revolt. Hyrcanus and Phasael were captured, and the latter killed himself. Herod was forced to leave Jerusalem secretly. He left his family in the strong fortress of Masada and fled to Petra; failing to win support there, he eventually made his way by Egypt and Rhodes to Rome, where he appealed to Antony. Antony, 'recalling Antipater's hospitality and filled with admiration for the heroic character before him, decided on the spot that the man he had once made tetrarch should now be king of the Jews'. However, it was not until 37 that Herod was able to enter Jerusalem, escorted to his capital by a force of Roman legionaries.

In 31 Octavian defeated Antony at the battle of Actium; this marked the end of the period of civil wars in Rome and is usually considered the starting-point of the Roman Empire. Herod, who had, of course, backed Antony, was lucky not to have been present at the battle; due to some intrigues on the part of Cleopatra, who envied his influence with Antony, he was campaigning against the Nabataeans at the time. Even so, his meeting with Octavian after the battle cannot have been easy and demonstrates once again the combination of daring and flexibility that enabled him to survive so long. He admitted his friendship with Antony, but, in Josephus' words, asked Octavian to consider 'not whose friend, but what a good friend I was'. Octavian confirmed him in his position and restored to Judaea certain territories which Antony had given to Cleopatra. Shortly afterwards, Herod also made the acquaintance of Octavian's chief minister, Agrippa; the two became firm friends, and it is after him that the later members of the family, mentioned in the Acts of the Apostles, were named.

Externally, Herod now found the situation easier; he based his policy on his friendship with Augustus (as Octavian now became known) and Agrippa, and they did not let him down. Thus, when Augustus visited Syria in 20 BC, he dismissed certain complaints against Herod – and so effectively that the complainants committed suicide –, increased his territory, made him one of the procurators of Syria, and appointed his brother, Pheroras, tetrarch of the area east of the Jordan. In 15 BC Agrippa, who had now become Augustus' junior partner in ruling the Empire, with particular responsibility for the east, paid a very successful visit to Judaea, and in the next year Herod travelled a thousand miles to join Agrippa in a naval campaign in the Black Sea. On their return together to Asia Minor, Herod was able to secure Agrippa's support for the Jews of the Dispersion, some of whom were being unfairly treated by the Greeks in whose cities they lived.

At this stage, as Josephus puts it, 'In Augustus' affections Herod was second only to Agrippa, and in Agrippa's second only to Augustus.'

Herod never enjoyed the same success in his relations with the Jews. He was an Idumaean and, therefore, could not combine the offices of king and high priest, as the Hasmoneans had done; the separation of the two offices served as a permanent reminder to his subjects of the fact that he was a usurper and the nominee of a foreign power and was, moreover, a lasting contradiction of what Josephus called the 'theocratic' tradition of the Jews. Nevertheless, his achievements, particularly on the material level, were far from negligible. He developed the economic resources of his kingdom, rebuilt the temple in Jerusalem, and founded two new cities – the port of Caesarea, which was on such a scale that it took twelve years to complete, and the city of Sebaste (the word is the Greek equivalent of Augustus) in Samaria. When severe famine struck Judaea in 25 BC, he acted promptly and vigorously, selling the gold and silver furniture from his palace to buy corn from the Roman governor of Egypt; he, of course, was a personal friend.

Furthermore, he took an active interest in the welfare of the Jews of the Dispersion, intervening, as we have seen, to secure for them free enjoyment of certain rights previously conceded by the Romans; notable among these were the right to contribute to the treasury of the temple in Jerusalem and the right of exemption from military service, which would have involved infringement of the strict laws governing the sabbath.

It is difficult to recognize in this vital and capable ruler the tyrannical monster who, in the story told in Matt.2.16 f., ordered the massacre of the innocents. This story is not recorded anywhere apart from the Gospel of Matthew. Herod was under severe pressure by reason of his chaotic family situation. He married ten wives and had fourteen children, nine of them male, but the struggle for the succession centred at first on the sons born to him by his first two wives.

Before Herod became king, he had married Doris, a commoner and, like himself, an Idumaean; their son, Antipater, was Herod's eldest child. Even before the Parthian invasion of 40 BC, Herod had realized that this marriage brought him no diplomatic advantage. The success of Antigonus on that occasion brought the matter home to him, and in 37 he married Mariamne I. Doris and Antipater were banished from the court. The new match seemed ideal. Not only was the bride strikingly beautiful, but she united in herself the two rival branches of the Hasmonean family, being the grand-daughter of both Hyrcanus and Aristobulus; Herod might reasonably hope that this marriage would seem in a sense to legitimize his position and thus bring peace and security to the kingdom. His hopes were soon disappointed, for Mariamne detested him from the start and constantly schemed against him for the benefit of her own family. Her chief rival at court was Herod's sister, Salome, who found natural allies in Doris and Antipater. In eight years these intrigues led through the murders of Mariamne's brother, Aristobulus, who had become high priest, of Herod's uncle, Joseph, and of several minor figures to that of Mariamne herself.

Nevertheless, Herod treated her children with great kindness, sending the two sons, Alexander and Aristobulus, to be educated in Rome. There they moved in the highest society and became well-known to the imperial family. In 18 BC, when Herod visited Rome, they returned to Judaea with him, were clearly marked out for the succession, and became very popular. The intrigues between the two families continued, and Salome took advantage of Herod's visit to Agrippa in 14 BC to suggest on his return that the young men were plotting against him. The charge seemed plausible, and Herod reacted by recalling Antipater to court and, a year later, by making him his heir. Augustus effected a reconciliation between Herod and the sons of Mariamne in 12 BC, but explicitly recognized Herod's right to dispose of his kingdom, whole or divided, as he pleased, provided that he retained sole control until his death. (This was, perhaps, not the concession it seemed. Augustus did not want to become involved in Herod's family affairs, and, for the rest, he was permitting Herod only the right to make what will he pleased, without in any way guaranteeing its enforcement. The brusque removal of Archelaus in AD 6 bears this out.) The reconciliation was short-lived, and, in an atmosphere of increasing tension, of plot and counter-plot, the scheming continued, until, in 7 BC, Alexander and Aristobulus were tried

in absentia before the governor of Syria. Given no chance to defend themselves, they were convicted and executed.

Antipater's position must now have seemed secure and was recognized in a second will, but he was not content to remain crown-prince for long and was soon scheming against his father. On this occasion the plot also involved Herod's brother Pheroras and another of his wives, Mariamne II. It was the death of Pheroras in 5 BC that occasioned its detection. Antipater was recalled from Rome, where he had been spreading rumours against his half-brothers, Archelaus and Philip, was accused in private before Varus, the governor of Syria, was condemned and imprisoned. Only the need to inform the Emperor of certain matters which had come to light during the trial delayed his execution.

By now Herod was seriously ill, both physically and mentally, and it was clear that he could not live much longer. (One diagnosis of his illness, based upon the description given by Josephus, is that it was arterio-sclerosis, among the symptoms of which are rapid changes of mood and delusions of persecution.) In 4 BC, amid mounting opposition from the Pharisees and only a few days before his own death, Herod had Antipater executed and issued his fourth, and final, will.

Under its terms the kingdom he had built up was to be divided between three of his sons, the eldest of whom was only eighteen. Archelaus was to be king of Judaea proper, of Idumaea, and of Samaria; his brother, Antipas, tetrarch of Galilee and Transjordan; their half-brother, Philip, tetrarch of Gaulonitis, Trachonitis, and Paneas, the areas in the north-east of the kingdom. To his sister, Salome, whose intrigues had done so much to darken his last years, Herod left large estates and a huge sum of money. An even larger sum was bequeathed to Augustus and other members of the imperial family. Archelaus was ordered to carry his father's ring and all state papers to Augustus and to request his confirmation of the will.

Tetrarchs and Procurators

1. *Archelaus*
The vigorous action of Salome ensured that Archelaus' succession was not contested, but he soon showed that he had little of his father's

political flair. An unwise speech of his just before the Passover led to rioting in the temple, and his attempts to check it veered from untimely concessions to unnecessary force; eventually he sent in the army, and three thousand worshippers were killed. Shortly after, he left for Rome to seek confirmation of his father's will, which was disputed by his brother Antipas.

During his absence there were further disturbances in Judaea. These were occasioned by the rapacity of Sabinus, the procurator of Syria (and so, the emperor's chief financial agent in the area), in attempting to take over Herod's property before knowing Augustus' decision as to the succession, and led through bitter fighting between Romans and Jews around the temple to full-scale rebellion directed as much against Archelaus as against the Romans. (Significantly enough, the only elements to remain loyal were the troops whom Herod had recruited from among the Greek population of his kingdom.) The governor of Syria was compelled to intervene in strength and, after a brief but bloody campaign – 2000 of the rebel leaders were crucified – order was restored.

This news cannot have made Augustus' decision in Rome any easier, and it was further complicated by the arrival of a deputation from Jerusalem – backed, we are told, by the large Jewish colony in Rome – requesting him to abolish the Herodean kingdom and either bring the area under direct Roman rule or leave it autonomous. Despite all this, Augustus largely confirmed Herod's will, only withholding from Archelaus the title of king; for the time being, at least, he was to be only ethnarch.

Back in Judaea he showed little interest in the welfare of his kingdom, and soon earned a reputation for cruelty, which is reflected in the statement that Joseph was reluctant to pass through Judaea on his return to Nazareth (Matt.2.22). Finally, in AD 6 Jews and Samaritans combined to denounce Archelaus to Augustus for marrying his dead brother's wife – forbidden by Jewish law – and for his treatment of his subjects. Augustus exiled him to France and decided to make a province of Judaea.

The complexity of the following years, during which Judaea itself was a province while Antipas and Philip continued to rule their tetrarchies, can be seen in Luke's painstaking attempt to date the start of John the Baptist's ministry:

> Now in the fifteenth year of the reign of Tiberius Caesar, Pontius Pilate being governor of Judaea, and Herod being tetrarch of Galilee, and his brother Philip tetrarch of Ituraea and of the region of Trachonitis, and Lysanias the tetrarch of Abilene, Annas and Caiaphas being the high priests, the word of God came unto John . . . (Luke 3.1 f.).

Two points here call for elucidation: the reference to Antipas as Herod and the mention of two high priests. On Herod's death, Archelaus and, on his banishment, Antipas assumed the name Herod, and, except in Matt.2.1–22 and Luke 1.5, all references to Herod in the Gospels are in fact to Antipas. The Romans had deposed Annas from office, appointing his son Caiaphas in his place, but according to the Law a high priest remained until his death, and many Jews refused to recognize the change.

2. *Philip and Antipas*

Philip continued to rule over his tetrarchy until his death in AD 34, when for three years it became part of the province of Syria. Most of his subjects were Gentiles, and his task was probably easier than that of Archelaus. He seems to have made an efficient and conscientious ruler.

Antipas, who also remained in power until his death (AD 39), is better known, from the references to him in the Gospels and perhaps particularly as the man responsible for the death of John the Baptist; moreover, his tetrarchy, of Galilee and Transjordan, was the scene of much of Jesus' ministry. On the death of Augustus in AD 14 Antipas did all he could to win the approval of his successor, Tiberius, and it may have been his scheming to this end that lies behind Jesus' reference to him as 'that fox' (Luke 13.32). One example of this policy was his foundation of a new capital city on the Sea of Galilee, which he named Tiberias in honour of the emperor.

On a visit to Rome he fell in love with Herodias, the wife of his half-brother, Herod-Philip. This presented a serious problem. First, Antipas was already married to a daughter of the king of the Nabataeans, and any move that jeopardized the security of the eastern frontier would be unpopular in Rome. Secondly, if he obtained Herodias by divorce, he would be infringing Jewish law. Nevertheless, Herodias and Antipas were determined to marry, and Antipas' wife returned secretly to Petra, her rejection reviving the dormant hostility between the Nabataeans and the family of Herod. It was for this marriage that John the Baptist denounced Antipas, a course which led to his death and the dramatic story of Herodias' daughter, Salome (Mark 6.14–29).

An incident showing Antipas in rather better light occurred during Pilate's governorship of Judaea. According to the Jewish writer Philo, Pilate wished to dedicate some golden shields, carrying the emperor's name, in the temple. A deputation consisting of Antipas, three of his brothers, and the leaders of the Sanhedrin protested unsuccessfully to Pilate, but a letter to Tiberius secured a more favourable reply: the shields should be dedicated in the temple of Augustus at Caesarea, where they would give less offence.

In AD 37 Tiberius died, and with him Antipas' fortunes. The new emperor, Caligula, made his friend, Herod Agrippa I, the grandson of Herod the Great, king of Philip's former tetrarchy. Herodias, angry at what she considered a slight to her husband, set off with him to Rome to complain, but an accusation by Agrippa that Antipas was in league with the Parthians sealed his doom. Antipas was banished, and his tetrarchy and revenues given to Agrippa (AD 39).

Meanwhile, Archelaus' region had been a Roman province for thirty-three years. It was administered from Caesarea, Herod's new city on the coast, which being largely Gentile in population had none of the limiting traditions of Jerusalem. In Caesarea, and on his visits to Jerusalem, the governor lived in the palaces built by Herod. He could call upon the services of a small garrison of auxiliary troops, under the immediate command of a tribune, such as Claudius Lysias (Acts 21.31); many of these were probably recruited inside Judaea, at first from the army of Herod and Archelaus, but the great majority of them would have been Gentile, not Jew. In times of crisis requiring larger forces the governor would look for help to Syria, whose governor commanded four legions as well as some auxiliary units.

Although the province of Judaea was small – only about the size of Wales – it was in a thoroughly unsettled condition. The Jews felt themselves to be a unique people, and, though the basis of this claim was religious, under conditions of unpopular foreign domination its manifestations were bound to be political. Each of the main religious sects thus had its own political 'line' – most obviously, the extreme nationalism of the Zealots (see Part IV, Section 3, pp. 232 f.). The governors of Judaea varied a good deal in type and origin – Pilate, for example, was probably by birth a provincial Italian, rather than a Roman, while Tiberius Alexander was a renegade Jew of the Dispersion – but one forms the impression that generally speaking they were men of insufficient calibre to cope successfully with the peculiar complexities of their office.

It is impossible to give a full narrative of the events occurring in each governor's term of office, but the disturbed situation of the province, with brigands – or nationalist insurgents – active in the countryside and frequent changes of high priest – now appointed by the Roman governor – increasing tension in Jerusalem, needs to be remembered as the background to the ministry of Jesus.

3. *Pilate, Procurator of Judaea*

Pontius Pilate was the fifth governor of Judaea, in office from AD 27 to 36. His picture in the Gospels is well-known, but we also have information about him from two other sources, Josephus and the Jewish writer Philo of Alexandria, who was a contemporary of Pilate. It is Philo who relates Pilate's behaviour in the matter of the golden shields already mentioned; he describes him as 'naturally inflexible and stubbornly relentless' and accuses him of 'arrogance, repeated murders of innocent victims, and constant and most galling savagery'. As Philo was arguing to prove a case, his evidence may be unreliable.

Neither is Josephus unbiased, for he was attempting to prove that the Jewish War of AD 66–73 was not started by irresponsible fanatics but by men who had already endured a succession of incompetent and cruel governors with the utmost patience and who only took to war reluctantly and as a last resort; it is thus in his interest, too, to blacken Pilate's character. He records three incidents in Pilate's governorship. The first was a tactless attempt to send troops into winter quarters in Jerusalem carrying standards bearing a representation of the emperor's head. The Jews protested; there must be no 'graven images' in the Holy City. Pilate attempted compromise unsuccessfully, and the matter was referred to Tiberius, who decided in favour of the Jews. The second incident underlines the extreme difficulty of Pilate's position. He used some of the temple money to improve the water supply to Jerusalem and to the temple itself. Although this use of the fund was specifically permitted by the Law, there was rioting in Jerusalem, which Pilate put down violently. Finally, Pilate massacred some Samaritans who were caught up in a messianic movement; a complaint to Vitellius, the governor of Syria, to whom Tiberius had entrusted a general oversight of eastern affairs, resulted in Pilate's removal from office and return in disgrace to Rome.

Apart from the Gospel descriptions of Pilate's part in the trial of Jesus, there is a reference to Pilate in Luke 13.1, 'Galileans, whose blood Pilate had mingled with their sacrifices'. It is just possible that this incident was the cause of the enmity referred to in Luke 23.12 between Pilate and Antipas, the tetrarch of Galilee.

4. *Pilate and the Trial of Jesus*

The accounts of Jesus' trial before Pilate provide a good example of a Roman governor's judicial powers and of the way in which these would operate. It is one of the chief differences between Roman and modern English law that in the former very few crimes were clearly defined and provided with a set range of penalties and that even in these the procedures laid down applied only to Roman citizens. In all other matters brought before a magistrate (in this case, the governor) it was his first task to decide whether to listen to the accusers, for his power to dismiss a case was absolute. If he thought the matter deserved his attention, he would hear the trial and decide upon the sentence and penalty; from these, too, there was no appeal, though, before proceedings started, a Roman citizen could claim the right to be tried in Rome before the emperor.

Cases concerning Jews would not usually come before the governor at all, for it was Roman practice to allow well-established communities as large a measure of self-government

as was consistent with good order, and the Sanhedrin thus retained wide judicial powers. It could not, however, inflict the death penalty – except in the quite exceptional cases of Gentiles trespassing in the temple – though it is sometimes argued that it could sentence a man to death and forward its decision to the governor for confirmation. This probably mis-states the position. It is more likely that when the Sanhedrin felt the death penalty would be appropriate, it would institute proceedings before the governor; the Roman government was always particularly careful to retain life and death decisions in its own hands. At the same time, the prestige of the Sanhedrin must often have made it successful in such actions, and it is easy to see how such a belief could have arisen.

All the Gospels make it clear that Jesus was first examined before the Sanhedrin and then taken to Pilate. The charge was one of sedition. It seems that Pilate would like to have dismissed the case, but, fearing to do so outright, availed himself of the fact that Jesus was a Galilean to send him to Antipas (Luke 23.7). As Antipas refused to deal with the case, he was sent back to Pilate. Pilate's reluctance to pronounce the death penalty remains clear, but, when he hesitated, the Sanhedrin played its trump card: 'If you let this man go, you are no friend to Caesar' (John 19.12). Pilate could not afford to provide grounds for an influential deputation to go from his province to Rome and accuse him before the emperor of unreliability. He submitted to this extra-legal pressure and gave orders for Jesus' crucifixion. Thus, though it is possible that the Gospel writers exaggerate Pilate's reluctance and Jewish guilt, the trial as recorded in the Gospels, with its curious laxity of procedure and combination of religious, political, and legal arguments, is exactly what one would expect in this situation.

Any final assessment of Pilate's character is made impossible by the scarcity of evidence, but it is perhaps worth mentioning that, in accordance with Tiberius' preference for long terms of office, Pilate was allowed to remain governor of Judaea for nearly ten years.

The Later Tetrarchs and Governors

Herod Agrippa I enjoyed the friendship of both Caligula and Claudius, the emperors who succeeded Tiberius. Caligula had made him king of the area which his uncle Philip had previously ruled as tetrarch and had then enlarged his kingdom by the addition of Antipas' tetrarchy. In AD 41 Agrippa had bravely used his friendship with Caligula to persuade him to countermand his orders for the erection of a large statue of himself in the temple. In the same year Caligula was assassinated, and Agrippa was largely instrumental in securing the succession of Claudius. He was handsomely rewarded. Claudius abolished the province of Judaea and added it to Agrippa's territory, thus reconstituting the kingdom of Herod the Great.

He reigned for only three years, but during that time he showed considerable ability. To demonstrate that Judaea was Jewish once more he made Jerusalem his official residence, and by remission of taxes and other conciliatory moves he became extremely popular with his subjects. His execution of James, the son of Zebedee, and arrest of Peter, two of the leaders of the growing Christian community (Acts 12.1–18), is hardly likely to have been widely unpopular. (Stephen, the first martyr, had been illegally executed by the Sanhedrin in AD 37 during the period immediately following Pilate's recall, in which Judaea had no governor.)

One of the main problems for the Jews of the Dispersion was the ill-feeling existing in many cities between the Greek majority and the Jewish community. Nowhere was this more true than in Alexandria. Matters came to a head once again in Claudius' reign, and rival deputations from the city appealed to the Emperor in Rome. Claudius' decree confirmed the traditional rights of the Jews and ordered the Greeks not to interfere with these; at the same time the Jews were not to try to increase their privileges and were not to seek converts.

On Agrippa's death, Claudius wished to appoint his son, Herod Agrippa II, to the throne of Judaea, but the boy was only seventeen, and Claudius was persuaded to make the area a province once more. (It now, of course, included the whole of Herod Agrippa's kingdom.) Four years later, Claudius made Herod Agrippa II king of Chalcis in the Lebanon.

The governors of the restored province seem to have continued the generally low standard set by their predecessors, although Josephus comments favourably on the first two, Cuspius Fadus and Tiberius Alexander, on the grounds that they 'left native customs alone and kept the nation at peace'. With the third, however, Cumanus, troubles began again, his governorship being marked 'by disturbances and further disasters to the Jews'. There was rioting at the Passover between the worshippers and the Roman garrison – which, if one may believe Josephus, led to the death of more than thirty thousand. There was trouble when Cumanus ordered his soldiers to sack some villages whose inhabitants he suspected of harbouring brigands, and there was a clash between Galileans and Samaritans, which ended in the now traditional way with each side sending a deputation to the emperor; the influence of Agrippa II with Claudius ensured a Jewish victory.

Of the next governor, Felix, the Roman historian Tacitus says that 'he indulged in every kind of barbarity and lust and exercised the power of a king in the spirit of a slave'. He was well connected at court – his brother was influential with Claudius and was said to be the lover of the Empress Agrippina, the mother of Nero – and clearly owed his position to this. Drusilla, described in Acts 24.24 as his wife, was the sister of Agrippa II and had been married to the king of Emesa, whom she had abandoned for Felix, although this was contrary to Jewish law. Among other injudicious acts, Felix procured assassins to murder the high priest Jonathan. In the atmosphere of terror that ensued many innocent men were killed. Others flocked to join various false prophets, of whom the most famous is the Egyptian, referred to in Acts 21.38, for whom Paul was mistaken; Felix crushed these with great severity. His high-handedness also shows in his dealings with Paul, whom he kept in custody for two years without bringing him to trial; Luke attributes this to his hope that Paul would offer him a bribe (Acts 24.26).

His successor, Porcius Festus, was more business-like, both in his dealings with Paul and in attempting to free the country of bandits. Unfortunately he died in office, and in the interval before a new governor could take office, the Sanhedrin once again took the law into its own hands and executed James, the brother of Jesus, who was the leader of the Christian community in Jerusalem.

Of the next governor, Albinus, Josephus says that he was 'guilty of every possible misdemeanour' – he mentions robbery, crippling taxation, and accepting bribes – and adds the significant detail that it was during his term of office that 'the revolutionary party in Jerusalem cast off all restraint'.

'Yet the endurance of the Jews lasted until Gessius Florus was governor.' So Tacitus; and Josephus comments that he made even Albinus seem an angel and claims that 'it was he (Florus) who compelled us to take up arms against the Romans, thinking that it was better to be destroyed at once than by degrees'. Florus took up office in AD 64, and the Jewish War – so named, typically, from the Roman angle – began in 66. What occasioned it?

The Jewish War and the Fall of Jerusalem

The first trouble was a clash in Caesarea between Jews and Greeks, in which Florus favoured the latter. Shortly afterwards, he provoked further antagonism in Jerusalem when he demanded a large sum of money from the temple treasury on the pretext that the emperor required it. Demonstrations followed, and, after failing to secure the arrest of those responsible, Florus allowed his troops to loot. Many innocent people were killed, including Jews who were Roman citizens. The Jews complained to Cestius Gallus, the governor of Syria, and he sent one of his officers to investigate the matter; no redress followed. At this stage Agrippa II, who happened to be in Jerusalem, and who realized that if war broke out his own position would be in danger, made a long speech to the inhabitants of the city urging submission. For a time it seemed as though he might be successful, but when he went further and advised them to obey Florus until a successor arrived, the people stoned him, and he returned to his own kingdom, clearly seeing that war was now inevitable.

The war began with seemingly unconnected acts of aggression against the Romans. Within a month the rebels had seized Jerusalem and the greater part of Judaea and had captured the fortress of Masada with its huge arsenal. The disturbances spread to the predominantly Greek cities of the Decapolis and the coast, and even to Alexandria; in all of them there was violent fighting between Greeks and Jews. Cestius Gallus was compelled to intervene and

marched south with an army of thirty thousand men, but, despite early success, he failed to press home his advantage.

Nero realized the need for rapid action; the fighting must not be allowed to spread to the frontiers and endanger his recently won settlement with the Parthians. He appointed an experienced general, Vespasian, to the command of Judaea. In AD 67 Vespasian reconquered Galilee, where the young Josephus was in command, and the next year pressed on into Samaria and Transjordan. Meanwhile, in Jerusalem, factional struggles which amounted to civil war were rife and must seriously have weakened the capacity of the inhabitants to resist.

This was the situation in Jerusalem in AD 70 when Titus, the son of Vespasian, who had been left in command when his father returned to Rome to become emperor, came to attack the city. The story of the siege is graphically told by Josephus. The natural position of the city was immensely strong, and it was impressively fortified. Attack was only possible from the north or north-west, where the assailants would have to breach three walls in turn; even then, there remained the temple itself and the upper city, both of which could serve as well-defended inner citadels. The siege began in May. The Romans employed all their skill in siege warfare, building huge ramps and towers, attempting to mine the walls or battering them with huge boulders thrown from their artillery, and eventually constructing a wall of five miles in length running right round the city, but the defenders resisted heroically. Not until the end of September was the whole city in Roman hands. City and temple were razed to the ground. (Titus' achievement was recorded on a triumphal arch set up in the forum at Rome; its sculptures show the temple treasures, including the seven-branched candelabra, being carried in procession through the streets of Rome.)

Mopping-up operations continued for a further three years, culminating in the long siege and heroic defence of Masada, the great fortress which towers over the western shore of the Dead Sea. (The site has recently been excavated, and Josephus' account of the siege can now be compared with the findings of the archaeologists in Y. Yadin: *Masada*.) When further resistance proved impossible, the surviving defenders – to the number of nearly a thousand – set fire to the fortress and killed themselves; two women are supposed to have hidden in the underground water cisterns and thus to have furnished Josephus with details of the siege.

The result of the war was the end of a specifically Jewish state. The Sanhedrin and the high priesthood were abolished, and worship at the temple was forbidden.

Even so, for the Romans the Jewish problem continued, and two further revolts must be mentioned. In 115, while the emperor Trajan was campaigning aginst the Parthians, a rising started among the Jews of Cyrene and soon spread to those resident in Egypt, Cyprus, and Mesopotamia. In origin this seems to have been another in the long series of inter-racial and inter-cultural clashes between Jews and Greeks. In Cyprus, for example, the revolt was marked by hideous atrocities; a quarter of a million Gentiles are said to have perished, and the Greek city of Salamis was destroyed. Trajan, probably remembering the Jewish War of 66–73, obviously feared its effects on his eastern policy and crushed the rising with great severity. On this occasion Judaea itself remained at peace.

The last great rebellion of the Jews occurred in 132, in the reign of Trajan's successor, Hadrian. When Hadrian visited Judaea in 130, he decided that it would be unwise to leave Jerusalem in its ruined state as a focus for Jewish nationalism and announced plans for its refoundation as a self-governing city with the name Aelia Capitolina (Hadrian's family name was Aelius); its inhabitants were to be Gentiles, and Jews were not to be permitted to enter it except on one day a year; moreover, on the site of the temple would be built a pagan temple dedicated to the worship of Jupiter and the emperor.

In 132, the Jews reacted to this insensitive decision by breaking out into revolt. They were led by Simon bar Kochba, whose recognition as Messiah by the Rabbis rallied support to him. At first the guerilla tactics of the Jews were successful, but the rebellion was finally crushed in AD 135, and Hadrian's new city was built.

The Roman Administrative System

The provincial system established by Augustus

after the battle of Actium (31 BC) lasted without essential change throughout the period covered in this section. Under it, the provinces were divided into two groups. The older-established and more peaceful provinces were governed by proconsuls appointed by and responsible to the Senate. An example is Achaea, where Gallio was proconsul (Acts 18.12), but the most important of them were Africa (Libya and Tunisia) and Asia (the Aegean coast of Turkey). The remainder came under the direction of the emperor, who appointed their governors himself. They included most of the frontier provinces and others where trouble might be expected and contained twenty-four of the twenty-five or so legions of the regular army. The most important of them in the eastern part of the empire was Syria.

An apparent exception to this division are the client kingdoms, of which Judaea under Herod the Great was the most important. Despite their title, these were not truly independent territories, for whatever internal autonomy they enjoyed might be withdrawn at any time by the emperor. However, the uniqueness of Judaea, a country with a well-established tradition of social organization quite different from that of the Greek cities in other parts of the East, made this the obvious solution in this case and the degree of freedom from ostensible Roman control must have been very considerable until the deposition of Archelaus.

The imperial provinces were themselves divided into two classes. The more important of them were governed by legates, men of considerable military and administrative experience. Their main functions were two – military and judicial. The legate of Syria, for example, commanded four legions and various auxiliary units. These guarded the frontier with Parthia, policed the mountains and cities of the province, and could be used to intervene in the client kingdoms or minor provinces surrounding Syria. We have already seen that the cities of the Empire often enjoyed wide judicial powers, and the governor's chief duty in this field was to serve as a court of appeal from the judgments of local magistrates. The governorship of Syria was regarded as the senior appointment in the imperial provinces and enjoyed enormous prestige throughout the East.

The smaller provinces of the second class, to

which Judaea belonged, were governed by officials of less experience and standing. They are usually called procurators, the title used by the Roman historian Tacitus, but until the reign of Claudius their correct title was prefect, as an inscription found at Caesarea and dating from Pilate's governorship shows. Although they did not usually command legions and certainly enjoyed less prestige, their powers were basically the same as those of the legates.

So far, no mention has been made of the third main administrative field – the financial. To ensure control of the revenues of his provinces and to prevent corruption among their governors, Augustus separated this field from the military and judicial and created a new class of officials to deal with it, also called procurators. They were concerned with collection of the two regular taxes – the *tributum soli*, levied on land, and the *tributum capitis*, levied on other forms of property. To ensure that they were levied fairly, the holding of an accurate census was one of the first acts upon formation of a new province and was regularly repeated thereafter. There were also certain indirect taxes, including, for example, import/export dues of five per cent and taxes on the sale of slaves. These were not collected by the pro-curator's staff, but under contract by companies of financiers, who usually employed local assistants – the 'publicans' of the New Testament. All these taxes had, of course, to be paid in Roman currency, and the use of this – carrying as it did a representation of the emperor's head – inevitably caused unrest in Judaea.

The Decapolis

The Decapolis was a league of cities created by Pompey in 62 BC, probably for mutual defence against the neighbouring Semitic tribes. The individual cities, however, were probably much older. The Roman writer Pliny (*Natural History* V, 74) gives a list of the members, but, as the membership fluctuated, they were not always ten in number. Together they formed a fairly continuous block of territory east of the Sea of Galilee and the Jordan.

Among the certain foundation members were Scythopolis (which Josephus describes as the greatest city of the Decapolis at the time of the Jewish War and which was the only one of the cities to be situated west of the Jordan), Pella, Gadara, Hippos, Dium, Canatha, Philadelphia (now Amman, capital of Jordan), and Gerasa

The Family Tree of Herod the Great*

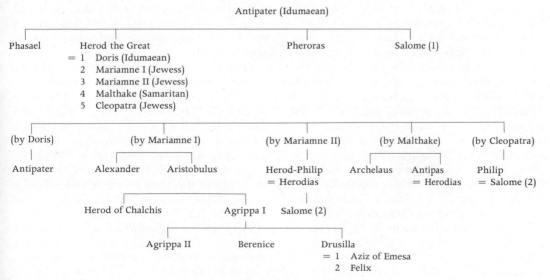

*The table is not complete. Only those names essential for an understanding of the Gospels, Acts and this article are included.

213

(modern Jerash, the best preserved of the cities and containing many fine buildings dating from this period). Abila was probably a foundation member. By the second century AD Damascus was also a member and had become the metropolis (chief city) of the League.

Jesus crossed the Sea of Galilee and visited the Decapolis on several occasions (Matt.8.28; Mark 7.31). He would have found in them a very different atmosphere from that in Galilee itself, for their population and way of life were Graeco-Roman.

2

Daily Life in Galilee

Phyllis Doyle

Geography and Climate

The climate and contours of Galilee today are the same as in the first century AD, but this area in the Mediterranean differs sufficiently from our own conditions to make it worthwhile to stress certain aspects. There are two main seasons, wet and dry. The winter is the cold rainy season, the summer hot and dry beginning early in May until the October rains bring in cooler weather. There are high mountains, such as Mt Meiron (3962 feet), in northern Galilee, and plains, such as the coastal plain, but the unique feature is the Jordan rift, where at the Sea of Galilee the land is 682 feet below sea level and further south at the Dead Sea it is 1292 feet below sea level. Jesus walking from Nazareth to Capernaum would descend from high windy moorland to the fierce heat of the Jordan valley. As Jerusalem is built on the high land of Judaea over 2000 feet high, the drop down to Jericho and the Dead Sea is over 3000 feet and one moves from the temperate zone into a tropical climate with tropical vegetation, palms and exotic flowers. Here, in the few miles from Jerusalem to Jericho, the contrasts of climate are experienced dramatically. The ministry of Jesus went on in this setting; tropical heat rising to 110 degrees Fahrenheit as a normal summer heat and in the high lands in the winter snow perhaps, while if, standing by the Sea of Galilee, he gazed towards Mt Hermon in the north, there snow lies perpetually. Now we can understand the constant references to the washing of feet, anointing with oil skins

dried by scorching winds, sudden storms swirling along the narrow cleft of the Jordan valley and whipping up the calm beauty of the Sea of Galilee in a matter of minutes into waves that endanger small fishing craft. They are all still there, these climatic conditions which any modern traveller can find in Israel today.

Roads and Hill-paths

The next feature to examine is the main routes that traversed Palestine in the time of Jesus, for along these routes came the wealth of the great civilizations of his day. Galilee, though small, was not isolated and the routes which converged on to this small territory gave it a key position which had been magnificently exploited by king Solomon.

The contours of the land determine the main routes. Palestine is a small country, some thirty-five miles broad, lying between the sea and the Jordan rift. There is a narrow coastal plain broadening into the plain of Esdraelon towards the north. Then, in the south, come the highlands of Judaea rising to an average of 2400 feet, which descend abruptly to the Jordan. On the other side of the Jordan rise the mountains of Moab, forming a barrier against the desert and also a high, but fairly level, route for caravans. Thus the main early roads, or trackways, tend to go in a north/south direction: one of the earliest of these, the so-called 'King's Highway', runs from Ezion-geber, at the head of the Gulf of Aqaba, where Solomon's copper mines were, northward through the desert, then along the eastern side of the Jordan to Damascus where it met the caravans coming south from the Euphrates with all their eastern wealth. Aerial photography shows this clearly as a trackway, somewhat similar to the trackways on the Downlands of southern England which have been worn by feet rather than made by skill.

The second great north/south route is the one leading from Egypt up the narrow coastal plain until it reaches the headland of Mt Carmel, then it must go through the narrow pass dominated by Megiddo and, passing into the plain of Jezreel, make its way south of Nazareth and eastward towards the Jordan, which it crosses just south of the Sea of Galilee, and on to Damascus. Another route from Damascus came north of the Sea of Galilee and Capernaum and met this Egypt-Damascus road *via* Tiberias. This, at the time of Jesus, was the famous Roman road, the Via Maris, the Road of the Sea. The Romans had built other paved roads in Palestine. One of these ran from Tiberias, the capital of Galilee under Herod Antipas (the Herod of the Gospels), westward over the steep rise from the lake into the hilly country around Nazareth. One branch went to the port of Acre, another went through the Megiddo gap to the coast at Caesarea. Along these routes the military could pass marching as many as sixteen miles a day; couriers could go by horse some twenty-five miles a day.

Galilee was thus not isolated from the traffic of ancient civilization. But Jerusalem was remote on its high perch among the Judaean mountains; there it could remain, a stronghold of Jewish tradition, though there was the Roman fortress of Antonia on the north-eastern wall of the city where it could overlook the temple, the holy sanctuary of the Jews.

Cities, Towns and Villages

The cities and townships of Palestine in the first century AD reflected three ways of life, glimpses of which inform the background of the New Testament. The all-pervading influence of Rome dominated certain cities, such as Caesarea, regarded as essential to the maintenance of the occupying forces. Certain townships, like Nazareth, remained essentially Jewish, while in the countryside of Galilee, around the lake and on the surrounding hills, the life of shepherd and fisherman went on even as it does today.

Roman life at this time was greatly influenced by Greece. The ten cities (the *Decapolis*) mentioned in Matt.4.25; Mark 5.20; 7.31 were out and out Greek cities, with temples, a forum, a theatre and public baths. Nine of these cities were on the eastern side of the Jordan: one – Scythopolis – was on the western side, a few miles from Nazareth (see Part IV, Section 1, p. 213). Caesarea and Tiberias had the same pattern and so did Jericho, the winter resort of Herod the Great.

Houses

The buildings and houses in the Romanized cities followed the Roman style. The ruins of Sebaste in Samaria, built by Herod the Great, reveal a city laid out in a rectangle of streets, each block containing four houses. The streets had colonnades which could be filled with shops, baths, theatres, etc. Jericho was built at the time of the Herods on a model of first-century Rome.

In such cities the houses for the well-to-do were built of brick or stone, some forty to sixty feet high, with very few windows looking on to the street and with a heavy street-gate which opened on to a passage or courtyard. Around this were the main rooms of the house; in smaller dwellings these were on the ground floor but in larger ones upstairs. There were summer and winter rooms, with the courtyard planted sometimes with trees and used as a pergola in summer. The bedrooms were small rooms off on one side, and there had to be a bathroom for the Roman steam bath. Heating was mainly by charcoal braziers or fires, the kind Peter sat in front of to warm himself in the courtyard of the high priest (Mark 14.54). In well-to-do houses there were beds, light structures of wood that lifted the bedclothes from the floor. The main rooms of these houses were paved with mosaics.

In contrast to the rich the houses of the poor were built of such perishable material that little remains today; they seem to have been of baked mud, which heavy rains would wear down. The saying of Jesus about the two houses, one built on rock and one on sand, indicates how important were the foundations (Matt.7.24–27). In Nazareth today one is taken to see the place where Joseph's carpenter's shop and his home are alleged to stand, but like many of the sites shown to pilgrims the identification is very uncertain. As any remains from the first century AD are always several feet below ground one descends some fifteen to twenty feet. For the dwelling is in two parts, the shop above and below it the living quarters. These again are on two levels, the floor being higher in one part than the other. In what remains of the house at Nazareth there are places for baking and for keeping the little oil lamp, but the unevenness of the floors obscures the normal pattern of the dwelling-house where one of the levels would be for the living quarters of the family and the other a craftroom, or for animals or for the children to play. The alleged birthplace of Jesus at Bethlehem is a good example of a dwelling with two levels: the actual place of birth is shown by an ornate star engraved on the ground radiating from a hollow, a little lower down in a small alcove where the animals were supposed to have been there was the manger. All of this is now below ground level and gains in mystery as one has to use an electric torch as a guide in the dim light. The poor houses were like boxes, flat roofed, made perhaps of rough rafters with branches laid across and plastered with mud. This could be removed easily (see Mark 2.4). The flat roof after rain was smoothed with a stone roller, which is still done today. The roof, surrounded by a parapet, was a useful adjunct to the house for drying vegetables, ripening fruit, sleeping and saying one's prayers. Poor people slept on the floor wrapped in their cloaks. In the house at Nazareth mentioned above there are little nooks and crannies which would have made lovely places for hide and seek for the children. The shepherds lived differently again, for they would be nomadic, out on the mountains of Judaea, or Galilee or Moab. To this day large caves remain, weather-proof and roomy though with low ceilings of rock, where fires can be built for warmth in the bitter cold of winter. Just outside Bethlehem is one such cave alleged to be the one in which the shepherds who heard the first Gloria from the angels lived. Bedouins still use it, as they do other caves in the vicinity.

Clothes

The Roman costume is well known for the military and the civilian. The soldier wore a short tunic, a coat of mail, a helmet, sandals on his feet, a belt with a sword and his shield – a description which is used by Paul in Eph.6.14 f. The *toga* could only be worn by Roman citizens and was generally used by city dwellers; it was a heavy woollen wrap, sometimes with a purple stripe round its margin for those who were free-born. Paul as a Roman citizen might have worn one. For state occasions, such as in the Senate or in court, togas were compulsory wear, so Pilate must have worn one when judging Jesus. Some of the togas could be very elaborate in decoration with gold embroidery as well as purple stripes. They must have been very hot wear in the summer of Palestine, and Roman citizens were relieved when they were allowed to discard them in the country.

The dress of the Jew can be deduced from mosaics and also from a very interesting document of later date which gives details of the Jewish garments which may be rescued from fire should it break out on a sabbath day. The poor people, like Jesus and his disciples, wore five garments including the distinguishing *tallith* or shawl. These consisted of a long cotton shirt, a leather or stuff girdle, shoes or sandals and a cloak, plus the *tallith*. The shirt would sometimes be almost a waist cloth wound tightly round the waist; it was worn by fishermen and workers. When stripped to this under-garment they might describe themselves as naked, as Peter is described in John 21.7 and as Jesus is always depicted on the cross. The cloak could vary, too, either sleeveless and of some coarse material, like goats' or camels' hair or sackcloth, or it could be a long-sleeved coat worn by officials, priests and educated persons. This cloak was like a cassock, open in front without a girdle and with wide sleeves; it was worn the same length as the undershirt which, for this costume, would be long. For indoor work this undershirt was worn with a girdle and could be tucked up. Perhaps this was what Jesus did at the last supper when he washed the feet of his disciples like a house-slave. The head-dress was important for it was distinctive for the Jew. He wore sometimes a small skull cap and over this would place his *tallith*, or he could use only the *tallith* with a cord, making him look rather like an Arab, whose head cloth, a *Kaffiyeh*, about a yard square, was folded diagonally and put on the head so as to screen the eyes and the nape of the neck; this, too, was kept in place with a cord, and may still be seen in Palestine today. The *tallith* needs special mention. It was a shawl which might be 'great' or 'small'. Every male Jew had to wear the small one next to the shirt, but often they were careless of this rule. It was of purplish-blue cotton with four tassels and marked the separation of the Jews from the Gentiles. The large *tallith* was the prayer-shawl proper, white, about two yards square, with a black border or stripes and a cord attached with eight threads and five knots, symbolizing the number of commandments in the Law (*Torah*). The women's dress was so like the men's that they could almost be exchanged, except for the head-dress. Instead of the *tallith* women would wear the veil so beloved by Paul! A widow might wear a black one. The women sometimes wore a kind of breastplate of colourful embroidery to brighten their dress. One can still see ladies with similar colourful addition on the sabbath in Jerusalem today.

The Roman men wore their hair short and were clean shaven. Their razors were of iron. The men of Palestine, on the contrary, wore their hair long and had beards. In the New Testament there are references both to growing the hair and to shaving it off to depict that a vow had been taken. Roman women had elaborate hair styles, unless as old-fashioned matrons they wore their hair piled high on the top of the head. Curls with a fillet of beads might be worn by a young woman. Both men and women dyed their hair and sometimes wore wigs, remains of which have been found in the catacombs. Rich women, as today, had elaborate cosmetics, painting their faces and their nails, both of hands and feet. Sweet smelling herbs were used for anointing hands and feet, as one notices with the woman who anointed Jesus' feet with costly perfume from a jar (Luke 7.36–50).

Where did these herbs come from? Many, such as cassia and cinnamon, came from the East along the caravan routes, but in Palestine itself many were cultivated, especially in the fertile gardens of Jericho. There in the time of the Roman conquest of Palestine was found the rare balsam, whose appearance in Israel smacks of romance. Josephus, the Jewish historian, states that the seeds were brought by the Queen of Sheba among her gifts of spices to Solomon, for the balsam was indigenous to Arabia. He also states that cuttings from these herbs were taken, with others, to a village called Mataria, six miles north of Cairo, when Cleopatra became the owner of Jericho and its gardens. Sir John Maundeville, the great mediaeval traveller, mentions these balsam bushes at Mataria as 'slender little trees which are no higher than the belt of your riding breeches and resemble the wood of the wild vine'. But when the Crusaders came to Palestine in the twelfth century there were no traces of these bushes at Jericho.

Foot-wear in this hot, dusty country had to be loose. Sandals were the usual wear, made of leather, wood or dried grass, with thongs passed through loops to bind them firmly to the feet. The Romans sometimes wore boots consisting of a sole and a closed upper, or this upper might consist just of thongs for coolness. Slippers or sandals were worn indoors. When at a meal, sandals were removed by slaves and so, at the end of the meal when going home, the guest would ask for his sandals to indicate his intention of leaving.

The dyes used for the wigs and for the bright coloured embroideries and cloaks were extracted from both vegetable and animal sources. Thus the famous purple used throughout the Mediterranean came from the murex snail living in the sea. Great quantities of empty snail shells have been found at Tyre and Sidon, which was a flourishing centre of this trade. Rich yellow came from both the pomegranate and the saffron, woad yielded a lovely blue, while the earth contributed ochre and red chalk. No wonder the Jews loved bright colours.

Food and Drink

In many of his parables Jesus mentions feasts; indeed, one of the expectations of the coming of the Messiah was that a great feast would be held in celebration. What were the everyday foods, and the luxuries and the ways of serving them? The Roman way of life differed considerably from that of the Jewish, though many of the Jews in Palestine had become, by the first century AD, very like their conquerors in their behaviour. The Romans had four meals a day, of which the first, early in the morning, and the third, served about four o'clock, were very light. For children the first consisted of just a pancake, for adults bread spread with honey or dipped in wine and a few dates and olives. The mid-day meal, known as *prandium*, was also a light one, though at times it might be quite elaborately dressed. The heavy meal of the day was in the evening and for special occasions might be three-course. This was called *cena*, and was often preceded by a bath. The food might be fish, fowl, butcher's meat, vegetables and fruit, brought in on wooden trays. The guests ate with their fingers, reclining at the semi-circular tables, which had to be wiped down between each course and the guests offered bowls of water and towels to wash and wipe their hands. Sometimes these meals went on for three hours.

The Jews lived a much simpler life, though the rich ones, like Simon the Pharisee (Luke 7.36–50), might ape the Romans in many ways. But the Jewish religion forbade eating certain foods and strict Jews were thus cut off from mixing with Gentiles. This was Peter's problem when Gentiles became Christians (Acts 10). Jews ate very little meat, usually only on festival days. It had to be specially killed, for they were forbidden to eat meat with blood in it. This was *kosher*. Roast lamb was compulsory at the Passover, but meat was usually boiled. Many vegetables were eaten raw, like small cucumbers, and the Jews liked onions and garlic in their food. The usual cereals eaten were corn and rice; horse-beans and lentils, various cucumbers and marrows were among the vegetables. There were many fruits: pomegranates, grapes, mulberries, dates, figs and various nuts. As there was no sugar, honey and dried dates, figs and raisins supplied the sweetness. Milk and wine were drunk and, above all, the olive was a staple element in the diet, for it supplied both its fruit and its oil.

The Jews only had two meals a day, one at midday and one in the evening, though they broke their fast with a snack in the morning. Every house would have its stone corn-mill where the corn, whether it were wheat or barley, had to be ground between two heavy stones requiring at times two women for the job, and a very noisy one it was, too. Similarly, every community would have some kind of press for pressing the oil out of the olives; some of the wealthy households had their own olive presses, as can be seen from the excavations which have been done at the house of Caiaphas the high priest.

Education

The curriculum in Roman schools imitated the pattern set up by the fifth century BC in Greece. Boys attended school from about six years old and were taught to read, write and count (this would be on the abacus); the reading matter in Gentile schools was often Homer and stories of the gods and goddesses, so that the children became knowledgeable about their origins, both mythical and religious, and were incidentally taught drama and poetry. Music was also considered very important by Plato and had early been incorporated into the schools of Greece, for performance on the lyre as accompaniments for poetry (hence the word lyrical), and for singing. 'To play the lyre' was the phrase used to denote a gentleman. Music was also important in the teaching of dance, which was part of religious education, as the services in the temples needed both boys' choirs and ritualistic dances. Every school had its gymnasium attached. Here the younger boys learned to wrestle and run and jump, while the older ones, over fourteen, joined with men in the more disciplined training of the body, for, to the Greeks, athletics were essential to keep the balance between body and mind which was the Greek ideal of perfection. Mathematics was also taught to the older boys, as well as rhetoric and logic. The teachers in these schools in the Roman empire had a low status, very often being slaves. In Greece they had been respected as free and learned men.

Education in Palestine was far more widespread than is generally supposed. Nearly every town had its school; the percentage of literate people was high, as evidence from first-century scribblings on walls seem to suggest. But Jewish religion gave a different slant to the content of the curriculum and to the position of teacher, which was revered. The child learned much in his home through his mother's teachings and the many ceremonies held in the home. The clearest example of this is the elaborate training in history and ritual associated yearly with the Passover, when the youngest boy must ask the leading questions about the reason for the ceremony of his elders

(Deut.6.20–25). Each child was taught a text of Scripture containing the same letters as his name; here we see an ancient stress on the significance of the name in Hebrew religion. He also had to know several psalms by heart and, in strict households, the 'Shema', the great statement from Deuteronomy (Deut.6.4), 'Hear, O Israel, the Lord our God is one Lord', was said at the beginning of the day. This text was often placed in a little container or called the *Mezuza*, which was inserted in the lintel of the door as a frequent reminder of the faith. The quotation from Ps.31.5, 'Into thy hands I commend my spirit', is also thought to be a prayer taught by mothers to their children as they go to sleep.

Between the age of five and six the child began school, which was held often in the synagogue though there might be a special school house. Teacher and pupils either stood or sat in a semi-circle on the floor. The curriculum was divided into three phases: up to ten the boys learnt exclusively from the Old Testament; between ten and fifteen they were taught the traditional Law; after fifteen they went on to study and discuss theology. It was essentially a religious training, comparable to what is given today in Burma and Tibet. There were no mathematics, nor physical education, nor music – elements considered essential by the Greeks. But the mode of teaching by question and answer, which is the Socratic method, was apparently followed, as can be seen when Jesus, in the temple, asked and answered questions from the doctors of the Law (Luke 2.46 f.). He had then reached the age to be accepted into the congregation and receive his *tallith*, his prayer shawl, the sign of his entry into the adult privileges of the synagogue. The ceremony performed today for Jewish boys of thirteen is called *Bar Mitzvah*. On the sabbath following it he puts on his *tallith* and reads the Law for the first time in the synagogue.

Flowers and Birds

One final word about flowers and birds which frequent this area. Palestine is noted for its spring flowers, of which the wild anemone is well known with its crimson flower. The flowers of pomegranate and citrus scent the air. In the modern garden of Gethsemane homely plants, like marguerites, marigolds and snapdragons, abound. Of the birds the stork can still be seen in the fields and the eagles hover far above, as do the hawks. In the first century AD mastic, produced from a pistachio bush, which has a lovely perfume and an intriguing flavour, was much sought after, as it is today, by children using it as chewing gum.

All these details are a background to the story of the Gospels. In the next section two examples are given orientating some of these facts around two centres, one at Capernaum and the other at Jerusalem. The first may be especially helpful in teaching juniors of about nine, the second for somewhat older children.

Two Centres of Jesus' Ministry

1. *Capernaum and its Neighbourhood*

Capernaum lies at the northern end of the Sea of Galilee where, in the first century AD, it was a good-sized town on one of the important highways leading to northern Transjordan; it had a custom-house and a military guard, as well as a well proportioned synagogue. The town had a beautiful position looking south over the Sea of Galilee, this lovely lake with its reedy edges and still water reflecting the blue sky. On the eastern side of the lake are the ranges of the Moabite mountains. In a curve of the land to the west lies the wooded bay of Magdala, or Migdal as it is now called, the home of Mary Madgalene, who became a most devoted follower. To the north the Jordan rift breaks the mountains so that the winds howl down it and whip up the sea into sudden storms. To the west the hills rise upwards steeply towards upper Galilee and Nazareth. Capernaum is a very ancient place, for in 1925 the skull of a man reckoned to be about 100,000 years old was found in a gorge of the brook 'Amud. After the death of John the Baptist Jesus came down from Nazareth, some twenty-five miles away and, according to Matthew, made this town his home (Matt.4.12 f.). Capernaum is redolent of incidents recorded in the Gospels.

The ruins of the synagogue, rebuilt in the second or third century AD on the foundations of the old one, stand close to the water's edge. Here Jesus began his public ministry and recruited his first apostles, Simon and Andrew, James and John, from the fisher-folk near

Capernaum, and Matthew from the custom-house itself (Mark 1.14–20; 2.14). Here he healed Jairus's daughter, whose father was a ruler of a synagogue (Mark 5.22–43). The centurion, whose servant he healed, was stationed here (Matt.8.5–13). When he returned home to Nazareth the inhabitants there demanded that he should perform miracles similar to those he had done at Capernaum, but he could not because the atmosphere was hostile (Luke 4.16–30). The town by the lake had become the centre from which he went forth on his mission.

Just about two miles away from Capernaum, moving westwards, another small area of land is crowded with memories from incidents in Jesus' ministry. Rising up from the lake, and now dominated by a church, is the hill alleged to be the mount from which the great sermon was preached (Matt.5–7). Whether the Sermon on the Mount is one long discourse or, as is more likely, a collection of Jesus' sayings, here, in this area, there rang out words that must have startled his listeners, for he announced that the happy people were the poor, not the rich; the happy were those who grieved and those who were gentle in a world where Roman soldiers paraded their strength. Today the Church of the Beatitudes commemorates the sermon on its eight-sided tower by having the eight 'Blessings' written there in Latin, each beginning with 'Beati'. Looking across the lake towards its western side, only sixteen miles away, is Tiberias, Herod's capital of Galilee, built in AD 20 in Hellenic Roman style and named after the Roman emperor as a compliment. Here luxury and vice, pomp and circumstance, contrasted with the simplicity of living among the fisher-folk and shepherds; a contrast that would give added point to the list of virtues which Jesus proclaimed as essential to happiness.

The material in the above section should enable teachers of young juniors to construct a centre of interest, with a pictorial map for class work; a frieze depicting perhaps the road from Damascus crowded with people and transport; scenes in the synagogue or on the shore, etc. It is intended to give location to stories and events from the Gospels.

2. Jerusalem: The Last Week

When Jesus took his last journey from Galilee to Jerusalem he spent a night with Zacchaeus in the rich city of Jericho (Luke 19.1–10). Zacchaeus, a rich man himself, small in stature, was so anxious to see Jesus that he climbed a tree to get above the crowd. He was a tax-collector, but Jesus' impact on him made him suddenly wildly generous and ashamed, and he offered half his ill-gotten gains to those he had wronged. Not far away, a few miles further along on the shores of the Dead Sea, was a settlement which some people think Jesus knew well, the Qumran community of the Essenes (see Part IV, Section 3, pp. 231 f.). The country would be full of memories for Jesus, but he was intent on his journey to Jerusalem, nineteen miles away and nearly 4000 feet to be climbed. So he went up the stark road, whose loneliness had given such point to his parable of the Good Samaritan; he knew the way; his disciples apprehensively followed behind.

At the highest point of the road, just behind the Mount of Olives, Jerusalem appears suddenly in all its beauty, dominated by the magnificence of the temple. With a facade 150 feet high, facing eastward, it was made of light marble with decorations of pure gold. Surrounding the main building were colonnaded courts and vestibules; in the very centre crowning the whole edifice was the Tabernacle, which, according to the historian Josephus, sparkled 'like a snow capped mountain'. The massive walls of the city, rising 250 feet high above the surrounding valley, embraced other well-known buildings: the Roman fortress Antonia on the north-east side, Herod's palace on the west with its three enormous towers, 130, 100 and 80 feet high, a little below that was the house of the high priest, also a stronghold with its own prison. These four buildings were to play their part in the drama that followed. Today none of them remain, for the city was destroyed by the Romans in AD 70, but the sites are there and modern archaeology has revealed evidence of their authenticity; while the breathtaking beauty of the city remains, for the Muslims erected on the site of the Jewish temple two magnificent mosques, which scintillate, the one with golden and the other with silver decorations, even as the original temple must have done. The first is 'The Dome of the Rock', the second 'The Mosque of Al-aqsa'. Christian pilgrims today are invited by their Arab guides to stop and praise God when they first set eyes on this most Holy City.

Jesus lodged at the house of his friends, Mary, Martha and Lazarus, at Bethany, which is at the foot of the Mount of Olives. There, today, one can go down into a dark room below the level of the ground to see the alleged dwelling, and nearby the tomb from which Lazarus is said to have been raised. From Bethany to Bethphage is a steep walk of about half-an-hour up a stony path. Here, at the top of the Mount of Olives, Jesus, on Palm Sunday, mounted the ass and rode down an equally steep path towards Jerusalem. A modern church, called *Dominus Flevit*, marks the spot where, according to a very old tradition, he paused and wept over the coming fate of the city. Further on he would pass the Garden of Gethsemane, and then down into the valley of the brook Kedron and so up the steep slope into the city itself. During this week he preached in the courtyards of the temple, where he challenged the authorities until they took active steps to get rid of him.

There is confusion as to the site of the house in which the Upper Room was located. Two places seem to have an equal claim and one of them is now marked on maps of the city as the Cenacle, that is, the Room of the Supper, which we call the Last Supper. It must have been a well-to-do house to have an upper room suitable for guests. Wherever the exact site may have been, there is no doubt that in order to get from that side of Jerusalem to the Garden of Gethsemane Jesus and his disciples must have passed close by a site on which stood, so it is claimed, the house of Caiaphas, the high priest. Archaeologists have uncovered a stone-paved path of the Roman period running just by the side of the house. Here has been found a large pile of coins of the kind used for paying the fine of *corban*, for exemption of certain religious duties. As Jerusalem is extremely hilly this path descends first towards the gate through which Jesus would have to go to reach Gethsemane. Outside the gate the surface of the path is even rougher and steeper; down it plunges towards the brook Kedron, but first past the monument commemorating the tomb of Absalom, and then to the refuge of the Garden and the agony, the betrayal and the arrest of Jesus. From there he would have to retrace his steps, as a prisoner, along the same path and now into the house of Caiaphas to face his accusers.

The church of Peter Gallicantu, the Cock-crow, nowadays stands over the site of the high priest's house, and modern archaeologists have discovered the levels appropriate to the Roman period. There is a large space where the examination could have taken place; in imagination one can almost identify the place where Peter sat and warmed himself and denied Jesus, and the spot where Jesus could have turned and looked at him, a look that drove him weeping from the hall. The prisons that have been unearthed add to the reality of the conditions of this fearful night. There is one prison just a little higher than the other. Here are stone pillars still with the holes bored in them where the prisoners could be stretched with arms and legs splayed out and fastened to the holes. A long narrow room provided a place for the prison guards. At the far end is a slit in the wall through which one looks into a dark dungeon, which had been cut out at a much lower level through solid rock. Here dangerous prisoners would be kept. The only way into it at that time was a hole, cut in the solid rock, through which the prisoner was lowered. Many people believe that the remnant of the night of Holy Thursday was spent by Jesus in this very pit, for where else could the high priest have placed so dangerous a prisoner? From the house of Caiaphas he was hurried early on Friday, through the narrow, hilly streets of Jerusalem, probably right across to the other side of the city to the fortress of Antonia.

The fortress Antonia is the place of the Roman Praetorium where the trial of Jesus before Pontius Pilate probably, but not quite certainly, took place. The site was scientifically excavated as recently as 1930, when Father Vincent, Professor at the French Biblical School of Jerusalem, and Reverend Mother Marie Godeleine studied and pieced together evidence to show that this was indeed the authentic site of the trial. The convent which now stands over this site is today called 'Ecce Homo' and the address, today, is Via Dolorosa. A model of the citadel has been reconstructed in the convent. Today one has to descend deep below the level of the street to get to the central court, or *Lithostrotos*, the Pavement. Here can be seen paving stones of the Roman period: on one of them is engraved a kind of dice board. This was probably used for the 'Game of the King' which was played by soldiers guarding a prisoner condemned to death. The mockery of the splendid robe, the crown and the sceptre, were all part of the game permitted to the soldiery, which at one time they played among themselves but, owing to its roughness, the authorities allowed it only to be practised on a condemned man. On the stone is a clearly engraved letter B, which probably stands for *basileus*, the Greek word for king. There has been unearthed a portion of the actual roadway, the original level of the Via Dolorosa, made of close packed stones which have been striated to make it easier for horses or donkeys to climb the steep gradient. At an even lower level than the Lithostrotos are the magnificent cisterns built by Herod. The surface of the courtyard is cut by parallel water channels to drain off the heavy winter rains into these immense reservoirs still in use by the sisters of the convent.

The hill of Calvary was not far off outside the city-wall; not far to go in normal circumstances. Nowadays the pilgrim can traverse the distance quickly through the narrow streets to the church of the Holy Sepulchre, which is within the present-day city-walls, and encloses not only the probable site of the crucifixion, but that of the tomb.

The details given in this section have been selected to introduce older juniors to the kind of evidence which establishes the background to the gospel story. The material could be used for models of Jerusalem, of the fortress Antonia; for scenes for dramatic incidents from Palm Sunday to Easter Day; for the making of a 'film' by the children; or perhaps an imaginative reconstruction of the last twenty-four hours of Jesus' earthly life with television commentators from the twentieth-century reporting events from strategic positions.

There is an abundance of material, such as postcards, colour transparencies, guide books with suitable plans and maps available for enthusiastic teachers, who may wish to make of the Gospels 'living history' for their pupils.

3

Jewish Religious Life in the First Century AD

John Bowden

Background and Sources

The Jewish scene in the New Testament period was a continually changing one. This is hardly surprising, in view of the earth-shaking events which took place between AD 1 and AD 100. In AD 70 the temple, the central symbol and focal point of Judaism, was destroyed, with many far-reaching consequences. During the first century the foundations of a new form of Judaism began to be laid with the emergence of the Rabbis, their codification of the tradition and their approval of an authorized canon of Jewish Scripture. There was constant conflict with Rome, to the point of a series of savage battles; and, no less important, there was an increasing conflict with Christianity, which arose from the heart of Judaism and with its growing success posed a great many urgent questions.

The Judaism that emerged from this turbulence was as unified as it had ever been. A council of rabbinic teachers, meeting at Jamnia about AD 90, managed successfully to reorganize the chaos with which they were confronted. Their measures led to the eventual elimination of a number of competing forms of Judaism and the predominance of a single version, Rabbinic Judaism, the Judaism of today. During the first century, however, these competitors were very much in evidence, so that as well as reckoning with a changing historical situation, we have to keep in mind that there were variations in Judaism from group to group and from place to place.

First, a distinction has to be made between Palestinian Judaism and the Judaism throughout the Roman Empire (the Judaism of the Dispersion), with its greater contact with the Hellenistic Greek atmosphere of the Mediterranean world. The distinction is by no means a clear-cut one, for Palestine, too, had been strongly influenced by Greek culture (see Part III, Section 15, pp. 191 ff.), but living in a foreign country, being at a considerable distance from the temple, and approaching the Torah in Greek and not Hebrew (to give only a few examples) all had their effect upon the Jews of the Dispersion.

Secondly, within these two broad categories there were more specific groupings. In Palestinian Judaism there were Pharisees, Sadducees, Essenes and Zealots, to mention the best known; and the obvious, though often neglected, split between the educated and the uneducated, those who could read and those who could not. Similar differences will certainly have existed in Hellenistic Judaism, with Hellenistic philosophy and religion exercising their attractions even perhaps to the degree where Judaism turned into gnosticism (see Part IV, Section 12, pp. 343 f.), but they are very hard to trace.

It is, in fact, difficult to document any of the groupings or to describe them in any great detail, even where we know that they existed. Our problem is the old one – lack of information. So thoroughly did Rabbinic Judaism carry out its work of unification that it is often almost impossible to see the views of the movements it replaced, particularly those with which it did not agree. A list of the sources of our information with their particular characteristics may give some idea of the problem:

1. The *Rabbinic writings* fall, roughly speaking, into four main groups. (*a*) The *Mishna* is a compilation of legal requirements, written down about the end of the second century AD, in the form of legal opinions; (*b*) the *Gemara* is a discussion of the Mishna. The two together form the *Talmud*, of which there are two versions, Babylonian and Palestinian, completed at the end of the fourth century AD. (*c*) The *Tosefta*

collects sayings which failed to be included in the Mishna (individual verses are known as *baraita*). (*d*) *Midrash* is a term used to describe commentary on the Scriptures; sometimes it is legal, but it can also be elaboration of the biblical text.

As material for historical reconstruction these writings are almost useless. They have no interest in historical sequence or relationships, nor do they offer any chronological detail. They certainly contain early material, handed down orally, but because they were compiled later than the council of Jamnia, their view of the past is selective, hazy and either partisan or idealistic. For example, there is nothing in them to suggest the Maccabaean revolt or the destruction of the temple. What clues they do offer are in the realm of Jewish religious thought and institutions.

2. For our knowledge of the history of the period we depend on the Jewish historian *Josephus* (see Part IV, Section 1, p. 203). Josephus lived between AD 37 and 100, and his two major works, the *History of the Jewish War* and the *Jewish Antiquities*, present a unique picture of developments in the first three-quarters of the century. These books do, however, have their drawbacks. Josephus was a client of the Flavian emperors and had to be tactful in his presentation of Judaism; he also had to come to terms inwardly with his own position, which other Jews regarded as treacherous. We therefore have to allow for some bias. Furthermore, Josephus is silent about Judaism after the end of the war of AD 66 and so leaves us completely in the dark about the developments which led to the council of Jamnia.

3. For much of our knowledge of first-century Judaism we are indebted, directly or indirectly, to Christianity. This is especially true of our knowledge of Hellenistic Judaism. It was the Christian church that preserved the writings of Josephus and of Philo of Alexandria (born *c*.20 BC). Otherwise they would have remained unknown, as would the Jewish books which go to form the Apocrypha (see Part III, Section 15, pp. 196 f.). Christianity also preserved the apocalyptic literature between the testaments; the Rabbinic writings are essentially non-eschatological. This, of course, raises the question how widespread apocalyptic hopes for the future were during the first century. Was it a popular way of thinking, or was it confined to

minority groups? Because we know so little about the authorship of the Pseudepigrapha, as this literature is called, the answer is not obvious.

4. Christian sources themselves tell us much about Judaism, and chief among them is the New Testament itself. Often it alone offers evidence for first-century Jewish practice and for some details of Roman administration. But historical reliability is difficult to decide. The pictures of Judaism in the second half of Acts are usually accepted as reliable, but the first half is more of a problem (see Part IV, Section 12, p. 336). In the Gospels, we have to allow both for bias and for lack of information. For example, the portrait of the Pharisees in Matthew is certainly conditioned by later opposition between Jews and Christians towards the end of the century (see Part IV, Section 12, p. 347). Similarly, it would be difficult to tell what the temple was like merely from the references to it in the Gospels and their accounts of Jesus' cleansing of it; one notable Jewish scholar has even remarked: 'It is difficult to believe the evangelists had ever seen the temple or had any clear understanding of what it was.' In the letters of Paul we have first-hand evidence of the mind of a first-century Jew – but what kind of a Jew was he?

5. Finally, and most vivid among all our sources, is Palestinian archaeology and its two most spectacular finds: the site of the Qumran community and its literature, and the citadel of Masada. Qumran and the Dead Sea scrolls have given us an extensive view of the life of a sect previously known only from occasional references. Masada illustrates two greatly contrasting times, the luxury of the desert palace of Herod at the beginning of the century and the tragedy of the last stand of the Zealots in AD 73; it has also provided the lost original Hebrew text of the book of Ecclesiasticus (preserved beforehand, by Christianity, only in Greek) and – a fragment from the Dead Sea scroll literature.

Here again we come to a problem. How far can we assume a connection between these two sites which by chance we know particularly well? Are there consequences for the wider picture of first-century Judaism? As one area is highlighted, the amount that we do not know about the rest stands out all the more.

Because of all these difficulties and imponderables, the brief pictures of Jewish society and religion which follow must be regarded as a series of very approximate reconstructions, in which much is disputed and uncertain. Reconstructions like this have to be attempted if we are to try to understand the background against which the early church grew up and the New Testament was written. But they must be recognized for what they are. Pharisees and Sadducees and scribes parade through modern classrooms as though we had substantial knowledge of them and could recognize and assess them for what they were. In reality, however, the reliable information we have is quite astonishingly small. To pretend it is more does not help. What inevitably become caricatures do not further either our understanding of Judaism in New Testament times or Christian relationships with Judaism today.

The Temple

Until it was destroyed by the Romans in AD 70, the temple at Jerusalem was the official centre of Jewish worship, a great place of pilgrimage and an immensely powerful symbol. Although Jewish theology had increasingly stressed the transcendence and otherness of God, the temple was still regarded as being in a special way a divine dwelling place: the scenes reported by Josephus immediately before its fall suggest a confidence, even then, that God would not allow it to be harmed.

The temple standing in the first century was in fact the third to be built, following Solomon's temple destroyed in 587 BC and the one that replaced it after the return from Babylon. Herod the Great began work in 20/19 BC on the same site but according to a different ground plan, in the prevailing Roman-Hellenistic style of architecture. Construction went on for a very long time: certainly until AD 64, and it may be that the temple was still unfinished at its destruction.

Nothing remains of the temple proper today, apart from the great platform now surmounted by the Moslem Dome of the Rock and the substructure of the massive surrounding walls. For an idea of what it was originally like we depend on two descriptions, one in Josephus and the other in the Mishna tractate Middoth; they do not always agree, but provide enough information for a general picture.

The site of the temple was on a hill in the south-eastern part of the present Old City. A great paved court was laid on the temple platform, surrounded by magnificent colonnades against the outside walls. This court was accessible to people of any race or faith, Gentiles included, and was by no means reserved for purely religious activities. In common with other ancient temples, the Jerusalem temple was used as a safe-deposit for valuables, and other quasi-commercial transactions were carried on there.

Within the court was an enclosure surrounded by an embankment, with steps going up to a wall with nine gates. Inscriptions, the Greek text of one of which has been found, warned Gentiles against going further:

No foreigner may enter inside the barrier and embankment. Whoever is caught doing so will have himself to blame for his ensuing death.

On the east side of the inner area was the Court of the Women, the regular place of assembly for public worship. Women were accommodated in a gallery round the court, which contained trumpet-shaped boxes to receive offerings. Fifteen semi-circular steps led up to a broad gate which gave on to the west side, divided into the Court of Israel and the Court of Priests, where the regular sacrifices were offered.

Finally, at the heart of the temple itself lay the Holy Place, again elevated by twelve steps. Within was a vestibule which gave on to the main doorway of the temple sanctuary. Here were the sacred objects in gold, the seven-branched lampstand, the table for the shew-bread and the altar of incense: a curtain screened the Holy of Holies, containing no furniture whatever, which only the high priest might enter, once a year, on the Day of Atonement.

Thus the elevation of the temple and its holiness increased progressively towards the centre, as did the elaborateness of its ornamentation. Built of great blocks of gleaming white stone and decorated with all possible splendour, it must have been a breath-taking sight. Josephus' praise is lavish; he remarks that the outside of the building was covered with so much gold that the onlooker could scarcely look directly at it in bright sunlight. He adds that after the sack of Jerusalem the market of gold for the whole province of Syria was completely glutted, so that the standard of gold was depreciated to half its value. Even allowing for exaggeration, we, too, can be impressed.

Temple Worship

The foundation of the worship offered at the temple was the daily sacrifice, offered morning and evening on behalf of the people. So fundamental was it that it was never interrupted once during the rebuilding of the temple. A positive understanding of the joy taken in the ritual sacrifice of animals and the significance attached to it is perhaps the hardest thing for modern Westerners coming to grips with the Bible to achieve, but there is abundant evidence of that joy and of the belief that sacrifice could bring forgiveness. The system was at its height in the last days of the temple, when probably more care and money was lavished on it than at any other time.

Public sacrifice was accompanied by a lengthy ceremonial and was followed by private sacrifices, both sin-offerings and votive offerings. The whole of Palestine was divided into twenty-four divisions, each of which was on duty in turn for one week (see Luke 1.8 f.). Priests and Levites from the course on duty were responsible for offering the sacrifices, and lay representatives were deputized to be witnesses on behalf of the whole people. A yearling lamb was killed and then followed a service of prayer; incense was offered and the lamb solemnly burnt; the priests pronounced a benediction and the choir of Levites sang the appointed psalm, the ceremony being accompanied by the blowing of trumpets.

More numerous sacrifices were offered on the sabbath and on major festivals. The most important of the latter were the Feast of Weeks (Pentecost), the Feast of Tabernacles (Succoth) following the Day of Atonement, and the Feast of Passover. Of great antiquity, these feasts had accumulated many overtones of meaning. The Feast of Weeks was a thanksgiving for the grain harvest, but also commemorated the giving of the Law on Mount Sinai; the Feast of Tabernacles, or Booths, recalled the time when the Israelites were wandering in the desert and lived in tents, but also contained an ancient prayer-ceremony for rain; the Passover, while commemorating the deliverance from Egypt, was also associated with the Feast of Unleavened Bread, which originally also had an agricultural significance.

Pilgrims came to all these festivals, often covering vast distances to be present. Passover was the annual peak; one estimate gives the total number of pilgrims likely at that time as about 125,000, compared with the approximately 55,000 permanent residents of Jerusalem. The Passover meal was eaten in domestic surroundings, in table-fellowships of between ten and twenty; pilgrims had by law to stay that night within the limits of Jerusalem itself, as they were ritually interpreted. Despite the flexibility of this interpretation, the crush must have been immense.

The Temple Staff

Just as the temple embodied in itself the aspirations of Jewish worship, the high priest stood as chief representative and symbol of the Jewish people. On paper, so to speak, he was a lofty and almost superhuman figure, set apart from his people and standing above them. His descent, his marriage, his whole way of life were to be of the utmost purity. Invested for life with the sacred garments, he alone could enter the Holy of Holies, on the Day of Atonement, as we have seen. Whenever he appeared, to take part in sacrifice or other ritual, as he willed or as custom prescribed, he was accompanied in state and accorded all due reverence.

In reality things were rather different. The Jewish people were not their own masters. Making theological prescriptions was one thing – keeping to them was another. Both Herod and the occupying Roman forces appointed and dismissed high priests quite arbitrarily, for political reasons. Nor was the failure entirely external. Simony, nepotism and rivalry between priests was all too common, and belonging as they so often did to the richest families, high priests could be harsh and politically self-seeking.

But the pendulum must not be allowed to swing too far in this direction. As sacred mediator between God and the people and representative of the people, the high priest was a supremely important figure. There was a long and sacred tradition behind him to counterbalance any personal failings, and his position gave him unique influence – religiously towards his people and politically even towards Rome. Even deposed high priests retained considerable authority.

(One problem connected with the high priest is that first-century documents, including the Gospels and Acts, regularly talk about 'the high priests' in the plural, although only one was in office at any time. Possible explanations for this are either that the references are to members of the high-priestly families, or that they denote a group of the chief priests of the temple who formed a well-defined body, including some of the officials to be mentioned below. Perhaps the latter suggestion is more plausible.)

Under the high priest there was an extensive temple staff, some of whom were permanently in residence, while others came to Jerusalem as their duty required. Chief among the permanent staff was the captain of the temple, who had overall responsibility for the routine worship of the temple and principal assistant to the high priest. He was chief of the temple police force, with power to arrest on temple property. A group of overseers (no less than seven) was responsible for the organization of the temple, and a group of treasurers (no less than three) administered its considerable income.

As has been said, the ritual was carried out by twenty-four courses of priests and the same number of courses of Levites, who were not in permanent residence. It has been estimated that there will have been some 7200 priests involved, and a rather larger number of levites. Specific duties were assigned to individual priests in turn; the climax of a priest's life came when he went into the sanctuary alone to make the incense offering. The Levites functioned as singers and musicians, servants and guards.

The Law

The temple and its priesthood may have been the most striking symbol of Judaism, but had they been its exclusive centre, Judaism would never have survived their fall. The way in which it adjusted to the situation after AD 70 shows that there were other strengths; these strengths had as their common basis the Law, and to a considerable degree the history of the different parties within Judaism is the history of different interpretations of the Law. Even while the temple still stood, even within Judaea itself, there seems to have been an increasing preoccupation with the scriptures and their implications, and this preoccupation will have been even more characteristic of the Jews of the

Dispersion. A movement like that found at Qumran is unthinkable without this development, which comes to full effect in Rabbinic Judaism.

The beginnings of the trend are to be found in the Babylonian exile and the period after the return; early stages can be seen reflected in Part III, Sections 13 and 14, pp. 173 ff., 182 ff. During this period the Pentateuch took final form and was accorded its place of honour as the *Torah, the* Law; the Prophets had taken a place beside it by the beginning of the second century BC and the Writings were recognized during the first century AD.

'Law' gives a wrong idea of this written basis of Judaism; the Hebrew, Torah, does not have quite the same significance. The word means 'instruction' or 'doctrine' rather than 'law', and of course the Pentateuch, to which it is applied, is by no means only a law-book. Nevertheless, that is what it became as it was made the object of more and more intensive study. The methods which were used sometimes seem bizarre in the extreme and the discussions over finer points interminable in their casuistry; but, as with sacrifice, it is essential to try to see the positive elements which such study was believed to bring and the enjoyment with which it was carried out.

Here, as well as in considering the parties within Judaism, it needs to be remembered once again that the Gospels – and Paul – present only one side of the picture; the other side also needs to be looked at sympathetically.

The Sadducees

Party lines within Judaism began to be laid down at the beginning of the second century BC, and the events which gave rise to the divisions are described in Part III, Section 15, pp. 193 ff. By the first century AD they were well established, though again too rigid a classification is dangerous. We know there were differences within particular groups, and familiarity with the make-up of modern church denominations ought to put us on our guard against supposing that groups were too uniform.

The Sadducees probably take their name from Zadok, the high priest in the time of David, but that is no more than a guess. They were the priestly, aristocratic party, whose interests centred on the temple. They were opposed to the new developments represented by the Pharisees, and with the destruction of the temple and its consequences became the losing party and faded away. As a result, we are more than usual in the dark about them, as our information comes from their opponents and gives an essentially negative account of their characteristics.

The high priest was usually a Sadducee, but this does not mean that all Sadducees were priests. It seems likely that the Sadducean party also included the Jewish lay nobility, landowners with considerable resources. By virtue of the character of its membership, the party was drawn from a select social background; for the same reason, it was essentially conservative in its outlook. The make up of the party and the conditions under which they lived kept them out of touch with developments in popular thought and their necessary involvement in the politics of their time will not have helped their standing with the people.

Sadducean interpretation of Scripture was literal in contrast to that of the Pharisees, whose oral tradition they rejected. From this basic position will stem their well-known denials of resurrection, future rewards and punishments, angels and spirits, and providence. These facts are recorded by Josephus, Matt.22.23 and Acts 23.8 – the way in which they are recorded is too terse for us to be able to generalize usefully from them. Perhaps they are less useful than they look; it may be that, like aristocrats and prominent church leaders of all times, the Sadducees were not particularly interested in theology.

The Sanhedrin

The supreme Jewish council was the Sanhedrin; the word is a version of an Aramaic transliteration of the Greek *synedrion*, assembly. It consisted of seventy-one members. It is not easy to see just who belonged to it because of the way in which it is portrayed in the sources: Josephus and the New Testament present a political side and the Rabbinic literature a religious side. This led some scholars to suppose that there were two Sanhedrins, one political and one religious. Such a solution, however, is rather drastic, and it is much more likely that the Rabbinic sources are reinterpreting the Sanhedrin and reading back into it features which it took on after the fall of the temple. The very nature of Judaism meant that political and religious questions were inextricably intertwined.

In the earlier post-exilic period the Sanhedrin will have consisted of senior priests and representatives from the aristocracy; later, Pharisees gained representation in it and increased their influence. The effective power it had varied considerably, depending on the regime of the time; the question becomes important in connection with the trial of Jesus. No firm conclusion can be drawn from the evidence, as is clear from the arguments which still continue.

The Scribes

The scribes were a new rising upper class, which increasingly replaced the old hereditary aristocracy in influential positions. Their power grew with the influence of the Law and the importance of its interpretation, and was based on the knowledge they had acquired through their study. To become a scribe required a long period of training both in methods of interpretation and in the material of the tradition. The aim of this training was for the scribe to be able to make his own personal decision on religious and judicial questions. Official recognition came with 'ordination', for which there was a minimum age limit. Later sources give this as forty years of age; this may be an exaggeration, but it shows the seriousness with which training was regarded.

The recognized scribe had an unrivalled reputation, as Ecclus.39.1–11 shows. He could hold key positions in the administration of justice, in government and in education; the Pharisaic representatives in the Sanhedrin will have been scribes. On the other hand, being a scribe was not necessarily a remunerative occupation; it seems that many of the scribes were quite poor and had to support themselves by working at a trade.

Scribe is the name of a qualification, not that of a party. Although the question is a confused one, it is unlikely that the scribes should be completely identified with the Pharisees; the Sadducees had their own traditions and their own scribes. Obviously, however, the Pharisee scribes would be the more predominant. (Here once more the terminology in the Gospels needs to be used with care.)

The Pharisees

If on the whole the scribes regularly appear in association with the Pharisees, there is of course a difference between the two. Not all Pharisees had a scribal education, for the Pharisees were a lay movement which set out ideally to embrace the whole of the Jewish people. The meaning of the name is again uncertain, but is probably best understood as 'the separated ones'; like the title 'Christian' (see Part IV, Section 12, p. 347), it may first have been given them by their opponents. The Pharisees developed out of the earlier movement of the Hasidim (see Part III, Section 15, p. 193); we can only guess at how organized a movement they formed and what changes took place between the Maccabaean period and the first century AD.

If we wanted to contrast scribe and Pharisee, it could be said that the scribe was essentially concerned with a theological emphasis whereas the Pharisee was preoccupied with ritual matters. Being a 'separated one' meant striving to be separated from impurity of all kinds. But of course a contrast like that will not do. For the Law and the understanding of the Law was the means of avoiding impurity, so that the work of the scribe was indispensable. The leaders of the movement will have been scribes. By 70 BC they seem to have gained entry to the Sanhedrin, and from then on they never altogether lost power, though they had many serious setbacks.

The Pharisaic movement was probably an association of closed groups with particular specified rules of conduct. Would-be Pharisees will have had to accept certain regulations before being admitted and then to serve a probationary period before being granted full membership. The Pharisees were engaged in a struggle on two fronts: on the one hand they had to fight to preserve the purity of Judaism in the face of the 'people of the land', those who sat lightly to the ritual laws – it was this fight that led to the rules and regulations of which the Gospels present so hostile and negative a picture. On the other hand, and at a different level, they opposed the Sadducees in the struggle for the leadership of the people.

As we saw, the Sadducees were essentially conservative and inflexible in their approach to the Law; as a result they were unable to cope adequately with new needs and changing situations. The Pharisees tended in the other direction. The essence of their position was a distinction between the written Law and the oral tradition. The written Law had to be understood and interpreted, to meet changing times and situations, in the light of the oral tradition. The tradition served to safeguard the Law by 'putting a fence' round it; the ten commandments became six hundred and thirteen; directives were worked out for all possible eventualities.

That is the negative way of looking at it. More positively, we might say that the Pharisees saw that if the Law was to continue as the living basis of Judaism it had to be interpreted in a flexible way; otherwise the time would come when it could no longer speak to the present. The danger here was that with their more flexible method of interpretation the basic material and intent of the Law would be submerged by its interpretation – and that is what tended to happen. With flexibility, too, came the inevitable consequence that disputes arose over variant interpretations. The later Rabbinic literature is full of this kind of discussion; the most famous arguments from an earlier period are those between the schools of Hillel and Shammai, teachers who flourished at the very beginning of the Christian era. Shammai was proverbially strict, conservative and irascible; Hillel patient, gentle and liberal. The most famous anecdote about him is typical of the best in the Pharisaic tradition. A proselyte wanted to learn the whole Torah while standing on one foot. After Shammai rebuffed him, the proselyte came to Hillel. 'Do not do to your neighbour what you would not want to be done to you,' Hillel told him, 'that is the Torah, the rest is commentary. Now go and learn it.'

Rabbinic Judaism

After the council of Jamnia, Judaism became known as Rabbinic Judaism, not Pharisaic Judaism, though the two are directly connected. Where Pharisaism ends and Rabbinism begins is almost impossible to say, and the question is more a modern one than one that a first-century Jew would ask. The change in name is connected with the use of the word 'Rabbi'.

At the beginning of the century, Rabbi was not a formal title, but a mode of address, 'My master', used as a mark of respect. It is used a number of times in this way in the Fourth

Gospel, in remarks to Jesus (e.g., 1.49; 6.25). By the end of the first century, however, it had taken on formal significance, as is indicated by Matt.23.7 f., a passage which dates from the time of the early church rather than that of Jesus. In the second century it was firmly established, and that is the way in which it is used in the Rabbinic literature.

It was the Pharisaic/Rabbinic development which shaped the future of Judaism; the heightened prominence of the Law after the fall of the temple was accompanied by an institution which had been increasing in importance for some time before AD 70, the synagogue and its worship.

The Synagogue

The Greek word *synagoge*, from which the synagogue takes its name, is used in the Greek Old Testament to translate the Hebrew word '*eda*, 'congregation'. In such cases it does not, of course, refer to a building at all. So when we investigate the beginnings of the synagogue we have in effect two separate questions to answer: first, when did groups of people begin to meet together for prayer and the study of Scripture; secondly, when did these meetings begin to take place in a building specially designed for the purpose?

There is unlikely to be any clear-cut beginning for the first process, which will have happened gradually from the exile onwards. Jewish sources, of course, trace the institution of the synagogue, like everything else, to Moses; the earliest beginning, however, is likely to be the movement with which Ezra was connected, and there will have been other contributory factors in different places. In Alexandria, Jews will have come across Greek religious associations, which met regularly once a week; in many places Jews may well have had regular meetings as part of municipal life. It is even possible that there may be some connection between the synagogue and the meetings of members of the course on duty at the Jerusalem temple – those who did not go to Jerusalem are thought to have met together at home for prayer when the sacrifice was being offered in the temple. The difficulty with this last suggestion is knowing when the practice to which it refers actually began. At any rate, by the first century there was certainly a strong tradition of regular meetings for prayer and study of the Scriptures – and probably there were also special buildings in which these meetings took place.

Archaeological exploration has revealed only one possible synagogue from the first century – spectacularly enough, on the site of Herod's palace at Masada. Strong reasons were found for supposing that one of the rooms there had been converted and used as a synagogue by the Zealots who occupied it for their last stand. Otherwise there are no remains of synagogues earlier than the second century AD. On the other hand, there is written evidence to suggest that even in the first century, synagogues were widespread. There may be some question whether the scene in the synagogue in Luke 4.16–30 is historical, but it is difficult to write off the many references in Acts to synagogues throughout the Mediterranean world (e.g., 9.2; 13.5; 13.14; 14.1; 16.13; 17.1). These references cover Syria, Cyprus, Asia Minor and Greece; Josephus makes special mention of synagogues in Caesarea and Tiberias; and Acts and Rabbinic writings both mention synagogues in Jerusalem itself.

One can no more speak of the typical synagogue than one can speak of the typical church. The ground plans of those which have been unearthed vary considerably, and no sequence of architectural development can be established. Under the influence of the Jerusalem temple, sometimes there will have been elaborate external decoration; in Babylon, attention was chiefly lavished on the interior.

The synagogue was more than a place of worship; it was also something of a social centre with secular uses, a place for judicial and political, as well as religious, gatherings. Some scholars even believe that the synagogue was used as a place where hospitality could be offered to travellers. It was certainly a centre for education, where children may have received elementary instruction and where teaching was given to adults who wanted help in reading the Scriptures. Above all, in the Dispersion the synagogue was an important factor in unifying the Jews who lived in a place.

There was no permanent 'minister' of a synagogue, as there usually is in a Christian church. The principal official was the 'head of the synagogue' (*archisynagogos*), who played a chief part in all synagogue functions, was ultimately responsible for the conduct of services, and at some stage may have chosen the lessons. He was assisted by the *hazzan*, an official the meaning of whose title is obscure: it is interpreted as anything from 'sexton' to 'overseer'. The *hazzan* seems to have performed most of the practical duties of the head of the synagogue and was responsible for much of its administration; the traditional idea that he was a kind of village schoolmaster seems to be incorrect. The synagogue also had its council of elders; in predominantly Jewish areas these will also have been civic officials.

Despite the variety of purposes it could serve, the synagogue was primarily a place of worship, and services were held on sabbaths and feast days. The central act of worship was the reading of Scripture, and the interior furnishing of the synagogue was directed towards this purpose. A special shrine contained rolls of the Torah (and also, perhaps, of the Prophets), which were treated with solemn reverence. Even when worn out they would be respected: a storeroom (*geniza*) in a Cairo synagogue containing worn-out scrolls provided some exciting discoveries, including a document also found at Qumran, at the beginning of this century. Near the shrine would be the dais from which lessons were read and sermons given. The main lesson was from the Torah, and was followed by one from the Prophets; it is thought that by the first century a triennial cycle of readings in the Torah had been established, but this is a matter of some dispute. In Palestine, the reading would be in Hebrew, sometimes accompanied by an Aramaic translation; in the Dispersion the Greek translation was read out. When a competent person was present, the reading of the lessons was followed by a sermon expounding them; there seems to have been a custom of inviting any visiting teacher who happened to be present to deliver this address (Acts 13.14). The service opened with the *Shema* ('Hear, O Israel'), and the reading and interpretation of the Scriptures will have been preceded and followed by prayer.

It is difficult to tell whether women were separated from men in synagogue services in the first century. Only Philo gives any explicit information, suggesting that women occupied a gallery in the synagogue at Alexandria; Rabbinic writings are silent, and architecture is little help. On the whole it seems likely that in view of the position of women in society at this time, silence is not to be interpreted in a positive way: women will either have been segregated or excluded.

Judaism in the Dispersion

During the first century, there were more Jews living outside Palestine than within it. Estimates vary, but a rough guess would be that there were rather more than two million Jews in Judaea and about four million elsewhere. The dispersion (Greek *diaspora*) had taken place gradually and for a number of reasons; there were, of course, the forced deportations to Babylon, where about a million Jews lived, but trade took Jews elsewhere round the Mediterranean almost from the beginning. There were particularly close connections with Egypt, where Alexandria had a great Jewish community; there were also Jews in North Africa, Syria, Asia Minor, Greece and Italy.

These Jews had to preserve their identity in a culture which was predominantly Greek. They were therefore organized into communities, living in separate quarters of a city and having the power of self-government to a considerable degree. Both the Hellenistic states and the Roman government allowed a great deal of freedom to religious associations, but the privileges of the Jews went well beyond this. They were on the whole in an excellent position towards the state, but had to pay for it by suffering the constant ill-feeling of their neighbours, which on occasion damaged official relations (for more details see Part IV, Section 12, pp. 346 f.).

Although the language of the Dispersion was Greek, these Jews still looked to the temple while it stood, and paid a great deal of money to support it. The synagogue, however, will have been a far more regular influence in their day-to-day life. The problem of knowing how far Greek culture affected Jewish beliefs has already been mentioned (see above, p. 223); we do not have enough evidence. The two writers from whom we have extensive works are very different in character, although they are almost contemporaries; Philo from Alexandria and Paul from Asia Minor.

Paul's life and thought is described in detail elsewhere (see Part IV, Sections 9 and 10,

pp. 301 ff., 313 ff.); in contrast, Philo seems calmer, more cultured, more philosophical – very much the traditional university don. His writings comprise some historical works, a set of questions and answers, almost in commentary form, on Genesis and Exodus, and a great number of essays on particular subjects in the Pentateuch. His principal tool is allegory, and he uses it to commend the Jewish Law to the Greek world. By reading the ideas of Plato and the Stoics back into the Old Testament in this way, Philo is able to present Moses as the great philosopher, whose ideas have been borrowed by the Greeks. He is helped by the Greek translation of Torah; the word *nomos*, law, already had many philosophical and scientific overtones. We do not know what sort of an audience Philo reached in his own time, but his works had considerable influence on early Christian writers.

If Pharisaic Judaism culminated in the Rabbinic tradition, Hellenistic Judaism gave way to Christianity. It had no future in the context of Judaism, just as Jewish Christianity had no future in the context of the church. A modern Jewish comment is apt: Jewish Christianity withered since it lacked survival power; Hellenistic Judaism withered since it lacked survival value.

Qumran

In one respect, the movement of which the community at Qumran formed a part may be seen as an extreme development of Pharisaism, which took the principle of separatism to new heights; it probably originated during the Maccabaean period.

The people of Qumran are almost certainly Essenes, a group mentioned by Philo, Josephus and the Roman naturalist Pliny the Elder, though the title is never used in the Dead Sea scrolls. There are some discrepancies between the ancient accounts and what we know at first hand, but the similarities are close enough to be convincing. Details of the life of the community are provided by the site itself and two documents containing regulations: the Community Rule, formerly called the Manual of Discipline, and the Damascus Rule, so called because it describes a group which migrated to Damascus and entered into a new covenant.

The latter document was found in a Cairo *geniza* (see above p. 230), but fragments have also turned up at Qumran; it probably represents a different stage of development from the Community Rule, as there are again some dissimilarities.

The larger movement of which the Qumran community was a part did not all live in isolation in the desert. It had representatives in communities in villages and towns all over Palestine who had closer contacts with day to day social life. The Qumran community represents the greatest degree of separation; the remains of its buildings show that it was virtually self-sufficient. Wherever they lived, members shared the same beliefs and hopes; they regarded themselves as the remnant of the true Israel, and they looked for a messianic age to come. Their beliefs were reflected in their organization, into clergy and laity and into twelve tribes and smaller subsidiary units.

The priests had ultimate authority, though there was a community assembly and a council of twelve laymen and three priests to show that the laity also had their share in decisions. The two chief officials seem to have been the Priest and the Guardian (or Inspector), responsible for ritual and community life; there is much dispute over the precise nature of their work.

Once their suitability had been established, new members entered into the 'new covenant' in the presence of the whole community. What happened after this is disputed. There is evidence of a progressive training: a two year probationary period, during the first year of which the candidate took no part in the more sacred activities and retained his possessions, followed by a second when his property was kept by the community until his training was complete, and when he was admitted to some sacred functions; finally, full membership was granted, possessions were renounced and he took a full part in meals and worship. The question is whether this sequence applied to all members, or only to a select inner group; the second alternative seems more likely. In that case there will have been a superior council within the community. Marriage was not forbidden, even to the inner group, and some female skeletons have been found at Qumran, but those looking for ultimate perfection are likely to have chosen celibacy.

Like other Jewish groups, the people of Qumran studied the Scriptures avidly, but their biblical commentaries show that they had their own special method of interpretation. They applied the texts of the prophetic books to their own history and future, using an approach not dissimilar to that found in apocalyptic and parts of the New Testament. The Commentary on Habakkuk is the best example of their work. From their reading of Scripture they expected two Messiahs, a priestly Messiah of Aaron and a Messiah of Israel (and also the Teacher of Righteousness, a mysterious figure who also played a part in their history?; here again the texts are puzzling and there is much argument). The War Rule describes the final battle between the spirits of light and the spirits of darkness which would be paralleled by a similar battle on earth before the final victory was won.

These future expectations helped to condition the day-to-day life of the sect and were an important reason for their continued purity. Their negative attitude to the rest of Judaism around them led to a rejection of the traditional calendar and a rejection of temple worship. Their own worship centred on the common meal, which probably represented the eschatological feast that would be celebrated in the last days.

The discovery of the Dead Sea scrolls and their contents at first led to some exaggerated ideas about the significance of the Qumran sect in relation to Christianity. In fact, very few direct connections between Qumran and the early church can be demonstrated, and none on matters of central importance. A reading of the scrolls alone will make it quite clear that their main importance is in the light that they shed on the different forms of Judaism to be found at the beginning of the Christian era.

(The most convenient introduction to the Dead Sea scrolls and translation of the texts is to be found in Geza Vermes, *The Dead Sea Scrolls in English*, published by Penguin Books.)

The Zealots

Politically, the Pharisees were quietists; they were advocates of non-violence in relationship with Rome. The chief characteristic of the Zealots, who had much in common with the Pharisees, was their approval of violence in defence of their faith.

There are probably connections between the Zealot movement and the Maccabees (see Part III, Section 15, pp. 193 f.), but its beginning is usually taken to be a revolt against the census of Quirinius in AD 6. Judas, the leader of the revolt, was a Galilean, the son of an Eleazar who was executed by Herod; his son led the last stand of the Zealots at Masada. The Zealots refused to pay Roman taxes; they take their name from their zeal for the temple and the Law, which is amply illustrated in the writings of Josephus. Josephus writes very disapprovingly of them and labels them *sicarii* ('assassins'); he could hardly do otherwise in his position.

Luke's list of apostles includes Simon, called 'the Zealot' (Luke 6.15; Acts 1.13); the parallel passages in Mark (3.18) and Matthew (10.4) have 'the Cananaean', which is the Aramaic form of the same word. The presence of a Zealot among Jesus' followers, coupled with recorded actions of Jesus like the cleansing of the temple and the fact that he was crucified by the Romans on a quasi-political charge has prompted elaborate theories about the connection between Jesus and the Zealots. It can only be said that there is just not enough evidence to make out a case – either way.

The Samaritans

Had it been prophesied around AD 30 that the only movements to survive the next two thousand years would be the successors of the Pharisees, the followers of Jesus and the Samaritans, the forecast would have been considered too ridiculous to be worth a second thought. Yet this is what has happened. A group of the despised Samaritans still lives and worships near Mount Gerizim, despite all the troubled history of Palestine.

The Samaritans were the inhabitants of what was once the northern kingdom of Israel. In New Testament times it is clear from both Jewish and Christian sources that there was hatred and hostility between them and the Jews. Unfortunately, beyond the recognition of this enmity there is much that is blurred and indistinct.

The Samaritans regard themselves as the true Israel, which was split off from the rest of the people when the latter were tainted by the sin of Eli, priest at Shiloh in the time of Samuel. Though they were deported at the fall of the northern kingdom in 722 BC, they returned fifty-five years later. The Jews, on the other hand, regarded the Samaritans as the descendants of the colonists who repopulated the northern kingdom after the Assyrian conquest. Because of this, they felt Samaritan religious observances to be fatally tainted.

The Samaritan view cannot be right, but the Jewish view is also exaggerated in the opposite direction. What the truth was has now been lost. Developments after the Jewish return from exile, with their new concerns, seem to have led to constant rivalry between Jews and Samaritans. How it began is obscure, but it reached its climax when the Samaritans built a temple of their own on Mount Gerizim. The date of its building is unknown; it was, however, there by the early second century BC, and does not seem to have been new then.

In 129 BC, John Hyrcanus destroyed the temple on Gerizim, adding to Samaritan hatred. Herod married a Samaritan woman, so relations may have become slightly easier during his reign; it is even possible that for a time Samaritans had access to the Jerusalem temple. However, Josephus reports that a new act of defilement, the scattering by Samaritans of human bones in the temple grounds, stirred up the old hostility again. The first century was a bad period: Jews on pilgrimage from Galilee, passing through Samaria, were set on and attacked; in the end Samaritans were treated by Jews as Gentiles.

Earlier references to the Samaritans contain a number of vivid sayings about their impurity; John 4.9 has an old comment about the practice of Jews and Samaritans not using the same vessels for this reason. Yet the Samaritans shared the same Torah with the Jews (without the Prophets and Writings, which they did not accept). These were the people whom Jesus chose to illustrate gratitude and love.

Accepted Ideas in First-Century Palestine

Margaret Thrall

All Jews had in common the religious beliefs expressed in the Old Testament. This is the first and most obvious thing that can be said about their outlook on life. They were educated in the Scriptures in the synagogue schools, and what they learned there would be consolidated later by their attendance at worship on the sabbath and also by means of the great festivals of the Jewish year which celebrated the mighty acts of the God they believed in. But religious thinking had not come to an end when the last book in the Old Testament had been written. The Pharisees, the Zealots, and the Qumran sect (see Part IV, Section 3, pp. 228 ff.) were all influential, and all of them produced ideas which gradually became popular among ordinary Jews who were not specifically attached to any religious party. Many of these ideas are reflected in the New Testament. In the minds of ordinary people they would tend to intermingle and coalesce, so that the general climate of thought was characterized by a mixture of them all.

To have been born a Jew meant that a man inevitably lived his life within some kind of a religious framework. He might or might not profess a high degree of individual piety. As a Jew, however, he believed himself to belong to a nation which had been specially chosen by God as the instrument of his divine purpose, and which was therefore protected and favoured by him. He believed that God had rescued the Israelites from slavery in Egypt, and that, if they obeyed his commands, he would regard them as his 'peculiar treasure', his 'kingdom of priests', and his 'holy nation' (Ex.19.3–6). This conviction was reinforced by the yearly celebration of the Passover, which commemorated the deliverance from Egypt. God was also naturally understood as demanding the exclusive loyalty of the whole nation. The worship of any other god was decisively to be condemned. In the past history of the Jews there had been occasions when they had indulged in heathen cults. But in the time of Jesus this was no longer true. Religious practice corresponded with official belief. Popular religion conformed to the words of the ancient prayer: 'Holy art thou, and thy Name is to be feared, and there is no God beside thee' (*The Eighteen Benedictions*). God was the Creator and Preserver of the world, and he was unique. Furthermore, the national way of life symbolized the conviction that God was to be obeyed as well as worshipped. The Jews believed that their function as a nation was to display the greatness of their God through their obedience to his law. In this way they distinguished themselves from other nations. They insisted on keeping the sabbath as a day of rest from work, and they insisted that certain foods, such as pork, were unclean and not to be eaten. By these and other means they symbolically demonstrated their belief in the uniqueness of their God, through their witness to the demands he made for their total devotion to his will. All this gave meaning and purpose to their national life. It was through them that God's plan for the whole world was to be carried out. They believed that the underlying purpose of world history was that the will of the God of Israel should be acknowledged and obeyed. They showed the rest of the world what this meant, and by their own obedience to the law they assisted in the fulfilment of the divine plan for humanity.

Evil and Suffering

This brings us to another important aspect of Jewish thought during the first century. The actual state of affairs in the world appeared to disprove some of their religious beliefs. There was a great deal of evil, sin and suffering which was surely contrary to God's intention, and yet the world's sole purpose was to conform to the divine will. They themselves were oppressed beneath the tyranny of a heathen government, and yet God had specially chosen them to enjoy his favour and protection. So there was a conflict between belief and reality. The Jews had to ask themselves what explanation there was. And they naturally indulged in hopes of a better future for themselves and their nation.

Why, then, did the God of Israel allow the Romans to continue to occupy Palestine, the holy land of his chosen people? Some of the Pharisees provided an answer. The Jews were in servitude to the Gentiles because they had sinned. The Roman occupation was a sign of God's wrath. This state of affairs would continue until the Jews repented. A similar explanation was often given of individual suffering as well, for it was a common belief that illness was a punishment for sin. The idea is reflected in the question asked by the disciples of Jesus in the story of the man born blind: 'Rabbi, who sinned, this man or his parents, that he was born blind?' (John 9.2). If one asked the further question, why do men sin, the Pharisees would probably have replied that there is within man an evil impulse, but that this can be held in check by keeping the law. Sin results from the failure to use the law as a remedy against the evil impulse.

Side by side with these explanations of sin and suffering, there is to be found a rather different way of looking at the situation. The present state of affairs is evil because the world and mankind are in the power of Satan, the prince of evil, and a host of lesser demons. The Qumran sect believed this (see Part IV, Section 3, pp. 231 f.). They regarded themselves as the children of light and the rest of mankind as the children of darkness. The children of darkness were under the dominion of the angel of darkness, who is also called Belial. All other evil powers were subordinate to this prince of evil. He was thought of as making war on the children of light and attempting to lead them astray. There are similar ideas in the New Testament. In the story of the temptation of Jesus (Luke 4.1–13), the devil is made to say that all the kingdoms of the world are in his power, and at the end of I John the writer says that the whole world lies under the sway of the evil one (I John 5.19). Jesus is accused of curing the demon-possessed by means of the diabolic power of the prince of the demons, and he asks in reply, How would it be possible for Satan to drive out Satan (Mark 3.22 f.)? In the background of this story there lies the idea of a kingdom of evil spirits ruled over by Satan. For Satan to assist in the exorcizing of demons would be for him to promote a state of civil war in his kingdom.

What was thought to be the function of the evil spirits? In the first place, they tempt men to evil conduct, such as idolatry, strife, and bloodshed, and set them against God. In the story we have already referred to (Luke 4.1–13), Satan is represented as trying to persuade Jesus to adopt courses of action which he knows to be contrary to God's will. Secondly, they do people physical and psychological harm. The idea that many illnesses were caused by demons was very common. The diseases themselves were spoken of as a 'spirit of leprosy', an 'asthma spirit', a 'spirit of heart disease', and the like. In the Gospels, the demon-possessed whom Jesus cures are variously afflicted. Some show symptoms of madness (Mark 5.1–20), some may be sufferers from epileptic fits (Mark 9.14–29), others may be dumb or blind (Matt.9.32–34; 12.22).

There were, therefore, two different ways of explaining the world's evil state. It could be regarded as the divine punishment for sin. Or it could be attributed to the activity of the demonic powers. Whichever way the Jews looked at it, the remedy, they believed, was ultimately in the hands of God. God alone would be able to bring about a radical alteration in the fortunes of their own nation and of the world at large. So they looked hopefully to the future.

The Presence of God

Before we discuss their future hopes, however, we must say something about their ideas of God's presence and God's activity in the interim period before the moment of his final intervention to put things to rights. Did they in fact believe that God was still present with his people and active to secure their welfare? Or was he absent from the world he had created and from the nation he had chosen as his own?

There is no single answer to this question, since there seem to have been varying ideas about the presence of God in the world – ideas which do not perhaps completely contradict each other, but which are difficult to combine in an entirely logical pattern.

In Pharisaic circles there was a strong conviction that God was present in the world everywhere in a quite direct way. No sin escaped his notice. Conversely, he cared personally for all his people, taking an interest in the ordinary joys and sorrows of everyday life. He was said to bless bridegrooms, to visit the sick, and to comfort mourners. He was believed to be present when men met to pray or to study the Law. He heard every prayer, however privately and quietly it might be uttered, as though he were taking part in a human conversation. Pious Jews addressed him in prayer as 'Our Father'. This shows that God was not thought to be wholly remote and unapproachable.

Nevertheless, there was a sense in which he was believed to be inactive, if not absent. In the past history of Israel, so the Scriptures related, God had bestowed his Spirit upon kings, warriors and prophets, and so had given them a dynamic divine energy and wisdom which was lacking in ordinary men. This gift of divine energy and insight now seemed to be no longer available. Of particular importance to the Jews of this period was the belief that the Spirit of God had inspired the prophets, and so had enabled them to understand and communicate their divine message. But by the time of Jesus prophecy had ceased. God no longer spoke by the Holy Spirit through the prophets.

Two qualifications are necessary at this point, however. God was believed sometimes still to speak to man directly, though not through the Holy Spirit. He spoke by means of a mysterious voice from heaven. We can see an example in Matt.3.17, where it is claimed that at the baptism of Jesus a voice from heaven declared him to be God's beloved son. Also, the members of the sect at Qumran believed that they were guided by a divine spirit which they spoke of as the spirit of truth.

Belief in angels was a more popular expression of the conviction that God was still present and active in the world. The angels are God's messengers, and members of his celestial court. They are spirits of fiery substance with the appearance of blazing light, but they appear to men in human form. Sometimes they appear in dreams (Matt.1.20), sometimes in visions experienced during the day (Acts 10.3). Gabriel is the angel who reveals God's plans to men – hence his appearance in the annunciation story (Luke 1.26–38). Michael is the champion of God's people against their enemies. In the Dead Sea scrolls he appears as the prince of light, or the angel of God's truth, and assists the children of light in their struggle against the prince of darkness. Often the individual was believed to have his own guardian angel, and, on a wider scale, different angels were regarded as responsible for the affairs of the different nations. The angels also administer the realm of nature. They regulate the movements of the stars, and control the sea, the rain, and the thunder.

Hopes for the Future

So much for belief in God's activity in the present. What kind of future did the Jews hope for? And how did they expect that it would come about? Again, there are several different answers. Some thought of the better time to come, and of the means of its achievement, in ordinary, this-worldly terms, while others indulged in hopes of a more supernatural kind. Often the two ways of looking at the future merge and intermingle.

The Zealots cherished this-worldly hopes (see Part IV, Section 3, pp. 232 f.). They looked for a time when God alone would rule Israel, and this meant that his holy land must be taken out of the hands of the Romans. Nor were they the only people to hope for the end of Roman rule in Palestine. In one of the Psalms of Solomon (composed in Pharisaic circles after the first conquest of Jerusalem by the Romans in 63 BC), we find the following prayer for the expected messianic king:

> And gird him with strength, that he may shatter unrighteous rulers,
> And that he may purge Jerusalem from nations that trample her down to destruction (Ps.Sol.17.24).

The conquest of Israel's enemies is a necessary prelude to the betterment of her situation. And high hopes may be entertained of her future glory. In another first-century work, the Assumption of Moses, we have this description of Israel after the punishment of the Gentiles:

> And God will exalt thee
> And he will cause thee to approach to the heaven of the stars,
> in the place of their habitation.

And thou shalt look from on high and shalt
see thy enemies in Gehenna (Ass.Moses
10.9 f.).

This means that Israel has reached 'the height
of national, political and spiritual success alike'.
In addition, it is expected that the Jews of the
Dispersion – those living outside the borders of
Israel – will return to Palestine, and that all
God's people will be endowed with the gift of
the Holy Spirit and purified from evil.

There are differing opinions about the fate
of the rest of mankind. In many descriptions of
the future the judgment and punishment of the
wicked is a prominent feature, together with
the judgment and vindication of the righteous.
The vindication of the righteous tends to be
synonymous with the restored fortunes of
Israel, which have just been described. The
judgment and punishment of the wicked is
often synonymous with the fate of the Gentiles
and their rulers. But other hopes are expressed
for the Gentiles as well. They are not necessarily
all to be destroyed. They may remain in existence and acknowledge the supremacy of the
Jews. They may even be converted to genuine
obedience to the God of Israel.

God's people are to be rescued from supernatural as well as from human enemies. The
hope is expressed that the power of Satan will
be destroyed:

And then his kingdom shall appear throughout all his creation,
And then Satan shall be no more (Ass.Moses
10.1).

In the Dead Sea scrolls, Satan is to be finally
and decisively defeated at the end of the war
between the children of light and the children
of darkness.

The Glorious Future

At this point we begin to approach the other-
worldly type of hope for the future. The sect at
Qumran believed that after the final battle the
earth would be miraculously renewed, and that
it would be restored to the state of perfection
which it had possessed at its original creation.
There would be a new temple in a new Jerusalem. God's people would inherit the glorious
nature which had once belonged to Adam in the
Garden of Eden, and they would enjoy the gift
of eternal life. In other writings of the period

similar ideas occur. In the book of Enoch, for
example, eternal life is granted to the righteous.
The distinction between heaven and earth will
disappear, and the saints will dwell with the
angels for ever.

The two forms of the future hope gradually
came to be distinguished more clearly, and the
one was thought of as the prelude to the other.
First there was to be a better state of affairs in
this world. The power of Rome would be van-
quished by the messianic king sent by God,
who would rule the whole earth, and there
would be no more evil, pain, or sorrow. This
period would be limited. It was a means of
transition to the second, and final, state of
existence. When it came to an end, the dead
would be raised to life and the great world-
judgment would take place. Then the righteous
would be received by the angels, become like
the stars, and dwell for ever in the heavens.

How did the Jews suppose that the better
situation of the future would be brought about?
As we have already said, they all took it for
granted that fundamentally it would be God's
doing. There were, however, different ideas of
how he would choose to act.

The Zealots believed in initiating political
and military action themselves. But they were
also convinced that if they themselves took the
first step in provoking a revolt against Rome,
then God would fight with them and for them,
and would win them a miraculous victory. Had
they not believed this, they would never have
taken up arms at all. A realistic appraisal of the
military situation in purely human terms would
make it obvious that a small subject nation,
such as the Jews, could not possibly hope to
stand out against the organized might of imperial Rome.

Other Jews believed that the initiative rested
with God alone. Sometimes he would act
without any human assistance at all. The
Assumption of Moses shows us God and his
angel acting to deliver Israel:

Then the hands of the angel shall be filled
who has been appointed chief,
and he shall forthwith avenge them of their
enemies.
. . . . . .

For the Most High will arise, the Eternal God
alone,
and he will appear to punish the Gentiles,

and he will destroy all their idols (Ass.Moses 10.2,7).

Elsewhere, however, a human agent of the divine will enters the picture. He is to be a king chosen and endowed with authority by God, and a descendant of the royal house of David. He is often called the Messiah, i.e., the anointed one. (Anointing with oil symbolized the choice of a man for high office.) He will secure both the political and the spiritual welfare of the nation of Israel. There is an impressive description of such a Messiah in the Psalms of Solomon. As we have seen (see above, p. 236), he will drive the Gentiles from Jerusalem. He will set up a great kingdom which will be the centre of the whole world, and all the heathen peoples are to serve him. All this suggests military might, and yet it is clearly stated that he will not put his trust in weapons of war but in God. There is some suggestion that he asserts his supremacy by means of moral and spiritual force:

> For he shall not put his trust in horse and
>   rider and bow,
> nor shall he multiply for himself gold and
>   silver for war.
> . . . . . .
> The Lord himself is his king, the hope of him
>   that is mighty through his hope in God.
> All nations shall be in fear before him,
> For he will smite the earth with the word of
>   his mouth for ever.
> . . . . . .
> He will rebuke rulers, and remove sinners by
>   the might of his word (Ps.Sol.17.37–39, 41).

He himself is righteous and holy, and rules justly, caring for his people like a shepherd for his flock. But he does all this because God has endowed him with the power of his Spirit.

The Qumran sect also believed in a Davidic Messiah who would conquer the heathen. He is to be the military head of the community in the final war against their enemies. This war, however, has a twofold character. It is certainly a war against earthly foes, the heathen nations, and here the Messiah, also called the prince of the congregation, has his part to play. But at the same time it is a war on the supernatural plane, between the prince of light and the angel of darkness. It is the archangel Michael who fights against Belial on behalf of God's elect. 'This is the day appointed by him for the defeat and overthrow of the Prince of the kingdom of wickedness, and he will send eternal succour to the company of his redeemed by the might of the princely angel of the kingdom of Michael. . . . He will raise up the kingdom of Michael in the midst of the gods, and the realm of Israel in the midst of all flesh.' It is just possible that the Messiah himself begins to take on a supernatural character, as he appears to be closely connected with the angelic hosts.

Whether or not this is so, there did exist in some Jewish circles the idea of a transcendent, supernatural being who would appear at the end and take part in the judgment, and with whom the blessed elect would dwell in the life of eternity. In the book of Enoch this being is called the Elect One and also the Son of man. He is a heavenly figure accompanying God himself:

> And there I saw One who had a head of days,
>   and his head was white like wool,
> and with him was another being whose
>   countenance had the appearance of a man,
> and his face was full of graciousness, like one
>   of the holy angels (I Enoch 46.1).

He is to be enthroned in glory and he will judge all the nations and their rulers. He will also judge angels, likewise the evil spirits and their chief Azazel. He will save the righteous, and dwell in their midst forever. Because he is himself close to God they also will enjoy the divine presence:

> And the Lord of Spirits will abide over them,
>   and with that Son of man shall they eat
> and lie down and rise up for ever and ever
>   (I Enoch 62.14).

This sort of discussion of Jewish hopes perhaps gives the impression that they were chiefly concerned with their own national misfortunes and chiefly preoccupied with dreams of future bliss for themselves as God's elect. It may be useful, in conclusion, to emphasize once again that what the best religious minds were concerned with was a genuine theological problem: if God is Lord of the whole world, why is the present state of affairs so obviously contrary to his will? And the fundamental hope was that in the end he would fully establish his authority and demonstrate his absolute sovereignty. This is what is meant in the New Testament by the coming of the Kingdom of God.

5

The Writing of the First Three Gospels

What Kind of a Book is a Gospel? · *C. F. Evans*

Literary criticism of any book rests on the belief that to know what a book is good for and what may be expected from it depends to some extent on knowing what sort of a book it is, and how it has come to be the kind of book it is. The same holds good for the Gospels. What kind of a finished article is each of the Gospels? In what category do they belong?

Supposing someone living towards the end of the second century AD had made a present of the four books we call Gospels to the famous library at Alexandria, which was the most scholarly place in the world at that time, what would the librarian have thought of these books, and how would he have set about cataloguing them? He might have considered putting them under the section headed *Bioi* or 'Lives'. These tended to be rather discursive accounts of philosophers, literary men or statesmen – the most famous to come down to us are Plutarch's *Lives* of famous Greek and Roman statesmen, which he arranged in pairs to illustrate some moral virtue. But the librarian might have been puzzled by the fact that two of these books, Mark's and John's, gave no account of the birth of Jesus, but started as it were in mid-stream. So he might have considered putting them under the section headed *Praxeis* or 'Acts'. These were narratives of the heroic deeds of notable people – for example, the Acts of Alexander the Great – and the title was eventually adopted rightly or wrongly for one of the books of the New Testament, the Acts of the Apostles. But the librarian might have thought that Jesus was not a sufficiently well-known public figure to have Acts – he is, after all, represented in these books as being put to death by the government – and that there was

too much teaching in them, and too much about God, to go under the title of Acts. So he might have thought of putting them under a category called *Apomnemoneumata* or 'Memoirs'. These were collections of individual anecdotes about, or sayings of, a famous figure, generally supposed to come from someone who knew him well, as, for example, the famous *Memoirs of Socrates,* written by the Greek historian Xenophon. There was in fact one early Christian writer who did speak of these Gospels in these terms. He was a man called Justin, a Christian teacher living in Rome about the middle of the second century, who in his Apology, or Defence of Christianity, addressed not to his fellow-Christians but to the general public, refers to what he calls 'The Memoirs of the Apostles'. Judging from what he quotes from these memoirs it looks as if he is referring to something like some of our Gospels. A sentence from his description of Christian worship, which is actually the earliest we possess, goes as follows: 'And on the day called Sunday there is a meeting in one place of those who live in cities or the country, and the memoirs of the apostles or the writings of the prophets are read as long as time permits.' In another place he writes of the 'memoirs of the apostles which are called Gospels . . .'. This shows that Justin, in using the word memoirs, was doing his best to give his non-Christian audience some idea of what the Gospels were like in terms with which they were familiar; *but,* he also indicates that the word for them among Christians was not memoirs, and indeed this title for them does not appear again in any Christian writing after Justin. What they were called among the Christians themselves was 'Gospels'.

This fact is remarkable in two respects. In the first place, it shows that the Christians had an instinctive feeling that these books did not fit into any of the current categories of literature. They were not *Bioi,* lives; they were not *Praxeis,* deeds; they were not even *Apomnemoneumata,* memoirs. A new genre of literature had been born, which required a new name. In the second place, the name is a very odd one and without parallel. The word 'gospel' was not often used in the plural anyhow, and it had never before been a name for a book. Of course the word 'gospel' in the singular was very common in the church – it is particularly common in Paul's letters – and it was not unknown outside the church. Its basic meaning was 'good news', especially the good news of salvation or deliverance from some threat of catastrophe. There is, for example, an inscription from Asia Minor dated 9 BC, which speaks of the birth of Augustus, who brought peace to the Roman Empire after its long and catastrophic civil war, as 'good tidings for the world'. But the word is much more frequent in the New Testament, where it has a precise meaning, and it is always used there in the singular; for the Christians it was axiomatic that there was, and could only be, one gospel. It was almost a synonym for what we would call Christianity. It is God's gospel, that is, it belongs to the God of the Old Testament, and it is the message of his final deliverance of his people from what threatened them, and it is in fulfilment of his promises in the Old Testament. But in the New Testament 'gospel' is never a book. It is always a spoken message and what that message says. The verbs used with it are never verbs like 'write' or 'read', but always verbs like 'announce', 'proclaim', 'speak' or 'receive', 'hear', 'obey'. When, therefore, it became a title describing a certain kind of book, the word was being put to a new use. This means that the first Christian readers had an instinctive feeling that these books were something which did not fit into any of the known types of literature. It also means that they had a feeling that what made these books new was their close relation with the original spoken gospel or message, which was also something new in the world. So the word was transferred from one to the other, and took on a new meaning as the title of a book.

External Evidence

What is the explanation of this development, and how did these books come to be what they are, and what are they good for? The quickest short cut to an answer would be, of course, if we had enough reliable information from the horse's mouth about who wrote the Gospels, and when and how and why they were written, and in what relationship the writers stood to the events that they were talking about. Suppose, for example, that the gospel writers had talked about themselves and their work in their own books, or others who lived near enough to the time of the writing of the Gospels to have reliable information had written about them, and their works had come down to us. This is what would be called external evidence about a book. But this short cut is denied to us, because very little indeed of this kind has been handed down to us, and what little has come down appears to be not very reliable – some would say it is largely guess-work and worthless. As to the Gospels themselves, Matthew and Mark are completely anonymous; the writer nowhere speaks of himself or his work. So is John, though at the end someone else, writing in the plural, says that the Gospel was written by the beloved disciple – but we do not know who he is; and when this note was added, and how reliable it is, we do not know. Luke does say something in the dedicatory preface he has attached to his two-volume work –the Gospel and Acts; he says that many had written before him, that their work had been based on traditions coming from eye-witnesses of the events and preachers, and that he himself had followed all things accurately. Unfortunately this tells us much less than we might at first sight imagine, because this preface is written in the somewhat stilted and conventional phraseology in which such prefaces were usually couched. It was the custom to refer to one's predecessors, and to say that one's information came from reliable sources and so on, and since the language is conventional we cannot press it too hard – for example, when he says that 'many' had written before him, we cannot take this as reliable information that there were already a considerable number of Gospels in existence.

As to the information coming from outside the Gospels themselves, it really reduces itself to little more than two quotations from a certain Papias, who was a bishop in Asia Minor round about AD 130 (his exact date is not known). These quotations have come down to us because they are preserved by Eusebius, the first church historian, writing at the beginning of the fourth century. Papias lived at a time when, in his own words, he still preferred oral tradition about the Christian message to books. Nevertheless the written Gospels of Matthew and Mark were already in existence and in use, and he made statements about them. About Matthew he said: 'Matthew drew up a compilation of the Lord's utterances in the Hebrew language (meaning either Hebrew or Aramaic), and everyone translated (or interpreted) them as he was able.' About the Gospel of Mark he made a longer statement, which he said he had got from a certain 'elder'. This was to the effect that Mark's Gospel was not written in an orderly fashion (he may mean it was not like Matthew's), and that the reason for this was that Mark was Peter's disciple and interpreter, and Peter did not preach in an orderly manner, but as the occasion demanded; thus Mark's lack of order is due to his exactly reproducing Peter's preaching. What is this information worth? That is a much disputed question. So far as his statement about Matthew is concerned it would seem to be worthless, since if Papias is talking about the Gospel of Matthew we know – and there is no good evidence that he is not – then it is quite clear that our Matthew is not a translation from anything, but his own book written in Greek from the start. Is Papias' statement about Mark's Gospel also worthless? Some would be inclined to say no, and that there may be some connection between Mark's Gospel and Peter, though perhaps not as precise as Papias makes out. Others would be inclined to say yes, and that Papias, or his informant, is making a guess to account for what he regards as the lack of smooth orderly writing in a book which had already become an accepted book in the church. Subsequent Christian writers who say anything on this matter do not add to our information. They would seem to be repeating what Papias said and embroidering it.

Internal Evidence

This point had to be discussed in some detail because it is precisely the dearth of reliable external evidence about the authorship and origins of the Gospels which compels us to embark on the long, delicate and difficult process of analysing the Gospels themselves. People do sometimes think of the gospel critic as a kind of wanton wrecker who pulls a Gospel to bits just for the fun of the thing. But this is not the case. His method of internal analysis is forced on him by the lack of reliable external evidence. To give another example, we have no precise information about the date at which each Gospel was written. We are not, of course, entirely in the dark. It is probable that the earliest was written somewhere about AD 65 – that is, later than Paul's letters, though not necessarily later than the other letters in the New Testament. We have seen that Papias, writing about 130, or earlier, refers to Matthew and Mark as established and accepted books in the church, and a piece of papyrus has been recently discovered containing a fragment of the Gospel of John, which the experts date with some confidence early in the second century. This shows that the Gospel of John was already current by that time. So we would not go far wrong if we put the date of the writing of all the Gospels somewhere between AD 65 and AD 100. But we have no more precise information than that, and therefore the critic is compelled to examine the Gospels themselves by any means to hand to see whether they can yield up their secrets about themselves, just as a literary critic does with a play of Shakespeare, or a historian with an ancient document, or even a scientist when he frames his hypothesis and constructs his experiments to test it.

How does the critic set about his work? First, there is a preliminary job to be done which can only be mentioned briefly. It is a well-known fact that when we copy anything of any length we make mistakes – we leave out words, we misspell, we make alterations and so on. This has happened down the centuries in the copying of the Gospels. As a result the text of the Gospels varies from manuscript to manuscript, varies very often in small ways, varies occasionally in bigger ways. It is the job of the textual critic to decide which are the most reliable manuscripts, and to judge in each case between two different versions of a word or sentence which it was that the evangelist actually wrote. Did Matthew write the Lord's Prayer with the doxology, as some manuscripts have it, or without it as others? In this way the textual critic attempts to get back to a purer form of the text, free from error – if we compare the Revised Version or the New English Bible with the Authorized Version we can see that they are translations of a Greek text which in many places is different from the Greek text behind the Authorized Version, and a purer one. The work is delicate and technical, but that is partly because there are so many manuscripts available for the New Testament, far more than for any other ancient text whatever. It is unlikely that we cannot restore what the evangelists actually wrote except in comparatively few cases of any importance.

The Synoptic Problem

Taking this for granted, how does the critic go about his work? It really begins from the point when a certain German scholar named Griesbach in 1776 printed the Gospels of Matthew, Mark, and Luke in columns alongside one another in such a way that the passages which were similar in all three stood opposite one another. This procedure was revolutionary. Already early in the second century we have evidence from Christian writers that the existence of four Gospels and not one single authoritative account was felt to be a problem, and the problem was all the more acute in that the four accounts were often different from one another. One way of getting over this problem was to

try to turn them into a single account by fitting them together, perhaps by taking John's as the framework, because he appears to have a ministry lasting three years, and then placing the material from all four to form as near as possible a single continuous story. It cannot really be done; it is like trying to make a jigsaw out of several different jigsaws. But this is how the Gospels were studied for centuries, and so it was impossible to look at each one critically on its own, and to ask questions about their origins and their relations to one another. But when Griesbach printed the Gospels in this way – incidentally he called his work a synopsis, and that is why the first three Gospels are called Synoptic Gospels – certain things came out into the light. The first was how different the Gospel of John was from the other three. This was shown by the fact that it was impossible to make a fourth column alongside the other three. There was hardly anything to go in it; only very occasionally does the Gospel of John overlap with the other three, so that it stands on its own, and has to be studied in a different way. The second was that the three Synoptic Gospels had a remarkable character. Although they differed from one another considerably, so that there was often material in one column which had nothing corresponding to it in the other two columns, it was also the case that again and again the material in all three columns was not only similar but almost identical in wording. Here is an example:

Mark 2.3–12	Matthew 9.2–8	Luke 5.18–26
3 And they came, bringing to him a paralytic carried by four men.	2 And behold they brought to him a paralytic, lying on his bed;	18 And behold, men were bringing on a bed a man who was paralysed, and they sought to bring him in and lay him before Jesus;
4 And when they could not get near him **because of the crowd,** they removed the roof above him; and when they had made an opening, they let down the pallet on which the paralytic lay.		19 but finding no way to bring him in, **because of the crowd,** they went up on the roof and let him down with his bed through the tiles into the midst before Jesus.
5 <u>And when</u> Jesus <u>saw their faith,</u> he said *to the paralytic,* 'My son, <u>your sins are forgiven.</u>'	and when Jesus <u>saw their faith</u> he said *to the paralytic,* 'Take heart, my son; <u>your sins are forgiven.</u>'	20 <u>And when</u> he <u>saw their faith</u> he said, 'Man, <u>your sins are forgiven</u> you.'
6 Now *some of the scribes* were sitting there, questioning in their hearts, 7 'Why does this man speak thus? It is <u>blasphemy</u>! **Who can forgive sins but God** alone?'	3 And behold, *some of the scribes* said to themselves, 'This man is <u>blaspheming.</u>'	21 And the scribes and the Pharisees began to question, saying, 'Who is this that speaks <u>blasphemies</u>? **Who can forgive sins but God** only?'

[Mark]	[Matthew]	[Luke]
8 And immediately Jesus, perceiving in his spirit that they thus questioned within themselves, said to them, **'Why do you thus question** in your hearts? 9 Which is easier, to say to the paralytic, "Your sins are forgiven," or to say, "Rise, take up your pallet and walk"?'	4 But Jesus, knowing their thoughts, said, 'Why do you think evil in your hearts? 5 For which is easier, to say, "Your sins are forgiven," or to say, "Rise and walk"?'	22 When Jesus perceived their questionings, he answered them, **'Why do you question** in your hearts? 23 Which is easier, to say, "Your sins are forgiven you," or to say, "Rise and walk"?
10 But that you may know that the Son of man has authority on earth to forgive sins' – *he said to the paralytic* – 11 'I say to you, rise, take up your pallet and go home.'	6 But that you may know that the Son of man has authority on earth to forgive sins' – *he* then *said to the paralytic* – 'Rise, take up your bed and go home.'	24 But that you may know that the Son of man has authority on earth to forgive sins' – he said to the man who was paralysed – 'I say to you, rise, take up your bed, and go home.'
12 *And he rose,* and immediately took up the pallet and went out before them all; so that they were all amazed and glorified God, saying, 'We never saw anything like this!'	7 *And he rose* and went home. 8 When the crowds saw it, they were afraid, and they glorified God, who had given such authority to men.	25 And immediately he rose before them, and took up that on which he lay, and went home, glorifying God. 26 And amazement seized then all, and they glorified God and were filled with awe, saying, 'We have seen strange things today.'

Words underlined are identical in all three Gospels; words in italics are common in Mark and Matthew; words in bold print are common in Mark and Luke; a broken line indicates close similarity.

Other examples which can be used in the classroom are: the baptism of Jesus: Mark 1.9–11 = Matt.3.13–17 = Luke 3.21–22; the healing of a leper: Mark 1.40–45 = Matt.8.1–4 = Luke 5.12–16; Jairus' daughter: Mark 5.21–43 = Matt.9.18–26 = Luke 8.40–56; Peter's confession: Mark 8.27–38 = Matt.16.13–27 = Luke 9.18–26. The phenomena here present a scientific problem. It arises because, as is well known, there are any number of ways of telling the same story, and no two people will use identical sentences and words. If a teacher found two essays with this amount of agreement, he would assume that one pupil had been cribbing from another.

What is the explanation of these phenomena? Is it sufficient to say – and this was the first solution to be offered – that the individual gospel stories had been so often repeated that in the telling they had become stereotyped in form and wording, so that when Matthew, Mark, and Luke, whoever they were, acting independently, at different dates, in different parts of the church, came to put down their traditions, their Gospels agreed at these points because the form and wording had become fixed? There is an important point to note here. The early church was a teaching body rather than a writing body, and the eastern memory is much more retentive than ours. Nevertheless,

as a solution this would not do, and for two reasons. First, the agreement in wording was so close, at times extending to even the most minute Greek words, that it was straining the evidence to say that wherever these stories were told in the church, perhaps over a period of forty years, they were always told with exactly this wording. And secondly, the stories which were so similar in wording were also told in the same order. This would not be surprising if the stories in the Gospels had a necessary order about them, and if they were closely connected with each other by a careful date, or by precise information as to where and when each incident took place. But this is not the case. Some of them are simply connected with phrases like 'and then . . .'. Again it would be straining the evidence to say that wherever these stories were told in the forty years they were always told in the order – A B C D E. If this solution had to be excluded, there was only one possibility left; someone must be copying somebody else. (In the ancient world it was not considered reprehensible for one man to use another man's work without acknowledgment. It was only the invention of printing which made it so, as then a man's writing became his possession, and had to be protected by copyright.) The question now was: which evangelist was borrowing from which?

243

After many years of trial and error, stretching over the best part of a century, in which one hypothesis after another was tried and rejected, the solution which has come to be almost universally accepted as best satisfying the evidence is that the first of the three Gospels to be written was Mark's, and that Matthew and Luke, independently of each other, used Mark's Gospel as the framework of their own Gospels. The grounds for this conclusion are basically three. First, while almost all the material in Mark, in column one in the synopsis, has an equivalent in column one or column three, the reverse is not the case. There is a great deal in Matthew's column and in Luke's which is not in Mark's. This, of course, is not conclusive in itself, but it points in a certain direction. Secondly, some of the words and phrases common to all three look like phrases characteristic of Mark's style, and where Matthew and Luke differ it looks as if they are altering and improving what is in Mark. And thirdly, the stories they have in common are either in the same order in all three, or when they are not it is either Matthew and Mark who agree together in having the same order and Luke not, or it is Mark and Luke who agree together and Matthew not. It is not the case that Matthew and Luke agree against Mark in the matter of order. The conclusion then is that Mark's Gospel is the common denominator of the other two, and the reason for the agreement in wording is the use made of Mark by Matthew and Luke.

This solution has immediate consequences. In the first place, it focuses attention on the Gospel of Mark for the first time in Christian history. Early Christian writers very seldom quote from Mark. It looks as if it was comparatively neglected in the church. Nobody wrote a commentary on it until the sixth century. It is almost a miracle that it has survived. But now it appears in a quite different light. We can see that Mark was the first to put the material together in this way, that he was probably the inventor of this new genre of literature which required a new name to describe it. In the second place we can see that Matthew's was not the first Gospel, and that it cannot have

been written by an apostle, for his Gospel now appears to be a fresh edition of Mark's with additions, and it is incredible that an apostle, who was an eye-witness of the events, should have used another book as the basis of his own. This discovery overturns a tradition of the church, which dates from soon after the appearance of the Gospel of Matthew, that it was the first to be written and came straight from the pen of an apostle. Then, thirdly, it is now possible to examine those passages where all agree, and to observe carefully the changes which Matthew and Luke make in Mark – how they improve his style, how they shorten him, correct what they think are his mistakes, how they tone down what they find offensive. For example, in the passage about Jesus blessing the children who were brought to him (Mark 10.13–16 = Matt.19.13–15 = Luke 18.15–17) the accounts are almost word for word the same, except that in Mark Jesus is angry when the disciples rebuke those who brought the children. In Matthew and Luke Jesus' anger is omitted. It is characteristic of Mark that he does not mind presenting Jesus as angry, and that he does not spare the disciples, while it is also characteristic of Matthew and Luke, from their later point of view, that they do not like referring to violent feeling on the part of Jesus and that they have a more reverential attitude towards the disciples. So we can now begin to get behind Matthew's and Luke's Gospels as finished articles, to peer in, as it were, through the window of the workshop where they are being made, and to see them in the making, and to get some idea of what went on in the minds of the editors, Matthew and Luke, as they reacted to Mark. The Gospels cease to be static, and we see them in the process of growth.

But the Synoptic problem is not finished with at this point; there is still something to be explained. For, if we take out of Matthew and Luke all they got from Mark, there are still some two hundred verses in which they agree with each other in wording, sometimes very closely. One example is the preaching of John the Baptist:

Matthew 3.7–10	Luke 3.7–9
7 But when he saw many of the Pharisees and Sadducees coming for baptism, he said to them,	**7** He said therefore to the multitudes that came out to be baptized by him,

'You brood of vipers! Who warned you to flee from the wrath to come? **8** Bear fruit that befits repentance, **9** and do not presume to say to yourselves, "We have Abraham for our father"; for I tell you, God is able from these stones to raise up children to Abraham. **10** Even now the axe is laid to the root of the trees; every tree therefore that does not bear good fruit is cut down and thrown into the fire.'	'You brood of vipers! Who warned you to flee from the wrath to come? **8** Bear fruits that befit repentance, and do not begin to say to yourselves, "We have Abraham for our father"; for I tell you, God is able from these stones to raise up children to Abraham. **9** Even now the axe is laid to the root of the trees; every tree therefore that does not bear good fruit is cut down and thrown into the fire.'

Words underlined are identical in the original; a broken line indicates close similarity.

Further examples for classroom use are: candidates for discipleship: Matt.8.19–22 = Luke 9.57–62; condemnation of Galilean cities: Matt. 11.20–24 = Luke 10.13–15; asking and receiving: Matt.7.7–11 = Luke 11.9–13. It will be seen that the agreement is very close indeed, but Matthew and Luke cannot have got this from Mark because Mark has nothing like it. What is the explanation? Here the answer is not so certain and not so widely accepted. We could say one of three things. Either Matthew, as well as having Mark in front of him, also had Luke, and got these verses from Luke; or Luke, as well as having Mark in front of him, also had Matthew, and took these verses from him. But the difficulty about either of these explanations is that Matthew and Luke use this common material in such different ways and put it in such different contexts in their Gospels. So the solution which is most widely accepted is that they were using a common source, largely made up of the sayings of Jesus, and that each used it in his own way as he fitted it into the framework supplied to him by Mark. Scholars denote this source by the symbol 'Q'. There are, however, considerable difficulties when it comes to reconstructing 'Q' out of Matthew and Luke, and in such a way that it carries conviction. Do we follow Luke's version when it differs from Matthew's? Do we follow Luke's order rather than Matthew's? So there are some scholars who still prefer to say that Luke used Matthew as well as Mark.

If now we take out of Matthew and Luke not only all they owe to Mark but also what they have in common which is not in Mark, then we are left with what Matthew alone has and what Luke alone has. For these two lots of material the symbols used are 'M' and 'L'. But it is very doubtful whether these two symbols should be used to denote single written documents. It is not at all clear, for example, that Luke got his stories of the birth of Jesus which he alone has from the same place as he got the parables of the Good Samaritan and the Prodigal Son, which he alone has. It is probable that at this point we get back to oral traditions which the evangelist was the first to put into writing when he included them in the pattern of his book. So we could represent the Gospel of Matthew by a kind of algebraical formula: the Gospel of Matthew = Matthew, the editor (Mark + 'Q' + 'M'), and the Gospel of Luke = Luke, the editor (Mark + 'Q' + 'L').

By such methods as these, which are called out by the nature of the evidence which demands to be explained, the critic is led on from one point to another and to test one hypothesis after another. He is able to make the Gospels begin to talk and to tell us something about themselves, and about how they came into being within the life of the church to express the gospel message which the church was preaching and living by. At this point the further question opens up, can we go any further back and get nearer to the point where the material which composes the Gospels and the spoken message of the gospel are closely related to each other? Can we, for example, get behind the Gospel of Mark as a finished product and break it down into component parts? If so, will these component parts show us anything of their relation to the single gospel? Can we do the same with 'Q', and with 'M' and with 'L'? If we are to be able to do this we cannot go any further along the lines of literary analysis I have been describing because there are no more agreements in wording in the Gospels to be explained. We shall have to come at the material by some different method.

What Actually Happened? · *D. E. Nineham*

Matthew and Luke were like most other historical writers, at any rate to this extent, that they used written sources. Indeed they seem to have drawn on previous writers for a very large part of what they had to say.

There is nothing particularly surprising about that, but it does tell us something important about them; namely that they had not themselves taken part in the events they describe. For a person who is talking about something that he has actually seen, though he may borrow a phrase, or even an occasional paragraph, from a previous account, will want to tell his story in his own words and not copy slavishly the words of others.

Once it was recognized that Matthew and Luke were, in this sense, secondary authorities, attention naturally switched to the sources on which they relied. What were the character, age, and origins of these sources? Were they, too, secondary or were they the work of eye-witnesses?

All except one of them seem to have disappeared, but luckily the one that has survived is the most extensive and important – the Gospel according to Mark, and as a result Mark's Gospel has been minutely studied in the past century. No one who is not a specialist in these matters can easily imagine the amount of attention scholars have lavished on the sixteen short chapters of the Gospel of Mark in the endeavour to find out how it came into existence and what sort of reliance can justifiably be placed upon it.

The Shape of Mark's Gospel

There is very little external evidence to help in answering these questions and what there is gives rise to some suspicion, so scholars have rightly felt that in the first instance, at any rate, they must rely on the internal evidence of the Gospel itself. What does that evidence tell us?

The first thing that was noticed, when the Gospel was studied from this point of view, was that it divided fairly sharply into a number of short paragraphs. There is nothing remarkable about that; but when these paragraphs were studied individually a fact of considerable importance emerged. Each one is a self-contained unit which tells of some one deed or saying of Jesus and can perfectly well be understood in isolation from its context. The point may be illustrated from a short section of Mark's Gospel, especially if attention is concentrated on the first and last parts of the paragraphs in question.

He went out again beside the sea; and all the crowd gathered about him and he taught them. And as he passed on, he saw Levi the son of Alphaeus sitting at the tax office, and he said to him, 'Follow me.' And he rose and followed him.

And as he sat at table in his house, many tax collectors and sinners were sitting with Jesus and his disciples; for there were many who followed him. And the scribes of the Pharisees, when they saw that he was eating with sinners and tax collectors, said to his disciples, 'Why does he eat with tax collectors and sinners?' And when Jesus heard it, he said to them, 'Those who are well have no need of a physician, but those who are sick; I came not to call the righteous, but sinners.'

Now John's disciples and the Pharisees were fasting; and people came and said to him, 'Why do John's disciples and the disciples of the Pharisees fast, but your disciples do not fast?' and Jesus said to them, 'Can the wedding guests fast while the bridegroom is with them? As long as they have the bridegroom with them, they cannot fast. The days will come, when the bridegroom is taken away from them, and then they will fast in that day.

No one sews a piece of unshrunk cloth on an old garment; if he does, the patch tears away from it, the new from the old, and a worse tear is made. And no one puts new wine into old wine-skins; if he does, the wine will burst the skins, and the wine is lost, and so are the skins; but new wine is for fresh skins.'

One sabbath he was going through the grainfields; and as they made their way his disciples began to pluck ears of grain. And the Pharisees said to him, 'Look, why are

they doing what is not lawful on the sabbath?'
And he said to them, 'Have you never read
what David did, when he was in need and
was hungry, he and those who were with
him: how he entered the house of God, when
Abiathar was high priest, and ate the bread
of the Presence, which it is not lawful for
any but the priests to eat, and also gave it to
those who were with him?' And he said to
them, 'The sabbath was made for man, not
man for the sabbath; so the Son of man is
Lord of the sabbath.'

Again he entered the synagogue, and a
man was there who had a withered hand.
And they watched him, to see whether he
would heal him on the sabbath, so that they
might accuse him. And he said to the man
who had the withered hand, 'Come here.'
And he said to them, 'Is it lawful on the
sabbath to do good or to do harm, to save life
or to kill?' But they were silent (Mark
2.13–3.4).

Each of the sections is a self-contained unit,
which can be understood without any reference
to what comes before or after.

Now contrast with that an ordinary piece of
biographical writing, for example, this page
from Lord Eustace Percy's *Life of John Knox*
(p. 208):

That, however, was not his destiny. He had
hardly installed himself and opened his books
when he received a letter from Mrs Bowes.
Sir Robert, presumably the chief obstacle to
Marjorie's marriage, had died in late Feb-
ruary or early March. Sir Richard, no longer
captain of Norham, had (we must suppose)
withdrawn his opposition. Let Knox therefore return. They could meet at Berwick;
and, if England could not offer a home to
Marjorie and him, perhaps Scotland would.

The venture did not at all appeal to Knox.
It was *most contrarious to his own judgment*.
Nevertheless he set out. If he had received
any communications from Scotland itself
suggesting his return, they did not weigh
much with him. Mrs Bowes alone, he said,
had *drawn* him *from the den of* his *own ease*.

His reluctance was natural. He had had
few influential friends in Scotland. His connections there had been only with the
Lothian lairds and with the company of St
Andrews. To the lairds he was known as little

more than an upper servant; but among the
company of St Andrews he had enjoyed a
rather surprising prestige.

Here it will noticed that each paragraph only
makes sense in the light of what comes before;
for example, one paragraph begins 'The venture
did not at all appeal to Knox'. What venture?
You only know if you have read the paragraph
before. The thing holds together, and that is
what you would expect, for a writer normally
constructs each paragraph as he goes along and
specially designs it to lead on from what he has
said before to what he plans to say next. Why
should this not apply to Mark? The obvious
explanation would seem to be that Mark's paragraphs were not specially constructed for their
present position in the Gospel; indeed that they
were not constructed by Mark at all, but simply
taken over ready-made. They each had a life of
their own before ever Mark put pen to paper.
Each one existed as a separate story, intended
to be understood on its own, without reference
to the others. What Mark in fact did was not to
write a book *de novo* but to string together a
series of already existing, originally self-
contained paragraphs. Scholars have a special
name to distinguish paragraphs of this kind –
they call them *pericopes* (which is simply the
Greek word for 'paragraphs' or 'sections').

The Purpose of Mark's Gospel

But now some obvious questions arise. How
came Mark to write in this extraordinary way
and how did the *pericopes* he incorporated come
into existence? If we take a closer look at these
pericopes, two further facts appear. First, every
pericope is designed to make some religious
point or to convey some religious impression.
You never feel that any of these *pericopes* is
meant simply to satisfy your curiosity or add to
your stock of historical knowledge for its own
sake. Some of them give us sayings about
religious and moral topics, sayings which
demonstrate Jesus' perfect wisdom, for example,
the *pericope* about the basis of Jesus' authority
(Mark 11.27b–33) or that about the rights and
wrongs of paying taxes to the Romans in Mark
12.13–17 (cf. also Mark 10.17–22 and 12.28–34).
Others describe deeds of Jesus, but they are
always deeds which impress us with his perfect
moral goodness or his supernatural power;
examples of this type of story are Jesus'
blessing of the children (Mark 10.13–16) or his

healing of a deaf-mute (Mark 7.32–37, cf. also Mark 1.23–27 and 4.35–41). When we have read one of these stories we are left feeling as people often felt in the stories themselves, 'Surely anyone who could do things like that must have stood in some very special relationship with God.' So in Mark we read: 'And they were filled with awe, and said to one another, "Who then is this, that even wind and sea obey him?"' 'In fact these stories all have a religious slant; they are all angled in such a way as to emphasize some aspect of Jesus' *religious* significance.

And that brings us to the second characteristic of these stories; every fact or detail, however interesting it might be, which does not contribute towards the religious theme of the story is omitted. An example will make that clear.

> Another time he entered a synagogue, and a man was there with a withered hand. And they watched to see if he would heal him on the sabbath, hoping to find a charge to bring against him.   Then he said to the man with the lame hand, 'Stand forth.' And he asked them, 'Should one do good on the Sabbath, or evil? Save life, or kill?' But they answered nothing. Then he looked at them with anger, grieved at their hardness of heart. And he said to the man, 'Stretch out your hand.' He held it out and it was restored (Mark 3.1–5).

You notice we are not told the day or time or the place. We are not told the crippled man's name, or age, or occupation. We are not told who the people were who tried to entrap Jesus, and at the end we learn nothing about their subsequent history or that of the man who had been healed. We are told only what is necessary to convince us that Jesus was totally in the right as against his opponents and that he was possessed of a power so remarkable that, at any rate in first-century eyes, it was nothing short of supernatural.

If we study Mark's gospel carefully we find that this story is typical of practically all the others, and so the question we have to ask is: In what circumstances are stories with these particular characteristics likely to have arisen? Is not the most likely answer: In church? When a preacher tells a story about Jesus, is not this exactly the sort of way he does it? When he is expounding a saying of Jesus he does not mind whether it was spoken at ten in the morning or six in the evening, at Capernaum or at Bethsaida, to a man called Benjamin or a man called Eleazar. What concerns him is simply the meaning of the saying and its relevance to his hearers; and he only deals with the historical background so far as it is important in making that meaning clear.

It is to this sort of context that New Testament scholars point us for an explanation of Mark's *pericopes*. No doubt in the years immediately after Jesus' lifetime, when his original friends and disciples spoke about him, their narratives came tumbling out with all the wealth of detail that filled their memories. But as the years went by and the stories were repeated in public contexts, in church sermons and catechism classes, and in Christian missionary work, often by people who had never seen Jesus themselves, all purely picturesque detail will have fallen away and the stories will have become progressively streamlined into a concise, severely practical form. And naturally, once a story had attained the form best adapted for such practical religious uses, it will have tended to become more or less stereotyped in that form, especially as the oriental memory, in those days before the wide dissemination of books, was very tenacious and accurate. In fact the form in which these stories were told was so largely governed by the purposes for which they were told, that we can still very often tell from the form in which a story has come down to us what particular impression the early preachers or teachers intended it to make, and for that reason the branch of New Testament study which deals with these *pericopes* has come to be known as *form-history* or *form-criticism*.

It is demonstrated by form-critical study, for example, that if the point to be brought out in connection with some incident was the comment the Lord made upon it, then, in the telling of the story, the comment itself would be reported in full and given prominence, while the rest of the incident would be related as briefly as possible, just the minimum being retained that was necessary to provide the Lord's words with an intelligible setting. A story of this kind about Jesus is usually referred to in English as a 'pronouncement-story'. The point will be clearly understood if Mark 2.18–20 (? and vv. 21 f.), for example, or 2.23–27 is contrasted with Mark 5.25–34. If, on the other hand, the aim was to stress the remarkable nature of some *action* of Jesus, as evidence of his supernatural power, then any words that might have been spoken in connection with it would be briefly reported and little emphasized, and the emphasis would be concentrated entirely on those features of the incident which underlined its supernatural character – for example, in the case of a healing, the chronic and deep-seated nature of the illness, the ease with which Jesus cured it, the impression of amazement made on the bystanders and the completeness of the cure as evidenced by the healed man's ability to run or shout or carry his own bed (see, e.g., Mark 5.25 f.; 9.20–22; 2.12). Such stories are usually referred to in England as 'miracle stories', although the actions they describe are not always miracles in the strict sense.

This suggestion about the origin of Mark's *pericopes* has a further fact to recommend it: it provides an explanation of the independent, self-contained character of the stories. For the natural thing would be for the preacher or teacher to repeat one such story at each service or instruction class, and not to confuse his hearers by adding other stories with a different moral or lesson. And so the tradition about Jesus would naturally tend to circulate in the form of a large number of short, separate, self-contained stories, each one relating a single incident and doing it in such a way as to make as clear as possible its religious bearing. At the earliest stage the stories circulated mainly by word of mouth. Probably by the time Mark came to write, a certain number had already been collected and committed to writing. For example, in the opinion of many scholars, the six stories in Mark 2.1–3.6 had already been collected and written down before Mark incorporated them in his Gospel.

For the most part, however, Mark probably knew the stories only in oral form, and what he did in effect was to collect and write down some of the stories about Jesus with which he had become familiar through hearing them repeated in his own and neighbouring churches.

The Stories in Matthew and Luke

If now we look at those sections of Matthew and Luke which they derived from sources other than Mark, we discover that they too are made up almost entirely of similar *pericopes*, presumably for similar reasons. This applies both to the material which Matthew and Luke appear to have derived from a common source, or sources, e.g., Matt.8.5–13 (cf. Luke 7.1–10); Matt.11.7–11 (cf. Luke 7.24–28); Matt.12.43–45 (cf. Luke 11.24–26) and to the material which is peculiar to each evangelist, e.g., Matt.2.1–12; Luke 2.41–50; 10.17–20. In reading these and the other *pericopes* referred to in this article it is important to remember that in the text as we have it the evangelist has sometimes added phrases at the beginning and end to link them with what precedes and what follows.

So we seem justified in formulating the conclusion that virtually all the material in our first three Gospels reached the writers or their sources in the form of the sort of short, separate, self-contained stories we have been describing. If the question is raised why Mark was no longer content to leave the stories in their oral form but committed some of them to writing; and why Matthew and Luke followed his lead, the answer must be that the evidence does not allow us to say with any certainty. The suggestion is sometimes made that it was because eye-witnesses were dying off and hopes for a speedy end of the world were dying out, but at any rate in the case of Mark and Matthew, that explanation will hardly bear investigation. More probably, Mark's church commissioned a written version of certain of the well-known stories to meet some specific liturgical or catechetical need no longer known to us, and then the resultant book of stories proved so valuable that other churches followed suit, though their needs, being somewhat different, gave rise to rather different Gospels. Indeed on one view Matthew's Gospel is essentially a new and expanded edition of Mark's.

Whatever the evangelist's motives, if we try to imagine him starting to work on the basis of a tradition of this kind, we are bound to ask: 'On what basis did he select the particular *pericopes* to be included and on what principles did he arrange them?' As far as arrangement goes, the answer that springs to mind immediately is that he arranged the stories in the order in which they occurred. But would he in fact know in what order they occurred? In view of what we have seen about the circumstances in which the individual stories were preserved, it does not seem very likely. New Testament scholars are not as yet entirely at one on this matter, but it is pretty generally agreed that to a considerable extent, at any rate, when it came to the arrangement of their *pericopes* the evangelists had to use their own judgment. In some cases the answer was obvious enough – for example, the birth narratives had to come at the beginning and the trial and crucifixion stories somewhere near the end; but for the most part, we have to reckon with the possibility that the arrangement of the material was the work of the individual evangelist, and what is more that it was largely governed by the same sort of practical considerations that had led to the preservation of the stories in the first place. One such practical consideration would be convenience of reference; this seems to have been what was in Matthew's mind, for example, when he collected the teaching of Jesus on the basis of subject matter and arranged it in five large blocks, each dealing with a single general topic (5–7; 9.3–11.1; 13.1–53; 18–19; 24–25. Professor G. Bornkamm denies that this five-fold arrangement is conscious or significant, but he is almost alone in that view). Matthew may also have been influenced by his belief that Jesus was a second Moses and a desire to show that the new law he brought was given in five blocks, corresponding to the five books of the Old Testament law.

Another consideration governing the evangelists' arrangement of their material will have been the light that one story can throw on another, if the two are placed side by side, just as a poem may gain new meaning if it is read alongside another poem in an anthology. For example, in Mark 8 the story of how the disciples gradually recognized the truth about Jesus comes immediately after the story of Jesus gradually restoring sight to a blind man. Probably what Mark had in mind was not that the one incident occurred immediately after the other as a matter of historical fact, but that if we read the two stories side by side, we may be brought to see that when people recognize the truth about Jesus they are not making a discovery by the exercise of their own unaided wits, but are having their eyes opened by God, just as the blind man had his physical eyes opened in the story.

Interpreting the Gospels

If all this is true about the origins of the Gospels, two conclusions follow – one positive, the other negative. The first is that in reading the Gospels we must always be on the lookout for the practical aims which controlled the writer's choice and arrangement of his material. We must always be asking: What truth did he mean to bring out by selecting this particular story and including it in this particular context in his Gospel? We must regard him in fact as an evangelist, a preacher, who sought to bring out certain vital religious truths about Jesus by the way he selected, formulated, and arranged his *pericopes*.

Negatively, all this means that we can draw only very limited historical conclusions from the order of events in the Gospels. We cannot really reconstruct from it the course of Jesus' life. And to that is added a further consideration: we saw that those responsible for preserving the *pericopes* in the early church were not interested in purely picturesque and personal detail. It is not only that they say nothing about Jesus' appearance or health or how he dressed or how long his ministry lasted: they were not interested in his *inner* development either. What concerned them was what Jesus' deeds and sayings meant to them and their contemporaries, not what they had meant to Jesus himself; and so they told nothing about how or why Jesus came to act or speak as he did, or how his thought and outlook developed. Obviously, what is absent from the *pericopes* must be absent from the finished Gospels, and that means that the Gospels afford no basis for a Life of Jesus in the sense of an accurate account of the outward course of events and a tracing of the inner spiritual pilgrimage which accompanied and controlled those events.

Before we pass finally to consider the significance of that, let us go back behind the finished Gospels and take another brief look at the individual *pericopes*. How far do these narratives correspond to incidents which actually occured? Clearly it is very difficult to generalize, and competent scholars are considerably divided on this issue. Some insist on the retentiveness of the oriental memory and point out that the early Christians believed their very salvation to depend on these historical events, so they would have had every ground for complete accuracy with regard to them. Accordingly, their accounts of Jesus can be regarded as generally trustworthy. unless in a particular case we have special indications to the contrary.

Other scholars are not so sure. They argue that stories handed on by word of mouth always get modified in the process and that that is especially likely to have happened in this case, where the tradition was handled by comparatively poorly educated folk, who were not accustomed to scholarly standards of accuracy, and in any case lived before the rise of modern scientific historical study.

In trying to decide on this issue, it is extremely important to preserve a sense of proportion. No one is accusing the early Christians of any dishonesty or intent to deceive. What the second group of scholars is suggesting is that any new insight about Jesus which came to the early Christians in the period after the resurrection was almost bound to be reflected, often quite unconsciously, in the way they narrated his earthly life. For example, if the early church became convinced that the Lord was (in their sense of the term) the Son of God, it was natural that some of the *pericopes* should come to be told in a way that implied as much, even if they had not done so in their earlier form (e.g., contrast Matt.14.33 with the earlier form in Mark 6.51; or Matt.16.16 with Mark 8.29 and Luke 9.20). And that may also be the reason why some *pericopes* suggest that Jesus claimed to be Son of man, while others suggest that he did not (on the one side, cf., e.g., Mark 2.10; Luke 7.34; 9.58; 22.48 and Matt.16.13 – even though the AV reading is the wrong one; on the other side cf. Mark 8.38; Luke 9.26; 12.8 f.; Matt.19.28, where 'Son of man' seems to refer to someone other than Jesus himself, see below, p. 252). In fact what the *pericopes* give us is not *directly* the life of Jesus but what the early Christians believed the life of Jesus to have been like. And in that connection we have to remember that their interpretation of a whole lot of things differed from ours. If, for instance, they heard of Jesus having cured a case of what we should call epilepsy, they unhesitatingly interpreted it (as no doubt Jesus did himself) as the casting out of a demon.

So there is no escaping the fact that these stories present us with an inextricable combination of history and interpretation. But that is not for a moment to say that they are pure fiction or that the interpretation they contain is worthless. In the first place, the interpretation is not the work of any eccentric individual or minority group. The first three evangelists drew their material from many sources and many parts of the church, yet the overall picture in all this material is remarkably consistent. And even if we date the Gospels later than many scholars would, the material was only circulating in oral form for fifty years or so, which is hardly long enough for even an oral narrative to get completely out of hand. When Mark's Gospel was written, there must still have been plenty of people alive who had known Jesus, though it is difficult to be sure that they had any *direct* influence on its composition. What is more, the picture of Jesus that the Gospels give is remarkably true to the conditions in Palestine in Jesus' time – and we now know quite a lot about Palestine at that time. The people, the institutions, the questions in the gospel stories, for the most part fit remarkably well with what we know – which is quite an impressive fact when we remember that many of those who passed on the tradition were living a good deal later and a long way from Palestine. We may feel sure that if they had simply been inventing, their inventions would have reflected much more closely the circumstances of their own times and places, in the same sort of way that mediaeval painters portray the Madonna in mediaeval clothes.

Still, the fact remains that what these stories, and the Gospels based on them, present to us is an inextricable interweaving of history and interpretation. About that two things may be said. The first is that it is not a matter simply for regret. If we are Christians and believe that the New Testament writers were in some sense inspired, we shall want to take their interpretation of Christ's life very seriously. We shall believe that their interpretation of him in the first century is meant to help us to interpret him in the twentieth century. Indeed some modern theologians have taken this line of thought a very long way. They argue that from the religious point of view the Christ of the early church's preaching, the *interpreted* Christ, is all that matters. According to them, God's way of saving us is to confront us, through the church, with this Christ of faith and to challenge us to accept and follow him. On such a view the question how far there was a historical figure corresponding to this Christ of faith is a comparatively unimportant one, but this is a position which seems to many people impossibly paradoxical, and in recent years a group of scholars in Germany have been examining this whole question in a quite novel way. These scholars fully accept the sort of account of the Gospels I have been giving and they agree that a Life of Jesus in the modern sense is impossible. But then, they say, a life in that sense is not what we want. We do not need for religious purposes to be able to trace Jesus' inner psychological development; what we are concerned about is Jesus' claims about himself and his will for us. What relationship did he claim to have with God, and what relationship did he desire that we should have with him? And this is precisely the sort of information the Gospel *pericopes* were intended to give.

But do they give it correctly? To put it simply, the way to find out is this. Take the interpreted picture of Jesus presented in the Gospels, and look for any passages which do not square with it – which have slipped through the interpretative net, so to speak. For example, according to the interpretation of the church, Jesus claimed to be Son of man, and yet we come across a passage like this: 'For whoever is ashamed of me and of my words in this adulterous and sinful generation, of him will the Son of man also be ashamed, when he comes in the glory of his Father with the holy angels' (Mark 8.38); at any rate, on the most obvious interpretation, Jesus here seems to *distinguish* himself from the Son of man. The early church will hardly have invented such passages, for they seem to contradict its general picture of Jesus, so they are presumably original and provide a starting-point for a historical reconstruction. Clearly there is no room for dogmatism here, but this is the *sort* of line along which a good deal of recent scholarship has been working; and the upshot so far appears to be something like this. Although the historical Jesus probably differed in certain quite important respects from the picture conveyed by the finished Gospels, he was in fact such that the gospel picture can justly be described as 'fair comment' – legitimate deduction from the genuine historical facts.

In order to fill that out, notice first the 'authority' or 'directness' of Jesus. In his teaching and activity he was not dependent on any support from outside himself. For example, he did not say, as the Rabbis tended to say, 'Things are thus and so because that is what the Old Testament means if properly interpreted.' Nor did he say, 'So and so is going to happen because if you add up the numbers in Daniel or Jeremiah that is how it works out'. He just boldly claimed, 'I tell you . . .'

And what did he tell them? That God's kingdom was coming and they would soon be finding themselves face to face with God – inescapably involved in dealing with God, in a situation in which his will prevailed completely, and everything had been brought into conformity with it. Jesus probably envisaged this in terms of the end of the world and God's appearing, with clouds descending and trumpets blowing, very much along the lines of contemporary thought; and he may have expected it very soon. But that, it is argued, is not really vital, because it was not the whole, or even the centre of Jesus' concern. He was not just concerned to point men to something God would do in the future – he believed God was *already* doing something in and through him. When he was able to cast out demons, for example, he interpreted that as God's power at work in him, starting the final overthrow of the forces of evil. And even more important, he believed that in his dealings with other human beings God was also at work. Jesus had certain attitudes and standards; he demanded honour, goodness, consecration, unselfishness, and love – what he called 'perfection' – from everyone, and he would settle for nothing less; he would not abate his demands by so much as a jot or tittle. But yet he welcomed people into his company and full friendship without their having come anywhere near meeting his demands. He freely gave his friendship to extortioners and prostitutes and all sorts of people who came nowhere near having attained the perfection he demanded. He called people to come and stand beside him, to adopt his relationship and attitude to others. They were to come without any pretence of having attained perfection; and yet without any fear of being rejected by Jesus. His principle seems to have been that his free acceptance of those who came into contact with him and the influence of his love on them would lead them to contrast their previous attitudes with his, and would create his attitude in them.

And all this he did *in God's name*. His attitude, he said, is God's attitude and if men have accepted his call and entered into relationship with him, then they are in that same relationship with God. Jesus' unconditional promise of love and acceptance was in fact God's promise made through him, so that in all he said and did he claimed to be confronting men directly and immediately with God. That was the meaning of his 'authority' and 'directness'. As one of the German scholars put it, 'His attitude is not that of a prophet or a sage; it is that of a man who dares to act in God's place.'

This means that as he saw it, people's relationship with God was essentially bound up with their relationship to him. To 'follow' Jesus, to accept his call and forgiving friendship *is* to partake in God's kingdom, to be in the true relationship to God. Therefore Jesus believed that with his appearance the time of salvation had arrived; the time, that is, when people can enter into a decisive relationship with God. Jesus' aim was not so much to introduce a new concept of God as to open for men a new relationship with God, a relationship which means the certainty of being accepted, and so freedom from anxiety; and thus sonship, liberty, simplicity, love.

And all this Jesus offered without being other than a man among men. The choice he offered was what is sometimes called an 'existential' choice. There was no 'proof' – no outward 'reason' on which people could base their acceptance of his claim or promise; they had to take it or reject it according as their own deepest being responded. 'What think you . . .', he said, and again, 'Blessed are they who are not offended – i.e. put off, moved to objection – by me.'

If there is any truth in all this – and it is of course still very much *sub judice* – it is obviously important. When New Testament writers spoke of Jesus as a supernatural figure who had come down from heaven to live on earth, they were only drawing out, in the ways of speaking natural to them, the basic truth which Jesus himself had affirmed in his own way. That is to say, while Jesus, so far as we can now reconstruct him, was not by any means identical with the figure portrayed in the finished Gospels, or in St Paul's epistles or in the creeds of the church, he was such – and his words and actions were such – that these later descriptions were legitimate ways, for their own respective periods, of saying about him what he would have wanted said in those periods. Which still, of course, leaves open the question: 'What would he want said today?'

The Gospel Makers and their Message · *C. F. Evans*

What was it that the writers of the Synoptic Gospels wanted to convey to their respective readers by the way they arranged and edited the materials they had to hand? This is a question which has to be kept in mind all the time a Gospel is being studied. A full answer would involve a detailed examination of all parts of a Gospel and of those parts in relation to the whole. What is set out below can only be in the form of brief guidelines.

The Gospel According to Mark

The Gospel according to Mark is the one of which it is the most difficult to trace the

pattern, and many different views are held about it. It has a kind of prologue (1.1–15) which gives some clue to the whole. It begins very abruptly, not with the birth of Jesus but with John the Baptist's preaching as the fulfilment of Old Testament prophecy and his promise of the mightier one who would baptize with Holy Spirit. This is Jesus, who is baptized by John, receives the Holy Spirit and is acknowledged by God as his Son and Servant. Jesus is tempted in the desert, but no details are given. A summary of his message, God's gospel, is given as 'the appointed time has come, the rule of God has drawn near' (1.15). From 1.15 to 10.31, Mark places nearly all the material in Galilee, perhaps because this is for him the chosen place of God's revelation where Jesus' ministry is received by crowds. The build-up of this ministry by Mark is through a succession of paragraphs, for the most part of two kinds: (*a*) stories of Jesus' work of power; (*b*) teaching through controversy with his opponents.

Mark's style

1. *The Acts of Power*

In one story after another (sometimes with little connection between them) Jesus is shown to be victorious over various kinds of physical and mental disorder – over demoniacs by exorcism, over fever, paralysis, haemorrhage, death, deafness, blindness. He is even in control of disorder in nature, and can multiply food. Occasionally a meaning is suggested, as when the healing of the paralytic is evidence of the forgiveness of sins, or exorcism a sign of the defeat of the rival kingdom of Satan. But for the most part these acts are unexplained, and sometimes, when Jesus demands silence and secrecy, a mystery is suggested about them.

2. *Controversy*

style

Interspersed with the works of power are controversial dialogues in which Jesus is the victor in debate with opponents (often Pharisees) in bringing to light God's will in relation to various aspects of life and religion – sinners and the righteous, fasting, the sabbath, what is clean and unclean, marriage and divorce, children, wealth. The effect of all this is to present a figure of tremendous and mysterious power and authority: in two places (2.10,28) he is referred to as 'the Son of man' (see Part IV, Section 8, p. 300 f.). This power and authority is also shown in Jesus' capacity to draw huge crowds and to detach men from their occupations to become his personal followers. He teaches these disciples, despite their inability to understand, and they share his power.

3. *Death and Resurrection*

style

In ch. 8 the disciples, in contrast with others, confess Jesus to be the Christ, but are told to be silent, and from this point the mysterious and unexplained title 'the Son of man' reappears. Now the Son of man must undergo a divinely ordained suffering and rejection and death at the hands of the authorities. This death will be followed by resurrection and glory. The dis-

ciples, three of whom see a glimpse of Jesus in his future glory at the transfiguration, must also expect suffering. From 10.32 ff. the story moves to Jerusalem, the scene of this rejection. Again, there is power and authority – in the entry into Jerusalem, the cleansing of the temple, the cursing of the fig tree; in controversies over taxes, resurrection, the commandments, the messiahship and in the words which will 'never pass away' in which Jesus instructs his disciples in advance of the trials that lie ahead and of the ultimate consummation of all things by God through the Son of man. But now this is a prelude to the condemnation of Jesus by the authorities for his acknowledgement of himself as the Christ and the coming Son of man, and his crucifixion by the agency of the Romans. The scene is one of total desertion by men and apparently by God, until a centurion confesses that Jesus was 'a son of God'. The Gospel ends as abruptly as it began with a visit by women to the tomb and their encounter with an angel there who gives them a message for the disciples that the risen Jesus is to go before them into Galilee.

. . . and they went out and fled from the tomb; for trembling and astonishment had come upon them; and they said nothing to anyone, for they were afraid (16.8).

author

4. *Authorship*

According to tradition, some of it going back to the second century AD, the author of this Gospel was a certain Mark, who was a companion of Peter, from whose preaching he derived his materials, and he wrote in Rome. (New Testament references to a Mark are Acts 12.12; 12.25; 15.37–39; II Tim.4.11; I Peter 5.13.) The tradition could be correct, at least in part, but it throws no light on the Gospel itself, unless it is that the stress in this Gospel on the suffering of the Son of man and his disciples is due to the situation of Christians at Rome under their persecution by Nero in AD 64. Mark's paragraphs do not read like first-hand transcripts from an apostle who was an eyewitness. The author could have written to stir up his church to a renewed mission to the Gentile world through the message of the powerful and authoritative Christ who broke with Judaism.

The Gospel According to Matthew

The Gospel according to Matthew is easier to analyse, as in general it has a clearer structure. It is like Mark, and has been called 'a fresh edition of Mark', but it is also very unlike Mark.

It is like Mark because there is little in Mark's Gospel which has not been taken over into Matthew. Thus the story from the entry into Jerusalem to the empty tomb (Matt.20.17–28.7) is a writing out of Mark's story with the addition of a few incidents and of much parable material. In the Galilean ministry (3.1–20.16) the narrative framework as well as some of the material is from Mark.

It is unlike Mark because Mark's narrative, with some slight alterations in order, is used as a framework for collections of largely non-Marcan material in the form of discourses on a theme. The result is that compared with Mark it lacks vigorous movement, and the story often stands still – e.g., in 8.1–9.34 most of the miracles are gathered together and are strung one after another, and so are the parables in 13.1–52. What stands out and gives this Gospel its special character is the five collections of teaching, each rounded off with the formula 'It came to pass when Jesus had finished . . .' (7.28; 11.1; 13.53; 19.1; 26.1).

1. *Shape and Contents*

The pattern of the Gospel appears to be somewhat as follows:

(*a*) It begins (chs. 1–2) not abruptly but with a theological genealogy, tracing the descent of Jesus from the father of the Jewish race, Abraham, in three periods of fourteen generations (perhaps the equivalent of six sevens, leading to Jesus as the beginning of the seventh seven, a perfect number), and with the birth of Jesus, five episodes each built round the fulfilment of an Old Testament text.

(*b*) The Marcan beginning of the Galilean ministry is expanded and leads to the first of the discourses in which Jesus is the giver of the new Law on a mountain (chs. 3–7).

(*c*) The Marcan miracles, with expansions, and his call of the twelve leads to a missionary charge to them (8.1–10.42).

(*d*) Marcan and non-Marcan material leads to an expansion of the Marcan section of parables by additional parables on the nature of the kingdom of heaven (11.2–13.52).

(*e*) Marcan incidents, including the confession of Peter (here the rock of the church), the transfiguration and a dispute by disciples over greatness, lead to instruction of the disciples on behaviour in and the discipline of the church (13.54–18.35).

(*f*) Matthew's re-telling of Mark's account of the entry into and the ministry in Jerusalem leads to an expansion of Mark's eschatological discourse (Mark 13) and to parables of judgment (19.1–25.46).

(*g*) The narrative of the passion and resurrection, ending not abruptly but with the command of the exalted Lord to go to the whole world and the promise of his permanent presence.

These collections of teaching are carefully constructed, especially the first, the Sermon on the Mount. Eight beatitudes express the grace of the gospel, leading to two addresses to disciples as salt and light, five illustrations of the statement 'I came not to destroy but to fulfil', each introduced by 'It was said . . . but I say', the three religious duties of almsgiving, prayer and fasting, etc. Behind these constructions may lie what the Jews called 'Targum'. This began as translation of the Old Testament out of Hebrew when people no longer understood that language, but it also came to include interpretation and application of the text, sometimes by the use of similar passages from elsewhere in the Old Testament. It may be that Matthew is a kind of 'Targum' of Mark, and that this kind of activity had been going on in Matthew's church before he began to write.

The result is that this Gospel assembles sayings on a particular subject and their application, and reads more like a manual of instruction for Christians on the Gospel and its demands, on the nature of the Christian life in the church, and the severe judgment upon belief without practice. It has been suggested that this Gospel was written for reading in church. For these reasons it certainly became from the first the most popular Gospel. But there is a further element. The fact that so much of Matthew's special material is Jewish in tone and is concerned with Jewish matters, and that the author appeals so much to the Old Testament to prove a point, may indicate that his church had lived close to Jewish communities. It may be that this teaching had been hammered out in the face of Jewish opponents who denied the

Christian claims about Jesus, and in order to show that Jesus was the Jewish Messiah, his disciples the true Israel or people of God, and the Old Testament and the Law, when interpreted by Christ, belonged to the Christians.

2. *Authorship*

The author is unknown. His dependence on Mark makes it unlikely that he was an apostle, and it remains a mystery how the name 'Matthew' became attached to this Gospel. It was probably written after the fall of Jerusalem (AD 70: Matt.22.7 seems to refer to this). There is evidence that it was known to Ignatius, the bishop of Antioch in the early years of the second century, which may indicate that it was written somewhere in Syria.

The Gospel According to Luke

The Gospel according to Luke is constructed to a considerable extent from the same or the same kind of material as Mark and Matthew, but the result is different from either. This is partly because, unlike them, it is not a complete work in itself, but the first volume of a two-volume work, Luke-Acts, which has been separated from its sequel in order to be brought into the Gospel section of the New Testament. Luke was the only one of the evangelists to think and plan in this way, or to speak about the origin and purpose of his work, as he does when he addresses Theophilus in a preface (1.1–4). The writing there is in the conventional literary language of prefaces, and for that reason cannot be pressed too hard. Thus in view of Luke's dependence on Mark, 'Q' and other material ('L'), made up of independent stories, it can hardly be the case that there were 'many' Gospels in existence when he wrote or that he had been in personal touch with events 'from the beginning'.

As generally translated, 1.4 gives the impression that Luke is writing to give Theophilus further instruction in his Christian faith. However, the NEB translation 'so as to give you authentic knowledge about the matters of which you have been informed' could mean that Theophilus was not a Christian, and that the whole two-volume work was being written to give an account of the origins of Christianity so as to commend it to the outside world, and to defend it against the charge of being treason-

able to the state (this theme appears in Luke's account of the Passion, and is dominant in the second part of Acts). In any case, the style of the preface shows that Luke thought of himself as a literary person writing to some extent like a Greek historian.

1. *The Pattern of the Gospel*

Luke is dependent upon Mark, but in a different way from Matthew. He places what he takes from Mark in blocks alternately with his non-Marcan material and does not mix them together, and in the non-Marcan material what he gets from 'Q' and what he gets from 'L' are not much mixed together. Scholars are divided over what this implies. Some hold that if all that he derives from Mark is taken out of Luke's Gospel, what is left still makes a continuous narrative from John the Baptist to the resurrection, and they conclude that this was Luke's first version (Proto-Luke= 'Q' plus 'L'), which Luke later filled out with blocks inserted from Mark, who was thus not a primary but a secondary source for him. Others hold that this is not so, and that Mark supplies the basic framework in the Galilean ministry and the passion narrative, but that Luke has used it and edited it more freely, and for his own purposes has chosen a non-Marcan in preference to a Marcan story (e.g., the call of Peter [5.1–9]; the visit to Nazareth [4.16–30]; the anointing by a woman [7.36–50]).

There is no clearly pronounced pattern as in Matthew, but the narrative is more flowing than in Mark. Luke intended to write 'in an orderly manner' (1.3), and by this he seems to mean the treatment of one subject at a time (e.g., all the material gathered in 3.1–20 makes up a little account of the career of John the Baptist), with smoother transitions from one section to another so that the whole is more intelligible. He can write vividly in more than one style, including that of the Greek Old Testament. This versatility, and the fact that some of his special material – parables of the Good Samaritan, Prodigal Son, Dives and Lazarus, and episodes such as the Call of Peter, the Visit to Nazareth and the Anointing, the Walk to Emmaus, etc. have a highly graphic character, gives his Gospel a special appeal.

The birth stories are quite different from Matthew's. They trace parallel births of John and Jesus; they are not written around Old

Testament texts as fulfilment of past prophecy, but in Old Testament style and as occasions of the revival of prophecy itself (the Canticles: 1.14–17, 32–34, 46–55, 68–79; 2.29–35). The Galilean ministry is largely Marcan, but Jesus is depicted more than in Mark as one who is on a journey (4.14 f., 16, 31, 44; 5.12; 7.1, 11; 8.1 f.). The journey from Galilee to Jerusalem, only briefly referred to by Mark and Matthew, becomes for Luke a framework for the whole middle section of his Gospel (9.51–19.28; cf. 10.38; 13.22; 17.11; 18.31), which as far as 18.14 is made up entirely of non-Marcan material. This concept of the journeying healer and preacher occurs again in Acts in relation to Philip, Peter and Paul, and is a common feature of Hellenistic literature. Luke's passion narrative has additional material and, like the rest of his Gospel, many human touches. It is rounded off by resurrection stories concerned not with Galilee but with Jerusalem, which also provide a bridge to the second volume, the Acts of the Apostles.

There are some threads which run through the two volumes and therefore affect the choice of material for the first volume and the way in which it is presented. One is the theme of the Spirit, through whose agency Jesus is conceived, which he receives at his baptism and which controls him in his temptations. By its power he heals and teaches (4.16 ff.). The same Spirit is his gift from the Father to the disciples (24.49; Acts 1.8) and directs the church throughout Acts. Also Luke is the only evangelist to say that Jesus named the twelve 'apostles' (6.13), and these are the chief recipients of his teaching and the nucleus of the church in Acts. Luke's version of this teaching is more immediately directed towards the moral guidance of men.

2. Authorship

According to tradition, Luke was Paul's travelling companion. This may be correct, but it may have been arrived at by deduction that among the 'we' mentioned in Acts was Luke the physician, referred to in Col.4.14; Philemon 23 f.; II Tim.4.9–12. Even if it is correct, it throws no light on the Gospel, as this is derived from Mark and other such sources, but not from Paul. The Gospel was written after AD 70 (the fall of Jerusalem is reflected in 21.20), but it is not known where.

6

The Miracles

John Bowden and Robert C. Walton

The Nature of Miracle

What is a miracle? Philosophers and theologians have argued long over the question and have produced some complex and sophisticated definitions. When it comes to classroom discussions, however, the starting-point is clear enough. A miracle is usually taken to be an action or event which apparently violates the accepted order of nature. The sea is suddenly turned back, the sun stands still, water is changed into wine, a small quantity of bread feeds a vast crowd, the sick are suddenly healed and the dead are revived.

Miracles like this are still discussed because they are to be found in the Bible; not only on its fringe, but at crucial points in the story which Old and New Testaments tell. Of course, they are not confined to the Bible. Miracle stories are also common in the ancient Near East outside the Old Testament and in the first-century Mediterranean world outside the New Testament. They appear in Buddhism, Hinduism and Islam, and in later Christian tradition, right down to the present day. But only the biblical miracles are generally thought to be a problem worth devoting attention to.

These biblical miracle stories belong to a pre-scientific outlook, and are part of a completely different approach to the world from the one to which we have become acclimatized (for some of its characteristics see Part IV, Section 4, pp. 234 ff.). This approach may best be called 'mythical', provided that the term is understood correctly. 'Myth' is a way of looking at the world which presents what we would be more likely to call dimensions of personality, of experience (including what man believes to be experience of the divine), in an objective, tangible, pictorial form. In a three-decker universe, with heaven above and the underworld below, with divine and demonic forces at work, the story, the description, the picture takes the place of abstract analysis or philosophical and psychological argument. This is the setting where miracle belongs.

Miracle and myth are by no means identical. What we would call miracle is often absent from a 'mythical' view of the world. But in such a view, where there is nothing like modern science to draw a line with a reasonable claim to authority between what is theoretically possible and what is theoretically impossible, the distinction between a factually correct historical account and a religiously significant symbol inevitably becomes blurred. Just how blurred this line could be is not easy to establish. How literally, say, the first-century world understood the language of myth and accounts of miracle is a puzzling question. Attitudes probably varied widely, just as do miracle stories themselves.

Even in a mythical setting, miracles appear in some places and not in others. They cluster round the exodus from Egypt, the lives of Elijah and Elisha, the ministry of Jesus and the work of the apostles as told, e.g., in Acts. On the other hand they are almost completely absent from the primary traditions of the great prophets, the wisdom literature, the apocrypha I Maccabees (but compare II Maccabees) and the letters of Paul and his successors. Outside the Bible, from the time of the early church, one might compare the more or less rational approach of Plutarch and Josephus and the scepticism of Lucian of Samosata with the excessive credulity of Philostratus, author of a life of the wonder-worker Apollonius of Tyana, and Antonius Diogenes, whose *Incredible Things beyond Thule* which included a trip to the moon was accepted even by quite respectable philosophers. Perhaps the most interesting example of different attitudes to miracle comes from the

eleventh century. The historian R. W. Southern, writing about Anselm and his biographers, notes how the famous Archbishop of Canterbury was at one time accompanied on his travels by two companions; of these, one regularly saw miracles, while the other did not!

This differentiation in the appearance of miracle also extends to the kind of miracle stories that are told. Not all of them have the same profundity. On the one hand, there are the miraculous legends or semi-edifying tales which great figures or events seemed to attract almost automatically. Many of these stories are popular in character; they are often unedifying and superficial, and reduce miracles almost to the level of the conjuring trick. Examples of this type are the elaborations of the plagues of Egypt, most of the Elisha stories, the incident of the coin in the fish's mouth (Matt.17.24–27), some of the miracles attached to Peter and Paul in Acts (5.12–16; 9.32–41; 19.11 f.; 20.7–12), and above all the stories of the boy Jesus in the apocryphal gospels. In the Infancy Gospel of Thomas, for example, Jesus becomes a little menace, cursing those who annoy him so that they die (and then reviving them). The apocryphal Acts of the Apostles take the biblical Acts even further, with talking animals, obedient bed-bugs and swimming kippers. By this stage miracle has virtually become popular entertainment.

On the other hand, miracle can be an attempt at representing the profound and the mysterious character of people or events through which a new dimension seems to be present, exhausting ordinary language and ideas. Something of this very different atmosphere can be seen in, say, the story of the burning bush at the call of Moses, in the central event of the exodus from Egypt which kindled the faith of a nation, and above all in the work of Jesus, at the centre of the New Testament.

Those who told miracle stories thus saw miracles as the working of supernatural power in the world. This power was not necessarily good; miracles could be worked by the devil as well as by God. For example, in the story of the Egyptian plagues (Ex.7–11) there is virtually a competition between Moses and Aaron and the Egyptian magicians; Jesus himself is accused of casting out demons by demonic power (Matt.12.24; for an amusing sideline on the whole question see Acts 19.13 ff.). So in the early days, the problem for Christians was not so much in establishing that miracles had happened as in demonstrating what they meant.

Miracles and Science

As we have seen, even against a mythical background, miracles were 'miraculous'. The first century AD was probably one of the most credulous periods of history, but even then the restoration to life of a corpse was not an everyday occurrence. On the other hand, when so many marvellous stories were going the rounds, such a happening would have been that much easier to credit. The problem of miracle really became serious when the growth of science provided rational explanations for hitherto unexplained happenings, reducing phenomena which might be attributed to divine intervention and establishing consistent 'laws of nature'. Once this scientific approach had been established, miracle tended to be detached from its context in myth and examined in physical terms.

How was a miracle possible? That was the key question, but alongside was another, equally important. Was the old view that what could not be explained in natural terms had to be supernatural still valid? Suppose a 'miracle' occurred; did it necessarily point to divine action? It might be a fraud or a misunderstanding. It might be explicable in other terms if all the facts were available. It might be explicable in the future, with an increase in scientific knowledge. It might be an oddity, a freak. In short, not only did the possibility of miracle seem more remote; because the whole world view of which miracles had been a part gave way to a new approach, miracles were no longer accepted as the kind of pointers which they once seemed to be.

This new situation led to three different approaches to miracle:

1. *Science and belief in miracle conflict: belief in miracle is to be retained.* In a famous book on miracles, C. S. Lewis defended the old, supernatural view of miracle against all objections. For him, Christianity itself was based on the Great Miracle, that God had become man; given this, was it not fitting that other remarkable happenings should follow? A 'naturalistic' approach was not enough; Christianity demanded a supernaturalist view

of the world. In its time, this attitude was very popular; it does, however, leave the Christian fighting rather a lone battle as the man who can believe 'eight impossible things before breakfast', and with more recent developments in theology as a whole is increasingly difficult to sustain. (Bruce Marshall's book, *Father Malachy's Miracle*, is a vivid fictional account of a similar point of view.)

2. *Science and belief in miracle conflict: miracles are to be rejected.* It is regularly argued that scientists have discovered enough to establish a system of natural laws which rule out the possibility of miracle. There is some truth in this argument. We do not see miracles happening, and our day-to-day life and our reconstruction of the past are based on the presupposition that nature is regular. On the other hand, with science has also come the insight that our knowledge is based on observation and experience and can never be absolute. So while scientists and historians may be very sceptical indeed, strictly speaking they can never rule out completely the possibility of miracle.

3. *Science and belief in miracle can be reconciled.* The discovery of quantum physics and the principle of indeterminacy appeared to some people to make science far more opentextured. The impossibility of predicting the behaviour of nuclear particles led to revised statements like, 'Scientifically speaking, a miracle is a highly improbable, statistically rare, but not impossible event.' Such a view builds heavily on the objections to the second view mentioned above, supported by the feeling that the categories of science cannot by themselves explain every dimension of human life. But this is an irrational combination of thoughts and is certainly a misinterpretation of recent scientific developments. While it is true that twentieth-century science is very different from that of the nineteenth century, responsible scientists (including many Christians) seem agreed that the new developments do not in themselves alter the problems of the relationship between miracle and science.

Do Miracles Happen?

Is it, then, possible to come to any provisional conclusions about miracle? One of C. S. Lewis' important points was that the ideas with which a person approaches a miracle story will determine what he makes of it: 'Those who assume that miracles cannot happen are merely wasting their time by looking into the texts; we know in advance what results they will find, for they have begun by begging the question.'

It is difficult to seem not to beg the question, for a straight answer to the question 'Do miracles happen?' is not easy. As we have seen, the historian can reconstruct the past only on the assumption that the world is regular and constant, i.e., that miracles do not happen. He naturally fears that excessive credulity will corrupt his judgment as a historian. On the other hand, he has to accept that his method, by its very nature, could not accept a miracle even on the strongest testimony. That is its limitation.

Perhaps the most satisfactory reply, under the circumstances, is to stress the need to look at particular miracles against their proper background and thought-world. Sometimes close examination of a miracle will show it to be of a kind that can reasonably be dismissed or explained in another way; sometimes the dimension of mystery will simply have to be acknowledged and it will have to be recognized that something really beyond our understanding may have taken place.

The more general issues are certainly relevant, but without detailed application they will only remain abstractions. This will become clear if we look more closely at the miracles in the Gospels; the principles applied here can be extended to the treatment of miracles elsewhere in the Bible.

Miracles in the Gospels

As we have seen, miracles were attributed to Jesus by later writers as they were to other famous men. Sometimes this wholesale attribution of miracles hinders our understanding rather than helping it. The Jesus who conjures a coin out of the mouth of a fish to pay his tax, who makes sparrows out of clay or stretches with his bare hands a piece of wood which is too short for Joseph's purpose is more grotesque than anything else. Nor are we really enlightened by the elaborations to Matthew's passion narrative, stories of saints appearing out of their graves and of angelic guardians at

the tomb. We can see why these stories were told, but they seem artificial; even the incident in Luke's Gospel, where Jesus heals the ear of the man wounded by Peter at the time of his arrest, strikes us as being little more than an embellishment.

On the other hand, there are other stories told about Jesus which seem to have much deeper roots. There are the miracle stories themselves (e.g., the stilling of the storm [Mark 4.35–41], the healing of the Gerasene demoniac [Mark 5.1–20], the healing of Jairus' daughter [Mark 5.21–43], the feeding of the multitudes [Mark 6.30–44; 8.1–10], the walking on the water [Mark 6.45–51]) which occur in the earliest tradition and focus interest in various ways on the power of Jesus and the impression he made. There are also incidental references to miracles in contexts where the miracle itself is of subsidiary interest. Thus in Mark 3.1–5, the healing of the man with a withered hand on the sabbath is secondary to the main controversy, what is permissible on the sabbath. Similarly, among the sayings of Jesus, the famous remark, 'If I by the finger of God cast out devils then is the kingdom of God come upon you' (Luke 11.20; cf. Matt.12.28), takes the miracles as its basic premiss; the dispute is over what the miracles mean (see above).

One of the firm facts in the tradition about Jesus therefore seems to be that he performed miracles. Is it then possible to go further and to say more closely what these miracles were?

Two categories are usually distinguished: the healing miracles and the 'nature' miracles. The first group includes exorcisms and the cure of the crippled, blind, deaf, dumb (and even the raising of the dead); the second comprises, e.g., the stilling of the storm, the walking on the water, the feeding of the five (four) thousand. The distinction is a useful one, not because the first group is less problematical for our modern views than the second (i.e., there might well be a psychological explanation for the cures), but because with the nature miracles the relationship between the story as we have it and an event behind it seems that much more complex.

With their overtones of Old Testament (and other?) imagery, the nature miracles in fact come quite close to stories like those of the temptation and the transfiguration, where the basic event (if there was a single event at all) lies buried under a very considerable amount of interpretation. Given this position, rather than trying to penetrate the interpretation, it is better to look for the meaning it is intended to convey.

It is, then, perhaps justifiable to see the healings and exorcisms as most characteristic of Jesus' own work, and the other miracles as above all ways of understanding him. But this is not, of course, a distinction which would have occurred to the evangelists themselves.

The evangelists have an important part in the miracle stories. They have selected these stories, arranged them and even retold them to fit their own wider purposes. This means that the same story may have a different emphasis from Gospel to Gospel.

Miracles have the most positive role in the *Gospel of Mark* (see also Part IV, Section 5, pp. 253 f.). Almost one third of Mark consists of miracle stories, immensely varied both in form and subject-matter. Some have a biblical flavour, but many are closer to the atmosphere of the first-century world. Mark uses these miracle stories to highlight Jesus as above all the destroyer of unclean spirits and the forces of chaos by his greater power of the spirit; Jesus is the victor who emerges triumphant from his contest with the demons – it is a case of the Holy Spirit (1.8) overcoming the 'unclean spirits'.

This dynamic use of the miracle tradition is absent from the other two Synoptic Gospels. *Matthew* takes over the Marcan miracles and adds some of his own. But by keeping them all together in a group and thus in essentials confining them to one part of his Gospel (8.1–10.42, see Part IV, Section 5, pp. 255 f.), he reduces their prominence so that the figure of Jesus is no longer predominantly that of a doer of mighty work, but that of a teacher. Where Matthew himself introduces miracles outside this section (e.g., 17.24–27; 27.52 f.; 28.2–4), they tend to be much more legendary in character.

In *Luke*, the opening scene of Jesus' ministry (4.18 f.) links the miracles directly with the Holy Spirit, which is such a prominent concern of Luke's throughout the Gospel and Acts. A summary of the ministry of Jesus in Acts 10.38 mentions 'how God anointed Jesus of Nazareth with the Holy Spirit and with power and how he went about doing good and healing all that were oppressed by the devil, for God was with him'. To a degree this resembles Mark, but there is a real difference: the element of mystery and awe which is so characteristic of Mark almost completely disappears; Luke's Jesus is a much more human figure, and comes much closer to the type of the first-century travelling wonder-worker.

The *Gospel of John* differs greatly from the Synoptic Gospels in its treatment of miracle, as in so much else. It only has a few miracles, which are called 'signs', a word which 'indicates that John has made a selection of those actions which for him were most significant because in their outward and physical circumstances they served as the clearest pointers to what in Christian experience believers had come to see Jesus to be and his gifts to be' (see Part IV, Section 11, pp. 328 f.). Signs by themselves are not enough. They need to be interpreted and understood properly. And in the end they can be dispensed with.

The different approaches of the Gospels to miracle indicates the kind of questions which should be asked of the stories they contain. Seen as part of a portrait of Jesus, what do the miracles convey? Are they cheap and superficial marvels, with a superficial view of God? Or are they part of a mythical approach in which writers are struggling to convey and interpret the mystery of an overwhelming experience which sometimes takes the form of miracle because it refers to something beyond common words and experiences?

The Resurrection

It is sometimes said that the resurrection is 'the greatest miracle of all'. This may, however, be a misleading way of putting it. For the resurrection of Jesus comes close to those stories, mentioned above, where interpretation and original occurrence are so intertwined that it is very difficult indeed to see what actually happened.

The customary ways of approaching the resurrection closely resemble the alternative approaches to miracle mentioned earlier.

1. *The traditional faith of the church in the physical resurrection of Jesus' body is straightforward, and to be accepted.* The tomb was empty; Jesus appeared to his disciples and

later ascended to heaven. The New Testament says so. Why complicate things further? Of course, there are discrepancies (both between individual Gospels and between the Gospels and I Cor.15.1–8), but these are only to be expected when the same event is told by several different people.

2. *The bones of Jesus lie buried somewhere in Palestine.* Bodies, once dead, cannot be revived. There can be no exceptions to the scientific law that all men must die. Furthermore, to insist on the physical resurrection of Jesus is to introduce at the wrong point a stumbling-block in the way of belief. What matters is not so much whether or not one has the capacity to believe in a physical resurrection of Jesus, but rather commitment to the way of Jesus, to the new life which is made possible in the fellowship of his church, where his spirit lives on.

3. *Both the preceding views are too simple.* For others, it is impossible to prove the question either way in definite terms. So the resurrection might be presented as John Hick presents it:

> We shall never know whether the resurrection of Jesus was a bodily event; or consisted instead in visions of Jesus; or in an intense sense of his unseen personal presence. But we do know the effects of the event and we know that whatever happened was such as to produce these effects. The main result was the transformation of a forlorn handful of former followers of an executed and discredited prophet into a coherent and dynamic fellowship with a faith which determined its life and enabled it to convince, to grow, to survive persecution and become the dominant religion of the Roman Empire.

This view takes from the first approach the conviction that *something* happened, and from the second the conviction that human reaction to Jesus was a constituent part of the event; but it is unwilling to go as far as either to their respective extremes.

A view of this kind would certainly seem to fit the evidence best. The resurrection is a complex event. New Testament writers talk about it in different ways and differ in more than detail. But they agree in including in this 'event' the consequences of the death of Jesus, up to and including the conviction of the church that Jesus, who had died, was the Risen Lord. What is to be singled out from all this complex as the essence of the resurrection is less easy to say. Paul, for example, shows no knowledge of the empty tomb, and his use of the phrase 'he appeared' (I Cor.15.5) allows of no conclusions as to the nature of the Risen Lord. An examination of the Gospel accounts of the resurrection will show a wide divergence: the contributions of the evangelists themselves seem to be considerable. Compare, for example, Matthew, Luke and John, the three Gospels with resurrection appearances; is it not significant that the Christ who appears is in Matthew a Matthaean Christ, in Luke a Lucan Christ and in John a Johannine Christ? The more deeply we penetrate the more mysterious it becomes.

There are indeed questions here. Nevertheless, the main fact, that those who doubted were transformed into a dynamic new movement, would still seem to be best explained by a recognition that this change had been produced by something which had happened, and which they knew to have happened, to Jesus of Nazareth.

Teaching the Miracles

There are obviously serious difficulties in using the miracle stories of the Bible in the classroom. They cannot be ignored or evaded; children will certainly hear them outside school, sometimes told with conviction, sometimes laughed at sceptically. It is plain that the miraculous element in Christian teaching which seemed to authenticate as God-given the work of Moses, Elisha or Jesus, now often distorts the picture. When the miracles which once promoted faith now provoke doubts and questionings, what can we honestly say to our pupils?

1. *Infant Classes*

Young children, being without the power of conceptual thought, obviously cannot grasp arguments about miracles. There is a danger, pointed out by Violet Madge, of building up a picture of Jesus as a conjurer (see Part II, Section 3, p. 40): 'He had strong magic.' Some teachers may feel that it is wiser to omit the miracle stories entirely; others believe that this would deprive children of experiences which are important to them.

Rigorous selection is clearly necessary. There is no point, for instance, in telling the legend of the talking donkey (Num.22.21 f.) or of the axe-head which floated (II Kings 6.5). What, then, of the favourite story of the drowning of the Egyptians at the Sea of Reeds and the escape of the Israelites? The question which a teacher must answer is this: Will this story enrich the understanding of God's power and goodness, or will it be lost in the excitement of drowning men and plunging horses and chariots stuck in wet sand? On the other hand, might it not be wise to tell young children the story of Moses and the bush which burned with fire but was not consumed (Ex.3.1–12)? This can convey (as in Rembrandt's well-known etching, which is reproduced in many books) not a magical trick but a sense of wonder and mystery. The story can be told so that the emphasis falls upon Moses' reverence and awe in the presence of God. It can be introduced by saying that this is a story which people loved to tell about Moses, and be followed, not by an attempt at explanation, or by moralizing, but by encouraging the children to express what they themselves feel by painting the story or writing a poem about it.

In telling the miracles of Jesus to young children, once again selection is necessary and the approach is all-important. No-one will be helped by the story of Jesus walking on the water if it is suggested that 'perhaps the boat was near the shore and Jesus waded out to the disciples'. It is equally wrong to draw an irrelevant moral: to emphasize, for instance, in telling the miracle of the loaves and fish, the generosity of the little boy who shared his dinner. (The boy with the 'five barley loaves and two small fish' in any case only appears in the version given in the Fourth Gospel [John 6.9].) The miracles of Jesus should be chosen and so told as to emphasize his power and his compassion.

2. Junior Pupils

Gordon Benfield in his article (Part II, Section 3, pp. 52 f.) makes three points about the teaching of miracle stories to junior children.

(i) Pupils are bound to ask, 'What happened?' and 'How did it happen?'. Often the only honest reply is that we do not know and cannot even guess at the answer to these questions. And the children, likewise, should be discouraged from guessing.

(ii) The important question is this: What did men know and experience of God to cause them to believe in the divine deliverance of Israel at the Sea of Reeds, and in the resurrection of Jesus?

(iii) Miracles – especially those told in the Gospels – are glimpses into the kind of world God wants. This child was ill and near to death. Now she is well again. Give her some food (Mark 5.21–24, 35–43). That is God's kind of world.

To these suggestions one other might be added. The world as we know it in the twentieth century through the discoveries of science is not magical and capricious, but it is certainly full of wonder and mystery. Scientific understanding which is not superficial but profound recognizes that wonder and mystery; poets seek to express it. This can be discussed and illustrated before going on to the next step. Junior children can begin, at least, to understand that in the past, when the scientific way of looking at the world was unknown, it was natural and inevitable that men should find explanations and express their sense of mystery and wonder by believing in miracle.

3. Senior Pupils

At this stage, in a spirit of honest inquiry, the points made in the preceding paragraphs can be explored at a deeper level.

With senior pupils some distinctions of importance can be made. Compare, for instance, the miracle of deliverance at the Sea of Reeds with the miraculous story of the three men in the burning fiery furnace (Dan.3). The first is in a historical document, the second is in an invented story told to encourage, with the hope of deliverance, Jews suffering outrageous persecution. Did anyone in the second century BC think that it actually happened? This lesson, or series of lessons, might begin with a study of the Jews under the Seleucid kings (see Part III, Section 15, pp. 191 ff.), and go on to discuss what such literature as the book of Daniel meant to people in Jerusalem under such a burning fiery trial. It could include extracts from the recording of Benjamin Britten's parable for church performance, *The Burning Fiery Furnace*. And the point to be made is that in the historical record of the book of Maccabees, in the imaginative story of the three men in the fire and in Britten's music, something is being said about the power of God and the faithfulness of his worshippers.

This indeed is the position we should strive to reach in all our teaching about the miracles. No doubt some were related because men love to hear of marvels, and because they offered an explanation of what was otherwise inexpli-cable. But in telling the miracle stories which belong to the great moments of history, such as the exodus and the life of Jesus, there was a more profound motive. To those who lived through such great moments, the miracles bore witness to a firm belief that what they had experienced was not a chapter of accidents, but a fresh unfolding of the loving purposes of God.

7

The Ministry of Jesus

Alan T. Dale

The most striking thing about Jesus is his immense influence over the heart and imagina-tion of ordinary men and women. He has shown a persistent and enduring power of haunting – to put it no higher – the minds of all sorts and conditions of men, contradicting the pre-scriptions of friends and surviving the criti-cisms of enemies. He has been profoundly involved in the rise and fall of civilizations. He has had more to do with the rise and attitudes of the modern world – its scientific inquiry and its secular convictions – than most of us are aware of. He has made himself at home in races other than his own. Whatever the problems – and they are not a few – with which the earliest records of his story present us, we must remind ourselves, as we set out to tell his story, that we are not dealing merely with a misty figure half-seen in debatable documents, but with a man whose three brief public years have left an indelible mark on all men's life and thought, and whose character and ministry and remembered words have an incredible power of awakening the imagination and opening the minds of men twenty centuries after his death, one Friday afternoon, some-where about the year AD 29.

Writing about Jesus can so often get lost in the bogs of the important but limited discussion of documents and of the uncertain events of the rise and spread of the Christian community in the first decades after his death, that we must remind ourselves of what we are now attempting. We are scrutinizing the earliest records to find a clue to the widespread and profound personal influence of Jesus. Who *is* he who can speak to us through the etchings of a Rembrandt or the sculpture of an Epstein, the paintings of a Spencer or a Rouault, the poetry of an Eliot or Auden, the work of a Gandhi or a Dr Luther King; and who, beyond this, can be the inspiration and guide of steel-workers, shop-keepers, farmers, house-wives today? Though, before we have finished, we may have other things to say about him, we must begin with an awareness of the public facts of his influence in the world. This is the man on whose story we are now embarking.

Those who have tried to write his story have often been charged with painting it in their own likeness. There is truth in this charge (it is true of all biographies); but we cannot escape this dilemma. We must be bold. We must not be frightened of asking our own questions and being ourselves in his presence. We must listen to historian and biblical scholar and take a proper note of what they have to say; but we must not be intimidated by them. We must constantly remember who it is whose story we are telling.

The Evidence for the Story

The evidence on which any account of Jesus must be founded has already been discussed in some detail (see Part IV, Section 5, pp. 239 ff.).

It is necessary, however, to make some comments about it here; we must keep in mind what kind of evidence it is.

Three things only need be said:

1. The indisputable fact with which we begin is the existence, in the later decades of the first century, of small Christian communities scattered throughout the Mediterranean world. Their records – Gospels, letters, the remarkable Fourth Gospel, The Revelation – have been subjected to the most intense scrutiny that has ever been given to any ancient documents. It is clear that they are religious documents – church books – 'reflecting in manifold ways,' as one writer has said, 'the experiences and reflections of the churches in the final decades of the first century and adapted to meeting the felt needs of these primitive communities'. What we find, then, in the letters as well as in the more apparently 'historical' Gospels, is *the memories of his friends,* set down in the way they needed them and as they understood them.

2. These are, therefore, not 'historical documents' in our twentieth-century meaning of the words. Historical investigation as we understand it is a recent discipline. But *this does not mean that their authors were indifferent to authentic information about Jesus.* Their conviction that in him 'God acted' required of them that, as far as they could, they should make sure that what they said had happened had really happened. They must get right 'the plain story of what had happened in the ministry of Jesus'. If they knew they were freely inventing a story, the very ground of their convictions would have been cut from beneath them. We have much sorting out to do and we must be careful how we use their evidence, but their reports are honest reports, not deliberate fiction.

3. What we have, therefore, before us in the letters and the Gospels are *portraits* of Jesus. There has been much discussion about what knowledge Paul had of Jesus, but no-one can read through Paul's letters without being aware of the portrait of Jesus which illuminated his mind – a portrait painted from knowledge, as his 'thumb-nail sketch' of Jesus in I Cor. 13.5–7 seems to imply. We meet different portraits of Jesus in the first three Gospels, and another bolder portrait in the Fourth Gospel. We are free to examine these portraits, question details

and comment on their broad strokes. But, finally, we must stand back from the portraits; when we do so, we become aware, as we note their different colours and pattern, of a recognizable figure, of a real person, at once strange and familiar, at once confirming and challenging our impressions and assumptions. Above and beyond the questions and hesitations which arise as we read, the total impression which these portraits make upon us is of a real story in a real world: that face was once seen, that voice was once heard.

The Presuppositions of the Story

But before we begin to sketch that story out, there are two other important questions to take note of – questions which perhaps more than others make this story seem to many people remote and unreal.

1. The reports about the events with which we are concerned belong to the pre-scientific world. Men's assumptions about the world they lived in and the way they thought and talked about it were very different from our assumptions and the way we think and talk about it (see Part IV, Section 4, pp. 234 f.). This is no insuperable obstacle to our understanding of them. Their different assumptions and idioms no more inhibit dialogue with them than a similar situation inhibits dialogue with present-day pre-scientific people, if we take the trouble to learn something of their language, idiom and approach. But it does mean that we must take trouble; we must not read the accounts in the Gospels as though they had been written in our own century by people who think about the world as we do. We have to ask about their reports – 'Why did they put it like this?' 'What happened to make them talk like this?' 'How would we put it today?' Anybody who has lived among civilized but pre-scientific people knows how inescapable these questions are. We have to ask them of the events before us.

2. But more important is another question. We have noted that the records in which the story of Jesus is found are religious records. Their writers were concerned with getting clear the meaning of their new religious experience which was rooted in events that had happened a few decades before in Palestine. They wanted to know what actually

happened; but they described the events that happened – and only so much of them as mattered to them, for they were not attempting a full historical account – in religious language. These events had evoked for those who were first involved in them a new awareness of God, and they used language which brought this character of the events out. For example, such a word is 'miracle' (see Part IV, Section 6, pp. 257 ff.), a word which has been in recent centuries a storm-centre of debate. It does not, as has been said, necessarily mean something which breaks 'the regularities and consistences of nature and history', as by many people then and now it has been assumed to mean. The characteristic word for 'miracle' in the New Testament is not 'wonder', but one of two other words – 'power' and 'sign'. Hence it may best be defined as 'an event which through its unusual character attracts our attention, but also awakens or deepens our awareness of, our faith in, and our assurance of, the love of God'. The question of what actually happened in what the New Testament writers describe as 'a power' or 'a sign' is open to inquiry, and we may have to admit that for many such occasions we have to say 'We do not know'; but what we cannot do is to dismiss it as if that was the end of the matter. This event awakened the sense of God's presence – made God real – for them. We must ask why. We must remember, then, what our authors are doing and what kind of language they are using.

The Background of the Story

We come now to the story of Jesus itself. It is a story we shall never begin to understand unless we place it firmly against the background of his day – a country occupied by Roman troops whose presence provoked not only a general feeling of resentment and frustration but also the bitter activities of a Resistance Movement, the Zealots (see Part IV, Sections 1 and 3, pp. 208, 232 f.). Jesus was no rootless individual. He grew up in Galilee where the Resistance Movement was very much alive; Nazareth was about two miles from Jaffa, 'the oldest and most important settlement in this part of the hill country . . . and a rallying point for the armed opposition to the invading Roman Army' in AD 66. Its bitter resistance must have had a long history behind it; and it is likely that Jesus grew up in a strong resistance atmosphere.

We have learned much in our own day about resistance movements – how they dominate and determine the mind and mood of a people under the apparent calm of ordinary life, and how their very secrecy gives them an indisputable authority over the activities of ordinary citizens. Their clandestine character offers room for a wide variety of opinions among ordinary people which only become acute when full-scale fighting breaks out. It is against such a background that the ministry of Jesus must be seen; his sayings and actions take on new meaning against it; the brevity of his ministry and his political murder outside Jerusalem become intelligible. For the fact is that he came to his convictions the hard way – he was not day-dreaming about some ideal world, but making a costly and dangerous attempt to ask real questions about a real world. His criticism of the common assumptions of his day, arising as they did from his own profound experience of God's presence and a life-time's meditation on the history of his people, made him, when his attitude became recognizably clear, suspect with Resistance Movement, people and government alike, and disowned by many of his friends (John 6.66).

Jesus' ministry falls midway in the story of the three hundred years' Jewish war for religious and political freedom. The war began with the Maccabaean rebellion of 168 BC (see Part III, Section 15, pp. 191 ff.) and ended with Bar Kochba's revolt in AD 132. Its story is the theme of Josephus' *The Jewish War,* a book to be used, indeed, with caution, but where we may find 'set down both clearly and accurately the main course of events . . . the long-drawn agony of the war (AD 66–70) and the happenings which preceded it, with such a wealth of detail that his work is a major contribution to the history of a critical century'. The reading of this book is a prerequisite for the proper reading of the Gospels.

The Gospels, as we have said, are church books, written for the guidance of the early Christian communities and concerned with their religious life. These communities, after AD 70, were predominantly non-Jewish in their membership; for many Christians then the incidents in Palestine from AD 29 to 70 were mere episodes in a far-off province on the eastern edge of the Roman Empire, as interesting to them as a colonial war in Africa probably was to an ordinary British citizen in the last century. But the brutal and violent story of what had happened pushes through even these religious records. It is the critical context against which the very meaningfulness of Jesus' 'Good News' is to be grasped – even his phrase 'The kingdom of God' may have been the watchword of the Zealots. What he did and said was meant for men and women there and then; only because this was so, could it also have a meaning for all mankind.

A story which Josephus tells about Pilate is a fitting quotation to give us the feeling of what it was like to live in Palestine in Jesus' day.

As procurator of Judaea Tiberius sent Pilate, who during the night secretly and under cover, conveyed to Jerusalem the images of Caesar known as *signa*. When day dawned this caused great excitement among the Jews; for those who were near were amazed at the sight, which meant that their laws had been trampled on – they do not permit any graven images to be set up in the City – and the angry city mob were joined by a huge influx of people from the country. They rushed off to Pilate in Caesarea, and begged him to remove the *signa* from Jerusalem and to respect their ancient customs. When Pilate refused, they fell prone all round his house and remained motionless for five days and nights.

The next day, Pilate took his seat on the tribunal in the Great Stadium, and summoned the mob on the pretext that he was ready to give them an answer. Instead he gave a pre-arranged signal to the soldiers to surround the Jews in full armour, and the troops formed a ring three deep. The Jews were dumbfounded at the unexpected sight, but Pilate, declaring that he would cut them to pieces unless they accepted the images of Caesar, nodded to the soldiers to bare their swords. At this the Jews as though by agreement fell to the ground in a body and bent their necks, shouting that they were ready to be killed rather than transgress the Law. Amazed at the intensity of their religious fervour, Pilate ordered the *signa* to be removed from Jerusalem forthwith.

We can imagine the talk and comment in the streets of Jaffa and Nazareth. Among such people Jesus had to think his own way to the truth about God and man; such were the people he attempted to persuade when he made his public appeal after the arrest of John the Hermit; and from such people came his first friends. He was living in a real world and dealing with real situations.

The Resistance Movement was not a bid for mere political freedom. Politics and religion were, for Jews, two sides of one coin. Hence among the people of the country, many different religious movements made a bid for their allegiance – Pharisees who were popular with the common people, groups such as we meet in the monastery of Qumran in the Jordan valley, Sadducees (wealthy priestly families) in Jerusalem, and followers of John the Hermit. The common people, as at all times, had their own varying, ambiguous attitudes. But it was the political situation which gave all these movements their focus; it is not an accident that Jesus was its victim.

The Outline of the Story

No biography of Jesus can be written; what we find in the Gospels, as we have said, are portraits of Jesus, painted some years later in a very different situation by people with deeply religious convictions. When we look at them we are looking at their portraits of their Master and Lord.

It has been widely held that, because this is so, we can know nothing of the actual story of Jesus and that it is impossible to separate the religious story from the originating incident which lies behind it. What is more, it is said, all we have are isolated stories strung together on a framework which is the creation of the evangelists themselves (this view is discussed in Part IV, Section 5, pp. 246 ff.). There is no questioning that the theological convictions of the writers – and of the communities they speak for – are deeply impressed on the stories they have given us. But is this all that can be said?

We have already emphasized that among the convictions of the early friends of Jesus was the conviction that the story which lay at the heart of all they most deeply believed was an authentic story – it had really happened. There is much evidence that they cared enough about the authenticity of their fundamental story to put down their memories of what Jesus actually did and said even when they themselves were puzzled about them and perhaps did not really understand why on these occasions he should have done and said what they reported. Is it likely that they did not remember also something of the broad outline of the course of his ministry?

Dr C. H. Dodd once wrote a famous article in the *Expository Times*, which is worth considering, though it has been questioned by some scholars. He looked at the editorial notes with which Mark linked his various stories about Jesus together ('generalizing summaries' which other more radical scholars admitted as such) and noted that, if we put them together, the striking thing 'is the way in which the summaries fall naturally into something like a continuous narrative'. Here they are:

After John's arrest Jesus came into Galilee proclaiming the Kingdom of God in the words, 'The time is fulfilled, and the Kingdom of God has drawn near: repent and believe in the Gospel.' He entered Capernaum; and on Sabbath days he would go to the synagogue and teach. All were in a state of astonishment at this teaching; for he used to teach them as one with authority, and not like the scribes. He went proclaiming in the synagogues throughout Galilee, and casting out demons. He went out to the seaside, and the whole crowd would come to him, and he would teach them. From Judaea and Jerusalem, from Idumaea and Peraea, and from the districts of Tyre and Sidon, a great throng hearing what he was doing, came to him. He told his disciples to have a boat waiting for him because of the crowds, so that they should not throng him; for he healed many, so that all who had plagues kept pressing upon him to touch him. The foul fiends, whenever they saw him, would fall before him, and cry out, 'Thou art the Son of God.' He would enjoin them not to make him known. He went up into the hill-country, and summoned those whom he himself wanted, and they came to him. He appointed the Twelve that they might be with him and that he might send them out to preach and to have authority to expel demons. So he appointed the Twelve (and here follows

their names). He summoned the Twelve and began to send them out two by two; he used to give them authority over foul fiends; and they went out and preached repentance. They kept expelling demons and anointing many sick folk with oil and healing them. The apostles gathered to Jesus and reported to him all that they had done and said.

So, if this argument is accepted, behind the individual stories (which came to Mark without any indications of time and place), behind the larger groups of material (genuinely continuous narratives, stories strung upon an itinerary, and stories connected by unity of theme), we can discern 'an outline of the whole ministry, designed, perhaps, as an introduction of the passion story, but serving also as a background of reference for the separate stories'.

What, then, is this broad 'outline' of the story of Jesus? We can mark these decisive moments:

His Call (the Baptism and Temptations)

The Proclamation of the 'Good News' ('Gospel') in Galilee

The Desert Meal ('The Feeding of the Five Thousand')

A Period of Retirement

The Incident near Caesarea Philippi and the Mountain Climb ('The Transfiguration')

The Journey to the South

The Last Days

Most of the older attempts to write 'the story of Jesus' took the whole structure of the gospel narratives as their pattern, beginning with the birth stories and proceeding to the stories of his death and resurrection. This procedure suits well if what we are concerned about is a meditation on the whole ministry of Jesus. But it gets the real story out of focus and blurs the edges of the dramatic and urgent quality of what seems actually to have happened. Let us approach the story in another way, and paint our own portrait of him, as far as the evidence permits.

The Climax of his Death

A cursory reading of the gospel material reveals the startling way in which the passion narrative – the story of the last few days – dominates the whole record. It was that death in the afternoon which not only haunted the imagination of his first friends but was for them the clue to the whole story.

The passion narrative (Mark 14 f.; Matt.26 f.; Luke 22 f.; John 18 f.) was probably the first account to be given permanent oral – and, later, written – form. From the earliest days, when his friends met to 'break bread' together and remember what happened on the night before he died, this story had been told as part of their meeting. Three different versions seem to have survived, those in Mark, in Luke (where it is now interwoven with Mark's account) and in John (where, if Dr Dodd is right, we find the third account). Some scholars, however, would explain the differences between the passion narratives as due simply to the extra-material the evangelists used and to their special theological views. This story of the passion dominates the whole account of the ministry of Jesus, occupying a predominant place in the telling.

Let us summarize it in its Roman version as we find it in Mark.

It begins a few days before the Passover feast with Jesus' sudden return, incognito, to the capital city. He had already apparently made arrangements for the hiring of a house. He sent two carefully chosen friends to a pre-arranged rendezvous, to be guided by a man 'carrying a water-jar' to an unknown house. Here they prepared a meal; here, after dark, came Jesus and his other friends.

The meal does not seem to have been a Passover meal, though this has been its association in Christian practice from earliest times. The evening meal had taken a prominent place in the common life which Jesus and his friends lived together; this was the last of such evening meals. Jesus gives it a unique meaning – giving himself, in the giving of the bread and the wine, to and for his friends, and through them, to all mankind. The earliest record we have of what happened is found in one of Paul's letters:

The Lord Jesus, on the night of his arrest, took bread and, after giving thanks to God, broke it and said: 'This is my body, which is for you; do this as a memorial of me.' In the same way, he took the cup after supper, and said: 'This cup is the new covenant sealed by my blood. Whenever you drink it, do this as a memorial of me' (I Cor.11.23–25 NEB).

Whatever the debates in Christian circles about the precise meaning of his words, their overwhelming significance is plain. His death was to make utterly clear all that he had lived for, and be the means by which his Father would 'reconcile the world to himself', at once the reality and hope of all humanity.

Meanwhile, Judas had left the company – a strange, enigmatic figure whose motives and intention have troubled the Christian conscience ever since. Whether it was his rigid loyalty to Jesus ('I know what he ought to do and I will force him to be himself'), his passionate belief that Jesus was the Messiah (but the Messiah of the Resistance Movement), his isolation from the others (he seems to have been the only southerner among them) can only be a matter of conjecture. Something like this, however, may be the explanation of his sudden suicide when all his dreams crashed about him and he realized the enormity of what he had done.

The others walk through the dark streets and out to the Olive Orchard, Gethsemane, perhaps on their way to Bethany where they may have been staying. Here they stayed, and here Jesus felt the crisis he was facing suddenly overwhelming him – 'horror and dismay came over him'. 'My heart is ready to break with grief,' he said. He felt, apparently, some contradiction between his own judgment and what he knew, deep in his heart, was his Father's will: 'Not what I will, but what thou wilt', he prayed.

Suddenly a posse of armed men break into the orchard. They seem to have thought that in the darkness they might arrest the wrong man; Judas makes identification unmistakable by kissing him.

The meeting of the Jewish Council and the trial before Pilate follow, with Peter's cowardly disavowal and the soldiers' horse-play, and by nine o'clock in the morning, he was crucified outside the city. The agony dragged on into the afternoon.

Then Jesus gave a loud cry and died. When the centurion who was standing opposite him saw how he died, he said, "Truly this man was a son of God."

It is a dramatic ending.

Whatever stories precede this plain and moving account of the death of Jesus are an exploration of how and why it ever happened.

For his friends, it was not just a brutal political murder – its political background counted least in their minds. It was its theological significance that mattered, and raised for them the whole character and work of God for all humanity. The reasons for their belief are found in their own accounts – in their selection of story and saying and their references to the Old Testament – and in other New Testament documents like the letters of Paul and the Fourth Gospel. But neither was it a mere political event for Jesus. It had long been clear to him that there was no escaping a brutal death (they are common in occupied countries); during the last months he had spoken of it to his friends to their consternation and bewilderment. It was bound up for him with what he believed was the whole work God was doing in and through him – the climax of human history.

That Jesus thought all this through in the light of the actual situation among his own people, their hopes and fears, their wild dreams and military preparations – asking himself how ordinary men and women can be persuaded to see what God is really like and what he actually is doing, criticizing their own assumptions and breaking the entail of their own history – is clear from the way in which the Desert Meal (Mark 6.30–44) was for him the great critical moment between his baptism and his death (see below, p. 273).

Such is the story which dominates the records. What brought him there?

His Call

The beginning of the story is the incident by River Jordan (Mark 1.9–11; Luke 3.21 f.; Matt.3.13–17).

The story of what happened by the river – and in the wilderness above it – must go back to Jesus himself. It is the story of his call – the first great crisis he had to face. It was a profound personal experience, not a public event as later it seems to have been thought (Matt. 3.14; Luke 3.22). No man talks easily of his profoundest experiences, and then only to his closest friends when some crisis demands it of him. The incident at Caesarea Philippi (Mark 8.27–30) was such a crisis for Jesus. His language and theme change after this – about God as 'Abba' ('Father'), about the kingdom of God and about his death. It is not improbable that his friends knew nothing about his experience at River Jordan and in the wilderness until Jesus, knowing they were completely misconceiving the work God had given him to do, for the first time told three of his closest friends on the Mountain Climb what had happened and what it meant to him in the light of the history of his people.

Jesus must have long pondered God's work among his own people and in the life of mankind during the years in Nazareth. His own deepening experience of God's presence, his prolonged study of the Scriptures, his participation in village debates led him to make up his mind about the nature of that work. News of the preaching of John the Hermit in the Jordan valley reached Nazareth. It was the moment when he must act. He went down to take his part in this moment of prophetic revival – and found himself face to face with his unique destiny.

Luke tells us that Jesus was praying after his baptism when he suddenly became aware of this unique destiny. In words reminiscent of a royal Psalm (Ps. 2) and one of the Servant Songs (Isa.42.1), he heard God calling him to his unique relationship with him and to the unique work he had to do. Whatever he may have thought before of his place in the renewal of God's real work to which John called men back, he knew now that into his hands was given its leadership. The words 'Son', 'the Beloved' (meaning 'Messiah' but not using the word), and 'Servant' were typical of his own thought and approach, revealing his intimate sense of God's presence ('Father') and his relationship to his fellow-men. They were to recur again and again, and they colour parable and poem.

He now knew his destiny, but he had again to think through what his destiny involved. This is the theme of the days he now spent in the loneliness of the wilderness of Judaea. The character of God's work among men was to be the principal point of disagreement between himself and his own countrymen, and· he summarized his thinking in this critical period in parabolic form – a form in which his mind was most at home – for his friends. His work was to be concerned neither with the dream of some earthly paradise ('bread alone') nor with political power ('all the kingdoms of the world') nor with browbeating the minds of men with wonders ('the pinnacle of the temple'). Persons can only be treated as persons ('You must love God with all you are, and your neighbour as yourself'); the intimate reality of God's love can only be made known in personal friendship. He chose to be a teacher and to wander through the villages – meeting people, talking to them, offering them his friendship, being their servant, proclaiming the Good News of the kingdom of God. There was no other way if God, whom, in the depth of his being, he knew as 'Father', was to be made plain to ordinary men and women – to men even of the Resistance Movement – not as an abstract truth but as a living experience changing their lives and refashioning the world they lived in. He was no dreamer. He knew well the complexity of human nature and the titanic task to which he was committed. He had his feet planted firmly on the ground. The range and depth of his thinking in the wilderness are distilled in the bold words in which Mark summarizes the theme of his Galilean campaign:

The time has come;
The kingdom of God is upon you;
Repent;
Trust in the Good News.

In Galilee

'After John had been arrested, Jesus came into Galilee proclaiming the Gospel of God' – so Mark (1.14 NEB); 'armed with the power of the Spirit' – so Luke (4.14 NEB).

Why Galilee? At first sight, this strikes us as a most unexpected decision for anyone who claimed to stand in the prophetic tradition. We can understand the fascination of the Jordan valley and the desert beyond (John's choice) with its symbolic harking-back to the desert traditions of the Jewish people and the story of their founder Moses. To Jesus, with his forward-looking mind, Jerusalem, the heart of the nation, would surely seem to be the one place where the 'Good News of God' should be proclaimed. We know how deeply the old city touched his imagination:

O Jerusalem, Jerusalem, the city that murders the prophets and stones the messengers sent to her!
How often have I longed to gather your

children as a hen gathers her brood under her wings! (Luke 13.34 NEB)

It was to the capital city he came to make his last and final proclamation to his people.

Why Galilee, then? It was the 'foreign province', suspect in the eyes of the more orthodox south, only recently – a hundred or so years before – reoccupied by a Jewish population. 'Are you a Galilean, too?' the Jewish authorities once rebuked Nicodemus. 'Study the scriptures and you will find that prophets do not come from Galilee' (John 7.52 NEB).

The answer may lie in the freshness, originality and imagination with which Jesus had thought out the strategy of his work. Galilee was, of course, his home territory, a countryside and people he knew and understood and loved – his precise observations of them gave him the imagery of parable and poem. But it was perhaps the independence and liveliness of its people, their unorthodoxy, that made him feel that here was the opportunity – which the rigid society of the south forbade – of his really being listened to. He was a northerner, and the north, which comes out so badly in the great southern histories of the Old Testament, had stubbornly held that there, rather than in the compromising south, the real religious traditions of the covenant had been maintained. Here, too, were large populations of foreigners – Greek cities, foreign landowners; such a mixed population was a more congenial centre for that public criticism of popular assumptions which he knew was to be part of what he had to say. All this is conjecture; we do not know. But we should note the boldness and originality of his decision.

Nazareth was no possible northern centre: 'A prophet will always be held in honour except in his own home town, and among his kinsmen and family.' The story of his visit there (Mark 6.1–6) is one of sullen resentment: 'What surprised him was that the people of his own village didn't trust him.' There is a story, too, of his mother's and brother's bewildered concern and his refusal to go outside to meet them. Looking round at those who were sitting in the circle about him he said 'Here are my mother and my brothers. Whoever does the will of God is my brother, my sister, my mother' (Mark 3.35 NEB).

Capernaum, the busy fishing-town on the north-west shore of the Sea of Galilee, became his centre. It was a customs station and an out-post of the Roman army, and close by passed the great road from Egypt to Damascus. Here he lived – he seems to have owned his own house – and from here he climbed the hills to the many villages and small towns.

Nobody remembered the details of these exciting months. Mark begins by giving us what we might call 'A Day in the Life of Jesus' (1.21–38), where the sort of man he was, his informal way of dealing with people, his concern with human need are clearly painted. It ends with a story that highlights the dilemma that constantly faced Jesus.

> Very early next morning he got up and went out. He went away to a lonely spot and remained there in prayer. But Simon and his companions searched him out, found him, and said, 'They are all looking for you.' He answered, 'Let us move on to the country towns in the neighbourhood; I have to proclaim my message there also; that is what I came out to do' (Mark 1.35–38 NEB).

We must come back to this dilemma; let us now look at the other memories of his friends.

The stories in Mark bring out vividly the character of Jesus' whole approach to his work – his profound concern with people, with 'all sorts and conditions of men'. No prejudices proscribed his meeting them; no taboos held him back. He would touch a leper in healing him (1.41) in spite of the irrational fears that popularly surrounded this skin disease. A madman, a little girl, an unknown woman in the crowd, a blind man stand witness to the quiet generosity of his spirit – a feature of his character that common people and artists and poets down the centuries have seized on as the most striking thing about him. The emphasis of these stories is not on their remarkable character (this they assume but do not enlarge upon) but on their power and concern through which the reality of God's presence made itself known. 'Power' and 'concern' are linked inseparably together and lie at the heart of his impact upon ordinary men and women. No better commentary on these stories can be found than what may be Paul's thumb-nail sketch of Jesus' character in his letter to the Corinthian church (I Cor.13.4–7): 'He was never in a

hurry and always kindness itself. He never envied anybody at all, never boasted about himself. He was never snobbish or rude or selfish. He didn't keep on talking about the wrong things other people do; remembering the good things was happiness enough. He was tough – he could face anything. And he never lost his trust in God, or in men and women. He never lost hope and he never gave in.'

Luke, who sets all these stories on a larger canvas, touches something of their deeper quality – the compassion of Jesus which crosses all the barriers which we so often, in a false self-defence, erect between one group and another, one person and another. His stories about Jesus and the Roman officer (7.1–10) and the woman 'who was living an immoral life in the town' (7.36–50) foreshadow that great concern for people of every race which dominates his Gospel. Here, in Jesus himself, we see the roots of that universality and catholicity which alone can match God's love.

Such overriding of the accepted religious taboos of orthodox society could only bring him into debate and conflict with the authorities. This is a developing theme of Mark's account. Here was a fundamental disagreement about the whole nature of real religion, and here is the explanation why, in the long run, Jesus' bitterest enemies were the good synagogue people. It is brought boldly out in the story of Jesus' evening meals in Capernaum. It makes utterly clear the divergence of concern:

> When Jesus was at table in his house, many bad characters – tax-gatherers and others – were seated with him and his disciples; for there were many who followed him. Some doctors of the law who were Pharisees noticed him eating in this bad company, and said to his disciples, 'He eats with tax-gatherers and sinners!' Jesus overheard and said to them, 'It is not the healthy that need a doctor, but the sick' (Mark 2.15–17 NEB).

There follow the stories about fasting and the disciples' plucking ears of corn as they walked through the cornfields. That Mark was clearly aware of the significance of these incidents is shown by the sayings of Jesus he associates with the stories: 'Fresh skins for new wine!' and 'The sabbath was made for the sake of man, not man for the sabbath' – which put their finger on the revolutionary nature of the whole ministry of Jesus. He adds at the end of this group of stories the words: 'The Pharisees . . . began plotting against him with the partisans of Herod to see how they could make away with him' (Mark 3.6 NEB). No wonder; what his friends seem to have been unaware of was increasingly clear to the authorities.

But it was not only the religious authorities who came into conflict with him; Galilee was one of the strongholds of the Resistance Movement, and at last the issues between them and Jesus had to be brought into the open. The whole Galilean campaign is brought to an abrupt end at the Desert Meal (Mark 6.30–44). This provoked the great crisis in the ministry of Jesus. After this, he never went back to Galilee again – except once when he passed through it incognito (Mark 9.30 f.). Before that last journey south, there intervenes a period of retirement where the whole struggle in the wilderness of Judaea is re-enacted, and Jesus seems to have been compelled to rethink through the principles and purposes of all that he was doing.

We are told that the incident of the Desert Meal happened almost by accident.

Jesus and his friends had set off in a boat to find a spot away from the crowds where they could find some rest from the incessant demands of the people. They were recognized in the boat and the crowds hurried along the coast. Jesus summed up the situation and put the boat into shore. The crowd was an organized crowd – five thousand men. Though this story had, by the time Mark was written, been the subject of much Christian meditation and preaching (in which its religious meaning had been predominant), it had not altogether lost touch with the original occasion. The grass was 'green' (it was spring) and at the common meal they sat down in military companies ('fifties' and 'hundreds'). The Fourth Gospel suggests that it was an informal meeting of members of the Resistance Movement ('They meant to come and seize him to proclaim him king' – 6.15).

We are not concerned at the moment with all the details of this story, but with its main intention. Jesus recognized what was happening – 'His heart went out to them, because they were like sheep without a shepherd.' The words have Old Testament echoes. They echo the story of the prophet Micaiah and King Ahab where Micaiah describes a vision he had seen: 'I saw all Israel scattered upon the mountains, as sheep that have no shepherd; and the Lord said, "These have no master; let each return to his home in peace"' (I Kings 22.17). Here the words 'sheep without a shepherd' mean a 'nation without a government, an army without a commander, a leaderless mob, a danger to themselves and to everybody else'. So the five thousand men in front of him seem to Jesus.

He now shows his superb ability to handle men. They shared a common meal together and the talk went on into the afternoon. Then he got the men to disperse without any outbreak of violence. 'After taking leave of them, he went up the hillside to pray.'

The aftermath was, at first glance, disastrous. 'From that time on,' says the Fourth Gospel, 'many of his disciples withdrew and no longer went about with him' (6.66 NEB). From now on Jesus is a lonely figure. Only a handful of his friends remained loyal; some months later, in Jerusalem, even they abandoned him. He died alone.

Such an event had to happen some time. Jesus had to make publicly clear that he could have no part in the Resistance Movement, that its ideals and his had no meeting place, that he was looking beyond the understandable political parochialism of his people to the wider world of God's whole work in the world of men.

Nothing is clearer from these stories than that Jesus had to come to his fundamental convictions and to hold them the hard way – as all of us have to win and hold our convictions. There is no royal road to certainty in these matters. The Desert Meal led inevitably to his obscure exile in the north, in alien territory across the borders of his homeland.

In Retirement

Jesus was not exempted from those inner struggles of the spirit which, in times of deep personal crisis, all men have to face. We cannot, with the evidence available to us – the memories of his friends – say very much about what he himself went through. But that he knew this darkness of the soul, the story of his wrestling in the wilderness of Judaea and the agony of

Gethsemane are evidence enough. The silence that now shrouds his story needs some explanation. His friends knew little of what happened – what he did and where he went. They tell us a story of his meeting with a foreign woman when he wanted to remain unrecognized (Mark 7.24–30). Then silence until they meet him again near Caesarea Philippi and three of them climb a mountain with him (Mark 8.27–9.13). What we notice about these last two stories is their echoes of the baptism and the temptations, evidence of what he had been struggling to get clear in his retirement in the northern hills.

With these stories in mind, remembering the crisis of the Desert Meal, we catch a glimpse of the inner debate which must have occupied him in those lonely days.

The Galilean campaign has apparently ended in disaster – his friends still uncomprehending, the religious authorities suspicious, the Resistance Movement hostile. This wide rejection made him re-examine his methods. Was the way he had followed in Galilee the way in which the work God had given him to do ought to be done? He had approached men as men; he had given himself to individual people; his only weapons – persuasion and the integrity of his own vision. Was this the only way – or was there some other? Can the care and love of his Father be brought home to anybody by any other way than by loving them, and in his love of them trying to help them to see that this alone was the reality through which human life can have the depth and richness and joy which is our native heritage? We put this in our own language; but this is the fundamental human issue that not only Jesus but all who are concerned with the remaking of human history have to face. He had settled it at the beginning in the Judaean wilderness; he now reaffirmed it in the northern highlands. There is no other way.

He takes up his work again, and meets his friends near Caesarea Philippi.

Near Caesarea Philippi

Now there is a new note, as we have already hinted, in what he has to say. The way of love is the way of suffering. The shadow of his own inescapable death falls across his path.

The incident at Caesarea Philippi is crucial:

On the way he asked his disciples, 'Who do men say I am?' They answered, 'Some say John the Baptist, others Elijah, others one of the prophets.' 'And you,' he asked, 'who do you say I am?' Peter replied, 'You are the Messiah.' Then he gave them strict orders not to tell anyone about him; and he began to teach them that the Son of man had to undergo great sufferings, and to be rejected by the elders, chief priests and doctors of the law; to be put to death, and to rise again three days afterwards. He spoke about it plainly. At this Peter took him by the arm and began to rebuke him. But Jesus turned round, and, looking at his disciples, rebuked Peter. 'Away with you, Satan', he said: 'you think as men think, not as God thinks' (Mark 8.27–33 NEB).

It was a great thing for Peter to say – when the desertion of Jesus by friend and foe alike was staring them in the face. But his words show that he still had little inkling of the radical newness of Jesus' own vision, a fact which Matthew's expanded account misses (Matt.16.3–23). His loyalty to Jesus was unshaken; his understanding of Jesus had yet to begin. We can see in this conversation Jesus' own suspicion of conventional language – he did not like the word 'Messiah'. But it was something other that was now dominating his mind – the cost of love, and his whole-hearted acceptance of what he knew this involved for him. Words alone were no longer enough to shake men out of their conventional obsessions and open their minds to the only truth that mattered. He must face love's ultimate demand.

A week later, he took three of his close friends and climbed with them upward to the snowline of Mt Hermon. That they shared with Jesus some exalted spiritual experience – such an experience as he had had alone by River Jordan – is clear. He took them into his confidence and opened his heart to them. It was perhaps on this climb, as we have suggested, that they heard for the first time what had happened by River Jordan. Moses and Elijah were the theme of his conversation – Moses the founder of the people and Elijah the representative of the prophets, the whole history of God's dealing with humanity and his place in that great, strange work.

Mark's account is this:

Six days later Jesus took Peter, James and John with him and led them up a high mountain where they were alone; and in their presence he was transfigured; his clothes became dazzling white, with a whiteness no bleacher on earth could equal. They saw Elijah appear, and Moses with him, and there they were, conversing with Jesus. Then Peter spoke: 'Rabbi,' he said, 'how good it is that we are here! Shall we make three shelters, one for you, one for Moses and one for Elijah?' (For he did not know what to say; they were so terrified.) Then a cloud appeared, casting its shadow over them, and out of the cloud came a voice: 'This is my Son, my Beloved; listen to him.' And now suddenly, when they looked round, there was nobody to be seen but Jesus alone with themselves.

On their way down the mountain, he enjoined them not to tell anyone what they had seen until the Son of man had risen from the dead. They seized upon those words, and discussed among themselves what this 'rising from the dead' could mean (Mark 9.2–10 NEB).

There was nothing more to do now, except to take up his work again in the only way he knew it could be done; but this time, not in Galilee but in the south. He passed through Galilee incognito.

In the South

The journey south and Jesus' movements until the last week in Jerusalem are shrouded in obscurity. Dr T. W. Manson has called our attention to the importance of the brief sentence in which Mark summarizes it:

On leaving those parts [in the north] he came into the regions of Judaea and Transjordan; and when a crowd gathered round him once again, he followed his usual practice and taught them (10.1 NEB).

Judaea and Transjordan, the countryside east of the river, are now the area of his southern campaign, and the quoted words seem to imply a wider ministry than the account that follows seems to allow for.

Did he move south in the late spring, passing down the east side of the river, and come to Jerusalem at the beginning of that last week? Such is the impression that the records give us; but we must remember that the account as we now have it had been used in the worship of the church where all the events of the Passion were celebrated together. Perhaps the journey took longer, and perhaps Jesus spent a much longer time east of the river (so Mark's brief words quoted above would seem to suggest) than a mere journey south would permit.

Dr Manson has suggested that Jesus came to Jerusalem in October when he entered the city on a donkey, dealt with the shopkeepers in the foreigners' court of the temple, and was engaged in open debate with the religious authorities. It was then that the authorities 'began to look for a way to arrest him, for they saw that the parable [of the Vineyard Tenants] was aimed at them; but they were afraid of popular feeling, so they left him alone and went away' (Mark 12.1–12).

Jesus had made up his mind to make his final appeal to his people when they gathered for the feast of Passover in the next spring. He did not intend to have his hand forced. So he spent the winter outside the jurisdiction of the Jerusalem authorities in Transjordan, and returned to the city a few days before he was arrested. It has always seemed that the elaborate preparations that were made to secure his secret arrest away from popular interference, to suborn one of his friends and to come to some agreement about all this with Pilate, would take far more time than a few days. If the course of events was as Dr Manson has suggested, there would be time enough.

The two incidents which need comment – whether they happened in the last week or whether the winter separated them from the supper in the upper room and his arrest – are Jesus' entry into the city and his action in the foreigners' court of the temple (Mark 11.1–10; 15–19). They are both, along with his giving of the bread and wine in the upper room, 'acted parables', a form of proclamation which can be noticed in the stories of the prophets, especially Isaiah, Hosea and Jeremiah (cf. Isa.8.1–4; Hos.1.2–9; Jer.18.1–12).

The entry into the city made clear his whole approach to God's work. He had made secret preparations for it – arranging for the hire of a donkey with a farmer in a village near the city, as he made secret arrangements for the hire of the house. He rode in to claim his right as God's Chosen Leader. Did he remember those days a thousand years before when his ancestor David, after the southern rebellion, rode back on a warhorse to reclaim the city along the same road? (II Sam.19.15–20.2). He was no such leader. The words of Zechariah's poem were probably in his mind:

> Lo, your King comes to you;
>   triumphant and victorious is he,
> humble and riding on an ass,
>   on a colt the foal of an ass (Zech.9.9).

All he had done and said in the preceding ministry was symbolized in this act. It must have been intended for his friends, as was the symbolism of the supper. If it happened in the October, he joined the pilgrims coming into the city for the feast of Tabernacles and used the occasion for his own purposes. Had it been a public claim to messiahship, it is strange that the authorities, looking round for evidence to incriminate Jesus, did not seize upon this occasion as the kind of evidence they were looking for. But the significance of the 'acted parable' is quite clear.

Jesus' 'Cleansing of the Temple' was the second acted parable, and was a public one. It is important to notice that the market was held in the foreigners' court. Jesus' action, taking the people by surprise, was a declaration of the universality of the Good News – 'My house shall be called a house of prayer for all nations,' he quoted, and added 'but you have made it a robbers' cave.' He was later asked by the authorities what right he had to act like this. It was on this occasion he told the story of Vineyard Tenants (Mark 12.1–9), whose unmistakable point precipitated the Jewish government's decision to get rid of him.

It was now clear that the Jewish leaders were going to stand no more nonsense. When Jesus returned in the spring, their plans were laid. They caught him at night in an orchard; his execution was now only a matter of time.

The Strategy of Jesus

We have sketched, in bold strokes, the course of the three brief years of Jesus' ministry as suggested by the 'framework' that lies behind the gospel material; the political and religious situation he had to deal with explains the brevity of that ministry and illuminates its pattern.

But one decisive aspect of his work – his strategy – must now be dealt with, an aspect which needs a broader background to bring its importance out into the open.

Jesus was a realist. God's work was, for him, not some ideal pattern forcibly super-imposed on the intractable material of human history; it was the inner pattern of history itself. God was 'Creator' as well as 'Father'; he was not, as it were, caught out by the recalcitrance of men and women. All history is the theatre of the drama of his love – he 'makes the sun rise on good and bad alike, and sends the rain on the honest and dishonest' (Matt.5.45). It is this conviction of Jesus which is brought out in the developing argument of the Fourth Gospel and is summarized in the words 'My Father has never yet ceased his work, and I am working too' (John 5.17 NEB).

How was God working out his purposes in the history of humanity? Jesus had the Scriptures of his people as his guide. He had meditated deeply on them and he quotes them with an originality and insight which surprises us with its freshness still. The theme of the Old Testament – its 'salvation-history' – is that God does not dragoon men, but wins them through his 'steadfast love', speaking to the world through 'his people'. This is the insight of Moses; it is embodied in the idea of the covenant. But who are his people? Moses welded the scattered tribes into a people, linked by their loyalty to Yahweh. The tribal confederacy was to be 'the people of God'. This proved politically unstable. David took the idea further by developing the tribal confederacy into a nation. Is then the 'nation' the instrument of God's active love in human history? The deviating story of the southern and northern kingdoms raised serious doubts. The theme of the prophetic debate was the frustrating inadequacy of the political unit, the nation, as a vehicle of God's love, and the proposal of a more informal group (the 'remnant' of Isaiah's phrase) whose fellowship should be founded simply on loyalty to God who would be the leader of nation and world alike. The disaster of the exile and the rebirth of the city, the Maccabaean rebellion and the political and religious situation as he found it in his own day, were the background of Jesus' own thinking – a background exemplified in the ambiguity of the Pharisees and the anger of the Zealots (see Part IV, Section 3, pp. 232 f.). Jesus went back to the heart of the Old Testament, the witness of the prophets, especially the books of Isaiah and Jeremiah – books some of whose profoundest words were in his mind at his baptism and at supper on the night before he died.

His reading of the Old Testament led him to the conviction that no *political* entity can be the effective vehicle of God's love, only a genuinely religious society the loyalties of whose members were to God alone, freely transcending and gathering up in themselves all the other loyalties of kin, race, nation, class. If his work was to go on, it would be through such a group or society. Hence his calling of disciples 'to be with him', with the 'twelve' as their centre. The very number 'twelve' recalls the tribal confederacy – they were to be the nucleus of God's 'people', to be in the wider life of mankind like 'salt' and 'leaven' and 'light', and to live, as he himself lived, as the 'servants' of their fellow-men. Through their life among their fellows, God's love, the fundamental fact of human history – the source of its reality and the principle of its existence – would be proclaimed and acknowledged. God's love would establish itself as the joyfully accepted way of life, not automatically or by threat, but through the gladly accepted sufferings of those who humbly received God's love themselves and, in its strength, lived for others, sharing their common life and being involved in their common destiny.

Two words bring out what Jesus intended their function in society to be. They were his 'apprentices' ('disciples') and they were to be 'mixers' ('apostles' – 'sent out'). They were to set the pace:

Don't judge and you won't be judged,
don't condemn and you won't be condemned;
forgive and you will be forgiven;
give and you will be given;
   good measure,
   pressed down,
   shaken together,
   running over,
   will be poured into your lap.
The measure you give
will be the measure you get (see Luke 6.37 f.).

We can see something of Jesus' working-out of these convictions even in the fragmentary accounts of the men he chose as his closest friends – 'the twelve' – and particularly in the man he marked out as their leader – Simon 'the Rock' ('Peter') as he nicknamed him. The four surviving lists of the twelve (Mark 3.16–19a; Matt.10.2–4 – a second edition of Mark's list; Luke's two lists, Luke 6.14–16 and Acts 1.13 [the eleven]; there are further traditions about three of them – Andrew, Philip and Thomas – in John) are perplexingly different from one another and show that, by the time Mark was written, the twelve were 'traditional figures of the past'. Of eight of them we know little or nothing. Four of them come to life in the memories of Jesus' friends: the two brothers, James and John, whom he nicknamed 'The Thunderers'; Judas Iscariot, 'the man from Kerioth' (a town either south of Hebron or in old Moabite country); and especially Peter, of whom many stories are told both in the Gospels and in Acts.

We note that they were all laymen – a fact which, in the light of the subsequent history of the Christian community, is surely significant. Four of them we know were fishermen, one a customs-officer. The presence among them of a member of the Resistance Movement – Simon the Zealot – and the lone figure of Judas Iscariot show the risks Jesus was willing, like all true teachers, to take. All ventures in genuine fellowship involve immense risks – anything can happen in the close companionship of men of independent minds (which Jesus encouraged) and of different backgrounds and assumptions. This, too, in the light of Christian history, is startlingly significant.

But it is Peter of Bethsaida (John 1.44) whose rough but loyal heart speaks for the common man in whom Jesus, under God, put his trust for the future of humanity. In the stories told of him he is painted 'warts and all': his impulsiveness and dogged loyalty; his courage – and the breaking of his courage; his qualities as a 'Beloved Captain' – and his lack of imaginative insight (Gal.2.11–14); his slowness to understand (Mark 8.27–33) – and his fearless quickness to act when the truth came home to him (Acts 10.1–11.18); and his manly love of his Master which held him to the end (John 21.15–19). In Peter we meet the kind of 'apprentice' Jesus wanted, and in Jesus' handling of him we see his greatness as a teacher. Into such hands as Peter's he was ready to commit the whole destiny of his work.

As Jesus realized the realities of the human situation in which he found himself – the rigid and conventional and unimaginative habits of organized religion, the passions and blindness of existing political societies – he set himself to the work of calling into existence the nucleus of a new community (but a community which had its roots in the past history of his people): the community of his 'friends' (cf. John 15.15) whose principle of existence is their humble acceptance, centred in their loyalty to himself, of God's 'amazing love' as the source and principle of their own life, and through whom the whole world might become his Father's family. We touch here Jesus' profoundest political and social insight; and we note that its ground and justification are to be found in his religious insight: God as 'Abba' ('Father').

The Man Behind the Story

When we stand back and look at the story of Jesus as a whole, as we see it shining through the 'portraits' his friends painted, he stands before us in unambiguous clarity. Nobody can be in doubt about what sort of man he was, though we can confuse ourselves with a too particular concern with the debatable details.

What strikes us most forcibly about him is his sanity and his maturity. As we watch him through these brief years moving towards his tragic destiny – his execution outside his capital city – he stands out among his fellows as the *real man*. His sense of God's presence ('Abba!'), his life lived for his fellow men, his steady and penetrating vision make us aware that we are meeting for the first time a man who was 'true man', showing us the fullness and richness and joy of being really alive. We watch him dealing with men and women – and children; we say 'This is how we ought to live among our fellows'. We watch him dealing with the evil that shatters our common life and makes us act as caricatures of men; we say 'This is the sort of person we ought to be'. We watch him assailed and hurt by the brutal realities of his immediate society – 'man's inhumanity to man' – and marvel at his freedom from its corrupting obsessions; we say 'We ought to be free like that.'

We note other aspects of his life which reveal his insights and 'soaring mind'. He chose to be a *teacher*. He is the only great religious leader who seems to have asked himself questions like these: 'How do ordinary people learn?' 'How do they become aware of God's presence and their own destiny?' and 'How can they be helped to make sense of their confusing experiences?'. He is 'the greatest teacher of the western world'; his ways of dealing with ordinary people as a teacher have come to their own only in the context of our modern debate about education. His parabolic method – his approach to the minds of ordinary men and women – is not an imitation of old illustrative methods found in past teachers, but a new venture in opening men's minds and encouraging them to think for themselves and be critical of their prejudices, challenging their conventions and provoking them to ask questions (see Part IV, Section 8, p. 286).

When we come to look more closely at his reported sayings, we become aware that he brought to his whole presentation of his convictions a great poetic imagination – he was a *poet*, holding his own with Dante and Shakespeare. His simplicity is deceptive. He created a body of sayings which have caught the imagination of the world and provided the greatest minds with an enduring stimulus. 'He is the greatest artist of us all', said van Gogh. It is not an accident that the profoundest commentary of his life and words is to be found, not in the works of theologians and scholars, but in the works of artists and in the lives of countless ordinary men and women. His parables and poems have a profound imaginative unity.

We may pause, for a moment, to consider one implication of the fact that Jesus was, in the technical sense, a poet. We know nothing – except the story Luke tells (2.41–52) – about Jesus' boyhood. But if he was a poet, and if his parables and poems are not just teaching devices but the way in which he habitually thought and in which he himself came to his insights, then the imagery of parable and poem take on a new meaning. We know, from the continuing debate about the nature of poetry initiated by Wordsworth and Coleridge, how deeply the experience of a poet's boyhood moulds his later poetry. The imagery of Jesus' parables have every mark of being largely what he remembered from boyhood, used, remade, then formed into vehicles of his profoundest insights – the raw material of his mature vision. They are a surer guide to what boyhood meant to him than much of the guesswork in which we indulge.

But more than this, he was a *leader of men*. Members of the Resistance Movement wanted to 'make him king' – that needs some explanation. The story of Peter walking with him through the darkened streets after that final supper speaks for countless others.

> Jesus said, 'You will all fall from your faith; for it stands written: "I will strike the shepherd down and the sheep will be scattered." Nevertheless, after I am raised again, I will go on before you into Galilee.' Peter answered, 'Everyone else may fall away, but I will not.' Jesus said, 'I tell you this: today, this very night, before the cock crows twice, you yourself will disown me three times.' But he insisted and repeated: 'Even if I must die with you, I will never disown you' (Mark 14.27–31 NEB).

Jesus had an extraordinary power of holding men. He was honest and direct and could be witheringly frank. He never played for popularity; his honesty cost him temporary rejection by many of his early friends. But immediately after his death five hundred of them (I Cor.15.6) gathered together; and from that moment the circle of followers spread over the known world. There is no magic about this (though many other things must be said about it); he knew how to speak to men and how to lead them.

There is something else to be said. His hold over men was more than 'leadership'. There was a strangeness about him that puzzled and held men – especially those who came to know him intimately. His 'mighty works' were not just the sort of things Pharisees and others could do (cf. Luke 11.19). 'If it is by the finger of God that I drive out the devils, then be sure the kingdom of God has already come upon you.' These 'mighty works' were moments when, for those who could recognize it, the reality of God was brought home to them. There are other moments recorded when the 'strangeness' of Jesus scared his friends. 'They were on the road, going up to Jerusalem, Jesus leading the way; and the disciples were filled with awe; while those who followed behind were afraid' (Mark 10.32 NEB).

Here we perceive that aspect of Jesus' total 'witness' which, vaguely apprehended in his life-time, was seen and recognized by his friends after his resurrection with unmistakable clarity. He was not only leader; he was *Lord*. There was a strange authority about him which they found both disconcerting and arresting. He not only spoke with authority and not as the scribes (Mark 1.22); there was an authority about his whole life – an authority which still speaks through his life and words, and overrides the stumbling attempts of his friends to describe or explain it. This is the essential Jesus. In the light of later Christian experience, this is the central thing about him.

The Heart of the Story

If any brief words could put what is the heart of the Christian faith, they might be these words: 'God is love . . . We love because he loved us first' (I John 4.8,19). Love – *agape*, to give the New Testament word – is the clue to our human story, because it is its originating fact and its enduring principle. The world is God's world; he is Lord of history; and he is love. Our awareness of this is supremely the work of Jesus; 'he made God real'. This is the heart of his story. For his story is the story of love in action. This is what it means to 'be human' – genuinely human: 'Jesus lived love; God is love and has made men for love'.

Love is not the weak and sentimental thing that we often make it. It is robust, venturesome, utterly open to the varied complexity of human relationships. It is tough, as Paul said – 'there is nothing that love cannot face' (I Cor.13.7). Jesus made this plain (cf. John 1.18).

The crowds of Galilee and Jerusalem pass through the stories which Jesus' friends told about him: farmers, fishermen, tax-collectors, housewives, children, religious leaders in village and city; members of the Resistance Movement and Roman soldiers; governor and high priest. Jesus meets them with openness and friendship; he is frank and critical and speaks in plain language; but behind agreement or disagreement, approval or reproof, stands his profound concern for people as people. He could mark insight and commend it – whether he met it in a doctor of the law or in a Roman officer.

His parables – and there are about sixty of them, whole or in fragment – are crowded with people. What marks them (if we could cease treating them as mere pious moral homilies) is the breadth of their sympathy (a rascal of a manager was the 'hero' of one of his stories) and their profound insight into human nature. Here are real people, and the situations in which we meet them are real situations. These stories are explorations of the meaning of love as the working principle of human action. Jesus expected ordinary men and women to see the point he was making – this was the only way in which human situations could be dealt with – and he put it so that hard-headed people could see what he was driving at and be in no doubt. He was revealing the way in which things actually work, situations actually develop, human meeting be really human meeting. His charge against the people of his time was that they were like 'children sitting in the market-place and shouting to one another' (Luke 7.32) – they were not grown-up. Love is really grown-up; it is the way of maturity.

But most of all we see what love means when we come to the story of his death. It was his concern for men and women that brought him to that lonely hill – and his refusal to let any other way have any part of his decisions. It was precipitated by the treachery of one of his closest friends, but he stood his ground. The cross, for Christian and non-Christian alike, is the symbol and reality of the supremacy and triumph of love.

So the heart of the story (this should guide us to the way we should deal with it in our teaching) is the exploration of love; its character, its manner, its ability to deal with an unpredictable world, its maturity and its cost, its source in God's love of us. 'We must pass through many hardships,' as Paul is reported to have once said – what mother or father or friend, what person who has ever loved, does not know that? There is no 'short cut' to dealing with human relationships; all our failures and disasters come from trying to take one. When we do so, we find ourselves driven to treat persons as less than persons – numbers, units, individuals. But we are persons; love is the only way persons can live as persons together.

This is the heart of the story of Jesus.

This is the point John is making when, at the very beginning of the Book of the Passion (John 13.1–9), the great conclusion of his dramatic presentation of the ministry of Jesus, he puts this story as the supremely characteristic story about Jesus:

> The Great Feast of the Jewish people was near. Jesus was having supper with his friends.
> He got up from the table and took off his long robe. He picked up a towel and tied it round him like a belt. He poured water into a basin, and began to wash his friends' feet.
> When he had washed their feet, he picked up his long robe, put it on and sat down again at table.
> 'I have shown you what you must do,' he said. 'You must do what I have just done for you. Believe me –
> A slave is not greater than his master,
> a messenger than the man who sent him.
> I hope you understand all this. You will be happy men if you live as I have shown you.'

Not the End but the Beginning

The death of Jesus, we now know, was not the end but the beginning. Indeed, the stories we have been examining are no cool historical accounts – they are all written in the light of the amazing new experiences which followed his death. It is this that gives them their peculiar elusiveness: they are about events that really happened, but events that had an original strangeness – a strangeness that could not be expunged from any record of them if they were to be honestly reported; and more, events that were the prelude to the new shared experience which was at once an awareness of God's love 'shed abroad in their hearts' and an inescapable sense of the continuing presence of the risen Lord. Paul's words give this experience its classic expression: 'The life I now live is not my life, but the life which Christ lives in me; and my present bodily life is lived by faith in the Son of God, who loved me and sacrificed himself for me' (Gal.2.20 NEB).

Let us consider the reports of the decisive experiences which brought into being the Christian community and revolutionized for his friends the way they remembered his ministry and death and made them describe the story not as though it was just something that had happened in the past but had an enduring contemporary quality for all who accepted Jesus as Lord. There would have been no such community without them; only, possibly, a dwindling Jewish sect, one among many, to be scattered and destroyed by the war of AD 66–70.

The earliest account we have is found in one of Paul's letters written in Ephesus somewhere about AD 56 – nearly thirty years after the death of Jesus. But it probably goes back to within a few years of his death, Paul's words suggest, to his own baptismal initiation in Damascus City, about AD 36, some seven years after Jesus died.

> I handed on to you the facts which had been imparted to me: that Christ died for our sins, in accordance with the scriptures; that he was buried; that he was raised to life on the third day, according to the scriptures; and that he appeared to Cephas, and afterwards to the Twelve. Then he appeared to over five hundred of our brothers at once, most of whom are still alive, though some have died. Then he appeared to James, and afterwards to all the apostles.
>
> In the end he appeared even to me; though this birth of mine was monstrous, for I have persecuted the church of God and am therefore inferior to all other apostles – indeed not fit to be called an apostle. However by God's grace I am what I am (I Cor.15.3–10 NEB).

We note the brevity and reticence of the report: 'he appeared' – a word which can describe visible sight or spiritual experience. Of the reality of what happened there was no doubt – the new life of his first friends was rooted in it; but to give an intelligible and coherent account of it was another matter. Paul's long discussion of the questions it raises that follows the account we have quoted, and the later records in the Gospels, are their attempt to do so.

The very divergences in the gospel reports bespeak their honesty – they give the stories that were current in the great centres of the Christian community and they do not try to make them fit. The ending to Mark is now lost; the present ending (16.6–20) is a much later addition, one among several added endings. The appearances they list are these: Matthew – to the women, to the eleven in Galilee; Luke – to two disciples (not of the 'twelve') on the road to Emmaus, to the eleven in the upper room; John – to Mary of Magdala; to the ten in the upper room, to the eleven a week later, again gathered there, to seven on the beach of the Sea of Galilee; the added ending to Mark – to Mary of Magdala, to two 'as they were walking on their way into the country', to the eleven 'at table' (this reads like a summary made from the earlier accounts). Paul's list is different still: to Cephas, to the twelve, to 'five hundred of our brothers at once', to James (Jesus' brother), to 'all the apostles', then 'to me'.

All the reports, except Paul's, agree that the tomb was empty (Paul did not mention the tomb). This was no proof of Jesus' resurrection – it was susceptible of several explanations, and it created its own problems – but it was a fact and they all report it. The account in the Fourth Gospel is supposed by some scholars to be a criticism of too naïve an understanding of what happened; at any rate, it calls attention, as Luke does, to another fact – Peter and the 'other disciple' were not deeply impressed by the discovery: 'As yet they did not know the scripture, that he must rise from the dead. Then [they] went back to their homes' (John 20.9 f.). 'The story appeared to them to be nonsense' (Luke 24.11 NEB; cf. also v. 21).

We note, too, if we read the reports in chronological order, an increasing emphasis on the materiality of the appearances. There is, further, a divergence among them as to where his appearances to the eleven took place; Matthew says Galilee; Luke Jerusalem; John Jerusalem and then (in the appendix to the Gospel) Galilee.

The debate among Christians as to what reportable events happened and what sort of events they were is obviously as old as our earliest records. It has been an intense debate in recent centuries; the rise of scientific inquiry and the later development of historical methods of research have brought it acutely before the minds of Christians and non-Christians alike. It is not likely to be concluded. For we are dealing with an event which is not a purely historical event. It is closely involved in the reality of Christian experience, not just another incident in the unfolding story. It was not the reports of what had happened to a limited number of witnesses that changed men's lives; it was the event itself. It was the revealing climax which made all the difference to the story. They could only say 'God raised him from death'.

The evidence suggests that in the few weeks following the death of Jesus some of his friends – some named, some not – had certain experiences of Jesus risen. Paul is careful to state that his own experience, which he lists with the others, fell outside this limited period. These special 'appearances' then ceased; the later experiences of the risen Christ, open to all who accepted him, were real but different. If we remember the uniqueness of this event (the resurrection of Jesus was not in the same category as other reported 'resurrections' of men; it was the defeat of death), these reports do not strike us, after the strictest historical scrutiny, as fictitious accounts that owe their existence to human imagination; they strike us as honest attempts to give some account of real experiences that defied all efforts to give a coherent account of them. Of their authenticity the early friends of Jesus had no doubt – their new experience of God, their new fellowship with one another, their new understanding of human life and history were not something they had struggled to achieve; they were 'given'. The spirit of Jesus was present with them; they were not just imitating him. The final evidence for them that these reports were reports of what had actually happened – 'Christ was raised to life' – and not reports of queer hallucinations, was the reality of their new life and fellowship which was open to public scrutiny.

It was in the light of this transforming experience of Christ risen that later in the century the stories of Jesus' birth came to circulate. These are not historical accounts, but stories which sing the wonder and glory of Jesus. They are beautiful and profound stories which haunt the imagination – the coming of Jesus to humble shepherds and eastern astrologers. But the birth of Jesus is wrapped in mystery. Even the place of his birth is open to question. Most probably it was Bethlehem (he was a descendant of king David – as many others in Palestine at the time must have been), but some historians would say it was Nazareth. The nature of his birth is a matter of theology not of history; Christians make different judgments. Our decisions on these matters are secondary to our decisions about the story of Jesus as a whole – the witness of his remembered ministry, what he did and said and how he died, and the witness of the resurrection and the Christian experience of God's love and all that this means in our living and thinking. The great claims made for Jesus – in the first century: 'God was in Christ reconciling the world to himself' (Paul), or in the twentieth century: 'Christ is the centre of life' (Bonhoeffer) – rest upon this broader foundation.

'Follow Me!'

No survey, such as we have attempted, of the whole ministry of Jesus – his life, his death, his resurrection – can be a mere historical inquiry. His story must be subjected to the strictest historical study; for us, as for the first friends of Jesus, it is a matter of utmost importance to be sure that what we claim happened really happened. Pious guesswork does him no service; too much is at stake. He invites our questions, and we are free to ask them and to seek, in the most rigorous way, the answers.

But we are not merely asking historical questions. Jesus pushes our questions back until we come to 'You – who do you say I am?'. Any retelling of his story must bring us to this point, and leave us to answer it.

If we now stand back and look at the whole story, we find that it faces us with three questions.

Isn't love the real human adventure? Men have looked in many directions for the fulfilling experience, the real adventure: to war, to self-enrichment, to wealth, to pleasure, to learning, to 'progress'. The brief story of Jesus puts a question mark against all our chosen ideals and ambitions, and faces us with this fundamental question.

Isn't love the clue? From the beginning of history men have tried to make sense of our strange and tangled human story – the kind of sense which enables a man to live in its light – and to find some meaning in our frustrating human experience; or they have given up any hope of making sense of it at all. Jesus was no glib dogmatist; he came to his convictions the hard way. Is not all he said and all he lived – his death itself – summarized in this question?

Isn't love the end? Men have dreamed all kinds of dreams about the future of humanity as a common society in a common world. Our very inventions preclude any ultimate isolation from one another. We seek, in economics, in scientific research, in education, the clue to a common world. All these are important. But the story of Jesus forces us back to ask what kind of world we really want and how we expect to make it. He subjects all our common assumptions – as he subjected the common assumptions of his own time – to a critical scrutiny, and provokes us to a bolder inquiry. Isn't love 'the clue to history', its meaning and its end?

It is important to get the questions right, but it is just as important to know how to go about finding the answers. Jesus' approach is summed up in his 'Follow me!' – the answers are to be found not only by hard thinking but also by bold living. Love is not a blueprint – it is a guide; its true meaning can only be found experimentally. God's world is a world in the making – to be explored, lived in, shared, en-

joyed together. How this is to be done can only be found in the doing – 'Follow me!'

Jesus' own account of his work comes to us through the minds of his friends, often in their language and circumscribed by their horizons. But what he was and what he had to say has an originality and freshness which transcends them both. Perhaps it is the experimental note in word and deed that has enabled him to survive the great changes in human society of the last two thousand years, and to exercise his widest influence in the modern world.

Love is the great *human* experience, the attitude which is the precondition of finding the real answers to our human questions. Jesus was the pioneer; the trouble is that we follow him so far behind.

8

The Message of Jesus

Robert C. Walton

The Needs of the First Christians

The Gospels in the form in which we possess them are church books. They were written in the second half of the first century AD to meet the needs of the early followers of Jesus gathered together out of a pagan environment in their Christian communities (see Part IV, Section 5, pp. 246 ff.). These early churches were not, for the most part, Palestinian, and after AD 70 when the country had been laid waste and Jerusalem destroyed, Christians in Galilee and Judaea must have been few and unorganized. The growing churches were in the great cities of the Graeco-Roman world, Antioch in Syria, Ephesus in Asia Minor (now south-west Turkey), Corinth, Philippi and Thessalonica in Greece and in Rome. The members of these churches were Greeks, Romans, Syrians, Egyptians and Asiatics, though not a few Jews had also been converted to the new religion. These centres of Christianity and these church

members were far away in distance from the world Jesus knew and very different from him in culture and upbringing.

The message of Jesus as it is presented to us in the four Gospels has three historical settings. Latest in time (c.AD 65–100) is the world of these established churches of the Roman empire; churches as far apart as Syrian Antioch in the east to Rome in the west, the world of the four Gospel makers, the men who compiled Mark, Matthew, Luke and John.

Earlier than this (c.AD 29–65) is the world of the first Christian communities. These were in Jerusalem, Samaria, Caesarea and other Palestinian cities and also, largely as the result of Paul's missionary activities, in Asia Minor, Greece and Rome. At this time the leaders of the new religion were mainly Jews and their understanding of the teaching of Jesus was partly coloured by their Jewish inheritance. These communities possessed no Gospels. Their knowledge came from oral traditions; from memories of what Jesus had said and done which were handed down by word of mouth in public addresses, instruction classes for converts, and, no doubt, also in private conversations. Some of the deeds and words of Jesus were probably written down quite early and the manuscript treasured in one of the local churches, but, for the most part, Christians at this time relied for their knowledge upon the shared memories of those who had known Jesus.

The third historical setting is Galilee and Judaea where Jesus lived, taught, died and triumphed over death: the brief period of time when the parables, the aphorisms and the proclamation of the kingdom of God were spoken for the first time.

It is necessary, therefore, to disentangle as far as possible the original message spoken by Jesus in Palestine from the meaning drawn out of it by Christian teachers and by the four evangelists. The Christian communities in both of the two later historical settings had a zeal for evangelism. They looked outward to a world which desperately needed the message of Jesus. They were missionary churches. Moreover, in the years *c*.AD 29–65 there was a particular reason why evangelism could not wait. The great decisive moment – the return of Jesus to earth in great power and glory – was, so they believed, imminent. To their disappointment the 'second coming' was delayed – in fact it never happened – but while they waited for the Day of Judgment and Reward the Christians evangelized fervently. An evangelist needs a message, and so the questions they asked were these: what did Jesus teach? What message from him must I declare to the pagans in this city? What promises and consolations, and what practical advice, did he speak for our help and comfort?

The task of separating the original message of Jesus from the later additions and interpretations is difficult and often uncertain. Biblical scholars frequently disagree and an element of personal judgment is inevitable. There are, however, many instances which a teacher can use in the classroom where it is quite easy to see evangelists using 'the preachers' technique'. They begin with an incident, a saying, a parable, like preachers announcing their text, and then expound it to meet the needs of their audience.

This process can often be detected where a parable is told in more than one Gospel. For instance, the parable of the Good Shepherd in Luke 15.3–7 ends by declaring that when one sinner repents there is rejoicing in heaven. God is the Shepherd (a frequent Old Testament metaphor) who searches out those who are lost. In the Gospel of Matthew (18.12–14) the same parable is told in slightly different language. Then at v.15 the parable is used to point out a Christian's duty towards an offending brother-Christian. As the shepherd searches for a lost sheep, so 'if your brother sins against you, go and tell him his fault, between you and him alone. If he listens to you, you have gained your brother . . .' (vv.15–18).

Another example is the parable of the Empty House told both by Luke and Matthew in almost identical language. Here is Luke's version:

> When the unclean spirit has gone out of a man, he passes through waterless places seeking rest; and finding none he says, 'I will return to my house from which I came.' And when he comes he finds it swept and put in order. Then he goes and brings seven other spirits more evil than himself, and they enter and dwell there; and the last state of that man becomes worse than the first (Luke 11.24–26).

Here in Luke's version the parable stands by itself, though it is preceded by the saying, 'If it is by the finger of God that I cast out demons, then the kingdom of God has come upon you', and by the parable of the Captured Castle. Since the story is about evil spirits we might say that it is an acute psychological analysis of the state of mind of people who, cured of mental hallucinations, slip back into their neurotic state because they can find nothing positive to live for. We could sharpen the interpretation by saying that Jesus himself must fill the house of life, if a man is to be creative and happy. The Gospel of Matthew adds its own interpretation: 'so shall it be also with this evil generation' (Matt. 12.45). The opponents of Jesus, the Pharisees and lawyers, are the houses inhabited by eight evil spirits, seven of whom are worse than the original occupier.

These are fairly simple examples. Our task, using the help which New Testament scholars provide, is to try to see, however imperfectly, Jesus the teacher as he was, and to understand his message.

'The Greatest Artist of us All'

This phrase from the painter van Gogh has been quoted by Alan T. Dale in the preceding article on the ministry of Jesus. He has written that 'Jesus was a poet holding his own with Dante and Shakespeare' (see above p. 278). Here are some of the poems of Jesus in Dale's translation.

Everybody who listens to me
and then does something about it
is like a sensible builder.

He builds his house –
and he builds it on rock.

Then winter comes.
The rain pours down,
the mountain torrents come tumbling down
  the hillside,
the great winds blow
and batter the house.
But it stands up to it all –
underneath it is rock (Matt.7.24 f.).

What did you go out on the moors to see?
Grass blown by the wind?
But what did you go out to see?
Somebody clothed in silk?
You must look in palaces for splendour and
luxury!

But what did you go out to see?
One of God's great men?

Yes! I tell you –
Somebody greater than God's great men of
  old (Matt.11.7–9).

To remember that Jesus was a poet with a poet's inward vision and a gift for handling words, using vivid images from everyday life, not abstract arguments, helps us in various ways to get to the heart of his teaching. For instance it is often a clue to those passages of the Gospels where someone has added an explanation of the words of Jesus. The parable of the Sower (Mark 4.3–9 = Matt.13.1–9) ends with the words, 'He who has ears to hear, let him hear', or as we might say, 'Now work out the meaning for yourself.' Then follows in both Gospels (vv. 10–20 in Mark; 10–23 in Matthew) a long and tedious explanation of the parable. Scholars can give their own reasons for saying that this is a later addition, but there is a sound common-sense reason as well. Poets do not explain their poems. They offer us their vision and leave us to discover the meaning.

If we take the teaching of Jesus as a whole we seem at first sight to be presented with deep-seated and irreconcilable differences. If the heart of his message is to be found in that collection of sayings which we call 'the Sermon on the Mount' (Matt.5–7 = Luke 6.20–49) then we shall think of him as an ethical teacher whose morality sprang from the imitation of God. 'You must be perfect, as your heavenly Father is perfect' (Matt.5.48). If, on the other hand, the heart of his message is in Mark 13 then Jesus is a visionary whose eyes are fixed upon a dramatic future. The old order of the world will disappear and a new order will take its place:

And then they will see the Son of man coming in clouds with great power and glory. And then he will send out the angels, and gather his elect from the four winds, from the ends of the earth to the ends of heaven (Mark 13.26 f.).

Could one man have thought in two such different and apparently inconsistent ways? Certainly it would be a defect in a systematic theologian, but Jesus was a poet. Think of William Blake who wrote in *Songs of Innocence* such lines as:

Little Lamb, who made thee?
Dost thou know who made thee?
Gave thee life and bid thee feed
By the stream and o'er the mead.

and who also wrote in a poem about John Milton:

Bring me my bow of burning gold!
Bring me my arrows of desire!
Bring me my spear! O clouds unfold!
Bring me my chariot of fire!

Poets are not usually interested in creating logical systems of thought in which each single part fits into the whole. They speak or write about that which at a particular moment captures their imagination and stirs their soul. They sing as birds sing. The message of Jesus has no tidy outward shape, but it has an inner unity centred upon the proclamation of the kingdom of God.

How did Jesus Teach?

We know from the Gospels that Jesus went regularly to synagogue on the sabbath and that sometimes he was invited to address the congregation (see Luke 4.16–30 and 13.10). Often, however, his teaching must have been his contribution to a conversation. He would stop to chat at the village well or in the market place, joining in ordinary friendly talk about fishing and farming, about housework and the care of children, and listening to wilder talk about the taxes and the Roman overlords and the state of the nation. Presently he would drop into the conversation a remark of profound meaning. 'Look at those children over there squabbling at their play – some won't play at weddings and the others won't play at funerals; nothing pleases them. And there are people in our nation whom nothing pleases. They didn't like John the Baptist and they don't like me. But you'll see. God will be proved right' (see Luke 7.31–35 = Matt.11.16–19).

Jesus frequently used a technique – well known to teachers – of making an inquirer answer his own question or puzzle out his own problem. 'What do you think about this?' he said and went on to tell without comment the story of two sons; one promised to work in the vineyard and did not go; the other, who at first refused his father, later changed his mind and went to work. Which of these two did as his father wished? (Matt.21.28–31). Again, when a Pharisee objected to a prostitute who knelt weeping at the feet of Jesus, and anointed them with myrrh, Jesus told a story about a money lender who wrote off the debts of two men, one for five hundred silver pieces, the other for fifty. Then came the challenging question: 'Which will love him most?' (Luke 7.36–50). When a lawyer, wishing as lawyers do to justify himself, asked 'Who is my neighbour?' Jesus told the parable of the Good Samaritan and said in effect to the lawyer, 'Now answer your own question' (Luke 10.25–37).

The Originality of Jesus

Jesus was a Jew brought up in an orthodox pious home, where religious festivals, the weekly sabbath and the yearly feasts were observed. We may safely assume that he learnt to read and write in the synagogue school at Nazareth. He spoke Aramaic and perhaps also Greek, but the language he learnt at school was Hebrew. His book was the Jewish Scriptures, the Old Testament.

Although the message of Jesus was continually illuminated by the faith and tradition of his nation, his thought was wider and owed much to his acute observation both of nature and of human behaviour. The background of his teaching was the daily life of men and women in Galilee, and it was also the needs and problems of his nation. He took sharp notice of what was happening in his world. We have not, for instance, fully grasped the significance of his temptations when we have traced back his three replies to the allurements of Satan to the book of Deuteronomy. The poverty – sometimes downright hunger – of some of his countrymen lies behind the temptation to turn stones into bread, and the problems of political power – the Roman grip upon the country and the mounting hatred and violence of the Zealots – is the background of his refusal to accept 'the kingdoms of the world and their glory' (see Matt.4.1–11 = Luke 4.1–13).

As we shall see later, many of the parables have their setting in actual events in the troubled life of Galilee, but one example may be given here:

> When a strong man, fully armed, guards his own palace, his goods are in peace; but when one stronger than he assails him and overcomes him, he takes away his armour in which he trusted and divides his spoil (Luke 11.21 f.).

The meaning seems to be that 'the strong man armed' represents the forces of evil which are overcome by Jesus who is stronger than the strong man in his castle, but what prompted the story and gave it immediate point for the listeners, may well have been one of the frequent Zealot raids on Roman garrison posts in order to capture weapons: 'he takes away his armour in which he trusted and divides the spoil.'

This realism was one reason why people said about Jesus that 'he speaks with authority – not like the lawyers' (Mark 1.22). It was an authority which he claimed explicitly. 'Years ago people said this and this, but I say to you', and the astonishing thing is that many people took this bold speaking without offence and approved of it.

Jesus was a Jew trained from childhood in the national religion and practising that religion throughout his life. Yet on certain issues he rejected the orthodox and accepted teaching of the Pharisees and lawyers. Mark, in the early part of his Gospel (2.15 to 3.6), has brought together four incidents in which Jesus defied the rules. First, at a supper party, he consorted with tax-gatherers, who either directly or indirectly were in the service of Rome, and also with 'sinners' – the outsiders of polite society whom the orthodox regarded as undesirable lay-abouts. In the second incident Jesus refused to fast as a sign of mourning for John the Baptist's imprisonment. In the third and fourth incidents he defied the strict regulations about working on the sabbath. He allowed his disciples to pluck ears of corn from a harvest field, to rub them in the palms of their hands in order to separate the kernel from the husk and to eat the kernels. This was not theft from the farmer's field, but technically it was working on the sabbath. Finally Jesus healed on the sabbath a man with a withered arm.

It is not necessary to suppose that these four incidents happened one after another at the same point in the ministry of Jesus. Mark grouped them together and put the spotlight upon them because they illustrate how Jesus consistently rejected the Pharisaic policy for Israel under the Roman occupation. That policy had its roots in Jewish theology, but the theology could hardly escape a political reference. Strict observance of the whole Law by the whole community was the only way to preserve Israel's distinctive and traditional way of life. Such observance made the sabbath and days of fasting into 'Independence Days'. So the Pharisees set up a barricade of rules and insisted that they should be kept. We can understand their reasons and respect their motives.

In place of the Pharisaic policy Jesus proclaimed a new way of life and a new kind of religion. He described himself as the bridegroom and his disciples as guests at the wedding. He likened his message to new wine and said that it would burst old wine-skins. When he was challenged about healing a man on the sabbath he forestalled hostile criticism by the direct question, 'Is it lawful to do good or evil on the sabbath, to save a life or to kill?' Mark ends this section of his Gospel by telling us that the Pharisees reacted by plotting with the partisans of Herod Antipas to destroy Jesus. This was a very odd alliance. The Pharisees had little use for a renegade like Herod who certainly did not practise strict obedience to the Mosaic Law. But they put their scruples in their pockets, as men will in a crisis, and began negotiations with Herod's supporters. At this moment, according to Mark, the shadow of Golgotha first fell across the pathway of Jesus.

To reject the policy of preserving national identity by strict obedience to the Law was, of course, only the negative side of the new religion. What was its positive message? To answer this question we must examine what Jesus said in parables and sayings and actions about God, about man's response to God, about the kingdom of God, about the fate of Israel; and what he said about himself.

The Parables

It is perhaps in the parables more than anywhere else in the Gospels that we realize the originality of Jesus. They are not, of course, unique. The Jewish Rabbis used parables and so did St Paul. But no other parables are comparable to those of Jesus in their terseness, their wit, their sharp observance of human behaviour and in their extraordinary power of conveying profound truth throughout a well-told story.

The background of the parables is the daily life of Palestine. The characters include farmers, fishermen, housewives and merchants; kings, landowners and judges; a woman searching for a lost silver piece; squabbling children, guests at a wedding and a family whose house had been burgled. Along with the parables are brief metaphors or similes which have no story line and which appeal to our imagination or our sense of humour. 'If one blind man guides another they will both fall into the ditch' (Matt.15.14 NEB). 'It is easier for a camel to pass through the eye of a needle than for a rich man to enter the kingdom of God' (Mark 10.25 NEB). 'Why do you look at the speck of sawdust in your brother's eye, with never a thought for the great plank in your own' (Matt.7.3 NEB)?

It is sometimes possible to detect an actual occurrence as the inspiration of the parable, though there must always be an element of uncertainty. For instance, in the parable of the burglar (Matt.24.43 = Luke 12.39) the past tenses suggest some recent burglary in the village which everybody was talking about. 'If the householder *had known* at what time of night the burglar was coming, he *would have* kept awake and *not have let* his house be broken into.'

It may be that we have another example in Luke's version of the parable of the Talents (19.11–27) which unlike Matthew's version (25.14–30) has, it seems, a double plot. The main part of the story as in Matthew tells how three servants were entrusted with differing sums of money while their master went on a journey. There is also a sub-plot which begins at Luke 19.12: 'A nobleman went into a far country to receive kingly power and then return.' At v. 27 the sub-plot reappears: 'But as for these enemies of mine, who did not want me to reign over them, bring them here and slay them before me.'

This sub-plot appears to be the beginning and ending of an entirely different story which became intermingled with that of the talents in the tradition used by Luke. It illustrates, however, how an event may have prompted a story. In the spring of the year 4 BC, Herod the Great died in Jericho. By his will his kingdom was divided among his three sons. Archelaus, the eldest, a young man of eighteen, was given Judaea and Samaria. Herod's will, however, had to be ratified in Rome by the emperor Augustus, and Archelaus left Palestine for Rome taking with him all the necessary documents and his father's signet ring – 'a nobleman went into a far country to receive kingly power'.

If Archelaus is the man of noble birth in the sub-plot it would throw light upon the closing verse (v. 27) in Luke's version: 'but as for these enemies of mine who did not want me to be king, bring them here and slaughter them in my presence.' Archelaus proved himself to be a stupid, cruel and vain-glorious ruler who in AD 6 achieved the unique distinction of uniting Jews and Samaritans in a joint denunciation to Augustus. Archelaus was summoned to Rome and never returned.

For many centuries and up to recent times the church turned the parables into allegories in which every detail was given a moral or a theological meaning. The beginnings of this process can be seen in the use made of the parables by the early church. The additions to the original parable of the Sower in Mark 4.10–20 show clearly what happened. The seed sown by the farmer is 'the word'; the birds which ate the seed falling on the foot-path represent Satan; the young corn which had no proper roots is allegorized into those Christians who easily fall back from their faith. The seed which yields the abundant harvest represents the faithful, stalwart Christians.

Later interpretations carried this kind of interpretation to more extravagant lengths. For instance, in the parable of the Labourers in the Vineyard (Matt.20.1–16), the landowner at harvest time goes to the market place on five separate occasions in the course of a single day to hire labourers. Christian theologians in the second and third centuries saw great significance in these five summonses to work. For one of them, Irenaeus, they symbolized the periods in the history of redemption from Adam onwards. For Origen they held a different meaning. The five summonses to work in the vineyard represented the different stages of human life at which men become Christians. What the parable of the Labourers in the Vineyard means is discussed below. These fanciful interpretations are still sometimes heard in sermons but biblical scholars have long since abandoned them and they should never be used in the classroom.

The parables, then, are vivid short stories rooted in everyday life. They are stories with meaning and many of the central themes of the message of Jesus are embodied in them. They are attractive material for telling to children, but often the parables chosen are a few firm favourites – the Sower, the Good Shepherd, the Prodigal Son, the Good Samaritan and the Talents. Overmuch repetition first in the primary and then in the secondary school can easily exhaust their interest. In the following paragraphs suggestions are made for using other, less well-known parables, especially in the top junior and secondary forms. In teaching them it is important to make clear that they were spoken by a poet, and that their background and immediate reference is first-century Palestine. Yet, like all great art, they have a timeless quality and can be used to illuminate modern issues.

1. *The Wheat and the Weeds* (Matt.13.24–30)
The Drag-net (Matt.13.47–50)
These two parables make the same point. Jesus says that at the time when he is speaking

it is impossible to tell who is, and who is not, a member of God's kingdom. The weeds (darnel: a poisonous plant which is closely related to bearded wheat and in the early stages of growth hard to distinguish from it) cannot be rooted up until harvest time. Fishing with a seine or drag-net, usually slung between two boats, was normally done at night, and you cannot sort good fish from bad in the dark. It is when the net has been dragged ashore in daylight that the catch can be sorted. There is a time when you cannot tell wheat from weeds; good fish from bad, and the time has not yet come when a man can know who is shut in and who is shut out from God's kingdom.

Compare with this the story of the healing of the centurion's servant (Matt.8.5–13). There was no doubt considerable astonishment among those who witnessed the interview between Jesus and the centurion, that Jesus should even be willing to talk to, let alone befriend, a hated Roman. In v. 11 Jesus says in effect, 'Wait. Do not judge now. Many people like this Roman officer may find a place in God's kingdom, feasting with the great heroes of Jewish history, and many Jews, "born to the kingdom" will be shut out from it.' These parables are a warning against making hasty judgments about people, and they are a plea for toleration. They are good material to use in class when questions arise about race-relations.

2. *The Labourers in the Vineyard* (Matt.20.1–15). Note: v. 16 is a later addition.

Some early fanciful interpretations of this parable have already been rejected (see above p. 288). One modern meaning imposed upon it may be swiftly dismissed. The story is not a blue-print for management in twentieth-century industry. Any employer of labour on a large scale who acted as did the owner of the vineyard would quickly find himself in trouble with the trade unions.

The parable is about the generosity of God: God who 'makes his sun to rise on good and bad alike and sends his rain upon the honest and the dishonest' (Matt.5.45 NEB): God who gives not what we deserve but what we need. The labourers who have hung about the market place from early morning to late afternoon, need a full day's wage (the Roman *denairus* 'a penny a day' AV if they and their families are not to go hungry. The owner of the

vineyard knows this and pays his men according to their need. The nearest earthly parallel to this action of God is the way loving parents treat their children justly, but with special consideration and generosity towards any member of the family who is in special need.

3. *The Mustard Seed* (Mark 4.30–32)
The Yeast in the Bread (Matt.13.33)
The Sower (Mark 4.3–9)
The Patient Farmer (Mark 4.26–29)

These four parables are grouped together because they are each in different ways 'parables of assurance'. They bid us have confidence in God. In each of them the kingdom of God is compared to what happens at the end of the process; the full grown mustard seed which by the lake of Galilee grows to a height of eight to ten feet; the tiny pinch of yeast which makes the bread to rise; the abundant harvest.

The people to whom Jesus told these stories were not interested in the slow processes of growth as a modern botanist will be. Their minds worked like that of an amateur gardener who plants tulip bulbs in the autumn, forgets about them during the long winter, and then, one morning in May, is suddenly excited by signs of colour in the buds. The patient farmer sows the seed and then loses interest. He sleeps and gets up, and the seed sprouts and grows, 'and he doesn't know how'. Nor does he care (Mark 4.27). His interest is only quickened when the grain is ripe because this to him is the miracle. From a seemingly dead seed comes the harvest; from a pinch of yeast the daily bread. It is a miracle of resurrection; life springing out of death. From the same miraculous process, from a small band of disciples with Jesus at their head, the kingdom of God grows.

4. *The Pearl Merchant* (Matt.13.45)

A merchant with a fine collection of precious pearls, which is his joy and delight, searches for one pearl of matchless beauty and, having found it, he sells all that he possesses to buy the one pearl of great price. In this parable the emphasis falls upon the great joy which the merchant experiences when he has made his choice, sold all his possessions, finally committed himself and become the owner of the supremely lovely pearl. So is the joy of the man who enters the kingdom of God. (See a similar parable *Hidden Treasure* [Matt.13.44].)

It is legitimate to use the parable of the Pearl Merchant when questions of moral choice are under discussion, provided that the elements of joy and of commitment are emphasized. Our moral choices are not always between actions which are bad and actions which are good. Often the choice lies between an action, or a way of life, which is good and one which is better: exchanging pearls for pearls. Less frequently, the choice is between a way of life which is in itself good and the best way of all: exchanging fine pearls for the one pearl of great price.

This truth can be illustrated from the life of Jesus, though it would be claiming too much to say that the parable is autobiographical. Jesus began as a carpenter at Nazareth. It is probable that Joseph was dead (he disappears from the story after the first visit to Jerusalem when Jesus was twelve years of age). If this is so then Jesus was the bread-winner for Mary and his brothers and sisters. It was a good thing to be; a good life to live. It was, you might say, a collection of pearls. Then at the age of thirty Jesus gave up that life to become a wandering teacher and healer. This, for him, was a better life to live; a finer collection of pearls. Three years later (or perhaps sooner) Jesus abandoned the life of teaching and healing. He 'stedfastly set his face towards Jerusalem', the stronghold of his enemies, where he was executed. This – again for him with his absolute confidence in God and knowledge of the divine purpose – was the best thing of all: the exchange of fine pearls for the one pearl of great price. And like the merchant and the man who found treasure in a field, he had great joy. 'He, *for the joy that was set before him*,' wrote one of his followers later, 'endured the cross, despising the shame' (Heb.12.2).

5. *The Unforgiving Servant* (Matt.18.23–35)

The lesson of this parable is obvious. Some of the details, however, can be used to build up an interesting lesson for secondary pupils.

The sum owed by the king's servant is enormous; 10,000 talents which was roughly equivalent to two and a half million pounds. Clearly the servant is not a bailiff on a private estate but the governor of a province; a pro-consul or procurator like Pontius Pilate. One of the main responsibilities of so important an official was to collect the taxes and transmit them to the royal treasury. This pro-consul had evidently been feathering his own nest on a tremendous scale. Even so, the vast sum of the debt is deliberately exaggerated. The Jewish historian Josephus records that in 4 BC the annual taxes imposed upon the districts of Galilee and Perea amounted to only 200 talents – a fiftieth of the sum owed by the pro-consul in the parable.

There are other details which show that Jesus gave a Gentile setting to this parable. Under Jewish law the sale of a wife (v. 25) was forbidden. Again, although torture was frequently employed upon a defaulting governor of a district or a province to compel him to disclose where he had hidden the money it was forbidden under Jewish law (in v. 34 'jailors' in RSV means 'torturers' as in AV and NEB).

The parable ends with the phrase, 'forgive your brother from the heart'. It is the only kind of human forgiveness which is genuine in the sight of God. To say, 'I forgive you but I never want to see you again', is forgiveness only with the lips (see Matt.15.8 f. which is a quotation from Isa.29.13).

Teaching about the Kingdom

A large number of the parables, including most of those discussed in the preceding section, begin with the phrase, 'The kingdom of God' (or 'of heaven' in Matthew) is like . . .'. The proclamation of God's kingdom is a dominant theme in the message of Jesus, but there is no clear-cut formal definition of its nature. Instead we are presented with a poet's rich confusion of similes and metaphors. What the kingdom is like and the evidence of its presence is conveyed in parables, short vivid phrases and sometimes in enigmatic sayings.

Those who first heard Jesus speak of the kingdom of God would not have found it an unfamiliar idea. The expectation that God's kingdom would come was a part of the Jewish faith. But the word 'kingdom' can mislead us. It suggests an area of territory like the 'United Kingdom', or the 'Kingdom of Norway' or 'the Hashemite Kingdom of Jordan'. 'God's kingship' brings us nearer to the meaning. What the Jews longed for and confidently expected was the vigorous and established power and activity of God in the world. In the time of Jesus, however, the world, from the point of view of the

Jews, had long been a disordered place. Rome, in the persons of Pontius Pilate and the puppet kings of Galilee and Transjordan, was in command. Classical historians write about the Roman peace, Roman justice, Roman law and order, but to the Jews Roman domination was a usurpation of God's kingship. Yet it was a temporary seizure of power which rightly belonged to God. The Lord's throne was set in heaven; his kingship ruled over all the world.

God was king. His own people – the Jews who knew this unalterable truth – must wait, and waiting, be obedient to the will of their King which was enshrined in the Law. They had been waiting for many long years, but the time would come when God would take decisive action. He would assert his authority, destroy those who resisted his kingship and welcome into his kingdom the Jews who had stedfastly remained his loyal subjects.

How startling then was the proclamation with which Jesus began his ministry in Galilee.

> The time is fulfilled and the kingdom of God is at hand; repent and believe in the Gospel (Mark 1.14).

This may be Mark's summary of the heart of the message preached by Jesus at the beginning of his public ministry, but there is no reason to doubt that it is an accurate summary. The phrase 'the kingdom of God is at hand' can be translated 'is upon you' as in NEB, but whichever translation is preferred the meaning is clear. God's kingship, Jesus declared, is a present reality here and now in Galilee. It has come or it is on the point of appearing like the rising sun coming up over the horizon.

> Blessed are the eyes which see what you see! For I tell you that many prophets and kings desired to see what you see, and did not see it, and to hear what you hear, and did not hear it (Luke 10.23 f. = Matt.13.16 f.).

Prophets and kings had desired to see the triumph of God's purposes; the sovereign rule of God and, said Jesus, 'you are seeing it now.'

Without doubt the announcement of the kingdom caused great excitement among the people of Galilee and to those who could believe it, it brought joyful expectancy and hope. 'After all these years of waiting,' they would say, 'it is going to happen in our time, before our very eyes.' We can sense this mount-ing excitement in the early chapters of the Gospel of Mark. 'The news spread rapidly.' 'Great crowds came to see him.' 'The large congregation (in the synagogue) were amazed.' But often the crowds must have been puzzled and some in the crowds were repelled. There was an element in the preaching of Jesus about the kingdom which seemed shocking and even blasphemous to the orthodox Jew. 'If it is by the finger of God that I cast out demons, then the kingdom of God has come upon you' (Luke 11.20; see Matt.12.28). The kingdom has come in the coming of Jesus. 'What! This workman from Nazareth?' He spoke, it is true, with conviction and authority, 'not like the lawyers'. He had magnetism and the gift of healing, but to men who expected that a king of the line of David, or a heavenly representative of God, would come to inaugurate the kingdom, the proclamation of this Galilean was, to say the least, perplexing. So, as Jesus himself recognized, his proclamation divided men. 'A man's foes will be those of his own household' (see Matt.10.34–39; 8.21 f.).

There was something else disturbing about this preaching of the kingdom. It was the sense of urgency. There was, said Jesus, a crisis and the crisis had been created by his own coming. Men must make a decision and act now, but his hearers were slow to recognize the immediacy of the crisis. 'The kingdom is upon you,' said Jesus. 'All the signs of its appearing are before your eyes!'

> When you see a cloud rising in the west, you say at once, 'a shower is coming'; and so it happens. And when you see the south wind blowing, you say, 'there will be scorching heat'; and it happens. You hypocrites! You know how to interpret the appearance of earth and sky; but why do you not know how to interpret the present time?' (Luke 12.54–56).

Yet in other parables and sayings the time scale is somewhat different. The crisis is building up but the decisive moment has not yet come.

> I have come to set fire to the earth and how I wish it were already kindled (Luke 12.49 NEB).

> Remember, if the householder had known what time the burglar was coming he would not have let his house be broken into. Hold

yourselves ready, then, because the Son of man is coming at the time you least expect him (Luke 12.39 f. NEB).

Be ready for action, with belts fastened and lamps alight. Be like men who wait for their master's return from a wedding-party, ready to let him in the moment he arrives and knocks. Happy are those servants whom the master finds on the alert when he comes (Luke 12.35–36a NEB).

In these stories the crisis though imminent has not yet come upon men. The master has not yet come home.

What is life like when God reigns? In the Gospels there is a rich profusion of metaphors, but we can separate out four main ideas.

1. The coming of the kingdom is compared to natural processes of growth. This is not a contradiction of the sense of urgency and crisis for the point is not slowness of growth but the small beginnings and the assurance of an abundant harvest. Jesus and his small band of followers must have seemed pitifully weak in contrast with the political and religious forces ranged against them, and the inertia of the ordinary man. Yet, like the tiny mustard seed which grows into a large bush or the pinch of yeast which makes the bread to rise, the kingdom grows and spreads and works in society (see above, p. 289).

2. When God reigns men receive what they need and not what they deserve (see above, The Labourers in the Vineyard, Matt.20.1–15, p. 289 f.). There will be justice but above all generosity, for God 'makes his sun to rise on good and bad alike, and sends rain on the honest and dishonest' (Matt.5.45 NEB).

3. When God reigns, forgiveness will be the paramount social virtue, and for those who have already recognized the coming of the kingdom, and have accepted God's rule it is the permanent moral obligation. 'Forgive us . . . as we have forgiven' (Matt.6.12 NEB).

4. When God inaugurates his reign there will be a time of separation. The wheat will be harvested and the weeds burned (Matt. 13.24–30. See pp. 288 f.). There will be – to use a favourite metaphor of Jesus – a great feast to which some who are invited will refuse to come, and the poor, the crippled, the blind and the lame, and the homeless who sleep along the hedgerows, will come to the banquet (Luke

14.16–24 = Matt.22.1–14). There will be a great Day of Judgment when the sheep will be separated from the goats; when the hard-hearted will be rejected and the compassionate will enter and possess the kingdom (Matt.25.31–46).

Teaching about God

When we speak about God in the classroom we face two problems. The first is particularly acute when teaching adolescents. 'But, sir, where's the proof?' 'Please, miss, how do you know there is a God?' There is, of course, no proof in the sense of a logical watertight progression of argument to an inescapable conclusion. There *are* reasons, some intellectual, some moral, some born of personal experiences, but probably no one single reason can withstand the corrosive acids of modern disbelief. Faith in God is like a rope in a gymnasium: it is made up of many different strands twisted together. No one single strand will bear the weight; only the rope will hold.

This problem did not confront Jesus in his teaching. No one in his day would ever have dreamed of asking the question, 'How do you know that there is a God?' It was as self-evident to Jesus and his contemporaries that God is, as it was self-evident that sun, moon and stars are.

The second problem which we face in the classroom is to make the word 'God' sound real, so that instead of being an emotive noise it conveys a mental picture with a clear outline and sharply defined details. This was a challenge to Jesus as it is to us, and he answered it in two ways.

1. All his preaching of the kingdom was, as we have seen, a declaration of God's universal power and of his purpose for the world.

2. He gave a rich meaning to the phrase 'God is Father'. In the Old Testament God is frequently spoken of as 'Father'.

As a father pities his children,
So the Lord pities those who fear him
(Ps.103.13).

The Jewish Rabbis used the metaphor. 'Be strong as a leopard,' one of them wrote, 'and swift as an eagle and fleet as a gazelle and brave as a lion to do the will of thy Father who is in heaven.'

Jesus himself did not use the word 'Father' as often as is sometimes thought. In the developed theology of the Fourth Gospel the word occurs 107 times, often in the phrase 'my Father', but in the Synoptic Gospels it occurs much less frequently: only four times in Mark, six in Luke, eight or nine in the 'Q' passages and twenty-three in Matthew. What is original in the teaching of Jesus and gave such clarity to the word 'Father' was the way he used it in his sayings and parables.

> Is there a man among you who will offer his son a stone when he asks for bread, or a snake when he asks for fish? If you, then, bad as you are, know how to give your children what is good for them, how much more will your heavenly Father give good things to those who ask him? (Matt.7.9–11 NEB. See Luke 11.11–13).

It is surprising that in a patriarchal society in which the authority of the father over his family was unquestioned, the emphasis in the teaching of Jesus falls not upon God's arbitrary power, but upon his watchful, loving care of men and women. This heavenly Father, whose name is to be used with reverence and whose will men must strive to do, is like a shepherd searching for a lost sheep, or a housewife looking for a lost coin, or an anxious father longing for his son's return (Luke 15).

In the narrative of Jesus' agony in Gethsemane (Mark 14.32–42) we catch a glimpse of his attitude towards God his Father. Here was a real struggle to maintain his faith and to keep to his purpose, but when the conflict was over he was back on the rock on which he had always stood; his absolute trust and unswerving obedience. For the sake of his Father's purpose he would endure physical torment and mental and spiritual suffering.

Teaching about Prayer

In the thought of Jesus religion was not ostentatious observance and prayer was the very opposite of a lengthy monologue (Matt.6.1–8). Sincerity was everything (Luke 18.10–14). The brevity of the prayer which Jesus taught to his disciples is significant. It is enough to acknowledge the holiness of God ('hallowed be thy name'), to desire his kingly rule on earth ('thy kingdom come'), to pray for everyday needs and for forgiveness, and for deliverance in every fiery trial (Matt.6.9–13).

There are two parables about prayer which can easily be misinterpreted. Both appear on the surface to emphasize that prayer consists of persistent begging. In the parable of the Friend at Midnight (Luke 11.5–9) a man knocks up his neighbour at night to borrow three loaves of bread. At once he gets a blunt refusal. 'Don't bother me. The door is locked, and we are all in bed.' But the man outside goes on hammering at the door until 'because of the very shamelessness of his request' (v. 8 NEB) he gets his three loaves of bread.

The clue to resolving the difficulty presented by this parable lies in the way we translate the opening words; 'Which of you . . . ?' (AV). The New English Bible has 'Suppose one of you . . .'. The three Greek words thus translated regularly introduce questions which expect emphatic replies, such as 'No one!', 'Impossible!', or 'Everybody, of course'. So the parable begins, 'Can you imagine that if a friend came to you at midnight to borrow three loaves of bread, you would answer,"Go away. We're all in bed."' The answer to this rhetorical question would be, 'Impossible! Of course I'd get up for a friend in need.' And can you imagine God not answering your cry for help? 'No! Of course not. It's unthinkable.'

The second parable, that of the Unjust Judge (Luke 18.2–8a), teaches the same lesson and should be interpreted along the same lines. A widow brings her case before a single judge, not before a tribunal, which suggests a dispute about money: a debt, a pledge, money due to her as her inheritance is being withheld and she seeks justice. She persists until the judge finally yields 'so that she will stop pestering me'. The meaning is in v. 7. God listens to the cries of the poor and the oppressed and suddenly he acts to befriend and rescue them. Perhaps those to whom Jesus told this parable were men who thought of the poor and the weak as 'outsiders', and assumed that God also had no time for them.

Teaching about Man

1. *Dependence upon God*

'Blessed are the poor in spirit, for theirs is the kingdom of heaven' (Matt.5.3). Luke's version of the first beatitude reads, 'Blessed are you poor' (6.20). There has been much argument as to which of these versions is the more original, but whichever we choose makes little difference to the meaning. 'Poor in spirit' does not mean 'poor-spirited', like a race horse that will not run; 'poor' has a wider connotation than material poverty. In Jewish thought the 'poor in spirit' and the 'poor' were those people who were much too wise to imagine that they were 'self-made'; isolated and entirely independent. They were those who recognized and lived by their dependence upon God – and this is not often the attitude of mind of very wealthy people. We catch a glimpse of the 'poor in spirit' in the first two chapters of the Gospel of Luke.

> My soul magnifies the Lord
> and my spirit rejoices in God my Saviour,
> for he has regarded the low estate of his handmaiden (Luke 1.46 f.).

According to the teaching of Jesus man is a dependent creature (see Matt.6.25–34). It is the reason why he said, 'Unless you become as children, you will never enter the kingdom of heaven' (Matt.18.3). Children are not innocent but they are dependent, and they have a great capacity for trusting others.

From this fundamental premiss about our human condition flow all the attitudes of the truly unaggressive person which are set out in the beatitudes – mercy, purity, peaceableness and so on. Such people are 'the salt of the earth' and 'the light of the world' (Matt.5.13 f.).

2. The Inward Springs of Action

In the collection of sayings which is known as 'The Sermon on the Mount' the emphasis falls not so much upon outward acts as upon inward desires and emotions; lust which leads to adultery, anger which may end in murder (Matt.5.21 and 27). Jesus speaks in other places in the Gospels of the contrast between outward observance and inward sincerity. Mark 7 begins with an explanation of a Jewish custom for non-Jewish readers. A strict Jew tried to avoid all social contact with Gentiles even to the extent of touching anything which had been handled by a Roman, a Greek or a Syrian. At the market a Jew might brush accidentally against a non-Jew, or handle a bunch of grapes which a Gentile had fingered. With the taint of the Gentile still on his hand he might touch a cup or a table when he returned home. That was why his wife was always washing the cups and pots. Jesus dismissed all this as nonsense. It is not outward contacts which defile a man but inward thoughts and desires (see vv. 1–8, 14–23).

It was this inward sincerity which Jesus commended in the generosity of the widow who put two small copper coins into a collecting bowl at the temple (Mark 12.41–44) and in the act of a woman who anointed his feet with precious ointment (Mark 14.3–9). It is commended also in the parable of the Lowest Seats at the Feast (Luke 14.7–11). Generosity and humility and gratitude, issuing in good manners, are marks of those who are poor in spirit and know their dependence upon God.

3. Reconciliation

Jesus was profoundly troubled and indeed alarmed by the deep divisions within the nation. The political and social climate of Galilee and Judaea in his day was one of hatred, suspicion and resentment. There was the fierce anger of the Zealots (and of many more who did not belong to that party) against the Roman occupying forces. There was the centuries old smouldering resentment against the Samaritans, and the social antagonism between the 'respectable' and 'not respectable'; between the Pharisees and lawyers on the one hand and the 'publicans and sinners' on the other. Jesus resisted this quarrelsomeness with all the force at his command. His parable of the *Good* Samaritan must have angered many who heard it, and his willingness to befriend a Roman centurion and tax-gatherers like Matthew who worked for Herod Antipas, that puppet ruler of Rome, brought him no popularity. 'Love your enemies,' he said, 'and pray for those who persecute you' (Matt.5.44). 'Pass no judgment and you will not be judged' (Matt.7.1 NEB).

Jesus pressed upon individuals, and especially upon his disciples, the need to offer forgiveness. 'How often am I to forgive my brother if he goes on wronging me,' asked Peter, 'as many as seven times?' 'Seventy times seven' was the answer, leaving Peter with a mathematical problem on his hands which he probably could not work out (Matt.18.21 f.). 'If when you are bringing your gift to the altar, you suddenly remember that your brother has a grievance against you, leave your gift where it is before the altar. First go and make your peace with your brother and then come back and offer your gift' (Matt.5.23 f. NEB). The only altars in first-century Israel were in the temple at Jerusalem. Suppose (as is most likely) that this saying was spoken in Galilee. Was the man expected to leave his gift unoffered in Jerusalem and to travel post-haste back to Nazareth or Capernaum? With such vivid and challenging statements Jesus proclaimed the necessity for reconciliation.

4. *Renunciation*

According to the Fourth Gospel Jesus said, 'I have come that men may have life and may have it in all its fullness' (John 10.10 NEB). There are many places in the Gospels which give the impression that Jesus was happy in the abundant, creative life which he led. Yet at the heart of his teaching lies the stern demand for renunciation. Broadly speaking, the demand takes two forms.

(i) *Worldly Possessions*

There is a romantic picture of the child born in poverty in a stable; but there is no evidence as to whether the family was poor, or whether Jesus himself had sufficient resources for his simple needs. In his teaching there is no idealistic praise of a life of complete poverty, but there is a demand that his followers should sit lightly towards the standards and values of the world. 'Do not lay up for yourselves treasures on earth . . . but lay up for yourselves treasures in heaven' (Matt.6.19). 'Beware of all covetousness,' he said in reply to a request to settle a property dispute, 'for a man's life does not consist in the abundance of his possessions.' And then he told the parable of the Rich Fool (Luke 12.13–21).

Jesus spoke of the way in which great wealth threatens a man's true and creative life, using the well-known simile of the camel and the eye of a needle. At the end of this discourse there is a difficult saying. Peter said, 'We have left everything and followed you,' to which Jesus, according to the Gospel of Mark, gave this long reply:

Truly I say to you, there is no one who has left house or brothers or sisters or mother or father or children or lands, for my sake and for the gospel, who will not receive a hundredfold now in this time, houses and brothers and sisters and mothers and children and lands, with persecutions, and in the age to come eternal life (Mark 10.28–30).

Any interpretation of this enigmatic reply is bound to be uncertain. Many scholars regard it as an addition, in whole or in part, by the early church which looked beyond persecutions, to its reward. The long list of benefits, 'houses, lands, brothers, sisters, mothers and children' may reflect the intimate fellowship of the first Christians and the ideal of sharing possessions and having all things in common. If the passage in any form is an authentic saying of Jesus, it may be that he was gently laughing at blundering Peter. 'What about us?', says Peter, 'We've given up everything.' 'Do you want your reward, Peter?', Jesus replies, 'Would you like a hundred houses; a hundred mothers, brothers and sisters? Well you can have them.' And then the sting in the tail – 'with persecutions!'

(ii) *'Take up the cross'*

The story of a man who ran up to Jesus and asked what he must do to win eternal life is reported in all three Synoptic Gospels (Matt. 19.16–22; Mark 10.17–22; Luke 18.18–23). It is Matthew who tells us that the man was young and rich, and Luke who describes him as 'a man of the ruling class': hence the familiar title of the incident 'the Rich Young Ruler'. Jesus loved this young man at sight and laid upon him the heaviest demand: to give away to the poor everything he possessed and to follow Jesus – which surely means to become one of the small intimate band of disciples.

When James and John asked for prominent places in the coming kingdom, what they were promised was a cup of sorrow and a baptism of death (Mark 10.35–40 = Matt.20.20–23). In a public utterance to the people as well as to the disciples Jesus said, 'Anyone who wishes to be a follower of mine must leave self behind; he must take up his cross and come with me' (Mark 8.34 = Matt.16.24 = Luke 9.23). Clearly 'taking up the cross' meant different things for different individuals both in the lifetime of Jesus and afterwards. For some it led to sufferings and hardship, for some martyrdom, and for many others faithful, unspectacular service. There is a saying of Jesus which, then and now, unites all who follow him in obedience:

You know that in the world the recognized rulers lord it over their subjects, and their great men make them feel the weight of authority. That is not the way with you; among you whoever wants to be great must be the willing slave of all. For even the Son of man did not come to be served but to serve, and to surrender his life as a ransom for many (Mark 10.42–45 NEB).

Time Present and Time Future

This section deals with a perplexing and controversial aspect of the message of Jesus. Much of his teaching was directed to the immediate needs and problems of the men and women to whom he talked in small groups in the market place, or in large crowds gathered to listen to him. This teaching was concerned with 'time present'. On the other hand, in all the Gospels there is teaching which seems on the face of it to refer to dramatic and even cataclysmic events in the future. The thoughts of Jesus moved not only in 'time present' but also in 'time future'.

1. *Time Present*

Alan Dale in the preceding article has written of Jesus as a man 'making a costly and dangerous attempt to ask real questions about a real world'. Jesus was not a visionary nor a spectator of life's scene: he did not dwell in an ivory tower. The backcloth of his message was the Roman occupation and the revolutionary movement directed against it. It was also the deep division between the Jewish hierarchy – the priests and Sadducees – and the ordinary people led by the Pharisees. The 'setting in life' of his teaching was the daily round and constant worries of farmers and fishermen, shopkeepers and merchants, housewives with their children. 'Don't be anxious,' he said constantly, 'and don't be afraid' (Matt.6.25 f.). He urged men to be generous towards each other as God is generous (Matt.5.43 f.), and to make courageous gestures of friendship even towards traditional enemies (Luke 10.29–37).

As Jesus spoke of men's daily needs and preached generosity, compassion and forgiveness there was always in his mind the reality of God's kingship. Don't be anxious or afraid; your heavenly Father knows what you need. 'Seek first his kingdom and his righteousness and all these things shall be yours as well' (Matt.6.31–33). As we have seen in many parables and sayings Jesus proclaimed that God's kingship was a present reality. It had come or it was very near, now in Galilee in the early years of the first century AD.

In Luke 17.21 there is a saying of Jesus which reads in the Authorized Version, 'the kingdom of God is *within you*'. Modern versions give the translation, *'in the midst of you'* (RSV) or *'is among you'* (NEB). Taken by itself the saying refers to 'time present'. The kingdom of God is actually here now. Luke, however, or the source which Luke used, placed this saying in a context which prophesies future events. The time of the Son of man will come and it will be a time of catastrophe and terror. 'Like the lightning-flash that lights up the earth from end to end, will the Son of man be when his day comes' (17.24 NEB). The arrangement of these verses in Luke is no doubt the work of someone in the early church, but it illustrates an important point about the teaching of Jesus. His thought moved easily from 'time present' to 'time future'.

2. *Time Future*

In the Gospels there are predictions; forecasts concerning the future. In Matt.23.37–39 = Luke 13.34–35 there is the well-known lament over the Holy City. 'O Jerusalem, Jerusalem . . . behold your house is forsaken and desolate.' Luke, however, included in his Gospel another and very different lament.

> When he came in sight of the city, he wept over it and said, 'If only you had known, on this great day, the way that leads to peace! But no; it is hidden from your sight. For a time will come upon you, when your enemies will set up siege-works against you; they will encircle you and hem you in at every point; they will bring you to the ground, you and your children within your walls, and not leave you one stone standing on another, because you did not recognize God's moment when it came (Luke 19.41–44 NEB).

This is a terse and vivid prediction of the siege and destruction of Jerusalem which began in May and ended in September of the year AD 70. Since this event took place some forty years after the time of Jesus, it is often argued that such a description of the great catastrophe must have arisen within the early church. This supposition can be neither proved nor disproved, but it seems unnecessarily pedantic. The prediction does not describe in detail the actual siege of Jerusalem, as the Jewish historian Josephus reported it many years later.

The words of Jesus describe a typical siege; a city encircled, siege engines battering at the wall and so on. Moreover, to one who like Jesus took a close interest in the political clamour and unrest of the Jews, and yet, standing apart from it, was not blinded by partisan emotions, it needed no special insight to realize that if the revolutionary elements continued to oppose the government by violent acts, the Romans would reinforce their troops in the country and drive straight towards Jerusalem.

There are other passages in the Gospels which may reflect the horrors of the war which began in AD 66, though scholars hold different views on the point. Mark 13 is clearly a collection of sayings which Mark himself may have put together, or which may already have been in existence as a separate document. It is probable that genuine sayings of Jesus are embedded in it, and some of these seem to be predictions of the great war between the Jews and the Romans. Here, for instance, is a prediction of the plight of war refugees. The editor's hand is evident in the opening phrases.

When you see 'the abomination of desolation' usurping a place which is not his (let the reader understand), then those who are in Judaea must take to the hills. If a man is on the roof, he must not come down into the house to fetch anything out; if in the field he must not turn back for his cloak. Alas for women with child in those days, and for those who have children at the breast! Pray that it may not come in the winter (Mark 13.14–18 NEB).

The Future of Israel

Did Jesus predict the rejection of Israel as the chosen instrument of God's purpose? It is clear that this view was held at least in some quarters in the early church. The part played by the Jewish authorities in the death of Jesus; the hostility displayed by some Jews towards the new Christian communities, both played their part in shaping the belief that the 'Old Israel' had been rejected and the 'New Israel' – the Christian church – had taken its place. This belief has certainly left its mark upon the form in which some of the sayings and parables of Jesus have come down to us.

In Matt.23 we have a sustained and bitter condemnation of the Pharisees and lawyers. This was certainly put together in its present form by an editor. It has a clear literary shape: an introduction (vv. 1–12); the seven accusations against the lawyers and Pharisees, each beginning, 'Woe to you' (vv. 13–36); and in conclusion a lament over Jerusalem, the centre of unfaithfulness, 'killing the prophets and stoning those who are sent to you' (vv. 37 f.). How far this stylized chapter truly reflects the teaching of Jesus is a difficult question to answer, but the evidence of the Gospels as a whole makes clear that he did attack the religious leaders of Israel and declare that they and the kind of religion for which they stood would be rejected. But did Jesus predict the rejection of Israel as the chosen people of God? The answer we give to this question depends largely upon the way we interpret two parables: the Vineyard (Mark 12.1–11 = Matt.21.33–43 = Luke 20.9–18), and the Marriage Feast (Matt.22.1–14 = Luke 14.16–24).

The vineyard is let by an absentee landlord to tenants. On three separate occasions at harvest time he sends a servant to receive the rent in kind, and each of the servants is shamefully treated and sent away empty-handed. Finally the landlord sends 'his beloved son', and the tenants seize him, kill him and throw him out of the vineyard. The parable ends with the question, 'What will the landlord do?', and the answer is that he will destroy the tenants and give the vineyard to others.

The parable of the Marriage Feast, which is a parable of the Kingdom, tells a similar story. The invited guests make various trivial excuses and refuse to attend the banquet, and their places are taken by people 'both bad and good' collected at random by the king's servants.

The parable of the Vineyard is unusual because unlike most of the parables each detail has a meaning. The vineyard stands for Israel, the owner for God, the tenants are the Jewish authorities, the servants are Old Testament prophets who had been despised and rejected, the 'beloved son' is Jesus. Mark's version ends with the words, 'and they (the Jewish authorities) tried to arrest Jesus . . . for they perceived that he spoke this parable against them'. The vineyard is given to others just as in the parable of the Marriage Feast the ordinary citizens take the place of the invited guests. 'The publicans and harlots,' said Jesus on another occasion, 'go into the kingdom of Heaven before you' (Matt.21.31). It seems clear that it is not the nation as a whole which is rejected but the religious leaders, the lawyers and the Pharisees.

The Day of Judgment

Another controversial question concerning 'time future' is this: did Jesus predict that he would come again in glory; that there would be a final Day of Judgment and the end of the world? This, as we have seen, was a belief strongly held by Christians during the early years of the first century (see I Thess.5.1–11; II Thess.1.5–12). The belief waned as the years went by and the risen Christ did not appear in glory, but in mediaeval times it gained great popularity and was a favourite subject for artists. The belief finds expression in Mark 13 and is expanded in Matt.24–25 and in Luke 21.5–36. Here the predicted events are dramatic and terrifying – wars, earthquakes, famine and persecution, the rise of bogus messiahs and false prophets precede the appearance of Christ as judge of the world. There is a different picture in Luke 17.22–37 which comes from the source 'Q'. Men and women are going about their daily routine, eating, drinking, sleeping, trading, marrying and then, suddenly, like a flash of lightning the Day of the Son of man is upon them.

The teaching which we have quoted from the Gospels and the Epistles has a technical name: *eschatology*. The language in which it is expressed is *eschatological language*. It is alien to our way of thinking. Many Christians quietly ignore this element in the New Testament, and some biblical scholars deny that Jesus ever thought in these terms, or expected his own second coming. What are we to make of it all?

1. Eschatological thinking arises when there is a contradiction between the harsh realities of life and man's faith in God's power and justice. In this kind of situation the religious man says with Paul that 'the sufferings of this present time are not worthy to be comparing with the glory that is to be revealed to us' (Rom.8.18). Eschatological teaching brings hope to men, and when present sufferings are severe then the hope of a glorious future is often expressed in imaginative pictures. Sometimes the language is poetic and pastoral:

The cow and the bear shall feed;
　　their young shall lie down together;
　　and the lion shall eat straw like the
　　ox (Isa.11.7).

Sometimes it is dramatic, 'technicoloured' language to match the drama of the moment. In the dark days of the second century BC when the Jews were engaged in a desperate struggle with the Seleucid rulers (see Part III, Section 15, pp. 191 ff.), this was written:

Behold, with the clouds of heaven
　　there came one like a son of man,
and he came to the Ancient of Days
　　and was presented before him.
And to him was given dominion
　　and glory and kingdom,
that all peoples, nations and languages
　　should serve him;
his dominion is an everlasting dominion,
　　which shall not pass away,
and his kingdom one
　　that shall not be destroyed (Dan.7.13 f.).

It was natural that the first Christians, often isolated from the rest of their fellow citizens because of their faith, usually under suspicion, taunted for worshipping a crucified Saviour, and at times persecuted, should rest their hopes on Christ's return in power and glory. They believed that this hope was founded upon the teaching of Jesus, and they made collections of sayings which supported their faith and included them in their church books – the Gospels.

2. Jesus faced opposition, slander and resentment, and seems to have known – at least in the final months of his life – that his enemies would turn the full force of their power against him. But more than this; he was alarmed and sorrowful at the political situation of his nation. He knew that armed rebellion could only end in national disaster. Yet his faith in the purposes of God and in the realities of God's kingship did not waver. He, too, was a man of hope, and it should not surprise us that sometimes he expressed this hope in vivid and dramatic language. He was, we have said, a poet, 'the greatest artist of us all', and poets dream dreams and see visions.

3. Whether or not Jesus believed in his own 'second coming', he knew that he had been chosen by God to fulfil a particular rôle in history. The sayings and parables which he used when he thought about the future were

his way of expressing his confident faith in God's undefeated purpose.

Who was Jesus of Nazareth?

A modern biographer, writing the life of a public or semi-public figure, can usually draw upon other material for his portrayal of character than the known facts of his subject's career. There may be family letters and documents, reminiscences of friends, published articles, newspaper cuttings and even, with luck, a personal diary kept over the years of public life. With such materials at hand the biographer can explore the inner life and private thoughts of the man or woman of whom he is writing. He can trace the development of ideas and convictions and often he can discern not only what his subject thought about public affairs and private concerns, but also what he thought about himself.

Such a biography cannot be written of Jesus of Nazareth. The materials just are not there. In the nineteenth and early twentieth centuries devout and scholarly authors often included in their books a chapter on 'the self-consciousness of Jesus'. But there are no private letters, and no diary and no published articles. There are reminiscences of friends and followers, but these, as we have them in the Gospels, have been interpreted to meet the needs of the early Christians (see pp. 283 f.). Moreover, in the Synoptic Gospels Jesus displays a marked reluctance to speak about himself or to disclose his identity. For instance, when the disciples of John the Baptist were sent to ask, 'Are you he who is to come or shall we look for another?' Jesus turned the question aside. 'Are you the Promised One: God's Messiah?' asked John's disciples, and Jesus replied obliquely by pointing to his ministry of healing and preaching (Matt.11.2–6 = Luke 7.18–22).

Many scholars of the present day, therefore, say that we cannot answer the question, 'Who was Jesus of Nazareth?'. We know nothing for certain of his inner life and private thoughts. We cannot explore his 'self-consciousness' or know what he believed to be the truth about himself.

On the other hand, some New Testament scholars have recently re-opened the question of what Jesus believed about himself. Their studies are concentrated upon a fresh exami-nation of three titles which occur in the Gospels: 'Christ', 'Son of man' and 'Son of God'. In this section the evidence provided by these designations is briefly reviewed.

1. *Christ*

This title is of course the Greek form of the Hebrew 'Messiah': in both languages it means 'the Anointed One'. It occurs several times in the Synoptic Gospels, two of the references being of particular importance. The first of these is in Mark 8.27–33 = Matt.16.13–20 = Luke 9.18–22.

> And he asked them (the disciples), 'But who do you say that I am?' Peter answered him, 'You are the Christ.' And he charged them to tell no man about him (Mark 8.29 f.).

Luke's version is identical with Mark's except that Peter's reply reads 'the Christ of God'. In Matthew's version, which is surely an extended version of the early tradition, Peter replies, 'You are the Christ, the Son of the living God', and this is followed by an enthusiastic response from Jesus. 'Blessed are you, Simon son of Jonah. Flesh and blood has not revealed this to you but my Father who is in heaven.' This is followed again by the promise that 'on this rock' Jesus will build his church and that to Peter, or to all his disciples will be given 'the keys of the kingdom of heaven'.

In the early church the title 'Messiah' or 'Christ' became the corner-stone of the new faith. Jesus was the Anointed One, the long promised Deliverer, but what does the reply of Peter, 'You are the Christ', tell us about the convictions of Jesus concerning himself? He does not take the title upon his own lips and in Mark and Luke he sharply commands secrecy and begins immediately to speak of his approaching sufferings and death. As with the question asked by John's disciples, Jesus seems to turn aside an awkward situation by speaking of the present realities of his life. 'The Son of man must suffer many things.'

The second key passage is Mark 14.61 f. = Matt.26.63 f. = Luke 22.66 f. The scene is the examination of Jesus before the Jewish High Council. Caiaphas the high priest asks Jesus, 'Are you the Christ, the Son of the Blessed?' According to Mark Jesus replied 'I am'; Matthew reports that he answered, 'You have said so', and in Luke he replies, 'If I tell you you will not believe.' What is significant, however, is that all three Gospels agree that Jesus went on immediately to speak of himself as the 'Son of man', as if the title 'Christ' was of little importance to him. On this evidence we may well hesitate before asserting that Jesus claimed for himself the title 'Messiah'.

2. *Son of Man*

In the two incidents discussed in the previous paragraphs Jesus, when named by others as the Christ, seems immediately to have substituted the designation 'Son of man'. It is a title which occurs frequently in the Synoptic Gospels, and only on the lips of Jesus. Apart from the Fourth Gospel, where it occurs nearly as often as in Mark, it is only found once in the rest of the New Testament (Acts 7.56). To some scholars this title is the clue to the hidden thoughts of Jesus concerning his own identity. Others reject most of the texts in which it occurs as later interpolations. It is a puzzling title which appears to carry different meanings in different sayings. There are, for instance, sayings in which it is uncertain whether Jesus is speaking of himself, of his future return in glory, or of some other One who is yet to appear. 'When the Son of man comes will he find faith on the earth?' (Luke 18.8). One writer who attaches considerable importance to this designation and examines it at length has written, 'Here all is obscure and hotly debated.'

In the Old Testament 'Son of man' usually means simply 'man'. In the book of Ezekiel, for instance, it is constantly used whenever God speaks to the prophet. 'Son of man, stand upon your feet and I will speak with you' (Ezek.2.1). This seems to be the usage in such a saying of Jesus as, 'Foxes have holes, and birds of the air have nests, but the Son of man has nowhere to lay his head' (Matt.8.20 = Luke 9.58). 'I have nowhere to lay my head.'

There are, however, sayings in which Jesus claims the title and gives it greater significance. Consider first the story told in Mark 2.1–12. Jesus has before him a paralytic lying on a mattress, and says to him, 'My son, your sins are forgiven.' A group of lawyers who witness the scene declare that this is blasphemous talk. Jesus then heals the paralytic man saying that he does so 'that you may know that the Son of man has authority on earth to forgive sins'. Again at Mark 2.28 Jesus declares that 'the

Son of Man is lord of ('sovereign over' NEB) even the sabbath'. In these two narratives, if they truly represent what happened, Jesus in taking the title Son of man claims in the first instance authority from God and in the second sovereignty over a sacred institution.

Perhaps the most significant occasion on which Jesus appears to have claimed the title Son of man is one which has already been mentioned, namely the examination before the Jewish High Council after his arrest in Gethsemane. Having replied to the high priest's question, 'Are you the Christ, the Son of the Blessed?' Jesus added, 'You will see the Son of man sitting at the right hand of power and coming with the clouds of heaven' (Mark 14.62 = Matt.26.64 = Luke 22.69). Clearly the reference is to the prophecy in the book of Daniel which has already been quoted (see above, p. 298).

> Behold with the clouds of heaven
> there came one like a son of man.

The title 'Son of man' appears in the Gospels in three contexts: the earthly ministry of Jesus, his sufferings and his future glory. What remains uncertain is whether all three uses of the term are authentic, or whether the church, looking back upon the past events of the cross and resurrection gave its own meaning – a messianic meaning – to the title so that it became almost a synonym for 'Messiah'.

3. *Son of God*

There is a saying preserved by Matthew and Luke which is highly characteristic of the Fourth Gospel but unique in the Synoptics.

> All things have been delivered to me by my Father; and no-one knows the Son except the Father and no-one knows the Father except the Son and anyone to whom the Son chooses to reveal him (Matt.11.27 = Luke 10.22).

Apart from this the title 'Son of God' is only spoken by supernatural voices at the baptism of Jesus (Mark 1.11 = Matt.3.17 = Luke 3.22) and at his transfiguration (Mark 9.7 = Matt.17.5 = Luke 9.35); it is also spoken by demons before their defeat at the hands of Jesus (see, for instance, Mark 5.6 f.). Jesus, of course, spoke of God as his Father, but on the evidence of the Synoptic Gospels it would be hazardous to assert that he thought of himself as 'the Son of God' in the sense in which the early church proclaimed him.

The questions discussed in this final section are difficult and complicated. The issues have been simplified, and for a fuller discussion reference should be made to the commentaries and other books suggested in the bibliography.

This discussion of the evidence has raised questions but has not provided answers. If now we extend our thought and look again at the central message of Jesus the three titles come into a different focus and we can make a more positive statement.

Jesus, as we have seen, proclaimed that the kingdom of God had come. God's kingship was already exercising sway in Galilee and Judaea. The kingdom was not yet come in all the fullness of its power. The disciples must still pray 'Thy kingdom come', but a new power and authority and benevolence had arisen to give new hope to the people of Palestine.

The evidence for this new assertion of God's kingship was Jesus himself. One of his most significant sayings was spoken after he had, to use the words of the Gospel, 'cast out a demon that was dumb'. 'If,' said Jesus, 'it is by the finger of God that I cast out demons, then the kingdom of God has come upon you' (Luke 11.14–20). 'By the finger of God . . . by the power of God himself I do my work . . . and God's sovereignty is established.' By the will of God he was at the centre of this new movement in history. The world had turned upon a new course and would never be the same again because he had come. Whether or not he, in the depths of his own mind, expressed this fact by thinking of himself as 'Messiah', or 'Son of man' or 'Son of God', for those who believed on him in Palestine and for those who in the wider world entered the Christian fellowship, these titles expressed the new reality which they had come to know in Jesus.

9

Paul and his World

C. H. Dodd

The Graeco-Roman World

When a reader of the Bible turns from the Gospels to the other books of the New Testament, one thing that cannot fail to strike him is the sudden enlargement of the stage of action. The events of the Gospel story have hardly taken him beyond the narrow confines of Judaea and Galilee (an area comparable with, shall we say, Yorkshire). But turn the page, and the scene changes. The action shifts rapidly over a great part of the Near and Middle East, and as far west as the Adriatic. Over this wide area travellers move freely by land or water, untroubled by national frontiers or language difficulties. This is the Hellenistic world; that is to say, that part of the world which, embracing many different nationalities, was bound together by the use of the Greek language, serving as a vehicle for Greek thought and Greek

social and political ideals. It was largely the outcome of the conquests of Alexander the Great, whose deliberate policy it was to permeate the conquered territories with the Greek spirit. The cultural unity which he promoted survived the break-up of Alexander's empire, but the kingdoms formed out of the fragments gradually sank into decline, until a great part of the region presented the spectacle of a society in dissolution.

Then Rome came on the scene. Appearing first as one more competitor in the scramble for power, and a brutal and ruthless one, it ended by imposing peace and good order on the Hellenistic world, and adding to its cultural unity a political cohesion which it had lacked. It now becomes appropriate to speak of the 'Graeco-Roman' world. The transformation of a predatory and aggressive power into the presiding genius of a highly civilized international society was in large measure the work of the emperor Augustus, whose reign covers the transition from BC to AD. The imperial rule was accepted willingly enough by most of its eastern subjects. No doubt there were pockets of discontent (Jewish Palestine was one), but with inherited memories of prolonged anarchy and misrule to which the strong arm of Rome had put an end, most of them knew when they were well off.

The Empire: Political and Social Structure

Augustus had emerged from the civil wars as undisputed master of the whole Hellenistic world as far east as the Euphrates. Within the imperial frontier a few puppet principalities were allowed to survive, as a useful 'buffer' or an administrative convenience, but the greater part of the annexed territories was given a provincial organization which amounted to a business-like and efficient bureaucracy. Frontier provinces were placed under military governors in command of legionary troops, with the title 'legate'. They were appointed directly by the emperor and were under his personal supervision. Peaceful provinces away from the frontiers had civilian governors with the title 'proconsul'. They were appointed, nominally, by the Roman Senate, but the emperor had them well in hand. Minor provinces (like Judaea) might be administered by governors of inferior rank appointed by the emperor, with the title 'prefect' or 'procurator'.

Within his province the governor was invested with all the authority of the empire, subject only to remote control by the emperor in Rome. He was responsible for every aspect of administration, but most particularly for the administration of justice, which he exercised by holding regular assizes at the principal cities of his province in turn. Roman rule, however, was not so severely centralized as to leave no room for a measure of local government. Throughout the eastern provinces there were numerous partly self-governing cities. They might be ancient Greek city-states, like Athens or Ephesus, or cities founded after their pattern by Hellenistic monarchs, like Antioch-on-the-Orontes, the capital of the province of Syria. Or they might be Roman colonies, like Philippi in Macedonia. The original colonists had been time-expired legionaries, who were given grants

of land in the conquered territories by way of pension. Their institutions were closely modelled on those of the mother-city, and they took pride in their Roman citizenship (see, e.g., Acts 16.21). All these cities continued to be administered by their own magistrates and senates, who were allowed to exercise a certain degree of autonomy. It was no more than a shadow of the sovereign independence of the Greek cities in their prime, and it shrank with the years. But in the New Testament period the cities could still feel a justified pride in their civic liberties.

In most cities there were colonies of Jews. The Hellenistic monarchs had encouraged them as valuable settlers, and the emperors continued to accord them favourable treatment. Among the populace in general there was at most times an undercurrent of anti-Semitism, sometimes breaking out in violence. On the other hand there was widespread interest in some aspects of the Jewish religion, and its influence on Hellenistic thought was by no means negligible.

The Greek cities and the Roman colonies alike had a democratic element written into their constitutions. In the New Testament period the popular assembly, or town's meeting, still had an active, even if a restricted, part to play. But democracy was not a plant to flourish in the climate of the empire. Municipal communities tended more and more to reproduce the rigidly stratified structure of imperial society as a whole. At its head was the Roman nobility, wealthy and amply privileged, with exclusive access to the highest offices of state. At its base was the slave class, upon whose labour the economic structure ultimately rested.

The lot of slaves was inevitably harsh, especially of those employed in industry or agriculture, though Roman law now gave some protection against the extremes of brutality which in former times had often provoked large-scale insurrections. Domestic slavery had its alleviations. Some masters were considerate, and treated their slaves as subordinate members of the family. Besides, a slave who was well educated, as many were, or qualified by native talent or acquired skill for some specialized employment, was too valuable a property to be handled recklessly. It was possible for a slave to earn and save enough to purchase his freedom, or he might hope for emancipation by testament on his master's death. A steady stream of emancipated slaves passed into the free community. Many were employed in (what we should call) the imperial civil service. Many were 'rising men'.

For the humbler orders of the free population, with little or no share in civic privileges, there were voluntary associations (*collegia*). Such voluntary associations, or clubs, had abounded among all classes in Greek and Roman society, but the emperors looked on them with a suspicious eye, and disallowed them except in so far as their activities could be directed into obviously harmless channels. Associations of tradesmen were permitted, under supervision, and poor men's 'friendly societies' were treated indulgently. They functioned as burial clubs, and could assure other benefits to their members, beside providing for social intercourse, especially on such occasions as the festivals of the deities which a club might have adopted as patrons. The 'friendly societies' included in their membership both slaves and free men of the poorest sort, and they must have done something to humanize the lot of a rootless proletariate. They seem to have provided in part the model on which the earliest Christian churches were organized. Their open membership, their regularly appointed officials, the common fund maintained by members' contributions, and their social meals with a religious complexion, are all features that reappear in adapted forms.

Philosophy and Religion

In the eastern provinces of the empire, with their strongly Hellenic heritage, intellectual life was vigorous. The lively interchange of correspondence, attested by papyri, among business men, farmers, soldiers, and all manner of ordinary folk, reveals a large literate public. Such a public, even if not highly educated, was open to the spread of ideas. It is characteristic of the period that philosophy was no longer the preserve of academics or gentlemen of leisure, but came out into the market place. The 'street-corner' philosopher became a familiar figure. Some acquaintance, however superficial, with philosophical ideas must have been widespread. The school of philosophy with the widest appeal was Stoicism. It was on the one side an elaborate and deeply thought system of logic and metaphysics, which incorporated the most advanced natural science of the time. It was not, however, on this side that it made its widest popular impact, but in its ethical teaching. However little the austere Stoic code might be honoured in the observance, at any rate it did much to inform a 'conscience' (the word itself is a Stoic coinage) in a society which had been notably without moral anchorage.

In earlier times Greek philosophy had been critical of popular religion and in general sceptical about belief in gods. It now came to terms with the return to religion which was a marked feature of the time. It has been described as a 'failure of nerve', shaking the old Greek confidence in reason under stress of the fearful insecurity which had long overshadowed Hellenistic society. It might more fairly be described as an awakening to the reality of dark forces in man and his world, not amenable to pure reason, which Greek rationality had tried to keep out of sight – never, indeed, with complete success. Men began to feel the need for redemption from the dark forces, however these might be conceived. This need was not met by the ancient gods of Greece and Rome, though their time-honoured and imposing ceremonies retained their appeal, and were a matter of pride and emulation among the cities. But the Hellenistic world was open to contacts with religions of another type, particularly those of Egypt, Iran, and the Semitic East, including Judaism. From such sources, often in a confused mixture, strange cults emerged. Many of them offered initiation into a 'mystery', which in one way or another assured to the initiate deliverance from the evils he most feared. The new popularity of these cults reminded the Greeks that they had their own ancestral 'mysteries', and these now acquired a new prestige – and acquired also meanings which might have surprised the ancestors.

Of these 'religions of redemption' we know little in detail; the secret of the mysteries was well kept. But it seems possible to draw some broad outlines. There were, it appears, commonly two main elements: the ritual action, or drama, and the tale, or 'myth', which underlay the action. The myth might recount, for example, how the god or hero who was the lord of the cult had died and come to life, or had penetrated into the dark underworld and won his way out into the light. The ritual action was designed to reproduce in dramatic symbolism

– often, it seems, elaborate and spectacular – the plot of the myth, and this made the initiate partaker in the experience of his lord, and guaranteed him a blessed immortality. What proportion of the population of the empire received initiation into these cults we cannot know; it was probably a very small minority; but the influence of this type of religion on the thought and ethos of the time is unmistakable.

Where popular philosophy and popular religion met, there emerged a widely diffused way of thinking which, with great variety, shows some constant features. It held that this world is a realm of darkness and death in which the soul of man is imprisoned. He can, however, escape into the world of light and life through the attainment of 'knowledge'. But this was not the rational or scientific knowledge that ancient Greek philosophy had valued. It was more like revelation, or esoteric vision; and here the influence of the 'mysteries' is evident. At its highest it might take the form of a 'mystical' experience of oneness with 'The Real', or with 'The All' – which was often spoken of as 'knowledge of God'. At its lowest it might be nothing better than abracadabra. Popular religion and popular philosophy alike were deeply infected with the enervating belief in the dominance of the stars over human destiny, and astrology flourished.

Christianity in the Graeco-Roman World

All this went to constitute the climate of thought and feeling in which people of the Graeco-Roman world lived. It is at any rate an index to the kind of spiritual need of which they were conscious. And these were the people to whom the early Christian missionaries made their approach. They brought a religion of redemption. It took seriously the reality and power of the dark forces that menace the human spirit, but it brought also a buoyant confidence in the victory gained over them once and for all by Christ, and now open to be shared by all who would put their faith in him. It had, like the 'mysteries', its rites of dramatic symbolism, but its rite of initiation was a simple washing in water, and the drama of its central 'mystery' was no more than the sharing of bread and wine in memory of the Lord. These rites had behind them a tale, or 'myth'; but the 'myth' was a true story of a real man who had lived not so long ago. The death-and-resurrection of which it told was an event that had occurred within living memory. Yet in the two symbolic rites, or sacraments – baptism and the eucharist, or Lord's supper – what was past became present, and the believer shared the virtue of the death and resurrection of the Lord, and entered into union with him. So the Christian gospel affirmed.

This reference to a Lord whose person, character and teaching were well attested gave a specific ethical stamp to the Christian religion of redemption. Social ethics had, so far as can be judged, little place in the popular religions. The new religion had behind it the strong Jewish tradition of ethical monotheism inherited from the Hebrew prophets. Its Founder counter-signed that tradition, and yet by what he taught, and through his own action, liberated it from the limitations of the existing Jewish system, and offered the possibility of life under a 'law of liberty'. Here Christianity met the aspirations of Stoicism at its best, along with the assurance (which Stoicism lacked) of divine assistance towards the attainment of its ideals. Much of the ethical teaching of the New Testament would be recognized by any Stoic. And yet in the end the Christian ethic came out very differently. The Stoic ideal, lofty and austere as it was, remained essentially self-centred, and there was about it a certain coldness and hardness, however attractive the character of some of its exponents. Christianity, following the teaching and example of Christ, placed the centre of the ethical life in a warm regard for others, using for it the almost untranslatable term *agape*, which has to be rendered into English as 'charity', or 'love'. Here was a deeper basis for genuine human fellowship than other associations in the Graeco-Roman world could offer, and it was certainly one reason for the strong appeal that the church made to those who hungered for true community and had failed to find it.

Paul: Jew and Roman Citizen

The pioneer leader in the Christian approach to the Graeco-Roman public was the apostle Paul. The fortunate preservation of a number of his letters has put us in a position to know him better than we can know most personages of the ancient world. The information they give can be supplemented from the account of his career given in the Acts of the Apostles. It is true that there are points where it is not easy to bring the two sources of our knowledge into complete harmony, and there are critical questions about the Acts which are still open. But in the parts of the book with which we are more particularly concerned – those which deal with the extended missionary tours undertaken by Paul – there is good reason to believe that the author was well-informed. In the later chapters the narrative is sometimes in the first person plural. It appears that the author has incorporated extracts from something like a travel diary – his own diary, likely enough. If so, then we are reading an account which emanates from one of Paul's travelling companions, who was at times an eyewitness of what he records. The 'diarist' is with much probability taken to be Luke, the Greek doctor whom we know from the letters to have been a close associate of the apostle (Col.4.14; II Tim.4.11; Philemon 24). His work may be used – so far as it goes, for there are large gaps – as an historical frame in which to set the letters, which are Paul's own account of himself.

Paul was born at Tarsus in Cilicia (Acts 21.39), an ancient Greek city, and now a strong centre of Hellenistic culture. His parents belonged to the Jewish colony there. They were orthodox and brought up their son in the Pharisaic persuasion (Acts 23.6; 26.5; Phil.3.5). At the same time, the father possessed the coveted status of Roman citizen, which meant that the family had a superior standing in the local community. The son was a Roman citizen by birthright (Acts 22.25–29). At home he was Saul, named after the first king of Israel; outside he was Paulus, citizen of Tarsus, citizen of Rome. He was bilingual, equally conversant with Aramaic and Greek. More exactly, he was trilingual, for he could read the Hebrew Scriptures in the original. Thus his mind had the freedom of two worlds of thought. Though it does not appear that he was deeply versed in Greek literature or philosophy, he had perhaps rather more than the educated man's general acquaintance with ideas that were in the air. His language quite often carries echoes of Stoicism. On the other hand his formal education seems to have been entirely within the native Jewish tradition. He was sent to study in Jerusalem, under Gamaliel (Acts 22.3), the most distinguished Rabbi of his time. The fruit of his education is everywhere apparent in his minute acquaintance with the Scriptures of the Old Testament, and the Rabbinic methods of interpreting them (which for his modern readers sometimes make difficulties). He was thus exceptionally equipped for the task to which in the end his life was devoted, that of mediating to the Hellenistic public a religion rooted in Judaism.

Saul the Pharisee and Paul the Roman, it seems, did not live in complete harmony inside the same skin. There are signs of psychological tension. In early life the Pharisee was uppermost. He recites with pride the privileges of the chosen people: 'They are Israelites; they were made God's sons; theirs is the splendour of the divine presence, theirs the covenants, the law, the temple worship, and the promises' (Rom. 9.4. In this article biblical quotations in general follow the translation in the NEB). And not only was he proud of his people (as is right and proper); he was also proud beyond measure of his own standing as a Jew: 'Israelite by race, of the tribe of Benjamin, a Hebrew born and bred: in my attitude to the law a Pharisee, in pious zeal a persecutor of the church, in legal rectitude faultless' (Phil.3.5–6). In another retrospect on his early life he adds a significant phrase: 'In the practice of our national religion I was *outstripping many of my Jewish contemporaries* in my boundless devotion to the traditions of my ancestors' (Gal.1.14). That tells us something important about the man; he had an irresistible urge to excel, to be distinguished. It was necessary to his self-respect that he should see himself as the perfect Pharisee: 'in legal rectitude faultless'. (This may partly account for something extravagant or abnormal which some Jewish readers have found in Paul's account of his pre-Christian phase.) But the time came when he was forced to confess to himself that this was fantasy and not reality. He was not faultless, and his efforts to be so were self-defeating. 'When I want to do the right, only the wrong is within my reach. In my inmost self I delight in the law of God, but I perceive that there is in my bodily members a different law, fighting against the law that my reason approves' (Rom. 7.21 f.).

It is a recognized fact of psychology that when an inward conflict becomes unendurable, the subject may seek relief by externalizing the conflict, and projecting the hatred he feels for something in himself upon some object outside himself. This is what Paul did, and it was this that made him a persecutor. His first contact with the new sect of the 'Nazarenes', it appears, was through one of its most radical and aggressive representatives, a Hellenistic Jew (like Paul himself) named Stephen, who was reported to be 'forever saying things against the holy place and the law', saying, indeed, 'that Jesus of Nazareth will destroy this place (the temple) and alter the customs handed down to us by Moses' (Acts 6.13 f.). This was to impugn the most sacred pledges of Israel's status as God's chosen people. And when it appeared that these sectaries hailed Jesus of Nazareth as God's Messiah, this was sheer blasphemy. Did not the Law say, 'cursed is everyone who is hanged on a gibbet' (Gal.3.13)? These people were dragging the glory of Israel in the mire: they were enemies of the temple and the Law, enemies of Israel, enemies of Israel's God. All the hatred (and fear?) that Saul felt for that in himself which was 'fighting against the Law' could now be directed upon overt enemies. Stephen was stoned to death, with Saul as an accessory. This was only a beginning. With characteristic energy and initiative – and, it may be added, with characteristic determination to outstrip everyone else in zeal for the Law – he obtained from the high priest a commission to hunt the heretics down wherever they might be found (Acts 9.1 f.).

The Conversion of Paul

It was in the pursuit of this grim mission, on the road to Damascus, that he met with that which changed the current of his life. There are three accounts of it in Acts (Acts 9.3–9; 22.4–11; 26.12–18); but it is little that any narrative of events can tell us about spiritual experience. It can only hint at what took place in the depths of the soul under the form of describing objective occurrences. We are told of a light and a voice. The voice identified itself: 'I am Jesus whom you are persecuting.' Paul never doubted that he had actually met with Jesus, risen from the dead. When he calls the roll of witnesses to the resurrection he adds, 'In the end he appeared even to me' (I Cor.15.8); and when his credentials were called in question he retorted, 'Did I not see Jesus our Lord?' (I Cor.9.1) – as if that settled the question. This is the kind of certainty it is useless to argue

with; it does not abide our question. What the meeting meant to Paul himself we have to gather from occasional allusions in his letter, where he partly breaks through his customary reticence on the subject. Perhaps he comes nearest to letting the secret out when he speaks of 'the revelation of the glory of God in the face of Jesus Christ' (II Cor.4.6).

The effects, however, of the experience in his career and in the passage of history in which he played his part are open to our observation. It is evident that it brought the solution of his personal problem. The attempt to solve it by externalizing the inward conflict had proved to be no solution at all. The new solution he now found did bring real reconciliation of the contending forces in his own soul, in reconciling him also to the enemies he was pursuing with a pious hatred. He threw in his lot with the persecuted, that is, with 'Jesus whom he was persecuting'. But to throw in his lot with Jesus meant standing in with one who was under the 'curse' of the Law: it was to become an 'outlaw'. 'I have been crucified with Christ,' he wrote (Gal.2.20). It was the most complete break possible with his past self. It took all meaning out of the desperate struggle to see himself 'in legal rectitude faultless'. He could accept himself as he was, aware of his weaknesses, but willing, such as he was, to stand at the disposal of his new Master. 'We make it our ambition,' he wrote, 'to be acceptable to him' (II Cor.5.9). This was a different kind of 'ambition' from that which had spurred him on to 'outstrip his Jewish contemporaries'. It was the displacement of self from the centre. And that proved to be the removal of a crushing burden. Above all it was a liberating experience: 'Christ set us free, to be free men' (Gal.5.1).

It shows itself in an expansion of the range of his interests and energies, no longer restricted by Jewish nationalism and orthodoxy. For an orthodox Jew who lived the life of a great Greek city the problem of relations with Gentiles must always have been difficult. With the lines of his temperament and character before us in his letter, we cannot doubt that Paul was repressing his natural instincts in maintaining the degree of separation from his Gentile fellow-citizens which 'legal rectitude' seemed to require. Now he could give those instincts free rein. From the moment of his meeting with Jesus on the Damascus road he knew that the 'dividing wall' (as he called it) was broken down, and that he must 'go to the Gentiles'. Thus the main direction of his new mission was decided from the outset, though it may have been some years before the required strategy was worked out.

About Paul's earlier years as a Christian we are scantily informed. The skeleton outline in the Acts tells us little, and the little it tells is not easily correlated with what Paul himself records – also in mere skeleton outline. Looking back upon his career after many years, he recalls some of the unpleasant situations into which his missionary activities had brought him: 'Five times the Jews have given me the thirty-nine strokes; three times I have been beaten with (Roman) rods; once I was stoned; three times I have been shipwrecked, and for twenty-four hours I was adrift on the open sea' (II Cor.11.23–33) – and so forth; and very few of these find a place in the narrative of Acts. There is much that we do not know.

By Paul's own account, it was not until three years after his conversion that he returned to Jerusalem (Gal.1.17–19). At that time he stayed for a fortnight with Peter (or Cephas, as he calls him, using his Aramaic name), and met also James 'the Lord's brother'. These two would be able to tell him much at first-hand about Jesus. His stay in Jerusalem, however, seems to have been cut short, and he then spent a period which can hardly have been less than twelve years in 'the regions of Cilicia and Syria' (Gal.1.21). We should gladly have heard more about his activities during that period. Perhaps some of the unrecorded adventures he recalls belong to those hidden years. But we do not know. The Acts records only his arrival at Tarsus, in Cilicia (Acts 9.30), and his removal to Antioch, in Syria (Acts 11.25 f.). It is with his arrival at the Syrian capital that the story of Paul's missionary career really begins.

The First Missionary Journey

In that important and populous city believers in Christ were already prominent enough in the public eye to be given a nickname – for that is what 'Christian' really was (Acts 11.26). The community included a substantial proportion of non-Jewish converts from paganism. The introduction of this Gentile element had no doubt acted as a stimulant, and it is not sur-

prising to be told that they soon felt themselves impelled – indeed divinely inspired – to reach out to a still wider public in the Graeco-Roman world. For this enterprise they selected a Cypriot Jew named Barnabas (Acts 4.36 f.; 11.22–24; 13.2), and an obvious choice for his companion was Paul, whom Barnabas himself had first introduced to the Antiochene church (Acts 11.25 f.). The junior colleague soon slipped into the leading role for which his vigour and decision marked him out.

Thus began what is commonly referred to as Paul's 'First Missionary Journey'. It brought the two first to Cyprus (Acts 13.4–12) and then as far as the interior of Asia Minor, and in particular to a group of towns in the southern corner of the province of Galatia (Acts 13.14,51; 14.6 f.). In the light of what happened afterwards, it can be seen to have disclosed a pattern of events which was to recur with almost monotonous frequency. The author of Acts has depicted it in a full-length description of what happened at the first of these towns, Antioch-towards-Pisidia, a description which he no doubt intended to be taken as typical (Acts 13.15–50). It began with an address in the synagogue, to a congregation which included both Jews and 'Gentile worshippers'. The latter is an almost technical term for a class of persons, fairly numerous in many Hellenistic cities, who were attracted by the Jewish religion and liked attending the synagogue services, without becoming regular 'proselytes' and members of the 'commonwealth of Israel'. The 'Gentile worshippers' showed a lively interest, which spread to circles without previous association with the synagogue. The kind of approach that Paul made to these people implied (as we can gather from his letters) that Gentiles could become full members of the people of God without submitting to the Jewish Law, by joining the Christian church. As this implication became clear, it provoked a violent reaction among the stricter Jews. Thereupon the missionaries put out a statement of policy: 'It was necessary that the word of God should be declared to you first, but since you reject it . . . we now turn to the Gentiles' (Acts 13.46). It was the principle that guided Paul's procedure all through: 'To the Jew first, and also to the Greek' (Rom.1.16, 2.9 f.), as he expresses it more than once in his letters. In his Letter to the Romans he has provided a theological justification for it (Rom.

11.1–27). The outcome of this tour was, on the one hand, the foundation of several communities, largely Gentile in membership, and, on the other hand, the unleashing of a Jewish hostility to Paul's mission which was to follow him wherever he went, and finally to bring his active career to an end.

The missionaries now returned to the church which had commissioned them, at Antioch-on-the-Orontes (Acts 14.25–28). The measure of success they were able to report made it evident that the initiative must be followed up (Acts 15.36). Plans for a further tour included a change of partners. Barnabas chose to return to his native Cyprus (Acts 15.39). Paul, who was evidently raising his sights, took as his new colleague Silas (or, in Latin, as Paul's letters have it, Silvanus). He was a member of the church at Jerusalem (Acts 15.22 f.), but, from his name, a Hellenistic Jew, and, just possibly, a Roman citizen, like Paul himself (Acts 16.37).

The Second Missionary Journey

The 'Second Missionary Journey' was to be marked by a momentous new departure, not, it would appear, premeditated. It began unadventurously enough, with a return visit to the young churches founded on the previous tour (Acts 15.40–16.5). After this the missionaries pursued a curiously devious and uncertain course, without, so far as we are told, finding any opening for work, until they reached the shore of the Aegean at Troas, not far south of the Dardanelles (Acts 16.6–8). It is at this point that we come upon the first extract from the 'travel diary' incorporated in Acts: 'We at once set about getting a passage to Macedonia, concluding that God had called us to bring them the good news' (Acts 16.10). The decision to cross from Asia into Europe proved a turning point, opening a new period in Paul's career, during which he may be said to have really found himself. It is a period, too, illuminated for us by the letters he wrote during it.

A comparatively short sea passage brought the party to the nearest port on the European side, and they made their way through Macedonia towards the province of Achaia, or Greece. Several churches were founded, though the tour was chequered, as usual, with opposition. At Philippi it came from pagans, not without overtones of anti-Semitism (Acts 16.19–24).

At Thessalonica and Beroea the old pattern reasserted itself: the Jewish opposition made mischief with the civil authorities, and Paul was obliged to move on, leaving his companions behind (Acts 17.1–14). He arrived at Athens alone (Acts 17.15), in great disquiet (as he tells us in letters to Thessalonica written about this time) about the new converts whom he had been compelled by police pressure to leave prematurely (I Thess.2.13–35; II Thess.3.6–16). For this and perhaps other reasons he was, as he tells us in retrospect (I Cor.2.3), in low spirits as he left Athens for Corinth, which was, as it turned out, to be the scene of his greatest success so far.

Corinth had been one of the most important of the old Greek city states. After its destruction by the Romans it was refounded by Julius Caesar, and became the capital of the province of Achaia. Situated on the isthmus which separated the Aegean from the Adriatic – and the eastern half of the empire from the western – it had become an immensely busy and prosperous emporium of trade, with a large and mixed population. It had the unsavoury reputation which cosmopolitan seaport towns seem to attract.

Here Paul, now reunited with his companions, spent not far short of two years, maintaining himself by working at his trade of tent-making (Acts 18.3, 11, 18). It was his longest stay anywhere since he had started on his travels. The inevitable breach with the orthodox Jews set him free for independent action. He left the synagogue, taking with him one of its office-bearers, and set up his headquarters – defiantly perhaps, rather than tactfully – in a house next door belonging to a 'Gentile worshipper' (Acts 18.5–8). The opposition, as so often, tried to embroil him with the civil authorities, but the proconsul refused to entertain the charges they brought, as being no more than 'some bickering about words and names and your Jewish law'. The case was dismissed, and this must have considerably strengthened Paul's position (Acts 18.12–17). He succeeded in building up a numerous and active, if somewhat turbulent, Christian community, predominantly Gentile in membership, before he left to return to Jerusalem and Antioch (Acts 18.18, 22), making a brief call on the way at Ephesus (Acts 18.19–21), which he had already marked out as his next centre of work.

The Third Missionary Journey

About all this the narrative in Acts is singularly reticent. We may take it that the 'diarist' was not of the party at this stage. The 'Third Missionary Journey', through the interior of Asia Minor, is also given the most cursory treatment (Acts 18.23; 19.1). The author seems to be in a hurry, as Paul himself probably was, to reach Ephesus. It is evident that he had formed definite ideas about the most effective way of conducting his mission. It was, not to cover ground by moving rapidly from place to place, but to settle (as he had done at Corinth) at a suitable centre from which he could reach a whole province. Ephesus was to be such a centre. It was one of the principal cities of the province of Asia, with excellent communications by land and sea. Settled by Greeks in remote antiquity, but always with something oriental about it, it had been a meeting place of East and West long before the conquests of Alexander had inaugurated the Hellenistic age. Its world-famous temple was dedicated to the native Anatolian fertility-goddess whom the Greeks chose to call Artemis (Diana to the Romans) (Acts 19.27, 34 f.), though she had little in common with the virgin huntress of the classical pantheon. From ancient time a seat of Greek philosophical thought, Ephesus was also hospitable to all manner of superstitions, and in Paul's time it was notorious as a centre of the 'black arts' of magic (Acts 19.18 f.).

Such was the place which for the next three years or so was to be Paul's headquarters (Acts 20.31). There are evident signs of a planned strategy. As usual, he first made contact with the synagogue. When his position there became impossible, he was fully prepared with a plan. He formally 'withdrew his converts', and established himself on neutral territory in a lecture-hall in the city. Here he held daily conferences, open to all comers, which attracted numbers of residents and visitors to the city (Acts 19.8–10). But this was not all. By this time Paul had built up an efficient 'staff'. Their names keep recurring in his letters – Timothy (Rom.16.21; I Cor.4.17; 16.10; Phil.2.19–23, etc.), Titus (II Cor.7.6, 13; 8.6–17, 23, etc.), Luke, Tychicus (Eph.6.21; Col.4.7; II Tim.4.12; Titus 3.12), and several others (Silas has now faded out). They were available either for work by his side at head-quarters, or to be sent where they could be useful in keeping touch with churches already founded or in breaking new ground. It was in this way that Paul's mission spread in the province of Asia. We happen to learn from his letters the names of three up-country towns where churches were founded without any visit from the apostle – Colossae, Laodicea, and Hierapolis (Col.1.7; 2.1; 4.13–16) – and there were certainly others. The author of Acts says, perhaps with pardonable exaggeration, that 'the whole population of the province of Asia, both Jews and pagans, heard the word of the Lord' (Acts 19.10).

Meanwhile, however, trouble was brewing. There was furious opposition from the Jews (Acts 20.19), and some from pagan quarters (Acts 19.23–27), though we hear also of 'some of the dignitaries of the province who were friendly towards him' (Acts 19.31). Of the opposition we have some record both in Acts and in the letters (e.g., I Cor.15.32; II Cor.1.8). From the latter we also learn, what the author of Acts has not told us, that Paul was at this time driven almost to distraction by disorders in the church at Corinth. He sent members of his staff to deal with them (II Cor.12.17 f.), but he found it necessary to interrupt his work and cross the Aegean himself (II Cor.12.14). There are two letters to the Corinthians in the New Testament, but these contain clear indications that the correspondence they represent was more extensive. They illustrate vividly the problems that arose when people of widely differing national origin, religious background, education, and social position were being welded into a community by the power of a common faith, while at the same time they had to come to terms with the secular society to which also they owed allegiance. These problems were threatening to split the church into fragments. It may have been about the same time that the very serious trouble broke out which provoked Paul to write his fiercely controversial Letter to the Galatians. The date of the letter is uncertain, as is also its precise destination, but if this is the time to which it belongs (as seems most probable) there would be a sharp point in Paul's *cri de coeur* in the Second Letter to the Corinthians: 'There is the responsibility that weighs on me every day, my anxious concern for all our congregations' (II Cor.11.28).

The difficulties at Corinth were eventually resolved, and Paul, having wound up his work at Ephesus, was able to re-visit a church now fully reconciled. It is at this point that he wrote the longest and most weighty of all his surviving letters, that addressed to the Romans. In this letter he takes a brief retrospect on the work that lay behind him, and sketches a plan for the future. He has now covered the eastern provinces of the empire, 'from Jerusalem as far round as Illyricum,' as he expresses it. 'Now,' he adds, 'I have no further scope in these parts,' and 'it is my ambition to bring the gospel to places where the very name of Christ has not been heard.' Accordingly, he is planning to open up work in the west, with Spain as his objective. On the way he will visit Rome, and hopes to find there support for his enterprise (Rom.15.19–29). He had to tread somewhat delicately. The church of Rome was not of his foundation, nor within his 'sphere of influence'. He knew there was some prejudice against him, and before presenting himself in Rome he sends a considered and comprehensive statement of his theological position, which should disarm prejudice and establish his standing as a Christian teacher.

The Judaistic Controversy

The visit to Rome, however, was not pending immediately. First he must go to Jerusalem. Significantly, he implores the Roman Christians to 'pray to God for me that I may be saved from unbelievers in Judaea and that my errand to Jerusalem may find acceptance with God's people' (i.e., the church) (Rom.15.31). He therefore not only apprehended danger from Jewish opposition, but also felt some doubt how far he would be welcome to his fellow Christians at Jerusalem. To understand this we need to look at the situation which had developed as a result of his startling success in building, all over the eastern empire, a close-knit Christian community which was fully supra-national, multi-racial, with no distinction (as he wrote) between 'Greek and Jew, circumcised and uncircumcised, barbarian, Scythian, slave and free man' (Col.3.11). This inevitably antagonized those who adhered to a stiff, nationally orientated type of Judaism – those, in fact, who stood where Paul himself had stood before his conversion. He had 'ratted' on them, and that could not be forgiven or forgotten.

But there were many Jews within the church itself who were uneasy about Paul's missionary policy. Admit Gentiles to the church, by all means, but why do away with the salutary restraints of the Law? The first demand of this party was that Gentile converts should submit to the rite of circumcision, which brought a man within the 'covenant' guaranteeing the privileges, and the obligations, of God's people (Acts 15.2). In other words, a man must become a Jew before he could be recognized as fully Christian. This matter was satisfactorily arranged – or at least Paul thought so – at a fairly early stage. He went up to Jerusalem, he tells us, and conferred with the leaders of the church there. There emerged a kind of concordat between Paul and Barnabas of the one part and Peter, James and John of the other part. It was agreed that they should respect each other's independence of action. Peter and his colleagues would be responsible for missions to Jews, Paul and Barnabas for missions to Gentiles. It was clearly understood that circumcision should not be imposed on Gentile converts, and Paul at least took the view that this carried with it freedom for Gentile Christians from the 'bondage' of the Jewish Law (Gal.2.1–9). In Acts we have another account of a conference in Jerusalem, which may be the same, viewed from a different angle, or may be a different one (Acts 15.4–29). According to this account also Gentile converts were dispensed from the need for circumcision, and from demands of the Law apart from certain minimum requirements about which there is some measure of ambiguity (Acts 15.28 f.); in any case, to judge from Paul's correspondence, they remained more or less a dead letter.

The controversy was by no means settled. It dragged on for years, and brought in various side-issues, such as that of Paul's own status as an apostle, about which he was sensitive. But in the main it seems to have been accepted that Gentile Christians were not obliged to conform to the Law, but that Jewish Christians should be expected to do so. This would appear to be the position of James, 'the Lord's brother', who had become head of the Jerusalem church, and was regarded as the leader of all law-abiding Jewish Christians, amounting (so he claimed) to 'many thousands' (Acts 21.20). Paul could hardly take exception to this in principle. He himself, he tells us, conformed to the Law when he was moving among Jews (I Cor.9.20). But such a position was essentially unstable. The majority of the churches of Paul's foundation had a mixed membership of Jews and Gentiles. Could they really live together while following different codes of conduct? The centre of Christian fellowship lay in the communal meals in which they joined. Could Jewish Christians, in practice keep their Law, with all its dietary regulations, while eating in common with fellow-Christians who did not observe it? Was 'inter-communion' possible without hurt to somebody's conscience on the one side or the other (Gal.2.11–13)? In his letters Paul is seen to deal with difficulties of this kind with conspicuous tact and consideration, but on the main issue he was adamant. The church could not be allowed to become a Jewish institution with Gentile Christians tolerated as second-class citizens. 'There is no distinction,' he repeated (Rom.3.22; 10.12). If he had been finally defeated, the church might have had as little impact on the great world as any other of the numerous Jewish sects. He was not defeated, but neither could he be said to have gained a decisive victory in his life-time. Advocates of the narrower view dogged his steps to the end, and sought to win over his converts. No doubt they were honest and conscientious men, who stood obstinately by their principles, as he did. But they were wrong. He speaks of them in his letters with a passionate indignation, for the issue was to him vital.

Jerusalem and Rome

And yet the journey which he was planning when he wrote to the Romans was essentially a peace-making mission. When the Jerusalem concordat was made, the leaders of the church there had stipulated – and as Paul understood the matter it was the only stipulation – that the Gentile churches should take some responsibility for the support of the poverty-stricken Jewish Christians of Jerusalem. Paul responded eagerly to this request (Gal.2.10). The leaders in Jerusalem may have had in mind something like an equivalent for the contributions which Jews living abroad made to the temple at Jerusalem. But for Paul (as we know from his letters) it was an opportunity to demonstrate the true fraternal unity of Christians, bridging any divisions

that arose among them. He set on foot a large-scale relief fund, to be raised by voluntary subscription from members of the churches he had founded; he recommended a system of regular weekly contributions (Rom.15.25–28; I Cor.16.1–4; II Cor.8.1–9.15). The raising of the fund went on for a considerable time and there was now a substantial sum in hand to be conveyed to Jerusalem. He was to be accompanied by a deputation carefully composed, it appears, so as to represent the several provinces (I Cor. 16.3 f.; Acts 20.4). The handing over of the relief fund was to be both an act of true Christian charity and also a formal embassy from the Gentile churches affirming their fellowship with Jewish Christians in the one church (Rom.15.27).

The goodwill mission miscarried. Paul's reception by the leaders of the church at Jerusalem, if not unfriendly, was cool. James was thoroughly frightened of the effect his presence in the city might have on both Christian and non-Christian Jews, in view of his reputation as a critic of Jewish 'legalism'. He urged Paul to prove his personal loyalty to the Law by carrying out certain ceremonies in the temple (Acts 21.20–24). Paul was quite willing. 'To Jews,' he had written, 'I became like a Jew, to win Jews; as they are subject to the law of Moses, I put myself under that law' (I Cor.9.20). Unfortunately he was recognized in the temple by some of his inveterate enemies, the Jews of Asia, who raised a cry that he was introducing Gentiles into the sacred precinct (Acts 21.27–29). This was a high misdemeanour. There ran across the temple court a barrier with an inscription (which can still be read) threatening with death any foreigner who should trespass beyond it. There was no truth in the charge, but it was enough to rouse the rabble, and Paul was in danger of being lynched. He was rescued by the Roman security forces, and put under arrest. Having identified himself as a Roman citizen, he came under the protection of the imperial authorities (Acts 21.30–39), and was ultimately transferred for safe custody to the governor's headquarters at Caesarea (Acts 23.23–33). There were wearisome wrangles over jurisdiction between the Jewish Council and two successive Roman governors, Paul meanwhile being kept in confinement. In the end, seeing the possibility that he might after all be sent back to Jerusalem and fall into the hands of his enemies, he exercised his citizen's right and appealed to the emperor (Acts 25.1–12). Accordingly he was put on board a ship sailing for Rome. The account in Acts of the voyage, with the shipwreck off Malta, is reputed one of the finest sea-pieces in Greek literature (Acts. 27.1–28.15).

And so Paul fulfilled his cherished plan of a visit to Rome, but as a prisoner. He was placed under something like house-arrest. He occupied his own private lodging, with a soldier constantly on guard (Acts 28.16) but with liberty to receive visitors, while awaiting trial, which was still continually delayed. It is probable, though not certain,* that the Letters to the Philippians, Colossians and Philemon, all of which refer to the writer as being in prison at the time of writing, belong to this period of confinement – as also Ephesians, if this is indeed from Paul's hand. They show him actively at work, even under these difficult conditions, keeping in touch with his churches by letter, receiving and dispatching messengers.

The period of house-arrest lasted, we are informed, for two years (Acts 28.30). Then the curtain comes down. We may presume that the case eventually came up before the imperial tribunal, but whether it resulted in acquittal and a further period of freedom to travel, or ended in condemnation and execution, we have no means of knowing. The Letters to Timothy and Titus have been thought to refer to a second imprisonment in Rome, but the evidence is at best ambiguous, and it is unlikely that these letters, in the form in which we have them, come from Paul's own hand. That he ultimately suffered martyrdom may be taken as certain, and there is no good reason to doubt the Roman tradition that he was beheaded at a spot on the road to Ostia known as Three Fountains, and buried on the site now occupied by the noble church of St Paul-without-the-Walls.

A Note on Chronology

The chronology of Paul's career cannot be fixed precisely, but fortunately we have one precise date to start from. The proconsul before whom Paul was cited at Corinth was Junius Annaeus Gallio, who is known to have held the appointment from July AD 51 to June AD 52. On the showing of Acts, therefore, Paul was in Corinth from early in 50 to late in 51. From this fixed point we can calculate backwards and forwards, making the best of such indications of time as are supplied in Paul's own letters or in the Acts. The results will inevitably be in part conjectural, but the possible margin of error anywhere can hardly be more than three or four years.

If Paul reached Corinth early in 50, then his 'Second Missionary Journey' must have begun in 49, and the visit to Jerusalem which preceded it, when he came to an understanding with the leaders of the church there, would presumably fall in 48. Paul dates his earlier visit to Jerusalem fourteen years before this. As he may be assumed to use the inclusive reckoning then customary, this probably points to AD 35. This was three years (or on our reckoning 2-*plus*) after his conversion, which may therefore be tentatively dated to AD 33.

Returning to our starting-point in AD 50–51, and working forwards, we have first a condensed summary of protracted journeys, including stays of unspecified length at various places, without any notes of time, until we find Paul established at Ephesus for three full years. At what date this three-year period is conceived to have begun we can only conjecture. All things considered, it seems more likely to fall in AD 54–57 than any earlier. If so, then he can hardly have arrived in Jerusalem before 59. He was then arrested, and spent two years in prison, ending in 61. At that point the governor Antonius Felix was succeeded by Porcius Festus. On the reckoning we have followed this would be in 61, and in fact this seems the probable date for the succession, on the (somewhat ambiguous) evidence of non-biblical sources. Accordingly, Paul will have started for Rome in autumn 61, wintered in Malta, and arrived in Rome early in 62. His two years of house-arrest would then bring us to AD 64. Beyond that we cannot go, but it may be significant that it was in the winter of 64/65 that the emperor Nero made his savage attack on the Christians of Rome.

10

The Thought of Paul

C. H. Dodd

Paul and his Letters

For the thought of Paul we naturally turn to his letters. Although the Acts gives a very fair account of his life and work, and a general idea of what he stood for, it is in the letters that his mind is revealed.

In the New Testament there are thirteen letters which mention Paul as the writer. A fourteenth, the Letter to Hebrews, is by long custom included with them, but it is in fact an anonymous work; in the early church it was admitted that no one knew who wrote it. Of the thirteen it is not certain that all are directly from the apostle's hand. In his time it was not unusual for the disciples of an outstanding teacher to compose books to propagate his teaching as they understood it, and to publish them under his name; nor was the practice considered discreditable. There are reasons for thinking that some of the 'Pauline' letters may have originated in some such way. The strongest reasons apply to the Letters to Timothy and Titus. On the other hand, the four Letters to the Romans, Corinthians and Galatians, to which we might add the short note to Philemon, carry the stamp of Paul's style and personality on every page. There is no question that he composed them. Most scholars, probably, would say as much for Philippians and the First (and perhaps also the Second) Letter to the Thessalonians. About the Letter to the Colossians there is more doubt, but the balance of probability seems to fall in favour of Paul's authorship, possibly with some collaboration. Whether the Letter to the Ephesians should be included is debatable. In some ways its style is curiously 'un-Pauline'. Yet if it was written by a disciple he must have been one with an almost uncanny insight into the apostle's mind, and whether or not it comes from his own hand we cannot go far wrong in using it to fill out our picture of his thought in its maturest form.

The letters were almost all called forth by some particular occasion, and none of them, unless it be the Letter to the Romans, makes any attempt to present the writer's thought in a systematic way. Written at intervals in the midst of an extremely busy life, they are the product of a powerful intelligence responding to the challenge of urgent situations; it may be the challenge of practical problems of Christian living in a pagan environment, as in the Corinthian correspondence, or of subtle propaganda which seemed to him subversive of the truth, as in Galatians and Colossians. We have to gather his teaching by combining what he says in different places.

Any man's thought is necessarily formed in part by his background and environment, as well as by his personal experience. With Paul we have to take account of his Jewish upbringing and of what he owed to the primitive Christian community which he joined at an early stage in its history.

The Jewish Heritage

Among religions of the ancient world the Judaism of the first century was unique in being strictly monotheistic. Its fundamental tenets were that there is, and can be, only one God; that he is good – good in the same plain sense in which he requires men to be good, that is, just, merciful, true and the like – and that he is a 'living God' who reveals himself in history through action, in which he is working out his purpose for his world. Such was the faith which Judaism had inherited from the prophets of Israel. In this faith Paul was brought up.

But there was a certain contradiction deeply embedded in this monotheistic faith. The one God is God of the whole world, Maker and Ruler of all mankind. Yet in a special sense he is the God of Israel, the nation bound to him in an 'everlasting covenant'. The charter of this

313

covenant was the Law, believed to have been dictated by the Almighty himself to Moses on Mount Sinai. It was held to be the perfect embodiment of the righteousness of the one God and the righteousness he requires of men. As such it was necessarily absolute and universal. And yet it was primarily Israel's law; no other nation knew it. Paul himself has given eloquent expression to the pride which the Jew felt in this unique privilege: 'You rely upon the Law and are proud of your God; you know his will; instructed by the Law you know right from wrong; you are confident that . . . in the Law you see the very shape of knowledge and truth' (Rom.2.17–20. In this article biblical quotations in general follow the translation in the NEB). The possession of the Law marked Israel out as God's chosen people. It was to this people that God had revealed himself in 'mighty acts', and through it his purpose went forward to fulfilment. This was the central motive of its history and the key to its destiny. Thus the highest moral idealism was wedded to an assertive nationalism.

Judaism and the Nations

In this perspective, what is the status and the destiny of 'the nations that know not God'? To this question the answers were various and uncertain. Some of them show a finely humane spirit which will go as far as possible – without prejudice to Israel's prior claim – in generosity to the Gentile. Others must seem to us to approach the limit of nationalist arrogance. But there was in first-century Judaism a strong 'missionary' movement towards the pagan world. On one level it was content to propagate the monotheistic idea and certain fundamental moral principles, but its ulterior aim was to bring Gentiles within the scope of the divine mercy by incorporation in the chosen people. The 'proselyte' submitted himself to the Law of God – that is, to the Jewish Law; he became a Jew.

On the other side the question arose, what is the status and the destiny of Jews who, knowing the Law, do not in practice observe its precepts? Here again the answers were uncertain and various. The Law itself pronounced a 'curse' on 'all who do not persevere in doing everything that is written in the Book of Law' (Gal.3.10), and prophets and Rabbis alike use

language of the utmost severity in castigating offenders. Yet there is a notable reluctance to admit that in the last resort any 'son of Abraham' could be rejected by God; 'for the sake of the fathers' he would come through in the end. For Paul, who looked at the matter with a wider knowledge of the outside world, this was not realistic; moreover, it was inconsistent with the principle of monotheism. 'Do you suppose,' he writes, 'God is the God of the Jews alone? Is he not the God of Gentiles also? Certainly, of Gentiles also, *if it is true that God is one*' (Rom.3.29). The conclusion is unavoidable: 'God has no favourites; those who have sinned outside the pale of the Law of Moses will perish outside its pale, and all who have sinned under that Law will be judged by the Law' (Rom.2.11 f.).

But while this clears the ground by setting aside any idea of preferential treatment, it is a negative assessment of the human predicament. 'There is no distinction; all have sinned' (Rom.3.22). While allowing that there may be some good Jews who keep God's Law (Rom.2.29), and good Gentiles who 'carry out its precepts by the light of nature' (Rom.2.14), Paul holds that in principle human society is in breach of the Law of God, and is therefore headed for disaster. It is subject, as he puts it, to 'the law of sin and death' (Rom.8.2). This universal human condition enters the experience of the individual in the desperate moral struggle which Paul has depicted with such psychological insight in the seventh chapter of Romans: 'When I want to do the right, only the wrong is within my reach' (Rom.7.21). (A Roman poet, some half-century earlier, had put it in similar terms: 'I see the better and approve it; I pursue the worse' – *Video meliora proboque; deteriora sequor*.) The problem which started as a domestic concern within Judaism has turned out to be a broadly human one. That is why Paul's controversy with his Jewish opponents, which at first sight looks like an antiquated and parochial dispute, has permanent significance.

The Divine Initiative

The problem is acute in any religion of ethical monotheism which takes itself with full seriousness. The more nobly the goodness of God is conceived, the stronger is the sense of man's moral distance from him, and, at the same time, the stronger the conviction that in communion with such a God lies man's highest good. It is this that lends poignancy to Paul's account of the moral deadlock in which he felt himself, and mankind in general, to be trapped. The only possible solution he could contemplate was a fresh initiative from the divine end, parallel, he might have said, to the initiative God had taken when he established the 'covenant' with Israel at Sinai. Such a new initiative he now saw to have been taken when Christ entered history: 'What the law could not do because our lower nature robbed it of all potency, God has done – by sending his Son' (Rom.8.3). This divine initiative is an entirely free and self-originated act of God, conditioned only by his love for the human race 'while we were yet sinners' (Rom.5.8). This is what Paul describes as the 'grace' of God. The response that is asked for from men is 'faith', or better – since the word 'faith' has accumulated a variety of meanings, not all of them true to Paul's thought – it is simply that they should trust God and let him have his way with them.

In speaking of the effect of this divine initiative in human experience Paul uses a variety of expressions. The most general expression is 'salvation'. In common Greek usage the word had a wide range of meaning. It could mean safety or security; it could mean escape from calamity, actual or threatened; or it could mean simply good health or well-being. In effect the word stood for a condition in which 'all is well', and the particular way in which all is well depends on the context in which it is used. In Paul, as in New Testament writers in general, 'salvation' stands for a condition in which 'all is well' in the absolute sense; a condition in which we are secure from all evils that afflict, or menace, the human spirit, here or hereafter. Thus the expression, while strongly emotive, is hardly capable of telling us what precisely, as Paul sees it, God does for us in Christ. More illuminating are some of the metaphorical expressions he uses. Three of these have played so large a part in the development of Christian doctrine that they need to be looked at carefully.

First, there is the legal, or forensic, metaphor of 'justification' (Rom.3.24, 26; Gal.2.15 f., etc.). Sin is here conceived as an offence against law. The sinner stands at the bar. No one but a judge with competent authority can condemn or acquit. Before the divine tribunal the defendant is unquestionably guilty. But 'God acquits (justifies) the guilty' (Rom.4.5). Of course it is a violent paradox, and Paul was quite aware that it was so. He is putting in the most challenging terms his conviction that God takes a man as he is, 'with all his imperfections on his head' (as in the Gospels Jesus received the 'publicans and sinners'), and gives him a fresh start. He can now undertake his moral task relieved of the crippling sense of guilt.

Secondly there is the metaphor of 'redemption' (Rom.3.24; I Cor.1.30; Eph.1.7; Col.1.14). The Greek word was used of the process by which a slave acquired his freedom; it means 'release', 'emancipation', or 'liberation' (and is translated accordingly in the NEB). For Paul, the condition of a man caught in the moral dilemma he has described is a state of slavery, since he is unable to do what he wishes to do. (An almost contemporary Stoic philosopher said much the same: 'No sinner is a free man.') But God, exercising his supreme authority, declares the slave free, and free he is. All that Christ did – his entry into the human condition, his life of service, his suffering and death – may be regarded (still in terms of the metaphor) as the price God pays for the emancipation of the slave. 'Christ set us free, to be free men' (Gal.5.1): this exultant note of liberation sounds all through the letters. It was, unmistakably, Paul's own experience.

Thirdly there is the ritual metaphor of sacrifice. Sin can be regarded not only as a crime against the law, bringing a sense of guilt, or as a state of slavery, bringing a sense of impotence, but also as 'defilement', which makes a man feel ashamed and disgusted with himself. In ancient religions defilement could be incurred in all sorts of ways, many of them having nothing to do with morals. The defilement (it was assumed) could be removed by the performance of the proper ritual, most commonly, and perhaps most efficaciously, by the sacrifice of a victim. This was called 'expiation' (less accurately, 'atonement'). The metaphor of expiation, drawn from a world of thought quite alien to us, was ready to hand for anyone, like Paul, who was familiar with the elaborate ritual of sacrifice laid down in the Law of Moses, and in his time still practised in the temple at Jerusalem – or indeed for anyone acquainted with the religious rituals of the Greek states. This is the background of what he says about the work of Christ: 'God designed him to be the means of expiating sin by his sacrificial death' (Rom.3.25; literally, 'by his blood'; when Paul speaks of the 'blood' of Christ, he is using a kind of shorthand for the idea of sacrifice). There is no suggestion, here or elsewhere, that Christ offered himself as a sacrifice to 'propitiate' an offended deity. In using the metaphor of sacrifice Paul is declaring his conviction that the self-sacrifice of Christ meant the release of moral power which penetrates to the deepest recesses of the human spirit, acting (if one may put it so) as a kind of moral disinfectant.

These are the metaphors which have most captured the imagination of Paul's readers. His thought has sometimes been obscured through taking one or another of them – justification, redemption, or expiation (atonement) – by itself, and then forgetting that it is after all a metaphor. What he is saying all the time is that in Christ God has done for us what we could never do for ourselves. The criminal could not pronounce his own acquittal, nor the slave set himself free, and God alone could 'expiate' the defilement we have brought upon ourselves.

In the course of a passage (II Cor.5.18 f.) which is perhaps the clearest and most succinct statement of his teaching on this theme Paul writes: 'From first to last this is the work of God. He has reconciled us men to himself through Christ . . . What I mean is that God was in Christ reconciling the world to himself, no longer holding their misdeeds against them.' In the idea of 'reconciliation' his thought has passed out of the realm of mere metaphor and adopted the language of actual personal relations. Many people know something of what it means to be 'alienated', or 'estranged' – perhaps from their environment or their fellow-men, perhaps from the standards of their society, perhaps, indeed, from themselves. The deepest alienation is from the true end of our being, and that means estrangement from our Maker, out of which comes a distortion of all relationships. The great thing that Paul had to say to the alienated is that God, from his side of the gulf that has opened, has put an end to the estrangement; he has reconciled us to himself. Nowhere does he suggest that God needed to be reconciled to us. His attitude towards his creatures is, and always was, one of unqualified goodwill (as Jesus said, he is 'kind to the unthankful and wicked'). Out of that goodwill he has provided the way to reconciliation.

God in Christ

The whole process turns upon the action of God in Christ, and that action took place in history – in that historical episode which is the life and teaching, the death and resurrection, of Jesus Christ. About his life the letters have comparatively little to say. There was little occasion for it; they were all addressed to Christian readers, who might be presumed to know the salient facts. That Paul had a definite conception of his character is clear enough (see below, p. 322). His sayings are seldom quoted directly, but many echoes and reminiscences of them, as they are known to us in the Gospels, can be recognized by the attentive reader. (And how many sayings which never found their way into the Gospels may have left their mark? Acts 20.35 is suggestive.) In short, behind the theology of the Pauline letters stands firmly the figure of the 'Jesus of history'.

Of outstanding significance are the circumstances of the death of Jesus: the facts that he gave his life willingly for the sake of others, and that he died under the 'curse' of the law on a Roman cross (Gal.3.13). That meant a decisive breach with the old order. All that followed was to be understood as the breaking-in of something new. Christ died, but he rose again, and thus inaugurated a new order of life. To establish the fact of his resurrection Paul calls a whole series of witnesses, including some of those who had known Jesus most intimately, besides adding that he could corroborate their testimony out of his own experience. The fact of the resurrection gave him the clue to the meaning of the whole historical episode.

It was entirely in harmony with the prophetic valuation of history as the field of the 'mighty acts' of God that Paul should see the life, death and resurrection of Jesus Christ as one more 'mighty act', the 'fulfilment' of all that God had purposed and promised in the whole history of Israel. In common Jewish belief the symbol of that fulfilment was the expected 'Messiah'. After his conversion Paul accepted what the followers of Jesus were saying, that in him the Messiah had come. But what Paul meant by 'Messiah' was something different from any of the variant forms of Jewish messianic expectation. The messianic idea had to be re-thought in the light of a new set of facts.

One invariable trait of the Messiah in Jewish expectation was that he should be the agent of God's final victory over his enemies. On the popular level that meant, quite crudely, victory over the pagan empires which from time to time oppressed the chosen people. In Paul's thinking the idea of the messianic victory is completely 'sublimated'. It is the 'cosmic powers and authorities' that Christ 'led as captives in his triumphal procession' (Col.2.15). Paul is here drawing upon a mythology which in one form or another belonged to the mental furniture of most men of his time. Man as part of the visible universe was conceived as subject to 'phantom intelligences' (to borrow a term from Thomas Hardy) which limit his freedom and thwart his purposes. (Paul has an extensive and varied vocabulary to describe them; see Rom.8.38; Gal.4.3; Eph.6.12; Col.2.8, 15, etc.) We do not readily think in that way. But the mythology stood for something real in human experience: the sense that there are unexplained factors working behind the scenes, whether in the world or in our own 'unconscious', frustrating our best intentions and turning our good to evil (for example, perhaps, perverting the achievements of science into the menace of racial destruction). As Paul saw it, Jesus was in his lifetime in conflict, not only with his ostensible opponents, but with dark forces lurking in the background. To all appearance he was worsted by them. It was, Paul says, 'the [superhuman] powers that rule the world' that crucified him (I Cor.2.8), perverting intended good to evil ends (for neither Pilate nor the priests and Pharisees, at bottom, meant ill, any more than we do). But in the outcome Christ was not defeated. Unclouded goodness prevailed. His resurrection was the pledge of victory over all enemies of the human spirit, for it was victory over death, which Paul personifies as 'the last enemy' (I Cor.15.26); and appropriately enough, since death is the final frustration of all human designs – if that were indeed the end. But we now live in a world where victory has been won in a decisive engagement. 'God be praised!' Paul exclaims. 'He gives us the victory through our Lord Jesus Christ' (I Cor.15.57).

How Christ's victory is also ours will become plainer at the next stage of our inquiry. But for the present we note that the victory was won on the field of history, on which our own 'battle of life' must be fought out. It is for Paul of high significance that Christ lived a truly human life, 'born of a woman, born under the Law' (Gal.4.4 – in other words, he was a man and a Jew). But that does not mean that he is just one more individual thrown up by the historical process. On the contrary, his coming into the world can be seen as a fresh incursion of the Creator into his creation. God, who at the beginning said 'Let there be light', has now given 'the light of the revelation of the glory of God in the face of Jesus Christ' (II Cor.4.6). In the act of creating, according to an influential school of Jewish thinking, it was the (half-personified) divine 'wisdom' that was at work; and Christ himself, Paul says, was 'the wisdom of God' visibly in action among men (I Cor.1.24). The wisdom manifest in creation, said the Jewish thinkers, is 'the flawless mirror of the active power of God and the image of his goodness' (Wisdom of Solomon 7.26); and so Christ, Paul says, is 'the image of the invisible God' (Col.1.15). Indeed, 'in him the complete being of God, by God's own choice, came to dwell' (Col.1.19). In such terms, employing, and indeed straining, the resources of traditional and contemporary language, Paul seeks to bring out the meaning of a new and unprecedented fact – the fact of Christ. Here, then, is one line along which the idea of messiahship is developing into something new. We shall presently observe another such line.

The People of God

Paul had first encountered Christ in the community of his followers. The voice he heard at his conversion had announced the identity of Jesus with the persecuted church (Acts 9.5; 22.8; 26.14). It is therefore not surprising that he was led from the first to understand the work of Christ, and of God in him, in terms of the community which had arisen out of that work. This was a new historical phenomenon, to be brought into relation with the history of Israel as the field within which the purpose of God was working

317

itself out. The formative motive of that history was the calling into existence of a 'people of God' – a divine commonwealth, we might say – in and through which the will of God might be done on earth, an 'Israel' worth the name. The distinguishing mark of such an 'Israel' Paul found (not without some warrant in the best prophetic teaching) in the promise said to have been made to Abraham, the founder of the Hebrew race, that in his posterity 'all nations shall find blessing' (Gal.3.8). This ideal had never yet been realized, though in successive periods there had been some who had it in them to become such a people, the 'remnant' of which prophets spoke (Rom.9.27; 11.5). In the emergent church of Christ Paul saw the divine commonwealth coming into active existence. 'If you belong to Christ,' he writes, 'you are the issue of Abraham' (Gal.3.29), i.e., you are the true Israel in whom 'all nations shall find blessing'. Here we have a pointer to one reason, at least, why Paul set such store by his mission to the Gentiles. Thus the church was the consummation of a long, divinely directed, history. It is a theme to which he returns again and again (particularly in the long and intricate discussion in Rom.9–11).

The new, supra-national Israel was consituted solely on the basis of 'belonging to Christ', and not any longer through racial descent or attachment to a particular legal system. 'There is no such thing as Jew and Greek, freeman, slave, male and female; for you are all one person *in Christ Jesus*' (Gal.3.28). That expression 'in Christ' is one which recurs with remarkable frequency throughout the letters of Paul. The doctrine for which it stands is a highly original product of his fertile mind. But the reality of it was present in the church from the beginning. It found its expression in the two rites, or sacraments, of baptism and the 'breaking of bread'. These were practised in the church before ever Paul became a Christian, but he found in them a hitherto unexplored range and depth of meaning.

It was through baptism that a person was incorporated into the community of Christ's followers. In its suggestive ritual, in which the convert was 'buried' by immersion in water, and came out cleansed and renewed, Paul saw a symbolical re-enactment of the death and resurrection of Christ: 'by baptism we were

buried with him and lay dead, in order that as Christ was raised from the dead in the splendour of the Father, so also we might set our feet on the new path of life' (Rom.6.4). Baptism therefore affirmed the solidarity of all members of the church with Christ.

So, even more clearly and emphatically, did the other primitive sacrament of the church. From the first, its fellowship had been centred in the solemn 'breaking of bread' at a communal meal. As the bread was broken, they recalled the mysterious words which Jesus had spoken when he broke bread for his disciples at his last supper: 'This is my body' (I Cor.11.23 f.). Reflecting on these words, Paul observed, first, that in sharing bread the company established a corporate unity among themselves: 'We, many as we are, are one body, for it is one loaf of which we all partake' (I Cor.10.17). But not only so; Christ himself had said, 'This is *my* body.' Consequently, 'when we break the bread, it is a means of sharing in the body *of Christ*' (I Cor.10.16). The church therefore is itself the body of Christ; 'he is the head, and on him the whole body depends' (Eph.4.16). It is in this way that the new people of God is constituted, 'in Christ'.

Life in Christ

In all forms of Jewish messianic belief it was common ground that the Messiah is, in some sense, representative of Israel in its divine calling and destiny. This idea of representation Paul presses further. Those who adhere to Christ in sincere faith are identified with him in a peculiarly intimate way, as if they were indeed included in his own being. He is the *inclusive* representative of the emergent people of God. Another way of putting it is to say that Christ is the 'Adam' of a new humanity, of which the church is the spearhead. In the Jewish schools where Paul had his training there was much speculation about the 'First Adam' (the name is simply the Hebrew word for 'man'), and about the way in which all men, as 'sons of Adam', are involved in his fortunes as depicted mythologically in Genesis. Paul takes up this idea: mankind is incorporate 'in Adam'; an emergent new humanity is incorporate 'in Christ'. 'As in Adam all men die, so in Christ all will be brought to life' (I Cor.15.22, see Rom.5.12–14). Once again we see a fresh expansion of the messianic idea.

This line of thought points to the way in which Paul would understand the whole work of Christ. His action is our action; we are involved in it. 'One man died for all, and therefore all mankind has died. His purpose in dying was that men, while still in life, should cease to live for themselves, and should live for him who for their sake died and was raised to life' (II Cor.5.14 f.). In other words, the displacement of self from the centre is indeed a kind of death, but a death which leads into a new kind of life; and this displacement is already effected when a man adheres to Christ by faith. For he is then identified with him in his living and dying, and the reality and power of Christ's moral achievement are communicated to him: 'In dying as he died, he died to sin, once for all, and in living as he lives, he lives to God. In the same way you must regard yourselves as dead to sin and alive to God' (Rom.6.10 f.). What this meant to Paul personally we may learn from some words he wrote to the Galatians: 'The life I now live is not my life, but the life that Christ lives in me; and my present bodily life is lived by faith in the Son of God who loved me and gave himself up for me' (Gal.2.20). The deep feeling that comes out in this and other similar passages should satisfy us that all he says about the solidarity of the church with Christ is not mere theological theory-spinning. He is speaking about what he knows in himself with immediate certainty.

Problems of the Church

On one side, then, life 'in Christ' is a deeply personal and inward experience. But Paul also drew from it principles of fruitful application to the church as a society living in the world. The period during which his letters were written saw an immense expansion of the Christian community. Largely through his own enterprise it spread, geographically, over a remarkably large area, at a surprisingly rapid pace. The very rapidity of the advance brought him problems.

The enthusiasm which his mission aroused had sometimes disconcerting effects. It acted as a stimulant to the innate individualism of the Greek genius, and led to rivalry and competition. Parties were formed, each party boasting the eminence of its chosen leader and depreciating his rivals (I Cor.1.10–12). The unity of the church was seriously threatened. To anyone acquainted with the history of the ancient Greek city-states it is all sadly familiar. They had been torn with chronic faction, which in the end cost them their independence. Paul saw the Christian community in a like danger. That the church, as the new 'Israel of God', is in its essential nature one was for Paul axiomatic, and this unity, he held, should be reflected in the life of each of its local congregations. He was dismayed to see it being disrupted.

Apart from the tendency to factiousness endemic in Greek society, there were two problems special to the church as such. The first resulted from the persisting influence, in the minds of converts, of ideas and practices – they might be Jewish or they might be pagan – which they had so recently disavowed. Some grew out of them quickly, others more hesitantly, with the result that different levels of opinion and practice became marked. The other problem was incidental to the fact that the community had as yet no agreed body of belief or doctrine, beyond a few very simple and fundamental convictions. Yet the new way of life demanded intellectual expression adequate to its real significance. Adventurous minds experimented with ideas, with an intellectual agility which again is typically Greek. In itself this was healthy enough; it was the way in which a Christian philosophy was hammered out over the years. Paul's own mind was as adventurous as anybody's. But for Christians of less maturity, extravagance and eccentricity lay in wait. Here again was a threat to the unity of the church.

In so far as the problem was an intellectual one, he attacked it positively by developing the implications of faith in Christ along lines which met the questions that were actually being agitated. It is indeed largely in reaction to what he regarded as unfortunate experiments in answering such questions that his own theology was built up. Some of the practical problems he attacked in detail and *ad hoc*. He discusses, for example, divergences among Christians about the continued observance of Jewish holy days and food regulations (Rom.14), and, on the other side, about the extent to which they might share in the social life of their pagan neighbours without sacrifice of principle (I Cor.8.1–13; 10.18–33).

But apart from such special discussions Paul sought to undercut the whole threat to unity by insisting on the idea of the church as a body, analogous to a living organism, in which the parts, while endlessly various, are interdependent and subordinate to one another, and each makes its indispensable contribution to the well-being of the whole. There is a passage in his First Letter to the Corinthians (12.14–27) which is a classical statement of the idea of the social organism. The idea in itself was no novelty in Greek thinking. But in Paul's hands it takes an original turn, because he develops it in relation to his governing conception of the church as the body *of Christ*. In all its members, however various their endowments and functions, it is Christ who is at work, and God in Christ, through his Spirit pervading the body. 'There are varieties of gifts, but the same Spirit. There are varieties of service, but the same Lord. There are many forms of work, but all of them, in all men, are the work of the same God' (I Cor.12.4–11). So he writes, and there follows a list of such 'services' and 'forms of work' – a list which can be supplemented out of similar lists in other letters (Rom.12.6–8; Eph.4.11 f.). We can see how manifold and complex the activities of the Christian society had already become. If its unity was to be preserved, the various talents thus brought out must be accepted as the means by which Christ's members were equipped to be the channels of his own life in his body, and the temptation must be resisted of regarding them as claims to distinction for those who possessed them.

The Spirit in the Church

It is in this setting that Paul develops his doctrine of the Spirit, which again is one of his most original contributions to Christian thought. It was indeed an innovation, and one of considerable consequence, but it was an innovation rooted in what he had taken over from his Jewish background and from the first Christians. In some forms of Jewish messianic expectation it was held that in 'the days of the Messiah', or in 'the age to come', the divine Spirit, which was believed to have animated the prophets and heroes of Israel's remoter past, would be 'poured out' afresh, and in larger measure (Acts 2.16–18). The early followers of

Jesus, when the realization broke upon them that he had risen from the dead, experienced an almost intoxicating sense of new life and power. It was accompanied, as often happens in times of religious 'revival', by abnormal psychical phenomena – visions, the hearing of voices, ecstatic utterance ('speaking with tongues'), and the like. The early Christians valued these as evident signs that God was at work among them through his Spirit.

These abnormal phenomena reproduced themselves in the new Christian communities which sprang from Paul's mission to the Gentiles, and here they created an excited atmosphere which he saw to be full of danger. The situation needed delicate handling. Paul did not wish to damp down the enthusiasm of which these strange powers were one expression (I Thess.5.19–21). Nor indeed did he wish to deny that they could be the outcome of genuine inspiration. He knew what it was himself to have visions and hear voices (II Cor.12.1–4), and he could (so he tells his correspondents) 'speak with tongues' (I Cor. 14.18). But there were other 'gifts of the Spirit', less showy, but in the end far more important to the community, such as wisdom, insight, powers of leadership, the teacher's gift, a gift for administration, and even such apparently humdrum qualities as those which enable a person to give effective assistance to others who are in need or distress (see Rom.12.6–8; I Cor.12.28). These are gifts which 'build up' the community (I Cor.14.12; the old translation, 'edify', here and in many similar places, is now misleading, for 'edification' in current speech means something different from what Paul had in mind). Paul has thus diverted attention from the abnormal and exceptional to such moral and intellectual endowments as any society would wish to find among its members. It is the devotion of such endowments to the common good that gives them real value.

The principle thus established is obviously of wide application. Paul's congregations were not unique as communities threatened with disruption because individuals exploited their abilities and privileges for their personal advancement. But in applying it within the Christian church he had a powerful leverage for attacking the evil. Those to whom he wrote were right at least in attributing the powers or abilities of which they were conscious to the work of God through his Spirit. They were in no sense achievements of their own. They were, strictly, 'gifts' (the word Paul uses is a strong one, meaning something like 'grace-and-favour gifts', the sheer, unmerited bounty of the Creator). Give this full value, and it goes very far towards correcting the false attitude to which these people were inclined. 'What do you possess,' he asks, 'which was not given you? If then you really received it all as a gift, why take credit to yourselves?' (I Cor.4.7).

But Paul was able to take the matter a good deal further than that. If, as he holds, the church is truly the body of Christ, then it follows that all the various activities by which the body is built up are the work of Christ himself in his 'members' (the limbs and organs of his body). Any gifts which they are able to devote to that end are indeed gifts of the Spirit, and they are the work of God, but, more immediately, they are the gifts of Christ to his church (this is set forth at length in Eph.4.4–16; note especially vv. 7, 11 f., 16). The expressions, 'Spirit of God', 'Spirit of Christ', 'Christ dwelling in you', can be used as if they were, for practical purposes, equivalent (Rom.8.9 f.; a similar equivalence is implied in I Cor.12.4–6).

This meant a re-thinking of the whole idea of the Spirit and 'gifts of the Spirit'. The Spirit is no longer to be thought of as some kind of impersonal force acting on a man to produce astonishing effects. It is now to be recognized as the mode in which Christ himself is personally present in his church, inspiring and directing his members and shaping the whole body to his own pattern.

The Law of the Spirit

This truly original concept of the Spirit as the mode of Christ's own presence in his church opens up a new approach to ethics. Here Paul found himself obliged to meet a formidable challenge to his whole position. It was central to his message that the Christian man is free from the 'bondage' of the law, since Christ 'annulled the law with its rules and regulations' (Eph.2.15). This kind of language ran the risk of being misunderstood. His Jewish critics, outside and inside the church, suspected that in sweeping away the discipline of the Mosaic Law he was leaving his Gentile converts without moral anchorage in a licentious environment.

Paul perhaps scarcely realized at first how open to misconstruction his language was. He soon discovered that he was widely understood to be advocating a purely 'permissive' morality, which was in fact far from his intention. People were saying, 'We are free to do anything' (I Cor.6.12; 10.23), in the belief that they were echoing his own sentiments. And the trouble was that he could not flatly deny what they were saying. He could point out that there were some obvious limitations on freedom: '''We are free to do anything,'' you say. Yes, but not everything is for our good. ''We are free to do anything,'' you say; but does everything help to build up the community' (I Cor.10.23)? And again, 'You were called to be free men, only do not turn your liberty to license for your lower nature' (Gal.5.13). But the matter called for more radical treatment.

On the central point he made no concession: Christian morality is not conformity to an external code; it springs from an inward source. 'Let your minds be remade,' he writes, 'and your whole nature transformed; then you will be able to discern the will of God, and to know what is good, acceptable, and perfect' (Rom. 12.2). This transformation is effected by the work of the Spirit within, and here is the true source of Christian character and action: 'The *harvest* of the Spirit is love, joy, peace, patience, kindness, goodness, fidelity, and self-control. There is no law dealing with such things as these' (Gal.5.22 f.). The church is under a 'new covenant', which is not, like the 'old covenant', guaranteed by a code of commands and prohibitions 'engraved letter by letter upon stone' (II Cor.3.7), but by the Spirit animating the whole body of the church.

Then is the Spirit simply an 'inner light', and, if so, how am I to distinguish the promptings of the Holy Spirit from the promptings of my own spirit, which may be far from holy? Paul's answer to this question is found by drawing the full logical consequences of his doctrine that the Spirit in the church is the Spirit *of Christ* working in the members of his body. 'Christ dwelling within you' is no other than the Christ who lived and taught, died and rose again. Christians who have received the Gospel and the teaching that went with it are in a position to know what is 'Christlike' in character and conduct, and this is an objective standard by which all inner promptings may be brought to the test. It may even be described as 'the law of Christ' (Gal.6.2; I Cor.9.21). Paul is indeed cautious of using such quasi-legal language; he would not like to be thought to be introducing a kind of new Christian legalism. But he does mean that the norm of what is 'Christlike' is no less objective, and no less binding, than any written code could be. The 'law of Christ', and the 'life-giving law of the Spirit' (Rom.8.2) are not two things but one; apprehended inwardly, but essentially *given* by an Authority beyond ourselves. To 'let your minds be remade' (Rom.12.2) is, ultimately, to 'possess the mind of Christ' (I Cor.2.16). Sometimes Paul speaks as if this reshaping of the mind took place all at once when a man became a Christian, but there are sufficient passages in his letters to show him fully aware that the process might be a gradual, and a long, one (e.g., Gal.4.19; Eph.4.13, and, reflecting directly his own experience, I Cor. 9.26 f.), a process, even, possibly never completed in this life (Phil.3.12–14). But when once the process is genuinely afoot, a man is 'under the law of Christ', and Christ himself – not the man's own ideas or ideals, not even in the end, his conscience – is the judge to whom he defers in all his actions (I Cor.4.3 f.).

The Law of Christ

The law of Christ, then, is no other than Christ himself working through his Spirit in the church to give ethical direction. And it is *all* that we know of Christ that comes into it – his teaching, the example of his actions, and the impact of his death and resurrection. To illustrate this, it will be worth while to look rather closely at one passage where Paul is dealing in a practical way with delicate questions on which there were acute differences within the church – the long discussion in Rom.14.1–15.6, about the observance of holy days and of dietary rules. First, the careful reader will be reminded time and again of sayings of Jesus known to us from the Gospels, though none are quoted verbally. They may be listed as follows:

	Romans	Gospels
on judging others	14.4, 10, 13a	Matt.7.1 f.
on 'stumbling-blocks'	14.13b, 21	Mark 9.42, see Matt.18.7
on 'clean' and 'unclean'	14.14	Mark 7.15,19

What is important here is not the verbal echoes, but the way in which the teaching of Jesus has lodged so deeply in Paul's mind as to establish a standard and a point of view which has become truly his own. Secondly, he appeals to the *example* of Christ: 'Each of us must consider his neighbour and think what is for his good . . . for Christ did not consider himself' (Rom.15.2 f.). There is no Gospel text that could be cited for this, but it seizes upon what was clearly central to the whole ministry of Jesus as the Gospels present it. And indeed the entire discussion, which is an application of the principle that the Christian should 'receive', or 'accept', people whom he might be tempted to reject, 'as Christ accepted us' (Rom.14.1; 15.7), recaptures the theme which is so prominent in the Gospels: how Jesus received 'little ones' (children, of course, in the Gospels, but to Paul it suggested the spiritually immature), and, still more, how he received 'publicans and sinners'. And finally, he appeals to the meaning and effect of Christ's death and resurrection: 'No one of us lives, and equally no one of us dies, for himself alone . . . Whether we live or die we belong to the Lord. That is why Christ died and came to life again' (Rom.14.7–9; the connection of thought may be illuminated from II Cor.5.14 f.; see above, p. 319). In sum, then, the teaching of Jesus, the example of his life, the impact of his death, have acted as influences on Paul's thought, not as from outside, but creatively from within. His ethical judgments are informed by the Spirit of Christ, and yet are intimately his own. That is why the law of Christ, while it commands him absolutely, can never be felt as a 'bondage', like the old law 'with its rules and regulations', but 'where the Spirit of the Lord is, there is liberty' (II Cor.3.17).

From this point of view, Paul's ethical teaching is the application, to actual situations, of what it means to be 'Christlike'. He himself, he says, follows the example of Christ in 'regarding not my own good but the good of the many' (I Cor.10.33–11.1), and he would have his converts do the same. They are to imitate the 'gentleness and magnanimity of Christ' (II Cor.10.1), his 'steadfastness' (II Thess.3.5), his readiness to forgive (Eph.4.32; Col.3.13), his humility and his unreserved 'obedience' to the will of God (Rom.5.19, etc.), even at the cost of his life (Phil.2.8). His death is the commanding example of self-sacrifice for the sake of others (Gal.2.20; Eph.5.2, 25), and it was the expression of his limitless love for men (Rom.8.34 f.; Gal.2.20; Eph.3.18 f., etc.).

It is this quality of love, above all, that Paul holds up as the essence of what it means to be 'Christlike', and as the basic and all-inclusive principle of Christian living (Rom.13.8–10; Gal.5.14; Col.3.14; Eph.1.4, etc.). The word he uses is the almost untranslatable Greek *agape*, a word first brought into common use in a Christian setting. We can hardly do other than translate it 'love' (unless we follow the older rendering 'charity'), but in doing so we have to think away the flavour of sentiment or facile emotion that tends to cling to the word in our common usage. *Agape* certainly includes feelings of affection (Rom.12.9 f.), but basically it is an energy of goodwill going out towards other people, regardless of their merit, or worthiness, or attractiveness. The eloquent passage in I Cor.13, which has the aspect of a hymn in praise of *agape*, contains pointers to the kind of attitude and behaviour it inspires, and in this context it is presented as the highest of all 'gifts of the Spirit' (I Cor.12.31; 14.1). Once again, the 'law of the Spirit' and the 'law of Christ' are indistinguishable.

Social Ethics

Agape, then, is the source of the distinctively Christian virtues and graces of character. It is also the constructive principle in society: 'It is love that builds' (I Cor.8.1). Thus the ideas of the building of the body and the centrality of love imply one another, and form the effective basis for Paul's teaching on social ethics. The whole of Christian behaviour can be summed up in the maxim, 'Love one another as Christ loved you' (Eph.5.1; see also Gal.5.13 f.; I Thess.4.9; Col.3.14).

This does not, however, mean that Paul is content to say, 'Love and do as you please.' Nor, on the other hand, does he undertake to show how detailed rules of behaviour could be derived deductively from a single master-principle (which was the method favoured by Greek moralists). Ethical behaviour is essentially a man's response to actual situations in which he finds himself in day-to-day living as a member of society. Paul envisages his readers in their actual situation, not in just any society,

but in this particular society in which their daily life must be lived, namely the Graeco-Roman world, which Paul knew so well, with its specific institutions, political, legal and economic and the rest, and within that world the young Christian communities with their distinctive ethos and their special problems. He casts his eye over the scene and indicates, by way of selected examples rather than exhaustively, and always in concrete terms, how this whole network of relations may be permeated with the Christian quality of living.

On one side of it, indeed, he sees pagan society as so deeply corrupted that the Christian can do nothing but repudiate it root and branch. Of this side he has drawn a sombre picture, possibly with some rhetorical over-emphasis, in Rom.1.18–32 (see also Gal.5.19–21; Eph.5.3–5; Col.3.5, etc.). How close these immature Christians stood to the corruptions of paganism, and how easily they could relapse into them, we can gather from some startling remarks which he lets fall about his converts (e.g., I Cor.5.1 f., 11; 6.8–10; Col.3.5–7; I Thess.4.3–8), as well as from the passion with which he insists that there must be a complete and final break with the past (Col.3.5–10). So alarmed was he at the possibility of infection that he sometimes speaks as if the only way of safety was for the church to turn in upon itself and withdraw from pagan society altogether (II Cor.6.14–18); but he had to explain that this was not his real intention: the idea that Christians should avoid dangerous contacts by 'getting right out of the world' he dismisses as absurd (I Cor.5.9–13); and in fact it is clear that he contemplated Christians living on terms of normal social intercourse with their pagan neighbours (I Cor.10.27 f.). Their task is the more difficult one of living as full members of the society in which their lot is cast, while firmly renouncing its corruptions.

There was in truth another side to Graeco-Roman civilization. Deeply corrupted it might be, but nevertheless it was not without moral ideals. A certain standard of what was 'fitting' was widely accepted, at least in theory. The Stoics spoke of it as 'the general feeling of mankind' (*communis sensus hominum*). And up to a point there was a genuine desire to see this standard observed in corporate life. Paul was well aware of this, as he shows when he enjoins his readers, 'Let your aims be such as *all* men count honourable' (Rom.12.17). Even after his fierce castigation of pagan vices at the beginning of his Letter to the Romans he goes on to say that the good pagan may do God's will 'by the light of nature'; his conscience bears true witness (Rom.2.14 f.). And there is a broad universality about what he writes to the Philippians: 'All that is true, all that is noble, all that is just and pure, all that is lovable and gracious, whatever is excellent and admirable – fill all your thoughts with these things' (Phil.4.8). The language would seem to be deliberately chosen to suggest that such worthy themes for contemplation are to be sought and found over the widest field possible, in the church or out of it.

It is thus not surprising that Paul is content to work out his sketch (it is hardly more) of Christian behaviour within the framework of Graeco-Roman society as it actually existed. The empire itself is for him part of the divinely given setting for a Christian's life in the world, and he will be following the law of Christ in obeying the Roman law, respecting the magistrates, and paying his taxes. This is 'an obligation imposed not merely by fear of retribution but by conscience'. In fact, the fulfilment of such obligations is an application of the maxim, 'Love your neighbour as yourself' (Rom.13.1–10).

Similarly, in dealing with family life he takes over a general scheme current among moralists at the time (it is found especially in Stoic writers), which assumes the existing structure of the Graeco-Roman household, with the *paterfamilias* as the responsible head, and the other members, including the slaves, having their respective obligations (Eph.5.21–6.9; Col. 3.18–4.1), and indicates how within this general structure Christian principles can be applied and Christian motives find scope.

His earliest treatment of family life and its obligations, in I Cor.7, is largely tentative. He is feeling his way through a tangle of discordant views and practices, and 'giving his judgment' as best he can (I Cor.7.25). The whole discussion is biased by the belief he then entertained that 'the time we live in will not last long' (I Cor.7.29); everything therefore is provisional. In spite of this, we can see how Christian principles and motives are beginning to remould the pattern. That marriage is indissoluble for Christians he knows because there is a saying

of the Lord to that effect (I Cor.7.10 f.; see Mark 10.2–9). Beyond that he can only give his honest opinion, guided, as he believes, by the Spirit (I Cor.7.12, 25, 40). In Christ there is neither male nor female (Gal.3.28), and therefore, although the husband is inevitably the head of the household, the marriage relation itself must be completely mutual as between husband and wife: 'The wife cannot claim her body as her own; it is her husband's. Equally, the husband cannot claim his body as his own; it is his wife's' (I Cor.7.4). So sacred is the bond that in a mixed marriage the heathen husband is 'holy', i.e., belongs to God, through his Christian wife, and the heathen wife through her Christian husband, and the children of such a marriage are 'holy', i.e., 'belong to God' (I Cor.7.14). The implication is that the natural ties of family relationship are valid within the Christian fellowship which is 'the body of Christ'. Thus, although Paul feels that 'in a time of stress like the present' married life is strictly an irrelevance (I Cor.7.26–29), the idea of the Christian family is beginning to push through. By the time he wrote to the Colossians he had fully accepted the principle that the family should be a part of life 'in Christ', though the brief hints given here of its distinctive character are meagre enough (Col. 3.18–21). In the Letter to the Ephesians (if we may take that as representing his mature thought, see above p. 313) he sets forth a high Christian ideal of marriage in which a man's love for his wife is an image of the sacrificial love of Christ, who 'loved the church and gave himself up for it' (Eph.5.25–33).

The Graeco-Roman household included the slaves, and here again we can see Christian principles and motives making their way. It is fundamental that in Christ there is neither slave nor free man (Gal.3.28; Col.3.11). Accordingly, there is a level on which their status is equal: 'The man who as a slave received the call to be a Christian is the Lord's freedman, and, equally, the free man who received the call is a slave in the service of Christ' (I Cor.7.22). In writing to the Colossians he urges slaves to give their service 'as if you were doing it for the Lord and not for men ... Christ is the Master whose slaves you must be'; and then he adds, 'Masters, be fair and just to your slaves, knowing that you too have a Master in heaven' (Col.3.23 f.; 4.1; see also Eph.6.5–9). The ideal of free mutual service transcends the legal relations of master and slave. As it happens, we have a letter, the short note addressed to Philemon, in which Paul deals with a particular case. Philemon's slave Onesimus had run away, having, apparently, helped himself from his master's cashbox. Somehow or other Paul came across him, and he was converted to the Christian faith. What was Paul to do? Under Roman law anyone harbouring a fugitive slave was liable to severe penalties, and a runaway recovered by his master could expect no mercy. Paul decided to send Onesimus back to his master, gambling everything on Philemon's readiness to take a fully Christian view of the matter. 'Perhaps this is why you lost him for a time,' he writes, 'that you might have him back for good, no longer as a slave, but as more than a slave, as a dear brother' (Philemon 12–16). The 'law of Christ', without disrupting the civil order, is transforming it from within.

Christ, the Church, and the Future

The permeation of the church, and ultimately of society, with the Christian quality of life gives actuality to Paul's doctrine of the indwelling of Christ, through the Spirit, in the body of his followers. This is seen to be no longer a bare theory, or, on the other hand, merely the inward experience of an individual. It is a force working in history. But if Christ is thus present in the church, then he is to be known not only through his historical life, supremely important as that is, but also in what he is doing in and through the church in the present, and in the future into which the present dissolves at every moment. His brief career on earth had ended, so far as the world in general could see, in failure. His disciples knew better. But how was the world to know? For many early Christians a sufficient answer to this question was that very shortly he would 'come again', and then 'every eye shall see him' (Rev.1.7). Paul began by sharing this belief. At the time when he wrote his earliest surviving letters (as they probably are), those to the Thessalonians, although he was concerned to damp down exaggerated expectations of an *immediate* 'second advent' (II Thess.2.1–3), he seems to have had no doubt that he and most Christians would live to see it (I Thess.4.15). Even when he wrote his First Letter to the

Corinthians he was still assured that 'we shall not *all* die' (I Cor.15.51). Before he wrote the Second Letter there was an occasion when his life was despaired of (II Cor.1.9), and it may be that for the first time he faced the likelihood that he would die before the Day, and in that way 'go to live with the Lord' (II Cor.5.8). At any rate, from this time we hear little more of the urgent, even impatient, expectation of earlier years.

He came to be less preoccupied with a supposedly imminent 'second advent', as he explored the range of Christ's *present* activity in the church. He saw the church expanding its influence abroad, and developing internally the complexity that marks the evolution of a living organism. If all this raised some problems, it was all part of the growth of the body – of Christ's body – and it was Christ's own work. 'It is from the Head that the whole body, with all its joints and ligaments, receives its supplies, and thus knit together grows according to God's design' (Col.2.19, cf. Eph.4.16). This, as he now saw it, is the way in which Christ is revealed to the whole universe (Eph.3.10). Nor is there any limit to this growth, 'until we all at last attain to the unity inherent in our faith' (Eph.4.13). In the church Paul saw men actually being drawn into unity across the barriers erected by differences of race or national tradition, language, culture, or social status. Naturally enough (since he had been personally involved) he was most powerfully impressed by the reconciliation of Jew and Gentile in the fellowship of the church (Eph.2.11–22). In this, as his horizons widened, he saw the promise of a larger unity, embracing all mankind (Rom.11.25–32). In this unity of mankind, moreover, he finds the sign and pledge of God's purpose for his whole creation. In a passage which has much of the visionary quality of poetry or prophecy, he pictures the whole universe waiting 'in eager expectation' for the day when it shall 'enter upon the liberty and splendour of the children of God' (Rom.8.19–21). In the church, therefore, can be discerned God's ultimate design 'to reconcile the whole universe to himself . . . to reconcile all things, whether on earth or in heaven, through Christ alone' (Col.1.20, cf. Eph.1.10). Such is the vision of the future which in the end Paul bequeathed to the church for its inspiration.

11

The Gospel According to John

C. F. Evans

Whether the Gospel of John should be taught to pupils at school, and if so at what age, are questions which call for careful consideration. Its simplicity of expression, its short sentences and limited vocabulary are deceptive. To penetrate its thought a certain sophistication is needed, and an appreciation of the symbolic use of language. Thus the mighty works of Jesus (miracles such as the feeding of the five thousand or the healing of a blind man) are here signs embodying spiritual truths. Much of the Gospel consists of discourses attributed to Jesus, and the movement of a discourse can depend upon the deliberate use of a phrase with a double meaning: in the conversation with Nicodemus, 'born afresh' or 'born from above' (3.3); to the woman of Samaria, 'running water' or 'living water' (4.10); speaking of his own destiny, 'elevated vertically from the earth (on the cross)' or 'exalted from the earth (to heaven)' (12.32 f.). The surprising fact that this Gospel does not contain a single parable of the Synoptic type probably means that the evangelist regarded all Jesus' utterances as parabolic (16.25). Moreover, he can write on more levels than one at the same time. For instance, is the reconstituted temple (2.19 ff.) the risen body of Jesus, or the body of Christ the church, or both?

If the Gospel is to be taught, it demands to be taken as a whole and in its own right; it is not to be used piecemeal to supplement, or to fill up supposed gaps in a Synoptic narrative. For, although the discourses may each have been constructed separately and then brought together (and perhaps added to by a later hand), and although certain breaks in the narrative have led some scholars to the view that there are sections which are not in their original order, the Gospel even as it now stands is a far more unified structure than any of the Synoptic Gospels, and it must be allowed to tell its own story in its own way. The form-critical method of separating out originally independent para-

graphs, and then considering them on the background of the oral tradition of the church through which they came to the evangelists (see Part IV, Section 5, pp. 246 f.), works for this Gospel only to a limited degree and with limited results. Thus, here, the feeding of the five thousand is no longer a separate episode standing on its own feet, but is the occasion for a discourse upon the bread of life. Even such a Synoptic-sounding and probably originally independent saying as 'He who loves his life shall lose it' (12.25) is now part and parcel of a discourse for the Greeks on the death of Jesus, and is inseparable from that context. The immediate background of this Gospel is not the oral tradition, but the highly distinctive type of Christianity reflected in the Epistles of John (whether or not these are by the same author as the Gospel), and Jesus utters throughout the thought and language of that type of Christianity. This gives the Gospel its unity and coherence, even at times its monotony, as does also the 'cyclic' method of writing characteristic of I John. The author introduces a subject, develops it, moves around it, and in doing so picks up something from a previous subject. For instance, the raising of Lazarus (11.1 ff.), with its climax, 'Lazarus, come forth', refers back to the saying in 5.25: 'The hour is coming, and now is, when the dead shall hear the voice of the Son of God, and those who hear shall live.'

Authorship and Date

Where the Gospel and its author are to be located in the spectrum of early Christianity, and at what place and date it was written are questions which do not admit of definite answers. The origin of the ascription of the work to a 'John' is unknown. There is evidence to suggest that the author may have stood closer than was later thought desirable to some form of that spiritual movement of 'salvation through knowledge' called Gnosticism (see below, pp. 343 f.) with which the churches were in conflict in the second century. Thus it is in Gnostic circles that we first know of the Gospel being used. The first commentator on it was a Gnostic named Heracleon (*c*.160). In the second century there were some 'orthodox' who bitterly attacked it and rejected it.

It is the theologian Irenaeus (*c*.185) who makes the identification of the author with the beloved disciple, the apostle, John, the son of Zebedee, resident at Ephesus to old age. This identification, while never proved to be impossible, is now generally rejected, chiefly on the grounds that apostolic authorship conflicts with, rather than illuminates, the particular character of this Gospel, and that it is hardly consistent with the early opposition to it in the church. The mysterious, unnamed 'disciple whom Jesus loved' is said to be the author in a note appended by a later hand (21.24), but in 19.35 he is referred to by the author as someone other than himself. In view of these and other difficulties most modern scholars have abandoned the search for the author's identity, and prefer to concentrate on the Gospel itself as indicating what kind of person he was. Ephesus as the place of origin rests on the same evidence of Irenaeus; other suggestions have been Alexandria, in view of the character of the Gospel's thought, and Syria, in view of similarities to that thought in writers like Ignatius of Antioch. Papyrus fragments of the Gospel belonging to the early part of the second century fix the latest time for composition at about the turn of the first century; there are no indications of a more precise date.

The Structure of the Gospel

While there is plenty of room for dispute over details there would seem to be a general plan, which might perhaps be compared to that of a great cathedral.

1. The approach to the cathedral through west front and portico is by way of a double introduction; first the religio-philosophical prologue (1.1–18), and then a prologue of a more traditional kind (1.19–51).

2. This opens into the nave with its pillars, which is the public ministry of signs and discourses, marked at one end by, 'This, the first of his signs . . .' (2.11), and at the other by, 'Though he had done so many signs before them, yet they did not believe in him' (12.37), and by quotations from Isaiah to characterize this ministry as one of rejection.

3. This is followed by the choir narrowing towards the sanctuary, which consists of a single discourse of Jesus in private to 'his own' issuing in a prayer of Jesus to the Father in their presence (13.1–16.33;17).

4. This in turn leads into the sanctuary proper, which is the narratives of the passion and resurrection (chs. 18–21).

1. *The Prologue (1.1–18)*

Unique in the New Testament in form and to some extent in content is a rhythmical composition, either from the author's own hand or taken over by him and interpolated by him with the two prose passages (1.6 f., 15) which are designed to underline the subordinate position of John the Baptist and his function as witness. While the key title 'the Logos' (Word) does not recur outside the prologue, the predicates of the Logos in the prologue – life, light, flesh, glory, only-begotten (Son) – provide principal terms for the portrayal of Jesus in the rest of the Gospel. The two divisions of the Gospel, at chs. 2–12 and chs. 13–17, may be said to be explications of two statements in the prologue, 'He came to his own home, and his own people received him not' (1.11), and 'But to all who received him, who believed in his name, he gave power to become children of God' (1.12). Thus the prologue is an overture, which in pregnant language places the works and words of Jesus in their widest cosmic setting as the revelation in action of the eternal relationship between the Father and the Son, between God and the creative Word. The second prologue (1.19–51) also emphasizes the subordinate position of John the Baptist – here and elsewhere the evangelist may be opposing claims of John's disciples current in his own day. John the Baptist bears witness both negatively by what he says that he is not, and positively by what he says Jesus is, namely the Lamb of God. This leads to a gathering by Jesus of personal followers, two being from among John the Baptist's disciples, and these make various (inadequate) professions of faith in terms of 'Rabbi', 'Messiah', 'Son of God', 'King of Israel', the climax being reached when Jesus refers to himself in terms of 'the Son of man' who spans heaven and earth.

2. *The Public Ministry (2.11–12.37)*

The public ministry is made up largely of signs and discourses. C. H. Dodd calls it the 'Book of Signs'. Rudolf Bultmann detects two separate sources, a 'Signs'-source and a 'Discourse-source', but the two elements appear to be too closely connected for that. The signs may be reckoned as six in number, three located in Galilee (water into wine, the nobleman's son, the feeding of the five thousand), and three in or near Jerusalem (the lame man, the blind man, the raising of Lazarus). Only the former are specifically called 'signs', but the latter also establish the reputation of Jesus as a performer of signs (9.16). By the use of the word 'sign', and by the way he uses the signs, the author indicates that he has made a selection of those actions which for him were the most significant because in their outward and physical circumstances they served as the clearest pointers to what in Christian experience believers had come to see Jesus to be and his gifts to be. This is evident when a sign gives rise to an interpretative discourse. For instance, the healing of the lame man on a sabbath day (5.1–47) signifies that Jesus is the Son who shares with the Father his continuing sabbath 'work', and who exercises by delegation the divine prerogatives of conferring eternal life on men and of judging them. Again the feeding of the multitude (6.1–65) signifies that Jesus as the Son of man both gives and is himself the heavenly manna, the living bread of God. So also the cure of the blind man (9.1–41) signifies that Jesus is the light of the world which both illuminates human life and exposes it for what it is. But sign and discourse can be related in a different way. Thus the first sign at Cana and the cleansing of the temple which follows (2.1–22) stand on their own, but they presage symbolically the new order of existence in the Christian gospel over against the Jewish dispensation, and these are themes which are taken up in the discourse with Nicodemus (3.1–21), a representative of Judaism, on the new birth of the Spirit to which the heavenly Son of man on earth testifies, and in the discourse with the heretical Samaritan woman (4.1–42) on the true and spiritual worship of God which is imminent through the Messiah who is the Saviour of the world.

How the discourses, which are without real parallel in the Synoptic Gospels, came into being is a difficult question to answer. They fall roughly into two classes.

(i) *Dialogues with Individuals or a Group*

In these dialogues Jesus introduces a theme by a paradoxical statement which is misunderstood by being taken literally; he then repeats the essence of the statement and elaborates the theme until it comes to rest in what he gives and who he is (chs. 3; 4; 6; 11). Sometimes the other persons fade into the background, and the dialogue becomes a monologue.

(ii) *Dialogues with the Jews and their Official Representatives*

These (chs. 5; 7–10) can also contain a misunderstood saying, but more often they are bitter controversies over the claims and status of Jesus arising out of his actions and words. They concern Jewish themes such as the sabbath, the Messiah, etc., and can include arguments which assume a Rabbinic method of interpreting Old Testament texts (7.23; 8.17; 10.34). It is these discourses which are principally responsible for the strong anti-Jewish flavour of this Gospel, in which 'the Jews' are constantly referred to without further discrimination as a single body and as the stock opponents both of Jesus and of the church (chs. 9–10).

What also orientates the Gospel in a Jewish direction is that the notes of time are largely provided by references to the feasts of the Jewish calendar (Passover, 2.13; 6.4; 11.55; an unnamed feast, 5.1; Tabernacles, 7.2; Dedication, 10.22). In some cases (e.g., chs. 6; 7; 10) part of the subject matter of the discourse corresponds with the special theme or commemoration belonging to the feast. Aileen Guilding has argued that this arises out of the special Old Testament lections prescribed for the feast. The discourses may thus be the results of a process of preaching, teaching and homily within that type of Christianity which the evangelist represents, and have been designed to present Christ as the fulfilment of the Jewish religion in its inner and deepest sense. In this way various themes are worked out. The 'glory' of Jesus as the revelation of the Father is displayed; the light is shown shining in the darkness and rejected but not overcome by it; the actions, words and person of Jesus give rise to belief or unbelief, and his ministry is the occasion of *krisis* in its double meaning of judgment and sifting by decision.

3. *The Private Discourse (13.1 to 16.33 and ch. 17)*

The foot-washing, which is both a powerful symbol of the death and resurrection of Jesus on behalf of his disciples and also a lesson to them of service, introduces a single esoteric discourse to an inner circle. This is distinctive in tone and content even in this Gospel, and it may have been shaped more by Greek models of the intercourse between a great teacher and his intimates. Speaking in full knowledge of his origin and destiny (13.1 ff.), and as it were from the further side of his death and resurrection, Jesus unfolds their inner meaning and their consequences for the believers. The fact that some of the themes occur first in chs. 13–14 and then recur in chs. 15–16 – e.g., the commandment of love, the necessity of abiding in Jesus as Jesus abides in the Father and of observing his commandments, prayer, the Paraclete, 'a little while', the defeat of the prince of this world, peace, the denial of Jesus by disciples – has led to the suggestion that two versions of the same discourse have been combined. Some of the subjects treated – e.g., warnings of persecution, of Jesus' departure, promises of divine assistance, the mission to the world – are in some measure parallel to what is found in the Synoptic Gospels, especially in the farewell speech in Mark 13, but they have been transposed into the Johannine idiom. What in the Synoptics belongs to the imminent future end of the age is here drawn into the present state of the indwelling of Jesus in the disciples through the Paraclete by virtue of his departure to the Father. The principal theme is that of love. This is all summed up in a last will and testament in the form of prayer, which is part declaratory of what Jesus has accomplished, and is part a petition in that he prays that the disciples and their converts may be maintained and perfected in the divine unity and truth through the efficacy of his own perfected work and self-consecration.

4. *Passion and Resurrection (chs. 18–21)*

Though inevitably covering some of the same ground as the Synoptics, the passion narrative is distinctive, and is highly dramatic. It is the first 'passion play'. It has a scenario in the form of the praetorium, with Jesus inside, the Jews outside, and Pilate as go-between. With dramatic irony the characters other than Jesus are made to speak better than they know, as when Pilate, ruler and judge, in two dramatic presentations of Jesus to those outside testifies that it is he who is 'the Man' (i.e., the Son of man, and hence judge, 19.5) and 'the King' (19.14); or when the Jews in demanding the Roman punishment of crucifixion unwittingly bring about the fulfilment of Jesus' own prophecy that he would die by being 'lifted up' (18.32; cf. 12.33) – cf. also 11.49 ff., where Caiaphas without knowing it utters prophetic words which to the believer describe the nature of Jesus' death. The Jewish aspect of the story has almost disappeared, being reduced to the perfunctory statement that the high priest interrogated Jesus about his disciples and his teaching (18.19). This is because in this Gospel the Jewish people has already passed judgment of death by the end of the public ministry (11.45–53). The whole weight falls on the Roman aspect. The Romans, a whole cohort of them, are introduced at the beginning to make the arrest, and the 'trial' takes the form of interviews between Pilate and Jesus on the nature of authority and kingship. Jesus is mocked in charade as a dummy king, and Pilate bears further witness by having the title over the cross written in three languages and by refusing to alter the wording. The choice is not, as in the Synoptics, between two individuals, Jesus and Barabbas, but a choice belonging to the evangelist's own time of Christ or Caesar, the one the king in the heavenly kingdom of truth and the other the representative of a this-worldly salvation. Jesus is condemned at the moment when the Jews turn their backs on Israel's vocation to testify that it is 'the Most High who rules in the kingdoms of men' and commit spiritual suicide with the cry 'We have no king but Caesar' (19.15). Jesus is represented as being in control throughout. From the cross he makes disposition for his family (19.25–27), brings about the fulfilment of Scripture (19.28), and announces the completion of his work (19.30), and from his completed death there flow symbolically the two sacraments (19.34).

After the presentation of the death of Jesus as itself his 'exaltation' and 'glorification', the resurrection comes as something of a surprise in this Gospel. The appearances of the risen Lord in ch. 20, like those in Luke, are confined to Jerusalem, but are distinctive and highly theological. In the first appearance Mary knows the Lord when, as the Good Shepherd, he calls her by name (20.16; cf. 10.3), and the message to be conveyed is that the resurrection is a stage not, as in Mark, on the way to Galilee, but on the way to the Father. In the second appearance in Jerusalem Jesus inaugurates the second creation by breathing on the disciples as God had breathed on Adam, and gives them the Spirit and power over sin for their universal mission. In the third appearance Thomas in face of the reality of the risen Lord utters the highest confession of faith, comparable with the opening words of the prologue, as the basis of the faith of future believers. What is probably an addition by a later hand (ch. 21) reflects the Galilean tradition of the resurrection in Mark and Matthew. Disciples whose work has been fruitless until the Lord appears make a perfect catch of fish under his direction – clearly a symbol of the apostolic mission to the world – and after a threefold interrogation corresponding to his threefold denial Peter is charged with the care of Christ's flock. A correction is made about 'the beloved disciple', a figure who makes his appearance in the Gospel at the passion narrative as companion and to some extent rival of Peter.

The Background of the Gospel

What factors of religious thought and environment have contributed to the construction of the Gospel? This is seldom an easy question to answer about any writing of the ancient world, since the surviving documentation from which to reconstruct that world is so limited. It is even less easy in the case of this Gospel, as the evangelist seems to be able to move easily in more than one realm of thought without being completely captured by any. Thus he is clearly at home in Judaism, though, so far as we can check it, this would appear to be the somewhat later Judaism of the Rabbis after AD 70, and so his book has been called 'the most Jewish book in the New Testament except Revelation'. On the other hand, some of his language is characteristic of the religious world of Hellenism, and his book has been called 'The Gospel of the Hellenists'. Moreover, except in the highly individual case of the Jewish philosopher Philo, we are insufficiently informed as to the extent to which, and the manner in which, these two types of religious thought, the

Jewish and the Hellenistic, had already intermingled with each other before the evangelist's own time. There is further the question of his relation to the Christian tradition before him and contemporary with him. Was he a relatively isolated figure, and his type of Christianity a relatively isolated type?

1. *Synoptic Gospels*

Whether he wrote in knowledge of any of the Synoptic Gospels is still debated. The common view has been that he certainly knew Mark and probably knew Luke. This view is supported by C. K. Barrett in his commentary on the ground of similarities not only of wording but of the order in which some groupings of events are narrated, and differences are accounted for by John's theological motives. On the other hand P. Gardner-Smith *(St John and the Synoptic Gospels)* concluded that John was ignorant of the Synoptic Gospels; the similarities, which are not sufficient to offset the great dissimilarities, are to be put down to the stereotyping effect of oral tradition. C. H. Dodd *(Historical Tradition in the Fourth Gospel)* has argued convincingly that behind this Gospel lies an historical tradition, including a passion narrative, which is independent of the Synoptists and which stems from southern Palestine, though this applies to only part of the material and hardly affects the discourses. It is noteworthy that in some instances where scholars are undecided on this matter they nevertheless frequently find themselves expounding a passage in John as though it did in fact lie on the background of something in the Synoptic Gospels, and especially in Mark (e.g., E. C. Hoskyns, *The Fourth Gospel*; J. Marsh, *St John*, Pelican Gospel Commentaries).

2. *Judaism*

The attitude to Judaism is ambivalent. On the one hand the Gospel is thoroughly Jewish in milieu and content. It is set within the scene of the Jewish festivals; it argues with reference to the main Jewish figures and types, Abraham, Moses, the prophets, the manna, the serpent in the wilderness; it treats of central Jewish matters, the temple, the law of Moses, the fathers, circumcision, purification, expectations of the Messiah and of the prophet. The author appears to be familiar with Rabbinic interpretations of Scripture, and with Rabbinic doctrines, formulae and legal procedure. On the other hand it is thoroughly anti-Jewish, and looks upon Judaism from a detached position as an episode in the past. 'The Jews' are constantly referred to as a single hostile people over against Jesus and his disciples, and the law of Moses can be referred to in a distant way as 'your law' (8.17). The Old Testament is quoted rarely and somewhat loosely. The Jewish doctrine of messiahship is mentioned only to be set aside, and the evangelist's 'doctrine of the Person of Christ is mainly worked out under other categories which are not those of Rabbinic Judaism' (C. H. Dodd). The manna in the desert serves to point to a pre-existent 'true' bread (6.32), which is not a Jewish conception. There are striking parallels between this Gospel and the heterodox Judaism of the Qumran scrolls. These are not sufficient to establish that 'John' was acquainted with the Qumran community or influenced directly by it, but such expressions as 'the children of light' and 'the children of darkness' found in the Qumran writings illustrate from Jewish sources a dualistic type of thinking found in this Gospel which has previously been put down to Hellenistic influences. The Qumran documents may also throw light on the sectarian character of the piety of this Gospel, in which the disciples are separated from the world, and are to be concerned with a love which is limited to the inner circle of the brethren.

3. *Philo*

Philo was a Jewish philosopher of Alexandria contemporary with the beginnings of Christianity (*c.*20 BC–AD 45), and he wrote a great deal. His aim was to commend Judaism and the Old Testament to Gentiles, and in doing so he made use of popular Hellenistic (i.e., Platonist and Stoic) philosophy, and expounded the Old Testament in a symbolic and allegorical fashion. It is not suggested that 'John' had read any of the voluminous writings of Philo, but that the mixture of Jewish and Hellenistic thought in Philo may illustrate how certain conceptions and expressions could come to be used in this Gospel. Thus Philo refers frequently to 'the Logos', and does so in a bewildering variety of ways, as the model or the medium of the creation of the world, as the sum of the heavenly world, as the means of communication between God and men, etc. He still speaks, however, in

a more Jewish manner of 'the Logos of God' or 'the divine Logos', whereas the evangelist refers to 'the Logos' simply without further definition. In Philo, as in this Gospel, 'light' plays a great part as a description of the divine, and so does the knowledge of God as man's true end and his eternal life. The adjective 'true' in the sense of 'heavenly' or 'divine', which is used in this Gospel of Jesus as the true bread and the true vine, is characteristic of Philo.

4. *Hellenistic Religion*

Philo is himself a pointer to a wider hinterland of Hellenistic religious thought with which the evangelist could have had some contact. There is, for example, the Hermetic literature. This consists of a number of tracts dating from the second to the fourth century AD, which in places may contain teaching from the first century. This teaching takes the form of a message to be preached to mankind; it is couched in a kind of philosophical mysticism, in which salvation from the earthly element in man and the realization of the heavenly element in him are brought to the individual through his knowledge of God as light and life, and sometimes this knowledge is mediated by a heavenly or essential man sent by God to earth. Some have maintained that the Gospel of John is the least institutional and sacramental of the New Testament writings and the most concerned with the faith and knowledge of the individual.

Then there is *Gnosticism*. In its second-century form it also exhibits in various shapes a scheme of salvation through knowledge. This is generally more cosmological and more pessimistically dualistic. The upper world of light and spirit is set over against a fallen world of matter and darkness. Men perish in this world because the light particles of mankind have been lost in the darkness until the redeemer gathers them together in a redeemed mankind which is his body. Did this second-century Gnosticism rest upon an earlier form of the same kind of belief in the first century with which the evangelist could have been in touch? Could this have been the source of this Gospel's dualism, where expressions like 'the above' and 'the below' (8.23) and 'the ruler of this world' (12.31; 14.30; 16.11) go beyond the ethical and eschatological dualism of Qumran? Does it throw light on the fresh use of the Jewish and Synoptic title 'the Son of man' to denote a pre-existent heavenly being who makes the double journey from heaven to earth and back? The evangelist would, however, have repudiated the Gnostic idea that matter was evil in itself (see below, pp. 343 f.).

Purpose and Thought

Along with Luke, but in contrast to Mark and Matthew, John states the nature and purpose of his book (20.31). It is summarized as a narrative of selected signs, and it has been written in order that its readers, who are here addressed, might believe that Jesus is the Christ, the Son of God, and that in so believing they might have life in his name (through him). This could mean that the book was intended for publication and was written for the conversion of unbelievers. C. H. Dodd holds that it was written for non-Christians. On the other hand the recipients of I John, who were undoubtedly already Christians, are addressed in the same way (I John 3.23; 5.1–5, 12 f.). A notable feature of the presentation of the ministry of Jesus in this Gospel is that the hard saying about the necessity of eating the flesh and drinking the blood of the Son of man brings about an acute crisis, and from that moment a great many cease to be disciples of Jesus (6.52–71). This may echo the situation reflected in I John where there has been a defection from the community, and many false prophets have gone out into the world because they denied that Jesus was the Christ and that he had come in the flesh (I John 2.19–22; 4.1–6). The Gospel may thus have been written to strengthen Christians who were faced with such a disturbing crisis of faith.

The statement in 20.31 does indeed summarize a good deal of the contents of the book, though not all. Although the author uses the thoroughly Christian expression 'Jesus Christ' (1.17; 17.3), he remains near enough to the original tradition to use 'the Christ' in its proper sense of the Jewish Messiah, and debate over messiahship in general and over the messiahship of Jesus runs through the Gospel (1.20, 25; 3.28; 4.25, 29; 7.26, 42; 9.22; 12.34). It is still important to confess that Jesus is the Christ (20.31; I John 2.22; 5.1), and in the Gospel this truth is revealed to the believer but concealed from the unbeliever. Nevertheless messiahship only touches the fringe of who Jesus is, and the deeper meaning of his work and person is indicated by other descriptions, and especially by 'the Son of God', 'the Son', 'the only-begotten' (i.e., unique), with their correlatives 'the Father' and 'my Father'. These terms provide the main thread of the Gospel, and the works and words of Jesus and his passion and resurrection are represented as the result of, and the unfolding of, an intimate relationship between the Father and the Son. While the term 'Son of God' has roots in the Old Testament as a description of Israel and of the king, and from there could have become a messianic term, it undoubtedly in this Gospel carries the Hellenistic sense of a supernatural being. As the Son of the Father and the Father's intimate Jesus is a pre-existent divine being whose day Abraham rejoiced to see (8.30–59), and who knows the divine secrets. He shares the divine glory (i.e., nature) and love from before creation (17.5, 24). He and the Father are a unity of purpose and action (10.30). He participates in the divine activities of conferring life and pronouncing judgment (5.17–29); belief in him is conjoined with belief in God (14.1), to have seen him is to have seen the Father (14.24). The opposition of the Jews in this Gospel arises from his claim to a unique sonship (5.18; 19.7). But while the term 'Son' in relation to the Father expresses the ego, even the egoism of Jesus, it also and at the same time underlines the contrary and complementary truth that Jesus is totally dependent on the Father, who is greater than he (14.28). The existence of Jesus is not a self-originated existence but derives from 'the Father who sent me' (a frequent term for God in this Gospel). He knows whence he comes and whither he is going (8.14). So also his words and actions do not originate in himself but proceed out of his knowledge of the Father (5.30–43; 6.37–40; 8.14–19, 26–29, 38–51; 10.17–38; 12.48–50; 14.10–24; 15.10–15). Hence the Jewish charge that he made himself 'independent of God' (this is the probable meaning of the words in 5.18) is the opposite of the truth. These complementary truths of the uniqueness of Jesus as the Son on the one hand and of his total dependence on the Father on the other hand are held in tension throughout the Gospel up to and including the prayer in ch. 17. Moreover, the passion and resurrection which follow are at one and the same time the result of the commandment and action of the Father and of the obedient will and action of the Son (10.17 f.; 14.30 f.; 17.4 f.).

The relation of Jesus to the world of men is expressed preeminently in the remarkable 'I am' sayings, which are without parallel in the Synoptics (6.35, 41, 48, 51, the heavenly, living bread; 8.12, the light of the world; 10.7, 9, 11, 14, the door of the sheep and the good shepherd; 11.25, the resurrection; 14.6, the way, the truth and the life; 15.1, the true vine). According to Rudolf Bultmann the majority of these are 'recognition' formulae, i.e., the 'I am' is to be taken as the predicate in the sentence, so that it should be rendered not by 'I am the true vine' but by 'the true vine, it is I'. If this is so, it means that behind such a statement lies the idea that there are certain perfect or ideal entities or figures which men are awaiting, and Jesus is identified with these over against any false claimants. Behind this in turn is the thought that men as created beings have certain vital needs – food and sustenance, drink to quench thirst, light to bring knowledge and to show the way to go, leadership along that way, community with one another and communion with the divine, and life itself. Only the 'true', living or divine form of these things is capable of satisfying human needs to the full, and that true form is Jesus, who both gives and is the true, living and heavenly bread, who gives the living water, who is the light of the world and the way to the Father, the good shepherd who leads and provides for his own, who is the true vine in whom believers abide and bear fruit, and who, as the resurrection itself, is the source of eternal life. In the prologue this is taken back to creation itself; the Word, who as Creator, is responsible for the world's existence, is the source of its true life, and this life throws light on all human life for good or ill.

Thus, whether in relation to God who is the Father or in relation to the world, Jesus is the unique and only revealer, and what he reveals and communicates in this Gospel is chiefly and almost exclusively himself and what he is. The function of everyone and everything else is to point to or bear witness to Jesus (an important theme; 1:7–3.33, John the Baptist; 4.39, the Samaritan woman; 5.39, the Old Testament; 10.25, the miracles; 15.26, the Paraclete; 19.35; 21.24, the beloved disciple). It follows that despite the evangelist's emphasis on the 'flesh' or humanity of Jesus (1.14; 6.51–63), no doubt in opposition to the spiritualizers or 'docetists' who were unable to accept that the divine and the material could ever be brought together (cf. I John 2.18–27; 4.1–6), he hardly escapes from some form of docetism himself. For the Johannine Christ is a heavenly man on earth; all his actions are highly symbolical; his discourses were never spoken in their present form; his feet barely touch the earth.

The most positive and inclusive term to describe what Jesus brings to men, according to this Gospel, is 'life' or 'eternal life'. In Judaism and the Synoptics, where it is to some extent a synonym for the kingdom of God, eternal life refers to what still lies in the future at the end of the ages; the phrase means 'the life of the age which is to come'. It is characteristic of the thought of this Gospel that it refers to what has become present here and now through the presence among men, first in the flesh and then through the Spirit, of the Son. It is almost a synonym for God. In I John 5.20 the true God, Jesus the Son and eternal life are conjoined. In the Gospel (17.3) a definition is given of eternal life as the knowledge of the one true God and of Jesus Christ as sent by him. It is not to be found in the knowledge of the Old Testament but only in Jesus to whom the Old Testament points (5.39); it is given now to him who hears (i.e., obeys) Jesus' word, becomes a believer, and therefore passes beyond the future judgment of the world (5.24 ff.; 6.47; cf. I John 5.11 ff.). This life is in the end life from the dead, and it is present through Jesus since he is himself already that which was believed to belong to the end of the world, namely the resurrection (11.25). This presence is made permanent by the Spirit. Here again the future is brought into the present. The 'second coming' or *parousia* of Christ is in this Gospel his return to his disciples to dwell within them by the Spirit. In four distinctive passages (14.15–17, 25 f.; 15.26; 16.7–15) the Spirit is called by a title, the Paraclete, which is unique in the New Testament (elsewhere only I John 2.1), and is difficult to translate. It is presumably meant to indicate the functions of the Spirit, which are described as glorifying and bearing witness to Jesus by teaching and bringing his words to mind, and so leading disciples into all truth, present and future, and as reproducing for them Jesus' own exposure of the sin and falsehood of the world. As the Son does not act independently of the Father, so the Spirit does not have a mission to men independent of that of the Son.

333

The passion of Christ is set in the context of his return to the Father after a completed work which is to be made available to men. It is hinted at several times in the Gospel as his (appointed) 'hour', and as soon as it begins the notes of time change, and the future 'not yet' gives place to 'now' (12.31; 13.31; 17.5). Jesus goes to his death in full knowledge of it (13.1 ff.), and is represented throughout as a royal figure who is in command of what is happening – there is no agony of doubt in Gethsemane in this Gospel, and the utterances from the cross are of fulfilment and triumph. On the negative side of 'salvation from', the death of Jesus is presented as that of the Passover lamb, which was the memorial of Israel's deliverance from Egypt (19.14, 36). On the positive side, by a play on the double sense of the verb 'to lift up', the vertical hoisting up of Jesus by crucifixion is interpreted as being his exaltation to God and his glorification, i.e., his return to, and disclosing of, the being of God (18.32, referring back to 12.32 f.; cf. 3.14; 8.28; 12.23; 13.31, etc). It is this because Jesus lays down his own life as an act of his will (10.17), and this is the supreme act of love for his friends (15.13). But behind the love of the Son is the love of the Father; it is love which governs the relationship between them (3.35; 14.31; 15.9, 17, 24 ff.). It is from love of the world that the Son descends into the world at the bidding of the Father (3.16). The deepest point of this descent in obedience to the Father is his death, which is therefore the point where the love of God is most clearly shown. Into this love Jesus desires to draw his disciples through his exaltation, and for this reason the commandment to love, which dominates the discourse in chs. 13–16 and 17, is the only new ethical injunction in the teaching of Jesus in this Gospel, and even this is limited to love for fellow believers. This love is defined as keeping Jesus' commandments, but there is no indication of what these commandments are (13.34; 14.15–21; 15.10–14; 17.23–26).

Finally, the means by which the Christian truth is appropriated is faith and knowledge, or, since the nouns 'faith' and 'knowledge' are never used but only the verbs, personal acts of believing and knowing, which are sometimes synonymous (6.69). John's use of 'to believe' is varied and profound. When the verb is used with the dative case of the thing or person it means to trust, as for example, Jesus, his words, the word of God or Scripture (2.22; 4.21; 5.38, 46 f.; 6.30; 8.45 f., 10.37 f.). But involved in this is often believing in the sense of accepting as true some statement which Jesus makes about himself – that he has been sent by the Father, is in the Father, has come from the Father, is the Son of God (8.24; 11.27, 42; 13.19; 14.10; 16.27–30; 17.8, 21; 20.31). Here to believe is to perceive God acting towards men in the words and acts and person of Jesus. This in turn leads to 'believing upon . . .', a use which is the most characteristic of this Gospel and very rare outside it. It means a moral and personal allegiance to Jesus in virtue of what he is, and so to be involved in what he is. Behind all these uses and related to them is the absolute use of the verb, 'to believe'. This belief can be of an unsatisfactory kind (4.48), or transient (16.31 f.), but in itself it denotes a whole attitude in which the unseen is grasped hold of as lying behind the visible, and it leads to knowing God. It comes into being through Jesus, because he is the one who consistently acts and speaks with reference to the invisible Father. In adhering to him the believer adheres to the Father who is behind him, and so comes to know God. Not to believe is to refuse to do this, to insist on adhering to what is visible, and therefore to remain in darkness and to be shown up by the light.

12

The Early Church

John Bowden

The Sources

Much of the life and history of the church during the first century or so of its existence is veiled in obscurity. The archaeological evidence of buildings, inscriptions and papyri, the writings of Jews, Greeks and Romans, historians, poets and philosophers, which tell us so much about the world of the time, hardly spare a word for the Christians. There is no sinister reason for this: the simple fact is that the first Christians were not noteworthy in such a way. There were not very many of them, they formed essentially a working-class movement, their worship was private and unspectacular, and they had very good reasons for not wishing to draw too much public attention to themselves.

There are one or two references to Christianity in non-Christian literature and one or two archaeological discoveries which have some bearing on it. These will be mentioned where they are relevant. But the main source of our knowledge of the early church comes from Christian writings. There are quite a number of these, some of which received official sanction and some of which did not. On the one hand, we have the New Testament itself and other writings which date from about the same time, but which were not given the same status. The latter include: the *Didache* or *Teaching of the Twelve Apostles, I Clement* and *Barnabas* (all probably first-century works); seven letters of *Ignatius of Antioch* (written about 115); the *Shepherd of Hermas* (an allegorical work from early in the second century) and *II Clement* (a homily by a different author from *I Clement*). Works from rather after the New Testament period, like the writings of Justin Martyr in the East and Tertullian in the West, also offer some help. All these writers are included among the 'Fathers' of the church. On the other hand,

there is now an increasing amount of material from the Christian underworld. Writings have survived, or have recently been discovered, from groups which were later regarded as heretical: discourses, poems, apocryphal 'Gospels' and 'Acts'. These writings, some of which are particularly important for our understanding of the development of gnosticism, seen alongside the more orthodox literature, indicate the great variety which Christian experience produced, almost from the very start.

Names and Dates

Most of the earliest Christian writing, especially the New Testament, raises two problems. First, it is difficult to know from what area a work comes and by whom it was written. Some New Testament documents were originally anonymous; it is more than likely that others were not written by the people whose names they bear: the Pastoral letters, the Johannine letters, the Petrine letters, James, Jude, all fall into this category. Reasons for this judgment will be given later, but since such 'pseudonymity', as it is called, is so frequent, it calls for a word of explanation here.

Under first-century conventions, pseudonymity was by no means a dishonest practice. It might be intended as a way of gaining a wider public (no commercial factors were involved!); as a token of homage to a master or to continue his work for a new age; it might spring from a feeling that the words were more than just the author's. Whatever the reason, the result is that we often have to guess at the true origin and nature of a work simply from its contents, regardless of the name to which it is attached. The same is true of books to which early tradition assigned authors: authorship was a puzzle even to Christians of the second and third centuries, and many of them then seem to have been as much in the dark as we are. (An added complication in this latter case is that the name attached to a work was important when the question of its inclusion in the New Testament was being discussed – hence a tendency to attribute as much as possible to an apostle.)

A similar problem arises over the dating of books. None of the New Testament books, even the letters, bears a date of composition, and again we must work out the most likely background from the contents. It is easy to fix the first documents of the New Testament period, the letters of Paul, and the last, II Peter, but almost a century separates the two, and fitting the remaining books into this space of time is a complex business.

Differences of Opinion

Where there are so many imponderables and so many possibilities of different reconstructions, it is very difficult to reach anything like widespread agreement. Pictures of the New Testament church have to be impressionistic; so much must be left to the individual who attempts one that a certain amount of subjectivity is inevitable. Perhaps the most important thing to remember is how much we do not know; any picture should therefore be open-textured, leaving room for alteration by new discoveries, without too much definition where definition is impossible. For with the kind of material that we have, the process of illustration is inevitably circular: the New Testament church has to be illustrated from the documents we possess and the documents have to be interpreted in the light of some picture of the New Testament church. It is a risky business, but there is no other way.

The Acts of the Apostles

Of all the sources for the history of the early church, the Acts of the Apostles is the most important – and the most tantalizing. Did it all really happen like this? How much fact and how much fiction? A hard question, for Acts is the only document of its kind for just on three hundred years. The best way of finding an answer is to look carefully at what it has to say.

1. *Date and Authorship*

Tradition has it that the Third Gospel and Acts (which beyond question belong together) were written by Luke the Physician, a companion of Paul (Col.4.14; II Tim.4.11). Recently, however, good reasons have been shown for questioning the tradition, which is not particularly strong. Fortunately, whichever side is taken in the debate, some conclusions are fairly clear. If Luke was the author of Acts, he was writing towards the end of his life, probably between 85 and 95, in different conditions from those in which the story he tells was played out. Furthermore, as will emerge, his knowledge of the earliest days of the Christian church was scanty: his account seems to be literary reconstruction based on a minimum of fact. His knowledge of the political and social conditions of the Roman world in the latter half of the first century AD may be excellent; Palestine before AD 70 was a harder scene to bring faithfully to life.

2. *Luke as a Writer*

Luke – as good a name as any for the author of Acts, whoever he was – was one of the great writers of the world, and Acts bears the stamp of his own particular brilliance. Unlike the Third Gospel, where fidelity to the sources is a dominant consideration, Acts is a work where the author has taken a free hand and has firmly shaped the material to his own design. The result is a unity in which the constituent ingredients are worked into shape with consummate skill. Luke must have used some sources, but where they leave off and his own work begins, or what relationship his own work bears to them, is extraordinarily difficult to see.

Legend has it that Luke was an artist: at the least, his word-pictures of the births of John the Baptist and Jesus, ascension and Pentecost, dominate the church's year. He is also a great story-teller, with a feeling for style and an ability to write so as not to weary his readers. For example, in the opening chapters of Acts, as at the beginning of the Third Gospel, his writing has a 'biblical', Old Testament flavour, in keeping with the solemnity of the first days of the church, so that at one time these chapters were even believed to be a translation of an Aramaic document; as he describes Paul's work in the Roman and Hellenistic world, his style changes in keeping with the subject-matter. Similarly, the beginning of the book is heavy with theological questions which have to be resolved; once these are settled the narrative becomes lighter, the pace quickens, and the story come to its climax with a great shipwreck scene.

The many speeches with which the story is interspersed are constructed with similar care. Whatever their origin, in their present form they are designed for their place in the book and fit into an overall pattern. For example, the story of Israel and its failings, begun by Stephen in Jerusalem (7.2–53), is carried to its conclusion by Paul at Pisidian Antioch (13.16–43); where the same story has to be repeated, as in the case of Paul's conversion, which is narrated three times (9.1–19; 22.3–21; 26.2–23), details are varied so as not to produce tedium. Even the basic outline of the book is simple and straightforward, so as to avoid confusion in the reader's mind.

3. *Historicity*

Now actual events are seldom simple and tidy, and a first question which arises is: in achieving this brilliant piece of story-telling, how far did Luke succeed in representing accurately the events that happened and the motives that lay behind them? What do we have to allow for?

It is obvious that Acts is selective. It is not a history of all the apostles; on the contrary, some of its clarity is achieved by a concentration on two main figures, Peter in the first half and Paul in the second. If we simply follow Luke, all is well; but if we cross-question him historically, all sorts of awkward gaps appear. What happened to the 'twelve'? How did James come to be leader of the church? How did Christianity reach, e.g., Damascus and Rome, where the chief missionaries of Acts find it already established? Why do we hear nothing of Egypt, which must have been an early stronghold?

There are two possible reasons for selectivity of this kind: the author may omit some things either because he cannot tell us (he has inadequate information) or because he does not want to (for one reason or another his information does not fit in with the picture he has chosen to present). Selection inevitably means

distortion – and both these motives seem to have been at work in Acts.

(i) If Luke was writing towards the end of the first century, his information on the earliest development of the church would be limited. There was some motive for the first Christians to preserve memories of Jesus' life; there was much less to do the same actively for their own history. They were more interested in their Lord and his coming than in their own affairs; the world was not expected to last long, and there was little reason for history writing. By the time Luke began his task, time had moved on. Jerusalem had fallen, and the first community there had been scattered. The days of Jewish Christianity were over; the future rested with the Gentile mission. Doubtless people at the important centres, Antioch, Caesarea, Ephesus, had traditions and memories, but little would have been written down. Luke would have had to travel about to glean information, and fitting the pieces of the jigsaw together can have been no easy task.

(ii) Writing a history under these conditions, Luke would have had to make up his mind about the guiding principles by which to organize his material. His chief concerns emerge clearly from what he writes, and an understanding of them will help us to assess his historical reliability.

4. *The Chief Concerns of Acts*

For Luke, God is firmly in charge and has always indicated the way the church is to go. At each decisive step forward, events are taken out of the church's hands, whether by direct divine guidance or by the pressure of outward events, until Jesus' saying in Acts 1.8 has been achieved:

You shall receive power when the Holy Spirit has come upon you; and you shall be my witnesses in Jerusalem and in all Judaea and Samaria and to the end of the earth.

Stage by stage the scene expands until it reaches its climax with the arrival of the gospel in Rome.

Acts opens with waiting, but then the Spirit is given at Pentecost to inaugurate the mission of the church (ch.2). At first, activity is limited to Jerusalem (chs.2–7), but as persecution drives the church further afield, so the Spirit indicates that its membership is to be extended, first to the fringe of Judaism (ch.8), and then through Peter's dream and the conversion of Cornelius to the Gentile world (chs.10; 11). This development, acknowledged by the Apostolic Council at Jerusalem (ch.15), is the foundation on which Paul's mission is based: according to Luke, Paul works essentially untroubled by controversy within the church. He, too, is constantly guided by the Spirit, in dreams and visions, so that he is in no doubt about the way he is to go (e.g., 16.9; 18.9; 21.4; 27.23 f.).

In addition to this main theme, there are several important subsidiary themes:

(a) *The church.* Because the Spirit is in charge, the church is united and harmonious (2.44; 4.32; 9.31; 11.18; 15.28; 16.5). One main development carries its growth forward, and people outside this main development are unimportant. The church is never confused or at a loss what to do, and its teaching is clearly God-given.

(b) *Jerusalem* is the focal point of the church's unity. Jerusalem is the Holy City, the place of the resurrection, ascension and Pentecost, and the headquarters of the early church. In Acts, everything seems to revolve around Jerusalem, and the Jerusalem church exercises careful supervision of what goes on elsewhere. It is Jerusalem that sends down envoys to Samaria to approve the action of Philip (8.14), Jerusalem that sets the seal on the conversion of Cornelius (11.18), Jerusalem that is the scene of the Apostolic Council (15.4) and Jerusalem to which Paul has to return, to his peril, to give account of his missionary journeys (20.16; 21.11, 15 ff.).

(c) *Rome* is more than the destination of the gospel. It is the seat of government of the first-century world. An important theme of Acts is that Christianity is respectable and not subversive; it deserves to be left unmolested. Christianity is the proper development of Judaism; it is the true Israel, whereas the Jews have taken a fatally wrong turning. When Christians are involved in disturbances, Jewish mischief-makers are usually found to be the cause of the trouble (e.g., 14.2; 17.5; 18.12; 21.27), and to the credit of the Roman authorities, they usually see this (16.35; 18.17; 26.30 ff.). Even more, distinguished and senior Roman officials are attracted to Christianity

and, indeed, are converted to it (10.48; 13.12; cf. 24.24).

5. *A Later Picture?*

Now all this produces rather a different impression from that given by documents from an earlier period and from a consideration of a wider cross-section of the evidence for earliest Christianity. The Acts picture is too uniform, and does not leave scope for the development of the great diversity which we saw to be characteristic of the early church. It is too assured; the crises which the church undoubtedly had to surmount are minimized. There is no hint of concern about the delay in the Second Coming, no memory of the bitter controversy over circumcision and the Gentiles, no trace of the important debate about the place of the Jewish law in Christianity. In Acts, the central issue between Jews and Christians is rather the resurrection of Jesus.

The letters of Paul witness to a different atmosphere; there we find Paul fighting for his beliefs and by no means certain of winning (the state in which his letters were left suggests that for a while he fell into neglect). It is not just that there are discrepancies between the Acts account of Paul's career and Paul's own writing (see Part IV, Section 9, pp. 307 ff.); the worlds of Paul and Acts are painted in different colours. It is as if Luke had equipped himself with a pair of rose-tinted spectacles.

Yet when all this has been said, Acts is still vital evidence. It may offer less guidance to the early period than we would like, but if we put ourselves in Luke's place and try to understand him, we shall learn a great deal about the church of his day and the problems it faced, problems which needed for their solution above all the answer that God was still in charge and that the church was called to be one, and to press on confidently.

The Ascension
Acts 1.1–11

Acts opens with a picture which is usually thought of as 'the ascension' of Jesus. It raises many problems, not just for our modern view of the world. But to ask directly on the basis of Acts what 'the ascension' was can lead to trouble, for only Luke, in the whole of the New Testament, presents it in this way. It is safer to approach indirectly, and above all to try to understand Luke against the background of the New Testament.

Other New Testament writers describe what happened to Jesus after his death and led to the birth of the church in two different ways, as resurrection and as exaltation. Resurrection and exaltation, and indeed the giving of the Spirit, are seen first as aspects of one complex event (cf., e.g., Rom.8.34; Phil.2.8 f.; Col.3.1; Heb.1.3; 10.13; Matt.28.16 ff.; John 20.22). Luke, however, splits the complex into three distinct parts and, following his practice of portraying divine action in the world in the form of vivid, objective pictures, has given each aspect (resurrection, ascension, Pentecost) a life of its own.

There is some doubt about the exact place of the ascension in Luke's sequence. According to the majority of ancient manuscripts, one ascension, on the day of the resurrection, is recorded at Luke 24.51, which clashes with the ascension after forty days in Acts 1.9. As the text between Luke 24.51 and Acts 1.6 has a number of peculiar features, it has been suggested that the passage between these two verses was supplied later, when the New Testament was given its present order and what was originally a single volume, Luke-Acts, was split. This removes some, but not all, of the difficulties.

It would be wrong, however, to emphasize these difficulties too much or, indeed, to lay too much stress on the physical feature of 'ascension' here. After all, the description of the two ascensions together occupies less than two verses. It is the message that accompanies them that is more important. For Luke, the ascension is a means to an end. It marks his recognition that the period of the church is not like the period of the earthly ministry of Jesus and that Jesus must take on a new status if he is to give the Spirit to the church. Luke depicts this transition in a way which was meaningful to the audience of his day and which had the stamp of 'biblical' authority.

Thus the way to teach the ascension is to concentrate on Luke's use both of first-century imagery to express what he wanted to say (e.g., in the three-storeyed universe, heaven, the home of God, was 'above': see Part IV, Section 4, pp. 235 f. etc.) and of Old Testament models (see especially Gen.5.24; II Kings 2.1–12).

The Twelve
Acts 1.12–26

Luke fills the interval between the ascension and Pentecost with an account of the election of Matthias to fill the vacant place in the twelve left by Judas' death. The Spirit is not yet given, so the time-honoured method of choice by lot is used (1.26). As often in these early chapters, there is much about this episode which is vague and puzzling if it is studied in depth. We have the impression that Luke has discovered it in isolation and is not quite certain how it fits in or what all its details mean. He therefore uses it primarily as a vehicle for his own purposes, to tell us what an apostle is (vv.21 f.: in his view, not in Paul's, cf. I Cor.9.1).

Matthias does not appear again, and the twelve as a group fade out of the subsequent narrative, except for a passing mention in 6.2. The list given in Acts differs from those in Matt.10.2 ff.; Mark 3.16 ff., which suggests that some of the twelve were soon forgotten. We have only legendary details about the later career of most of them. It is probable that they were chosen not so much as potential leaders of a future church, but rather as partners in the coming kingdom proclaimed by Jesus, where they were to sit on twelve thrones judging the twelve tribes of Israel (Matt.19.28; Luke 22.30: see further below, on 'Church Order', pp. 345 f.).

Pentecost
Acts 2

The story of the giving of the Holy Spirit is another of Luke's pictures and is evidently the end-product of a process which has mixed reminiscence, symbol and legend. Whatever happened, the basis can hardly have been a conjuring trick with languages; that goes against both our theological and our scientific understanding. We know from Paul that 'speaking with tongues' was a phenomenon in the early church (I Cor.12.10, 28, 30; 14.2 ff.), but it does not seem to have been like this. It probably died out later and Luke, while knowing of it, is somewhat confused about its nature (cf. Acts 10.46; 19.6).

It is possible that Luke intends the picture to suggest that Pentecost reversed the confusion of tongues at the tower of Babel (Gen.11); this is a hope for the last days held by some Jews ('Ye shall be the people of the Lord and have one tongue', *Testament of Judah*, 25.3). In the first century, too, Jews observed Pentecost above all as a commemoration of the law-giving on Sinai. Perhaps the wind and tongues of fire here derive from that.

If we may be doubtful about the accuracy of the picture, we may be sure that its symbolism reflects the experience of the first community. The church began with something which outstripped the expectations of the first followers of Jesus, dispelled their doubt, created a community of love, began to forge a unity which could eventually overcome barriers of race and endowed Christians with a strong sense of mission. This Jerusalem crowd is still Jewish, but there could hardly be a more vivid illustration of Paul's memorable words:

> There can be neither Jew nor Greek, there can be neither bond nor free, there can be no male and female: for you are all one in Christ Jesus (Gal.3.28).

The Early Church
Acts 3–5

Luke's picture of the life of the Jerusalem church is made up of two main ingredients, supplemented with speeches: particular incidents and more general comments in summary form. All the signs point to this being a way of carrying forward the story with a minimum of available material rather than summarizing an embarrassingly large amount of information. Luke may well be right in much of the general drift of his interpretation, but there is probably also exaggeration and the kind of uncertainty we noticed in the story of the choice of Matthias.

Public preaching and mass conversion may well have had less prominence in the early mission than Acts suggests (see below, p. 349). Luke's figures in Acts 2.41 (5000) and 4.4 (3000) must be exaggerated; at the time the total population of Jerusalem was less than 30,000, and to suppose such a high proportion of Christians already goes against all the rest of our evidence. Other features of the summaries seem to derive from the incidents involving individuals. The 'many wonders and signs' (2.43) is illustrated only by Peter's healing of the lame man. The theme of communism seems to grow out of the episode of Joseph Barnabas (4.36), who sold a field and gave the proceeds to the church.

How far did the first members of the church have possessions to sell (2.44 f.; 4.32 ff.)? Might Barnabas be remembered because he was a welcome exception to the rule? Some explanation like this would help to elucidate the difficult story of Ananias and Sapphira, which, as it stands, is almost inexplicable (5.1–11). It makes slightly better sense if we suppose that their fault was not so much being dishonest in a situation where everyone else was relinquishing their property as seeking special status by a striking gift which was not completely honest. Some scholars believe that, as at Qumran, so in the early church there was a group of *perfecti*, an inner circle of whom special sacrifices were demanded. To these Ananias and Sapphira would have aspired to belong.

In addition, these chapters show the church surviving its first persecution; the theme of resurrection is brought out for the first time in the apostolic preaching to the peril of the preachers (this pattern occurs often later: 4.2, 33; cf.17.18, 32; 23.6 ff.; 24.15, 21; 26.23).

The Seven
Acts 6

Most strain between Luke's picture and the material he uses is evident in the story of the appointment of the seven. On the surface, there is tension between Hellenists and Hebrews over the daily distribution (6.1). To obviate this, seven men are chosen as administrators, 'to serve tables', headed by Stephen (6.2 f.). But some questions are unanswered. Who are these Hellenists, and where do they come from? Why should *Hellenist* widows be neglected? If the seven are chosen to look after poor relief, why do they all come from the same group (they all have Greek names)? Would we not expect half of each? Furthermore, when the seven are chosen, Stephen, who holds the centre of the stage immediately afterwards, seems more a preacher than an administrator.

One interesting suggestion is that what we have here is a trace of the first serious division in the church, between the (more conservative) original Jerusalem church and a (more liberal) Hellenistic wing, which was causing increased tension with the Jewish authorities over its views and practices. The seven would be the leaders of this wing of the church. Certainly, according to Acts, when persecution breaks out over Stephen's death, only part of the church is affected (8.1; 11.19); we next find the Hellenistic group as the basis of the church at Antioch (11.19; 13.1). Whatever the explanation, only guesswork is possible, but this guess seems quite a good one.

Philip
Acts 8

Acts 8 is a kind of half-way house; a step forward in the Christian mission, but by no means a clear one. The activity connected with Philip takes place in a kind of twilight zone. First, he works among the Samaritans, who are not fully Jews, nor yet fully Gentiles either. Then he is directed to meet an Ethiopian official. Is this man a Gentile? He could be, but he is reading the Old Testament; that might make him a proselyte. After all, he has come to Jerusalem to worship. Luke does not bother to inform us further, but he conveys that things are moving, short of the decisive step of the Gentile mission.

The way in which Jerusalem is involved in this further step is in keeping with Luke's approach: Peter and John are sent to ensure that Philip has done everything in due order. The story of Simon, like that of Ananias and Sapphira, is obscure. In later tradition Simon became an arch-enemy of the church and was associated with gnosticism (see below, pp. 343 f.).

The Conversion of Cornelius
Acts 10; 11

The turning point in the Christian mission is the conversion of Cornelius, which is directly associated with Peter. Paul has been brought on the scene by the vivid account of his conversion (ch.9), but the Gentile question is essentially settled without him. Does Luke mean to suggest that the Jerusalem church was directly responsible for the development of the Gentile mission without the requirement of circumcision? Paul's later struggle (particularly Gal.2.7 f.: 'I had been entrusted with the gospel to the uncircumcised, just as Peter had been entrusted with the gospel to the circumcised') points in a very different direction.

A second problem is that during the reign of Herod Agrippa, no Roman troops were stationed in his territory. How, then, does Cornelius come to be there? Luke's predilection for prominent Roman figures and his particular approach to the Gentile mission may have led him to develop his story along the lines of the incident of the Roman centurion in Luke 7.1–10.

In any case, the length at which the story is treated shows how important Luke felt this development to be, and suggests that the final version is very much his own work. The approval given to Peter by the church as a whole indicates that any further danger to the church will meet with a united response.

(The part of Acts which relates to Paul is discussed in Part IV, Section 9 pp. 30 ff.).

Life in the Early Church

Following the narrative of Acts is one way of looking at the life of the early church; an alternative one is to ask specific questions of all the sources at our disposal and to see what answers they provide.

1. *The Spread of the Church*

As we have seen, the picture of the expansion of Christianity in Acts is a simplified one, and in any case it only covers a short period. Other sources offer a wider view.

Jerusalem, at first the centre of the church, held its position only for a limited period. According to a report in the fourth-century historian Eusebius, Jewish Christians withdrew from Jerusalem in AD 66, before its fall, and settled at Pella, a city of the Decapolis. Jerusalem did not regain its importance until the fourth century, when it became a place of pilgrimage. Jewish Christianity lived on, but became increasingly a backwater, of little more than historical significance.

Although the New Testament is silent about it, Christianity must have spread south to Egypt at an early date. Our earliest scrap of New Testament text, a papyrus fragment of the Fourth Gospel dated about 100, comes from Egypt, and the strength of the church, particularly in Alexandria, in the second century points to an early mission.

To the north-east, the boundary of the Roman empire and a difficult language barrier proved an early obstacle, so that the main thrust of Christianity was northwards and westwards. The mission consolidated itself through Syria and Asia Minor, with sizeable churches in Antioch, Smyrna, Miletus, Ephesus and Sardis, and from there moved north to Thrace, northern Greece and Bulgaria. It had little influence in the south of Greece, where only Salonika and Corinth had noticeable Christian communities.

Rome, of course, was soon a powerful church, despite persecution, and rapidly became the most important Christian city. The church there seems to have had some rich and influential members. Settlements were also made early in southern Italy and Provence. Finally, while Paul himself did not succeed in his plan to visit Spain, the signs are that Christianity was not long in arriving there. If we allow, as again is probable, for early missions on the north African coast, during the second century Christian influence will in some way have circled the entire Mediterranean sea.

Evidence for precise dating of these movements is diffuse and sometimes difficult to assess: some of the archaeological remains are particularly ambiguous. For example, a cross-shaped sign has been found on a wall at Herculaneum, in southern Italy – but is the cross to be associated with Christians at this time, and is the sign any more than the mark of a shelf-bracket? A famous word-square turns up twice at Pompeii, at Cirencester and at Dura Europos on the Euphrates:

```
R O T A S
O P E R A
T E N E T
A R E P O
S A T O R
```

As they stand, the words make insignificant sense, but rearranged they can be formed into A PATERNOSTER O (the first two words of the Latin Lord's Prayer, framed by Alpha and Omega), both vertically and horizontally, the two lines forming a cross over the central N. Pompeii was destroyed by an eruption of Vesuvius in AD 79; could there have been Christians there using Latin in this sophisticated way so early? Might the square have another significance?

With its rapid spread, and with many crucial questions still unsolved, Christianity must have adopted many different forms. Its kaleidoscopic panorama has been vividly illustrated by Professor Moule:

A traveller soon after the middle of the first century – say about AD 60 – going from Jerusalem to Ephesus, would encounter a wide range of doctrine and practice among communities who all, nevertheless, claimed some attachment to Jesus of Nazareth. Somewhere in Judaea he might have found the circle of James the Lord's brother still worshipping in a Christian synagogue consisting of practising Jews who also believed in Jesus as God's Messiah, but who may have gone only a very little way towards formulating a doctrine of Jesus as divine . . . In Samaria, who knows what kind of Christian colony there might be? One, possibly, which highly honoured the name of John the Baptist (whose mission had been vigorous in those parts and whose tomb, perhaps, they boasted), and which treasured traditions many of which are now embodied in the Fourth Gospel . . . Cosmopolitan Antioch (even to judge from no more than the references to it in the New Testament, let alone its later history) would present a strange amalgam of oriental astrology, Jewish legalism and Christian beliefs. By journey's end he would be prepared for the seething diversity of Ephesus, where the Pauline churches were to be quickly invaded by antinomianism, Judaizing Christianity and influences of a Johannine type. If he then took ship from Miletus to Alexandria, he might there find himself confronted with yet other types of Christian colony, or, if he had already met them at Ephesus or elsewhere, they would be even more concentrated and more clearly defined. Finally, in Rome, all sorts and kinds would jostle one another – Judaizing Christian synagogues, the most liberal of liberal gnosticizing sects, looking more like a mystery cult than the Israel of God, Petrine congregations, Pauline congregations and the rest.

Extend that picture across the Mediterranean northwards and westwards, over a century in time, and the true characteristics of early Christianity begin to emerge. It has to be extended, too, in terms of social class and literacy. Our knowledge of the church comes predominantly from written records, the thoughts and expressions of those who could put across their faith coherently, orthodox or not. But these would be only a small part of the Christian communities, which then, as now, would consist of many different kinds of people. Under these circumstances, a first necessity was a gradual striving towards discipline and clarification of belief, particularly against the onset of the creeping menace of gnosticism, that amalgam of religions which misled so many early Christian congregations, taking them along paths that it would have been better for them not to tread.

2. *Gnosticism*

Christian thinkers borrowed many ideas, symbols and concepts from the intellectual world of their time to explain the significance of Jesus and what had been done through him. Their approach to worship and to practical questions was also influenced by their environment. But how much outside matter can Christianity absorb before it ceases to be Christianity and turns into something else? This was the problem of the first two centuries, and the answer had to be discovered almost by trial and error. For quite some time, satisfactory and unsatisfactory ideas existed side by side, and it was only when their consequences were taken past a certain point that it was clear what would do and what would not do. Gnosticism is a convenient term for describing much of what eventually would not do.

Gnosticism took many forms, so a short definition of it is far from easy. Perhaps the easiest way to describe it is to begin at the end of the second century, when it had developed fully enough to reveal its inadequacies (this form of Gnosticism is usually given a capital G), and to trace its growth backwards from there.

For a long time, much of our knowledge of it was derived from attacks made by the church fathers, particularly Irenaeus of Lyons (*c*.180). From these attacks we see that Gnostic writers differed from each other in their views, but held several points in common in their explanation of the world and their offer of redemption:

(i) The world is not the creation of the true God, but was made by a subordinate being (Demiurge), often identified with the God of the Old Testament. Matter is therefore less than good.

(ii) Man is essentially akin to the divine; he is a spark of light imprisoned in a material body because of some kind of 'fall', and yearns for release.

(iii) Salvation is brought by saving knowledge (*gnosis*) which gives Gnosticism its name. Man is to be awakened and freed – by a saviour who descends from the true realm of light. But his deliverance will bring chaos to the present world and is therefore strenuously opposed by its powers.

Here is a blend of Christianity with elements of many different philosophies, elaborated to such an incredible degree that some scholars wondered whether the polemic of the church fathers did their opponents justice. However, the discovery of an extensive Gnostic library at Nag Hammadi in Egypt, with more than a thousand pages of Coptic texts, has so far shown that while Irenaeus and others disagreed, they did not seriously distort.

At its best, Gnosticism had much that was attractive, but it was fatally flawed. It was too dualistic, separating the Redeemer God from the Creator God. Its negative attitude to matter (and to what actually happened in the past) diminished the significance of Jesus. Above all, it had disastrous ethical consequences. If matter was evil, then the only alternatives were extreme asceticism or extreme libertinism: paying too much or too little attention to the physical element.

These comments, of course, relate to the end of the second century, after the New Testament period. But this approach hardly sprang up overnight. A less developed form of gnosticism (without the capital G) may therefore have existed in the New Testament period and before. Whether gnosticism is pre-Christian is debated; but the problems which Christians faced in explaining the world also troubled Jews, and later Gnosticism certainly contained Jewish elements.

Because gnosticism is not developed in the New Testament period, it is not at all easy to see what was gnosticism and what was not. Paul was troubled with a problem of this kind (e.g., I Corinthians, Galatians, Colossians; see also Ephesians). He had a constant fight against what seem to be gnostic tendencies, some of them arising from misunderstandings of his own teaching. He lost the battle in the short term; by the end of the first century most of Asia Minor seems to have gone gnostic. The

Johannine writings face a similar difficulty: I John and the Fourth Gospel both attack a form of gnosticism, while themselves having a close affinity with it. In the Pastoral letters we see an appeal to tradition and sound doctrine in the face of 'gnostic' ideas. The approach typified in the Pastorals was continued; it is out of this kind of response to gnosticism that the later fixed form of church order and the canon of the New Testament came about.

What these writings were combating can be seen from e.g., *The Gospel of Truth, The Gospel of Thomas, The Epistle to Rheginos* and other documents collected among the New Testament Apocrypha.

3. *Places of Worship*

It was only in the third century that churches began to purchase property for their own use, and 'churches' proper date from towards its end. Before that, worship took place in private houses (Acts 2.46; I Cor.16.19; Philemon 2). Because of the relative poverty of the first Christians, most of these houses would have been of the kind lived in by the lower and middle classes.

In Palestine and Asia Minor these were one-family buildings, anything up to four storeys high. The only large room, the dining room (upper room), was at the top of the building, and as the central element in Christian worship was a meal, meetings will have taken place there. The room usually contained a simple table and three couches (the *triclinium*); where there was a particularly large crowd, other seating had to be pressed into use (Acts 20.8!).

In Rome, on the other hand, the tenement was the norm. Tenements had apartments horizontally across them, and would not necessarily have boasted a dining room. Churches still standing mark the sites of tenements which in the fourth century were remembered as having been house-churches.

A Christian house-church has conveniently been preserved at Dura Europos on the Euphrates. It is later than the New Testament period, dating from the early third century, but gives a good indication of what a house-church will have been like. A dividing wall was demolished to make a room large enough for a congregation of about fifty; earlier congregations may well have been smaller.

4. *Baptism and Eucharist*

Baptism was the universal form of initiation into the church. By the time of the earliest literature that we have, the letters of Paul, it is firmly established, though there is much about its origin that is obscure. Christian baptism was doubtless connected with Jewish proselyte baptism and more specifically with the baptism of John, with which a strong tradition associates Jesus. There is a remark in the Fourth Gospel that Jesus himself did not baptize, and the command to baptize in the threefold name at the end of the Gospel of Matthew is agreed to have been read back on to the lips of Jesus. Whether the twelve were baptized (presumably not) and under what precise circumstances baptism was introduced remains a mystery. Candidates were, of course, primarily adults. When infant baptism was introduced is again disputed, but it may well have been early. Much depends on the interpretation of the phrase 'the house of' (e.g., I Cor.1.16).

The house-church at Dura Europos has been modified by the addition of a baptistery, but this provision would have been rare in the early period. Baptism seems to have been administered, by immersion, wherever there was water: in the desert between Jerusalem and Gaza (Acts 8.38), in a river at Philippi (Acts 16.15); later accounts show it to have been performed in public baths, in fountains, and in the sea.

The earliest celebration of the eucharist probably followed the pattern of the Last Supper. First would come the blessing, breaking and distribution of bread; then followed a meal, probably of bread, salt and fish; at its conclusion wine was taken, blessed and distributed. The pattern closely resembles Jewish table-custom.

A development has taken place by the time Paul writes I Corinthians. In I Cor.11, the two acts of the sacrament seem to have found a place together at the end of the meal. Abuses of the celebration have begun: the rich stuff themselves, while the poor, who were customarily invited as an expression of charity, starve. This disruption of common life led to a complete separation of meal and sacrament by the time of Justin (*c*.150). The meal continued for a while as a separate observance and was given a title of its own, *agape*, or love feast (see Jude 12). Eventually it fell into disuse. Later, more detailed descriptions of the eucharist show that portions of the consecrated elements were sent to those unable to be present.

The eucharist was probably celebrated weekly, on Sunday evening. In addition, from an early period Christians also seem to have had a morning gathering. In a famous letter to the emperor Trajan in 112, Pliny, governor of Bithynia, writes:

> They maintained that it was their habit on a fixed day to assemble before daylight and recite by turns a form of words to Christ as a god.

Jewish prayers were held at this hour, as a reinterpretation of and counter to sun-worship, and this pattern may have influenced Christians. Early in the second century the eucharist itself seems to have been transferred to the morning. The suspicion which fell on meetings of 'clubs' within the Roman empire made it impossible for Christians to assemble in the evening as they had done, and so the eucharist and this 'ministry of the word' were united.

How the two were related at an earlier time is not always clear. The analogy of synagogue worship suggests that there may long have been a service apart from the eucharist, to which, of course, only baptized members of the church were admitted. From the letters of Paul we hear of varied activities in worship. Paul knows that his letters will be read out there; worship will also have included prayers, sermons, singing, extempore prophesying and praying. By the time of Justin we hear of the reading of Scriptures, and of course one of the presuppositions of form criticism is the regular use of parts of the Gospels in worship (see Part IV, Section 5, p. 248).

5. *Sabbath and Sunday*

Pliny's letter also has an undoubted reference to the observance of Sunday, a Christian innovation. Jewish Christian churches in Palestine will have observed the sabbath, following custom here as in the practice of fasting, circumcision, food laws, temple tax and temple worship. But from the start there will have been some tension in the observance. Jesus was remembered to have broken the sabbath on a number of occasions; and the increasing Gentile influence on the church will have helped to lessen its significance.

At the same time, Sunday begins to take on a special meaning. Paul singles it out in I Cor. 16.1 ff. As he does not explain it in any way, it may well have been established for some time by then. The title 'the Lord's day' is first mentioned in Rev.1.10, and can be found in the writings of some of the Apostolic Fathers. The passages in which it occurs all come from Asia Minor and Syria, so the expression may have originated there.

'Lord's day' suggests a connection with the Lord's supper. Sunday was in fact primarily a day of worship. It seems to have a direct connection with the resurrection of Jesus; an added factor will have been the practical need of a regular day for meeting. Christians did not observe Sunday as a holiday. First, most of them will not have been able to afford the luxury of not working on that day. Secondly, to have called attention to themselves by not working then could well have invited persecution. Only in 321, when Constantine had officially sanctioned Christianity as a state religion, was Sunday rest introduced.

6. *Church Order*

Jesus' preaching was concerned with the kingdom of God and the Son of man; he left no instructions and made no arrangements for a church to follow him. As we saw, the twelve were not chosen as potential leaders of a future church; the very few passages in the Gospels which point to a detailed church order are almost certainly the work of the early church and do not come from Jesus himself.

Organization and ministry in the church was therefore something that the first Christians had to work out as they went along, in the light of changing circumstances. Answers seem to have differed according to time and place; the one thing that is clear is that for the New Testament period there is no settled church order. The threefold hierarchical pattern of bishop, priest and deacon was adopted throughout the church at a later time.

As the twelve (or most of them) disappear from view, the increasing prominence of James the brother of Jesus, comes as something of a surprise. Some scholars believe that the resurrection appearance reported in I Cor.15.7 was a special commissioning, others that the 'caliphate' principle of dynastic succession was at work. But there is insufficient evidence to tell.

345

Jesus' own following was more than twelve. Both the Gospels and Acts mention others, including Jesus' mother and brothers. But again, what happens to them is impossible to trace.

Although the phrase 'the twelve apostles' is so familiar, in the New Testament the *apostles* and the twelve are not always identical. The origin and meaning of the word apostle are hard to establish; 'apostle' means different things to different New Testament writers. For Luke, an apostle is one who 'accompanied us during all the time that the Lord Jesus went in and out among us' (Peter: Acts 1.21), thus excluding Paul. But for Paul himself, apostleship is something to be proud of; he is very anxious to defend his own (I Cor.9.1). For him, the apostles are those who have been commissioned by an appearance of the risen Lord, larger than himself and the twelve. Later, in the Pastoral letters, Paul is '*the* Apostle', the guardian of the faith. The one point of agreement is that apostleship is not something that can be passed on.

A famous passage, I Cor.12.28, mentions in succession apostles, prophets and teachers, and Eph.4.11 has a similar list. It is doubtful, however, whether these can be regarded as different classes of ministry. Rather, they are different activities, more than one of which might be practised by a single individual.

Deacon is usually a general term, describing any form of ministry or service ('deaconess', which occurs in Rom.16.1, is probably to be understood in this general way). In two passages, however, the deacon seems to be a particular minister, subordinate to the bishop (Phil.1.1; I Tim.3.8–13). If the two terms are used technically in Phil.1.1, this is the only evidence we have of such a formal ministry from the Pauline letters, so the terms may be general even there. In I Tim.3, the more formal use is certain.

Elders are not mentioned at all by Paul, but they are to be found as ministers throughout Acts, appointed by Paul and Barnabas 'in every church' (Acts 14.23; cf. 15.2 ff.; 16.4; 20.17; 21.18). Here Jewish practice is followed. Villages and towns had their groups of Jewish elders, seven in a village, twenty-three in a town and seventy in Jerusalem. When a place fell vacant, it was filled by the laying on of hands. This is the pattern to be found in Acts.

It may be that the word *bishop* occurs in a technical sense at Acts 20.28, but as in Phil.1.1 the word may be used generally ('overseer'). Bishop is a definite office in I Tim.3.1–7; Titus 1.7–9. The relationship between elders and bishops is a classic problem, as at times the two terms seem to be synonyms. The difficulty is to find an explanation accounting for the situation at the end of the second century when each particular area was in the charge of a single bishop ('monarchical episcopacy'). The most likely answer is that all bishops were elders, but not all elders were bishops.

We have even less evidence about the ministry at this time than about other important matters, and what is said in the Apostolic Fathers does little to help Clearly the pattern varied from place to place, and development was by no means uniform.

7. *Persecution*

To become a Christian was to join a group with a different attitude to society and government from that of others. In a world which had many different religions, membership of this group was probably not too dangerous as long as Christians were not forced into the limelight. Nevertheless, a flashpoint was never far away, particularly in relationships with Judaism and Rome.

Jesus had been a Jew, and many of his followers were Jews. But while they borrowed much from Judaism, Christians were reacting against it, too: the result was a love-hate relationship. On the one hand, Christians claimed to be the true Israel; on the other, they made light of the distinctive features of the chosen people – the law, circumcision, the temple, the sabbath.

Rome was the world power, and was tolerant provided that religion did not interfere with public order; it had even exempted the Jews from taking part in official religion. But Jesus had been crucified on at least a semi-political charge, and his followers took to meeting together and adopting what were regarded as anti-social attitudes. A word of complaint to the local governor from an offended neighbour, and even the most benevolent regime would have to take action.

(a) *Jewish persecution.* During the first century, relations between Jews and Christians seem to have got steadily worse. One reason will undoubtedly have been the great pressure under which Judaism suffered as a result of the first Jewish war and the fall of Jerusalem. Christians, as hybrid Jews, cannot have been looked on with much favour in that difficult period.

Before AD 70, as far as we can tell from the evidence, which is largely that of silence, the Jews showed remarkable restraint. Acts pictures them stirring up trouble for Paul wherever he goes, but it will be the active missionary, like Paul, who will have been most open to danger. In any case, we do not know how much Luke's mention of constant Jewish trouble-making is one of the stereotypes he uses to further his own purposes. At least, Paul escaped with his life. Only three martyrdoms are recorded at Jewish hands for this period: Stephen, James, the son of Zebedee, and James, the brother of Jesus. There would have had to be particular reasons for extreme measures.

By the end of the first century, on the other hand, there are signs of a clear break between church and synagogue. The remarks in the Fourth Gospel about 'putting out of the synagogue' (John 9.22; 12.42; 16.2) are puzzling in the light of other contemporary evidence, but it was certainly at this period that the *Birkat ham-minim*, the 'Heretic Benediction', was added to the other petitions of the Jewish Eighteen Benedictions. It read (in part):

May the Nazarenes (Christians) and the *minim* (heretics) perish as in a moment and be blotted out from the book of life.

The Gospel of Matthew, with its particularly harsh sayings against Judaism, seems to have been hammered out in this kind of situation.

(b) Roman persecution. Not only Jewish – Christian but also Roman – Christian relationships were affected by the position of Jews in the Roman Empire. This was inevitable, because of the close connection between the two and the Christian attempt to win the same favoured position as Judaism. It is interesting to note that the charge made against Christians by Tacitus, among others, is exactly that levelled by the populace against Jews: they are guilty of *odium generis humani*, hatred of the human race. They are anti-social, unpatriotic. And, of course, because of their attitude towards the state religion and their lack of outward ceremonial, Christians were soon regarded as 'atheists'.

To begin with, Christians did not even have a special name to distinguish them. For Paul, the phrase 'in Christ' does duty instead. The word 'Christian' appears only three times in the New Testament: in Acts 11.26 we are told that it was first used in Antioch. 'Christian' is a Latin form, not a Greek one, and a plausible suggestion is that it arose almost as a joke. Nero had a following of youths, so to speak a permanent fan club, who were known as the *Augustiniani*, followers of Augustus. He visited Antioch with this group in AD 60, and, Antioch being a sophisticated place, it may just have been that the followers of Christ were dubbed *Christiani*, to mock both them and Nero's claque. Certainly, to begin with the word is used far more by outsiders than by Christians themselves.

Be this as it may, the first Roman persecution of which we have any reliable details was launched by Nero after a fire had destroyed two entire quarters of Rome. Nero himself was thought to be responsible for the fire as a savage piece of slum clearance, but, as Tacitus records:

Nero fastened the guilt and inflicted the most exquisite tortures on a class hated for their abominations, called Christians by the populace. Christus, from whom the name had its origin, suffered the extreme penalty during the reign of Tiberius at the hands of one of our procurators, Pontius Pilate, and a deadly superstition, thus checked for the moment, again broke out, not only in Judaea, the first source of the evil, but also in the City.

The savagery of Nero's measures, also reported by Tacitus, is well known.

This may not be the first time that Christians were in trouble in Rome. In his life of Claudius, the historian Suetonius writes:

He expelled the Jews from Rome for continuously rioting, *impulsore Chresto*.

The last two words are to be translated 'at the instigation of Chrestus'. Is this a reference to Christians? It is impossible to be sure. 'Chrestus' is certainly a frequent spelling of Christ in the West, but it is also a common Greek personal name.

If Tacitus' account is fuller, there is still much that is obscure. In particular, it is hard to discover what subsequent consequences Nero's persecution had. It does not seem to have given rise to any general proscription of Christians (at any rate, we know nothing of such a move); apparently it was a temporary police measure carried out personally by Nero. Unfortunately, however, it did bring the church into prominence in an unwelcome way and put it on the wrong side in any troubles that might arise later.

There is little to illuminate more general Roman – Christian relations in the first century. Acts and the Pauline tradition are concerned to be on as good terms as possible with Rome; I Peter and Revelation show signs of persecution. Revelation, especially, is full of a bitter hatred.

Revelation is thought to have been written in the reign of Domitian and to bear witness to persecution then. But although the author is exiled on Patmos, he has not suffered a particularly harsh penalty. There is nothing to support the common view that Patmos was a penal colony; John's punishment was probably *relegatio in insulam*, a form of banishment which did not even involve the loss of property or rights. His one reference to past martyrdom, the mention of Antipas (2.13), gives no indication of how Antipas met his end. Recent persecution seems to have been limited and local; John's fears are for the future.

Other available evidence hardly adds up to the fourth-century picture of Domitian as the second great persecutor of the church. Admittedly, Domitian was despotic and megalomaniac, but his only specific action which may have been anti-Christian was his arrest of a prominent Roman, Flavius Clemens, his wife Flavia Domitilla, and Acilius Glabrio, consul for 95. The charge was 'atheism', 'in that they had slipped into Jewish customs'. The men were executed and Flavia Domitilla exiled. The charge may indicate Christianity, and Flavia Domitilla was regarded as a Christian in the fourth century, but early accounts do not actually use the word.

The last detailed piece of evidence from the New Testament period shows just how fluid and uncertain the situation was even in the early second century. Pliny's letter to Trajan (see above, p. 345) was written because Pliny was uncertain how to deal with Christians:

In investigations of Christians I have never taken part; hence I do not know what is the crime usually punished or investigated, or what allowances are made . . . whether pardon is given to those who repent or whether a man who has once been a Christian gains nothing by having ceased to be such; whether punishment attaches to the mere name apart from secret crimes, or to the secret crimes connected with the name.

He goes on to describe his method of questioning and comments how, once it became known that Christians were being prosecuted, the charge became commoner. He proudly notes that his firm action has increased attendance in the 'almost deserted temples'.

Trajan approves Pliny's approach and replies:

Nothing can be laid down as a general ruling involving something like a set form of procedure. They are not to be sought out; but if they are accused and convicted, they must be punished – yet on this condition, that who so denies himself to be a Christian, and makes the fact plain by his action, that is, by worshipping our gods, shall obtain pardon on his repentance, however suspicious his past conduct may be.

He adds that too much notice is not to be taken of anonymous denunciations.

It emerges from all this that Christianity is for some reason an offence, but that the official policy is to 'let sleeping dogs lie'. If Christianity is brought to the notice of the authorities, they have to act, but they are not actively hostile.

In short, the main threat to Christianity in the New Testament period, before the later, classic persecutions, came from the possible hostility or malice of the people among whom they lived. Tertullian put the position in his usual witty way: 'If the Tiber rises too high or the Nile too low, the cry is: "The Christians to the lion".' Some relief was brought by Hadrian's rescript to Minucius Fundanus, proconsul of Asia in 124–125, which Justin attached to his first *Apology*. According to this, Christians had to be accused of definite crimes under due process of law, and if the charge failed, they had the right to cross-charge their accusers.

8. *The Appeal of Christianity*

Why did anyone think of becoming a Christian at this time? Much tends to be said about early Christianity without consideration of this vital question.

The Christian mission was far from being a saturation programme of mass evangelization, though vague memories of a few general statements in Acts sometimes produce such a misconception. Of course, at certain times and in certain places there was public preaching of a missionary kind, but it was probably less widespread than we imagine.

Usually, most Christian activity was semi-private, and this led to prejudice and misinformation. The Christian vocabulary gave rise to suspicions of incest, human sacrifice and other forms of immorality. The books written to contradict such ideas in the first two centuries or so probably had few readers outside the church: then as now, it seems unlikely that religious publishing reached many uninvolved laymen.

Causes for further inquiry might be the sight of (or news of) a martyrdom, curiosity, friendship. Above all, the care taken by Christians of the needy was a strong point. Tertullian's 'See how these Christians love one another!' is not ironical. On proof of his faith, any Christian was guaranteed up to three nights' hospitality with no questions asked; there was, too, an elaborate system of care for the poor. Again, with its claims of equality, Christianity obviously had an appeal to women, even if the full consequences (as with slavery) were not drawn for centuries.

Above all, Christianity answered the vague, helpless, speculative interest, so widespread in the first century, that had been fostered by the shallow talk of philosophers: the desire to feel at home in the world, resentment of Fate, the need for security. It was probably in these terms, rather than in presenting the character of the human figure of Jesus, that it made its mark, for outside the Gospels (and only to a limited degree even in them), little attention is paid to the personal traits of Jesus of Nazareth, except to affirm that he *was* human. In a fine study of conversion, A. D. Nock gives an attractive summary of the appeal of Christianity:

The success of Christianity is the success of an institution which united the sacramentalism and the philosophy of the time. It satisfied the inquiring turn of mind, the desire for escape from fate, the desire for security in the hereafter; like Stoicism, it gave a way of life and made man at home in the universe,

but unlike Stoicism it did this for the ignorant as well as for the lettered. It satisfied also social needs and it secured men against loneliness. Its way was not easy; it made uncompromising demands on those who would enter and would continue to live in the brotherhood, but to those who did not fail it offered an equally uncompromisng assurance.

Literature from the Growing Church

1. *The Pastoral Letters*

This is the name given to two letters to Timothy and one to Titus written in the name of Paul. Modern scholars, however, agree almost unanamously that Paul is not their author. Reasons are: the style and vocabulary of the letters differs widely from the authentic letters of Paul; it is very difficult to fit them into what we know of Paul's life; in several ways they indicate a different situation, later than that of Paul's day. The letters may possibly have genuine fragments of Paul's work in them, but even if they do, the fact has little bearing on their general content.

The three letters belong in a group, though their subject-matter differs slightly: *I Timothy* and *Titus* have a good deal about the ordering of the church; in *II Timothy* false teaching is vigorously attacked. They are not a very exciting part of the New Testament; it is often claimed that they are hortatory, monotonous and unmemorable. There is no argument, and the thought is all too often kept within the bounds of a paragraph. One scholar has remarked that they seem to be the work of someone with no real thoughts of his own. But this should not blind us to their positive significance.

The Pastorals come from a church which has to cope with the problems of living an everyday life in the world; they present a Christianity for the ordinary man when the first excitement has worn off. Part of the trouble is that there are far too many misleading excitements about (II Tim.2.14 ff., 23; 3.6). Some form of early gnosticism (see above, pp. 343 f.) lies in the background. Against this, the characteristic phrases of the Pastorals stress 'the faith' (I Tim.4.6), 'sound words' (I Tim.6.3), 'the truth' (II Tim.1.14), though this faith is presupposed rather than outlined. The practical virtues enjoined are those widely approved in the Hellenistic world: 'godliness with contentment' (I Tim.6.6); 'self-discipline' (Titus 2.6); 'good conscience'(I Tim.1.18). A more formal ministry is developing in the church (see above). All this suggests a date right at the beginning of the second century.

2. *Hebrews*

Unlike the Pastorals, the Letter to the Hebrews was not thought to be Pauline even in the early church; its place in the New Testament was disputed up to the fifth century. Pauline authorship is, in fact, impossible; style, language and argument are quite different.

Not only is Hebrews not by Paul; it is doubtful whether we should really call it a letter. Comparison with the letters of Paul shows that it lacks the characteristic opening greetings; the final ch. 13, which contains closing greetings, may not be part of the original. It is better understood as an unusually long sermon, with a coherent argument making a series of theological points followed by related exhortations.

This argument is: God has spoken through a Son, in a superior revelation to that to the prophets (chs. 1; 2). The Son is Jesus, who is superior to Moses and his own namesake Joshua (3.1–4.13: Jesus is Greek for Joshua, hence AV). Jesus is the great high priest who has passed through the heavens, but at the same time he is completely human (4.14–7.28). He is no shadow, but true, and offered his own blood; so Christians may have boldness to enter the holy place (chs. 8–10). The work concludes with a long account of the power of faith (ch. 11), its consequences and implications (chs. 12; 13).

Hebrews sometimes looks Platonic, but is not directly so; the pattern of Jewish sacrificial worship is the strongest influence, and the work of Jesus is described in these terms. His career is presented more in the form of exaltation than of resurrection.

A subsidiary theme is that of the people to whom Hebrews is addressed, and may even account for its name. They are the wandering people of God, on pilgrimage through the world with no lasting rest or city, but seeking one that is to come.

Place and date of authorship are uncertain. Alexandria has often been suggested; as the allusions to the temple are literary, it cannot be placed definitely before AD 70.

3. *The Catholic Letters*

'Catholic' means 'intended for the whole church', but this later title for the group comprising I-III John, I and II Peter, James and Jude is hardly apt. It does not really fit at least I Peter and II and III John, which in their present form have specific destinations; nor are all the group properly letters.

The *Johannine letters* come from the same circle as the Fourth Gospel; some slight differences may mean that their author is not exactly the same, but his approach is remarkably similar. Thus the section on the Fourth Gospel should be read in close conjunction with this paragraph (see Part IV, Section 11, pp. 326 ff.).

I John points to a defection from the community: false prophets have gone out, denying that Jesus was the Christ and that he had come in the flesh (2.19). They say they have no sin (1.8) and claim to know God. Here, again, is a form of gnosticism. In countering these opponents John comes near to gnosticism himself. But the dominant feature of his letter is his stress on the claim of love within the community, in imitation of the act of God in Jesus Christ.

II and III John are slighter. Whether they are addressed to one community is unclear, but the situation is much the same. Again there is a form of gnosticism, coupled in III John with a power struggle.

If the Johannine letters belong together, the *Petrine* ones do not. They come from very different periods: II Peter is probably the latest book in the New Testament and has affinities, rather, with Jude.

It is doubtful whether *I Peter* was written by the apostle Peter. Its form alone raises suspicion. At present it is a letter, but it is obviously made of other elements. There is a clear break at 4.11. Before this the letter was written in general terms; because of the many references to baptism, this part has been thought to consist of an exhortation or exhortations connected with baptism: to take it as an actual liturgy, as some scholars do, seems to be going too far. 4.12–5.11 is much more specific, and seems to be directed to Christians undergoing persecution. The thought often seems post-Pauline, and the instruction on the nature of Christian life and the use of the word 'Christian' indicates a period nearer to that of the Pastorals.

II Peter styles itself a second letter of Peter and therefore presumably knows of I Peter; but the two have nothing in common. Chapter 2 is a revised edition of the brief Letter of Jude, *Jude* is a brief exhortation contending for 'the faith once for all delivered to the saints' (v.3) against false teachers who 'defile the flesh' (v. 8). It treats the apocryphal *I Enoch* (vv. 14 f.) and the *Assumption of Moses* (v. 9) as Scripture. These references are changed by II Peter, which has strict views and is very concerned about the interpretation of Scripture (1.20; 3.14; cf. II Tim.3.16 – an important anti-gnostic point). II Peter 1 is a farewell discourse by 'Peter' and ch. 3 is an explanation of the delay in the Second Coming. There are other features here which recall the Pastorals, especially the concentration on one authoritative figure.

James is more a homily or series of homilies, though it has the form of a letter. Its date and background are much disputed. At first sight it is so Jewish as to appear hardly Christian. But it can be seen to presuppose Paul's theology, misunderstood (2.14–26). Closer study shows other remarks more characteristic of Christianity than Judaism (1.18; 1.21; 1.25; 5.8, 12). The argumentative presentation of its thought recalls the Hellenistic form known as the diatribe. All this makes it doubtful whether the author was the brother of the Lord.

4. *Revelation*

This book, to many the most enigmatic in the New Testament, was written by a certain John on Patmos, possibly during the time of Domitian (see above on 'Persecutions', p. 348). We know no more about its authorship. It consists of a brief preface (ch. 1), letters to seven churches (chs. 2; 3), the revelation or 'apocalypse' proper (4.1–22.5) and an epilogue (22.6–20). It is thus Christian apocalyptic literature.

Despite many resemblances to Jewish apocalyptic, it has distinct characteristics of its own. It is not attributed to a figure of the distant past (Enoch, Daniel, Ezra), nor does it survey past ages in the guise of prediction. It is prophetic in the best sense of the word and Jewish apocalyptic is transfigured by the influence of Christianity.

Imminent persecution by Rome is expected; Revelation is written to strengthen and advise those who face it. The message is given symbolically. Pages are filled with symbols and numbers: swords, eyes, trumpets, horns, seals, crowns, white robes; 7, 12, 1260 days, 42 months, 666: the number of the beast. As a result it has been searched down the centuries for hidden knowledge of the future. But there are no secrets of this kind in Revelation. It is poetry, a continuous meditation on the Old Testament, with reading and vision inextricably combined. It may seem strange, savage and barbarous to us, but understood in its own terms, as a picture of the situation of the Christian church in a hostile world in which the power of Christ was still at work, it has as much to tell us about what it was like to be a first-century Christian as many other books of the New Testament.

13

Has the Bible Authority?

Robert C. Walton

Should the Bible be a Source Book in the Classroom?

Why should the Bible be a source book in a twentieth-century classroom? Certainly teachers need information and also inspiration unless the material for school assembly and religious education is to be spun like a spider's thread out of themselves, and few of us would claim that our own unaided ideas and our limited knowledge are a sufficient basis for teaching. Might there not be, however, better alternatives to a source book of the *Bible*?

It has been suggested, for example, that the source of contemporary moral and religious education should be found in the thoughts of philosophers and wise men, of scientists, historians and poets, of artists and visionaries from many cultures and many periods of history; and in the example of men and women who in their lives have displayed nobility, courage and compassion. There is value in this suggestion. It is no part of the argument of this article that the Old and New Testaments along with selections from church history should be the sole basis of religious education. Such a source book, however, – from Plato to Schweitzer – would be highly intellectual in content, valuable in a good sixth form but not much help to the 'Newsom child' who is 'half our future'. The Bible may be a difficult collection of literature but much of its material is not abstract. In part its value lies in the fact that it reflects so fully the problems and preoccupations of quite ordinary human beings and relates these problems to the purposes of God.

Another suggestion is that schools need a symposium drawn from the sacred scriptures of the major religions of the world: Judaism, Buddhism, Hinduism, Christianity and Islam. In an increasingly multi-racial society it is important that British children should be aware that many of their neighbours and class-mates inherit a different religious tradition and worship in forms different from those of Christianity. It is equally important that immigrant children should feel that their own religion is respected and their sacred books are used at their school. But one stubborn fact has to be faced. The Bible is an integral part of that Western culture which we have all unconsciously absorbed. In contrast, the cultures and thought-forms, which alone would enable us to enter imaginatively into the religion of a Buddhist or a Muslim, are strange to us. Without long years of study and sojourns in a Buddhist or Islamic country we must inevitably look at that religion from the outside. It will not become part of us. It will remain a school subject: it will not be a living experience.

None of this, however, answers the question of why the Bible should be used as a source book in school. An important reason, though by no means the only one, lies in the historical facts. Since the time when barbarian tribes, which from the late fourth century AD threatened to overrun western Europe, were stopped and driven back, and since the time when the conquests of Islam were halted at Poitiers at the end of the eighth century, our civilization has been shaped by Christianity and by the Christians' sacred book. Our political institutions, our social morality and our culture alike have been inspired by the teachings of the Bible. The great arguments of the Middle Ages about the source of authority in the state, no less than nineteenth-century social action in Britain, drew their inspiration from Christian thought and often from the words of Scripture itself. We cannot, apart from the Bible, understand our past or our present condition: moreover, we cannot understand ourselves. The Bible is 'the rock from which we were hewn and the quarry from which we were dug'. One needs overwhelmingly strong reasons for ignoring one's heritage.

The 'Canon' of Scripture

Why should a source book used in religious education consist of the thirty-nine books of the Old Testament and the twenty-seven in the New Testament? Parts of the Bible obviously have no more than an antiquarian interest, and it would be absurd to use them in the teaching of children. No Agreed Syllabus proposes a study of the book of Leviticus in the Old Testament or of the Epistle of Jude in the New Testament.

The 'canon' of Scripture means the list of books which Judaism and later Christianity accepted as authoritative. The 'canonical Scriptures' are authorized books. The reasons why these thirty-nine and twenty-seven books form the canon lie in the historical facts. For the Old Testament the important historical events are the exile and the return from Babylon in the sixth and fifth centuries BC and the fall of Jerusalem to the Romans in AD 70. These crises in Jewish history, when the ordered pattern of the nation's life broke in pieces, produced the need for a new authority (see Part III, Section 14, pp. 182 ff.), which was found in the canon of its Scriptures. The process was a gradual one. Ezra seems to have brought to Palestine from Babylon the Law of Moses (Genesis to Deuteronomy), though it was many years before its absolute authority was fully recognized. The 'prophetic' canon (Joshua to II Kings and the written versions of the prophetic utterances) was also fixed by about 200 BC. The third division of the Old Testament – the 'Writings' – was not integrated into the canon until about AD 100. The capture of Jerusalem by the Romans some thirty years earlier had produced a new crisis for Judaism. There was now no temple to be the focus of the nation's life. Only the sacred Scriptures remained as a cohesive force. The canon was revised; the three divisions of Law, Prophets and Writings were established. The Jews became the people of a Book.

The formation of the New Testament canon was also the result of the processes of history. The first centuries of the Christian era witnessed an astonishing growth of Christian communities in many parts of the ancient world. In cities, towns and villages men and women entered the church, persuaded by the preaching of the Christian message, attracted by the life of the Christian community. They were instructed in the beliefs of the church and baptized into its faith. The question inevitably arose: what was the basis for this new community and for its life and teaching? The answer, as for the Jews, was an authorized list of books. From about AD 200 in important Christian centres there was a canonical New Testament, though it was not necessarily the same in each place. The Epistle to the Hebrews was not, at first, admitted to the canon of the western churches, and the eastern churches had reservations about the 'catholic' epistles – James, Peter, John and Jude. From the sixth century onwards, however, both east and west accepted as canonical the twenty-seven books of the New Testament.

There was, however, another feature of the Christian canon. 'Christianity', it has been said, 'is unique among the great religions in being born with a Bible in its cradle'. That Bible was the Old Testament. Jesus had been trained in its teaching from boyhood: so had the twelve apostles and Paul and nearly all the leaders of the early church. Inevitably it took its place alongside the canon of the New Testament. The Christians, like the Jews, became the people of a Book.

The Nature of Biblical Authority

Whether or not the Bible has authority in the lives of men and women today depends in large measure upon the way we use it and upon the way it is taught in school.

The first axiom is that we should accept the Bible for what it is; a selection of the literature of the people of Israel over a thousand years of their history, and a selection of the literature of the Christian church in the first hundred years of its existence (see Part I, Section 1, pp. 3 f.). A great many stumbling-blocks disappear as soon as we obey this rule. For example, the historical books of the Old Testament record some blood-thirsty deeds by Israel's kings.

Saul has slain his thousands
    And David his ten thousands (I Sam. 18.7).

An exaggeration, no doubt, for these tribal battles were small-scale skirmishes compared with twentieth-century wars, but none the less it was blood-thirsty killing. Read as history they present no problem. To slaughter one's enemies in battle was an accepted practice of warfare in the tenth century BC as it is in the twentieth century AD. The trouble only arises if we try to extract moral lessons or theological arguments out of such incidents. You cannot judge the violence of Saul and David, any more than you can judge Charlemagne's occasional lapses into ferocity, by the moral sensitivity of a modern pacifist.

A second axiom is that we use the Bible wrongly when we read out of it whatever we will. A famous example of this error can be found in a series of sermons based on the Song of Solomon composed by Bernard who was Abbot of the monastery of Clairvaux from 1115 until his death in 1153. The Song of Solomon consists of a number of erotic love poems of no spiritual significance. They have their place in Israel's national literature because (like many poems in the English language) they reflect a widespread human passion. Bernard, however, in his sermons read out of them an extravagant panegyric on the love of Christ for men.

> O love, headlong, vehement, burning, impetuous, that can think of nothing beyond thyself, detesting all else, despising all else, satisfied with thyself . . . . Everything which the soul-bride utters resounds of thee and nothing else; so hast thou possessed her heart and tongue.

We are not likely to emulate the eloquence of St Bernard, but the temptation to make a passage of the Bible mean what we want it to mean is an insidious one for teachers and parsons alike.

A third axiom which follows from the first two is that we must start with the biblical writer himself, with what he actually wrote, and study his words until we understand what they meant to him, and what they meant to his contemporaries. The phrase 'the kingdom of God' so frequently used by Jesus is a case in point (see Part IV, Section 8, pp. 290 f.). It is, however, legitimate to go further than this. Where a biblical writer enunciates a moral argument or a religious truth of permanent significance (using, of course, the situations and the thought-forms of his own time) we may, having first grasped what the statement meant to him, explore what he says in terms of our own situation. For instance, Paul in I Cor.8 discusses a moral problem which seriously troubled the Christians at Corinth. The meat sold in the markets at Corinth, or provided at a banquet or a friend's dinner party had, as a general rule, first been consecrated to pagan gods. Could a Christian eat such meat with a good conscience? Paul's opinion was that a Christian who was strong in the faith would suffer no harm. 'A false god,' he wrote, 'has no existence in the real world' (I Cor.8.4 NEB). But an immature Christian, 'a weak character' (v.10) seeing other Christians eating 'consecrated' meat, might fall a victim in many moral temptations. 'Therefore, if food be the downfall of my brother, I will never eat meat any more' (v.13). Today Christians in the west do not have to face this particular issue, but the question of our moral responsibility for the welfare of others, and particularly for the protection of the 'weak' members of our society, is a living issue as it was in ancient Corinth. We may rightly use Paul's teaching to throw light upon our contemporary situation.

The fourth and last axiom is that our task as teachers is finished when, over the years, we have introduced boys and girls to the Bible. This 'introduction' involves many things. It includes helping our pupils to grasp the true nature of the biblical literature, weaning them away from prejudice and false notions, encouraging them to explore the Bible for themselves, and dealing patiently not only with their many problems and difficulties, but also with their periods of scepticism. The teacher is in the position of one who introduces a friend to another. He will describe the friend, and may with modesty speak of the relationship between them both which has been built up. But the friend is self-authenticating. The friend alone, and no other, can call forth the response of friendship. So, too, the Bible is self-authenticating. Its authority cannot be imposed, its significance cannot be demonstrated by using time-honoured phrases like 'Holy Scripture' or 'the word of God'. It may, like a friendship, be rejected. Yet it has been the experience of millions in the past and today that the Bible has the power to transmit to men the mystery and majesty, the power and loving-kindness of God: and also the mystery, and majesty, the power and loving-kindness of Jesus. It makes its own claims upon men's minds and imaginations and consciences, but this self-authentification, like that of a wise and patient friend, is often built up slowly; it may take years, decades or perhaps a whole lifetime.

FOR FURTHER READING

Paperback edition available

A. General

*Baker, T. G. A., *What is the New Testament?*, London: SCM Press, 1969.

Davies, W. D., *Invitation to the New Testament*, London: Darton, Longman & Todd, 1967.

*Filson, F. V., *A New Testament History*, London: SCM Press, 1965.

*Grant, R. M., *A Historical Introduction to the New Testament*, London: Collins, 1963.

Hooker, M. D., and Hickling, C. J. A., *What about the New Testament?*, London: SCM Press, 1975.

*Hoskyns, Sir E., and Davey, F. N., *The Riddle of the New Testament*, Faber, 1931.

*Hunter, A. M., *Introducing the New Testament*, London: SCM Press, 1957.

*Jones, C. M., *New Testament Illustrations*, London: Cambridge University Press, 1966.

*Moule, C. F. D., *The Birth of the New Testament*, 2nd rev. ed., London: A. & C. Black, 1966.

*Neill, S., *The Interpretation of the New Testament 1861–1961*, London: Oxford University Press, 1964.

*Perrin, N., *Introduction to the New Testament*, New York: Harcourt, Brace, 1974.

Reicke, Bo, *The New Testament World*, London: A. & C. Black, 1955.

The *Torch Bible Commentaries (London: SCM Press, various dates and authors) and *Cambridge Bible Commentaries on the New English Bible (Cambridge: Cambridge University Press, various dates and authors) provide an introduction and an explanation of the text of most of the books of the New Testament.

B. Background Material

*Barrett, C. K., ed., *The New Testament Background: Selected Documents*, London: SPCK, 1957.

*Jeremias, J., *Jerusalem in the Time of Jesus*, London: SCM Press, 1969.

*Josephus, J., *The Jewish War*, trans. G. A. Williamson, London: Penguin Books, 1959.

Perowne, Stewart, *The Later Herods: the Political Background to the New Testament*, London: Hodder & Stoughton, 1958.

Perowne, Stewart, *The Life and Times of Herod the Great*, London: Hodder & Stoughton, 1956.

Sandmel, Samuel, *The First Century in Judaism and Christianity*, New York: Oxford University Press, 1969.

*Smith, George Adam, *The Historical Geography of the Holy Land*, London: Fontana Books, 1966.

*Vermes, Geza, *The Dead Sea Scrolls in English*, London: Penguin Books, 1962.

Williamson, G. A., *The World of Josephus*, London: Secker & Warburg, 1964.

C. The Gospels

*Audrey, Sister, *Jesus Christ in the Synoptic Gospels*, London: SCM Press, 1972.

*Barclay, W., *The Gospels and Acts*, 2 vols., London: SCM Press, 1976.

*Barrett, C. K., *Jesus and the Gospel Tradition*, London: SPCK, 1967.

Beare, F. W., *The Earliest Records of Jesus*, Oxford: Basil Blackwell, 1962.

*Bornkamm, G., *Jesus of Nazareth*, London: Hodder & Stoughton, 1960.

*Caird, G. B., *Saint Luke* (Pelican Gospel Commentaries), London: Penguin Books, 1963.

*Dale, Alan T., *New World*, vols, 1–3, London: Oxford University Press, 1966 (for class use).

*Davies, W. D., *The Sermon on the Mount*, London: Cambridge University Press, 1966.

*Dodd, C. H., *The Founder of Christianity*, London: Fontana, 1973.

*Dodd, C. H., *The Interpretation of the Fourth Gospel*, Cambridge: Cambridge University Press, 1953.

*Evans, C. F., *The Beginning of the Gospel*, London: SPCK, 1968.

*Fenton, J. C., *Saint Matthew* (Pelican Gospel Commentaries), London: Penguin Books, 1963.

*Fenton, J. C., *What was Jesus' Message?*, London: SPCK, 1971.

*Jeremias, J., *New Testament Theology Vol. 1: The Proclamation of Jesus*, London: SCM Press, 1971.

*Manson, T. W., *The Sayings of Jesus*, London: SCM Press, 1949.

*Marsh, John, *Saint John* (Pelican Gospel Commentaries), London: Penguin Books, 1967.

*Nineham, D. E., *Saint Mark* (Pelican Gospel Commentaries), London: Penguin Books, 1967.

Reumann, John, *Jesus in the Church's Gospels*, London: SPCK, 1970.

Trocmé, E., *Jesus and his Contemporaries*, London: SCM Press, 1973.

*Vermes, G., *Jesus the Jew*, London: Fontana Books, 1976.

The Parables

*Dodd, C. H., *The Parables of the Kingdom*, London: Fontana Books, 1961.

*Hunter, A. M., *Interpreting the Parables*, London: SCM Press, 1960.

*Jeremias, J., *The Parables of Jesus*, 3rd ed., London: SCM Press, 1972.

Miracles

Fuller, R. H., *Interpreting the Miracles*, London: SCM Press, 1963.

Keller, Ernst and Marie-Luise, *Miracles in Dispute: a Continuing Debate*, London: SCM Press, 1969.

Moule, C. F. D., *Miracles*, Oxford: Mowbrays, 1965.

*Richardson, Alan, *The Miracle Stories of the Gospels*, London: SCM Press, 1960.

D. *The Early Church*

Cadbury, H. J., *The Book of Acts in History*, London: A. & C. Black, 1955.

*Conzelmann, H., *A History of Primitive Christianity*, London: Darton, Longman & Todd, 1973.

*Dale, Alan T., *New World*, vol. 4, London: Oxford University Press, 1966 (for class use).

*Downing, F. G., *The Church and Jesus*, London: SCM Press, 1968.

Haenchen, E., *The Acts of the Apostles*, Oxford: Blackwell, 1971.

Paul

*Barrett, C. K., *The Epistle to the Romans*, London: A. & C. Black, 1957.

*Barrett, C. K., *The First Epistle to the Corinthians*, London: A. & C. Black, 1968.

*Barrett, C. K., *The Second Epistle of Paul to the Corinthians*, London: A. & C. Black, 1973.

Beare, F. W., *St. Paul and his Letters*, London: A. & C. Black, 1962.

*Bornkamm, G., *Paul*, London: Hodder & Stoughton, 1971.

*Dale, Alan T., *New World*, vol. 5, London: Oxford University Press, 1966 (for class use).

*Davies, W. D., *Paul and Rabbinic Judaism*, 2nd ed., London: SPCK, 1955.

Dibelius, Martin, *Paul*, London: Longmans, 1953.

*Dodd, C. H., *The Epistle of Paul to the Romans*, London: Fontana, 1959.

*Hunter, A. M., *Interpreting Paul's Gospel*, London: SCM Press, 1960.

*Knox, John, *Chapters in a Life of Paul*, London: A. & C. Black, 1954.

Nock, A. D., *St Paul*, London: Oxford University Press, 1946.

*Scott, C. A. Anderson, *Christianity according to St Paul*, Cambridge: Cambridge University Press, 1927.

PART FIVE

For Quick Reference

For Quick Reference

Compiled by Jean Holm

Agriculture

Farmers lived in cities and villages and went out to their fields (the 'country') by day. Sometimes, when the ripening crops needed to be guarded, they built booths in the fields and slept there.

An inadequate water supply and stony ground combined to make agriculture a difficult occupation.

Cereals

Mainly *wheat* and *barley*.

The land was ploughed after the 'former rains' in October, and the seed was sown by hand.

The beginning of the barley harvest was associated with the Passover festival, and the wheat harvest with Pentecost, in the months April–June.

Reaping was done by hand with a sickle. On the threshing floor (of rock or beaten earth) oxen tramped round and round, pulling a threshing-drag (a wooden board with pieces of stone or metal set in its underside) to separate the grains from the ears of corn.

Winnowing, tossing the grain in the air with a wide pronged fork ('fan'), was done when there was just enough breeze to separate the chaff from the grain.

Fruit

Olive: This was the most important fruit. It flourished on the almost barren hillsides.

Cultivation was a long slow process, involving grafting when the tree was three years old. (In Rom.11.17–24 Paul describes something which is 'contrary to nature', not the normal grafting process.)

Olives were eaten fresh or pickled in brine, and olive oil was used in the preparation of food, for lamps, for anointing (both ritual and cosmetic use), and as a medicinal ointment (see Luke 10.34).

Fig: The crop ripens in the summer but very small fruits appear in March with the new leaves. These early figs, however, do not ripen, and drop before the main crop develops.

Grape: The cultivation of the grape, like that of the olive, was a long process, requiring several years before a new vine bore fruit.

Vines were planted on terraced hillsides and trained over trees or supported by wooden poles.

During the harvest the vine-grower, and probably his family as well, would live in booths or watch-towers in the vineyard.

The harvest, in late summer, followed by the treading of the grapes, was a time of rejoicing, and was associated with the feast of Tabernacles, the festival of Ingathering.

Wine was made by putting the grapes into the upper of two troughs dug in the rock. The grapes were trodden by bare feet and the juice ran through a channel into the lower trough.

New wine could be drunk immediately, but it was usually allowed to ferment and stored in wine-skins (made from the skins of goats or oxen).

Other Crops

They included dates, pomegranates, melons, almonds and *vegetables* like lentils, beans, leeks, onions and cucumbers, and *herbs* like garlic, chicory, endive, radish, mustard, cummin, mint and anise.

The fig-mulberry (the 'sycamore' of Amos 7.14) was not a cultivated tree. It grew wild, producing a rather inferior kind of fruit, and requiring attention only for a short time in the year.

Craftsmen

By the post-exilic period craftsmen had organized themselves into guilds, and in cities and towns they were grouped according to their craft in certain streets or quarters.

Weavers

Weaving was one of the oldest crafts. It was normally done by the women, who wove goats' hair fabric on their wooden looms for cloaks and tents, and wool, linen and silk cloth for garments and hangings. When weaving was done by men it was a despised trade.

Dyers

Materials were dyed bright colours with vegetable dyes or murex – a shellfish which produced a rich purple colour.

Fullers

New cloth was 'pre-shrunk' and made watertight by soaking it in a bleaching mixture and matting the fibres. The bleaching agent was an alkaline substance, known as 'fullers' earth'.

Soiled clothes were cleaned by soaking in a similar bleaching mixture and treading out the dirt.

Tanners

The preparation of animal skins was considered to be an unclean occupation, and tanneries had to be outside cities.

Leather was used for such things as sandals, shields, helmets, 'bottles' – usually goatskin – for carrying wine or water, and scrolls (see Writing Materials, below, p. 368).

Potters

Pottery, like weaving, was one of the oldest crafts. The potter's wheel was probably known in Palestine (Canaan) from before Abraham's time.

The finished articles were hardened by being sun-dried or fired in a 'furnace'.

The potter made such essential articles as bowls, jugs, water pots, storage jars and lamps.

The Hebrew word used to describe the potter's moulding or forming of his clay is also used in Gen.2.7 to describe God's forming of man from the dust of the ground.

Metal Workers

Tools included hammer, anvil, tongs and bellows. The main metals were:

Gold: This was a plentiful metal in the Near East in the biblical period, and was widely used for decoration. It was also a medium of exchange (see Money, below, p. 363).

The candlesticks of Solomon's temple were of solid gold, and there was lavish use of gold in Herod's temple.

Silver: It was called 'white gold', was used less frequently, especially in buildings.

Goldsmiths and Silversmiths: Craftsmen beat gold and silver into thin sheets for brooches, necklaces, rings, etc., or they plated objects by dipping them into molten metal.

Figurines were also made in the Mediterranean world (see Acts 19.24), though not within Judaism because of the prohibition against 'graven images'.

Copper and the stronger alloy, *Bronze* (copper mixed with tin): Sometimes misleadingly translated 'brass' or 'steel' in English versions.

Used for making weapons, helmets, etc., or fastened to wooden shafts to strengthen weapons, tools and farming implements.

The two great pillars and many of the ornaments of Solomon's temple were made of bronze.

Smelting works, dating from Solomon's time, have been found at Ezion-geber on the Gulf of Aqabah.

Iron: Probably wrought iron, produced by a more primitive process than was later used for cast iron.

Used, like bronze, for weapons, tools and farming implements, and for strengthening the wooden war chariots ('chariots of iron').

The Iron Age followed the Bronze Age, but it was not until David defeated the Philistines in the tenth century BC that the Israelites were able to learn the closely guarded secret of the smelting process (see I Sam.13.19 f.).

Carpenters

Tools included adze, saw, hammer, wooden mallet, chisel, sandstone (for planing), measuring reed and plumbline.

Carpenters made and repaired almost anything wooden – city gates, doors and window frames, roof beams, ploughs, yoke for oxen, and furniture for the homes of the well-to-do. Under Roman rule carpenters would be expected to make crosses for crucifixions.

Stonemasons

Tools included stone hammer, chisel, plumb-line, measuring reed, square, and trowel (used when mortar was put in between the layers of stone).

There was an ample supply of soft limestone in Palestine (in contrast to the scarcity of wood). Stone was often hewn and dressed at the quarry and taken to the building site ready for use (see I Kings 6.7).

Public buildings and large houses were usually built of stone, but even mud-brick houses often had a stone foundation.

Before the exile most important building was done by foreign craftsmen, but by New Testament times stonemasonry had become a skilled and highly respected Israelite craft.

Dress

See Part IV, Section 2, pp. 216 f. and below, p. 369.

Education

See Part IV, Section 2, pp. 218 f.

Food

See Part IV, Section 2, pp. 217 f. and above, pp. 359 f.

Games

We have little information about the games played by Jewish boys and girls. We do, however, know something about the games played in other Mediterranean countries in the first century AD, and it is quite possible that these were also played in Palestine.

Children's Games

In Old Testament times we hear of boys and girls playing in the streets of Jerusalem (Zech. 8.5). They probably imitated adult activities and played at 'weddings' and 'funerals' as the children did in New Testament times (see Matt.11.16 f.).

It is also likely that children enjoyed riddles as much as their elders did (see Judg.14.12 f.).

Other games were hop-scotch, blind man's buff, hide and seek, bowling hoops and spinning tops.

Terracotta dolls and dolls' furniture have been found. Some of the dolls have jointed arms and legs and holes for strings, showing that they were used as puppets. It is unlikely though that Jewish children had dolls, as this would be considered to be breaking the second commandment (Ex.20.4).

Games of Skill

Pebbles game: Pebbles were thrown from a distance into a hole in the ground.

Ball games: The balls were either thrown and caught or struck with the hand. There is no mention of any bats or racquets, and there was certainly nothing like football or tennis or cricket.

Other games, played by adults as well as children, included draughts, solitaire, knuckle-bones and throwing dice.

Athletics

The Greeks were enthusiastic about physical education and athletics, and in New Testament times there were gymnasiums and sports stadiums in most cities in the Mediterranean countries. Some young Jewish men took part in the 'games', but this shocked devout Jews, partly because the athletes ran naked, and partly because the games were dedicated to one of the Greek gods, and to take part in the games was to associate oneself with the worship of the god (Ex.20.3).

Justice

Early in Israel's history the administration of justice became the responsibility of the elders of the community and, in spite of developments in the system, in New Testament times the elders still had a dominant role.

In the pre-exilic period the elders would sit at the gate of the town or village, and individuals would bring their problems or disputes to them.

Priests also gave judgments (*toroth*, plural of *torah*) at the local sanctuaries. It is impossible to distinguish clearly between the legal functions of priests and elders, and some tension may well have existed between them, but it is known that difficult cases could be referred to the priests by the elders, and the 'decision' given was regarded as expressing the divine will.

During the period of the monarchy the king was recognized as the supreme judge, and Solomon had a 'porch of judgment' built in his palace. However, a centralized system of justice must have presented many problems (see II Sam.15.1–6), and it is likely that local administration continued to be the rule rather than the exception.

A system of local courts had developed by the end of the fifth century BC. The courts in the larger towns had twenty-three members, and in the smaller towns seven.

In New Testament times the Roman authorities were content to leave the administration of civil and religious law in Jewish hands, retaining control over matters of sedition or treason.

The provincial courts dispensed justice locally, but the highest Jewish authority in the land was the *Sanhedrin* at Jerusalem (see also Part IV, Section 3, pp. 227 f.). In theory if not in practice its decisions were binding on Jews everywhere, and difficult legal cases would be referred to it by the provincial courts.

The Sanhedrin had seventy-one members, and included the reigning high priest, past high priests who were still living, the chief priests (members of the priestly aristocracy who held important offices in the temple at Jerusalem), elders (leading members of the lay aristocracy), and scribes (members of the powerful professional class concerned with the interpretation of the law).

The chief priests of the temple (including the high priest) formed a small permanent 'court of priests' to deal with matters affecting the priests (e.g., marriage regulations) and the cultus.

The *Roman legal system* was highly organized, and ordinary citizens had right of access to the local courts (see Acts 18.12). In addition, Roman citizens had the right of appeal to the Emperor.

Witnesses

In Jewish law the evidence of two witnesses was required. If it was not possible to produce witnesses, those involved in the case had to go to the sanctuary and give their testimony under oath.

When the death sentence was passed it was the witnesses who had to begin to carry it out.

If a witness gave false testimony he had to undergo the same punishment that would have been meted out to the accused man.

Punishments

Fines were never imposed, but in cases such as theft or damage to property recompense had to be made; in the case of theft it might involve repaying a sum equal to four times the value of the goods stolen.

Imprisonment is not known until the fifth century BC, but men could be put in the stocks. Under the Romans there were public gaols, in which prisoners were chained, but an alternative method involved a convicted man being chained to a soldier but otherwise having freedom of movement.

Branding on the forehead could be part of the punishment of a thief or a runaway slave. A thief could be sold into slavery.

Scourging was common. The Jews used rods or leather thongs, and limited the number of strokes to thirty-nine. The Romans used thongs tipped with bone or metal.

Excommunication was practised by the Jews, for offences like the failure to observe the feast of the Passover.

Hard labour: The Romans sentenced prisoners to period of hard labour in the mines or in labour camps.

Death penalty was meted out for a large number of crimes. In Jewish law these included murder, blasphemy, idolatry, and such offences against the sanctity of family life as adultery, sodomy and incest. The death penalty was carried out by stoning, outside the city walls, or in some cases by burning.

In the Roman empire the death penalty was carried out by execution by the sword for Roman citizens, but for slaves, foreigners and criminals of the lowest classes it was by crucifixion.

Languages

See below pp. 368 f.

Marriage

Marriage was enjoined upon every Israelite and was one of the 613 precepts of the Jewish law.

Polygamy

It was practised to a limited extent in New Testament times as well as in the earlier period, though it tended to be disapproved of, and the high priest was forbidden to marry more than one wife.

In the patriarchal period, in northern Meso-potamia, it was customary for a wife who was barren or who had ceased bearing children to give her hand-maid to her husband in order to produce more children, as Sarah, Rachel and Leah are recorded as doing (see Gen.16.1–4; 30.1–4, 9).

Betrothal

Usually took place about a year before mar-riage, but it was legally binding. The marriage contract was made at this time. A girl was often betrothed when she was twelve years old.

Dowry

A gift to the bride from her father, usually augmented by gifts from the bridegroom. The husband had the right to use the dowry, but in the case of a divorce he had to give it, or its equivalent value, to his wife.

The dowry was separate from the *marriage payment* which the bridegroom paid to the bride's father.

Levirate Marriage

If a man died without having had a son, his brother was expected to marry the widow, and their first-born son became the dead man's heir (see Deut.25.5–10; Mark 12.18–23).

Restrictions

It was normal for the Hebrews to marry relatives (though there were some prohibitions, including incestuous marriages). Marriages with foreigners, however, were frowned upon, even in early times, and by the end of the fifth century BC they were forbidden.

By New Testament times the racial purity of the Jewish community had become so important that the whole population was classified into groups, and only specified groups were allowed to intermarry. The greatest restrictions applied to the priestly families.

Divorce

There were many grounds on which a man could divorce his wife. She was regarded as his property and therefore disposable, but he had to make a formal charge ('write her a bill of divorcement'), and by New Testament times he had to give her her dowry, the sum of money agreed when the marriage contract was made. A woman had no right to divorce her husband.

Money

Old Testament Times

The earliest known use of coins in Israel is in the fifth to fourth centuries BC. Before this precious metals, measured by weight, were used for money. The names of units of weight, therefore, came to represent money values, though these were eventually expressed almost entirely in terms of shekels (and half-shekels and quarter-shekels) and talents.

One gold shekel equalled ten silver shekels; but unless otherwise specified, 'shekel' refers to the silver shekel.

3,000 shekels = 1 talent

New Testament Times

Gold coins: Not specifically referred to in the New Testament.

Silver coins, Denarius ('penny' or 'piece of silver'): A Roman coin. It is impossible to give money equivalents, but at a very rough approximation a denarius was a day's wages for an agricultural labourer (a low paid job), and 1/12 of a denarius would provide bread for one person for a day.

4 denarii	=	1 shekel
100 denarii	=	1 mina ('pound')
6000 denarii	=	1 talent

Copper coins:
24 assaria (plural of assarion, 'farthing')
= 1 denarius
120 lepta (plural of lepton, 'mite')
= 1 denarius

The annual temple tax payable by every Israelite was a half-shekel.

Names – The Land and the People

The Land

Canaan: The early name of that part of the Fertile Crescent which was later known as Palestine and Syria.

Palestine: Derived from the word 'Philistine'. The Philistines, 'sea peoples' probably from Crete, invaded and over-ran Canaan during the twelfth century BC and gave their name to the country. During David's time they were con-fined to the southern coastal strip, known thereafter as *Philistia*.

Israel: In the eleventh century BC, the name of the united kingdom under Saul, David and Solomon. After the division of the kingdom at Solomon's death, the northern kingdom was called *Israel*.

Judah: The southern kingdom, so called because it consisted mainly of the tribe of Judah.

Judaea: The Graeco-Roman form of Judah, The name was used mainly for the region round Jerusalem, and probably dates from the fourth century BC.

Samaria: The region lying between Judaea and Galilee. It took its name from the city Samaria, the capital of the northern kingdom.

Israel and Jordan are the names of the two countries into which the state of Palestine was divided in 1948.

The People

Hebrews: A gentile name, used to describe the group of Semitic peoples who eventually established themselves in Canaan. Possibly connected with the *Habiru*, semi-nomadic tribes found in a number of areas in the Near East in the second millennium BC.

Israelites: A name with religious significance, emphasizing membership of the covenant community (see Gen. 32.28). It is most appropriately used after the foundation of the nation and its religion during the period of the exodus.

Jews: Literally, members of the tribe of Judah. The name was used after the exile (sixth century BC) for any adherent of Judaism, whatever his tribal affiliation.

Samaritans: Originally Israelites, and partly the survivors of the destruction of the northern kingdom, Israel. When Judaism developed in Babylon during the exile, the religion of the Jews diverged from that of the Samaritans. Excluded from the temple in Jerusalem, the Samaritans built their own temple on Mt Gerizim (see John 4.20).

Slavery

Slavery was practised in Israel throughout the biblical period, though it was less common by New Testament times.

Although the slave was considered to be completely the property of his master there were many laws governing the possession of slaves which made the actual practice more humane than in most other countries of the ancient world.

Gentile Slaves

Both male and female slaves were either captured in war, or brought to Palestine by slave traders, or born in the home of their masters.

The average price for a Gentile slave in New Testament times was twenty minas, 2000 times as much as a labourer was paid for a day's work (see *Money*, above, p. 363).

Gentile slaves had to become Jewish proselytes, that is, to accept baptism and, for males, circumcision. This was probably done so that they could handle food without making it ritually unclean.

They did not, however, have to observe the whole of the Jewish law. They observed only those parts of it which were not limited to specific times, and which therefore did not interfere with their work for their master.

Although they had been converted to Judaism they had few of the rights which membership of the Jewish community would normally confer, e.g., they were not allowed to marry an Israelite, and male slaves were not permitted to read the Law in the synagogue or to make up the number required for public prayer.

A Gentile slave could obtain his freedom if it were bought for him by someone else (he could not buy it himself as he could own no possessions), if his master decided to free him, if he suffered certain injuries at the hand of his master, or if his master died without leaving a male heir.

Hebrew Slaves

Male Israelites could sell themselves into slavery because of poverty or debt, or they could be made slaves as punishment for theft. Israelite girls under the age of twelve could be sold into slavery by their fathers, but only to another Jew. They often later married their master or his son.

The average price for a Jewish slave in New Testament times was about five minas. Jewish slaves were cheaper than Gentile slaves because their term of slavery was limited.

A Jewish slave had to be freed at the end of six years, unless he voluntarily relinquished this right and agreed to serve his master for life (see Deut. 15.12–18).

He could be freed before the end of six years if his master chose to free him, or if he redeemed himself or was redeemed by someone else.

A female slave had to be freed when she reached the age of twelve, but she then probably married her master or his son.

A Jewish slave had more rights than a Gentile slave. He could own possessions, he had to be treated in the same way as his master's elder son, and he was not given the most menial tasks to perform.

Taxes

Taxation in Israel appears to go back to the early days of the monarchy, and payment may have been in kind or by forced labour (see I Kings 4.7; 5.13–15), though we have no definite knowledge of systems of taxation in Old Testament times. The situation by New Testament times is more clear-cut.

Roman Taxes

Every Roman subject had to pay two direct taxes: a *land tax*, paid in kind, and a *poll tax*, paid in Roman money.

In addition, there were indirect taxes – *customs* – payable on the value of goods, e.g., on farm produce taken to the market for sale or on exported goods.

Tax-gatherers (publicans): The collection of Roman taxes throughout the empire was organized by financial companies in Rome, and they employed agents in the provinces.

The post of tax-gatherer went to the highest bidder, and the system encouraged bribery and corruption.

Those Jews who were willing to enter the employ of the Romans as tax-collectors were despised by their fellow-countrymen, and the money they handled was considered to be tainted and could not, therefore, be accepted as alms for the poor.

Jewish Taxes

The *temple tax* of a half-shekel (see *Money*, above, p. 363) had to be paid annually by every male Jew.

Tithes:

(a) The *priests' tithe*: One per cent of the harvest belonged to the priests as part of their income. There were those who observed the law scrupulously (see Luke 11.42; 18.12), but it appears that many were lax in their payment of the tithe.

(b) The *second tithe*: This tithe had to be spent in Jerusalem. The owner either brought the tithe in kind to Jerusalem, or sold it and brought the money to be spent in Jerusalem. It was not a tax in the sense of having to be paid to someone else, but it contributed to the prosperity of Jerusalem. (See also Part IV, Section 1, p. 213.)

Travel

Land Travel

On foot: Throughout the biblical period long as well as short journeys were commonly made on foot.

Asses: The earliest known beast of burden. Used for riding and for transporting heavy loads.

Camels: Probably not domesticated until the twelfth century BC. Camel caravans were used especially by merchants for long journeys.

Horses: Introduced to Israel in the time of David and Solomon. Used almost entirely to draw war-chariots and thus came to be a symbol for war.

Chariots: In early times the chariot was a wooden cart, drawn by two horses. First used in Israel in the time of David and Solomon. Used mainly in war, but also for peace-time travel by kings and other men of high rank.

Roads and Footpaths

See Part IV, Section 2, p. 214.

Sea Travel

Small wooden boats, with oars and one sail, were used on the Sea of Galilee in New Testament times for getting from one lakeside village to another as well as for fishing.

Larger, timber-built ships transported cargoes and passengers across the Mediterranean. These varied in size and construction but included galleys, with upturned prow and stern, and with one, two or three banks of oars.

Ships of war had very sharp prows, like beaks, for ramming enemy vessels.

Most ships carried one large square sail, but by New Testament times, when ships were often sailed rather than rowed, there could be a small foresail and even a small topsail as well as the mainsail. Two oars or paddles at the stern of the ship acted as rudders.

Sea travel was seldom undertaken in winter, partly because of the danger from storms, and partly because cloud often obscured the stars, by which the sailors navigated.

Warfare

Army

Old Testament Times: The first standing army in Israel was established by David. Before this the different tribes contributed their levy of soldiers when the need arose.

Captain of the host: In command of the whole army.

Captain: In charge of a division of 1000 men.

There were further sub-divisions of hundreds, fifties and tens.

The army consisted only of infantrymen until the introduction of chariots in Solomon's time.

New Testament Times: Roman soldiers were stationed in Palestine as in all other parts of the empire. Four legions, including the famous Tenth Legion, were stationed in the province of Syria, which included Palestine.

Local men from the provinces might also serve in the Roman army.

Centurion: In command of a *century*, or 100 soldiers.

There were six centuries in a cohort ('band') and ten cohorts in a legion.

Quarternion: A guard of four soldiers.

Temple Guard: This was a small force of Levites under the command of the *Captain of the Temple* in Jerusalem. This Jewish police force carried out guard duties at the temple, but could also be used by the Jewish authorities to make arrests and to execute punishments.

Weapons

Stones: Stones of all sizes could be hurled on the enemy from above. Smaller stones could be shot from a sling. This was a narrow length of woven cloth or leather, held by its two ends, with a stone in the middle. It was whirled round the head and then one end was released.

Darts, javelins: Light, tipped weapons to be thrown at the enemy.

Spears: A wooden shaft, tipped with flint in early times, and later with bronze or iron.

Swords: Short, dagger-like weapons with an iron blade. Sometimes two-edged.

Bows and arrows: Used from earliest times. Bows usually of wood, strung with ox-gut. Arrows of tipped wood or reed.

Battle-axes: Clubs of hard wood, studded with iron spikes.

Armour

Coat of Mail: Bronze for the leaders, leather for ordinary soldiers.

Helmet: Also bronze for leaders, leather for ordinary soldiers.

Shield: Leather stretched over a wooden frame. Either small and circular or large and rectangular.

Fortifications

An important factor in the siting and construction of every city and village. Cities in key positions, like Megiddo, commanding the pass in the Carmel Range, would have extra strong fortifications.

Fortified cities often had double walls, with projecting bastions and angled entrances. The walls were usually constructed of stone (occasionally of brick), and the gates were wooden, though sometimes covered with bronze.

Siege-craft

Methods used to capture a fortified city include:

Climbing the walls by means of *scaling-ladders*.

Breaking down walls or gates with *battering rams*.

Catapulting large stones, arrows or burning objects over the walls by means of *siege artillery*. Josephus describes the Romans in the siege of Jerusalem as catapulting stone missiles weighing half a hundredweight over a distance of 400 yards.

Building a *ramp* of earth to the height of the walls or constructing a *wooden tower* on which to mount siege engines.

Water Supplies

Climate and topography in Palestine combined to make the provision of water supplies essential for life.

Rainfall

Average is thirty inches a year, though in the south and east it may be four inches or even less.

No rain falls from May to September.

The *former rains* (October) and the *latter rains* (April) mark the beginning and end of the rainy season, but amounts vary and the rains may even fail altogether.

Wells

Springs ('fountains'): Some dried up in summer. Those which did not were greatly prized, and were described as 'living water'.

Cisterns: Hewn out of the rock to store rain-water drained from roof tops or gullies, or channelled from a spring. They had a narrow opening, and widened downwards to a square or circular chamber.

The mouth of a well had to have a cover on it (see Ex.21.33). A large stone was often used as a cover for wells in open country.

Domestic supplies: Large houses or groups of houses would have their own cistern. Humbler village homes depended on the common well. Women were responsible for the menial task of fetching water in large water pots.

Animal skins were used for carrying water on long journeys, and for the supply carried by the water-seller in times of scarcity. On these occasions the water was carried by men.

Public supplies: Very large cisterns or series of cisterns were constructed as underground reservoirs in towns and cities.

In *Jerusalem:* Enormous reservoirs have been found underneath Jerusalem. The only spring, Gihon, was in the Kidron valley, outside the city walls. From early times water was brought into the city by means of a watercourse hewn through the rock cliff which formed the boundary of Jerusalem. In the eighth century BC Hezekiah had a tunnel dug through the rock to take water from the spring Gihon to the Pool of Siloam inside the city walls.

In the first century BC Herod the Great had aqueducts built to bring water from reservoirs several miles outside Jerusalem.

In *Masada:* Huge underground cisterns stored water from the rare but heavy rain of the area. These cisterns held enough water for the needs of the hundreds of people associated with Herod's palace on this rock fortress in the wilderness near the Dead Sea.

Weights and Measures

There were no standard units of measurement in Old Testament or New Testament times. A unit might be greater in one country or region than in another, and a royal unit was greater than the corresponding common unit. All equivalents are therefore only approximations.

Length

Cubit: Approximately 20 inches (half a metre).

4 fingers' breadths	= 1 palm
3 palms	= 1 span
2 spans	= 1 cubit
6 cubits	= 1 reed
4 cubits	= 1 fathom
100 fathoms	= 1 furlong
$8\frac{1}{2}$ furlongs	= 1 mile (1·4 km)

Area

Indicated either by stating the length of the sides, or by the use of expressions like the amount of seed required to sow a given area, or the area that could be ploughed by a yoke of oxen in a day.

Weight

(see also *Money*, above, p. 363).

Shekel: Approximately 12 grammes (half an ounce).

10 gerahs	= 1 beka
2 bekas	= 1 shekel
50 shekels	= 1 mina ('pound')
60 minas	= 1 kikkar ('talent')

Units of weight have the same names as monetary values because before the introduction of coins precious metals, measured by weight, were used for money.

Capacity

Dry	Liquid	Dry and Liquid	Approximate equivalents*
$\frac{1}{8}$ cab			$\frac{1}{2}$ pint
$\frac{1}{4}$ cab	log		1 pint
$\frac{1}{2}$ cab	$\frac{1}{6}$ hin		2 pints
	$\frac{1}{4}$ hin		3 pints
		cab	4 pints
	$\frac{1}{2}$ hin		6 pints
omer	$\frac{1}{10}$ bath		$7\frac{1}{2}$ pints
$\frac{1}{6}$ ephah	hin		$1\frac{1}{2}$ gallons
		seah ('bushel')	$1\frac{1}{2}$ pecks
ephah	bath ('firkin')		9 gallons
lethech			$5\frac{1}{2}$ bushels
homer	cor		11 bushels

* 1 pint = 0·57 litre
 1 gallon = 1·2 US gallon = 4·5 litres

Writing

Writing is known to have been used in the Near East as far back as 4000–3000 BC.

The earliest surviving example of Hebrew writing (the Gezer calendar) is dated about 1000 BC.

Writing Materials

Influenced largely by the materials available in a given region, for example, clay tablets in Mesopotamia where there was an abundance of suitable clay.

Stone: Used especially when the inscription was intended to be permanent and public, e.g., law codes and commemoration of royal victories or other achievements. Seals, used as signatures, were also made of stone.

Clay: Used especially in Mesopotamia. Marks were impressed on damp clay which was then hardened by being sun-dried or fire-baked. This material lent itself most easily to the kind of wedge-shaped writing known as Cuneiform (from 'cuneus' – wedge). Sometimes the tablet was enclosed in a clay 'envelope' and the contents repeated on the outside.

Wood: Wooden writing tablets. Sometimes the surface was covered with wax or clay before the writing was done.

Leather: The tanned skins of animals, usually sheep or goats. A finer material was produced if the skins were treated by being washed, scraped, stretched and rubbed with pumice stone to produce a smooth surface.

Vellum is technically the material made from calf-skin, but it came to be used for any fine leather writing material.

Parchment is another name for vellum, derived from Pergamum, the city in Asia Minor which is credited with the invention of this writing material.

Skins were sewn together to form a continuous roll for longer documents.

Papyrus: Made originally by the Egyptians from the papyrus, a tall reed growing in the Nile swamps. The pith of the reed was cut into thin strips which were soaked, placed side by side, and covered with a layer of strips at right angles to the first layer. The two layers were then 'glued' together and hammered to form a smooth surface.

Sheets of papyrus were fastened end to end to form rolls.

Our word 'paper' comes from the word 'papyrus'.

Papyrus, which deteriorates with age or dampness, is a more perishable material than leather.

Pottery: Potsherd or *ostraca* are pieces of broken pottery, used for a variety of purposes – notes, lists, receipts, etc., and even letters.

'Books'

Scroll ('roll'): A continuous roll, made of leather or papyrus. The writing was done in vertical columns, which could be read progressively as the scroll was unrolled.

Codex: Separate sheets placed one on top of the other, folded and stitched together, as in modern books.

Writing Tools

Stylus ('pen'): Made from a reed.

For clay tablets the end of the reed was cut so as to produce a wedge-shaped mark.

For papyrus or leather the end of the reed was crushed so that the fibres formed a brush. Later, a reed with a sharpened end was used, more like the modern nib.

Ink: Normally black. Either non-metallic, made from soot mixed with gum and a little oil or water, or metallic (known at least from the first century AD) made from nut-galls, sulphate of iron and gum.

Ink-wells: Scribes carried ink in horn containers, which could be hung from the belt. Ink-stands of bronze or clay were used on writing benches. Palettes were used for 'mixing' ink, i.e. moistening the solid block of ink ready for use.

'Rubbers': A sponge was used for washing away writing which was done in non-metallic ink or a pen-knife was used for scraping a little off the surface of the writing materials.

Types of Writing

Uncial: Using entirely large capital letters.

Cursive or *minuscule:* A flowing script, with the letters joined.

Biblical Languages

Hebrew: One of the Semitic languages, related to Phoenician, Babylonian, Assyrian, etc.

A form of Phoenician script was used in Old Testament times but it was replaced in the second century BC by the 'square' script used in modern Hebrew.

Aramaic: Also Semitic. Originally the language of Syria, it was made the official language of the western part of the Persian empire in the fifth century BC.

By New Testament times it had become the common language of Palestine, though Hebrew remained the language for reading and studying the Jewish Scriptures.

Targums are Aramaic paraphrases of the Scriptures, made for use in public worship.

Greek: By New Testament times a simplified form of Greek had become the *lingua franca* of the Mediterranean world. The New Testament was written in this *Koine* (literally 'common') Greek.

Scribes

In Old Testament times there was a professional class of scribes, highly educated, who manned the 'Civil Service' and the 'Foreign Office', and who were part of the international Wisdom Movement.

By New Testament times scribes were still an important professional class, but their main concern was now the study, copying and interpretation of the Law.

There were Sadducaic as well as Pharisaic scribes. (See also Part IV, Section 3, p. 228.)

Miscellaneous

The Date of Jesus' Birth

The Christian era was probably first suggested in the sixth century AD in Italy. The birth of Jesus, which was to divide all history into BC (before Christ) and AD (*anno domini* – 'in the year of our Lord'), was reckoned to have taken place 753 years after the foundation of the city of Rome. However, Jesus' birth is recorded as preceding the death of Herod the Great, and Herod died in 750 AUC (i.e. after the foundation of Rome) at the latest.

The exact date of Jesus' birth is unknown but it is usually put at 6 BC or 4 BC.

The actual birth day of Jesus is also unknown. In the early centuries the birth and baptism of Jesus were celebrated in the eastern part of the Roman Empire on January 6. During the fourth century the church in Rome combined the commemoration of the birth of Jesus with the winter solstice and the Roman festival of the unconquered sun on December 25.

The High Priest's Dress

This consisted of an elaborate and distinctive set of eight garments. Each of the garments had symbolic significance and by New Testament times each was considered to have atoning power for specific sins. No records give us an exact account of the high priest's dress; this is one possible reconstruction (see Ex.28).

Four of the garments were the same as those worn generally by priests:

(*a*) White linen *drawers* or breeches.

(*b*) A white linen *robe*.

(*c*) A richly embroidered *waistband* ('girdle') wound two or three times round the waist with the ends left hanging.

(*d*) A *turban* of fine linen wound into a conical headdress.

In addition the high priest wore:

(*a*) A sleeveless tunic-like blue *robe* with a border of bell and pomegranate embroidery.

(*b*) The *ephod*, an apron-like vest with straps over the shoulders.

(*c*) The *breastplate* (called the 'breastplate of judgment'), a double square of linen on to which were set twelve precious stones, with the name of a tribe engraved on each. The Urim and Thummim (see below) were possibly in a small pouch in the breastplate. The breastplate was fastened to the ephod.

(*d*) The *mitre* ('diadem'), a flat gold ornament fastened to the front of the turban by blue ribbons.

N.B. The ephod in the high priest's vesture is to be distinguished from the garment of the same name, worn by priests in the early period of Israel's history. This was a short, kilt-like undergarment which did not reach to the knees. It was replaced after the exile by drawers.

Jot and Tittle

Jot translates the Greek word *iota*, the smallest letter in the Greek alphabet, similar to the 'i' of the English alphabet.

Tittle (literally 'horn') refers to the corner or stroke of a letter, possibly the mark distinguishing one letter from a similar one.

Phylacteries

Two small leather boxes, made from the skin of a clean animal.

One was worn on the forehead ('frontlets') and one on the forearm during the recital of the Jewish morning prayer.

Inserted in the boxes were small pieces of parchment with the following passages written on them: Ex.13.1–10; 13.11–16; Deut.6.4–9; 11.13–21.

The phylacteries were bound to the forehead and the forearm with long leather bands.

Urim and Thummim

Lots used as part of an oracle to discover the divine will. Probably two small stones differentiated by shape, size or marking. They were thrown to obtain an answer to a specific question.

The original meaning of the words is obscure, but may imply contrasts, e.g., 'Yes' and 'No' or 'Innocence' and 'Guilt'.

In later Old Testament writings they are said to be placed in the high priest's 'breastplate of judgment' (see High Priest's Dress, above, p. 369). The reason for this is uncertain but it suggests the association of the priestly office with the knowledge of the divine will.

Maps

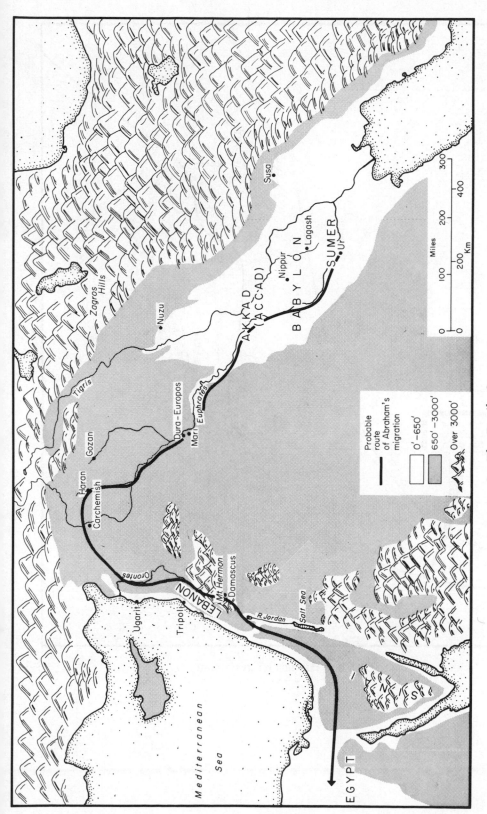

1 The Fertile Crescent

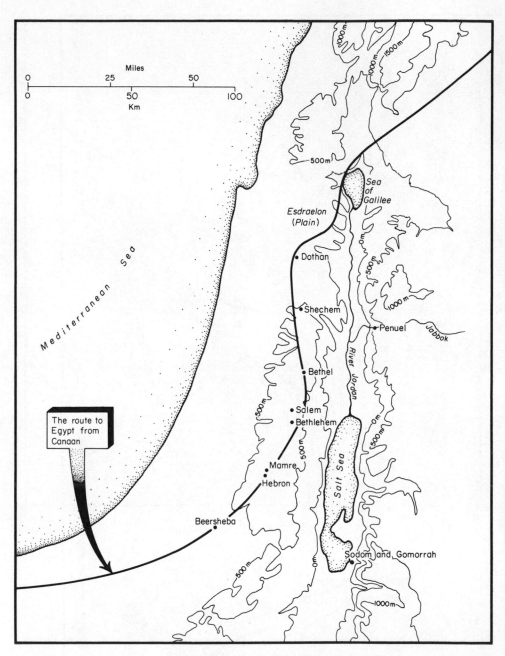

2   The Patriarchs in Canaan

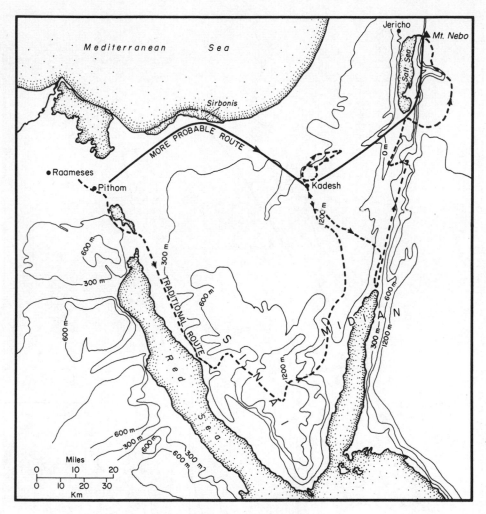

Mediterranean Sea

Sirbonis

MORE PROBABLE ROUTE

Raameses
Pithom

Kadesh

1200 m

TRADITIONAL ROUTE

600 m

300 m

600 m

600 m

300 m

Red Sea

600 m

300 m

600 m

600 m

300 m

600 m

300 m

S I N A I

M I D I A N

1200 m

1200 m

1200 m

300 m

600 m

Jericho

Mt. Nebo

Salt Sea

Miles
0   10   20
0 10 20 30
Km

3   From Egypt to Canaan

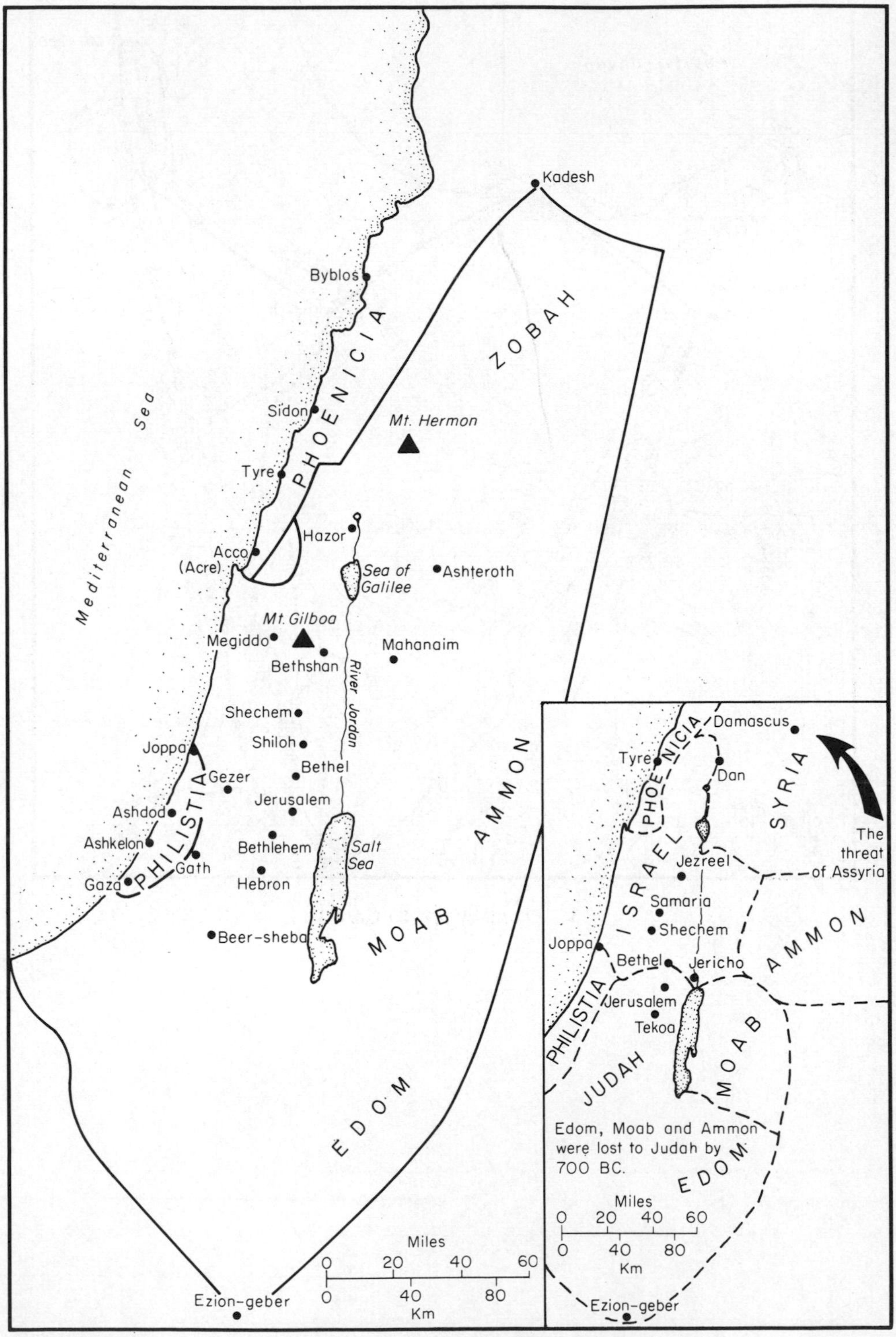

Kadesh
Byblos
PHOENICIA
ZOBAH
Mediterranean Sea
Sidon
Mt. Hermon
Tyre
Hazor
Acco
(Acre)
Sea of Galilee
Ashteroth
Mt. Gilboa
Megiddo
Mahanaim
Bethshan
River Jordan
Shechem
Shiloh
Joppa
Bethel
Gezer
Jerusalem
Ashdod
AMMON
Ashkelon
PHILISTIA
Bethlehem
Salt Sea
Gaza
Gath
Hebron
MOAB
Beer-sheba
EDOM
Miles
0 20 40 60
0 40 80
Km
Ezion-geber
Damascus
Tyre
PHOENICIA
Dan
SYRIA
The threat of Assyria
ISRAEL
Jezreel
Samaria
Shechem
AMMON
Joppa
Bethel
Jericho
PHILISTIA
Jerusalem
Tekoa
MOAB
JUDAH
Edom, Moab and Ammon were lost to Judah by 700 BC.
EDOM
Miles
0 20 40 60
0 40 80
Km
Ezion-geber

4 The Empire of David and Solomon
(*Inset*) The Kingdoms of Israel and Judah

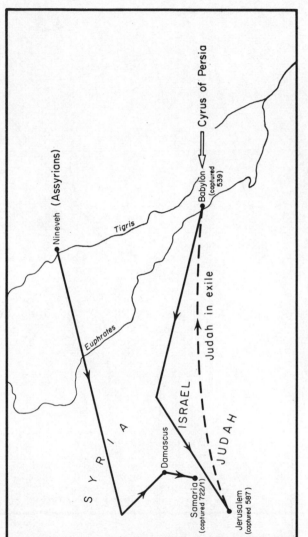

5   The Threat of Great Empires (Diagram)

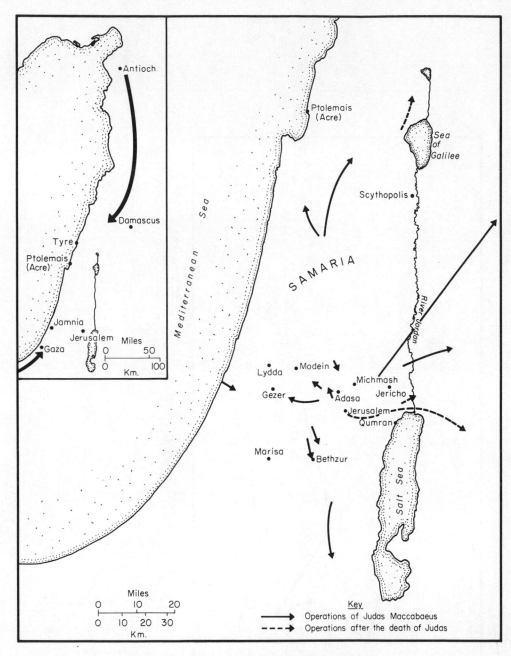

Key

→ Operations of Judas Maccabaeus
⇢ Operations after the death of Judas

6   The Struggle of the Maccabees
(*Inset*)   The Kings of the North and the Kings of the South

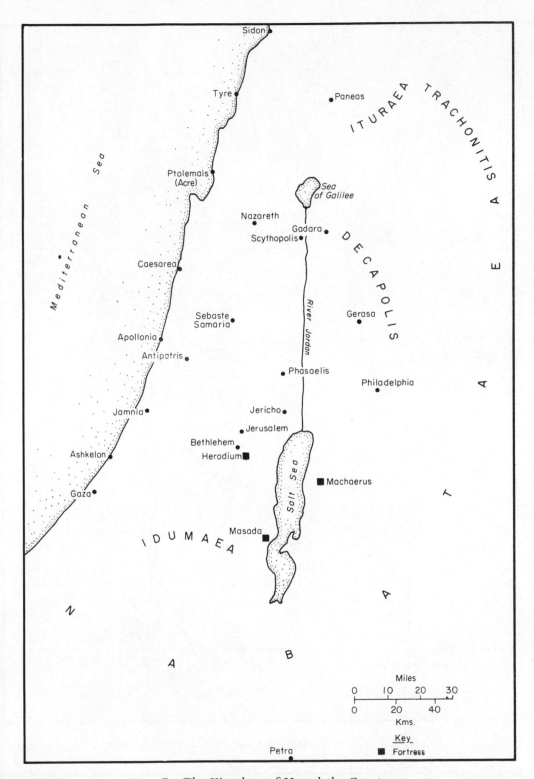

Sidon

Tyre

Paneas

ITURAEA

TRACHONITIS

Ptolemais
(Acre)

*Sea
of Galilee*

M e d i t e r r a n e a n   S e a

Nazareth

Gadara

Scythopolis

D E C A P O L I S

Caesarea

River Jordan

Sebaste
Samaria

Gerasa

Apollonia

Antipatris

Phasaelis

Philadelphia

Jamnia

Jericho

Jerusalem

Bethlehem

Herodium ■

S a l t   S e a

Machaerus ■

Ashkelon

Gaza

I D U M A E A

Masada ■

N

A

B

A

T

A

E

A

Miles

| 0 | 10 | 20 | 30 |

| 0 | 20 | 40 |

Kms.

<u>Key</u>

■ Fortress

Petra

7   The Kingdom of Herod the Great

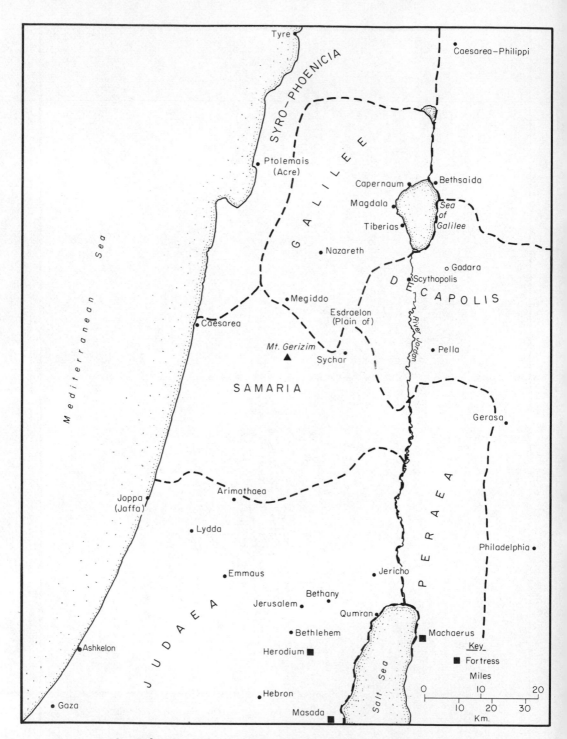

8   Palestine: The Gospels and the Acts of the Apostles

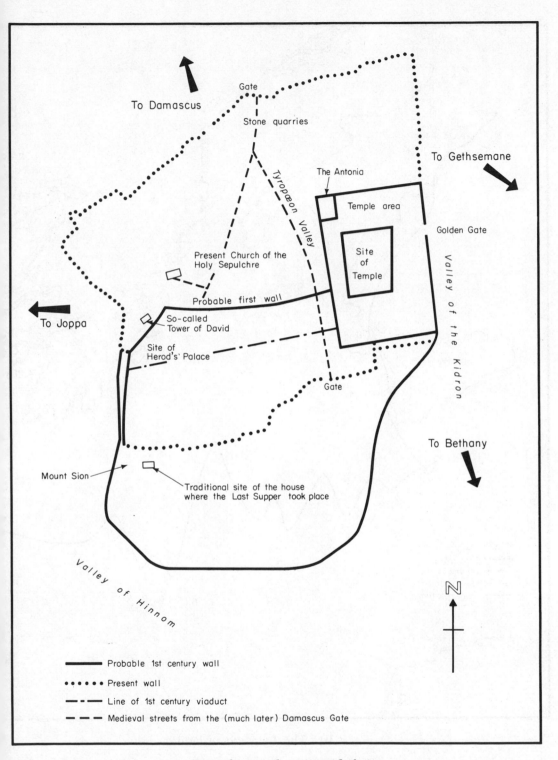

To Damascus

Gate

Stone quarries

To Gethsemane

The Antonia

Temple area

Golden Gate

Tyropœon Valley

Present Church of the
Holy Sepulchre

Site
of
Temple

Probable first wall

So-called
Tower of David

To Joppa

Valley of the Kidron

Site of
Herod's' Palace

Gate

To Bethany

Mount Sion

Traditional site of the house
where the Last Supper took place

Valley of Hinnom

N

——— Probable 1st century wall

•••••• Present wall

—·—·— Line of 1st century viaduct

— — — Medieval streets from the (much later) Damascus Gate

9   Jerusalem in the Time of Christ

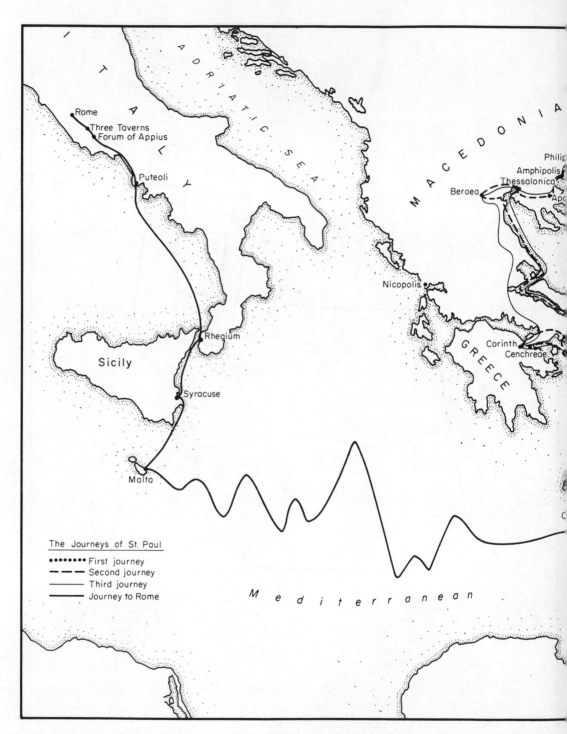

The Journeys of St. Paul

•••••• First journey
--- Second journey
—— Third journey
—— Journey to Rome

10   The Journeys of Paul

RACE

PONTUS

BITHYNIA

MYSIA

GALATIA

Troas
Assos• Adramyttium
Pergamum
Lesbos• • Thyatira
Mitylene

PHRYGIA

LYCAONIA

LYDIA
Sardis
hios• •Philadelphia
Smyrna ASIA •Hierapolis
•Ephesus •Colossae PISIDIA
Samos• •Laodicea
Patmos •Miletus CARIA

Antioch• •Iconium
•Lystra
•Derbe Tarsus•
CILICIA

Antioch•
Seleucia•
SYRIA

Attalia• •Perga
Cos LYCIA
Cnidus •Patara
Rhodes •Myra

Cyprus •Salamis
Paphos

C. Salmone

Sidon• •Damascus
Tyre•
Ptolemais
○(Acre)
Caesarea•

Jerusalem•

Alexandria•

Miles
100   200
0
0   100   200   300
Km

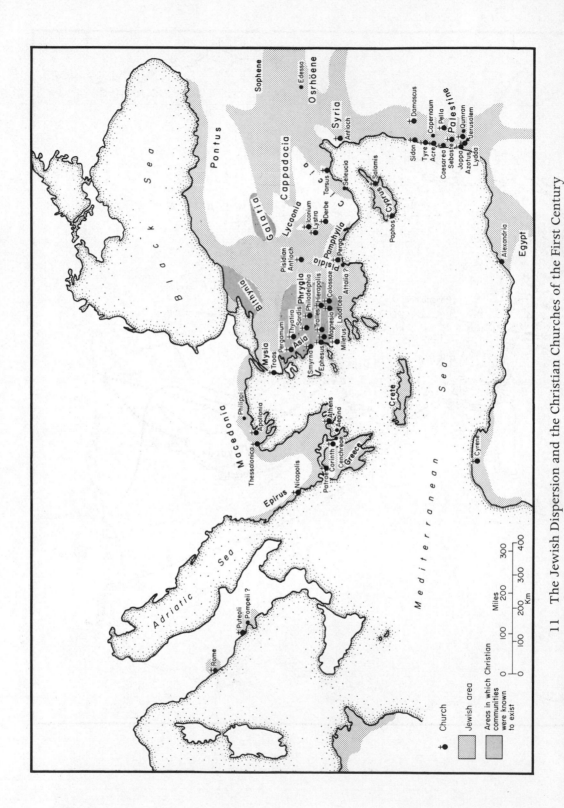

11 The Jewish Dispersion and the Christian Churches of the First Century

Black Sea

Pontus

Sophene

• Edessa
Osrhoene

Cappadocia

Galatia

Lycaonia

Iconium
Lystra
Derbe

Tarsus
Seleucia

Pisidian
Antioch

Pisid.

Pamphylia

Perga
Attalia

Cyprus

Salamis

Paphos

Damascus

Syria

Antioch

Sidon
Tyre
Acre
Caesarea
Sebaste
Joppa
Azotus
Lydda

Capernaum
Pella

Qumran
Jerusalem

Palestine

Mysia

Troas

Asia

Pergamum
Thyatira
Sardis
Smyrna
Ephesus

Phrygia

Philadelphia
Hierapolis
Tralles
Colossae
Magnesia
Laodicea
Miletus

Bithynia

Macedonia

Philippi
Apollonia

Thessalonica

Epirus
Nicopolis

Patroe
Corinth
Cenchreae

Athens
Aegina

Greece

Crete

Mediterranean Sea

Alexandria

Egypt

Cyrene

Adriatic Sea

Puteoli
Pompeii ?

Rome

400
300
300
200
200
Miles
100
100
Km
0

✝• Church

▨ Jewish area

▨ Areas in which Christian communities were known to exist

384

Indexes

INDEX OF NAMES AND SUBJECTS

Abel, 99, 152
Adolescence, 22, 24, 27 f., 53 f., 68
Agreed syllabuses, 22, 44, 52, 64 f.
Abraham, 48, 49, 102 f., 152
Absalom, 125, 126
Acts of the Apostles, 305, 307 ff., 336 ff.
Adam, 97, 99
Agrippa
  friend of Herod the Great, 205 ff.
  See also Herod Agrippa I
Agriculture, 78, 82 f., 115
Ahab, 60, 129 f.
Ahaz, 131 f., 140, 164
Ahaziah, 129, 130
Alexander, 206
Alexandria, 239, 341, 342, map 11
Amarna letters, 116
Amaziah, 137
Ammon, 79, 124, map 4
Amorites, 115
Amos, 136 f., 139
Amphictyony. See Tribal league
Ananias, 340
Anathoth, 142 f.
Andrew, 219, 277
Angels, 236
Antioch
  (Syria), 79, 191, 283, 302, 307, 308, 342, map 10
  (Pisidia), 307, map 10
Antiochus IV ('Epiphanes'), 62, 192 f., 195 f.
Antipas. See Herod Antipas
Antipater
  father of Herod the Great, 195, 203 f.
  son of Herod the Great, 205 f.
Antonia, Fortress, 220, 221, map 9
Apocalyptic, 61 f., 177, 195 f., 223
Apocrypha, 194, 196 f., 258, 335
Apostles, 277, 346
Archaeology, 7, 12 f., 102 f., 114, 121, 127 f., 173 f., 183, 224, 230
Archelaus, 206 f., 288
Aristobulus
  high priest, 194, 203
  son of Herod the Great, 206 f.
Ark, 109 f., 120, 124, 139, 147, 153 f., 157, 159

Artaxerxes
  I, 183, 185 f.
  II, 183, 186
Asa, 124
Ascension, 338 f.
Asshurbanapal, 132
Asshur-nasir-pal, 129
Assyria, 129 ff., 136, 139, 140 f., 143, map 5
Athaliah, 130
Athens, 308, map 10
Augustus (Octavian), 205, 302

Baal, 115, 135, 138, 143
Baasha, 129
Babylon, 18, 132 f., 144 f., 174 f., 192, maps 1 and 5
Balaam, 134
Balak, 135
Baptism, 62, 304, 318, 344 f.
  of Jesus, 62, 270
Barnabas, 307, 340
Baruch, 142 f., 144
Beersheba, 81, map 4
Benhadad of Damascus, 129
Bethany, 221, map 8
Bethel, 104, 114, 128, 136, 138, 148, 152, 183, maps 2 and 4
Bethlehem, 81, 216, maps 4 and 8
Bethshan, Beisan, 80, 192, map 4
Bible
  as a library, 3 f., 65
  as word of God, 3, 5
  authority of, 353 f.
  background to, 6, 12, 34, 47, 96 f., 102 f., 108 f., 114, 183 f., 191 f.
  canon of, 353
  language of, 32 f.
  nature of, 3 f., 5 ff., 31 f., 46 f.
  relevance of, 4 f., 13, 54 f., 66
  teaching of, 25, 28 f., 30 ff., 34, 40 ff., 44 f.
  truth of, 4 ff., 35, 55, 66 f., 146
  versions of, 8 f., 46 f., 54 f.
Bildad, 166 ff.
Bishop, 346
Blake, William, 285
Blessing, 101
Boaz, 188

Caesarea, 81, 205, 208, 215, 283, 311, map 8
Caesarea Philippi, 274, map 8
Caiaphas, 221, 299, 329
  See also Priests
Cain, 99, 152
Calvary, 222
Canaanites, 115, 124 f.
Capernaum, 215, 219 f., 272 f., map 8
Carchemish, 78, 133, map 1
Carmel, Mt, 76, 80, 215
Children
  experience of, 17, 19 f., 23, 29, 35, 38, 43, 44 f.
  growth of, 17, 21 f., 24 f., 29, 54
  questions of, 23, 25 f., 27 f., 29, 31, 36 f., 49 f., 68 ff.
  thinking of, 25, 35 ff., 44 f.
Christ. See Messiah
Chronicler, 189
Church, early, 243, 283 f., 288, 318 ff., 341 ff.
Circumcision, 94, 106, 174, 310
Cities, ancient, 83, 125, 215
Computers, 13
Conquest of Palestine, 84, 114 ff.
Climate of Palestine, 81, 214
Corinth, 283, 308, 309, 354, map 10
Covenant, 58 f., 84, 87, 91 f., 100, 105 f., 111 f., 114, 138, 160 f., 177, 313 f.
  Book of the Covenant, 82 f., 107, 118
Cox, E., 31, 65, 66, 68
Creation, 87 f., 95, 98 f., 159 f., 180
Criticism
  form, 11 f., 246 ff., 326
  nature of, 6, 241 f.
  redaction, 12
  source, 10 f., 85 f., 241 ff.
  textual, 7 ff.
Cursing, 101
Cyprus, 307, 308, map 10
Cyrus, 174, 176 f., 180, 183, 185

D Document, 85 f., 91 f.
Damascus, 79, 124, 126, 129, 130, 131, 140, 306, map 4 inset
Dan, 128, 148
Daniel, 61, 191, 195 f.

Darius I, 183, 184
David, 4, 34, 48, 123 ff., 134 f., 157
Deacon, 346
Dead Sea Scrolls, 9, 12, 13, 46, 224, 232 f., 237
Debir, 108, 114, 115
Decalogue. *See* Ten Commandments
Decapolis, 80, 213, 215, map 8
Devil, demons, 235, 261, 279
Disciples, 254, 257, 277
Discussion, 68 f.
Dodd, C. H., 268, 328, 330, 332
Domitian, 348
Doris, 205 f.
Dura Europas, 342, 344, map 1

E Document, 85 f., 89 ff.
Ebal, Mt, 81, 153
Ecclesiastes, 169 ff.
Ecclesiasticus, 196 f.
Edom, 79, 124, 126, 131, map 4
Education
  ancient, 218
  child centred, 19 f., 44 f., 55 f.
  primary, 17 f., 35 ff.
  religious, 18 f.
  secondary, 27, 53 f.
  sixth form, 64 ff.
Ego-ideal, 21 f.
Egypt, 85, 108 f., 129, 133, 136, 145, 176, 191, 341
Elders, 119, 346
Election, 92, 104 f., 110, 139 f., 145, 270
Elephantiné Papyri, 176, 183, 185
Elihu, 166 ff.
Elijah, 34, 59, 60, 130, 135, 274
Eliphaz, 166 ff.
Elisha, 130
Empty tomb, 56, 255, 261, 281
Ephesus, 283, 309, 327, 342, map 10
Esarhaddon, 132
Esau, 103
Eschatology, 177, 223, 237 f., 298
Esdraelon, 80, 214, map 8
Esdras
  I, 182
  II, 197
Essenes, 231
Esther, 197
Eucharist, 304, 318, 344 f.
Euphrates, 76, 77 (map) 79, map 1
Evidence
  external, 9, 240 f., 246
  internal, 9 f., 241, 246
Exile, 94, 173 ff., 227
Exodus, 84, 93, 107 ff., 114, 258, 263
Exploration, teaching as, 31, 36, 49
Ezekiel, 177 ff.
Ezion-geber, 80, 83, 121, 126, 214, map 4
Ezra, 182, 183, 185 f., 353

Felix, 210
Festivals, Jewish, 153 f.
  Day of Atonement, 154, 225
  Hannukkah, 61, 150
  Harvest, 67, 86, 104, 111
  Ingathering (Tabernacles), 83, 97, 104, 111, 119, 149 f., 160, 225
  New Year, 97, 149, 154 ff., 175 f.
  Passover, 58, 94, 110 f., 120, 149 f., 225 f., 234, 269
  Purim, 150
  Unleavened Bread, 83, 104, 111, 119, 149, 225
  Weeks, 83, 104, 119, 149, 225
Flood, The, 12, 88, 97, 100
Forgiveness, 294 f.
Fulfilment, 57, 62 f., 88 f.

Gad, 134
Galatia, 307, map 10
  Letter to, 309
Galilee
  Sea of, 80, 214, map 8
  District, 214 ff., 271 f., map 8
Gamaliel, 305
Geography of Palestine, 77 ff., 214
Geology of Palestine, 76 ff.
Gerizim, Mt, 81, 147, 153, 194, map 8
Gethsemane, 219, 293, 334, map 9
Gibeah, 121
Gideon, 80, 117
Gilboa, Mt, 81, 123, map 4
Gilgal, 147, 152
Gnosticism, 12, 326 f., 343 f.
God
  acts of, 84, 96, 236, 314
  name of, 93 f., 109
  nature of, 26 f., 50, 109 f., 113 f., 167 ff., 172 f., 179, 180, 234, 253, 292 f., 314 f.
  presence of, 106, 109 f., 235, 278
Golding, W., 67
Goldman, R., 25, 44
Gomer, 137 f.
Gospels, 8, 9, 12, 65, 239 ff., 261, 283 f., 330
  and history, 250 f., 265

Hadrian, 212
Haggai, 182, 184, 190
Haran, 77, map 1
Hazael, 130
Hazor, 80, 83, 114, map 4
Hebrews, Letter to, 350
Hebron, 81, 104, 115, map 2
Hermon, Mt, 214, 274, map 4
Herod
  the Great, 203 ff., 213
  Antipas, 206 f., 209, 287, 294
  Agrippa I, 209 f.

Hezekiah, 132
Hiram, 126
History
  and Jesus, 251 f.
  and the Bible, 33, 58 f., 67, 84 f., 95, 97, 103, 107 f., 250 ff.
  and the New Testament, 337
  and the prophets, 145 f.
  sense of, 6 f., 66 f.
Hodgson, L., 6
Holiness Code, 94
Holy Spirit, 236, 320 ff., 337
Holy War, 120
Horeb, Mt, 111, 112
Hosea, 137 f., 143
Hoshea, 131, 132
Houses, 215 f.
Hyrcanus, 194, 203 f., 233

Indoctrination, 20
Isaac, 105
Isaiah, 139 ff., 164
  Deutero-Isaiah, 173, 179–182, 185
  Trito-Isaiah, 183, 189

J document, 85 f., 87 f., 98 ff.
Jacob, 102, 103, 104, 106, 152
James
  son of Zebedee, 210, 219, 277, 295, 347
  brother of Jesus, 310, 345, 347
  Letter of, 351
Jehoiada, 130
Jehoiakim, 133, 144
Jehoiakin, 133
Jehoram, 129, 130
Jehoshaphat, 129
Jehu, 128, 130, 131
Jephthah, 117
Jeremiah, 142 ff., 164
Jericho, 83, 108, 116, 153, 214, maps 7 and 8
Jeroboam
  I, 126, 128 f.
  II, 130, 137
Jerusalem, 81, 83, 124 f., 139, 145, 155 f., 184 f., 209, 215, 220 f., 275 f., 283, 307, 310, 311, 329, 338, 341, maps 4, 8 and 9
  destruction of, 211, 297, 353
  See also Temple
Jesus
  birth of, 255, 256 f., 282, 369
  baptism of. *See under* Baptism
  message of, 283–301
  ministry of, 264–283
  resurrection of. *See under* Resurrection
  temptation of, 270 f.
  transfiguration of, 274 f.
  trial of, 209, 269, 329
  See also 69, 70, 316, 322 *and under* Passion story

Jezebel, 130
Joanna, 70
Joash, 130
Job, 166 ff.
Joel, 189
John
    disciple, 219, 277, 295, 327
    Gospel of, 240, 241, 261,
        326–334
    Epistles of, 326, 350
John the Baptist, 207, 287, 327
Jonah, 183, 187, 190
Joppa, 81, map 4
Jordan River, 80, 214, map 4
Joseph
    the Patriarch, 104
    of Nazareth, 290
Josephus, 183, 203, 208, 211, 223,
    266
Joshua, 114 ff., 152
    high priest, 184 f.
Josiah, 85, 132 f., 143
Jotham, 131
Judaea, 212, 214, map 8
Judaism, 222 ff., 234 ff., 313 ff.,
    330 f.
    Christian controversy with
        310 ff.
    Dispersion (Diaspora), 205, 210,
        223, 231, map 11
    Hellenistic, 222 f., 340 f.
    Palestinian, 222
Judas Iscariot, 277
Jude, 351
Judgment, 137 f., 141, 143, 145 f.,
    298
Judith, 197

Kadesh
    Wilderness, 111, map 3
    Northern Israel, 376, map 4
Kingdom of God, 71, 238, 252,
    289, 290 ff., 301

Lachish, 108, 114, 141
    Lachish letters, 128
Last supper, 221, 269
Law, 3 f., 61, 65, 94, 107, 118 f.,
    186, 187 f., 226 f., 228 f., 237,
    287, 310 f., 313 f.
Lazarus, 326
Lebanon, 79
Legends, 4, 46 f., 60, 108
    aetiological, 104
    cult, 104, 152 f.
Levites, 151, 186, 225, 226
Lewis, C. S., 259
Love, 23, 31, 39, 43, 56 f., 64, 70,
    276, 278 ff., 282 f., 323 f.
Luke
    evangelist, 257, 305, 336 f., 346
    Gospel of, 240, 242 ff., 249 f.,
        256 f.
    See also Acts of the Apostles

Maccabees, 191 ff., 276
    First book of, 191, 196
    Second book of, 191, 196
Maccabaeus, Judas, 61, 62, 193 ff.
Machaerus, Fortress, 194, map 7
Malachi, 190
Man, nature of, 98 f.
Manasseh, 132, 133
Manson, T. W., 275
Manuscripts, types of, 7 f., 241 f.
Mari, 78, 102, map 1
Mariamne I, 206 f.
Mark
    John, 254
    Gospel of, 240 f., 242 ff., 246 ff.,
        253 f., 261, 269
Masada, Fortress, 194, 204, 211,
    224, 230, map 7
Mary of Magdala, 70, 219, 329
Massoretes, 9
Mattathias of Modein, 193
Matthew
    disciple, 220, 295
    Gospel of, 240 f., 242 ff., 249 f.,
        255
Matthias, 339
Megiddo, 12, 80, 81, 133, 144, 183,
    map 4
Menahem, 131
Messiah, 56, 60, 238, 274, 299,
    316 f., 332 f.
Micah, 142
Miracles, 6, 58 f., 107, 249, 257 ff.,
    266, 272 f.
    teaching the miracles, 52 f., 63,
        262 f.
Mishna, 223
Mizpah, 147
Moab, 79, 124, 131, 188, map 4
Modein, 193, map 6
Monarchy, 121 ff.
    nature of, 125 f., 128 f., 161 f.
Morality, 57, 64, 69 ff., 113, 136 f.,
    167 f., 170 ff., 179, 304, 315,
    321 ff.
Moses, 34, 58, 59, 84, 107 f., 258,
    263, 274, 276, 314, 315
Myths, 4, 19, 46 f., 66 f., 97, 258,
    265, 303 f.
    aetiological, 98 f.

Nabonidus, 174, 176
Naboth, 130
Nahum, 146
Naomi, 188
Nathan, 134, 135, 136, 139
Nazareth, 215, 220, 271, map 8
Nebo, Mt, 79, 107, map 3
Nebuchadnezzar of Babylon, 133,
    175, 191, 196
Neco II of Egypt, 133
Nehemiah, 34, 183, 185 f., 187
    book of, 182
Nero, 347

Nicodemus, 328
Noah, 97, 100 f.
Nomads, 82
Northern Kingdom, 90 f., 127 ff.,
    137, 271
Nuzu, 103, map 1

Obadiah, 182
Omri, 128, 129
Onesimus, 325
Oral tradition, 11, 249 f.

P document, 85 f., 93, 98 ff.
Papias, 241
Parables, 27, 55, 245, 256, 280,
    284, 287 ff., 297 f.
    teaching the parables, 63, 288,
        290
Passion story, 53, 250, 254, 268 ff.,
    329, 334
Patriachs, 87 ff., 90, 93, 96, 102 ff.
Paul
    conversion of, 306 f.
    life of, 301–312
    thought of, 313–325
    See also, 34, 265, 346
Pekah, 131
Pella, 213, 341, map 8
Pentateuch, 10 f., 84 ff., 107
Pentecost, 62, 337, 339 f.
Persecution, 346 f., 351
Persia, 183, map 5
Personal relationships, 24, 27, 38 f.,
    70, 253
Peter, Simon, 210, 215, 219, 241,
    277 f., 295, 307, 310, 330
    Letters of, 350 f.
Petra, 203, 204, map 7
Pharisees, 69, 193, 228 f., 287,
    294, 297
Philip
    tetrarch, 206 f.
    disciple, 277, 341
Philippi, 283, 302, 308, map 10
Philistines, 79, 121 ff., map 4
Philo, 191, 208, 223, 331
Pithom, 108, map 3
Pliny, letter to Trajan, 345, 348
Poetry
    of Jesus, 278 f., 285
    of the Bible, 3, 19, 34 f., 36 f.,
        154 f., 189
Pompey, 195, 203
Pontius Pilate, 208 f., 267, 291,
    329, 347
Poverty, 295
Priests, 150 f., 226
    high priest, 151, 154, 163, 187,
        193, 205, 208, 226, 227
    See also Caiaphas
Promise, 88 f., 105
Prophets, 11, 59 f., 60, 130 f.,
    134 ff., 151, 160, 164, 177 ff.,
    189 ff.

Proverbs, 12, 164 ff.
Psalms, 12, 46, 151, 154 ff.
Pseudepigraphy, 224
Pseudonymity, 335 f.

Q source, 245
Qumran, 13, 80, 194, 224, 231 f., 235, 237, 331, map 8

Raamses, 108, map 3
Rabbis, 222 f., 229
Rehoboam, 128
Religion
  Babylonian, 175, 180
  Canaanite, 90 f., 93, 104 f., 106, 111, 115
  Hellenistic, 331
    mystery, 303
  Persian (Zoroastrianism), 184
Revelation, book of, 351
Resurrection, 254, 261 f., 280 ff., 329 f.
  teaching the resurrection, 63
Rezin of Damascus, 131
'Rich Young Ruler', 295
Roads, 214
Rome
  Empire of, 203 ff., 301 f.
  city of, 204 f., 283, 310, 338, 342, map 10
  Roman administration, 212 ff., 224, 302 ff., 347 ff.
  Emperor, 203 ff.
  Governor (of Judaea), 208 ff., 302, 311
Ruth, 187, 188

Sabbath, 58, 98, 150, 174, 219, 365
Sacrifice, 99, 105, 148, 151 f., 175, 179, 225, 315
  human, 105
Sadducees, 227
Sagas, 3, 66, 103, 152
Salome, 206
Samaria, 76, 81, 132, 138, 141, 192, 283, 342, map 8
Samaritans, 148, 188, 209, 233, 294
Samson, 81, 117
Samuel, 121 f.
Sanhedrin, 209, 212, 227 f.
Sarah, 103, 105
Sargon II of Assyria, 132
Saul, 114, 121, 122 ff., 135

Scribes, 162 f., 187, 228, 297
Sea
  of salt (Dead Sea), 80, 214, map 4
  of Reeds, 110, map 3
  of Galilee. *See under* Galilee
Sebaste, 205, 215, map 7
Second coming of Christ, 284, 298, 325
Seleucids, 191 f.
Sennacherib (Assyrian), 132, 141
Sermon on the Mount, 255, 294
Servant, suffering, 181 f.
Shalmaneser (Assyrian)
  III, 129, 130
  V, 132
Shechem, 81, 104, 115, 117, 147, 153, map 2
Sheshbazzar, 185
Shiloh, 115, 120, 147, 153, map 4
Shishak of Egypt, 129
Silas, 308
Sin, 99 f., 114, 157, 167
Sinai, 84, 109, 111, map 3
Slavery, 302, 324 f.
Social injustice, 131, 142 f.
Solomon, 4, 126 f.
Son of God, 254, 300, 332 f.
Son of man, 238, 252, 255, 300, 328
Song of Songs, 183, 189
Southern kingdom, 127, 132 ff.
Speaking with tongues, 320
Stephen, 340, 347
Stoicism, 303, 304
Stories, in teaching, 32, 34, 40, 46, 53
Suetonius, 347
Suffering, 24, 37, 62, 166 ff., 234 f., 274 f.
Sunday, 345
Synagogue, 58, 61, 176, 187, 219 f., 229 f.
Synoptic problem, 242 ff.
Syria
  Kingdom of, 129 f., map 5. *See also* Damascus
  Roman Province, 208, 212, map 10

Tacitus, 347
Talmud, 223
Tarsus, 305, map 10
Temple (Jerusalem)
  Solomon's 95, 121, 127, 134, 143, 147 f.

post-exilic, 148, 154, 182, 184 f.
  Herod's, 149, 211, 220, 224 f.
  organization of, 226
Ten Commandments, 112 f., 156
Tertullian, 348, 349
Thessalonica, 308
Thomas, 277, 330
Tiberias, 80, 207, 215, map 8
Tiglath-pileser II (Assyrian), 131
Tigris, 76, 78, map 1
Timothy
  follower of Paul, 309
  Letters to, 349 f.
Titus
  follower of Paul, 309
  Letter to, 349 f.
  Roman general, 211
Tribal league, 87, 89, 96, 115 ff., 119 f., 121, 124, 150, 153
  assembly of, 117, 153
  central sanctuary of, 120, 147
Troas, 308, map 10
Twelve, The, 277, 339
Tyre, 126, 130, map 4

Understanding, 6, 22 f., 29, 33, 45
  greater than articulation, 25, 45
Universalism, 187 f.
Ur, 12, 77, map 1
Uzziah, 130, 131

Vespasian, 211
Vocation, 58

Wisdom, 162 ff., 197
  personified, 165, 197
Wisdom of Solomon, 197
Wise men, 162 f.
Worship, 97, 118 f., 137, 151 ff., 225 f., 344

Yahweh, 109 f.

Zealots, 208, 232 f., 236 f., 266 f., 273, 286, 294
  Simon the Zealot, 277
Zechariah
  king of Israel, 131
  prophet, 182, 184
  book of, 190
Zedekiah, 133, 144
Zerubbabel, 183, 184 f.
Zophar, 166 ff.
Zoroastrianism. *See* Religion

INDEX OF SELECTED BIBLICAL REFERENCES

OLD TESTAMENT

Genesis
1–11	88, 93, 95, 96 ff.
1–3	85, 93, 98 ff.
4.1–24	99
4.25 f.	99
6.1–9.29	100 f.
11.1–9	101
12–50	103 ff.
12.1 f.	88, 104 f.
15.7–21	105
22.1–19	105, 152
37; 39–50	85, 104

Exodus
1.11	108
2.11–21	109
3	109 f., 263
6.3	93
7–12	90, 107
12.1–20	94, 111, 149
13.3–22	58
14–15	59, 110 f.
19–20	58, 111 f.
21–23	82 f., 118 f.
24.10–18	111 f.
34	111 f.

Leviticus
17–26	94, 187
23; 42 f.	111

Numbers
10.35	120

Deuteronomy
5.6–10	112
5.15	58
6.4 f.	58, 93
6.21 f.	118
16.3	111
26.5–10	86
27.1–26	153
31.9–13	119, 120
34	107

Joshua
1–24	114
1–9	116
6.34	117
10.36–39	115
24.19–22	113
24.30	116

Judges
1.1–36	115
1.8–15	116
7.22	120

Ruth
1–4	188
1.16 f.	188

I Samuel
1.1–28	120, 153
4.4–8	120
7.7–14	121
8.5–20	122
9.1–10.16	122, 134
13.8–15	122
18.6–9	123
22.11–19	122
31	123

II Samuel
2.2–4	123
5.6–9	124
5.17–25	123
8.16–18	125, 163
12.1–15	134, 135
15.18–22	125
20.23–25	163

I Kings
2.1–46	126
4.1–7	163
4.7–19	126
5.13–18	126
11.26–40	127
12.1–20	128
15.18–21	129, 130
17–19	130
18.20–40	135
21	60, 130
22	130

II Kings
11.1–3	130
14.25, 28	130
15.29 f.	131
16.5–9	131
17.5 f.	132, 141
18.4–16	132, 141
21.1–20	60, 132
22–23	85, 91, 132

23.30–35	133
25.1–21	133, 173

I Chronicles
10–29	121
27.32–34	163

II Chronicles
1–9	121
20.1–19	154

Ezra
1–6	182, 185
4.7–23	186
7.7	185
7.25 f.	186

Nehemiah
1–13	182 ff.
1.1	183, 185
4.1–23	186
6.1–14	186
8.1	186

Job
1–2	166 f.
5.17 f.	168
6.1 f.	168
9.32 f.	169
13.21–23	169
28	169
31	168
32–37	166, 167
42.7–17	167

Psalms
2	161
15	156
21	161
24	159
46	141, 158
48	141, 148, 158
51	157
65	160
76	141
78.67–72	139
81	160
84	156
87	158
93	159
95	160

101	162
122	155
126	161
130	156
132	139, 157

Proverbs

1–9	164
1.20 f.	165
8	165
22.17–23.11	164

Ecclesiastes

1.12–18	171
2.1–11	171
3.1–22	171
4.1–3	171
7 f.	172
12	172

Isaiah

1–39	139 ff.
1.2	59
1.4, 21–23	131, 140
2.2–4	142
3.16 f.	131
5.8–12	131
6.1–13	139
7.1 f.	131, 140, 164
9.2–7	142
10.7–19	141
11.1–9	142
14.24–26	141
17.12–14	141
29.13–16	131
31.4 f.	141
36–37	132, 141
41.21–29	180
42.1–9	181
42.18–20	181
44.26	181
45.1–13	180

46.1 f.	177
49.1–6	181
50.4–9	181
51.1–23	180
52.13–53.12	181
55–66	189
56.3–8	189
57.14–20	189
58.3–12	189

Jeremiah

1–52	142–145
1.4–10	143, 146
2.2 f.	146
7.1–20	143
11.18–23	143
12.1–6	143
15.10–12, 15–21	143
20.7–12	144
26.10 f.	143
27.1–11	144
30–31	145
37–38	144
39–44	173, 176
40.1–12	144 f.
42.1–17	145

Ezekiel

1–4	178
8.1	175
12.1–16	178
14.1	175
20.1 f.	175
33.1–9	178
33.10–20	179
37.1–14	179
37.23–27	61
40.1 ff.	178
44.9	61

Daniel

1–13	195 ff.

7.13 f.	298
9.26	192
11.1 ff.	191, 192
11.31 ff.	193

Hosea

1–14	137 f.
2.8, 13	138, 146
2.15	139
2.17	138, 146
2.22 f.	139
4.12–17	138
5.9	138
8.5	138
11.1–9	139
13.10 f.	139

Amos

1–9	136 f.
2.6 f.	136
5.4 f.	137
5.10 f.	136
5.21–24	131, 137
7.7–9	136
7.10–13	137

Micah

1–7	142
3.9–12	131
4.1–4	142

Haggai

1–2	182
1.6	184
2.6–9	184
2.16	184
2.21–23	184

Zechariah

1–8	182
4.9 f.	184
8.1–17	184

APOCRYPHA

I Maccabees

1.4 ff.	193
1.20 ff.	192

1.54	193
1.63	193
2.1–48	193

4.36–61	193
7	194
9.73	194

NEW TESTAMENT

Matthew

3.7–10	244
4.1–11	286
5–7	285
5.3	293

5.13 f.	294
5.45	276, 292
6.1–13	293
7.3	287
7.9–11	293

7.24 f.	285
8.5–13	289
9.2–8	242
11.7–9	285
11.27	300

12.45	284	3.1 f.	207	11.25	333
13.24–30	288 f., 292	3.7–9	244	12.32 f.	326
13.33	289	3.21–22	270	13.1–9	280, 329, 334
13.45	289	4.1–13	235, 286	14.1–24	332 f.
13.47–50	288 f.	4.16–30	286	14.28	332
15.14	287	5.18–26	242	15.1 f.	333
16.13–20	299	6.37	277	15.15	278
18.3	294	7.1–10	272	15.26	333
18.21 f.	294	7.31–35	286	16.7–15	333
18.23–35	290	7.36–50	217, 272, 286	17.3	333
19.13–15	244	9.18–22	299	17.5, 24	332
19.16–22	295	10.22	300	18–19	269, 329
20.1–16	288, 289	10.23 f.	291	18.32	334
21.28–31	286	10.25–37	286	19.12	209
21.33–43	297	11.5–9	293	20.1–31	329, 332
22.1–14	292, 297	11.19	279, 301	21.1–25	330
23.37–39	296	11.20	291		
24.43	287	11.21 f.	286	*Acts of the Apostles*	
25.31–46	292	11.24–26	284	1–28	336 f.
26–27	269	12.39	287, 292	1.8	337
26.63 f.	299, 300	12.54–56	291	1.1–11	338 f.
		13.34	271	1.12–26	339
Mark		14.7–11	294	2.1–47	339
1.1–15	253, 270, 271, 291	14.16–24	292, 297	2.16–18	320
1.21–38	272	15.3–7	284, 293	3–5	340
2.3–12	242, 300	17.21–24	296	4.36 f.	307
2.13–3.4	246 f., 272, 287	17.22–37	298	6.13 f.	306, 340
3.1–5	248	18.2–8	293, 300	7.2–53	337
3.13–17	270	18.15–17	244	8.5–8, 26–40	
3.35	271	18.18–23	295		341
4.3–9	289	19.11–27	288	9.1–9	306, 317, 337
4.10–20	288	19.41–44	296	9.30	307
4.26–29	289	20.9–18	297	10–11	341
4.30–32	289	22–23	269	11.18	338
5.1–43	260, 263	22.66 f.	299, 300	11.22–24	307
6.1–6	271	23.7	209	11.25 f.	307
6.30–44	260, 270, 273			11.26	347
7.1 f.	294	*John*		14.23	346
8.27–30	270, 274, 299	1.1–18	327	14.25–28	308
8.38	252	1.19–51	327	15.1–30	310, 338
9.2–10	275	2.19 ff.	326	15.40–16.5	
10.13–16	244, 247	2.22	334		308
10.17–22	295	3.3	326	16.6–10	308
10.25 f.	287	3.28	332	16.19–17.15	
10.28–30	295	4.10	326, 328		308, 338
11.1–10	275	4.25	332	17.5	338
11.27b–33		5.1–47	328	18.3–21	308
	247	5.17	276	18.23–20.31	
12.1–12	275, 297	5.30–43	332		309
12.41–44	294	6.1–65	328	20.28	346
13	298	6.15	273	20.35	316
13.14–18	297	6.35 f.	333	21.20	310
13.26 f.	285	6.66	266	22.3	305
14–15	269	7.23	328	22.4–11	306, 317
14.3–9	294	7.26	332	22.25–29	305
14.27–31	279	8.12	333	23.6	305
14.61 f.	299, 300	8.17	328	23.23–33	311
16.8	254	8.30–59	332	24.24–26	210
16.9–19	8	9.1–41	328	25.1–12	312
		9.2	235	26.5	305
Luke		10.7 f.	333	26.12–18	306, 307
1.1–4	256	10.30	332	27.1–28.15	
1.8 f.	225	10.34	328		312
1.46 f.	294	11.1 f.	326	28.16, 30	312

Romans
1.18–32	323
2.11 f.	314
2.17–20	314
3.22	311, 314
3.24	315
3.25	316
4.5	315
5.8	315
6.10 f.	319
7.21 f.	305, 314
8.2	314, 322
8.3	315
8.34	323
8.38	317
11.1–27	307
11.25–32	325
12.2	321, 322
12.6–8	320
13.8–10	323
14.1–15.7	322
15.19–29	310, 311

I Corinthians
1.10–12	319
1.24	317
1.30	315
2.8	317
2.16	322
4.7	321
5.1 f.	323
5.9–13	323
6.8–10	323
6.12	321
7.1–40	324
8.1–13	319
9.1	306
9.21	322
9.26	322
10.16–17	318
10.18–33	319
10.23	321

10.27 f.	323
11.20–34	269, 318, 344
12.14–27	320
13.1–13	323
13.5–7	265, 272
14.12	320
15.3–10	281, 306
15.22	318
15.26, 57	317
16.1 f.	345

II Corinthians
3.7	321
3.17	322
4.6	306, 317
5.9	306
5.14 f.	319
5.18 f.	316
10.1	322
11.23–33	307
12.1–4	320
12.17	309
12.28	320

Galatians
1.14	305
1.17–19	307
2.10–13	311
2.15	315
2.20	306, 319, 323
3.8	318
3.10	314
3.13	316
3.28, 29	318, 324
4.3	317
4.4	317
4.19	322
5.1	306, 315
5.13	321
5.14	323
5.22	321
6.2	322

Ephesians
1.4	323
1.7	315
1.10	325
2.11–22	325
2.15	321
3.10	325
3.18 f.	323
4.4–16	318, 321
4.11	320
4.13	325
4.32	322
5.1, 2, 25	323
5.21–6.9	324
6.12	317

Philippians
1.1	346
2.8	322
4.8	324

Colossians
1.14	315
1.15, 19	317
1.20	325
2.8	317
2.15	317
3.5–7	323
3.13	322
3.14	323
3.18–4.1	324
4.14	305

I Thessalonians
4.3–8	323
4.15	325
5.19–21	320

II Thessalonians
2.1–3	325
3.5	322